SHANGHAI

Transformation and Modernization under China's Open Policy

SHANGHAI

Transformation and Modernization
under China's Open Policy

Edited by

Y. M. Yeung and Sung Yun-wing

The Chinese University Press

ISBN 962–201–667–7

THE CHINESE UNIVERSITY PRESS
The Chinese University of Hong Kong
SHA TIN, N.T., HONG KONG
Fax: +852 2603 6692
E-mail: cup@cuhk.edu.hk
Web-site: http://www.cuhk.edu.hk/cupress/w1.htm

Printed in Hong Kong

Contents

Part III: Urban and Social Infrastructure

Part IV: Topical Perspectives

Illustrations

Figures

Tables

Preface

The successful publication of *Guangdong: Survey of a Province Undergoing Rapid Change* not only marked the launching of a new regional series of scholarly treatises on China by The Chinese University Press, but also confirmed the ongoing commitment to regional development issues in China by the Urban and Regional Development in Pacific Asia Programme of the Hong Kong Institute of Asia–Pacific Studies at The Chinese University of Hong Kong. Indeed, this book project on Shanghai began in mid-1994 and was inspired by the enthusiasm of some of the original contributors to the *Guangdong* volume.

After *Guangdong*, it was easy to understand why a book on Shanghai should be high on the research agenda of the programme. True, Shanghai has always held a special status in the history of modern China, harking back to its days of spectacular economic growth and social inequities/excesses in the early decades of this century. Its re-energized dash for bold economic reforms and social transformation since 1990, when Pudong was declared an open region to spearhead development for Shanghai, has warranted systematic documentation, analysis and evaluation. Even a casual visitor to Shanghai is able to detect the breath-taking physical and social transformation that has occurred since 1990.

The organization of this volume follows largely that of the *Guangdong* book. An attempt has been made to achieve comprehensive coverage, but such topics as customs and culture, finance and banking, and legal development, were not included due to a lack of suitable contributors. With the exception of only several chapters, all contributors are from Hong Kong. Lynn T. White III, of Princeton University, held a visiting academic appointment in Hong Kong in 1994. In addition to his chapter in this volume, he offered many valuable ideas and contacts. The present volume has made one obvious improvement on the *Guangdong* book, that is the inclusion of Chinese characters to permit easy reference and further scholarship.

We are indebted to many organizations and individuals for the successful completion of this project. First, sincere thanks are due to the Lippo Group which has supported the programme with an annual grant since 1993. A Lippo Urban Research Fund has been established, and it has been the primary source of funding for this project. We wish to express our appreciation to J. P. Lee (李澤培), of the Lippo Group, for his personal encouragement and interest in this project. The Department of Geography of East China Normal University, to which the senior editor has been serving as an advisory professor since 1990, has provided helpful logistical and other support during his visits to Shanghai for research purposes. In particular, the assistance provided by Professors Liu Junde 劉君德 , Mei Anxin 梅安新 and Ning Yuemin 寧越敏 during his visits are highly appreciated. A special note of appreciation should also go to Professor Hu Zhaoliang 胡兆量 of the Department of Geography at Peking University for furnishing the editors over the years a constant flow of up-to-date publications on China, including Shanghai. At the University, we have enjoyed excellent support from the Institute and the Department of Geography. Specifically, we owe much to Janet Wong (汪唐鳳萍), who handled with devotion and finesse correspondence with the contributors, liaison with The Chinese University Press and the general administration of the project. Lui Siu-yun (呂少忻) and Joanna Lee (李慧瑩) provided capable research assistance and ably carried out other tasks related to the production of this book. Most of the figures have been drawn or redrawn by S. L. Too (杜仕流) of the Department of Geography. Wong Kin-wai (王建慧) lent her professional editing skills to ensure the quality of this publication. We are grateful for the insightful comments from four anonymous referees, and every effort has been made to respond to their queries. Finally, our heart-felt thanks are reserved for all the contributors who have shared with us their expertise and experience and who have responded to our deadlines and repeated requests with understanding and forbearance. We are responsible for any remaining errors and shortcomings.

The Editors
June 1996

Abbreviations

APEC	Asia Pacific Economic Cooperation
ASEAN	Association of South East Asian Nations
CBD	central business district
CCP	Chinese Communist Party
EEC	European Economic Community
EJVs	equity joint ventures
ETDZ(s)	Economic and Technological Development Zone(s)
FDI	Foreign direct investment
GATT	General Agreement on Tariffs and Trade
GDP	gross domestic product
GNP	gross national product
IMR	infant mortality rate
JFRB	*Jiefang ribao* (Liberation Daily)
MOFERT	Ministry of Foreign Economic Relations and Trade
NCNA	New China News Agency
NICs	newly industrializing countries
NIU	National Income Utilized
NMP	Net Material Product
NMR	neonatal mortality rate
PECC	Pacific Economic Cooperation Council
PLA	People's Liberation Army
PRC	People's Republic of China
RMB	*Renminbi*
ROI	return on investment
SAR	Special Administration Region
SASS	Shanghai Academy of Social Science
SERC	Shanghai Economic Research Centre
SEZ(s)	Special Economic Zone(s)
SJD	*Shijie jingji daobao*
SO_2	Sulphur dioxide
SOEs	state-owned enterprises

TFR	total fertility rate
TNCs	Transnational Corporations
TSP	total suspended particulates
UNEP	United Nations Environment Programme
WHB	*Wen hui bao*
WHO	World Health Organization
WTO	World Trade Organization
XMWB	*Xinmin wanbao* (New People's Evening News)
XWRB	*Xinwen ribao* (News Daily)

1

Introduction

> The name summons up a world of compradors and foreign concessions, gunboat diplomacy and opium, afternoon tea at the Cathay Hotel and death by starvation in the streets outside Western cantonments. It recalls a landscape of gangsters, sweatshops, strikes and revolution, fierce intellectuals and vengeful Red Guards.[1]

Shanghai, literally meaning "on the sea," which is vividly described in the above quotation, is China's largest city. It symbolizes the clash between Western and Chinese civilizations. After it was named one of five open cities, provided by the Treaty of Nanking in 1842 following the Opium War, Shanghai was opened to Western trade and residence. It was a combination of unfettered Western capitalism, boundless Chinese entrepreneurial spirit and an unrivalled geographical location that witnessed more than a century of unprecedented and dramatic growth at the mouth of the Yangzi River (長江).

Yet Shanghai is a city of anomalies and paradoxes, because, as a semi-colonial city under Chinese soil, it marked the triumph of Western mercantilism and its most successful incursion into Asia in the nineteenth century.[2] The result was truly startling and remarkable, as in less than a century Shanghai had transformed itself from a third-class, local town to a thriving and leading metropolis of the world. In 1936, Shanghai was the seventh largest city in the world, with a population of 3.81 million. What is more, in its prime in the 1930s and 1940s, Shanghai was China's most urbane conurbation, a metropolis that exhibited all the hues of the human character. It was "as crowded as Calcutta, as decadent as Berlin, as snooty as Paris, as jazzy as New York" — in short, a giant among cities. No modern Asian city, not even Tokyo or Hong Kong, has been able to match Shanghai's cosmopolitan and sophisticated reputation from these vintage years.[3]

Development in Shanghai since 1949, after the PRC was established, was radically different. The record of growth prior to the economic reforms and open policy initiated in 1978 is well summed up by Rhoads Murphey:

> During the first three decades of Communist rule, Shanghai was periodically viewed officially as more problem than promise, an unwelcome leftover from a humiliating and resented semicolonial past. There was official talk in the early 1950s of dismantling Shanghai and distributing its factories and experts over the previously neglected rest of the country. Shanghai was never dismantled completely, but skilled workers, technicians, machine goods and tools, and some whole factories were reallocated from the city to aid in

developing new inland industrial centres, and Shanghai's own growth was sharply restricted.[4]

Indeed, even after 1978, when certain parts of southern China, particularly Guangdong 廣東 and Fujian 福建 , surged ahead in economic transformation, Shanghai experienced rather modest growth. However, with the announcement, in April 1990, of Pudong 浦東 , the land to the east of the Huangpu River (黃浦江) measuring some 350 sq km, as an open area for development, attention in China and, in fact in the world at large, is focused again on Shanghai. In just five years, massive physical and economic transformation has occurred, propelled by the dynamism of Pudong. Officially, Shanghai has been designated as the "dragon head" to lead the Yangzi Delta and Basin, and, more broadly, China, into the twenty-first century through rapid economic growth and a new phase of openness, modernization and development.

This volume was conceived to be as a concerted effort to document, analyze and interpret the development and change that have occurred in Shanghai since 1978. It relies largely on the expertise available in the tertiary institutions in Hong Kong. As in the companion volume on Guangdong, it adopts a largely comprehensive approach to the understanding different dimensions of life in Shanghai.[5]

In setting the stage for the subsequent chapters, this chapter is divided into three parts. First, it will provide a short overview of Shanghai, with a focus on some of its key elements. Thereafter, highlights of Shanghai's ongoing reforms in the 1990s are presented and, inevitably, they are traced back to the beginning of the open policy in 1978. Finally, the importance of the current reforms in Shanghai is discussed, focussing on whether they will rejuvenate the city to such an extent that it will recapture some of its former glory and on the relative roles of Hong Kong and Shanghai in the future. These are some of the questions addressed in the concluding section. In the course of this chapter, there are numerous references to the other chapters in order to enhance the continuity and consistency of this project.

Overview of Shanghai

Located strategically at the mouth of the Yangzi River, Shanghai lies expansively together with the island of Chongming 崇明 , on a large deltaic plain formed by centuries of alluvial sedimentation. The city constitutes, for the most part, the southeastern quadrant of the Yangzi River Delta, fringed on the north by the Yangzi River and on the south by Hangzhou Bay (杭州灣). Bordered by Jiangsu 江蘇 province on the north and west and by Zhejiang 浙江 province on the south, much of the boundless deltaic plain has an average elevation of 3 m to 4 m. The deltaic plain centred around Shanghai is crisscrossed with a dense network of canals and water-ways, most of them man-made, that connect the city to Tai Lake (Tai Hu 太湖) in the west.

Shanghai enjoys a mild climate, due to its subtropical latitude (30°23′ to 31°27′N) and its maritime location. The average January minimum temperature is 3°C. and the average July maximum is 27°C. Shanghai's winter temperatures are markedly higher than Nanjing's 南京 because of the moderating maritime influence on the former, notwithstanding their similar latitudes. Similarly, Shanghai is spared the extreme high summer temperatures in the Yangzi River Basin, for which Nanjing, Wuhan 武漢 and Chongqing 重慶 are infamous. Shanghai has plentiful rainfall, amount-ing to 1,143 mm a year, with a good spread throughout the year and a maximum in June and a minimum in December. Over the years, farmers in the area have been more fearful of floods than of droughts for their har-vests. Floods result from the heavy rains and sluggish drainage along the level and meandering waterways.[6]

The importance of Shanghai is to a large degree due to its location midway along the China coast. It serves as an effective link not only between the port cities of North and South China, but for cities in Japan and Korea and in the Asia–Pacific region as well. In air transport, Shang-hai is approximately one hour's travel time to Tokyo, Seoul, Taipei and Hong Kong. While Shanghai's own market is already quite sizable, its hinterland is enormous and unequalled in China. It is estimated to reach 77.7 million inhabitants in the Yangzi River Delta and 360 million in-habitants in the Yangzi River Basin. Shu Peijun, Lin Hui and Liang Jinshe (Chapter 20) point to the recent developments in infrastructure, such as the completion of the missing links in the rail link between Shanghai and Wuhan and the launching of the Three-Gorges Dam project, as positive factors which enhance the regional importance of Shanghai. Likewise, the recent easing of international relations will enable Shanghai to play a more active role in China's continuing open policy and to engage in economic interactions with countries in Northeast Asia and beyond.

Administratively speaking, Shanghai, with a population of 12.99 mil-lion in 1994, is one of the three special municipalities in China with a status equivalent to a province. From an area of only 636.18 sq km in 1949, the city has successively expanded, most notably in 1958, to its present area of 6,340 sq km, of which 280 sq km are occupied by the central city and 6,060.5 sq km by suburban districts and counties. The city is made up of three parts: the central city with its ten urban districts, namely, Huangpu 黃浦, Nanshi 南市, Luwan 盧灣, Jing'an 靜安, Xuhui 徐匯, Changning 長寧, Putuo 普陀, Hongkou 虹口, Zhabei 閘北 and Yangpu 楊浦; the four suburban districts of Baoshan 寶山, Minhang 閔行, Jiading 嘉定 and Pudong New Area (浦東新區); and the six suburban counties of Songjiang 松江, Qingpu 青浦, Jinshan 金山, Fengxian 奉賢, Nanhui 南匯 and Chongming (Figure 1.1 and Figure 1.2).

As the cradle of the Chinese Communist Party in 1921, Shanghai is inextricably part of China. For the past 150 years, the history of China has often been associated with Shanghai. Much has been written about the historical highlights[7] of the development of Shanghai, which Kerrie L. MacPherson (Chapter 19) describes. In particular, the context of Shanghai's development as a special city, in comparison with some of the world's largest and most famous cities, is traced from the nineteenth century to the reform period. The "Shanghai model" is unique in the history of China.

A major factor that sets Shanghai's development apart from other cities in modern China is its entrepreneurial spirit and its bold drive for innovation. Wong Siu-lun (Chapter 2) emphasizes entrepreneurship as the driving force for the economic dynamism and maintains that Shanghai still lacks an external pattern of entrepreneurship as found in Hong Kong. While Hong Kong and Shanghai each display their own style of entrepreneurship, in this respect his prognosis for Shanghai is mixed. This may be contrasted with Shanghai emigrant entrepreneurs in Hong Kong, who have been highly successful and have helped launch Hong Kong's postwar transformation into the vibrant economic entity in the Asia-Pacific region it is today.[8] Arguing similarly for the importance of the entrepreneurial spirit, Peter T. Y. Cheung (Chapter 3) ascribes Shanghai's slower development than Guangdong in the reform period since 1978 to its lethargy, or at least its erosion, after decades under the command economy.

In the past, Shanghai was noted for its *penchant* for keeping abreast of technology and of new ways of economic or social life. Lucian Pye's observation aptly drives home this point:

> Historically Shanghai was quick to adopt innovations: it first encountered trains only seven years after the completion of the first transcontinental

Figure 1.1   The Administrative Division of Shanghai

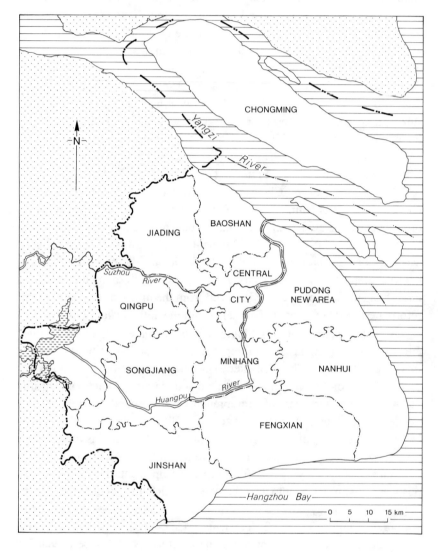

Figure 1.2   Urban Districts of Shanghai's Central City

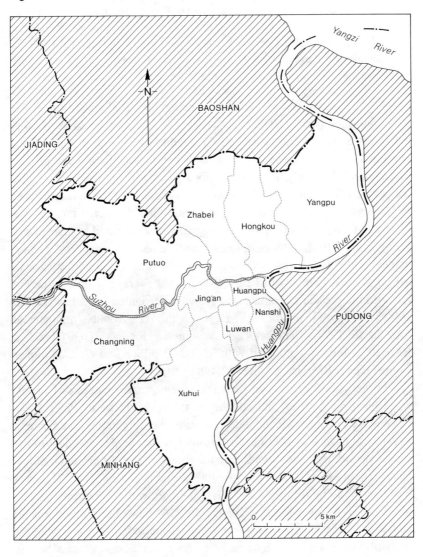

railroad in America; its first textile mills were built before any in the American South, and by 1930 it had, according to some methods of calculation, the largest mill in the world; its first cinema opened only five years after San Francisco got its first large movie house; and by the late 1930s its Commercial Press was publishing each year as many titles as the entire American publishing industry — most of which were, of course, pirated.[9]

A recent study divides Shanghai's economic development under the PRC into three periods. The first period 1953–1978, over 26 years, was one when Shanghai was under the command economy, with the societal distribution of resources being a decisive factor. Economic growth averaged 8.8%, clearly above the national average. This was followed by the period 1979–1990, over 12 years, when economic growth raced ahead in Guangdong and other southern areas and Shanghai acted merely as a "rearguard" in economic reform. Shanghai's manufactured products were losing ground in the domestic market and the lack of vitality of Shanghainese enterprises was becoming evident. Annual economic growth averaged 7.5%, which was below the national average. The third period refers to the present phase of rapid growth after Pudong was launched in 1990 as a growth platform for Shanghai, with average double digit annual growth. In 1994, Shanghai's gross domestic product (GDP) reached RMB197.2 billion (compared with RMB27.3 billion in 1978), and a per capita GDP of RMB15,206 (RMB2,498 in 1978).[10]

In the history of modern Shanghai, politics and economics have always been intertwined. Indeed, this is the main theme of Peter T. Y. Cheung's chapter, in which he demonstrates the importance and meaning of political change against the backdrop of economic development in the reform period. He draws attention to the emergence of the present political leadership in Shanghai and its close links to Jiang Zemin 江澤民, China's president, and Zhu Rongji 朱鎔基, vice-premier, who were former mayors of Shanghai. In any event, Xu Kuangdi 徐匡迪, Shanghai's present mayor and Huang Ju 黃菊, the party secretary, are representatives of the new class of technocrats who tend to be better educated and professional in their orientation. Moreover, Lam Tao-chiu (Chapter 5) traces the progressive articulation of local interest in Shanghai in the 1980s by quasi-officials and intellectuals. The vehicles were seminars, conferences, academic journals and the local media. By the 1990s, Shanghai had effectively changed from the situation of the late 1970s, when its political leaders, as noted by a renowned China scholar, consistently failed to assert the special economic and cultural interests of their city. During that period, it was not uncommon for leaders to advocate policies and programmes diametrically opposed to the interests and the welfare of the people whom they were supposed to represent.[11]

During much of the period since 1949, a point of strained relations between Shanghai and the central government has been the allegedly unfair distribution of revenues that originated in Shanghai. Several of the contributors point to the seemingly unfair burden Shanghai had to bear for decades by remitting the bulk of its revenues to the central government. Peter T. Y. Cheung shows that, between 1949 and 1983, as much as 87% of Shanghai's revenue of RMB350 billion was remitted to Beijing 北京 , leaving only 13% for its own utilization. In contrast, Lam Tao-chiu notes the revenue for local spending in Beijing and Tianjin 天津 averaged 30%. Ho Lok-sang and Tsui Kai-yuen (Chapter 6) explore in detail the implications of the fiscal relations between Shanghai and the central government. In the reform period, as much as one-sixth of the revenue of the central government has been derived from Shanghai. Consequently, Shanghai is described as the "golden milk-cow" of the planned economy by the editor of a local progressive journal.[12]

However, in 1988 Shanghai was granted a fiscal contracting system that previously was exclusively enjoyed by Guangdong and Fujian. In 1994, China adopted a "tax sharing system" whereby a uniform formula was put in place across the nation to substitute for the hitherto bilateral bargaining.[13] As Ho and Tsui have elaborated, Shanghai was still going through a period of difficult transition in the early 1990s, when local expenditures rapidly expanded while old responsibilities remained and the profitability of state-owned enterprises, traditionally a major source of revenue, was sharply reduced. As a consequence, budget deficits skyrocketed since 1985. The paid transfer of land-use rights that began only in 1988 has since greatly improved the local budget situation, particularly in Pudong.

In fact, starting with fewer encumbrances, Pudong New Area, as King K. Tsao (Chapter 4) demonstrates, has been able to pursue more effective institutional and administrative reform since 1990. It has effected a higher degree of functional consolidation by adopting a market-oriented approach to economic development. To expedite development by foreign investors and in the interest of operational effectiveness, the hierarchical levels of government and bureaucratic red-tape have been reduced.

The Quickening Pace of Reform

Although China adopted an open policy in 1978 and Shanghai was designated one of 14 open cities in 1984, it essentially took a back seat in the
economic reforms and rapid growth that had occurred in the southern
provinces. As Peter T. Y. Cheung highlights, the Tiananmen incident
(天安門事件) in 1989 and its spillover resonance in Hong Kong resulted in
the choice of Shanghai as the launching pad for the next phase of rapid
growth and economic reform in the 1990s. Thus, for almost every year in
the 1990s, Shanghai registered a GDP growth rate in excess of 14%,
maintaining a 14.1% growth in 1995.[14] While the recent growth rates have
been impressive, Shanghai has, in fact, achieved comprehensive and solid
progress in many sectors since 1978.

In economic development, Shanghai has experienced significant structural change, with an ever increasing emphasis on the development of the
tertiary sector. Since 1978, the tertiary sector has been growing the fastest,
picking up speed notably since 1990. By 1994, the value of the tertiary
sector had reached RMB78 billion, accounting for 39.6% of GDP.[15] However, Shanghai remains a nationally eminent industrial base, with industries accounting for more than 56% of Shanghai's GDP in 1993.[16]
Industrial development is heavily concentrated in six "pillar industries,"
namely, steel, automobiles, petrochemicals, energy, telecommunications
and computer products, with an increasing emphasis on technological
sophistication. In 1993, these industries yielded RMB31.4 billion in gross
industrial output, accounting for 47% of Shanghai's total value. Most of
these industries still focused on import-substitution, with a relatively scant
orientation towards exports.[17]

Four of these pillar industries are located in Shanghai's satellite towns,
whereas most of the traditional, inefficient and small-scale factories are
intermingled with residential and other land uses in the central urban area.
The 1990 Population Census revealed that in Shanghai's old city with 6.39
million inhabitants, there were 4,700 industrial enterprises, averaging 34
plants per sq km. The urban area had 53.5 sq km, or 20.5% of the land,
devoted to industrial use, which is much higher than the usual 15% for
industrial use in comparable cities in Western countries.[18] Thus, an extreme functional mixture and land-use fragmentation, in part a result of
historical and environmental factors and of the administrative apportionment of land after 1949, have been a hindrance to urban optimization.
Rupert Hodder (Chapter 9) shows that, since 1978, the new policies have

failed to produce any dramatic change in the entrenched chaotic pattern of industrial location. Various solutions to the seemingly intractable problems are being sought.

One of the daunting tasks faced by Shanghai, indeed by China as a whole, in its effort to restructure and modernize its industries is the magnitude of change required to reform state-owned enterprises. Victor Mok (Chapter 8) systematically traces the growth of industrial development in Shanghai in the 1980s, showing how new institutions such as enterprise groups, independent commodity producers and "horizontal linkages" appeared to open up markets and renovate industries. The formation of *get in Hockler.* "horizontal linkages" is cited by Rupert Hodder as one way of avoiding duplication of industrial activities by separate and administrative units, whereas the same theme forms a major focus of Lynn T. White III's Chapter 17, where the exchange of manpower is discussed. In an effort to promote flexibility and change within industrial enterprises, it has been reported that parts of some factories in Shanghai are run along quasi-capitalist lines, using a "one factory, two systems" formula.[19]

During the 1980s, Shanghai was able to attract a total of US$3.3 billion in foreign investment. After Pudong was established as a new open area in 1990, the amount of foreign investment in 1992 alone was equivalent to the entire preceding decade. Utilized direct foreign investment reached US$3.2 billion in 1994, which can be compared with US$2.3 billion in 1993.[20] Shanghai's investment environment is the subject of a purposeful survey that forms the core of Chapter 10 by Nyaw Mee-kau. According to the survey results, the "hard" investment environment is generally satisfactory, but the "soft" environment needs improvement in specific ways. Consequently, Shanghai is attractive to multinational corporations (MNCs) to be the base of their China operations. By August 1994, 146 MNCs with a total of 281 projects had invested in Shanghai. Of the world's 100 top MNCs, 37 are represented in Shanghai, for the most part bringing with them high technology.[21] Shanghai opened the first of two stock exchanges in China in September 1990 and now it has at least nine commodity exchanges.

In order to improve Shanghai's investment environment and to enable it to carry forward its reform programme, Shanghai's urban and suburban areas underwent momentous changes. To begin with, much of urban Shanghai is a historical artifact, a product of colonial rule that left a legacy of unbalanced development, incompatible infrastructure and difficult north–south access between districts. Roger C. K. Chan (Chapter 12) reviews the progress in urban development and redevelopment since the 1980s. Of special importance has been the massive investment in infrastructure development over the past five years, spurred on by the opening of Pudong. The Nanpu Bridge (南浦大橋) and the Yangpu Bridge (楊浦大橋) were completed, respectively, in 1991 and 1993, improving circulation between the banks of the Huangpu River. The 16-km Line One of the subway system, linking north and south Puxi 浦西 at a cost of US$680 million, was opened in December 1994, making it the largest municipal project in Shanghai's history. The inner ring road was opened to traffic in December 1994, linking Puxi and Pudong. During the period 1988–1993, Shanghai devoted more than RMB26.4 billion to infrastructure development, which was 1.4 times the total infrastructure expenditures for the preceding 10 years.[22] Many of the urban development and renewal problems stem from decades upon decades of land use dictated by politics and whim rather than logic and efficiency. Fortunately, the revenues from leased land for the past few years have put the government in a more favourable position to pursue urban change and reform.

K. I. Fung (Chapter 13) shows that an active satellite-town programme, for a variety of planning goals, has been implemented in Shanghai since 1958. Seven satellite towns — Wusong 吳淞 , Minhang, Wujing 吳涇 , Anting 安亭 , Songjiang, Jiading and Jinshanwei 金山衞 — have undergone rapid growth since 1984. However, heavy industry has been promoted in these towns at the expense of light industry, and residential infrastructure has been neglected. As a result, they are of relatively little interest to residents in the central city. After all, the urban bias of "better a bed in the city than an apartment in the suburbs" is pervasive.[23] Fung's caveat regarding Pudong's development is that it may jeopardize the growth of the satellite towns. One way likely to speed up development in these towns is to open them to foreign investment, as has already occurred in Minhang.

In light of Shanghai being China's largest city with a huge population, population control has been a prominent feature of its development since 1949. Lynn T. White III provides a broad interpretation of population control over the years, linking it to labour mobility, in particular to Shanghai's export of trained manpower to other parts of China. While Shanghai sent, as part of the *xiafang* 下放 movement, 829,000 educated and youthful residents to the countryside during the 1950–1964 period, they returned *en masse* in the late 1970s. Between 1977 and 1982, 498,700 educated youths returned, 264,900 in 1979 alone.[24] Compounding this was the problem during the 1980s of the temporary population. A 1988 survey of temporary migrants in large Chinese cities revealed that Shanghai had 2.09 million such inhabitants, who presented the city with both challenges and opportunities.[25] Thus, Shanghai's population has grown more from immigrants than from births. Temporary migrants now account for about one-third of the total population. Shanghai's low fertility predates public reforms, reaching birth rate lows of 10/1000 in 1972–1977, and its life expectancy is the highest of all the provinces.

The changing population dynamics have direct implications for some social sectors. Wong Tze-wai, Gu Xingyuan and Suzanne C. Ho (Chapter 16) describe the remarkable advances in health services during the past four decades. As a result of the increasing affluence of the rural population, there has been a shift in patient demands for health services from rural to county and city hospitals. A growing ageing population implies changing health care and social needs. In education, Grace C. L. Mak and Leslie N. K. Lo (Chapter 15) highlight changes since 1978. The content of education has veered towards more vocational education and an emphasis on utilitarianism in tertiary education. The supply of graduates from tertiary institutions cannot meet demand. A variety of measures have been taken to improve the quality of education. The shared goal for many in Shanghai is "first-rate education for a first-rate city." One tangible piece of evidence of social progress in the reform period is housing. Rebecca L. H. Chiu (Chapter 14) shows significant improvements on all fronts. For example, the per capita living area almost doubled from 4.4 sq m in 1980 to 7.3 sq m in 1993. The housing system reform programmes have proceeded apace with good results. By the mid-1990s, the provision of housing is no longer confined to the government. A secondary housing market, albeit limited and small in many ways, has emerged. To further develop in this direction, foreign developers have been allowed to develop mass housing in Shanghai, as they have in Guangzhou 廣州 and Wuhan. This has attracted more than 4,000 foreign companies, including 100 large overseas corporations.[26]

Since 1990, the biggest boost to Shanghai's development has been the policy initiatives adopted for Pudong. Anthony G. O. Yeh (Chapter 11) describes Pudong as a vehicle for Shanghai's re-emergence as a world-class city and he traces its recent development, with an emphasis on planning strategies and socioeconomic planning. By 1994, the ten large infrastructure projects launched in 1990 had been completed and achievements were notable in every respect.[27] After five years, Pudong has become the most important area for economic growth in Shanghai, accounting for one-third of its growth in 1994. Pudong's GDP of RMB6 billion in 1990 (constituting 8% of Shanghai's total) soared to RMB29.1 billion in 1994, accounting for 15% of Shanghai's total. In the first half of 1995, Pudong recorded a 20% growth rate over the same period in 1994, with its GDP totalling RMB17.3 billion.[28] During the past five years, RMB25 billion has been invested in Pudong's infrastructure.[29] Lujiazui 陸家嘴 is being developed as a new Chinese Wall Street, with the Shanghai Stock Exchange scheduled to move in in the autumn of 1996. Lujiazui's status as a financial district in relation to the Bund in Puxi is yet to be clarified, for 37 Western-style buildings in the latter are being leased out.[30] Looking ahead, Pudong has been accorded 18 new priority policies for the Ninth Five-year Plan, covering a wide spectrum from taxation, to finance, foreign exchange control, etc.[31] All in all, there is considerable expectation that Pudong will turn Shanghai from an industrial dinosaur into an economic dynamo and will lead Shanghai into the twenty-first century as an ultra-modern, externally-oriented and technologically sophisticated world city.

Notwithstanding the impressive growth Shanghai has been able to attain during the past few years, Shanghai's relative importance in China has been reduced markedly. Both Peter T. Y. Cheung and Sung Yun-wing (Chapter 7) compare Shanghai's economic position in China between 1978 and the 1990s and show dramatic declines. Primarily as a result of the rapid economic growth in many parts of coastal China, in South China in particular, Shanghai no longer enjoys its pre-eminent position as an economic, trade and transport centre. Table 1.1 attempts to show Shanghai's changing position in some select indicators during the reform period. Its relative decline in national importance is most obvious in government revenue, gross output value of industry, values of export and amount of cargo handled. To be sure, in all these sectors massive growth has been realized since 1978, but other parts of China have grown even faster.

The Future of Shanghai

While the open policy since 1978 has greatly transformed Shanghai in every way, especially since 1990, what fascinates Shanghainese and concerned observers most is the vision for its future. They are acutely conscious of its past achievements and, given its prevailing favourable political and economic climate in relation to the country and the Asia–Pacific region, Shanghai is building for an even grander future.

Table 1.1 Shanghai's Declining Shares in National Totals in Selected Indicators, 1978–1994

	1978			1985			1994		
	Shanghai	National	Sha/Nat %	Shanghai	National	Sha/Nat %	Shanghai	National	Sha/Nat %
Population and labour force									
Year end population (10,000)	1,098	96,259	1.14	1,217	104,532	1.16	1,356	119,850	1.13
Total employment (10,000)	697	39,856	1.75	764	49,873	1.53	763	61,470	1.24
Employment in urban state-owned units (10,000)	336	7,451	4.51	383	8,990	4.26	357.5	11,214	3.19
Economy									
Gross domestic product (RMB100 million)	312*	4,518*	6.91	467	8,964	5.21	1,971.9	45,006	4.38
Total investment in fixed assets (RMB100 million)	45*	911*	4.94	119	2,543	4.68	1,086.24	16,370	6.64
Government revenue (RMB100 million)	190.7	1,121	17.01	264	1,866	14.15	440†	5,088†	8.65
Gross output value of industry (RMB100 million)	545	4,237	12.86	830	9,716	8.54	4,255.23	76,909	5.53
Per capita consumption (RMB)	410	184	222.83	961	437	219.91	4,162	1,737	239.61
Foreign capital and trade									
Foreign capital actually utilized (US$100 million)	—	—	—	1.09	46.47	2.35	25.8	432	5.97
Direct foreign investment (US$100 million)	—	—	—	1.07	16.61	6.44	24.7	339	7.29
Total value of export (US$100 million)	29*	181.2*	16.00	33.6	273.5	12.29	99.4	1,210.4	8.21
Transport and communication									
Volume of freight traffic (100 million ton km)	1,487*	12,026*	12.36	2,015	18,365	10.97	3,777†	30,325†	12.46
Cargo handled at principal ports (10,000 ton)	7,955	19,834	40.11	11,291	31,154	36.24	16,581	74,370	22.30

Notes: * 1980 figures;   † 1993 figures

Sources: Guojia tongjiju 國家統計局 (ed.), *Zhongguo tongji nianjian 1986* 中國統計年鑑 1986 (Statistical Yearbook of China 1986) (Beijing: Zhongguo tongji chubanshe, 1986); Guojia tongjiju (ed.), *Zhongguo tongji nianjian 1995* 中國統計年鑑 1995 (Statistical Yearbook of China 1995) (Beijing: Zhongguo tongji chubanshe, 1995); Shanghaishi tongjiju (ed.), *Shanghai tongji nianjian 1986* 上海統計年鑑 1986 (Statistical Yearbook of Shanghai 1986) (Shanghai: Shanghai renmin chubanshe 1986); Shanghai shehuikexueyuan *Shanghai jingji nianjian she* (ed.), *Shanghai jingji nianjian 1995* (see note 10 below).

One area Shanghai needs to devote more attention and resources to is the environment. As Lam Kin-che and Tao Shu (Chapter 18) show, Shanghai remains poor in environmental quality in absolute terms and in comparison with other Chinese cities. The Huangpu River is but "a chemical cocktail composed of raw sewage, toxic urban wastes, and huge amounts of industrial discharges."[32] As recently as 1992, only 14% of the domestic sewage in Shanghai was treated prior to discharge. Lam and Tao advocate the adoption of cleaner production technologies but, with the rapid economic growth, the pressure on the environment will only exacerbate the dilemma.

A strategic objective at the 14th Party Congress held in October 1992, it was set as was for Shanghai to develop as a "dragon head and three centres" to lead the Yangzi River Basin and China at large into the twenty-first century.[33] The three centres refer to Shanghai as an economic centre, a financial centre and a trading centre.

Sung Yun-wing provides a balanced analysis of how likely Shanghai will be able to perform its "dragon head" role. As an economic centre, Shanghai's relative importance in the national picture is diminishing, despite impressive absolute gains. For example, Guangdong has overtaken Shanghai in share of national GDP, foreign investment and exports. Shanghai's role as an economic centre in the future is well described by Urban C. Lehner:

> Just as Guangdong was the showcase for China's economic reforms in the 1980s, Shanghai will be the laboratory in the years ahead for an even more important set of reforms — converting loss-ridden state enterprises into profit-making businesses and making the banking system solvent.[34]

To establish itself as a financial centre, Shanghai has a long way to go to catch up. Sung Yun-wing notes that, after eighteen years of economic reform, China's banking system is largely unreformed. Refusal in China to move the headquarters of the specialized banks from Beijing to Shanghai has slowed Shanghai's aspirations to become the financial centre of the country. The way ahead is fraught with difficulties if Shanghai and China as a whole are to win the confidence of foreign investors. Jesse Wong candidly projects this viewpoint:

> They see no quick way forward as long as China insists on its vision of a socialist market economy, which requires investors to accept the state sometimes as a partner, sometimes as a competitor and always as the final legal and regulatory arbiter.[35]

In trade, as Table 1.1 shows, Shanghai's relative share in the total value of exports and of cargo handled at ports has dramatically declined, being halved in terms of percentage between 1978 and 1994. Sung Yun-wing is also not optimistic about the future growth of Shanghai's trade, as a growing proportion of China's trade is handled by Guangdong and Hong Kong. As the Shanghai port is largely a river port, it cannot handle fourth and fifth generation container ships and 10,000-ton vessels. There is little hope that it will become a hub port in the global container network. Therefore, it comes as little surprise that Shanghai handles only about one-tenth of Hong Kong's yearly container traffic.[36] To remedy Shanghai's inadequacies in ocean transport, the central government approved, in early 1996, a 10-year project to establish Shanghai as a transport centre through the construction of a 100-km deep-water embankment and other facilities.[37] This is one of several options being considered.

In planning for and speculating about Shanghai's future, the often raised question is, will Shanghai overtake and replace Hong Kong, and, if so, when?

To begin with, one should be aware of the increasingly close and growing economic links that have been established between Shanghai and Hong Kong in recent years. In 1992, Shanghai's exports to Hong Kong amounted to US$1.1 billion, whereas its imports from Hong Kong totalled US$700 million.[38] Hong Kong is, in fact, the largest investor in Shanghai, with a cumulative investor stock totalling US$12 billion up to 1994 and another US$5 billion in the first three quarters of 1994 alone.[39] While Hong Kong has the advantage of being blessed with, among other assets, a natural and deep-water port, modern infrastructures, world-wide trading connections and a sound legal system, Shanghai has an unrivalled geographical position *vis-à-vis* Northeast Asia and the Yangzi River Basin, a huge hinterland, a strong science and technology base stemming from its numerous universities and research institutes, a vast city region with a large population, and a more diversified and balanced economy. Clearly, they both have strengths and weaknesses. In the course of rational decision making in China and in the spirit of the "one country, two systems" formula that has been designed for Hong Kong, as a Special Administrative Region under China after 1997, the territory should continue to play a critical role in the regional economy of Asia and beyond.[40] Two contrasting positions may be summarized concerning the relative roles of Shanghai and Hong Kong in the years ahead.

In the worst case scenario from Hong Kong's perspective, Shanghai's future is envisaged by Jim Robwer as follows:

> Sometime in the first decade of the 21st century it [Shanghai] will displace
> Hong Kong as China's main financial-service centre and shortly after surpass
> Tokyo as the most sophisticated and open financial market in the East Asian
> time zone — and so join London and New York as one of the indispensable
> big three of world finance.[41]

This is probably an overly optimistic projection of Shanghai's future.
However, in twenty years' time, some of Hong Kong's functions probably
will be taken over by Shanghai, which will be supported by a strong
industrial base, and will most likely achieve more balanced growth than
Hong Kong.

On the other hand, two contributors of this volume have come to a
more realistic assessment of Shanghai's future in relation to Hong Kong.
Wong Siu-lun maintains that both cities will retain their distinctiveness in
entrepreneurship which will guide their different styles of economic
development. In a similar vein, Sung Yun-wing foresees Hong Kong as
China's foremost port and a centre of foreign trade for a long time to come,
and Shanghai as the domestic financial centre of China, with Hong Kong
remaining a regional and international financial centre. Rather than seeing
one city replacing the other, a respected banker in Hong Kong perceives
Shanghai and Hong Kong metaphorically to be like the eyes of a dragon
which will spearhead China's huge and rapidly growing economy to
greater strength and diversity.[42]

Whatever the relative positions of Shanghai and Hong Kong in the
future, Pudong is viewed as a window of opportunity to shake off the
shackles of constraints and conflicts inherent in Puxi's pattern of development and to achieve a new world of miracle growth and modernity.
Pudong will be one of three cross-century mega-projects in China, the
other two being the Three-Gorges Dam Project (三峽大壩工程) and the
South Water North Diversion Engineering Project (南水北調工程). They
are all located in the Yangzi River Basin, which means they all will have a
positive reinforcing influence on the future of Shanghai.

In discussing prospects for Shanghai's future, Murphey was most
perspicacious about its true worth during the tumultuous early 1950s when
he maintained:

> Great cities do not arise by accident but they are not destroyed by whim. The
> geographic facts which have made Shanghai will prosper in the future once
> peace has been restored in East Asia.[43]

Murphey was proven right. When more peaceful conditions returned in the 1980s, Shanghai did make fundamental and favourable changes across a broad range of social and economic life. Murphey describes Shanghai of the late 1980s, as follows:

> Shanghai has not come full circle. The revolution has made a permanent change, but the radical decades are over, and the city's character and function are again being shaped by circumstances, location, and vital role it can perform for the new China.[44]

While the future of Shanghai is anybody's guess, it is beyond doubt that the present circumstances are the most propitious in more than fifty years for it to reassert the advantages of its geographical location and to play a vital role leading China and the Yangzi River Basin powerfully and purposefully into the twenty-first century.

Notes

1. James Walsh, "Shanghai," *Time*, 5 October 1992, p. 19.
2. The rise of Shanghai in its semi-capitalist and semi-colonial open mode of trade, as opposed to one of an agrarian empire only semi-open to the world personified by Guangzhou 廣州, is well analyzed by Yue Zheng 樂正, "Jindai Shanghai de jueqi yu Guangzhou de shiluo" 近代上海的崛起與廣州的失落 (The Rise of Modern Shanghai and the Decline of Guangzhou), *Twenty-first Century* 二十一世紀, No. 24 (August 1994), pp. 29–38.
3. Editorial piece —— "Shining Shanghai," *Asiaweek*, 24 November 1995, p. 28.
4. Rhoads Murphey, "Shanghai," *The Metropolis Era: Mega-cities*, vol. 2, edited by Mattei Doggan and John D. Kasarda (Newbury Park: Sage Publications, 1988), p. 158.
5. Y. M. Yeung and David K. Y. Chu (eds.), *Guangdong: Survey of a Province Undergoing Rapid Change* (Hong Kong: The Chinese University Press, 1994).
6. For detailed accounts of the physical environment of Shanghai, refer to introductory chapters in Yan Zhongmin 嚴重敏 and Yang Wanzhong 楊萬鍾 (eds.), *Shanghaishi jingji dili* 上海市經濟地理 (Economic Geography of Shanghai) (Beijing: Xinhua chubanshe 新華出版社, 1987); and Yan Zhongmin, Zhang Wudong 張務棟 and Tang Jianzhong 湯建中 (eds.), *Shanghaishi* 上海市 (Shanghai) (Shanghai: Shanghai renmin chubanshe 上海人民出版社, 1993).
7. For a general survey of the recent history of Shanghai, see Betty Peh-T'i Wei, *Shanghai: Crucible of Modern China* (Hong Kong: Oxford University Press, 1987). The introduction of manufacturing and various urban services with the attendant labour problems in the early part of this century is the theme of a

fascinating treatise, namely, Elizabeth J. Perry, *Shanghai on Strike: The Politics of Chinese Labor* (Stanford: Stanford University Press, 1993). There are other important studies covering different periods of Shanghai. A classic geographical study of Shanghai providing an understanding of its role and importance in the period immediately prior to 1949 is: Rhoads Murphey, *Shanghai: Key to Modern China* (Cambridge: Harvard University Press, 1953). Christopher Howe's edited volume, *Shanghai: Revolution and Development in an Asian Metropolis* (Cambridge: Cambridge University Press, 1981), covers much of salient developments from social science perspectives in the post-1949 period to the beginning of the open policy in the late 1970s. The early results of economic reforms to the mid-1980s is covered, with statistics as well, in Shanghai tongjiju 上海統計局 and Zhonggong Shanghai shiwei xuanchuanbu 中共上海市委宣傳部, *Shanghai shengli de shinian* 上海勝利的十年 (Ten Years of Victory in Shanghai) (Shanghai: Shanghai renmin chubanshe, 1986).

8. See Wong Siu-lun, *Emigrant Entrepreneurs: Shanghai Industrialists in Hong Kong* (Hong Kong: Oxford University Press, 1988).

9. Foreword to Howe (ed.), *Shanghai* (see note 7), p. xv.

10. Gao Ruxi 高汝熹 and Yu Yihong 郁義鴻, "Shanghai jingji: Tingji yu zaifei" 上海經濟：停滯與再飛 (Shanghai's Economy: Stagnation and Re-emergence), *Twenty-first Century*, No. 24 (August 1994), pp. 148–57; Shanghaishi tongjiju 上海市統計局 (ed.), *Shanghai tongji nianjian 1995* 上海統計年鑑 1995 (Statistical Yearbook of Shanghai 1995) (Beijing: Zhongguo tongji chubanshe 中國統計出版社, 1995); and Shanghai shehuikexueyuan *Shanghai jingji nianjian* she 上海社會科學院《上海經濟年鑑》社 (ed.), *Shanghai jingji nianjian 1995* 上海經濟年鑑 1995 (Shanghai Economy Yearbook 1995) (Shanghai: Shanghai shehuikexueyuan *Shanghai jingji nianjian* she, 1995).

11. See Lucian Pye's Foreword in Howe (ed.), *Shanghai* (see note 7), p. xiv.

12. Lynn T. White III, *Shanghai Shanghaied? Uneven Taxes in Reform China* (Hong Kong: Centre of Asian Studies, University of Hong Kong, 1987), p. 23. White III's whole study centred on the uneven taxes in reform China and how the tax regime had drained the spirit of enterprise from Shanghai more than from other places. Thus, Shanghai was "Shanghaied," meaning being "tricked or forced into something." Shanghai has been forced to pay very much more into state coffers than the political system has required of other places. In this sense, the city was unusually fettered and left with meagre resources to pursue development.

13. For a detailed description of the new fiscal arrangement, see Christine Wong, "Fiscal Reform in 1994," in *China Review 1995*, edited by Lo Chi Kin, Suzanne Pepper and Tsui Kai Yuen (Hong Kong: The Chinese University Press, 1995), pp. 20.1–13.

14. See "Shanghai Economy Seen to Grow to 12%," *Eastern Express*, 25 January

1996; between 1991 and 1994, Shanghai's GDP grew at 14.7% annually, with 1994's GDP of RMB197.2 billion, 50.9% over the 1991 figure. See *Shanghai jingji nianjian 1995* (see note 10), p. 51.

15. *Shanghai jingji nianjian 1995* (see note 10), p. 48.

16. Shanghaishi "Maixiang 21 shiji de Shanghai" keti lingdao xiaozu 上海市 "邁向21世紀的上海" 課題領導小組 (ed.), *Maixiang 21 shiji de Shanghai: 1996–2010 nian Shanghai jingji, shehui fazhan zhanlüe yanjiu* 邁向21世紀的上海：1996–2010年上海經濟、社會發展戰略研究 (Shanghai: Striding towards the 21st Century) (Shanghai: Shanghai renmin chubanshe, 1995), p. 127.

17. Yang Jianwen 楊建文, "Shanghai gongye jiegou zhanlüe tiaozheng" 上海工業結構戰略調整 (Adjustment of Shanghai's Strategy for Industrial Structure), *Hua qiao ribao* 華僑日報 (Overseas Chinese Daily News), 9 September 1994.

18. He Xinggang, "Development of Pudong and Optimization of Urban Area Structure in Shanghai," *Chinese Environment and Development*, vol. 4, no. 3 (Fall, 1993), pp. 68–88.

19. Willy Wo-lap Lam, "All Eyes on Shanghai," *South China Morning Post*, 2 November 1995.

20. Shanghai shehuikexueyuan *Shanghai jingji nianjian* she (ed.), *Shanghai jingji nianjian 1994* (Shanghai: Shanghai shehuikexueyuan *Shanghai jingji nianjian* she, 1994) and *Shanghai jingji nianjian 1995* (see note 10). In 1994, contracted, as opposed to utilized, foreign investment reached US$10 billion. Similarly, in the first ten months of 1993, Shanghai had foreign investment amounting to US$6 billion. See Yang Guosen 楊國森, "Shanghai —— weilai de 'dongfang Wanhadun'" 上海 —— 未來的「東方曼哈頓」 (Shanghai —— Future 'Eastern Manhattan'), *Hua qiao ribao*, 3 August 1994.

21. Xie Kang 謝康, "Shijieji kuaguo gongsi luxu jinjun Shanghai" 世界級跨國公司陸續進軍上海 (World-class MNCs Advanced towards Shanghai), *Hua qiao ribao*, 10 January 1995.

22. Shanghaishi renmin zhengfu jiedai bangongshi 上海市人民政府接待辦公室 (ed.), *Shanghai: Jueqi zhong de guoji dadoushi* 上海：崛起中的國際大都市 (Shanghai: Emerging International Mega-city) (Shanghai: Kexue chubanshe 科學出版社, 1993), p. 4.

23. He, "Development of Pudong" (see note 18). For an updated analysis of urban and suburban development in Shanghai, see United Nations Centre for Human Settlements, *Metropolitan Planning and Management in the Development World: Shanghai and Guangzhou, China* (Nairobi: Habitat, 1995).

24. He, "Development of Pudong" (see note 18).

25. Li Mengbai 李夢白 and Hu Xin 胡欣 et al. (eds.), *Liudong renkou dui da chengshi fazhan de yingxiang ji duice* 流動人口對大城市發展的影響及對策 (Temporary Population and Its Impact and Implications for Development in Large Cities) (Beijing: Jingji ribao chubanshe 經濟日報出版社, 1991).

26. Peggy Sito, "Waiver Raises Keen Interest in Shanghai," *South China Morning*

Post, 7 September 1994.

27. For an account of development results in the first five years, see Pudong gaige yu fazhan yanjiuyuan 浦東改革與發展研究院, *Pudong fazhan baogao 1991– 1994* 浦東發展報告 1991–1994 (Pudong Development Report 1991–1994) (Shanghai: Shanghai renmin chubanshe, 1994).

28. "Pudong Records 20 per cent Growth," *South China Morning Post*, 20 July 1995.

29. Foo Choy Peng, "Foreign Banks to be Appointed for Pudong Trade," *South China Morning Post*, 19 September 1995.

30. Foo Choy Peng, "High Rollers Queue for Chance of Place in 'Asian Wall Street'," *South China Morning Post*, 8 December 1994.

31. "'Jiuwu' qijian Pudong huo 16 xiang xin youwai zhengce"「九五」期間浦東 獲16項新優惠政策 (Pudong Awarded 16 New Priority Policies in the Ninth Five-year Plan), *Ming bao* 明報 (Ming Pao), 7 September 1995.

32. Murphey, "Shanghai" (see note 4), p. 176.

33. Shanghaishi "Maixiang 21 shiji de Shanghai" keti lingdao xiaozu (ed.), *Maixiang 21 shiji de Shanghai* (see note 16), p. 150.

34. Urban C. Lehner, "As Goes Shanghai, So Goes China," *The Asian Wall Street Journal*, 22 November 1994, S-9.

35. Jesse Wong, "Long Way to Go," *The Asian Wall Street Journal*, 22 November 1994, S-4.

36. Huang Renwei 黃仁偉, "Nianyi shiji 'dongfang da gang' zhanlüe shexiang" 廿一世紀「東方大港」戰略設想 (Strategic Plan for 21st Century 'Eastern Big Port'), *Hua qiao ribao*, 20 December 1994.

37. "Zhongyang pizhun Shanghai jian shenshuigang yu Tai jingzheng" 中央批准 上海建深水港與台競爭 (Central Authorities have Approved Shanghai to Build a Deep-water Port and Compete with Taiwan), *Ming bao*, 23 January 1996. See also Lana Wong, "Shanghai Port Plan Masks Wider Issues," *South China Morning Post*, 9 May 1996.

38. Sir Quo-wei Lee, "Shanghai and Hong Kong: Glowing Eyes of the Dragon," *South China Morning Post*, 6 October 1994.

39. "Hong Kong Biggest Investor in Shanghai," *Hua qiao ribao*, 5 November 1994.

40. A detailed discussion of Hong Kong's future position may be found in Zhu Jianru 朱劍如 (David K. Y. Chu) and Yang Ruwan 楊汝萬 (Y. M. Yeung), "Mianlin 1997 nian huigui Zhongguo de Xianggang diwei yu zuoyou" 面臨 1997年回歸中國的香港地位與作用 (The Position and Role of Hong Kong beyond 1997), in *Huanan diqu jingji fazhan fangxiang ji yu Xianggang, Taiwan, Riben jingji guanxi zhanwang* 華南地區經濟發展方向及與香港、台 灣、日本經濟關係展望 (Prospect of South China's Economy and Its Future's Interdependent Relationships with Hong Kong, Taiwan and Japan), edited by Ma Hong 馬洪 and Shinyasu Hoshino (星野進保) (Shenzhen 深圳: Haitian

chubanshe 海天出版社, 1995), pp. 206–34.

41. Jim Rohwer, "In the Region of Asian Greatness," *South China Morning Post*, 1 December 1995. A similar conclusion is derived from a Hong Kong academic, as found in Chen Wenhong 陳文鴻 (Thomas W. H. Chan), "Xianggang de diwei jiang bei Shanghai quti" 香港的地位將被上海取替 (Hong Kong's Position Will Be Replaced by Shanghai), *Guangjiaojing yuekan* 廣角鏡月刊 (Wide Angle Monthly), December 1993, pp. 46–49.

42. Lee, "Shanghai and Hong Kong," (see note 38). See also Huang Jianzhong 黃建中, "Shanghai neng qudai Xianggang ma?" 上海能取代香港嗎？ (Can Shanghai Replace Hong Kong?), *Xinbao caijing yuekan* 信報財經月刊 (Economic Journal Monthly), No. 224 (November 1995), pp. 54–57.

43. Murphey, *Shanghai* (see note 7), p. 205.

44. Murphey, "Shanghai" (see note 4), p. 181.

2

The Entrepreneurial Spirit
Shanghai and Hong Kong Compared

Wong Siu-lun

Almost as a matter of course, Shanghai and Hong Kong invite comparisons. They are both key urban centres on the China coast. They have both played important roles in the modernization of China. Before the Communist victory in 1949, there is no doubt that Shanghai was head and shoulders above Hong Kong as the leading metropolis. In its glamour, it outshone the British Crown Colony. Its economic prowess dwarfed all other Chinese cities. It had the highest concentration of modern factories and industrial work force in the country. Its manufacturing output made up half of China's foreign trade.[1] It was the cradle of nascent Chinese entrepreneurs, nurturing the largest number of economic innovators.[2]

Matched against such accomplishments, Hong Kong paled in comparison. Before the Second World War, it was essentially an entrepôt with limited industrial resources. As a former Governor of the Colony, Alexander Grantham observed, "Shanghai in pre-communist days was a great cosmopolitan centre; a sort of New York–Paris in an oriental setting. Hong Kong, by comparison, was a small village."[3]

Half a century later, in the 1990s, the economic fortunes of the two cities are reversed. Hong Kong has transformed itself into a thriving metropolis. It prospers as one of the successful "four little dragons" in Asia. Shanghai, on the other hand, has lost its lustre and lagged behind. This reversal of fortunes was initially denied by the Chinese Communist leaders. Resorting to ideological rhetoric during the Maoist era, they extolled Shanghai as the shining model of socialist development and dumped Hong Kong into bourgeois darkness. But as ideological fervour receded and was replaced by Deng's economic reform, the stark disparities between the two cities could no longer be denied.

In 1987, Jiang Zemin 江澤民 , as party secretary of Shanghai, published an article in the party organ *Hongqi* 紅旗 on the development of Shanghai and the necessity to persist on the socialist path. Besides adopting the standard official approach of highlighting Shanghai's accomplishments through a vertical comparison in time, Jiang also attempted a horizontal comparison by placing Shanghai's development alongside that of Hong Kong and Taiwan. He did so apparently because the popular frame of reference had changed as a result of the open policy. Such comparisons were unavoidable, posing threats to the legitimacy of the Communist regime. As Jiang acknowledged in the article, "when we discuss the superiority of socialism, some comrades raise this question: the territory of Hong Kong was originally behind the city of Shanghai. Why are so many of its economic indicators above those of Shanghai now?"[4]

But he sidestepped the issue by proceeding to underscore Hong Kong's special circumstances and its inherent problems and weaknesses as a capitalist economy. He was not prepared to engage in a frank comparison.

Some scholars in Shanghai were more forthright. In 1991, a research group at the Shanghai Academy of Social Sciences published a comprehensive comparison between the two cities. The chief editor of the volume, Yao Xitang 姚錫棠, wrote in the preface:

> If, historically speaking, Shanghai was more prosperous than Hong Kong, then at present, Shanghai is lagging far, far behind Hong Kong in terms of modernization and development. In 1987, the gross national product of Shanghai was US$14.66 billion, with a per capita GNP of US$1,174. The corresponding figures for Hong Kong were US$42.97 billion and US$7,673 respectively. In terms of total GNP, Hong Kong was 2.9 times that of Shanghai. In per capita terms, it was 6.5 times. In the period after the Second World War, particularly in the last 20 years, Hong Kong's economy has attained such rapid development not just because of its superior geographical location and favourable international factors owing to specific historical conditions. Its own successful experience must also play a part. Therefore, it is necessary for Shanghai to learn from the Hong Kong experience during the process of Shanghai–Hong Kong co-operation.[5]

By openly acknowledging Hong Kong's successful experience, Yao implicitly raised the awkward question: what accounts for Shanghai's laggardness? The reasons are varied, as Yao and his associates show in their book. They range from differences in investment milieu, industrial structure and export strategy, to local legislative mechanism, social welfare provision and urban management. However, they have not given due weight to one critical factor — the entrepreneurial spirit as the driving force of economic dynamism.

Shanghai, even in the heyday of Maoism, was not devoid of the innovative drive. But that was a special brand of entrepreneurship which I have called the mainland pattern.[6] It featured the dominance of the party–state in economic affairs, a restrictive supply of innovative agents and the adoption of a bureaucratic form of large managerial hierarchies. As the pillar of the socialist planned economy, Shanghai was the very embodiment of this style of entrepreneurship which has been sorely tested during the reform era. When Shanghai's party leaders initiated a mass campaign in 1992 in an attempt to renew the image of the Shanghainese and to revitalize the pioneering spirit of the city, the managers and party secretaries of state enterprises were still given pride of place in the anticipation that they would transform themselves into bold entrepreneurs.[7]

What was lacking in Shanghai, however, was the external pattern of entrepreneurship found in Hong Kong. That was a style of economic innovation propelled by competitive family firms and flexible sub-contracting networks. During the reform era, this external pattern has spread to Guangdong 廣東 and other parts of southern China, generating forces of dynamic growth. Now that Shanghai has been designated as the spearhead of the next phase of economic reform, will it be receptive to this external pattern of entrepreneurship? Will there be a similar fruitful blending of the mainland and external patterns as seen in Guangdong? To answer these questions, we have to examine the interaction between cultural values and institutional arrangements which shape the wax and wane of the entrepreneurial spirit in Shanghai.

Cultural Values

Anti-traditionalism was a key motif of Maoism, which came to a climax during the Cultural Revolution. As Maoism receded, there was a revived recognition of the importance of traditional values in Chinese economic life. In her book, *The Golden Age of the Chinese Bourgeoisie 1911–1937*, Marie-Claire Bergère demonstrates how the growth of the nascent entrepreneurs in early Republican China was rooted in traditional familial and regional solidarities. "The modernity of this bourgeoisie," she points out, "was thus not based on a break with tradition but on its ability to make tradition serve new objective."[8]

This view finds resonance in Chinese academic circles. In an article, Zhang Xinhua 張新華 of the Shanghai Academy of Social Sciences forcefully endorses the value of traditional culture. He writes,

> Culture is the spiritual pillar of the political structure, the economic system, and social relations; it is the well-spring of social cohesion. The loss of a people's cultural legacy can evoke the destruction of a traditional social structure and a deterioration or loss of national cohesion, leading to social turbulence and confusion. And once traditional culture and social structure undergo turbulence and destruction, a very long time will pass before another stable order can come about. And a new order must be accompanied by the continuity, rebuilding, and flourishing of the traditional culture under new conditions.[9]

The importance of tradition is not only acknowledged intellectually. There is ample evidence of its resurgence on the Chinese mainland, leading to a reinvigoration of entrepreneurship. However, such a resurgence is not "a simple return to the status *quo ante*."[10] As I have argued in the case of Hong Kong, traditional Chinese values are first adapted to a special social context before they become the wellspring of the entrepreneurial drive. That adaptation is a selective process which brings the values of familism, pragmatism, autonomy and personal trust to the fore.[11]

It should also be borne in mind that these values are by no means free of ambivalence and tension. Like other core values in traditional Chinese culture, they are often poised in a state of delicate balance with competing norms, forming pairs of dualistic ethical codes, such as familism vs. statism, pragmatism vs. idealism, autonomy vs. authority and personal trust vs. universalistic trust. Whether they become ascendant depends a great deal on the social and historical milieu.

In pre-liberation Shanghai, they apparently flourished in the milieu of "an enclave culture" or "the other China."[12] In present day Shanghai of the 1990s, these values of familism, pragmatism, autonomy and personal trust are re-emerging, still strong and resilient despite suffering decades of ideological attack. Recent social surveys conducted in the city, notably the study on cultural change by Godwin C. Chu and Yanan Ju,[13] and the biennial social indicators surveys carried out by Lu Hanlong 盧漢龍 of the Institute of Sociology of the Shanghai Academy of Social Sciences,[14] provide clear evidence for such a revival.

Familism

Like their counterparts in Hong Kong, residents in present-day Shanghai still attach great importance to family life. In a volume reviewing the social development of Shanghai in the past forty years, the authors cite survey findings regarding goals in life which show that 93% of the respondents upheld the pursuit of family harmony, 79% valued filial piety, 67% prized children's education, while only 64% subscribed to devotion to the prosperity of the nation and 61% chose to serve the people and the country.[15] Similar results were obtained in the Chu and Ju study. After analyzing their own survey findings, they conclude that "[a] close and warm family and successful children have always been high on the list of desirable ends for Chinese, and they still are."[16]

The norms of mutual assistance and economic reciprocity among family members and close relatives remain strong in Shanghai. In the Chu and Ju survey, they asked their respondents the question: "What will you do if a relative wants to borrow RMB200 from you?" The sum involved was the equivalent of about two month's salary of an average worker. More than half of the respondents, 61.8%, said they would lend the money unconditionally. Only a tiny minority, 2.5%, said no. Significantly, the younger respondents were found to be more willing to lend to their relatives than the older ones. In contrast, when the sample was asked whether they would lend the same sum to their friends, less than half of the respondents, only 43.9%, said they were prepared to do so.[17] When it came to actual assistance offered in times of emergency and misfortune, the 1987 Shanghai social indicators survey discovered that such help was mainly sought within the familial circle. The usual pattern was for those of the older generation to offer assistance and support to their juniors.[18]

Concern for the continuity of the family line constitutes a powerful motivating force for economic endeavours in Chinese families. Such a concern is expressed structurally by the emphasis on the parent–child bond as the core social relationship in the Chinese domestic group. This cultural preference is very much alive in contemporary Shanghai. In the Chu and Ju survey, they discover that a large majority of their respondents endorsed divorce as a solution to marital problems when no children were involved. But once children came into the picture, the endorsement for divorce dropped sharply to a low 34.8%. The supreme importance of children in the family is unmistakable. The parent–child bonds clearly take precedence over husband–wife relations.[19] In another study on family strategies and housing provisions, Deborah Davis has found in her interviews that residents show a clear preference for sons when competing for scarce resources. During the reform era, they sought to provide for needy sons before needy daughters in housing matters, and they were more likely to enter into co-residence arrangements with their male offspring. As Davis observes, "it appeared that after many decades of CCP hegemony in which one might have presumed that ideological supports for traditional preferences would disappear, the onus of providing shelter continued to be a male or patriline responsibility."[20]

Thus, it is evident that familism has revived in Shanghai. But it is not yet clear whether it has regained its full vitality as a social force. Compared with the entrepreneurial form of familism found in Hong Kong,[21] the Shanghai variant appears to be rather weak and inward-looking. Residents in Shanghai seem to treat the family more as a refuge than as a spring board for action. In the 1987 social indicators survey, Lu discovered that the respondents tended to spend most of their leisure time inside the family, either watching television or doing nothing in particular.[22] Very few of them were venturing outside to participate in social forms of recreation and exchange. This inward-looking tendency also attracted the attention of Chu and Ju in their study. "There seems to be a wide discontinuity between what happens within the family and what happens in the society at large," they observed.[23] Such an orientation is probably an adaptation of familism to the specific institutional environment of present-day Shanghai which we shall examine below.

Pragmatism

Prior to 1949, Shanghai provided fertile breeding ground for the development of a pragmatic mentality. A Shanghai ethos, *haipai* 海派 , flourished in the city extolling flexibility and innovation, in contrast to the Beijing ethos, *jingpai* 京派 , which glorified rectitude and traditionalism. The former embodied the brash vitality of the market, while the latter represented the genteel refinement of the court. The pragmatism of the Shanghai ethos found its most vivid expression in the adoption of the hybrid mode of *Pidgin* English in business transactions.[24] In the special environment of Shanghai as a treaty port, as Rudolf Wagner observes, two important elements of mainstream Chinese culture, the honest pursuit of profit and legitimate remonstrance, were accentuated and blossomed.[25]

The rise of Maoism as an ideological orthodoxy after 1949 led to the suppression of the Shanghai ethos. But once Maoism declined, the pragmatic orientation re-emerged. In a survey conducted in 1982, a group of college students in Shanghai was asked about the proper standards for a good youth in the 1980s. Over half of the students said that a good youth should have talent and dedication to work. Only a quarter of them believed that the yardstick should be the possession of Communist ideals.[26] More recently, there have been press reports about a poll conducted about which popular idols are most familiar to Shanghai school pupils. It was found that most of the youngsters knew about the Hong Kong singer, Liu Dehua 劉德華 [Lau Tak-wah], but few were aware of the Communist role model, Lei Feng 雷鋒 .[27]

The pragmatic strain in Chinese culture has religious underpinnings. The absence of an omnipotent god in Chinese religion has led to an incorporative attitude that emphasizes orthopraxy, the importance of practice and behaviour, rather than orthodoxy, the importance of belief and conviction.[28] Seen in this light, we can understand why the adoption of Catholicism in China took the form of blending with rather than rejecting the indigenous tradition of fidelity to family bonds,[29] and why the fervour of Maoism was very much a cultural deviation.

In the environs of Shanghai in the pre-liberation period, we witness a rich and diversified religious life. Buddhist temples and Taoist shrines coexisted with Islamic mosques and Christian churches. There were estimated to be nearly 3,000 such religious institutions in the city, involving more than 9,000 professional religious personnel. This religious diversity was sharply curtailed and suppressed when Maoism became the ruling orthodoxy in China. During the reform era, a more relaxed religious policy was implemented, and 72 religious institutions had been restored in Shanghai by the end of 1988.[30] Though the religious revival is still limited in scale, it is clear testimony to the resurgence of the pragmatic orientation.

Another manifestation of renewed pragmatism in Shanghai can be found in popular attitudes towards work and employment. In the 1987 Shanghai social indicators survey, it was found that among the various factors affecting job satisfaction, respondents were mainly concerned about material rewards and they cared little for work creativity. As Lu Hanlong notes, Shanghai residents show a strong utilitarian attitude in their occupational pursuits, putting material incentives well ahead of spiritual ones.[31] His observations are corroborated by similar survey findings obtained by Chu and Ju. When Chu and Ju asked their respondents to specify their top priority in choosing a new job, high income was the most popular, opportunity for career accomplishment came second, and interest was third.[32]

The Shanghainese have evidently become money-minded again. But it would be superficial to conclude that the renewed pragmatism is nothing more than crass materialism. As recent research in the sociology of economic life has shown, the phenomenon of money is laden with social meaning and thus calls for careful cultural analysis.[33] In this regard, the appearance of the term "Confucian businessmen" (*Rushang* 儒商) as a self label for entrepreneurs in Shanghai and other parts of China is intriguing. This term is not derived from Hong Kong where it has never enjoyed currency. It has apparently been lifted out of the recent intellectual debate about the role of Confucianism in economic development. Whatever its origins, it indicates a felt need to search for a moral framework as a legitimation of entrepreneurial activities. It also represents a conscious attempt on the part of the intelligentsia in the PRC to transform themselves into modern businessmen, through the blending of the literati and mercantile traditions, itself a collective act of pragmatism tinged with considerable ambivalence.[34]

Autonomy

In Hong Kong, the entrepreneurial impulse is sustained by a powerful urge to achieve the goal of becoming an owner, *dang laoban* 當老闆 . The desire is to attain autonomy of action and to avoid being subordinate to others.[35] In Shanghai, a strong achievement motivation is also palpable. There is also a discernible urge for autonomy. However, that urge is channelled mainly towards the pursuit of professional expertise rather than self-employment.

Despite three decades of socialist egalitarianism, the ethic of hard work has not diminished in importance as a normative value among Shanghai residents. When respondents in the Chu and Ju survey were asked about the key elements for career success, they attached the greatest importance to diligence, followed by personal qualifications and drive and ambition.[36] The work ethic is translated into remarkably high educational aspirations for one's children. More than 80% of the Chu and Ju sample said they were prepared to support their sons and daughters through university or graduate school.[37] Another survey of 1,141 households conducted in 1988 came up with similar findings. About 71% of the parents stated that they hoped their children would obtain university degrees, and they were actually investing heavily for their children's education as shown in the pattern of their household expenditures.[38]

What jobs do Shanghai parents want for their children when they join the workforce? The answer is clear: professional and technical occupations. In the 1988 survey, 53% of the parents chose scientific researcher, engineer and scientific technician as ideal jobs for their offspring.[39] In the Chu and Ju study, they find a similar enthusiasm for scientific and technical jobs which were endorsed by 33% of the respondents as ideal for their sons.[40]

The underlying rationale for such a choice is apparently a craving for autonomy and freedom from authority, since the survey findings reveal an equally clear rejection of the exercise of power as a desirable career path. Chu and Ju find that very few of their respondents, just a tiny 3.4%, wanted their sons to become party or government cadres.[41] In the Shanghai social indicators survey, respondents were asked to specify the main factors they would like their children to consider in their choice of occupations. The most important factor, in their view, pertained to the work environment and conditions. The least important factor turned out to be the amount of power attached to the position.[42]

Thus, it is evident that the political route of advancement, or "cadrefication," has suffered a sharp devaluation in Shanghai. However, unlike the case in rural Hungary under the economic reform,[43] the decline of the political route has not led to a commensurate rise in the attractiveness of the entrepreneurial path of upward mobility. Self-employment is hardly a favoured option in Shanghai. In the Chu and Ju survey, self-employed occupations are least preferred by the respondents as desirable jobs for their sons, with less than 1% of the sample choosing them. In contrast, when Korean respondents were asked the same question in a recent survey, 30% of the sample indicated a preference for self-employment for their sons.[44] In the case of Hong Kong, the desire for self-employment was also very strong. The 1988 social indicators survey discovered that "starting one's own business," chosen by 41% of the sample, ranked first as the best upward mobility route.[45]

The weak urge for self-employment found in Shanghai is striking and calls for an explanation. The cause probably does not lie in the realm of values, as the general desire for autonomy seems to be alive and well, but rather in the realm of the institutional arrangements, an issue we shall discuss after we have examined the core value of personal trust.

Trust

The ethic of trust is central to entrepreneurial activities. In the Chinese case, business trust is mainly built on the basis of personal connections (*guanxi* 關係) and mutual obligations (*renqing* 人情). During the Maoist period, this particularistic form of personal trust was severely criticized. Attempts were made to replace it with the universalistic ethic of comradeship based on common ideals. As ideological fervour receded during the reform era, personal trust resurfaced and *guanxi* proliferated.

Chu and Ju find that the overwhelming majority of their respondents in Shanghai attached importance to network connections. Only a few, less than 8%, said that connections were not important. Significantly, they found that the young people in their sample tended to attach greater importance to connections than the older ones, indicating that reliance on *guanxi* is probably a rising trend. When they probed the issue of *renqing* by posing the question: "Suppose a friend wants your help to ask someone to do something. You are able to do it, but it will give you some inconvenience. What will you do?" — about two-thirds of the respondents expressed a willingness to help.[46] Clearly both *guanxi* and *renqing* are regarded as important by Shanghai residents.

Personal connections and obligations are usually lubricated with gifts and favours. In the Shanghai social indicators survey, Lu discovers that the great majority of the respondents had monthly expenditures for gifts and entertainment which used an average 6.3% of their household budgets. Such expenditures were only slightly less than the sum spent on clothing, which was 7.3%.[47] Other commentators have also noted that giving gifts has become an important part of social life in Shanghai. Wedding gifts went up in monetary value from the puritanical level of RMB5 just after 1949 to the lavish level of RMB200 to RMB300 in the late 1980s. For various reasons, cigarettes have emerged as the major currency in the exchange of gifts and favours. As one Shanghai author observed wryly, "In matters big and small, whether they be doing business or finding your way, you need to have cigarettes to smooth the path. On social occasions, you can hardly get anything done without cigarettes."[48]

Though Shanghai residents clearly endorse the importance and utility of personal trust, they do so not without ambivalence. An undercurrent of mistrust and suspicion exists. There is suspicion about leaders who rely on *guanxi*. When respondents in the Chu and Ju survey were asked about what qualifications a good leader should have, having "good outside connections" was evaluated negatively and relegated to the bottom of the list.[49] Such a response is probably a reflection of the fact that personal trust is not a form of public good generating benefits for all. It is basically particularistic in nature, with rewards accruing to specific individuals and cliques.

There is also popular suspicion about strangers. In the Chu and Ju survey, an overwhelming majority of the respondents, about 85%, said they would not trust someone they met for the first time until they got to know him better.[50] Such mistrust is widely shared among the sample, with no significant variations found in terms of age, education or other variables. Another manifestation of mistrust can be detected in the remote neighbourhood relationship. Nearly half of the sample revealed that they hardly ever chat or spend leisure time with their neighbours.[51] Therefore, it is not surprising to find that the social networks of Shanghai residents are, in fact, rather limited and seldom extend beyond the immediate circles of kin and work units,[52] in spite of their expressed belief in the importance of the ethic of trust in principle.

This discrepancy between actual behaviour and expressed belief is the product of adaptation to a special social context. In many ways, the resurgent values of familism, pragmatism, autonomy and trust are not thriving as robustly as they are in Hong Kong because of social structural constraints existing in Shanghai today. The revival of cultural values conducive to entrepreneurship is still hindered by institutional fetters.

Institutional Fetters

The fetters which restrain the entrepreneurial spirit in Shanghai are not just economic ones. Obviously, the rigidity imposed by central economic planning plays a part. But the barriers created by attempts at social engineering since 1949 are equally important. After Liberation, the Chinese Communist Party (CCP) tried to overhaul the social order and to create a new form of social integration. It sought to impose an omnipotent mode of social control. However, just as in the economic realm, such control never really succeeded in becoming all powerful and pervasive. Unevenness in implementation existed, for instance, between the cities and the countryside. Among the large cities, Shanghai was singled out for special treatment. It was put under particularly tight rein, apparently because it was the symbol of bourgeois capitalism in the pre-liberation days. The CCP was bent on taming the shrew. The draconian social policies adopted for this purpose, such as purging the city of its old sins, restricting migration, transforming the occupational structure and controlling fertility, served wittingly or unwittingly to dampen the entrepreneurial spirit among Shanghai residents.

Damaged Identity

Since its rise to power, the CCP has pursued a relentless policy of instilling collective guilt in Shanghai by stigmatizing its past. Even during the reform period, CCP leaders have continued to harp on the negative stereotype which they had created for old Shanghai. For example, Jiang Zemin started his 1987 article on Shanghai's development with the standard refrain, "Before Liberation, it was a microcosm of old China. It reflected in a concentrated form the major contradictions and various pathologies of the colonial, semi-colonial and semi-feudal society. After Liberation, as the important economic centre and industrial base of our nation, its development fully manifested the vitality and superiority of the socialist system."[53]

In order to cleanse the guilt of a degenerate past, the Shanghainese demonstrated repentance by devoting themselves collectively to serving the nation, particularly through tangible financial contributions to the central coffers. When scholars at the Shanghai Academy of Social Sciences touched on the subject of Shanghai's fiscal burden in their comparative study of Shanghai and Hong Kong, they adopted the emotive language of pride mixed with implied guilt:

> After Shanghai's economic take-off [in 1949], Shanghai citizens with high patriotic spirit selflessly offered 86.3% of the wealth they had created to the socialist motherland, propelling the development of the entire national economy. According to the statistics, in the forty years since 1950, out of a total gross national [regional] product of RMB476.9 billion, about RMB411.7 billion has been directed to aiding construction of the whole nation.[54]

Thus, Shanghai has become the cash cow of the Chinese economy, and the heavy fiscal extractions from the city have clearly blunted its entrepreneurial responses during the reform era.[55]

More recently, Shanghai scholars and opinion leaders have been taking cautious steps to repair the damaged identity of their community by reconstructing its history and by casting its past entrepreneurial activities in a more positive light.[56] However, it will take considerable time to put the damaged identity together again. The terror of the various anti-bourgeois purges culminating in the Cultural Revolution have left deep scars in the psyche of the Shanghai community which is instilled with an ingrained inclination to seek self-preservation. It is little wonder that most of the Shanghainese have been found to be risk aversive and low in pioneering spirit when the Chinese economy is being reformed.[57] It would be the height of folly for them to take the lead in treading the tightrope between socialism and capitalism.

The former entrepreneurial identity of Shanghai cannot be quickly restored not only because of past traumas. Another contributing factor is the establishment of a new pattern of power distribution in the city which perpetuates a hostile stance towards the bourgeois past. For a long time, regional tension and social discrimination existed between the majority of the Shanghainese hailing from Jiangnan 江南 and the minority coming from Subei 蘇北 .[58] The Subei people formed the underclass in pre-war Shanghai. Their fortunes changed after 1949 and many of them became members of the new political élite. They were unlikely to be sympathetic to the old economic élites who used to look down upon them. As Emily Honig points out:

> The communist soldiers who crossed the Yangzi River and liberated Shanghai, members of the New Fourth Army, came mostly from Subei. After Liberation, many were appointed officials and cadres in the city government. So well recognized is the political prestige of Subei people (currently both the Mayor and Communist Party Secretary of Shanghai hail from Subei) that when citizens are dissatisfied, they commonly say, "No wonder we have so many problems — our leaders are all from Subei!"[59]

Migration Control

Similar to Hong Kong, pre-war Shanghai was a city of sojourners.[60] Its vitality was sustained by a massive movement in and out of the city of people searching for economic opportunities. After the establishment of the PRC, this freedom of geographical mobility was sharply curtailed. Migration was subject to stringent controls, particularly after the imposition of the household registration system in the late 1950s. While inward migration to the city was officially discouraged, the government implemented several large-scale outward migration programmes which reduced the size of the urban population. On the whole, it is estimated that Shanghai experienced a net loss of about 384,000 persons in the past forty years as a result of regulated internal migration.[61]

Pre-war Shanghai was also a cosmopolitan city. It had a sizable foreign business community composed of more than fifty nationalities. At its height, there were estimated to be nearly 150,000 foreigners living there.[62] After Liberation, most of the foreigners left. Shanghai then became essentially a Chinese city. International migration, including the emigration of Shanghai residents to foreign countries, was reduced to a minimum. During the climax of the Cultural Revolution, from 1966 to 1970, only 80 persons were granted permission to emigrate from Shanghai.[63]

This strict control on migration has had several repercussions on entrepreneurship. First, it has led to a loss of social diversity and pluralism. Deviant groups and those with bourgeois class backgrounds were banished from the city. For instance, most former prostitutes were sent back to their native villages or assigned to state farms in remote rural areas.[64] Second, it

resulted in a dissipation of skilled manpower and educated talent. As Lynn
T. White III points out in Chapter 17, a total of about 1.4 million Shanghai
people, of whom about 30% were technicians, emigrated to help other
regions during the last thirty years. Therefore, by the mid-1980s, in comparison with other major cities, Shanghai had fewer scientists and technicians employed in its state sector. Also a lower proportion of its
population held university degrees.[65] Third, it created a stationary urban
population with weak external networks. As Chu and Ju point out, "An
overwhelming majority of Chinese spend their entire lives in the same
general area where they were born. People born in Shanghai live their
entire lives in Shanghai. People born in Qingpu 青浦 stay in Qingpu."[66]

During the reform era, official controls on migration have been
relaxed. Geographical mobility in and out of Shanghai has quickened and
generated an emergent entrepreneurial momentum. But the scale of the
mobility is still quite limited relative to the huge size of the city's population which stood at 12.8 million in 1990. Three groups of recent migrants
are particularly noteworthy. The first group consists of the emigrants who
are given permission to settle abroad. Between 1980 and 1989, an estimated 175,300 persons applied for passports to leave Shanghai. The rising
trend of emigration from the city is confirmed by the 1990 Population
Census which records 66,336 persons from Shanghai residing abroad
when the census was taken. The Shanghai figure is the highest in the
country, making up 28% of the total legal emigrants from China. These
emigrants tend to have higher educational backgrounds than the general
population in Shanghai. As such, they represent an immediate brain drain
from the city.[67] But in the longer term, as in the case of Hong Kong,[68] it is
likely that these emigrants will contribute to the creation of external business linkages with their native home.

The second group includes the legal migrants who have been allowed
to transfer their household registrations into Shanghai. Between 1985 and
1990, these legal migrants amounted to about 407,000 persons. The
majority were highly educated, and they tended to be recruited into Shanghai to become administrators and professionals in the state and other public
sectors.[69]

The most entrepreneurial is the third group who have moved into
Shanghai without transferring their household registration. They are the
semi-legal or illegal migrants who are tolerated by the state, amounting to
488,000 persons in 1990. In many ways, they are similar to the illegal
immigrants who escaped from Guangdong to Hong Kong after 1949 and

who later became small factory owners.[70] Because they were barred from entering most of the stable occupations in Shanghai, these tolerated migrants had to find livelihood in fluctuating industrial and commercial pursuits. They were forced to seek advancement by the risky entrepreneurial path. But because they originate predominantly from rural areas and have a low level of education,[71] they are handicapped by a lack of both physical and human capital. Thus, it is unlikely that they will constitute a vigorous entrepreneurial force at least for some time to come.

Occupational Inertia

After Liberation, the CCP transformed Shanghai into the foremost industrial centre of the country, with a high concentration of heavy industries in addition to light manufacture. As the core city in the national planned economy, Shanghai was both the cash cow as well as the major beneficiary of the socialist economic system. In return for its large financial contributions to the central budget, Shanghai enjoyed various implicit subsidies in the form of state regulated prices and supplies.[72] With its vested interest in the system of central planning, it was not keen to champion the economic reforms towards a market economy. Thus, even in the 1990s, the state sector remained dominant in Shanghai and still overshadowed the non-state sector. For example, in the 1993 Shanghai social indicators survey, Lu finds that the great majority of the respondents, about 77.8%, were employed in state-owned enterprises. Only 16.7% and 5.5% were working in collectively owned and marketized enterprises, respectively.[73]

Most residents in Shanghai, as workers in state enterprises, used to enjoy a high level of job security, in addition to various political and economic benefits. As members of the labour aristocracy, they formed the political base supporting the rule of the CCP. The mutual dependency of the Shanghai proletariat and the CCP is shown in the pattern of job allocation. As late as 1991, Shanghai workers still relied heavily on the system of state allocation. In a survey conducted by Lin Nan 林南 in the three cities of Beijing 北京, Shanghai and Tianjin 天津, it was found that Shanghai had the highest percentage of respondents, some 87.1%, whose first jobs were obtained through state allocation.[74]

In China's state sector, enterprises were organized in the form of *danwei* 單位 or work units. These *danwei* functioned as self-sufficient entities that catered to virtually every need of its members. They created urban villages in large cities such as Shanghai, which workers joined for life. As a result, occupational mobility was kept to a minimum. For instance, Lu discovers in the 1993 social indicators survey that two-thirds of the Shanghai respondents never changed their work unit.[75] Even though market reforms progressively diminished the value of the benefits that state-owned work units could provide, the welfare benefits remained substantial enough to keep the majority of Shanghai workers in their fold. One of the critical resources still controlled by these work units was highly subsidized housing. Occupational mobility tends to yield a negative return in this regard. As Deborah Davis finds, among the twenty-one families with the worst housing whom she had interviewed, 24% of the male heads of household were highly mobile, having worked in four or more units between 1950 and 1987. But among the ten families that lived in the most spacious quarters, none of the fathers were occupationally mobile.[76]

Thus, the cost for Shanghai workers of venturing out of their work units for self-employment or other entrepreneurial pursuits was very high. Faced with the growing attraction of the market sector, they resorted to the strategy of "the integration of two systems" which represented an attempt to derive maximum benefits from both the planned and the marketized sectors, while avoiding the associated costs. As noted by Lu, the adoption of such a strategy pervaded the Shanghai economy.[77] At the enterprise level, work units were retaining state-owned operations while trying to forge joint ventures with foreign investors. At the family level, husband and wife tended to go separate ways occupationally, with one venturing out to the marketized sector and the other remaining in the security of the state sector. At the individual level, more and more workers were taking up multiple jobs, moonlighting, or taking extended leave from state employment in order to test the waters in the market. The proliferation of these hybrid modes of economic activities had its own dynamism. But by clinging to security blankets and safety cushions, these hybrid activities were not particularly conducive to the single-minded pursuit of entrepreneurial opportunities.

Birth Control

When the reform policy was initiated in the late 1970s, it led to a reduction of state intervention in the economy. But in at least one crucial area of social policies, that of fertility planning, the state actually increased its control tremendously. Through legislation and other strict measures, each couple was permitted only one child. The one-child policy met with various forms of resistance and difficulties throughout the country, but it was implemented very successfully in Shanghai.

The 1990 Population Census reveals that among all the administrative regions, Shanghai had the highest rate of singletons among its new-born babies and the lowest birth rate. Since 1983, over 96% of the infants born in the city annually have been the only children in their families. This led to a rapid decrease in the natural growth rate of Shanghai's population. In 1989, the rate of natural population growth in Shanghai was 4.96 per thousand, much lower than the rate of 9.70 per thousand in 1981. It is estimated that by 1997, if the variable of migration is held constant, Shanghai will begin to experience a negative rate of natural population growth at about −0.5 per thousand. This decrease in population will continue and will reach a rate of −1.7 per thousand by the year 2000.[78]

The success of the one-child policy in Shanghai has been welcomed by Chinese political leaders as it reduces the immediate economic burden imposed on the state through demographic pressures. But it may not bode well for the rise of entrepreneurship in the city because of several unintended consequences of the policy. First of all, as a result of the strict birth control measures, the population of Shanghai is ageing rapidly. The number of old people aged 60 and above will increase from about 1,891,000 persons in 1990 to 2,378,900 in 2000, an increase of 25.8% within one decade.[79] An ageing population is not conducive to entrepreneurial activities, as studies have shown that economic innovations are essentially youthful activities undertaken by people in their prime. The expanding proportion of the elderly in the population will also lead to a high dependency ratio that will constitute a drag on economic risk-taking. Second, the policy tends to produce a young generation of singletons who are more home-bound and less likely to migrate to seek economic opportunities elsewhere. As the only children in their families, their parents will be extremely reluctant to see them leave home. Like the eldest sons in the past, they will have a particularly heavy filial duty to take care of their parents. But worse than in the past, there will be no other siblings to share the responsibility. Then, lastly, the young generation of Shanghai residents will have very few relatives in their kinship networks. The opportunities for obtaining financial and other forms of assistance to start business ventures will be greatly reduced.[80]

Conclusion

In pursuing the reform policy since the late 1970s, Chinese leaders such as Deng Xiaoping 鄧小平 have emphasized the need to create inside the PRC several economic centres modelled after Hong Kong. When Shanghai was recently designated to assume the role of the "dragon head" in the economic reform and development process, there was widespread expectation both within and without China that it would soon be rejuvenated and surpass Hong Kong again as a metropolis.

But as far as entrepreneurship is concerned, as I hope to have shown in the above analysis, the prospects for Shanghai are mixed. There are clear signs of the resurgence of the core cultural values supporting innovative endeavours. But there also exist strong institutional barriers constraining the entrepreneurial spirit. As a result, we tend to find many enterprising Shanghainese as individuals, but not an enterprising Shanghai as a community. The innovators are flourishing outside of Shanghai, either in the rural enterprises in the Yangzi River Delta, or in the Special Economic Zones, such as Shenzhen 深圳, that were created from scratch. But it is important to bear in mind that the Hong Kong style of private entrepreneurship is not the only path towards economic innovation and prosperity. Given an institutional heritage that cannot be dismantled overnight, it is quite natural for Shanghai to be attracted to the Singapore model, with an emphasis on state-directed entrepreneurship. Therefore, at least in the foreseeable future, it is most likely that Shanghai and Hong Kong will retain their distinctiveness as economic centres, each displaying its own style of entrepreneurship.

Notes

1. Rhoads Murphey, *Shanghai: Key to Modern China* (Cambridge: Harvard University Press, 1953), p. 3.
2. Marie-Claire Bergère, *The Golden Age of the Chinese Bourgeoisie 1911–1937* (Cambridge: Cambridge University Press, 1989), pp. 99–139.
3. Alexander Grantham, *Via Ports: From Hong Kong to Hong Kong* (Hong Kong: Hong Kong University Press, 1965), pp. 104–105.
4. Jiang Zemin 江澤民, "Cong Shanghai de fazhan tan bixu jianchi shehuizhuyi daolu" 從上海的發展談必須堅持社會主義道路 (From Shanghai's Development to the Need to Persist Following the Socialist Path), *Hongqi* (Red Flag), No. 11 (1987), p. 8.
5. Yao Xitang 姚錫棠 (ed.), *Shanghai Xianggang bijiao yanjiu* 上海香港比較研

究 (A Comparative Study of Shanghai and Hong Kong) (Shanghai: Shanghai renmin chubanshe 上海人民出版社, 1990), p. 2.

6. Wong Siu-lun, "Chinese Entrepreneurship and Economic Development," in *China after Socialism: In the Footsteps of Eastern Europe on East Asia?*, edited by Barrett McCormick and Jonathan Unger (New York: M. E. Sharpe, 1996), pp. 130–148.

7. Zhonggong Shanghai shiwei xuanchuanbu 中共上海市委宣傳部 (ed.), *Jiushi niandai Shanghairen xingxiang* 九十年代上海人形象 (The Image of the Shanghainess in the 1990s) (Shanghai: renmin chubanshe, 1993), pp. 143–49.

8. Bergere, *The Golden Age of the Chinese Bourgeoisie, 1911–1937* (see note 2), p. 185.

9. Zhang Xinhua 張新華, "Lun yi chuantong wenhua wei yuanquan jianshe shehuizhuyi xin wenhua" 論以傳統文化爲源泉建設社會主義新文化 (On Using Traditional Culture as a Wellspring to Build a Socialist New Culture), *Shehui kexue* 社會科學 (Social Sciences), No. 3 (1990), p. 104; quoted in Lucian W. Pye, "How China's Nationalism was Shanghaied," *The Australian Journal of Chinese Affairs*, No. 29 (1993), p. 129.

10. Deborah Davis and Stevan Harrell, "Introduction: The Impact of Post-Mao Reforms on Family Life," in *Chinese Families in the Post-Mao Era*, edited by Deborah Davis and Stevan Harrell (Berkeley: University of California Press, 1993), p. 21.

11. Wong Siu-lun, "Modernization and Chinese Culture in Hong Kong," *The China Quarterly*, No. 106 (1986), pp. 306–25; and Wong Siu-lun, "Chinese Entrepreneurs and Business Trust," in *Business Networks and Economic Development in East and Southeast Asia*, edited by Gary G. Hamilton (Hong Kong: Centre of Asian Studies, University of Hong Kong, 1991), pp. 13–29.

12. Lucian W. Pye, "China's Nationalism"; Marie-Claire Bergere, "The Other China: Shanghai from 1919 to 1949," in *Shanghai: Revolution and Development in an Asian Metropolis*, edited by Christopher Howe (Cambridge: Cambridge University Press, 1981), pp. 1–34.

13. Godwin C. Chu and Yanan Ju, *The Great Wall in Ruins: Communication and Cultural Change in China* (Albany: State University of New York Press, 1993) (hereafter cited as *Great Wall in Ruins*). Chu and Ju conducted a survey in 1987 on a probability sample of 2,000 respondents, including 1,199 from metropolitan Shanghai and the rest from Qingpu 青浦, a rural county outside Shanghai.

14. Lu Hanlong 盧漢龍, "Laizi geti de shehui baogao — Shanghai shimin de shenghuo zhiliang fenxi" 來自個體的社會報告 — 上海市民的生活質量分析 (Social Report from the Individuals: Analysis of the Shanghai People's Quality of Life), *Shehuixue yanjiu* 社會學研究 (Sociological Studies), No. 1 (1990), pp. 71–91 (hereafter cited as "Shanghai shimin de shenghuo zhiliang

fenxi"); Lu Hanlong, "Yingxiang shimin shenghuo suzhi zhi zhu yinsu fenxi" 影響市民生活素質之諸因素分析 (An Analysis of the Various Factors Affecting Citizens' Quality of Life), in *Huaren shehui shehui zhibiao yanjiu de fazhan* 華人社會社會指標研究的發展 (The Development of Social Indicators Research in Chinese Societies), edited by Liu Zhaojia 劉兆佳 (Lau Siu-kai), Li Mingkun 李明堃 (Lee Ming-kwan), Yin Baoshan 尹寶珊 (Wan Po-san) and Huang Shaolun 黃紹倫 (Wong Siu-lun) (Hong Kong: Hong Kong Institute of Asia-Pacific Studies, The Chinese University of Hong Kong, 1992), pp. 101–18; Lu Hanlong, "Zhiye xuanze yu jiuye shenghuo zhiliang" 職業選擇與就業生活質量 (Choice of Occupation and Quality of Life in Employment), paper presented at the second conference on Social Indicators Research in Chinese Societies held at The Chinese University of Hong Kong, 27–29 April 1995.

15. Deng Weizhi 鄧偉志, Wu Xiuyi 吳修藝 and Hu Shensheng 胡申生 (eds.), *Shanghai shehui fazhan sishi nian* 上海社會發展四十年 (Forty Years of Social Development in Shanghai) (Shanghai: Zhishi chubanshe 知識出版社, 1991), p. 46.

16. Chu and Ju, *Great Wall in Ruins* (see note 13), p. 195.

17. Chu and Ju, *Great Wall in Ruins* (see note 13), pp. 87–89. For similar findings concerning financial help among parents and married children who were living apart in Tianjin 天津 in 1984, see Jonathan Unger, "Urban Families in the Eighties: An Analysis of Chinese Surveys," in *Chinese Families in the Post-Mao Era*, edited by Deborah Davis and Stevan Harrell (see note 10), p. 41.

18. Lu, "Shanghai shimin de shenghuo zhiliang fenxi" (see note 14), p. 73.

19. Chu and Ju, *Great Wall in Ruins* (see note 13), pp. 77–79.

20. Deborah Davis, "Urban Households: Supplicants to a Socialist State," in *Chinese Families in the Post-Mao Era*, edited by Davis and Harrell (see note 10), p. 64.

21. Wong Siu-lun, "The Applicability of Asian Family Values to Other Socio-cultural Settings," in *In Search of an East Asian Development Model*, edited by Peter L. Berger and Hsin-huang Michael Hsiao (New Brunswick: Transaction Books, 1988), pp. 134–52.

22. Lu, "Shanghai shimin de shenghuo zhiliang fenxi" (see note 14), p. 83.

23. Chu and Ju, *Great Wall in Ruins* (see note 13), p. 314.

24. Zhang Zhongli 張仲禮 (ed.), *Jindai Shanghai chenshi yanjiu* 近代上海城市研究 (Urban Studies on Modern Shanghai) (Shanghai: Shanghai renmin chubanshe, 1990), pp. 1148–49.

25. Rudolf G. Wagner, "The Role of the Foreign Community in the Chinese Public Sphere," *The China Quarterly*, No. 142 (1995), p. 431.

26. Cited in Stanley Rosen, "Value Change among Post-Mao Youth: The Evidence from Survey Data," in *Unofficial China: Popular Culture and Thought in the People's Republic*, edited by Perry Link, Richard Madsen and

Paul G. Pickowicz (Boulder: Westview Press, 1989), p. 201.

27. *Hong Kong Economic Journal*, 17 September 1995, p. 3.

28. See Wong, "Modernization and Chinese Culture in Hong Kong" (see note 11); James L. Watson, *The Renegotiation of Chinese Cultural Identity in the Post-Mao Era* (Occasional Paper No. 4) (Hong Kong: Social Sciences Research Centre and Department of Sociology, University of Hong Kong, 1991).

29. Richard Madsen, "The Catholic Church in China: Cultural Contradictions, Institutional Survival, and Religious Renewal," in *Unofficial China*, edited by Link, Madsen and Pickowicz (see note 26), pp. 103–20.

30. See Deng, Wu and Hu (eds.), *Shanghai shehui fazhan sishi* nian (see note 15), pp. 212–18.

31. Lu, "Shanghai shimin de shenghuo zhiliang fenxi" (see note 14), pp. 76–77.

32. Chu and Ju, *Great Wall in Ruins* (see note 13), p. 109.

33. See Viviana A. Zelizer, "The Social Meaning of Money: 'Special Monies'," *American Journal of Sociology*, Vol. 95 (1989), pp. 342–77.

34. Gu Yingchun 谷迎春, "'Rusheng xianxiang' xi" "儒商現象" 析 (An Analysis of the Phenomenon of "Confucian Businessman"), *Shehuixue yanjiu*, No. 4 (1995), pp. 13–18.

35. See Wong, "Modernization and Chinese Culture in Hong Kong" (see note 11). For similar findings in Taiwan, see Stevan Harrell, "Why Do the Chinese Work So Hard?" *Modern China*, No. 11 (1985), pp. 203–27; and Richard W. Stites, "Industrial Work as an Entrepreneurial Strategy," *Modern China*, No. 11 (1985), pp. 227–45.

36. Chu and Ju, *Great Wall in Ruins* (see note 13), p. 183.

37. Ibid., p. 204.

38. Deng, Wu and Hu (eds.), *Shanghai shehui fazhan sishi nian* (see note 15), p. 30.

39. Ibid., p. 30.

40. Chu and Ju, *Great Wall in Ruins* (see note 13), p. 206.

41. Ibid., p. 206.

42. Lu, "Shanghai shimin de shenghuo zhiliang fenxi" (see note 14), pp. 77–78.

43. Ivan Szelenyi, *Socialist Entrepreneurs: Embourgeoisement in Rural Hungary* (Cambridge: Polity Press, 1988).

44. Chu and Ju, *Great Wall in Ruins* (see note 13), pp. 296–97.

45. Thomas W. P. Wong, "Inequality, Stratification and Mobility," in *Indicators of Social Development: Hong Kong 1988*, edited by Lau Siu-kai, Lee Ming-kwan, Wan Po-san and Wong Siu-lun (Hong Kong: Hong Kong Institute of Asia–Pacific Studies, The Chinese University of Hong Kong, 1991), p. 164.

46. Chu and Ju, *Great Wall in Ruins* (see note 13), pp. 151, 190.

47. Lu, "Shanghai shimin de shenghuo zhiliang fenxi" (see note 14), pp. 79–80.

48. Deng, Wu and Hu (eds.), *Shanghai shehui fazhan sishi nian* (see note 15), p. 258.

49. Chu and Ju, *Great Wall in Ruins* (see note 13), pp. 133-34.
50. Ibid., p. 100.
51. Ibid., pp. 93, 100.
52. Lu, "Shanghai shimin de shenghuo zhiliang fenxi" (see note 14), p. 73.
53. Jiang, "Cong Shanghai de fazhan tan bixu jianchi shehuizhuyi daolu" (see note 4), p. 6.
54. Yao (ed.), *Shanghai Xianggang bijiao yanjiu* (see note 5), p. 23.
55. See Lynn T. White III, *Shanghai Shanghaied? Uneven Taxes in Reform China* (Hong Kong: Centre of Asian Studies, University of Hong Kong, 1989) (hereafter cited as *Shanghai Shanghaied?*).
56. See Zhang Zhongli (ed.), *Jindai Shanghai chengshi yanjiu* (see note 24); Yue Zheng 樂正, *Jindai Shanghairen shehui xintai 1860-1910* 近代上海人社會心態 1860-1910 (The Social Ethos of the Modern Shanghainese 1860-1910) (Shanghai: Shanghai renmin chubanshe, 1991); and Zhonggong Shanghai shiwei xuanchuanbu (ed.), *Jiushi niandai Shanghairen xingxiang* (see note 7).
57. Chu and Ju, *Great Wall in Ruins* (see note 13), pp. 296-97; and Zhonggong Shanghai shiwei xuanchuanbu (ed.), *Jiushi niandai Shanghairen xingxiang* (see note 7), p. 5.
58. Jiangnan includes the Ningbo 寧波 / Shaoxing 紹興 area of Zhejiang 浙江 and the Wuxi 無錫 / Changzhou 常州 area of Jiangsu 江蘇, while Subei refers to the part of Jiangsu north of the Yangzi River.
59. Emily Honig, "Pride and Prejudice: Subei People in Contemporary Shanghai," in *Unofficial China*, edited by Link, Madsen and Pickowicz (see note 26), p. 144.
60. See Frederic Wakeman, Jr., and Wen-hsin Yeh (eds.), *Shanghai Sojourners* (Berkeley: Institute of East Asian Studies, University of California at Berkeley, 1992).
61. Deng, Wu and Hu (eds.), *Shanghai shehui fazhan sishi nian* (see note 15), p. 15.
62. See Zou Yiren 鄒依仁, *Jiu Shanghai renkou bianqian de yanjiu* 舊上海人口變遷的研究 (A Study of the Changes in Population of Old Shanghai) (Shanghai: Shanghai renmin chubanshe, 1980), pp. 66-84; Wakeman and Yeh (eds.), *Shanghai Sojourners* (see note 60), p. 1.
63. Miao Jianhua, "International Migration in China: A Survey of Emigrants from Shanghai," *Asian and Pacific Migration Journal*, Vol. 3, Nos. 2-3 (1994), p. 448.
64. Christian Henriot, "'La Fermeture': The Abolition of Prostitution in Shanghai, 1949-58," *The China Quarterly*, No. 142 (1995), p. 483.
65. White III, *Shanghai Shanghaied?* (see note 55), p. 24.
66. Chu and Ju, *Great Wall in Ruins* (see note 13), p. 276.
67. Miao, "International Migration in China" (see note 63), pp. 449-50; 453-54.
68. See Ronald Skeldon (ed.), *Emigration from Hong Kong* (Hong Kong: The

Chinese University Press, 1995).

69. Zhou Zugen 周祖根, "Da chengshi qianyi renkou yanjiu" 大城市遷移人口研
    究 (A Study of Population Migration in a Large City), in *Jiushi niandai
    Shanghai renkou* 九十年代上海人口 (Shanghai's Population in the 1990s),
    edited by Shanghaishi renkou pucha bangongshi 上海市人口普查辦公室
    (Shanghai: Zhongguo tongji chubanshe 中國統計出版社, 1992), pp. 55–62.

70. See Victor Fung-shuen Sit and Siu-lun Wong, *Small and Medium Industries
    in an Export-oriented Economy: The Case of Hong Kong* (Hong Kong: Centre
    of Asian Studies, University of Hong Kong, 1989).

71. Zhou, "Da chengshi qianyi renkou yanjiu" (see note 69), pp. 56–63.

72. See White III, *Shanghai Shanghaied?* (see note 55), pp. 9–12.

73. Lu, "Zhiye xuanze yu jiuye shenghuo zhiliang" (see note 14), p. 13.

74. Quoted in Ibid., p. 6.

75. Ibid., p. 6.

76. Davis, "Urban Households" (see note 20), p. 75.

77. Lu, "Shanghai shimin de shenghuo zhiliang fenxi" (see note 14), p. 5.

78. See Shanghaishi renkou pucha bangongshi (ed.), *Jiushi niandai Shanghai
    renkou* (see note 69), pp. 115, 180; Deng, Wu and Hu (eds.), *Shanghai shehui
    fazhan sishi nian* (see note 15), p. 13.

79. See Shanghaishi renkou pucha bangongshi (ed.), *Jiushi niandai Shanghai
    renkou* (see note 69), p. 120.

80. For a more extended discussion of the ramifications of the one child policy,
    see Wong Siu-lun, "Consequences of China's New Population Policy," *The
    China Quarterly*, No. 98 (1984), pp. 220–40.

3

The Political Context of Shanghai's Economic Development

Peter T. Y. Cheung

Shanghai is unique. Not only does the city stand out in Chinese cultural and economic development, but it is also distinguished in modern Chinese politics and history. Some scholars call Shanghai, as opposed to other provinces or cities, the "key" to modern China.[1] Others characterize Shanghai during the 1919–1927 period as "the other China" — an alternative development model which epitomized cosmopolitanism, enterprise and urbanism, and at the same time Chinese and even nationalistic.[2] Shanghai was also the "cradle" of Chinese communism. After the Chinese Communist Party was founded in Shanghai in 1921, the party used the city as a base to organize students and workers in their anti-imperialist and anti-capitalist struggle.[3] The Kuomintang's (Guomindang 國民黨) conquest of Shanghai in 1927 and its liquidation of the Communists ushered in a period of authoritarian rule, which was soon followed by the brutal Japanese occupation and growing social and economic chaos during the civil war between 1946 and 1949. Shanghai is intriguing as well. Before 1949, the city was China's capitalist enclave as well as the hub of the communist-led workers movement in the 1920s and underground communist activities in the 1930s and 1940s. Shanghai was soon transformed from a glamorous financial and commercial centre into a leading socialist industrial base after the establishment of the People's Republic of China (PRC) in 1949. Even more dramatically, Shanghai was also the political bastion of radical politicians like the "Gang of Four."[4]

Shanghai's recent fate is equally telling. Despite its enormous intellectual and technological might, Shanghai's economic growth was mediocre during most of the reform era. Its fortunes turned for the better only since the late 1980s, notably after the 1990 decision of the central government to develop the Pudong 浦東 area into China's future commercial and financial centre. Shanghai soon became a new site, after Guangdong 廣東 and Fujian 福建, that rekindled the interests of foreign investors in the aftermath of

---

Research for this chapter was supported by a grant from the Research Grants Council in Hong Kong. The author would like to register his thanks for the research assistance provided by Veronica Sze, Patty Tse and Patrick Wong. Further, he would like to express gratitude to four scholars for their valuable comments on an earlier draft of this chapter: (in alphabetical order) Professors John P. Burns (The University of Hong Kong), Jae Ho Chung (Seoul National University), Zhimin Lin (Valparaiso University) and Lynn T. White III (Princeton University). Any errors are the author's sole responsibility.

the bloody Tiananmen incident (天安門事件) in 1989.[5] By 1995, with its former and incumbent leaders at the apex of the Chinese Communist Party and state apparatus, Shanghai's role in Chinese politics and economic development again attracted intense attention at home and abroad. The twists and turns in Shanghai's contemporary history pose important questions that cannot be easily explained by socioeconomic factors, demographic characteristics, or geographical endowments. Given the high degree of involvement of Shanghai in national politics, no survey of Shanghai can ignore the political factors that have shaped its economic development.

Politics and economics are closely intertwined in contemporary China. On the one hand, Shanghai's economic might has made it an especially important actor in Chinese politics. On the other hand, the economic significance of Shanghai has made its role in the Chinese political economy a highly political issue because of its tremendous impact on national stability. The political context of Shanghai's development is thus shaped by a multitude of factors. First, the relations between the central government and Shanghai are obviously a crucial determinant of the city's political and economic fate. However, Shanghai's role in China's political economy also constantly influences how the central government deals with it. Second, the type of leaders appointed in Shanghai is equally important. While central policy may dictate the candidates to be appointed, the personalities, skills and political orientation of these leaders ultimately shape their management of relations with the central government and their administration of the city. Third, the impact of social forces, such as workers and students, on Shanghai's development cannot be ignored. Since the other contributions in this volume deal extensively with the economic, administrative, physical and other dimensions of Shanghai, this chapter, therefore, chooses to focus only on three issues: the political implications of Shanghai's role in China's political economy, the evolution of its political leadership and the politics of its recent economic development.

The significance of these issues is obvious. The city's unique position in the Chinese economy and its particular structure have offered both a strong foundation and some inevitable constraints for sustained economic growth. In particular, the city's economic structure, inherited from three decades of socialist industrial development, presented a set of thorny economic and political problems to its government in the reform era. Shanghai's potential to become a key economic centre in China, however, cannot be fully tapped unless there is a slate of energetic and effective leaders who can deal effectively with the central government, formulate a viable development strategy, and lead the city through economic and political difficulties. Politics at the national level has also intervened in Shanghai's economic development from time to time. The interplay of these factors has thus weaved an intriguing story of how a Chinese, and Asian, metropolis struggles strenuously to modernize in this last half century.

Shanghai in China's Political Economy

Shanghai occupies a unique position in contemporary China's political economy. Since 1949, despite the atrophy of its role as a financial and commercial centre, Shanghai has evolved into a key industrial city in China, supplying industrial products, skilled personnel, as well as a huge amount of revenue. This section explores the political implications of Shanghai's role in China's political economy by examining its shifting economic fortunes, the political consequences of its economic difficulties, as well as the relations between politics and society.

Shanghai's Shifting Economic Fortunes

Any study of the politics of Shanghai's economic development must confront the dramatic rise and decline of its economy since 1949. Shanghai was China's undisputed economic centre for almost three decades after 1949. In 1978, Shanghai alone accounted for one-seventh of the industrial output, one-sixth of the revenue and one-third of the exports of the entire country.[6] In the 1953–1978 period, the annual growth rate of Shanghai's national income amounted to almost 9%, which was not only the fastest in the country, but also higher than that of the other leading coastal provinces (see Table 3.1). In 1978, its share in China's national income and gross output value in industry were 8% and 13%, respectively, both the highest among the provinces.[7]

Shanghai's ranking and share in the national economy, however, fell rapidly during the reform era as its economic dominance was increasingly challenged by other thriving coastal provinces. In 1978, China's top five contributors to its national income were Shanghai, Jiangsu 江蘇, Liaoning 遼寧, Sichuan 四川 and Shandong 山東 respectively; by 1990, the list instead comprised Shandong, Jiangsu, Guangdong, Sichuan and Liaoning.[8] Shanghai had fallen from number one on the list in 1978 to number six in 1985 and, worse still, number ten in 1990. Shanghai's share in China's national income was also halved from about 8% in 1978 to only 4% in

Table 3.1   Growth of National Income in Selected Provinces, 1953–1989

	Shanghai	Shandong	Jiangsu	Zhejiang	Guangdong	China
1953–1978	8.7	5.7	5.6	5.6	5.3	6.0
1979–1989	7.6	10.4	11.0	12.8	11.6	8.7

Sources: Guojia tongjiju (ed.), *Quanguo gesheng, zizhiqu, zhixiashi lishi tongji ziliao huibian* (see note 7 below), p. 47.

1990. If the growth rates in national income of various fast-growing provinces in the 1979–1989 period are compared, Shanghai's performance was not only much slower than areas like Shandong, Jiangsu, Zhejiang 浙江 and Guangdong, but also below the national average (see Table 3.1). Shanghai was once the leading industrial producer in China, but, even in this important role, it was now being overshadowed by the emergence of new industrial bases. To be sure, the city remained a major manufacturer of industrial products, ranging from steel and chemicals to domestic electrical appliances, yet its share of China's gross industrial output was cut almost by half, from 12% in 1978 to only 5.5% in 1994.[9] On the other hand, the share of competing provinces like Guangdong and Shandong in China's total industrial output had each risen from about 5–6% in 1978 to about 9–11% in 1994. Jiangsu had already surpassed Shanghai as China's leading industrial base, contributing 13% of the national industrial output in 1994. In sharp contrast to its envied position as China's leading exporter in the pre-reform era, Shanghai's share in the nation's total exports fell precipitously from about 30% in 1978 to a mere 7.5% in 1994 and, after 1986, Guangdong replaced Shanghai as China's foremost exporting province.[10]

Implications of Shanghai's Relative Economic Decline

Much of Shanghai's economic difficulties in the 1980s can be traced to its role as a key industrial base for socialist China. Due to the national policy that discouraged commerce and foreign trade, Shanghai was the beacon of socialist industry for three decades after 1949. Despite its rapid growth record in the pre-reform era, both Western scholars and Chinese observers agree that the command economy sapped Shanghai of its once vibrant entrepreneurial spirit because of its dependence upon the state for the allocation of funds and materials on the one hand, and its development of industry at the expense of commerce and foreign trade on the other.[11]

Unlike businessmen from its main rival of Guangdong who were noted for their commercial acumen, Shanghai's managers often first looked at the books and waited for policy guidance before doing anything, even in the 1980s.[12] One indicator of the conservative thinking in Shanghai was the slow growth of the private sector. In 1994, the share of people employed in individually-owned (*geti* 個體) and privately-owned (*siying* 私營) businesses of the total urban employment constituted only 2.8% in Shanghai, but 3.3% in Tianjin 天津 and 9.8% in Guangzhou 廣州 .[13]

More importantly, Shanghai's economic structure, inherited from three decades of socialist industrialism, had serious administrative and fiscal consequences for Shanghai. First, the difficulties of the state sector were a heavy burden on Shanghai. In 1994, the state sector contributed over 42% of industrial output in Shanghai, but only 20 to 25% in other coastal provinces like Guangdong, Jiangsu and Shandong.[14] In particular, the state industrial sector in Shanghai experienced great problems in the reform era. For instance, the lower labour costs of rural enterprises, the rising prices of raw materials and fuel caused by price reform, the heavy extraction of the state-owned enterprises (SOEs) by the central government as well as the bureaucratic management style and rigidity of the state sector all contributed to Shanghai's economic difficulties. The amount of subsidies used to support ailing SOEs increased substantially over the years and ate away at resources that would otherwise have been more productively used elsewhere. In Shanghai, the amount of subsidies for SOEs increased almost six times, from RMB588 million in 1987 to a record of RMB3.35 billion in 1993, a sum actually higher than the total budgetary spending on education, health and science, the largest category of its budget.[15] In the fall of 1994, about one-third of Shanghai's large and medium-sized SOEs were already suffering losses.[16] The number of workers employed in the state sector was also higher in Shanghai than in other large cities in China. In 1994, the state sector still accounted for over 72% of total urban employment in Shanghai, but only 58% in Guangzhou.[17] The concomitant need to provide housing, medical insurance and other services added up to a huge bill which affected the profitability of the SOEs. For instance, the provision of medical benefits, housing and other welfare costs amounted to RMB10,000 per capita for SOEs, but only RMB4,000 for rural enterprises in Shanghai.[18]

Second, Shanghai was on the verge of a fiscal crisis in the 1980s, especially before the introduction of a more favourable fiscal regime with the Centre in 1988.[19] Shanghai had been China's largest revenue generator, but the central government's fiscal dependence on Shanghai became problematic in the 1980s. Between 1949 and 1983, about 87% of Shanghai's RMB350 billion revenue was remitted to the central government; only 13% was left for the city.[20] Shanghai's total local revenue experienced negative growth in six out of the sixteen years since 1978, namely, during 1981–1983 and 1986–1988.[21] Having been the nation's largest revenue producer for decades, Shanghai's total local revenue as a part of China's total revenue fell from 15% in 1978 to only 4.8% in 1993.[22] The difficulties in generating revenue caused great concern not only for the Shanghai authorities, but also for the central government. With the exception of 1985 and 1986, Shanghai's local revenue did not surpass the record figure of RMB17.47 billion in 1980 until 1991.[23] Moreover, as one expert put it, Shanghai was "revenue-rich but cash-poor" because the central government, not the city, determined how the revenue would be deployed.[24] Since most of the city's revenue was used for economic construction before 1978, it had to devote about 21% to 25% of its total revenue for social spending, such as education, science, as well as public health in the 1980–1993 period.[25] Shanghai's fiscal difficulties forced its officials and researchers to plead for changes in its fiscal relations with the central government and to ask for more local retention, additional powers to raise new taxes and novel ways to raise funds.[26]

Third, the lack of adequate investment for urban renovation and other infrastructural facilities in Shanghai became not simply a matter of popular concern, but also a drag on economic growth. Such urban decline was mainly caused by the chronic lack of investment. In the 1949–1983 period, less than 4% of Shanghai's total expenditures, was spent on urban maintenance. Of the total spending on basic construction in the same period, two-thirds was spent on industry, whereas only 5% was spent on education and social welfare, 9% on urban utilities, and 10% on telecommunications and transportation.[27] Such public spending and investment priorities evidently reflected more the preferences of the central planners in Beijing than that of the city.[28] According to a famous article published in *Jiefang ribao* 解放日報 on 3 October 1980, Shanghai had five infamous records among China's large cities: the city was the most densely populated; its buildings were also the most densely built, its factories were the most crowded, its roads the narrowest, and the environment least covered by trees; the lack of housing for the needy was the most acute; the number of deaths from traffic accidents was the highest; and the instances of cancer were also the highest because of environmental pollution![29] To be sure,

Shanghai's leadership since 1985 had made an effort to deal with some of these problems. For instance, the amount of investment for Shanghai's urban infrastructure rose from RMB700–900 million in the 1980–1984 period to RMB2.3–3.7 billion in the 1985–1989 period.[30] The revamping of the city's infrastructure is still a daunting task. Given the severity and complexity of the above problems and Shanghai's special role in China's political economy, the state of its economic health has become a major economic as well as political issue for the central government since the mid-1980s.

Politics and Society in Shanghai

Shanghai's role as one of China's key cultural centres has also placed it squarely at the heart of political tempests. Beijing 北京 has always been the centre of political and ideological battles in contemporary China because of its cultural prominence and its status as the national capital. Shanghai's significance, however, comes immediately after Beijing in this regard. If political leadership is necessary to provide solutions to the many problems posed by Shanghai's unique political economy, even Chinese leaders, powerful as they are in a one-party state, cannot shape politics with a complete free hand. Cultural and social forces play an equally powerful role in limiting their menu of choices. The following discussion on the potential for radical political change in Shanghai aims to offer a corrective to a rather prevalent view that the city has simply become a capitalists' or investors' haven.[31] The conditions that provide fertile ground for radical politics have not entirely disappeared in Shanghai. Rather, with the move towards more market reform and perhaps political relaxation, the city may re-emerge as a centre for political change in post-Deng China.[32]

Whether before or after 1978, Shanghai has proved to be an ideological arena too important to lose in any major political battle in China. Shanghai's cultural status and resources made it an ideal place from which Chairman Mao Zedong 毛澤東 launched the Cultural Revolution in 1965. Even during the reform era, for instance, the Shanghai-based *Shijie jingji daobao* 世界經濟導報 (World Economic Herald) emerged as a fountain of new ideas in encouraging economic as well as political reform in the 1980s, including the propagation of ideas of technocracy.[33] More recently, Shanghai's ideologues served as ghostwriters for Deng Xiaoping 鄧小平 in his battle against ideological conservatives in Beijing in 1991, just before his southern tour in early 1992. Further, Shanghai has been a key arena for collective political actions as workers and students have at times turned the city into a centre of radical politics in twentieth century China.[34] In addition to Beijing's bend of officials and intellectuals, Shanghai boasts a heavy concentration of intellectuals and workers second to none except the capital. In 1994, the number of university teachers and university students in Shanghai amounted to 21,863 and 140,396, respectively, ranking second only after Beijing among China's major cities.[35] In 1994, a total of 4.78 million staff was employed in urban Shanghai, with 3.39 million working in the state sector.[36] The concentration of intellectuals and workers together in China's cradle of the proletariat may easily turn Shanghai into yet another political arena which will influence national level politics.

While the Cultural Revolution witnessed the most intense phase of student and worker activism since 1949, student protests did not abate in the reform era. For instance, student demonstrations which began in Shanghai in December 1986 and spread to other cities like Wuhan 武漢 , Changsha 長沙 and Beijing ultimately led to the downfall of the liberal general secretary Hu Yaobang 胡耀邦 . During the political crisis of 1989, Shanghai was also turned into a leading centre of action after Beijing.[37] Only lagging behind Beijing's record 56 days of protests, Shanghai ranked second among China's cities with 46 days of demonstrations.[38] If students provide idealism and sometimes leadership in political protests, workers often constitute the main force in confronting the state with strikes and more militant forms of political actions.[39] Given the long history of worker politics, the concentration of the working class, and the rapid socio-economic change expedited by fast-paced economic reform in the city since the 1990s, the Shanghai working class might once again become politically resurgent. Should Shanghai's economy enter into a protracted recession after the rapid growth that began in 1991 because of domestic and overseas economic fluctuations, workers may have to endure an extended period of minimal subsistence. Discontent among workers during such difficult times would provide a fertile ground for collective political actions unless the government can continue to deliver rapid growth, employment, or sufficient social security support. Similarly, students and intellectuals, when hit by economic hard times, may also turn their frustration with the existing political order into demands for greater political relaxation, especially if a precarious economic and political situation emerges after Deng Xiaoping passes away. To be sure, whether politics in Shanghai will turn radical depends not only on the emergence of student or worker-related issues, the availability of leadership among these social groups, and the possibility of alliances with other social forces, but also on the coercion and counter strategies of the party and the state. If the history of the last century provides any guide, it seems unlikely that the role of Shanghai workers and students in shaping Chinese politics will disappear once and for all with further marketization of the Chinese economy.

To sum up, Shanghai's role in the Chinese political economy is unique. While other provinces such as Guangdong are more marketized and economically larger in size than Shanghai, their political impact on Chinese politics are more limited because of their peripheral locations, lack of cultural clout, and absence of a critical mass of intellectuals and workers crowded into an urban setting. These political consequences of Shanghai's unique economic, social and political status have made it a place of major concern for all rulers in Beijing. Consequently, they have to deal with Shanghai, and its leaders, in a careful manner in order to facilitate the utilization of the city's economic and human resources while at the same time to avoid any unpredictable social and economic crises that may emanate from this largest metropolis in China.

Shanghai's Political Leadership

Shanghai is one of the three centrally administered cities in China, with an administrative status equal to that of a province. However, since 1949, the city's political leadership has been far more active and influential in national politics than most other provinces, especially during critical periods in contemporary Chinese political history. The involvement of Shanghai's leaders in Chinese politics provides an important cue to the city's fate in economic development. The following section examines the intricate relations between the Centre and Shanghai's leaders, the city's leadership and its changing political status, as well as the politics of its recent economic development.[40]

The Centre and Shanghai's Leadership

The appointment of Shanghai's leadership has always been a critical political decision that is not taken lightly by central leaders. Bearing in mind the case of the ambitious Gao Gang 高崗 , the leader from Northeast China who threatened the unity of the Communist party in the early 1950s, the central government tends to pick compliant officials to economically important areas in order to prevent them from using their local bases to challenge central authority. Hence the selection of provincial level leaders in China has always been a prerogative of the Centre, not the provinces. Aside from maximizing popular support for central policies and minimizing resistance, however, these leaders inevitably have to deal with problems confronting the locality and its people. China's provincial party secretaries have thus been aptly conceptualized as the "political middlemen" between the Centre and the locale.[41] While the engagement of provincial élites in Chinese politics varies significantly from case to case, the heavy involvement of Shanghai's leaders in national politics and their high representation in central party and state organs testify to the intricate relations between the Centre and the Shanghai leadership since 1949.

The pattern of leadership in Shanghai indicates complex calculations on the part of the Centre and their potential appointees. On the one hand, representation of Shanghai leaders in important central positions apparently reflects the personal ambitions and skills of individual leaders to climb the ladder of success and to participate in the struggle for power and policy at the national level. In a major study of élite mobility in contemporary China, David M. Lampton argues that moving ahead in China depends upon a host of contingent factors, including policy preference, organizational fate, visibility, seniority and luck.[42] At least three broad strategies for achieving political power can be identified. Put simply, a patron–client strategy depends on "personal or clientelistic ties," a regional strategy depends on territorial power bases, and a bureaucratic strategy depends on support from central state, party and military bureaucracies.[43] Shanghai has indeed offered fertile ground for cultivating a Chinese politician's career because it possesses all the important attributes of a territorial power base: "regional prosperity, a large-scale economy, and strategic location."[44] Since the city can serve as an excellent stepping stone for ambitious politicians to reach the top echelons at the Centre, those who have national ambitions might sacrifice Shanghai's interests for the sake of their own careers. To be sure, depending on their own political orientation and whether their own interests are served, these leaders may also fight for the localities under their governance. Commenting on Shanghai's leadership in the pre-reform era, Lucian W. Pye even argues that:

> since the founding of the People's Republic, Shanghai's political leaders have consistently failed to assert the special economic and cultural interest of the city ... they had over considerable periods advocated policies and

programmes diametrically opposed to the interests and the welfare of the people they presumably represented.[45]

Given Shanghai's political and economic significance and its fiscal contribution to the nation, the Centre's main concern is to appoint leaders who can effectively accomplish central objectives rather than promote local interests.

On the other hand, a higher representation of Shanghai leaders in the central party–state hierarchy suggests the significance that the Centre attaches to the city. Powerful provincial leaders have been appointed into the party's highest level from time to time. For instance, leaders from provinces that were becoming economically powerful were co-opted into the Centre so that they would be under tighter central monitoring and supervision.[46] Aside from Shanghai (1977–1982 and since 1987), incumbent leaders from only five coastal provinces and cities have been co-opted into the Politburo in the post-Mao era, including Beijing (1976–1980 and 1987–1995), Tianjin (1987–1993), Shandong (1992–1994), Guangdong (since 1992) and Sichuan (1987–1992). Further, central leaders might appoint provincial supporters to the Centre in order to marshall their support in the struggle for power and policy. In the pre-reform era, when class struggle and mobilization were the major themes of Chinese politics, Chairman Mao often appealed to provincial leaders to support his radical political and economic campaigns. In return, some of these provincial leaders were rewarded with positions in the party's hierarchy, as exemplified by the promotion of provincial party secretaries like Li Jingquan 李井泉 from Sichuan and Ke Qingshi 柯慶施 from Shanghai into the Politburo in 1958.[47] Similarly, in the reform era, reformist leaders from Sichuan and Anhui 安徽, namely Zhao Ziyang 趙紫陽 and Wan Li 萬里, were promoted by Deng Xiaoping to the Centre in order to act as the architects of his reform programme.[48] In short, the Centre tended to appoint compliant leaders to Shanghai who would put the interests of the central government above the city's interests. At the same time, most of them also advanced their own careers by using the city as a base in their struggle for power.

Shanghai's Leaders and Its Changing Political Status

Shanghai, in addition to Beijing, has always been a key locality that has enjoyed strong political representation in the Chinese Communist Party and state hierarchy since 1949. One important indicator of the rise and decline of Shanghai's political status is its leaders' command of important positions at the central level. While providing invaluable access to the Centre, the engagement of Shanghai leaders in national politics inevitably diverts their attention and energy from the city's own affairs and they are often compelled to think about and act upon national, rather than local, concerns. Shanghai's changing political status is thus reflected in the credentials and status of its top leaders as well as in its representation on the Central Committee and the Politburo. If membership on the Central Committee signifies a qualifying credential for incorporation into the élite corps in China, membership on the Politburo suggests the ultimate ascent of local leaders into the party's powerful decision-making core. Information on the political status of Shanghai's leaders is presented in Table 3.2 to Table 3.4. Table 3.2 is a list of top party and state leaders of Shanghai since 1949, Table 3.3 is a tally of Shanghai's party and state leaders elected to the Central Committee at each Party Congress, and Table 3.4 identifies Shanghai leaders who sat concurrently on the party's highest decision-making body — the Politburo.

Table 3.2　Shanghai's Party and State Leadership

Party secretary	Mayor
Rao Shushi 饒漱石 (1949.3–1950.1)	Chen Yi 陳毅 (1949.5–1958.11)
Chen Yi 陳毅 (1950.1–1954.10)	Ke Qingshi 柯慶施 (1958.11–1965.4)
Ke Qingshi 柯慶施 (1954.10–1965.4)	Cao Diqiu 曹荻秋 (1965.12–1967.2)
Chen Pixian 陳丕顯 (1965.11–1967.2)	Zhang Chunqiao 張春橋 (1967.2–1976.10)
Zhang Chunqiao 張春橋 (1967.2–1976.10)	Su Zhenhua 蘇振華 (1976.10–1979.1)
Su Zhenhua 蘇振華 (1976.10–1979.1)	Peng Chong 彭冲 (1979.1–1980.3)
Peng Chong 彭冲 (1979.1–1980.3)	Wang Daohan 汪道涵 (1980.10–1985.7)
Chen Guodong 陳國棟 (1980.3–1985.6)	Jiang Zemin 江澤民 (1985.7–1988.4)
Rui Xingwen 芮杏文 (1985.6–1987.11)	Zhu Rongji 朱鎔基 (1988.4–1991.4)
Jiang Zemin 江澤民 (1987.11–1989.8)	Huang Ju 黃菊 (1991.4–1995.2)
Zhu Rongji 朱鎔基 (1989.8–1991.3)	Xu Kuangdi 徐匡迪 (1995.2–　　)
Wu Bangguo 吳邦國 (1991.4–1994.9)	
Huang Ju 黃菊 (1995.2–present)	

Note:　For the sake of simplicity, party secretary in this table refers to the top party leader and mayor refers to the top state leader. Nonetheless, the party's top leader was called first party secretary from 1950 to the mid-1980s, and the top state leader was called chairman of the Municipal Revolutionary Committee from 1967 to 1979.

Source:　Chen Yi (ed.), *Dangdai Zhongguo de Shanghai* (see note 2), pp. 644–59; *Wen hui bao* 文匯報 (Hong Kong), 29 September 1994, p. A2.

Table 3.3   Number of Shanghai Party and State Leaders on the Central Commitee (CC), 1949–1995

	(A) Full mem.	(B) Alt. mem.	(C) CC total	(D) Shanghai in CC total (%)
7th CC (1945.4–1956.9)	3	3	6	7.8
8th CC (1956.9–1969.4)	2	1	3	1.8
9th CC (1969.4–1973.8)	6	4	10	3.6
10th CC (1973.8–1977.8)	9	1	10	3.1
11th CC (1977.8–1982.9)	6	1	7	2.1
12th CC (1982.9–1987.10)	3	—	3	0.86
National Party Conference (1985.9)	1	1	2	—
13th CC (1987.10–1992.10)	1	4	5	1.8
14th CC (1992.10–1995.9)	2	2	4	1.3

Note: The list includes those who were (first/second) party secretaries, deputy secretaries, mayors or deputy mayors, chairmen or vice-chairmen of Revolutionary Committees, and chairmen or vice-chairmen of Municipal People's Congresses from Shanghai elected into the CC at the beginning of the respective CC meetings. Column C refers to the sum of columns A and B.

Source: Ma Qibin et al. (eds.), *Zhongguo gongchandang zhizheng sishinian* (see note 47) pp. 587–89; *Wen hui bao* (Hong Kong), 29 September 1994, p. A2.

Table 3.4   Shanghai Leaders Who Were Concurrently Members of the Politburo

Maoist era	Post-Mao era
Chen Yi 陳毅 (1956.9–1958.11)	Su Zhenhua 蘇振華 (1976.10–1979.1)
Ke Qingshi 柯慶施 (1958.5–1965.4)	Ni Zhifu 倪志福 (1976.10–1979.1)
Zhang Chunqiao 張春橋 (1969.4–1976.10)	Peng Chong 彭沖 (1976.10–1980.3)
Yao Wenyuan 姚文元 (1969.4–1976.10)	Jiang Zemin 江澤民 (1987.11–1989.8)
Wang Hongwen 王洪文 (1973.8–1976.10)	Wu Bangguo 吳邦國 (1992.10–1994.9)
	Huang Ju 黃菊 (1994.9–present)

Note: This table identifies all Shanghai party secretaries (first party secretaries), chairmen of Municipal Revolutionary Committees, and mayors and their deputies who were concurrently members of the Politburo. The dates inside the brackets indicate the period of overlapping appointment. Zhang Chunqiao, Yao Wenyuan and Wang Hongwen were arrested in October 1976, but they were officially dismissed from the party in July 1977.

Source: Ma Qibin et al. (eds.), *Zhongguo gongchandang zhizheng sishinian* (see note 47), pp. 587–89; *Wen hui bao*, 29 September 1994, p. A2.

The Pre-reform Era

In the pre-Cultural Revolution period, most officials appointed to Shanghai's top positions were political heavyweights, hence reflecting the concern of the Centre towards the administration of China's most important economic centre.[49] Rao Shushi 饒漱石 , the former political commissar of the Third Field Army, became socialist Shanghai's first party secretary in March 1949, but his term lasted only for eleven months. He then concentrated on his post as the head of party, state and military organs in East China. In 1953, Rao became the head of the party's highly important Organization Department, but his partnership with Gao Gang, the leader in northeast China, in power struggle led to their downfall in 1954 as the first major case of factionalism since the founding of the PRC.

Chen Yi 陳毅 , the Commander of the Third Field Army who took over the city in 1949 and who was a close associate of Premier Zhou Enlai 周恩來 , was appointed Shanghai's first mayor in May 1949. Not only was he a decorated war hero and one of the ten Marshals honoured in 1955, but he was also a prominent and skilful politician who later became the PRC's second foreign minister in 1958. Chen's political stature was reflected in his appointment as a vice-premier in 1954 and as a member of the Politburo in 1956. During his tenure, Shanghai underwent a largely smooth socialization of private industry and commerce, which was no mean achievement given the fact that the city had the largest concentration of capitalists in China.

Since the 1950s, Shanghai's economic policy has been mainly dictated by the Centre. As early as 1953, the East China Bureau of the party not only severely criticized efforts to re-vitalize Shanghai's industries but also adopted a policy of using the city's industries to support economic development in other parts of the country.[50] In other words, despite the prominent status of Shanghai leaders, their primary task was to carry out central policies rather than to address local concerns. After Chen's departure from his posts as first party secretary in 1954 and then mayor in 1958, Shanghai came under the leadership of Ke Qingshi, which lasted for more than a decade, from 1954 to 1965.

Although less prominent than either Chen Yi or Rao Shushi, Ke Qingshi was a highly influential national politician not only because he enjoyed a close personal relationship with Chairman Mao Zedong, but also because he actively championed Mao's revolutionary cause. Having served as Jiangsu province's first party secretary since 1949, Ke was transferred to Shanghai in the fall of 1954 and became the longest serving party leader and mayor there until his death in April 1965.[51] Ke was an early and ardent supporter of a number of Chairman Mao's key political campaigns in the 1950s, such as the Hundred Flowers and the ensuing Anti-rightist Campaign.[52] He was also the key driving force that convinced Mao to launch the overly ambitious steel production campaign during the Great Leap Forward in 1958. Together with Li Jingquan from Sichuan, another Mao favourite, Ke was one of the two provincial party secretaries inducted into the Politburo in May 1958 because of their close ties with the pre-eminent leader. During 1949–1966, there were only a few territorial units that enjoyed membership in the Politburo: namely, Shandong under Kang Sheng 康生 from 1949 to 1954, Sichuan under Li Jingquan from 1958 to 1965, and Beijing under Peng Zhen 彭眞 from 1949 to 1966.[53] Ke was promoted to a vice-premier in January 1965, but he unexpectedly died from a serious illness in April. Two veteran officials from Shanghai, Chen Pixian 陳丕顯 and Cao Diqiu 曹荻秋 , were promoted respectively to be the city's party secretary and mayor. As both opposed the radicalism of the Maoists, they fell victim to their left-wing colleagues, Zhang Chunqiao 張春橋 and Yao Wenyuan 姚文元 . Both were purged during the Cultural Revolution. Despite the chaos caused by the Cultural Revolution, Shanghai also suffered from external policy changes. For instance, as China began to prepare for a possible war with the United States, a total of 411 factories employing over 150,000 staff were relocated to other parts of the country between 1964 and 1971.[54]

The power and status of Shanghai leaders in pre-reform China were also reflected by their concurrent appointments to other important positions. For instance, in addition to membership on the Politburo, Chen Yi, Ke Qingshi and Zhang Chunqiao served briefly as vice-premiers of the State Council.[55] Aside from Inner Mongolia, Shanghai was the only provincial unit that had a leader with vice-premier status during the pre-Cultural Revolution era. Ke and Zhang also served concurrently as the first political commissar of a regional People's Liberation Army (PLA) command, the Nanjing Military Region, during their tenure as Shanghai's top leaders. Further, both Rao and Ke served as the first party secretaries of the Communist Party's regional bureau — the East China Bureau — in the early 1950s and 1960s.

During the Cultural Revolution era, the political power of Shanghai's leaders in national politics reached a peak. The alliance between Shanghai's leaders and the increasingly radical Chairman Mao began during Ke Qingshi's tenure. Since Beijing's party and state apparatus were under the conservative party leader Peng Zhen, the Chairman and his wife turned to Shanghai's radical cadres for help in the mid-1960s.[56] The first salvo of the Cultural Revolution was fired by Shanghai's Yao Wenyuan when he published a commentary on a historical play by Beijing's vice-mayor and historian, Wu Han 吳晗 , in 1965. During the course of the Cultural Revolution, Shanghai leaders became Chairman Mao's staunch supporters. In January 1967, Zhang Chunqiao, a former official in charge of propaganda in Shanghai, orchestrated the "January Tempest," a seizure of political power by rebels against the Party Committee in power, which marked the capturing of power from the existing party establishment nationwide. Shanghai actively promoted a radical line over a wide variety of policy areas, ranging from the militia and the PLA to education, industrial management, and economic development strategy.[57] In 1974–1975, Shanghai's radical leadership also launched various ideological campaigns that established their hegemony over Chinese ideology and culture, targetting Premier Zhou Enlai and Deng Xiaoping.[58] As the power base of the Maoists, Shanghai did not suffer as much from social and economic disorder as other areas in the early and mid-1970s.

Shanghai leaders' occupation of key central positions increased significantly after the late 1960s. At the 9th Party Congress held in 1969, Shanghai's representation on the Central Committee increased from two to ten, including Zhang Chunqiao and Yao Wenyuan, both full members of the Politburo. By the 10th Party Congress held in 1973, the total number of Shanghai leaders with Central Committee membership reached an historic high of ten, yet Wang Hongwen 王洪文 , the worker rebel, was added to Shanghai's contingent on the Politburo (see Table 3.3). Together with Mao's wife Jiang Qing 江青 , Zhang, Yao and Wang were later labelled the infamous "Gang of Four."[59] Like his predecessor Ke Qingshi, Zhang Chunqiao served concurrently as the head of Shanghai's Party Committee and Revolutionary Committee as well as a member of the Politburo. Despite his conspicuous lack of party seniority, Wang Hongwen was even made a vice-chairman of the party and a member of the Standing Committee of the Politburo with Mao's support in 1973. As David S. G. Goodman has aptly pointed out, "there is little to indicate that the Gang of Four took the position they did because of developments in Shanghai" and hence "the reasons why they are identifiable as a group is not because of the city of Shanghai, but because of their position in Chinese politics since 1969."[60] Nonetheless, if not for the special political, economic and cultural resources of Shanghai, the radical group would not have been able to help Mao launch the Cultural Revolution through the use of the city's propaganda machine, nor would they have been able to carry out his revolutionary experiments as they did by using the city as a radical model. Shanghai provided a powerful ideological, political and organizational base for the "Gang of Four" not because they articulated the territorial interests of the city, but because they used the city for their own national political ambitions. In a sense, Shanghai was a pawn rather than an active player in national politics during the Cultural Revolution.

The Reform Era

After the death of Chairman Mao and the fall of the "Gang of Four" in 1976, the city suffered tremendously due to its lack of access to the highest reach of the party and state apparatus. Owing to its exceptionally influential role during the Cultural Revolution, Shanghai was understandably put under tighter central control. A central work team led by three senior cadres was sent to Shanghai in October 1976 after the fall of the "Gang of Four."[61] Su Zhenhua 蘇振華, a senior naval official, and Ni Zhifu 倪志福, head of the national trade union federation, were made the first and second party secretaries of Shanghai, respectively, in October 1976. Both Su and Ni were elected alternate members of the Politburo in 1973. Peng Chong 彭冲, a former party secretary from Jiangsu and an alternate member of the 10th Central Committee, was appointed third party secretary. The primary task of these three leaders was to eradicate the political and ideological influence of the "Gang of Four" and to reconstitute the party and state apparatus in Shanghai. The background of these leaders seemingly reflected central priorities. Su's military background was useful in dealing with the issue of public order and other security related issues. Ni, a Shanghainese who had spent most of his career in the union system in Beijing, was appropriate to deal with the workers and their concerns.[62] Peng, who had extensive experience in East China, especially Jiangsu, was the specialist in local administration among the three. The 11th Party Congress held in August 1977 again elected Su, Ni and Peng as full Central Committee members, while three other members of the Shanghai leadership were made alternate Central Committee members.

The radical legacy of the "Gang of Four" constituted major ideological and organizational constraints on the launching of the economic reform in the early 1980s. On the one hand, the impact of the purge of the "Gang of

Four" on the cadre corps in Shanghai was enormous. Between the fall of the "Gang" in October 1976 and 1978, almost one-third of the cadres at the district, county and bureau level or above were reshuffled in order to weed out radical remnants.[63] The rapid reshuffling of the cadre corps suggested that personnel and political problems dominated the tasks of the municipal administration during the first two to three years after Mao's death. On the other hand, the entrenchment of leftist thought in Shanghai not only slowed its involvement in the debate on the criterion of truth but also frustrated Deng Xiaoping's efforts to re-orient party policy towards economic reform and to deal with the cult of Chairman Mao and the reversal of verdicts on cadres.[64] Even in 1979, not only were there cadres in Shanghai who opposed Deng's reversal of Maoist policies, but Peng Chong, in particular, wanted to stop the national campaign debating the criterion of truth in the entire country.[65] Finally, given the extensive connections between the radicals and Shanghai, the indispensable fiscal remittances from the city, as well as the unstable situation of the city in the late 1970s, it was unlikely that the central government would give the city more prerogatives in economy policy.

These three leaders did not act as pioneers in launching reform in Shanghai for a number of reasons. On the one hand, these leaders were politically and ideologically closer to Mao's hand-picked successor, Hua Guofeng 華國鋒 , than the emerging Deng Xiaoping. On the other hand, both Ni and Su did not seem to have the time or energy to tackle Shanghai's economic difficulties, possibly because of their other portfolios.[66] Consequently, these leaders could not devote all their attention to the revitalization of Shanghai or act as its effective spokesmen. As Su and Ni were unable to focus on their work in Shanghai, Peng Chong became the *de facto* leader in Shanghai and, after the departure of Su and Ni in January 1979, he was formally made the first party secretary and later the chairman of the Shanghai Municipal Revolutionary Committee.[67] While Peng's tenure (July 1976 to March 1980) was long enough for him to spend more energy on the development of Shanghai, his performance was disappointing. One obvious reason was Peng's ideological and political affinity to the "whateverist" (凡是派) line of his patron, Hua Guofeng, but his "team-player" leadership style also probably made him reluctant to push for economic reform.[68] As Hua lost his positions as premier and chairman of the party, respectively, in 1980 and 1981 to Deng Xiaoping's associates, Zhao Ziyang and Hu Yaobang, Peng was transferred from Shanghai in April 1980 and later became one of the five vice-chairmen of

the Standing Committee of the National People's Congress. Although he
kept his seat on the Central Committee, Peng lost his position on the
Politburo and the Secretariat when the 12th National Party Congress convened in September 1982.

With Peng's departure, Shanghai's political status reached a nadir in
the early 1980s. Chen Guodong 陳國棟 and Hu Lijiao 胡立敎 were appointed first and second party secretaries, respectively, in 1981. Chen
Guodong, a Jiangxi native born in 1911 and a member of the 11th Central
Committee elected in August 1977, succeeded Peng Chong as first party
secretary in April 1980. Chen's career was mainly in the financial sector,
having served in various positions in East China including deputy director
of its financial department and director of its grain department. Prior to his
appointment to Shanghai, he was president of the All-China Federation of
Supply and Marketing Coops, as well as head of the State Council's small
group on finance and trade.[69] As evident in his work experience in the
financial sector, Chen was widely known to be conservative in his
economic views and close to the party elder, Chen Yun 陳雲 .[70] In addition
to the leftist legacies of the "Gang of Four," the lack of central status for
Shanghai's leaders and the absence of strong ties with top central leaders
were not auspicious for its quest for better treatment from the Centre in the
first half of the 1980s. Chen's counterpart, Wang Daohan 汪道涵 , was not
a member of the Central Committee when he was appointed Shanghai's
mayor in 1980 and he failed to be admitted to the new Central Committee
elected in 1982. Wang, an Anhui native born in 1915, served in East China
for an extended period of time before being promoted to be a vice-minister
of the First Ministry of Machine-building Industry.[71] In the post-Mao
period, he served as a first vice-minister of the Commission for Foreign
Economic Relations (and later the Ministry for Foreign Economic Relations),
as well as deputy director of the State Import–Export Administration Committee and the State Committee of Foreign Investment Administrative. However, Wang was more an open-minded leader who had many good ideas
about Shanghai's development than a decisive leader like some of his suc-
cessors. Despite Wang Daohan's eagerness to re-invigorate Shanghai, his
lack of political stature did not help his endeavours. Hu Lijiao, a Jiangxi
native who was born in 1914 and became a full member of the 11th Central
Committee, was appointed Shanghai's second secretary and later elected
chairman of the Shanghai Municipal People's Congress in 1981. Hu served
as a vice-minister of the Ministry of Finance in the 1950s and as vice
president of the People's Bank of China since 1962 as well as in various

positions in East China and Heilongjiang 黑龍江 before the Cultural Revolution.[72] Before his appointment to Shanghai, he worked in party and government organs in Henan 河南 . In other words, both Chen and Hu were outsiders coming from the financial and banking system which was very much under the shadow of conservative party leader Chen Yun. The party secretaries and mayors of Tianjin and Beijing, the other two centrally administered cities, as well as Shanghai's neighbours, Jiangsu and Zhejiang, were usually full members of the Central Committee, as were the leaders of most of the important provinces. In the 12th Central Committee elected in 1982, Shanghai's leaders no longer enjoyed a seat on the Politburo; Chen and Hu were the only two with Central Committee status. Even though Guangdong and Fujian did not enjoy strong representation on the Central Committee or the Politburo, their reform programmes were personally endorsed by Deng Xiaoping and they maintained good ties with top leaders like Zhao Ziyang.

At the National Party Conference held in September 1985, a reshuffling of the Shanghai leadership was set in motion. Both Chen Guodong and Hu Lijiao joined 64 other older cadres in retirement, and 56 officials were made full Central Committee members and 35 were made alternate members, including Shanghai's leaders-designate. Jiang Zemin 江澤民 , who was already a Central Committee member, was appointed the city's mayor in July 1985 and Rui Xingwen 芮杏文 , who was appointed the city's party secretary in May 1985, was made a full Central Committee member and one of his deputies, Wu Bangguo 吳邦國 , was made an alternate member at this September conference. By the end of 1985, only three members in Shanghai's leadership core enjoyed Central Committee status.[73]

The Centre's change in policy towards Shanghai was aptly reflected in the appointment of leaders since the mid-1980s.[74] Compared with their predecessors, the new batches of leaders sent to Shanghai were not only younger (in their late 50s and early 60s) and university-educated, but also politically ambitious and better connected with the Centre. Jiang Zemin's age (61 in 1987), educational and technical qualifications, experience in industrial management and foreign trade, and previous working experience in Shanghai all favoured his posting. Jiang, a native from Yangzhou 揚州 , Jiangsu, born in 1926, was a graduate of Shanghai's prestigious Jiaotong University (交通大學) with study experience in the Soviet Union in 1955-1956. Not only did he possess working experience in various enterprises in Shanghai after 1949, but he had also served in the central ministries.

Before his appointment as the minister of Electronic Industry in 1983, he had also worked, like his predecessor Wang Daohan, as vice-chairman of the State Council's State Import–Export Administrative Committee and on the State Committee of Foreign Investment Administration. Jiang was also one of the central officials who had studied various export processing zones abroad in order to offer advice to the Centre on the Special Economic Zones (SEZs).[75] Rui Xingwen, a Jiangsu native born in 1927, was a close associate of Premier Zhao Ziyang and a former vice-minister in various ministries. But Jiang Zemin and Rui Xingwen were known to have difficulties working together, hence Rui was promoted in November 1987 to secretary of the Central Committee's Secretariat. After Rui Xingwen's departure from Shanghai, Jiang took over the post of party secretary in November 1987 and the mayorship was taken by Zhu Rongji 朱鎔基 in April 1988. The reshuffling of Shanghai's leadership in 1987 was especially crucial because it marked the revival of its leaders in Chinese politics as well as a change in central policy. Shanghai's representation in the central party bodies increased steadily after 1987, with Central Committee membership rising to five in 1987. In particular, Jiang's promotion to the Politburo renewed the pre-reform pattern of putting Shanghai's party leader on the Politburo, which obviously reflected the city's growing political status as well as a change in the Centre's policy towards the city.[76]

The new leaders appointed since 1985 undertook major efforts to confront Shanghai's economic problems, bargained ardently with the Centre, and formulated new strategies to mobilize resources in developing the city.[77] In particular, both Jiang Zemin and Zhu Rongji made a mark in governing Shanghai, something which also greatly helped their political careers later. Jiang Zemin attempted to cultivate a populist image by trying to deal with problems that deeply concerned ordinary people, such as food supplies, housing shortages and environmental pollution.[78] He also made an effort to attract and utilize foreign investment in order to finance Shanghai's development. For instance, the amount of actual foreign investment used by Shanghai in 1986, 1987 and 1988 grew by 110%, 120% and 88% respectively.[79] Zhu, a Hunan native born in 1928, was a graduate in electric motor engineering from Qinghua University (清華大學). Having served in various positions in the State Planning Commission and the State Economic Commission, he had extensive working experience in industrial economy, but almost none in local administration.[80] Nonetheless, he had proved to be not only a capable administrator who exercised his authority in a determined and decisive manner which, nonetheless, made many enemies among his colleagues and subordinates, but also a skilful politician who could please his clients in Shanghai as well as his bosses in Beijing.[81] During his tenure, he scored major successes in dealing with a wide range of difficult social and economic problems confronting Shanghai, including the smooth handling of popular protests in the summer of 1989, an increase in the supply of vegetables, the improvement of administration, as well as the promotion of foreign investment and the securing of central support for the Pudong project. His performance caught the attention of Deng and his appointment reputedly received support from party elder Chen Yun as well.[82] According to one China observer, although Zhu Rongji, who was already promoted as a vice-premier in April 1991, was a key supporter of Deng Xiaoping in the preparation and publication of a series of articles in Shanghai's *Jiefang ribao* in 1991, which paved the way for Deng Xiaoping's political offensive in early 1992.[83] The involvement of Shanghai's propaganda apparatus and the support given by its leadership to the launching of the ideological battle preceding Deng's early 1992 southern tour not only reflected the reliance on a local power base by a central politician in an ideological struggle akin to Mao's launching of the Cultural Revolution, but also the important cultural and political resources that the city could lend to contenders in Chinese politics. Zhu Rongji was promoted to vice-premier of the State Council in April 1991 because of his accomplishments in Shanghai and because of the support of Deng and other party elders. Only an alternate member of the Central Committee when he was appointed mayor of Shanghai, he was made a full Central Committee member and more importantly, a Standing Committee member of the Politburo of the 14th Central Committee in October 1992. Similarly, Jiang Zemin was appointed general secretary of the party in late June 1989, chairman of the Central Military Commission in early November 1989, and later president in March 1993. The status of ex-Shanghai leaders at the Centre indeed reached an apex in the history of the PRC.

Wu Bangguo and Huang Ju 黃菊 , who succeeded Zhu Rongji as party secretary and mayor, respectively, in 1991, had a somewhat easier job as the most difficult task of securing preferential policies from the Centre was secured. What was especially important about the appointment of Wu Bangguo and Huang Ju was that they were not only the first batch of veteran Shanghai cadres who were promoted to the highest municipal positions, but also the high-flyers promoted by Jiang Zemin in the 1990s.[84]

Since the Cultural Revolution, all of Shanghai's top leaders had been sent there from outside rather than being promoted from within. Even though Wu and Huang were not Shanghainese, they both spent their entire careers in the city. Wu, an Anhui native born in 1941, was only 51 years old when he was made a member of the Politburo of the 14th Central Committee in October 1992, which made him the youngest member of the highest policy-making body. Wu was only an alternate member of the 12th and 13th Central Committees, but was rapidly promoted as a full member of the Central Committee and a Politburo member by the 14th Central Committee. Similarly, Huang was not a Shanghainese, but a Zhejiang native born in 1938, and he was only 56 years old when he was promoted to the Politburo in late September 1994. Both Wu and Huang share many important similarities. Like Jiang and Zhu, both graduated from engineering from a prestigious university (Qinghua), both had worked in enterprises and industrial bureaus before their promotion to the Municipal Party organs, and both were made deputy party secretaries in 1985. Their education, technical expertise and youth made them radically different from Shanghai's leaders in the early 1980s, but much more similar to the technocratic generation that has taken over Shanghai's leadership since 1985. However, unlike both Jiang and Zhu, both Wu and Huang are veteran Shanghai cadres, even though they are not Shanghai natives.

The political status of Shanghai's leaders has advanced further since 1992. Wu Bangguo was appointed to the Politburo by the 14th Central Committee held in October 1992. Former mayor Huang Ju, who succeeded Wu as party secretary, was also elected to the Politburo and Wu was promoted to a member of the Secretariat at the Fourth Plenum held in late September 1994, a conference which endorsed stronger party discipline and obedience towards the Centre with Jiang Zemin as its core. Despite a tally of negative and abstention votes totalling 16%, Wu Bangguo was elected vice-premier by the National People's Congress in March 1995.[85] Whether these negative votes were against Wu himself or against Jiang's effort to recruit more Shanghai-based cadres into the Centre is hard to determine, both might well be contributing factors for such unprecedented voting behaviour. However, the intimate relations between Jiang and his Shanghai associates like Wu and Huang were amply revealed. Starting from 1987, all party secretaries from Shanghai concurrently occupied a seat on the Politburo (see Table 3.4). While there were only four Shanghai members in the 14th Central Committee in 1992, the much higher representation of ex-Shanghai leaders in the top echelons continued to reflect their dominance over the Centre since 1989. In the view of the other provinces, it could hardly escape suspicion that leaders like Jiang and Wu would often be more sympathetic to Shanghai than to other provinces. Of the provincial units represented on the Politburo, only Shanghai and Guangdong remained by June 1996. The death of Tianjin's party secretary, Tan Shaowen 譚紹文, resulted in the loss of that city's "seat" on the Politburo, while Beijing's former party secretary, Chen Xitong 陳希同 was relieved of his positions in the Central Committee and the Politburo in September 1995.[86] The reorientation of China's focus of development to Shanghai since 1990 largely coincided with the rise of former and incumbent Shanghai leaders, who became the largest grouping among any locality at the highest levels.

Since the mid-1980s, an increasingly technocratic leadership had emerged in Shanghai.[87] On the 13-member Standing Committee of Shanghai's Municipal Party Committee elected in December 1992, the average age of the members was only 52 years and 85% of the members had a university education.[88] In fact, 6 of the 13 members were engineers and senior engineers, while 5 were associate research fellows or professors in the natural sciences. In February 1995, Xu Kuangdi 徐匡迪, a Zhejiang native born in 1937 and a former president of Shanghai's Polytechnic University, was elected mayor, while Huang Ju became Shanghai's party secretary. An accomplished scholar in metallurgy and the recipient of many academic awards, Xu was the only mayor in China who was awarded membership in the prestigious Chinese Academy of Sciences in July 1995.[89] Although he was an alternate member of the 14th Central Committee, he did not have a lot of experience in either politics or administration until 1989 when he took a number of positions, such as head of the Higher Education Bureau, vice-mayor, and director of the Municipal Planning Commission. Indeed, the rise of Xu, as well as of his colleagues in Shanghai, symbolizes a new type of technocrats who are now emerging in China.

Observations about Shanghai's Political Leadership

The evolution of the careers of Shanghai's leaders shows a distinct pattern since 1949. First, with the exception of Beijing, the level of involvement of Shanghai leaders in national politics since 1949 has been much higher than most other localities.[90] After a lapse of several years in the early 1980s, since 1989 Shanghai's leaders have again become actively involved in national politics. Jiang Zemin's lack of an extensive political network in the central party–state hierarchy apparently prompted him to rely upon Shanghai and his former colleagues as his power base and network. During his tenure as general secretary and later as state president, more and more Shanghai officials were promoted to the capital in order to strengthen Jiang's political position as the post-Deng succession unfolded. In addition to Wu Bangguo and Huang Ju, other well-known examples include Jiang's promotion of Zeng Qinghong 曾慶紅 , the son of Zeng Shan 曾山 and a former deputy party secretary of Shanghai, to be the head of the important General Office of the Party's Central Committee, and Gong Xinhan 龔心瀚 , a former Shanghai official in charge of propaganda, as a deputy director of the Propaganda Department of the Central Committee.[91] Jiang also seems to rely upon research institutes in Shanghai to carry out policy research and make policy recommendations.[92] Similarly, Zhu Rongji recruited former staff members from Shanghai to Beijing, including, for instance, the promotion of Zhu Xiaohua 朱小華 , a former vice-president of the Shanghai Branch of the People's Bank, to the post of vice-governor of the People's Bank of China in 1993, and the appointment of Lou Jiwei 樓繼偉 , a former vice-director of Shanghai's Economic System Reform Office, as the department head of the State Commission for Restructuring the Economic System in 1992.[93] The current mayor, Xu Kuangdi, is also considered a Zhu protégé.

While some China observers have coined the term "Shanghai Faction," to describe such officials, it should again be emphasized that Jiang and Zhu recruited these cadres in order to shore up their political base in Beijing rather than to fight for Shanghai's interests. Nonetheless, their long association with Shanghai should help the city, just like Zhao Ziyang's generally sympathetic relations with Guangdong before his downfall in 1989. While such connections might be greatly helpful for the city in the short run, they may also backfire because the city's political status may be affected if its patrons fall from grace at the Centre.

Second, while most of Shanghai's leaders in the pre-reform era acted more like agents of the central government, the leadership since the mid-1980s has become more active in promoting and defending the interests of the city. For instance, Shanghai's leaders have voiced strong support for highly controversial central policies, such as the revenue sharing reform in 1994, while at the same time bargaining for central support for their pet project, Pudong. Repeating the compliant behaviour of his predecessors, Wu Bangguo openly stated Shanghai's position on revenue sharing at a press meeting in Beijing during a session of the National People's Congress in March 1994:

> Shanghai will resolutely carry out anything that has been decided on by the central authorities; Shanghai will not be exceptional to things that apply to the whole country; Shanghai will make more contributions to the central authorities annually while developing its economy.[94]

On the same occasion, however, mayor Huang Ju reported that:

> In deciding the sharing relationship between the central authorities and Shanghai, the central authorities once again assured that the policy of developing and opening up Pudong will not change and that the original mechanism with which Shanghai repays its own foreign debts will not change. All these show the Party Central Committee and State Council's support for Shanghai's work.[95]

The bargain between the Centre and Shanghai could not be more clearly revealed. By taking advantage of their connections at the Centre, recent Shanghai leaders have thus both pleased their Beijing bosses and bargained for Shanghai.

Finally, Shanghai has also served as the grooming and testing ground for potential national level leaders. In the post-Mao period, the most prominent promotions were, of course, Jiang Zemin, Zhu Rongji and Wu Bangguo. Other lesser examples include, for instance, Lin Hujia 林乎加, a former vice-chairman of the Shanghai Municipal Revolutionary Committee (1977–1978) who later became the mayor and party secretary of Beijing, Chen Jinhua 陳錦華, a former vice-mayor (1979–1983) who later became the minister of the State Planning Commission, and Ruan Chongwu 阮崇武, another former vice-mayor (1983–1985) who later became minister of Public Security, minister of Labour and the current party secretary and governor of Hainan province.[96] The promotion of Jiang and Zhu by Deng Xiaoping reflected the pre-eminent leader's calculation to introduce into the leadership core technocrats from Shanghai who can manage the economy and balance different political forces at the top echelon.

The Politics of Shanghai's Development

Several developments in the 1980s examined earlier are crucial to understand Shanghai's resurgence in the early 1990s. First, Shanghai's economic decline was beginning to spell fiscal difficulties for the central government.[97] Shanghai's leaders, on the other hand, were able to capture the attention of the central government to its fiscal crisis, which compelled a re-examination of Shanghai's economic predicament.[98] Second, the state of Shanghai's economic health had become as much an economic as a political problem for the Centre. Third, Shanghai's problems epitomized the difficulties of economic reform of the state sector in China, especially of the SOEs. No successful economic reform could ignore the difficulties of reforming SOEs, of which there were plenty in Shanghai. An awareness of these concerns among the top central leadership paved the way for policy adjustments towards Shanghai since the mid-1980s, but the critical move was not made until 1990.

Gradual Adjustments in Central Policy towards Shanghai

Attempts to revitalize Shanghai started first in the early 1980s inside the city itself before it became an issue for the Centre. Despite mayor Wang Daohan's efforts to revitalize Shanghai, he met with a great deal of frustration, not only because of bureaucratic inertia and the lack of central support, but also because of the lack of adequate resources. As early as 1981–1982, there was debate about the future development of Shanghai.[99] Grandiose visions for Shanghai were articulated by local policy researchers in the early 1980s, but few concrete measures were undertaken and not much material support was offered by the central government. One of the early central efforts to reconceptualize Shanghai's role in China's economy since 1978 was the plan in 1982 to build up a Shanghai Economic Zone comprising the city and five other nearby provinces, but it quietly ended in failure.[100]

Central policy thinking about Shanghai began to undergo important changes in the mid-1980s when top central leaders began to expand China's open policy. After Deng's first southern tour to Central and South China in early 1984, fourteen coastal cities, including Shanghai, were granted preferential policies akin to the SEZs. At a special meeting of the central Finance and Economics leading group held in mid-August 1984, Shanghai's party secretary Chen Guodong and mayor Wang Daohan presented a proposal to reinvigorate the city by upgrading its technology, building new industries, as well as by developing the tertiary sector. Soon afterwards, a central research and study group was sent to the city to draft, in co-operation with its party and state organs, a development strategy for

Shanghai.[101] This strategy led to the granting of perferential policies modelled after those given to Guangdong and Fujian. The preferential treatment included raising the revenue retention ratio and fixing this favourable arrangement for six years, increasing the foreign exchange retention ratio, and decentralizing more financial and foreign trade power to Shanghai.[102] In 1988, Shanghai was even granted a fiscal contracting system that had previously only been enjoyed by such provinces as Guangdong and Fujian.[103]

The shifting of China's focus of reform and development from South China to Shanghai in the early 1990s can thus be traced to a series of policy adjustments that began in the mid-1980s. In the early 1980s, most top central leaders, like Deng Xiaoping, Li Xiannian 李先念, Zhao Ziyang and Hu Yaobang, had already visited Shanghai.[104] Hu, the general secretary of the party, even suggested that Shanghai become a pioneer in China's modernization. Policy suggestions made by Zhao Ziyang, then premier, also preceded the Pudong development initiative in the early 1990s. For instance, in January 1985, Zhao declared that the "transformation and revitalization of Shanghai should be put on the agenda of the central authorities." In particular, he argued for a comprehensive re-examination of Shanghai's role in the Chinese economy:

> Shanghai plays an important role because it is China's biggest economic centre, and such a role cannot be played by any other province or municipality … Shanghai is one of China's biggest and oldest industrial bases but, at the same time, it is also the biggest port and international and domestic trade centre, a scientific and technological centre, and a banking centre. It should become our country's biggest information centre. We must proceed from all these to transform and revitalize Shanghai.[105]

One month later, in February 1985, the Centre decided to open three of China's most important deltas, including the Yangzi Delta, for foreign investment as part of a broadening of the open policy. Zhao's efforts to extend preferential policies to China's most dynamic coastal areas culminated in his proposal for a coastal development strategy in 1988 which, among other things, emphasized economic links between coastal China and the world economy. The efforts by Shanghai's leadership since 1985 were fairly successful in reinvigorating the city within the existing policy constraints and catching the attention of the Centre, yet these new ideas and policy adjustments did not lead to a large-scale effort to build up Shanghai as China's leading economic centre until 1990.

The Politics of Pudong's Development

Shanghai's resurgence came only after direct, central level intervention by China's pre-eminent leader in the early 1990s. While Deng Xiaoping agreed to approve the requests for special policy treatment by Guangdong and Fujian in April 1979, other central leaders, especially Chen Yun and Hu Qiaomu 胡喬木, were much less enthusiastic about such preferential policies because of their ideological and political implications. At the Centre, in December 1981, Chen Yun categorically ruled out an extension of SEZ policies to other areas. In Shanghai, however, mayor Wang Daohan, after consulting with experts in early 1980, was trying hard to put forward a proposal to build up Pudong. Despite objections from more conservative elements of the Shanghai leadership who thought this idea to be an reinstatement of the foreign settlements, both Wang and party secretary Chen Guodong withstood such criticism and put forward a report to the Centre.[106] Since the central government did not approve of the plan, Wang scaled down his proposal and instead suggested the construction of two smaller economic zones in Hongqiao 虹橋 and Minhang 閔行, with Caohejing 漕河涇 later added to this list. After extensive lobbying by the Shanghai leadership, the establishment of these three zones was finally approved in 1986, seven years after the SEZs in Guangdong and Fujian were approved by the central government.

As China remains a unitary party–state, initiatives by top leaders still constitute one of the most important ways to open the doors for bold economic reform. The establishment of the Pudong area to the east of Shanghai's city proper serves as an excellent example to show how politics, rather than simply economic planning, has been the key to the city's future.[107] Similar to the opening of Guangdong and Fujian in the late 1970s, Shanghai's recent Pudong development initiative was launched after support came from the top central leaders as well as after intensive lobbying efforts by the city. Despite repeated requests in the 1980s, the development of Pudong took off only after a "final push" by none other than Deng Xiaoping himself.[108] To Shanghai leaders' surprise, Deng wanted to speed up the development of Pudong during his spring festival visit there in February 1990.[109] Soon afterwards, Pudong received a package of special policies in April 1990 and later became the national focus of economic reform and development.

As a huge country with enormous geographical diversities, China is constantly looking for useful local experience that can serve as a

developmental model for the whole nation. Similar to the opening of
Guangdong and Fujian in 1979, Deng attempted to use Pudong to stimulate
China's economic reform and, at the same time, to establish another success story to boost his stature and to strengthen his own political power in
the aftermath of the 1989 political crisis. Again, just like the opening of
Guangdong and Fujian in the Chinese strategy of national unification,
Deng might also have contemplated using Shanghai to replace the increasingly recalcitrant Hong Kong when he advocated fast growth for the city
in the early 1990s.[110] This view merits serious attention, although it is
difficult to find official policy documents as substantive proof. *The
Economist*, for instance, argued that:

> What kicked Shanghai back into the forefront of China's modernisation was
> in part Mr. Deng's renewed itch for speedy growth, but more directly his
> distrust of Hong Kong — a sense that had been quickened in 1989 when
> Hong Kong staged huge demonstrations of popular support for the democracy
> protests in Beijing that culminated in the Tiananmen massacre ... From
> Beijing's point of view, Shanghai would make a safer powerhouse for
> Chinese development than Hong Kong ever could, because it can be con-
> trolled more easily — or so it is hoped.[111]

Deng's worry was probably proven correct in the eyes of the Chinese
government, especially in view of the deterioration of Sino–British relations after the arrival of the new Hong Kong Governor, Chris Patten, in
mid-1992. Patten's introduction of political reform, which was considered
contrary to the Basic Law and various diplomatic understandings between
the British and the Chinese governments, only served to reinforce the kind
of concerns that Deng and other leaders might have about the colony.

The future of Pudong's and Shanghai's development hinges, therefore,
very much on the support of the political coalition that commands the
Centre. A number of conditions still favour Shanghai. First, the development of Pudong did not seem to arouse as much élite disagreement as the
establishment of the SEZs in the early 1980s. Most of the key central
leaders, both retired and incumbent, have voiced their support for Shanghai and Pudong, most notably as a long-term strategy for reinvigorating
Shanghai and for developing the hinterland along the Yangzi River (長
江).[112] Much like his earlier imprimatur of the SEZs in Guangdong and
Fujian, Deng Xiaoping commented frequently on Shanghai's development
and hence tied himself closely to Pudong. In fact, the Pudong project
might appeal to diverse, competing political interests, ranging from eager

Shanghai leaders who had wanted central support for years, to the conservative party elder Chen Yun who was after all a Shanghainese himself and a patron of the state sector of the Chinese economy.[113] Chen, who passed away in April 1995, told mayor Huang Ju that he very much agreed with the opening of Pudong.[114] Hence the case of Shanghai contrasted most sharply with the opening of Guangdong and Fujian in the early 1980s when support came mostly from Deng Xiaoping, Hu Yaobang and, in particular, Zhao Ziyang. There was much less élite consensus about the special policies granted to these two provinces and their SEZs.[115] Second, Deng Xiaoping's move was not only economically sensible but also politically shrewd because the shift to Shanghai as the new focus of China's economic development served his goal of stimulating another phase of economic reform and high speed growth in the aftermath of the June 4 crisis in 1989. In his report to the 14th Party Congress held in mid-October 1992, Jiang Zemin pointed out that Shanghai should be built into an international economic, financial and commercial centre as soon as possible.[116] In sum, the opening of Pudong reflects not only Deng's political skills to stimulate fast-paced reform in the aftermath of 1989 and possibly his long-term strategic considerations to incorporate Hong Kong back into the motherland, but it also reflects the interplay of the political interests of Shanghai's leaders and the local community in Shanghai who longed for an answer to the physical and policy constraints of the city's development.[117]

Whither Shanghai?

Shanghai has played a critical role in contemporary Chinese politics and economic development because of its economic might and the political opportunities that may stem from such strength. Several tentative observations about Shanghai's future stand out in this overview of the political context of Shanghai's economic development. Forecasting Chinese politics has been proven to be a risky enterprise, but two scenarios about Shanghai's political and economic future might be contemplated.[118]

The first scenario is that, as China's future centre in finance, commerce and technology, Shanghai will probably act more as a leading member of an emerging coastal coalition rather than as an economic centre overshadowing all others in China's political economy. In fact, Shanghai's share in China's gross domestic product, gross industrial output and total retail sales is still only about 5% to 6%, but its potential is more easily discerned if examined in the context of China's "gold coast".[119] If Shanghai is grouped together with the five other leading provinces in eastern and southern China, namely, Guangdong, Fujian, Zhejiang, Jiangsu and Shandong, then the combined economic might of these six areas, which account for only one-quarter of the nation's population, would contribute over 40% of the gross domestic product, over 50% of the gross industrial output, and about 40% of total retail sales of the entire country. Should these provinces act together to bargain with the Centre on behalf of the more affluent coastal areas over social and economic policy, they would constitute a powerful lobby. In fact, during the deliberations over the Ninth Five-year Plan in Beidaihe in August 1995, one Hong Kong press report even suggested that Shandong, Shanghai, Zhejiang, Guangdong and Hainan had joined together and wrote to the Centre asking for a relaxation of macroeconomic control.[120] Shanghai, given its special economic and political status in China, will likely play a leading role in any such coalition.

The second scenario is that while the coastal provinces still compete fiercely with one another, the Centre will play off some provinces against the others. Indeed, political tradition and style as well as economic interests divide China's provinces and any future provincial coalitions might comprise changing sets of provinces rather than a stable group, with the exact composition depending upon the issues at stake. Hence the Centre may form alliances with some against the others over different issues. For instance, Shandong and Shanghai traditionally toe the Centre's line more closely than the others, and recent leaders from both areas have been co-opted into the central government.[121] On the other hand, Guangdong and Hainan 海南 are often more innovative in intrepreting and implementing central policies. Shanghai is, of course, part of the provincial grouping favoured by the Centre. This scenario is made more credible by developments in Chinese politics in 1995. Chen Xitong, the powerful former party secretary of Beijing, was sacked in May and officially expelled from his positions on the Politburo and other organs at the Fifth Plenum held in September 1995 because of his alleged corrupt lifestyle, negligence over rampant corruption committed by his subordinates and other questionable conduct.[122] His sudden fall was, however, obviously not a simple case against corrupt officials, but also a victory of the Centre under Jiang Zemin in dealing with a recalcitrant local strongman. Further, despite repeated assurances given by Jiang Zemin towards the SEZs in Guangdong since he took power, an open debate about the fate of the zones broke out in 1995 between policy researchers with close connections with the central government and officials in the SEZs.[123] Owing to the prevalence of corruption among Guangdong's local cadres and other social evils which are easily picked up by the Centre, one might wonder whether this star of China's reform era might well become the next victim in the divide-and-rule strategy of the Centre, which is now dominated by former and incumbent officials from Shanghai.[124] At the same time, however, Shanghai continues to receive support from the Centre, and immediately before the convening of the Fifth Plenum of the 14th Central Committee in late September 1995, its Pudong area was granted another package of favourable policies by the central government, especially to attract foreign investment in China's banking sector.[125] One Machivallian interpretation of these events is that these attacks against Guangdong might be a means to let off the grievances of the poor provinces, while ever more preferential policies will be offered to Jiang Zemin's power base, Shanghai.

It is too early to tell which of these scenarios will become the dominant trend in post-Deng China, although it is also possible that both scenarios will be played out in succession. The Fifth Plenum of the 14th Central Committee held in late September 1995 still confirmed central support for Pudong and the SEZs, yet there were hints that concrete policies might be adjusted.[126]

Shanghai's economic rebound since 1990 was undoubtedly spectacular. The annual growth of its gross domestic product rose from 3.5% in 1990 to 14–15% per annum in the 1992–1994 period. The increase of its gross industrial output again rose from 4% in 1990 to 20% in 1992–1993 and 17% in 1994.[127] The growth of foreign capital actually utilized also increased from 11% in 1991 to 42% per annum in 1992–1993 and 23% in 1994.[128] While Shanghai will become China's prime commercial and financial centre in the coming century, it will not be the only "key" to post-Deng China. Important as it is in Chinese politics and economics, Shanghai is unlikely to resume the domineering role it once enjoyed in the early part of this century since during the eighteen years of reform and opening to the outside world, other dynamic coastal provinces have already established themselves as economic powerhouses. Moreover, the heavy involvement of Shanghai's former and present officials in central level politics might introduce risks to its economic future. Undoubtedly, once unleashed in the 1990s, Shanghai will become a powerful political and economic force to be reckoned with in post-Deng China, but its role as China's most populous city, major cultural centre and largest urban economy will ensure that it can never escape the watchful eyes of the central government, no matter who is in power.

Notes

Works frequently cited have been identified by the following abbreviations:

QGZZLTZH *Quanguo gesheng, zizhiqu, zhixiashi lishi tongji ziliao huibian* 全國各省、自治區、直轄市歷史統計資料匯編
ZGJTZ *Zhongguo gongye jingji tongji ziliao* 中國工業經濟統計資料
LZZWRC *Lijie Zhonggong zhongyang weiyuan renming cidian* 歷屆中共中央委員人名詞典
SSJJFJ *Shanghai shehuizhuyi jingji jianshe fazhan jianshi* 上海社會主義經濟建設發展簡史

1. See, e.g., Rhoads Murphy, *Shanghai: Key to Modern China* (Cambridge: Harvard University Press, 1953).
2. See Marie-Claire Bergere, "'The Other China': Shanghai from 1919 to 1949" in *Shanghai: Revolution and Development in an Asian Metropolis*, edited by Christopher Howe (Cambridge: Cambridge University Press, 1981), chapter 1; Lucian W. Pye, "How China's Nationalism was Shanghaied," *Australian Journal of Chinese Affairs*, No. 29 (January 1993), pp. 107–33. Books on the social, economic and political development of Shanghai in the twentieth century are too numerous to cite. Aside from works cited in this volume, useful studies of modern and contemporary Shanghai include: J. Bruce Jacobs and Lijian Hong, "Shanghai and the Lower Yangzi Valley" in *China Deconstructs: Politics, Trade and Regionalism*, edited by David S. G. Goodman and Gerald Segal (London: Routledge, 1994), chapter 8; Betty Peth-T'i Wei, *Shanghai: Crucible of Modern China* (Hong Kong: Oxford University Press, 1987); Lynn T. White III, *Policies of Chaos: The Organizational Causes of Violence in China's Cultural Revolution* (Princeton: Princeton University Press, 1989), and *Shanghai Shanghaied?: Uneven Taxes in Reform China* (Hong Kong: Centre of Asian Studies, University of Hong Kong, 1991). General overviews by mainland Chinese researchers include, e.g., Chen Yi 陳沂 (ed.), *Dangdai Zhongguo de Shanghai* 當代中國的上海 (Shanghai in Contemporary China), vols. I, II (Beijing: Dangdai Zhongguo chubanshe 當代中國出版社, 1993); Zhongguo gongchandang Shanghai shiwei dangshi yanjiushi 中國共產黨上海市委黨史研究室 (ed.), *Zhongguo gongchandang zai Shanghai (1921–1991)* 中國共產黨在上海 (1921–1991) (The Chinese Communist Party in Shanghai, 1921–1991) (Shanghai: Shanghai renmin chubanshe 上海人民出版社, 1991).
3. Chen Yi (ed.), *Dangdai Zhongguo de Shanghai*, vol. I (see note 2), p. 41.
4. For an analysis of how the "Gang of Four" used Shanghai as a base in Chinese politics before and after the Cultural Revolution, see Parris Chang, "Shanghai and Chinese Politics: Before and after the Cultural Revolution," in *Shanghai*, chapter 3, edited by Christoper Howe (see note 2), pp. 66–90.

5. See, e.g., the special issue entitled "Shanghai: China's Financial Capital?", *Asian Wall Street Journal*, 22 November 1994, pp. S1–S16.

6. Hua Jianmin 華建敏 (ed.), *Kuashiji de gongcheng: Shanghai jingji, shehui yu chengshi fazhan guihua yanjiu* 跨世紀的工程：上海經濟、社會與城市發展規劃研究 (An Engineering Project Straddling across the Century: An Economic, Social and Urban Development Planning Study of Shanghai) (Shanghai: Shanghai renmin chubanshe, 1995), p. 6.

7. Guojia tongjiju gongye jiaotong wuzisi 國家統計局工業交通物資司 (ed.), *Zhongguo gongye jingji tongji ziliao 1949–1984* 中國工業經濟統計資料 1949–1984 (Industrial Economic Statistical Data of China, 1949–1984) (hereafter cited as *ZGJTZ 1949–1984*) (Beijing: Zhongguo tongji chubanshe 中國統計出版社, 1985), p. 145; Guojia tongjiju 國家統計局 (ed.), *Quanguo gesheng, zizhiqu, zhixiashi lishi tongji ziliao huibian* 全國各省、自治區、直轄市歷史統計資料匯編 (A Compendium of Historical Statistical Data of the Nation's Provinces, Autonomous Regions and Municipalities) (hereafter cited as *QGZZLTZH*) (Beijing: Zhongguo tongji chubanshe, 1991), p. 5.

8. *QGZZLTZH* (see note 7), various pages; Guangdongsheng tongjiju 廣東省統計局 (ed.), *Guangdong tongji nianjian 1991* 廣東統計年鑑 1991 (Statistical Yearbook of Guangdong 1991) (Beijing: Zhongguo tongji chubanshe, 1991), p. 36.

9. The following figures on industrial production came from *ZGJTZ 1949–1984*, p. 144; Guojia tongjiju 國家統計局 (ed.), *Zhongguo tongji nianjian 1994* 中國統計年鑑 1994 (Statistical Yearbook of China 1994) (Beijing: Zhongguo tongji chubanshe, 1994), p. 376.

10. Shanghaishi tongjiju 上海市統計局 (ed.), *Shanghai tongji nianjian 1995* 上海統計年鑑 1995 (Statistical Yearbook of Shanghai 1995) (Beijing: Zhongguo tongji chubanshe, 1995), p. 22; Guojia tongjiju (ed.), *Zhongguo tongji nianjian 1995*, 中國統計年鑑 1995 (Statistical Yearbook of China 1995) (Beijing: Zhongquo tongji chubanshe, 1995), p. 37.

11. White, *Shanghai Shanghaied?* (see note 2), p. 23; Yang Dongping 楊東平, *Chengshi jifeng: Beijing he Shanghai de wenhua jingshen* 城市季風：北京和上海的文化精神 (City Monsoons: The Civil Spirit of Beijing and Shanghai) (Beijing: Dongfang chubanshe 東方出版社, 1994), pp. 330–37.

12. For a highly readable account of Shanghai's economic predicament and its struggle to modernize in the reform era, see Yu Tianbai 俞天白, *Shanghai: Xingge ji mingyun* 上海：性格即命運 (Shanghai: Her Character = Her Destiny) (Shanghai: Shanghai wenyi chubanshe 上海文藝出版社, 1992).

13. Guangzhoushi tongjiju 廣州市統計局 (ed.), *Guangzhou tongji nianjian 1995* 廣州統計年鑑 1995 (Statistical Yearbook of Guangzhou 1995) (Beijing: Zhongguo tongji chubanshe, 1995) p. 389 and *Guangdong tongji nianjian 1991* (see note 8), pp. 84–85.

14. Guojia tongjiju (ed.), *Zhongguo tongji nianjian 1995* (see note 10), pp. 378–

79.

15. Beijing also suffered a similar fate as Shanghai. Such losses in Beijing rose from RMB1.2 billion in 1987 to RMB6 billion in 1993. Zhonghua renmin gongheguo caizhengbu *Zhongguo caizheng nianjian* bianji weiyuanhui 中華人民共和國財政部《中國財政年鑑》編輯委員會 (ed.), *Zhongguo caizheng nianjian 1994* 中國財政年鑑 1994 (Finance Yearbook of China 1994) (Beijing: Zhongguo caizheng zazhishe 中國財政雜誌社, 1994), pp. 355, 367.

16. United Investigation Group, "An Investigation into Shanghai State Enterprise's Profit and Losses," *Management World*, No. 3 (May 1995), p. 138.

17. *Guangzhou tongji nianjian 1995* (see note 13), p. 389; *Shanghai tongji nianjian 1995* (see note 10), p. 52.

18. United Investigation Group, "An Investigation into Shanghai State Enterprise's Profit and Losses" (see note 16), p. 139.

19. For an excellent analysis of Shanghai's fiscal relations with the Centre, see Lin Zhimin's chapter in Jia Hao and Lin Zhimin (eds.), *Changing Central-local Relations in China: Reform and State Capacity* (Boulder, CO: Westview, 1994), chapter 10.

20. Chen Minzhi 陳敏之 (ed.), *Shanghai jingji fazhan zhanlüe yanjiu* 上海經濟發展戰略研究 (A Study of Shanghai's Development Strategy) (Shanghai: Shanghai renmin chubanshe, 1985), p. 243.

21. *Shanghai tongji nianjian 1995* (see note 10), p. 25.

22. Ibid., p. 21; *Zhongguo tongji nianjian 1994* (see note 9), p. 213.

23. *Shanghai tongji nianjian 1995* (see note 10), p. 21.

24. Lin's chapter in Jia and Lin (eds.), *Changing Central-local Relations in China* (see note 19), pp. 240–41.

25. Only in 1985 and 1986 that such spending's share in total expenditure fell to 18%–19%, *Shanghai tongji nianjian 1995* (see note 10), p. 29.

26. Chen Mingzhi (ed.), *Shanghai jingji fazhan zhanlüe yanjiu* (see note 20), pp. 248–58.

27. Ibid., pp. 243–44.

28. Lin's chapter in Jia and Lin (eds.), *Changing Central-local Relations in China* (see note 19), p. 242.

29. *Jiefang ribao*, 3 October 1980, p. 1.

30. *Shanghai tongji nianjian 1995* (see note 10), p. 21.

31. See, e.g., the special issue of *Asian Wall Street Journal*, 22 November 1994. Such a prevailing view ignores the critical roles played by major classes and groups in Shanghai that had changed the course of Chinese politics.

32. I am not arguing that Shanghai is on the verge of major political change; rather, my point is that the historical experience of Shanghai should not be completely ignored. Major cities in China and other developing countries have all played critical roles in political change in this century, and they are

likely to do so in the future as China's economy modernizes.

33. Li Cheng and Lynn T. White III, "China's Technocratic Movement and the World Economic Herald," *Modern China*, 17 (July 1991), pp. 342–88.

34. This cursory discussion of such an exceptionally important topic, of course, cannot do justice to the subject matter. For specialized studies, see, e.g., Elizabeth Perry, *Shanghai on Strike* (Stanford: Stanford University Press, 1993); Jeffrey Wasserstrom, *Student Protests in Twentieth-century China* (Stanford: Stanford University Press, 1991); White III, *Policies of Chaos* (see note 2).

35. Guojia tongjju (ed.), *Zhongguo tongji nianjian 1995* (see note 10), pp. 601, 604.

36. *Shanghai tongji nianjian 1995* (see note 10), p. 52.

37. There are many eye-witness accounts of the 1989 crisis in Shanghai, see, e.g., Part V in Jonathan Unger (ed.), *The Pro-democracy Protests in China: Reports from the Provinces* (Armonk, New York: M. E. Shapre, 1991). For a spatial analysis, see James Tong, *The 1989 Democracy Movement in China: A Preliminary Spatial Analysis* (Hong Kong: Hong Kong Institute of Asia-Pacific Studies, The Chinese University of Hong Kong, 1994).

38. Tong, *The 1989 Democracy Movement in China* (see note 37), pp. 20, 32–35.

39. This section cannot offer more analysis of this important issue because of the lack of systematic and reliable data on collective political actions by workers in the reform era.

40. The "Centre" (*zhongyang*) refers to the "State Council and its commissions, ministries and leadership small groups in Beijing as well as the Party Politburo, Secretariat and the organs of the Central Committee." However, the term "central government," "central authorities" and "Centre" will be used interchangeably in this chapter. See Kenneth Lieberthal and Michel Oksenberg, *Policy Making in China* (Princeton, New Jersey: Princeton University Press, 1988), p. 138. The impact of local politics on Shanghai and its economic development is, of course, an important issue, but it deserves a separate treatment beyond the scope of this chapter.

41. See David S. G. Goodman, *Centre and Province in the People's Republic of China: Sichuan and Guizhou, 1955–1966* (Cambridge: Cambridge University Press, 1986), especially pp. 177–94.

42. David M. Lampton, *Paths to Power: Élite Mobility in Contemporary China* (Ann Arbor, Michigan: Center for Chinese Studies, University of Michigan, 1979), especially chapter 1.

43. Ibid., pp. 6–8. Peng Chong 彭冲, one of Shanghai's leaders in the initial post-Mao era, was one of his six cases, see ibid., chapter 3.

44. Ibid., p. 7.

45. See Pye's Foreword in Howe (ed.), *Shanghai* (see note 2), p. xiv.

46. See, e.g., *Jiushi niandai* 九十年代 (The Nineties) (Hong Kong), (December

1994), p. 33.

47. Unless otherwise specified, data on personnel changes in this chapter draws from Liu Jintian 劉金田 and Shen Xueming 沈學明 (eds.), *Lijie Zhonggong zhongyang weiyuan renming cidian* 歷屆中共中央委員人名詞典 (A Biographical Dictionary of Central Committee Members) (hereafter cited as *LZZWRC*) (Beijing: Zhonggong dangshi chubanshe 中共黨史出版社, 1992); the appendix in Ma Qibin 馬齊彬 et al. (eds.), *Zhongguo gongchandang zhizheng sishinian* 中國共產黨執政四十年 (The Chinese Communist Party in Power for Forty Years) (Beijing: Zhonggong dangshi chubanshe 中共黨史出版社, 1991), pp. 587–618. Editorial Board of *Who's Who in China* (ed.), *Who's Who in China: Current Leaders 1994* (1st edition, 1989, Beijing: Foreign Languages Press, 1994).

48. According to Susan Shirk, Deng Xiaoping and his associates also used fiscal decentralization to buy provincial support for Deng's reform and open-door policy. See Susan Shirk, *The Political Logic of Economic Reform in China* (Berkeley: University of California Press, 1993), chapter 9.

49. By Cultural Revolution, this chapter follows the official definition of the 1966–1976 period for the sake of simplicity.

50. Sun Huairen 孫懷仁 (ed.), *Shanghai shehuizhuyi jingji jianshe fazhan jianshi, 1949–1985* 上海社會主義經濟建設發展簡史, 1949–1985 (A Concise History of the Development of Shanghai's Socialist Economic Construction, 1949–1985) (hereafter cited as *SSJJFJ*) (Shanghai: Shanghai renmin chubanshe, 1990), p. 207.

51. A short biography of Ke Qingshi can be found in Liu and Shen (eds.), *LZZWRC* (see note 47), pp. 262–63.

52. Andrew Walder, *Chang Ch'un-ch'iao and Shanghai's January Revolution* (Ann Arbor: Center for Chinese Studies at the University of Michigan, 1978), pp. 6–7.

53. Another Politburo member Gao Gang was the secretary of the Northeast Bureau and Northeast People's Government Committee, later called Northeast Administrative Committee, but he reputedly committed suicide in 1954 after he and Rao Shushi failed to win in the first major factional struggle in the party since the establishment of the PRC.

54. This removal project was completed only in 1973; see Sun (ed.), *SSJJFJ* (see note 50), pp. 467–70. In order to preserve their power base, the "Gang of Four" did ensure adequate provisions of materials to Shanghai during the Cultural Revolution.

55. Chen was in office from September 1954 until the completion of his tenure in Shanghai in November 1958; Ke from January 1965 until his death in April 1965 and Zhang from January 1975 until his downfall in October 1976.

56. See Parris Chang's chapter in Howe (ed.), Shanghai (see note 2); for a Chinese account, see *ZGS* (see note 2), chapter 7.

57. See Goodman's chapter in Howe (ed.), *Shanghai*, chapter 5.

58. Merle Goldman, *China's Intellectuals: Advice and Dissent* (Cambridge: Harvard University Press, 1981), chapter 6.

59. Other radical cadres were also promoted to the Centre. For instance, although not formally a leader from Shanghai, Yu Huiyong 于會泳, a former music teacher from Shanghai who joined the camp of the "Gang of Four," was also promoted to become a Central Committee member in 1973 and later became the minister of Culture in 1975. Yu was not counted in Table 3.3.

60. See Goodman's chapter in Howe (ed.), *Shanghai* (see note 2), pp. 148–49.

61. Sun (ed.), *SSJJFJ* (see note 50), p. 589.

62. Liu and Shen (eds.), *LZZWRC* (see note 47), pp. 302–3.

63. Chen Yi (ed.), *Dangdai Zhongguo de Shanghai*, Vol. II (see note 2), pp. 292–93.

64. On the difficulties of dealing with such ideological problems in Shanghai, please refer to a collection of articles by a former deputy party secretary and director of the propaganda department in Shanghai. Chen Yi, *Shinian licheng* 十年歷程 (A Ten-year Journey) (Shanghai: Baijia chubanshe 百家出版社, 1990); also see *ZGS* (see note 2), pp. 604–605.

65. Chen Yi (ed.), *Dangdai Zhongguo de Shanghai* (see note 2), p. 102.

66. With the exception of Peng, both Su and Ni had important duties in addition to their posts in Shanghai: Su was the first political commissar of the Navy of the People's Liberation Army since 1973 while Ni had served as the chairman of the All-China Federation of Trade Unions since 1978.

67. Su passed away in April 1979; Lampton, *Paths to Power* (see note 42), p. 94.

68. The comment on his team-player style was suggested in Lampton, *Paths to Power* (see note 42), p. 101.

69. *Who's Who in China 1989* (see note 47), p. 40; Liu and Shen (eds.), *LZZWRC* (see note 47), p. 230.

70. Gao Xin 高新 and He Pin 何頻, *Zhu Rongji chuan* 朱鎔基傳 (A Biography of Zhu Rongji) (Taibei: Xin xinwen wenhua shiye youxian gongsi 新新聞文化實業有限公司, 1993), pp. 86–87.

71. *Who's Who in China 1994* (see note 47), pp. 617–18; for a biography of Jiang by a Hong Kong-based China watcher, see Zheng Yi 鄭義, *Jiang Zemin zhuanqi* 江澤民傳奇 (A Biography of Jiang Zemin) (Hong Kong: Ming chuang chubanshe 明窗出版社, 1992).

72. Liu and Shen (eds.), *LZZWRC* (see note 47), pp. 264–65.

73. Ruan Chongwu 阮崇武, another deputy secretary and vice-mayor from Shanghai, was made a full Central Committee member, but he was transferred to become a minister of Public Security in September 1985.

74. For an excellent analysis of the relationship between Shanghai's leadership and reform strategy, see Zhimin Lin, "Shanghai's Big Turnaround since 1985: Leadership, Reform Strategy, and Resource Mobilization." Paper

delivered at the Centre of Asian Studies, University of Hong Kong, 21 October 1995.

75. Some observers suggested Wang Daohan was the key person that highly recommended Jiang for the mayorship. Zheng Yi, *Jiang Zemin zhuanqi* (see note 71), p. 84–89. Jiang has maintained close relationship with Wang since the mid-1980s and it is widely known that Wang still exercises strong influence over policy making in Shanghai.

76. In addition to Jiang Zemin and Ruan Chongwu, four other leaders from Shanghai, namely, Wu Bangguo, Huang Ju, Gu Zhuanxun 顧傳訓 and Chen Zhili 陳至立 were elected alternate members of the Central Committee in the 13th Party Congress held in 1987.

77. Please refer to Zhimin Lin's paper, "Shanghai's Big Turnaround since 1985" (see note 74).

78. Zheng Yi, *Jiang Zemin zhuanqi* (see note 71), chapter 7.

79. *Shanghai tongji nianjian 1995* (see note 10), p. 26.

80. Zhu did serve very briefly in the Industrial Department of the Northeast China People's Government in 1951–1952, *Who's Who in China 1994* (see note 47), p. 943.

81. Such an assessment was widely shared among his observers, see, Zheng Yi, *Jiang zemin zhuanqi* (see note 71) and Gao and He, *Zhu Rongji chuan* (see note 70).

82. Gao and He, *Zhu Rongji chuan* (see note 70), pp. 92, 216.

83. Ibid., pp. 218–27; also see Suisheng Zhao, "Deng Xiaoping's Southern Tour: Élite Politics in Post-Tiananmen China," *Asian Survey*, 33 (August 1994), pp. 739–56.

84. For their background, see *Wen hui bao* 文匯報 (Wen Wei Pao) (Hong Kong), 29 September 1994, p. A2.

85. Of the 2,752 NPC deputies present in the voting over his nomination, Wu received 2,366 supporting votes, 210 votes against and 161 votes abstained, and another 15 people's deputies did not participate in the voting. Jiang Chunyun 姜春雲, his counterpart from Shandong who was also elected a vice-premier, received a total of 996 negative and abstained votes, and only 1,746 votes in favour, see *South China Morning Post*, 18 March 1995, p. 1.

86. *Hong Kong Economic Times*, 30 September 1995, p. A11.

87. By technocrat, I refer simply to officials who had a professional qualification as scientists, engineers, or professional managers. For a more detailed analysis of the technocratic tendencies in China, see Li Cheng and Lynn T. White III, "The Thirteenth Central Committee of the Chinese Communist Party: From Mobilizers to Managers," *Asian Survey*, 28 (April 1988), pp. 371–99.

88. Biographical details in this section draw from Shanghai shehuikexueyuan *Shanghai jingji nianjian* she 上海社會科學院《上海經濟年鑑》社 (ed.),

Shanghai jingji nianjian 1994 上海經濟年鑑 1994 (Shanghai Economic
Yearbook 1994) (Shanghai: Shanghai shehuikexueyuan *Shanghai jingji
nianjian* she 上海社會科學院《上海經濟年鑑》社, 1994), pp. 25–29.

89. *Hong Kong Economic Times*, 17 August 1995, p. A12.

90. Owing to the lack of comparable data and studies, I am unable to compare
systematically the pattern of political involvement of Shanghai with the other
provinces. My observations do not touch upon the role of the military in
politics.

91. Willy Wo-lap Lam, *China after Deng Xiaoping* (Hong Kong: PA
Professional Consultants, 1994), p. 336.

92. While acknowledging the difficulty of pinpointing the impact of such
researchers and their output, it is clear that many of the Shanghai analysts
wrote their reports with Beijing's concerns right at heart. For examples of
such writings, see, e.g., Fudan fazhan yanjiuyuan 復旦發展研究院 (ed.),
Goujian xintizhi —— 1994 Zhongguo fazhan baogao 構建新體制 —— 1994
中國發展報告 (Establishing a New System —— China's Development Report
1994) (Shanghai: Shanghai renmin chubanshe, 1994).

93. Information from *China Directory 1995* (Tokyo: Radio Press, 1995), pp. 72,
101. Lou was later made a vice-governor of Guizhou 貴州.

94. Reported in *Jiefang ribao*, 11 March 1994, in *Foreign Broadcast Information
Service, FBIS-CHI-94-074*, 18 April 1994, pp. 56–57.

95. Ibid.

96. Chen Yi (ed.), *Dangdai Zhongguo de Shanghai*, vol. II (see note 2), pp. 657–
59.

97. Please refer to Lin Zhimin's chapter in Jia and Lin (eds.), *Changing Central–
local Relations in China* (see note 19), chapter 10 and White III, *Shanghai
Shanghaied?* (see note 2).

98. Lin's chapter in Jia and Lin (eds.), *Changing Central–local Relations in
China* (see note 19), p. 247.

99. See Chen Yi (ed.), *Dangdai Zhongguo de Shanghai*, vol. I (see note 2), p. 335
and Lam Tao-chiu's, "Local Interest Articulation in the 1980s" (Chapter 5),
in this volume.

100. For an account of this issue, see *SSJJFJ* (see note 50), pp. 613–15.

101. For an account of these developments, see Chen Yi (ed.), *Dangdai Zhongguo
de Shanghai*, vol. I (see note 2), pp. 336–39.

102. For details, see ibid. and Lin's chapter in Jia and Lin (eds.), *Changing
Central–local Relations in China* (see note 19), pp. 247–48.

103. Ibid., pp. 250–52.

104. See Chen Yi (ed.), *Dangdai Zhongguo de Shanghai*, vol. I (see note 2), p.
326.

105. *Foreign Broadcast Information Service*, (see note 94), 16 January 1985, p.
K1.

106. Yu Tianbai, *Shanghai: Xingge ji mingyun* (see note 12), p. 199.
107. The following analysis of Pudong aims only to illustrate the significance of political intervention in Shanghai's development. Anthony G. O. Yeh's "Pudong: Remaking Shanghai as a World City" (Chapter 11) in this volume, however, provides a more detailed analysis of this new development area.
108. Please refer to Anthony G. O. Yeh's "Pudong: Remaking Shanghai as a World City" (Chapter 11) in this volume as well as Lin Zhimin and Wang Jiangwei, "Politics of SEZs: The Case of Shanghai's Pudong" (unpublished paper, October 1992). I would like to thank Professors Lin and Wang for sharing their paper, and this section is indebted to their insights.
109. Lin and Wang, "Politics of SEZs: The Case of Shanghai's Pudong" (ibid.), p. 9.
110. Whether Shanghai will eventually replace Hong Kong is another issue that has been touched upon in Y. M. Yeung's "Introduction" (Chapter 1) of this volume.
111. *The Economist*, 24 December 1994–6 January 1995, p. 26.
112. For instance, in the summer of 1995, Li Peng suggested that while some concrete measures might be adjusted, central policy support for Pudong would not be changed. He also reiterated his support to develop Pudong and to build up Shanghai into one of the international economic, financial and trading centres. *Xinhua Monthly* 新華月報, May 1995, p. 72.
113. Also see Lin and Wang, "Politics of SEZs: The Case of Shanghai's Pudong" (see note 108), pp. 10–18.
114. For excerpts on speeches and policy documents by party elders and current leaders in favour of Pudong's development, please refer to Zhao Qizheng 趙啓正 (ed.), *Xin shiji, xin Pudong* 新世紀，新浦東 (New Century, New Pudong) (Shanghai: Fudan daxue chubanshe 復旦大學出版社, 1994), pp. 320–32. Nonetheless, no satisfactory explanation of Chen Yun's calculations in supporting Pudong was offered yet. Some China observers argued that Chen supported Pudong in order to pre-empt Deng Xiaoping, Gao and He, *Zhu Rongji chuan* (see note 70), p. 147.
115. On the case of Guangdong, please refer to Peter T. Y. Cheung's chapter in Y. M. Yeung and David K. Y. Chu (eds.), *Guangdong: Survey of a Province Undergoing Rapid Change* (Hong Kong: The Chinese University Press, 1994), chapter 2.
116. *Xinhua Monthly*, October 1992, p. 12.
117. Lin and Wang, "Politics of SEZs: The Case of Shanghai's Pudong" (see note 108), pp. 10–13.
118. This discussion, of course, does not preclude other scenarios, nor are these two scenarios mutually exclusive.
119. Statistics calculated from *Zhongguo tongji nianjian 1994* (see note 9), pp. 32, 35, 60, 376, 377, 496.

120. *Ming bao*, 24 August 1995, p. A2.
121. For an excellent analysis of Shandong's reform and development strategy, see Jae Ho Chung's paper, entitled "Shandong's Strategies of Reform and Opening," delivered at the annual meeting of Association for Asian Studies, Washington, D.C., on 8 April 1995.
122. *South China Morning Post*, 3 October 1995, p. 8.
123. For analyses of this debate, see *Jiushi niandai*, October 1995, pp. 49–51 and *South China Morning Post*, 20 September 1995, p. 21.
124. *South China Morning Post*, 15 August 1995, p. 8 and 20 September 1995, p. 21.
125. *Wen hui bao* (Hong Kong), 19 September 1995, p. A2.1
126. The text of the communique can be found in *Da gong bao* 大公報 (Ta Kung Pao) (Hong Kong), 5 October 1995, pp. A5–A6.
127. *Shanghai tongji nianjian 1995* (see note 10), pp. 24–26.
128. Ibid., pp. 23–26.

4

Institutional and Administrative Reform

King K. Tsao

Before the adoption of China's open policy in the late 1970s, Shanghai was a typical large city under the planned economy which had been introduced in the 1950s under the Soviet development strategy. In this development strategy, the large city was an industrial centre, producing industrial goods, for which the countryside supplied agricultural products. At the time, China was primarily divided into two distinct parts. The first included the cities which were the base for industrialization, supplying expensive capital goods. The second included the countryside which supplied cheap agricultural raw materials or semi-materials to the cities. This strategy enabled the cities to function as centres for collecting revenue to support the state's industrialization programmes. By this mechanism, the state could extract the surplus value from the countryside to subsidize industrial production and to maintain workers' living standards in the cities.[1] Nonetheless, this division was also complicated by the institution of the household registration system which forbade the migration of the peasantry to the cities.[2]

Parallel to this development strategy, the Shanghai municipal government was fully equipped organizationally to meet its economic needs and tasks. The municipal government had multiple layers of bureaucracy and institutions to manage the economic system in accordance with the plan. All inputs and outputs of production were allocated and dictated by the bureaucrats in these multi-layered departments.[3] There was no market. Bureaucrats carried out all the minute and detailed planning, allocations, distribution and, above all, co-ordination.[4] Bureaucratic red-tape, overstaffing, inertia, functional overlapping, inefficiencies and other related bureaucratic problems plagued the system.[5] Additionally, many bureaux and administrative organs merely reflected the overall design of the planned economy and the tasks set by it. The administrative structure was

Research for this chapter was supported by two research grants: the Hong Kong Research Grants Council and the South China Programme of The Chinese University of Hong Kong. This financial help enabled the author to make three separate field trips, in August 1994, January 1995 and May 1995, to conduct in-depth interviews with scholars and officials in Shanghai. The author wishes to thank professors Zhou Shiqiu 周世逑 and Wu Zhihua 吳志華 for their expertise in the preparation of this chapter. The encouragements, suggestions and comments made by professors Jon Elster, Nina Halpern, Tang Tsou (鄒讜), Yue-man Yeung (楊汝萬), John Worthley and the views by an anonymous reviewer are also appreciated.

based on the principle of sectoral management, and subsequently it was divided into the metallurgy, chemical, railways, communication, posts and telecommunications, water resources, construction, geology, agriculture, forestry, mineral resources, energy resources, electrical power industry, coal, machine-building, electronics, materials and equipments sectors, to name a few.

With the reform of the state and the economy in the post-Mao era, administrative and institutional changes followed as well in Shanghai. The questions to be addressed here are: To what extent have these institutional and administrative changes occurred? What are their significance, prospects and limitations? And how is this related to the larger political and economic picture? These are the focus of this chapter, which is organized in three parts. First, it traces some of the formal institutional and administrative reform of Shanghai both in the 1980s and 1990s to map out changes and continuities. Second, it evaluates the extent, scope and degree of change in light of the national context. Finally, a few concluding remarks summarize this chapter.

Administrative Changes

The 1980s

Shanghai established many non-permanent administrative bodies to deal with matters as they emerged. The municipal government had to follow the directives and issues of prime concern of the central government. Within the context of the central–local relationship, more than 40 non-permanent organizations were formed in 1983.[6] This number increased to over 80 in 1985.[7] Such non-permanent committees were usually headed by a vice-mayor who could add authority to the administrative body. As a result of this proliferation of organizations with unclear boundaries of responsibility, the city government created additional institutions to co-ordinate the various functions of these committees. This was done by the setting up of a "joint conference" (*lianxi huiyi* 聯席會議) system which could bring different hierarchical and administrative units together.[8] The rationale was to include all the leaders in the departments concerned, who could hold meetings to resolve their differences. This would achieve consensus among various agencies, cutting across the boundaries of multiple bureaux,[9] in order to formulate coherent policies on important issues. The advantage of this *ad hoc* "joint conference" was to reduce the number of non-permanent organizations in the governmental structure. Furthermore, it was incorporated into the existing bureaucratic structure without creating any new organizations. However, its existence was an indication of the organizational redundancy and of the lack of clear functional delineation. In short, there were many organizations and staff at the municipal level.[10]

Shanghai was slow in implementing administrative and institutional changes in the early 1980s, despite the national institutional reform in 1982. As the emphasis of the national institutional reform indicated at the time, Shanghai followed suit by incorporating more younger and educated cadres into the municipal government. There was a concern over the issue of succession. Older revolutionary cadres had to retire so that the younger and the educated cadres could have the jobs. This was primarily a political consideration which had institutional implications as well. In sum, administrative problems were compounded by the setting up of more organizations on issues of finance, trade and auditing in order to meet the economic changes of the time.[11]

Additionally, the policy priority for development pursued by the central government was to emphasize Guangdong province and the Special Economic Zones. Shanghai was the traditional base for providing a lion's share of the national coffers and the risks of reducing Shanghai's contribution would have been serious.[12] However, there was a vocal urge for change in Shanghai as a result of the unequal financial arrangements between Shanghai and the Centre.[13]

The year 1988 was a significant year for Shanghai.[14] A national institutional reform was launched in that year, as well. The political environment was very favourable for institutional and administrative reform.[15] A few strong and consolidated steering committees were set up to strengthen, streamline and centralize the various tasks which had been performed by different agencies. These were not *ad hoc* in nature like the "joint conference." They were matrix organizations,[16] with functional co-ordination within the overlapped and fragmented authoritarian system.[17] They could enhance organizational effectiveness. These improvements were particularly noticeable in the fields of city planning, construction and foreign investment.

The Municipal Integrated Economic Leading Group was formed to improve macro management and co-ordination of various departments. It served to formulate the development strategies on issues of personnel, capital and materials, and to implement economic policies.[18] All these could enhance the overall planning capacity of the city and the long-term strategic co-ordination of various departments by developing coherent and consistent policies.

The Municipal Construction Fund was set up to raise and make use of funding for the promotion of real estate business, and for the construction of basic infrastructure within the city.[19] Shanghai was short on capital for infrastructure building as most of its profits and revenues had been remitted to the central government since 1949.[20] The formation of the Fund was to rectify the relative backwardness of the city's infrastructure provisions. Gradually, policies were enacted to encourage private investments in real estate development by both domestic and overseas investors.

Above all, the establishment of the Shanghai Foreign Investment Working Commission on 10 June 1988 represented the most important institution-building effort. Before the creation of this Commission, foreign investors needed to go through 5 commissions and offices, and 20 bureaux of the government (or at least 40 official seals and a maximum of 126 official seals) in order to get approval for an investment project.[21] This newly created commission consisted of four components to promote administrative authority and institutional effectiveness.[22] Then Mayor Zhu Rongji 朱鎔基 was the director of the Commission. Committee members included vice-directors of the Planning Commission, Foreign Economic and Trade Commission, Economic Commission and the Construction Commission. New investment regulations were also issued to clarify the investment procedures and to make the process more transparent. Finally, an official seal was needed to approve investment applications,[23] substantially cutting the red-tape and bureaucratic layers. For instance, before the establishment of this Commission, direct foreign investment grew 44% annually from 1985 to 1987. The 1988 figure, however, increased by 72% in comparison with the 1987 data. Other forms of foreign investment also increased dramatically, 55 times more in 1988 as compared with 1987.[24]

The 1990s

Institutional and administrative changes stagnated momentarily after the 1989 Tiananmen incident (天安門事件), including the agenda for functional delineation and streamlining set in the 1988 national institutional reform package. However, the momentum for changes in Shanghai continued as China opened up and reformed the economic system. At the 14th Party Congress held in October 1992, China further reoriented the economy in the fundamental direction of a socialist market. The strategy was to have a market system economically, but a socialist system politically.[25] The new orientation of the economy guided the tactics of the institutional reform package in 1993. The mechanisms were to convert some economic departments into commercial entities and to strengthen the roles of others in their regulation, co-ordination, supervision and formulation capacities for mid- and long-term plans.

First, the separation of politics from the enterprise is to make the enterprise run as a commercial entity, eliminating the intervention of politics at the enterprise level. It involves a reduction in the power of the government by enlarging the role played by the market. Thus, by 1995, some industrial bureaux were turned into stocks companies.[26]

Another feature of the institutional reform is functional consolidation. The merging of two or more administrative units which perform similar tasks into a single agency has been the norm. This is done to streamline the bureaucracy by reducing overlapping functions and hierarchical redundancy. Take the Educational Commission as an example. The educational functions in the Municipal Education and Health Office, the Higher Education Bureau and the Education Bureau have been combined and merged into the Municipal Educational Commission.[27] An overarching commission has been set up to deal with all related educational matters. This differs from the previous practice of setting up two or more bureaux to deal with the functional areas of adult education and higher education. This is also true in the real estate and land sectors. The Bureau of Real Estate and Land Administration has been created to replace the administrative units of the Bureau of Real Estate, the Land Administration Bureau and the Office of Housing Reform.[28]

The final approach is a middle course to commercialize most of the activities of the bureaux by setting up companies, while retaining some of their administrative functions. For instance, the former Architectural Materials Industry Bureau and the Architectural Engineering Administration Bureau of the Construction Commission have been turned into commercial companies, while maintaining two administrative offices in the Construction Commission to carry out the necessary administrative tasks.[29] The newly-created Architecture Administration Office and the Architectural Materials Administration Office are lower in hierarchical rank and have less power than that of the previous two bureaux.[30]

Comparing the current municipal government structure (Appendix I) with that of 1986, some departments still remain intact — retaining the basic functions of the government. These include the Civil Affairs Bureau, Judiciary Bureau, Archives Bureau, Establishment Committee, Personnel Bureau, Organizational Affairs Bureau, Nationalities Affairs Committee, Religious Affairs Administration and the Overseas Chinese Affairs Office. They are the fundamental units of the municipal government. New organizations have also been created or strengthened to deal with issues, including the Aerospace Bureau, Bureau of Power Construction, No. 2 Light Industry Bureau, the Social Security Administration Bureau, Supervisory Bureau, Railways Bureau, Posts and Telecommunications Bureau, Geology and Mineral Resources Bureau, Afforestation Committee, Marine Security Supervisory Bureau and Channel Bureau. All these reflect the changing economic and social environment. Some obsolete institutions such as the Handicraft Industry Administration Bureau, Aviation Industry Office, and Supply and Sales Cooperatives were abolished as they have not met the goals of or adapted to the pace of reform.

Shanghai has established the Textile State-owned Assets Administration Company. This is to be in charge of all the state-owned textile enterprises. At the national level, the Textile Industry Association has been set up. Shanghai has not followed suit, however. The Textile Bureau is still in the government structure.[31] The State-owned Assets Administration Company does not have the formal power of a bureau. It is an intermediary institution (*zhongjie jigou* 中介機構), or a quasi-public organization, to replace the formal functions of the bureau. This is one of the most important institutional changes, though this change is not fully reflected in the formal organizational chart of the municipal government.

The setting up of intermediary organizations implies that the society and economy have more autonomous power.[32] Tasks performed by the quasi-public organizations include accounting, legal affairs, adjudication and other consultancy services.[33] For example, in the Hongkou 虹口 district of Shanghai, there were 44 quasi-public organizations by the end of 1993.[34] The intermediary organization is different from the traditional dichotomy between private and public organizations.[35] Formal governmental power has been shifted to the quasi-public organizations, which are not yet commercial organizations.[36] These organizations still perform some management functions. In sum, this represents a restructuring of intergovernmental relationships within a wider theoretical perspective.[37] However, the Pudong 浦東 government has undergone, by far, the greatest institutional and administrative changes.[38]

Pudong New Area

The development of Pudong New Area can be traced back to 1984 when the "Outline on the Economic Development Strategies of Shanghai" was drafted. That was the earliest mention of the planning and development plan for Pudong.[39] A position paper on the development strategies of Shanghai was formally proposed, and it was eventually accepted by the State Council in February 1985.[40] The development strategies included the direction, goals, and the necessary conditions and policies to achieve these aims.[41] In 1986, the municipal government, along with many research institutes and universities, conducted research on the economic conditions in Shanghai. In May 1988, an international conference on the development of Pudong was held.[42] In early 1989, the Party Centre decided to develop Pudong.[43] Finally, the declaration to set up Pudong New Area was formally announced by Li Peng 李鵬 on 18 April 1990.[44] Pudong has since accelerated its development with unparalleled momentum, with most of the infrastructure works being set up within the last five years.

The salient features of Pudong's intermediary institutions are particularly relevant to a study of institutional changes. Administratively, the Pudong government is under the direct jurisdiction of the Shanghai municipal government and the director of the Pudong Management Committee is also a vice-mayor of Shanghai municipal government.[45] The structure of the Pudong government is described as follows (see also Appendix II).

In comparison with the Shanghai municipal government, the Pudong government has a simplified institutional arrangement, with only ten bureaux.

1. Industrial and Commercial Administration
   To deal with the administration of industrial and commercial activities, and the registration of new enterprises in the district.

2. Bureau of Finance and Tax
   Power to fix the budget for the district, and manage state-owned capital and taxes.

3. Bureau of Social Development
   Instead of setting up many organizations to deal with such issues as culture, health, science and technology, education, medicine, sports, civil affairs, and community management, there is only one bureau to deal with all these issues.

4. Urban Construction Administration
   In charge of public facilities, environmental sanitation and traffic issues.

5. Bureau of Rural Development
   To handle all issues related to the rural economy, village and county construction, and water resources.

6. Bureau of Economy and Trade
   Responsible for industry, commerce, external trade and economic co-ordination.

7. Integrated Planning and Land Bureau
   To deal with the issues of social, economic and city planning, and matters pertaining to land and real estate management.

8. Commission for Disciplinary Inspection/Supervisory Bureau
   This is a combination of two units from the party and the government. It deals with the party's disciplinary inspection, and the government's administrative supervision and auditing.

9. Organization Department/Labour and Personnel Department
   To handle all issues relating to civil service reform, personnel issues in the party and government, and the labour market.

10. Party Committee/Administration Office
    To handle all supporting services such as secretarial, administrative and service-related works. Such issues as external and foreign affairs relationships, promotions and the united front are also included.[46]

Pudong New Area has administrative power equivalent to the vice-provincial level. It has jurisdiction in areas of planning, approving of projects, finance and banking, foreign affairs, external trade, labour and personnel matters. However, issues related to the overall development of Shanghai and its relationship with Puxi 浦西 area are not within its jurisdiction. Furthermore, if proposals and policies must be approved by the Party Centre or the State Council, then the Pudong government must get approval from the municipal government first.[47] Pudong has much power in comparison with the 11 other districts in Shanghai. The structure of Pudong New Area is different from that of the traditional Puxi area. It takes a market-oriented approach to economic affairs by reducing the hierarchical layers of the government.[48]

The institutional structure of the Pudong government also displays the following characteristics. First, the overall design is based on the principle of "small government and big society."[49] As stated previously, the Shanghai municipal government still sets up bureaux to run community affairs. In Pudong, however, the Bureau of Social Development deals with all these issues. The Integrated Planning and Land Bureau handles issues related to social, economic and city planning, and matters pertaining to land and real estate management, as does the Bureau of Rural Development.

Second, there are no specialized economic bureaux in Pudong, as for example, the Chemical Industry Bureau, Machinery and Electrical Industry Administration Bureau, and the Instruments and Telecommunications Industry Bureau, to manage these economic activities. Such tasks have been completely delegated to the enterprises.[50] The government does not manage the specific sector and industry, but maintains some control over the flow of capital and over issues of macro management.

Third, the Pudong government was deliberately created without direct reference to the old municipal structure. The old structure was constrained by its inability to cut the staff size and to adopt radical institutional restructuring.[51] The Pudong government represents a radical departure from previous practices. It is not only an experimental site, but it also indicates future possible directions for institutional changes.

Fourth, the existence of intermediary institutions and the civil service reforms have enabled the Pudong government to keep down the number of staff. Pudong has been ahead of Shanghai in implementing civil service reforms, Young civil servants have been openly recruited to sit for competitive and open examinations. There is a total of about 800 staff in the Pudong government.[52]

Significance, Implications and Limitations

In this section, some theoretical issues revolving around institutional and administrative reform, within the larger political context, are addressed. These include partial reform, the relationship between the party and the government, intergovernmental relationships and the linkage between factional politics and development.

Partial Reform

Shanghai has adopted a partial reform strategy, or piecemeal reform, for institutional and administrative reform. A partial reform is different from the comprehensive reform introduced in the former Soviet Union and Eastern European countries. The Pudong government, as an experimental site, exhibits some radical elements by using the principle of "small government and big society." However, in Shanghai proper, large-scale staff reduction or the extensive abolition of institutions has not taken place. This is also true for the national institutional and administrative reforms. The Textile Industry Bureau and Light Industry Bureau have been abolished, yet guild associations have been created to retain some of the administrative functions of the previous bureaux.[53] Textile workers still receive payments from the government even though their enterprises continue to lose money. This reflects a concern about stability by the reform élite. If workers lose their jobs, they will have no protection. However, laying off staff will reduce financial burdens and enhance competitiveness. This is a trade-off between efficiency and stability. After all, the goal of the institutional and administrative reform is stability. There are contradictory elements, both old and new, in the administrative system.[54] This is consistent with the overall partial reform strategy at the national level; in this respect, Shanghai is no exception.

Party and Government

To a certain extent, the relationship between the party and the government in Pudong also manifests the pattern of partial reform. It represents the unity and combination of the party's organizations with the governmental departments. The party's Organization Department and the government's Labour and Personnel Department are combined, as are the Party Committee and the Government's Administration Office. This practice is in line with the anti-corruption efforts in the post-Mao era. In combating corruption, the tendency has been to marshall resources by merging the party's Disciplinary Committee and the government's Supervision Unit. They share the same office, but organizationally they remain separate. This combination strengthens the organizational capacity to have more resources to tackle rampant corruption. Yet, this organizational integration is inconsistent with the decision made at the 13th Party Congress, held in October 1987, that there should be party and government separation. Until now, the party still holds a dominant position to formulate governmental policies. This indicates the limitations of the partial reform and of the separation between the party and the state.

Intergovernmental Relations

The emphasis on the development of Pudong raises concern not only in other parts of the country, for instance, in the Shenzhen Special Economic Zone (深圳特區) (SEZ), but it also raises conflicts within Shanghai as well.[55] The conflict is not confined to central–local relationship. It is a conflict between different districts in Shanghai. The stress on the development of one particular administrative unit has implications for resources allocations to other districts as well. Each district wants to develop and to benefit from the locating of the most lucrative projects and enterprises in its region. This is a zero-sum game in the sense that the preferential treatment of Pudong will hamper prospects of attracting foreign investment to other districts of Shanghai, let alone to other parts of the country.[56] Also, the interests and the development of the hinterland will be put aside temporarily, as the comparative economic advantages of Shanghai are exploited.[57] To resolve such differences, a compromise has been made mandating that the current policies towards the SEZs and Pudong will not be changed. Their importance is further stressed, along with the emphasis on the development of the hinterland, in the recent document of the Fifth Plenum of the 14th Party Congress.[58] In sum, conflicts between governmental units, both vertically and horizontally, have been a salient feature of the post-Mao era.

Linkage between Factional Politics and Development

Last, there is the assumption about the development of Shanghai in general and Pudong in particular that there is a direct relationship between development and the predominant influence of factional politics. To put it bluntly, the Shanghai faction at the Centre has contributed to the development of Shanghai and Pudong. To probe this question more deeply, it suggests the importance of factional politics and its influence on the formulation of public policy. More resources have been channelled to Shanghai as a result of the leadership from Shanghai.[59] As the argument goes, this is even the case in a period of economic readjustment to cool down the inflationary economy. Shanghai continues to receive special treatment or privileges from the Centre, for example, by having authority to issue bonds, receive credits, and rights to export and import goods, just to name a few.[60] Thus, the Centre has given preferential policies to Shanghai. This linkage has a wide appeal and it is very popular in the perceptions of the people as they are influenced by the mass media. To a certain extent, it is influential in China studies circles as well. Further examination of the fact that the Centre has supported Shanghai in the process of development does not describe the extent of the influence exerted by the Shanghai faction. This explanation is not without flaws.

Instead of tracing the personal backgrounds and career paths of the Shanghai élite, this author asks several questions to guide the discussion and to offer some observations about this linkage.[61] These questions must be clarified and addressed before a definite answer can be offered. The questions are: Has the Shanghai group at the Centre played a pivotal role both in the beginning or in the later development stage of Shanghai and Pudong? Was the entire process initiated and promoted by this group? To what extent has the change of leadership at the Centre contributed to the development of Shanghai and Pudong? And to what degree has the change of the overall developmental strategy in China contributed to the development of Shanghai and Pudong? Is it necessarily the case that the policy proclaimed by the Centre merely reflects the narrow local vested interests of the Shanghai élite?

From a historical perspective, the foundation for the development of Pudong began in 1980s. This was before any Shanghai élite was promoted to the Party Centre. The development of Shanghai was also in line with the spirit and policy at the time, as large coastal cities were used as engines for economic development, though the role of Shanghai was not singled out particularly. The development of the 14 coastal cities, including Shanghai, did have the support and consensus of the then liberal reformers Hu Yaobang 胡耀邦 and Zhao Ziyang 趙紫陽 .

In the 1980s, the Centre emphasized development in the south. In the 1990s, the focus has shifted from Guangdong 廣東 to Shanghai as a change in development strategy.[62] The further opening up of Guangdong has been limited as it has been integrated into the South China Economic Zone.[63] The Centre needed to find another economic, banking and finance centre for China, and Shanghai was its choice. Shanghai's traditional role as a financial centre before 1949 is particularly significant. The development of Shanghai can have a radiation effect, benefiting the Yangzi region and the eastern part of China.[64] It can be a catalyst for economic development in China. In this respect, some foreign financial giants have expressed optimistic views concerning the financial role of Shanghai.[65]

The role played by the supreme leader Deng Xiaoping in developing Shanghai is also crucial. From 28 January to 18 February 1991, Deng conducted an inspection tour to Shanghai and he made the following remarks:

It is late for us to be developing Shanghai, so we have to work hard.

When we decided to establish the four special economic zones in 1979, we chose them mainly on the basis of their geographical advantages.... However, we did not take the intellectual advantages of Shanghai into account. Since the people of Shanghai are clever and well educated, if we had decided to establish a special economic zone here, the city would look very different now.

The 14 open coastal cities include Shanghai, but these have no special status. It would have been better to develop the Pudong district a few years ago, like the Shenzhen Special Economic Zone. Development of the Pudong district will have a great impact, not just on the district itself, but on all of Shanghai, which in turn will serve as a base for the development of the Yangzi delta and the whole Yangzi basin. So we should lose no time in developing the Pudong district and persevere until construction is completed ...[66]

By quoting Deng's remarks in length, the importance of the learning experience in policy making and the geographical implications for developing Shanghai and Pudong are fully revealed. Deng regretted that "it would have been better to develop Pudong district" much earlier. In 1992, one year later, he even criticized himself by admitting that it was one of his "biggest mistakes" not to have included Shanghai as one of the SEZs to develop in the late 1970s.[67] Deng's endorsement added unparalleled weight and hence accelerated the development of Shanghai and Pudong. This can explain why additional resources have been channelled and preferential policies have been provided to Shanghai and Pudong, even during the period of economic readjustment.

To conclude, it is not primarily the support of the Shanghai faction that has led to the development of Shanghai and Pudong. The plan for the development of Shanghai and Pudong was already in place in the 1980s. Furthermore, the decision by the Centre to develop Pudong came in early 1989, even before Jiang Zemin moved to Beijing 北京 after the June 4 Tiananmen incident.[68] Needless to say, the development of Shanghai and Pudong is beneficial to Shanghai, and the Shanghai élite has tried to make use of the development of Pudong to accelerate the development of Puxi, in Shanghai proper. Pudong can be used as the "locomotive" for the economic development of Shanghai.[69] However, the Centre needs to have an international economic, finance and trade centre, and Shanghai is the obvious choice because of its location and its traditional heritage.[70] Furthermore, other political considerations are involved, though they are difficult to be substantiated.[71] The development of Shanghai has the support of both Shanghai and non-Shanghai élites.[72] Above all, Deng Xiaoping, the supreme leader, supports the development. In sum, the development of Shanghai and Pudong cannot be accounted for solely by the factional politics variable. Its development hinges on a number of factors, such as the role played by the supreme leader, the learning experience in policy making, the merits of the policy, the international environment, historical conditions and other political considerations.

Concluding Remarks

The underlying assumption of this chapter is that the reorientation of China's economic system, from plan to market, resulted in institutional and administrative changes in the 1980s and 1990s. In the 1950s, the planned economy dictated the functions and the administrative tasks of the municipal government. In the 1990s, the reform of the economy guided the institutional and administrative reform.[73]

Another assumption is that institutional changes are important. Institutions do play an independent role that influences the behaviour of the people. Institutional changes and innovations can provide possibilities and constraints for decision-making agents.[74] Institutions matter a lot. The reduction of bureaucratic red-tape, inertia, overlapping functions, unclear functional responsibilities and ambiguities can increase the effectiveness of the organization and facilitate the operational process. The setting up of the Foreign Investment Commission is an example whereby as a result of which foreign investment increased in Shanghai. Caution is needed, however. There are still many institutional and administrative problems in Shanghai. Reform of the system under the principle of market socialism only began in 1993. It will take a long time to observe positive results from such changes. Institutions need time to consolidate and forge new administrative arrangements.

The restructuring of governmental institutions and the organizational integration in Shanghai are intended to promote the benefits of non-duplicative structures so that efficiency and the advantage of smooth and nearly-frictionless action can be attained.[75] However, a wide array of societal problems have emerged which will further challenge, compound and even pose a threat to the existing institutional arrangements and their administrative practices. Can the recent efforts at institutional change based on scientific management[76] upgrade the organizational capacities in order to cope with the political and economic challenges? Will the current institutional and administrative arrangements meet the needs and demands of the people, particularly on the issue of accountability? How does the élite deal with the mounting problems and pressing issues of rampant bureaucratic corruption, for instance? All in all, the Shanghai élite, as well as the national élite, need to respond to these important challenges in the concluding chapter of the twentieth century, and, perhaps, even far beyond in the future of the twenty-first century.

Appendix I

Shanghai Municipal Government in 1995

Economic Commission
  Aerospace Bureau
  Bureau of Goods and Materials
  Labour Bureau
  Pharmaceutical Administration Bureau
  Textile Industry Bureau
  Chemical Industry Bureau
  Machinery & Electrical Industry Administration Bureau
  Metallurgical Industry
  Light Industry Bureau
  No. 2 Light Industry Bureau
  Agricultural Mechanization Administration Bureau (previously known as Agricultural
    Machines Industry Bureau)
  Instruments and Telecommunications Industry Bureau
  Bureau of Power Construction
  Railways Bureau
  Posts and Telecommunications Bureau
  Geology and Mineral Resources Bureau

Planning Commission
  Price Bureau
  Statistics Bureau
  Labour and Wage Committee

Science and Technology Commission
  Standardization and Metrology Administration

Foreign Affairs Office

Foreign Economic Relations and Trade Commission

Finance and Trade Office
  Aquatic Products Bureau
  No. 2 Commerce Bureau
  No. 1 Commerce Bureau
  Finance Bureau
  Tax Bureau
  Grain Bureau
  Audit Bureau
  Collective Enterprises Office
  Industry and Commerce Administration

Educational Commission

Health Office
  Family Planning Commission
  Patriotic Health Campaign Commission
  Sports Commission
  Health Bureau

Social Security Administration Bureau

Urban and Rural Planning Construction Commission
  Environmental Protection Bureau
  Afforestation Committee
  Bureau of Real Estate and Land Administration
  Urban Planning Bureau

Construction Commission
  Bureau of Public Utilities
  Municipal Engineering Administration
  Bureau of Power Construction
  Gardens and Forestry Administration
  Architecture Administration Office
  Architectural Materials Administration Office

Agricultural Commission
  Agricultural Bureau
  Water Resources Bureau
  Farms Administration

Traffic Office
  Harbour Bureau
  Channel Bureau
  Marine Security Supervisory Bureau
  Communication and Transportation Bureau

Industry and Technology Commission

External Economic and Trade Commission

Broadcasting & TV Administration
Film Bureau
Bureau of Culture
Bureau of Press and Publication

Bureau of National Security
Public Security Bureau
Judiciary Bureau
Civil Affairs Bureau
Supervisory Bureau
Fire Bureau

Tourism Administration Bureau
Archives Bureau
Air Defense Office
Coordination Office
Establishment Committee
Personnel Bureau
Organizational Affairs Bureau
General Office
Research Section
Attaché

Nationalities Affairs Committee
Religious Affairs Administration
Overseas Chinese Affairs Office

Municipal Advisory Bodies
  Economic Laws Research Centre
  International Issues Research Centre
  Economic Research Centre

(This list of bureaux in the Shanghai Municipal Government is based on the following sources: First, it is based on the 1986 Municipal Chart published by the Shanghai municipal government and the Ministry of Personnel. At that time, there were 77 departments and bureaux [For details, please refer to Shanghaishi bianzhi weiyuanhui bangongshi 上海市編制委員會辦公室(ed.), *Shanghai dangzheng jigou yange: 1949–1986* 上海黨政機構沿革 1949–1986 (The History of the Shanghai Party and Governmental Organizations 1949–1986) (Shanghai: Shanghai renmin chubanshe, 1988) and Renshibu difang jigou bianzhi guanlisi 人事部地方機構編制管理司 (ed.), *Zhonghua renmin gongheguo sheng, zizhiqu, zhixiashi dangzhengqun jiguan zuzhi jigou gaiyao* 中華人民共和國省、自治區、直轄市、黨政群機關組織機構概要(The Outlines of the Party and Governmental Administrative Organizations of the Provinces, Self-authonomous Regions and the Municipalities Directly Under the Jurisdiction of the State Council of the People's Republic of China) (Beijing: Zhongguo renshi chubanshe 中國人事出版社，1989). To the best of my knowledge, there has not been any external publication which charts the organization of the municipal government since 1989. Second, it is based on my three separate field-trips to Shanghai during which I was able to document some changes. Third, information has been provided by the following books and journals: *Zhongguo zhengfu jiguan minglu* 中國政府機關名錄 (Directory of Chinese Governmental Organizations); *Shanghai dianhua haobu 1995* 上海電話號簿 1995 (1995 Shanghai Telephone Book); *Zhongguo dianhua haobu* 中國電話號簿(China Telephone Book) and the *Bianzhi guanli yanjiu* (see note 27).

Appendix II

Pudong Development District

1. Industrial and Commercial Administration
2. Bureau of Finance and Tax
3. Bureau of Social Development
4. Urban Construction Administration
5. Bureau of Rural Development
6. Bureau of Economy and Trade
7. Integrated Planning and Land Bureau
8. Commission for Disciplinary Inspection/Supervisory Bureau
9. Organization Department/Labour and Personnel Department
10. Party Committee/Administration Office

Source: *Pudong yanjiu baogao 1993* (see note 38 below), p. 75.

Notes

1. Alexander Eckstein, *China's Economic Revolution* (Cambridge: Cambridge University Press, 1977), pp. 50–51.
2. William L. Parish and Martin King Whyte, *Village and Family in Contemporary China* (Chicago: The University of Chicago Press, 1978), pp. 53–54.
3. In 1949, there were only 21 governmental organizations in Shanghai. In 1952, the number jumped to 29. By 1956, it further increased to 62 departments, 34 of which were primarily dealing with economic and social affairs. See Diao Tianding 刁田丁 (ed.), *Zhongguo difang guojia jigou gaiyao* 中國地方國家機構概要 (A Brief Account of the Chinese Local State Institutions) (Beijing: Falü chubanshe 法律出版社, 1989), p. 181.
4. Janos Kornai, *The Socialist System: The Political Economy of Communism* (Princeton: Princeton University Press, 1992), pp. 97–100; Chen Yi 陳沂 (ed.), *Dangdai Zhongguo de Shanghai* 當代中國的上海 (Shanghai in Contemporary China), vol. 2 (Beijing: Dangdai Zhongguo chubanshe 當代中國出版社, 1993), pp. 386–92; see also Alec Nove's characterization about the former soviet-type regimes in his *The Soviet Economic System* (London: George Allen and Unwin, 1982).
5. Deng Xiaoping lucidly summarized all these kinds of bureaucratic problems in 1980. Please refer to: *Deng Xiaoping wenxuan* 鄧小平文選 (Selected Works of Deng Xiaoping) (Beijing: Renmin chubanshe 人民出版社, 1983), p. 287.
6. These included: Family Planning Commission, Sky Defence Committee, the Traffic Leading Group and the People's Armed Committee, among others. See the book edited and published by Shanghaishi renshiju, Shanghaishi keji ganbuju and the *xingzheng yu renshi* bianjibu 上海市人事局、上海市科技幹部局和《行政與人事》編輯部 (ed.), *Shanghai renshi gongzuo wenjian huibian* 上海人事工作文件匯編 (The Compilation of Documents about Shanghai Personnel Management) (internal circulation), 1987, vol. 1, p. 271.
7. Ibid., p. 285.
8. Starting from 1985, this "joint conference" (*lianxi huiyi* 聯席會議) consisted of Planning Commission, as the convenor, Finance Bureau, Tax Bureau, People's Bank (Shanghai Branch), Bureau of Goods and Materials, Labour Bureau, Industrial and Commerce Administration Bureau, Price Bureau, Statistics Bureau and the Labour and Wage Committee. This was to co-ordinate the various functions of these departments to make coherent policy. See Shanghaishi jingji tizhi gaige lingdao xiaozu bangongshi 上海市經濟體制改革領導小組辦公室 (ed.), *Shanghaishi jingji tizhi gaige wenjian huibian* 上海市經濟體制改革文件匯編 (The Compilation of Documents of the Reformation of the Shanghai Economic Structure) (Beijing: Qiye guanli chubanshe 企業管理出版社, 1986), vol. 2, p. 90.

9. Departments still handled their own affairs. See *Shanghai renshi gongzuo wenjian huibian* (see note 6), p. 285.

10. Zhang Wenshou 張文壽 (ed.), *Zhongguo xingzheng guanli tizhi gaige —— yanjiu yu sikao* 中國行政管理體制改革 —— 研究與思考 (Reforming the Chinese Administrative Management System: Research and Reflection) (Beijing: Dangdai Zhongguo chubanshe, 1994), p. 104.

11. See Cao Jingjun 曹景鈞 (King K. Tsao), "Jigou gaige yu renyuan xiaojian" 機構改革與人員削減 (Organizational Reform and Staff Reduction) in *Xingzheng jigou gaige touxi* 行政機構改革透析 (The Penetrative Analysis of the Reformation on Administrative Organizations), edited by Zhao Baoxu 趙寶煦 (Suzhou: Suzhou daxue chubanshe 蘇州大學出版社, 1995), pp. 149–56.

12. From 1949 to 1987, Shanghai surrendered about 85% of her total income deriving from revenues, taxes and other kinds of profits to the national coffers. This is akin to the strategy of "drying the water to fish" in order to squeeze and extract more resources from Shanghai by the Centre. See Zhang Zhongli 張仲禮 and Yuan Enzhen 袁恩楨, "Jiushi niandai Shanghai jingji de gaige, kaifang he fazhan" 九十年代上海經濟的改革、開放和發展 (Reform, Open-door and Development of Shanghai Economy in the 1990s), in *Huigu yu zhanwang* 回顧與展望 (Retrospect and Prospect), edited by Zhang Zhongli and M. Jan Dutta (Shanghai: Shanghai shehui kexueyuan 上海社會科學院, 1991), p. 470.

13. See Ho Lok-sang and Tsui Kai-yuen, "Fiscal Relations between Shanghai and the Central Government" (Chapter 6) in this volume.

14. In 1988, Shanghai was under the financial contract system and could retain a few billion RMB more for development purposes. See Zhang Zhongli and Yuan Enzhen, "Jiushi niandai Shanghai jingji de gaige, kaifang he fazhan" (see note 12), p. 471.

15. This was due to the extremely favourable conditions for change and reform in the nation at the time. The 13th Party Congress was held on 25 October to 1 November 1987, which led to the subsequent political reform process. There was even the price reform proposal advocated by Deng Xiaoping 鄧小平 in May 1988, though it was postponed as a result of chaotic and excessive consuming by the people. In short, from late 1987 to early 1989, the political environment was favourable for administrative and institutional reform both at the national and Shanghai levels. During this period, the author of this chapter was at Peking University (北京大學) to conduct his dissertational research.

16. This is akin to the matrix organization in the field of public administration. This is not to create a formal organization, but to develop a project-oriented task force to solve a specific problem. The fundamental difference between the matrix organization and the Chinese one, however, is that the Chinese one is at the super-organizational level and the former is at the sub-organizational level. For a definition of matrix organization, please refer to Ralph C. Chandler and Jack C. Plano, *The Public Administration Dictionary* (New

York: John Wiley & Sons, 1982), pp. 194–95.

17. This has been the theme developed by Kenneth G. Lieberthal and Michel Oksenberg in their study of the Chinese bureaucratic system. See Kenneth G. Lieberthal and Michel Oksenberg, *Policy Making in China* (Princeton: Princeton University Press, 1988).

18. This leading group was formed in 1987. *Shanghai jingji tizhi gaige shi nian* bianjibu (ed.), *Shanghai jingji tizhi gaige shi nian* 上海經濟體制改革十年 (Ten Years Reformation of Shanghai Economic Structure) (Shanghai: Shanghai renmin chubanshe 上海人民出版社, 1989), p. 50.

19. Shanghai shehuikexueyuan *Shanghai jingji nianjian* bianjibu 上海社會科學院《上海經濟年鑑》編輯部 (ed.), *Shanghai jingji nianjian 1988* 上海經濟年鑑 1988 (Shanghai Economy Yearbook 1988) (Shanghai: Sanlian shudian 三聯書店, 1988), p. 406.

20. See note 12.

21. *Shanghai jingji tizhi gaige shi nian* bianjibu (ed.), *Shanghai jingji tizhi gaige shi nian*, p. 682; and *Shanghai jingji nianjian 1988* (see note 19), p. 41.

22. These included (1) projects approval; (2) management and co-ordination; (3) grouping of similar facilities and (4) services provided. See *Shanghai jingji nianjian 1988* (see note 19), p. 41.

23. *Shanghai jingji tizhi gaige shinian* (see note 18), p. 683.

24. Foreign direct investment still grew 16% in 1989 as compared with 1988, although the Tiananmen incident occurred in 1989. Other forms of direct investment grew 5% in 1989, as compared with 1988. Changes of percentages are calculated by author. The 1985 data come from Shanghaishi tongjiju 上海市統計局 (ed.), *Shanghai tongji nianjian 1987* 上海統計年鑑 1987 (Statistical Yearbook of Shanghai 1987) (Shanghai: Shanghai renmin chubanshe, 1987), p. 299; 1986 and 1987 data come from Shanghaishi tongjiju (ed.), *Shanghai tongji nianjian 1988* 上海統計年鑑 1988 (Statistical Yearbook of Shanghai 1988) (Beijing: Zhongguo tongji chubanshe 中國統計出版社, 1988) p. 311; the 1988 data come from Shanghaishi tongjiju (ed.), *Shanghai tongji nianjian 1989* 上海統計年鑑 1989 (Statistical Yearbook of Shanghai 1989) (Beijing: Zhongguo tongji chubanshe, 1989), p. 386; and the 1989 data come from Shanghaishi tongjiju (ed.), *Shanghai tongji nianjian 1990* 上海統計年鑑 1990 (Statistical Yearbook of Shanghai 1990) (Beijing: Zhongguo tongji chubanshe, 1990), p. 310.

25. The concept of market socialism was originally expounded in Oskar Lange's "On the Economic Theory of Socialism" in *On the Economic Theory of Socialism*, edited by Oskar Lange, Fred M. Taylor and Benjamin Lippincott (Minneapolis: University of Minnesota Press, 1938), pp. 55–143.

26. Interview with an official in Shanghai, January 1995.

27. See *Bianzhi guanli yanjiu* 編制管理研究 (Organization Administration Research), No. 2 (1995), p. 35; Interview with a Shanghai visiting scholar at

The Chinese University of Hong Kong, October 1995.

28. Ibid., No. 2 (1995), pp. 38-39.

29. Ibid., No. 1 (1994), p. 40.

30. In the Chinese hierarchical structure, it is divided into the ranks of *bu* 部 (ministry), *si* 司 (department), *ting* 廳 (department or office), *ju* 局 (bureau), *chu* 處 (division) and *ke* 科 (section). See King K. Tsao's "Civil Service Reform" in *China Review 1993*, edited by Joseph Cheng and Maurice Brosseau (Hong Kong: The Chinese University Press, 1993), p. 5.13; and also Yan Huai, "Organizational Hierarchy and the Cadre Management System" in *Decision-making in Deng's China*, edited by Carol Lee Harmin and Suisheng Zhao (Armonk, New York: M. E. Sharpe, 1995), p. 42.

31. As all the municipal governments have the autonomous power to set up some organizations which are in critical need for local purposes, Shanghai has this flexibility to keep the Textile Bureau and the Light Textile Bureau as there are many textile enterprises. And most of the employees of the former Ministry of Textile Industry, now the China Textile Industry Association, are still paid by the public coffers. Interview with an official in Shanghai, August 1994.

32. This is a justification as Shanghai is located within the context of the newly industrializing countries (NICs). Some authors try to rationalize the use of intermediary organizations as the necessary component for the success of the NICs such as Hong Kong and Singapore. In addition, the existence of these organizations in Shanghai before 1949 is also used for historical justification. See Wang Jiangang 王健剛, "Lun shehui zhongjie zuzhi" 論社會中介組織 (Comment on the Social Intermediary Organizations), *Bianzhi guanli yanjiu* 編制管理研究, No. 2 (1994), p. 27; Chen Wenchao 陳文朝, "Liangge zhuanye jingji guanliju gaizhi de qishi" 兩個專業經濟管理局改制的啓示 (Revelations of the Reformation of the Two Specialized Economic Management Bureaux), *Bianzhi guanli yanjiu*, No. 1 (1994), pp. 40-41, and Fang Gou 方構 and Zhu Guoxiang 朱國祥, "Shichang jingji tiaojian xia de shehui zhongjie zuzhi" 市場經濟條件下的社會中介組織 (The Social Intermediary Organizations under the Conditions of Market Economy), *Bianzhi guanli yanjiu*, No. 1 (1994), pp. 28-36.

33. Document on the decision of the establishment of socialist market economy adopted by the 14th Party Congress, held on 12 October 1992, can be found in *Wen hui bao* 文匯報 (Wen Wei Pao) (Hong Kong), 13 October 1992.

34. 19 organizations still have administrative capacities. They are the Traffic Transportation Management Centre (交通運輸管理所), Medical Inspection Centre (葯品檢驗所), Construction Quality Supervision Centre (建築質量監督站), Cultural Market Investigation Centre (文化市場檢查所), Property Rights Supervision and Management Centre (產權監理所), Labour Service Company (勞動服務公司), Retirement Fees Coordination Centre (退休費統籌管理所) and Marriage Management Centre (婚姻管理處), to name a few.

Another 14 organizations have a mixed administrative duties and consultancy services including the Family Planning Centre (計劃生育指導站), Environmental Protection and Inspection Centre (環境保護監測站) and Investment Management Company (投資管理公司). For the remainder, 11 organizations are service-oriented and they do not possess any administrative duties at all. They engage in real estate, legal affairs, accounting and consultancy services. See Hong Bian 虹編, "Guanyu Hongkou qu shehui zhongjie jigou qingkuang de diaocha" 關於虹口區社會中介機構情況的調查 (Concerning the Investigation of the Conditions of the Social Intermediary Organizations in Hongkou District), *Bianzhi guanli yanjiu*, No. 3 (1994), p. 33.

35. There is the dichotomy between the public and private organizations in the literature of public administration. However, this boundary is becoming blurred as a result of many factors including: (1) the decision made by the private organization has direct and indirect impacts upon the public organization, and (2) public organization has adopted and employed a number of policy tools such as privatization and marketizaion to improve efficiency and have cost-reduction. See Graham T. Allison, "Public and Private Management: Are They Fundamentally Alike in All Unimportant Respects?" in *Classics of Public Administration*, edited by Jay M. Schafritz and Albert C. Hyde (2nd edition, Chicago, Illinois: The Dorsey Press, 1987), pp. 510-29.

36. It is close to the public dimension within the Chinese context.

37. For a comparative analysis, the current situation in the US is to restructure government organizations in terms of adding or altering an organization. This will affect inter-organizational relationships, or intergovernmental relationship, to meet the public interests. See, Charles R. Wise, "Public Service Configurations and Public Organizations: Public Organization Design in the Post-privatization Era," *Public Administration Review*, March/April (1990), p. 149.

38. A number of books about the economic and trade dimensions of Pudong New Area have been published, and those issues will not be discussed here. Readers can consult, for example, *Pudong yanjiu baogao 1993* 浦東研究報告 1993 (Pudong Research Report 1993) (Shanghai: Xinqu shangwu zixun fuwu zhongxin 新區商務諮詢服務中心, 1993) and *Maixiang 21 shiji de Pudong xinqu* 邁向21世紀的浦東新區 (The Pudong New Area: Striding towards the 21st Century) (Shanghai: Shanghai renmin chubanshe, 1994).

39. *Shanghai jingji nianjian 1990* 上海經濟年鑑 1990 (Shanghai Economy Yearbook 1990) (Shanghai: Sanlian shudian, 1990), p. 10.

40. *Shanghai jingji tizhi gaige shinian* (see note 18), p. 50.

41. *Shanghai jingji nianjian 1990* (see note 39), p. 5.

42. Ibid., p. 10.

43. See Zhang Zhongli and Yuan Enzhen, "Jiushi niandai Shanghai jingji de gaige, kaifang he fazhan" (see note 12), p. 471.

44. Ibid., p. 3.
45. See note 38.
46. *Pudong yanjiu baogao* 1993 (see note 38), pp. 74–76.
47. *Shanghai jingji nianjian 1992* 上海經濟年鑑 1992 (Shanghai Economy Yearbook 1992) (Shanghai: Shanghai shehuikexueyuan *Shanghai jingji nianjian* she 上海社會科學院《上海經濟年鑑》社, 1992), p. 80.
48. There are only 10 bureaux in Pudong, but there are over 40 bureaux in Puxi. In comparison, it is a substantial reduction of organization and staff. However, those staff in Pudong are well-equipped with advanced technology such as personal computers, cars and cellular phones. Author's interview, January 1995.
49. *Bianzhi guanli yanjiu*, No. 3 (1994), p. 36; and Cai Laixing 蔡來興 (ed.), *Shanghai: Chuangjian xin de guoji jingji zhongxin chengshi* 上海：創建新的國際經濟中心城市 (Shanghai: Creating a New International Economic Centre City) (Shanghai: Shanghai renmin chubanshe, 1995), pp. 240–41.
50. *Bianzhi guanli yanjiu*, No. 3 (1994), p. 40.
51. Author's interviews, May 1995 and October 1995.
52. The municipal government has not fully implemented the Civil Service Provisional Regulations as it was proclaimed on 1 October 1993. Until September 1995, there were only five departments to carry out the reform. They were: the Religious Affairs Administration (宗教局), the Overseas Chinese Affairs Office (華僑辦公室), the Legal Office (法制辦公室), the External Propaganda Office (外宣辦) and the Price Bureau (物價局). *Xinmin wanbao* 新民晚報, 25 August 1995; and author's interview, October 1995.
53. They are: China Light Industry Association and China Textile Industry Association. Author's interview, August 1994.
54. See John McMillan and Barry Naughton, "How to Reform a Planned Economy: Lessons from China," *Oxford Review of Economic Policy*, No. 1 (1992), pp. 130–43.
55. Ibid. For comparative purpose, see Paul E. Peterson, *City Limits* (Chicago and London: The University of Chicago Press, 1981).
56. Even if someone argues that it is not a zero-sum game, the following questions are still needed to answer. How long does it take for Shanghai to develop? Will Shanghai return and help other underprivileged regions in the hinterland in the future? And to what extent? See Jon Elster, *Rational Choice* (Oxford: Blackwell, 1986).
57. The concerns of the Shenzhen Special Economic Zone (SEZ) are that the privileged policies enjoyed by the Shenzhen SEZ might be taken away. See *Ming bao* 明報 (Ming Pao) (Hong Kong), 11 August 1995, p. C6. There has been a debate about whether the Shenzhen SEZ should continue to receive special treatment as a result of the comments made by Hu Angang 胡鞍鋼. This is not the space to go into details about the debate concerning whether the

privileges of the SEZs should be taken away and more priority should be given to the hinterland for bridging the development gap. For the debate, please refer to: *Ming bao*, 21 August 1995, p. C1 and 22 September 1995, p. E3.

58. See "Concerning the Proposal of Formulation of the Ninth Five-year Plan and the Long-term Goals of Year 2010" of the Chinese Communist Party, adopted and approved by the Fifth Plenum of the 14th Party Congress held on 28 September 1995, in *Wen hui bao*, 5 October 1995, pp. A6–A7. Particularly Item 29 of Section Four of the Document deals with this issue, p. A7.

59. This kind of approach has been widely reported and popularized in newspapers and journals. See, for example, *Ming bao*, 17 January 1995, p. A2; and *Kaifang* 開放 (Open Magazine) (Hong Kong), No. 11 (1995), pp. 34–36. Some commentators have tried to broaden the factional base by including Jiangsu 江蘇 province. Thus, the Jiangsu–Shanghai group includes Jiang Zemin 江澤民, Zhu Rongji 朱鎔基, Wu Bangguo 胡邦國, Huang Ju 黃菊, Zeng Qinghong 曾慶紅, Ba Zhongtan 巴忠倓, Gong Xinhan 龔心瀚, Zhou Ruijin 周瑞金 and Liu Ji 劉吉. See *Asiaweek*, 26 May 1995, p. 38. For a theoretical elaboration and debate about the factional politics, please refer to a number of articles published recently in *The China Journal*. Particularly see Tang Tsou's "Chinese Politics at the Top: Factionalism or Informal Politics? Balance-of-Power Politics or a Game to Win All?", *The China Journal*, No. 34 (July 1995), pp. 95–156.

60. Many rights and powers have been given to Shanghai in comparison with other regions. One can consult, for instance, the following reports. *Renmin ribao* 人民日報 (People's Daily) (Overseas edition), 12 March 1992, p. 1; *China Trade Communiqué*, Vol. 9 (1993), pp. 11–13, *Xinbao caijing yuekan* 信報財經月刊 (Hong Kong Finance and Economic Monthly), No. 3 (1994), pp. 17–18; and *Lianhe bao* 聯合報 (United Daily News) (Hong Kong), 27 September 1995, p. 8.

61. For an alternative inquiry, see Peter T. Y. Cheung, "The Political Context of Shanghai's Economic Development" (Chapter 3) of this volume.

62. The recent concerns of the mayor of the Shenzhen SEZ are that the privilege and status of the city may be taken away as a result of policy change. See *Ming bao*, 11 August 1995, p. C6.

63. See Y. M. Yeung and David K. Y. Chu (eds.), *Guangdong: Survey of a Province Undergoing Rapid Change* (Hong Kong: The Chinese University Press, 1994).

64. See Shi Peijun, Lin Hui and Liang Jinshe, "Shanghai as a Regional Hub" (Chapter 20) of this volume for the wider geographical implications.

65. John Wadswoth Jr., managing director of Morgan Stanley Asia Ltd., said, "I think Shanghai is capable of becoming the financial centre (in Asia–Pacific) by the year 2000." This remark about the success of Shanghai is in fact a shortening of 10 years earlier than what the Chinese had estimated and

predicted that Shanghai can be an international finance centre by the year 2010. Stephen Stine, "The Dragon's Head," *Asia, Inc.*, vol. 2, no. 12 (December 1993), p. 42; and the special report by *Yazhou zhoukan* 亞洲周刊 (Asiaweek), 8 May 1994, pp. 28–31.

66. *Deng Xiaoping wenxuan*, vol. 3 (see note 5), p. 366. The translation of his remarks comes from *Selected Works of Deng Xiaoping*, vol. III (Beijing: Foreign Languages Press, 1994), p. 353.

67. From 18 January to 21 February 1992, Deng had a southern tour and talked to the Shanghai leaders. He said, ". . . Shanghai is another example. . . . In retrospect, one of my biggest mistakes was leaving out Shanghai when we launched the four Special Economic Zones. If Shanghai has been included, the situation with regard to reform and opening in the Yangzi Delta, the entire Yangzi River valley and, indeed, the whole country would be quite different." in *Deng Xiaoping wenxuan*, vol. 3 (see note 5), p. 376. The translation of his remarks comes from *Selected Works of Deng Xiaoping*, vol. III (see note 66), pp. 363–64.

68. See Zhang Zhongli and Yuan Enzhen, "Jiushi niandai Shanghai jingji de gaige, kaifang he fazhan" (see note 12), p. 466.

69. Zhao Qizheng 趙啓正, the director of the Pudong New Area Management Committee and the vice-mayor of Shanghai municipality, made the following comment: "The development of Pudong is to make Shanghai as the economic locomotive, and let the Chinese economic express train run faster." See *Xinbao* 信報 (Hong Kong Economic Journal), 14 March 1995, p. 30.

70. The development of Pudong can be traced back to Sun Yat-sen (孫逸仙) who had a plan to develop Pudong, too, as Thomas Gold suggested. See *Lianhe bao* (Hong Kong), 18 February 1994, p. 10.

71. There are bascially three major categories. First, a former official in the Shanghai Foreign Economic and Trade Commission stated that the development of Pudong was not simply for the pure consideration of developing Pudong. The Beijing and Shanghai élites have used Pudong as a way out for Shanghai and the nation. See *Lianhe bao* (Hong Kong), 18 February 1994, p. 10. Second, one of the often cited reasons is that Shanghai can gradually replace Hong Kong in the future as Hong Kong will be a Special Administrative Region (SAR) of China after 1 July 1997. There may be some justifications about this speculation. However, China is big enough geographically to have two international centres on trade, finance and banking. Their relationship may be a complementary and supplementary one in the future, and it is not necessarily a zero-sum relationship. Additionally, this concern or fear about the replacement of Hong Kong by Shanghai may in part due to the uncertainties of the change of sovereignty in the run-up of 1997. Third, other considerations such as the consequences of the Tiananmen incident of 1989 and the collapse of the former regimes of the Soviet Union

and the Eastern European countries may play some roles in developing Pudong. See *Lianhe bao* (Hong Kong), 18 February 1994, p. 10.

72. Shanghaishi "Maixiang 21 shiji de Shanghai" keti lingdao xiaozu 上海市 "邁向21世紀的上海" 課題領導小組 (ed.), *Maixiang 21 shiji de Shanghai* 邁向21世紀的上海 (Shanghai: Striding towards the 21st Century) (Shanghai: Shanghai renmin chubanshe, 1995), pp. 100–19.

73. This is the thesis developed in the article co-authored by King K. Tsao and John Worthley in their "Chinese Public Administration: Change with Continuity during Political and Economic Development," *Public Administration Review*, March/April (1995), pp. 169–74.

74. There is a large literature on this important issue. See the following books for theoretical reference: James G. March and Johan P. Olsen, *Rediscovering Institutions: The Organizational Basis of Politics* (New York: Free Press, 1989); and Walter W. Powell and Paul J. DiMaggio (eds.), *The New Institutionalism in Organizational Analysis* (Chicago: The University of Chicago Press, 1991). For the application of institutional analysis to some specific cases, refer to Susan L. Shirk, *The Political Logic of Economic Reform in China* (Berkeley: University of California Press, 1993).

75. This is what Louise G. White calls it the institutional design of the orthodox public administration. Please refer to "Public Management in a Pluralistic Arena," *Public Administration Review*, November/December (1989), pp. 522–32, particularly p. 525.

76. See Frederick W. Taylor, *Principles of Scientific Management* (New York: Harper & Row, 1911) and Luther Gulick, "Notes on the Theory of Organization," in *Classics of Public Administration*, edited by Jay M. Shafritz and Albert C. Hyde (Chicago, Illinois: The Dorsey Press, 1987), second edition, pp. 79–89.

5

Local Interest Articulation in the 1980s

Lam Tao-chiu

Although the decade of the 1980s in China has generally been characterized as one of increasing fiscal decentralization to the provincial-level
administration,[1] there has been no uniform pattern of development.[2] In
Shanghai, as noted by Zhimin Lin, "the path towards greater local control
of fiscal resources was complicated."[3] In 1980, when the policy of "appor-
tioning revenues and expenditures between the central and the local
authorities, while holding the latter responsible for their own profit and
loss," colloquially called "eating in separate kitchens" (*fenzao chifan* 分灶
吃飯), was introduced, Shanghai, together with Beijing 北京 and Tianjin
天津 was left out.[4] These three municipalities were required to adhere to
the old fiscal arrangement with the Centre which left them with little
autonomy as well as with a small revenue base.[5] Shanghai, in particular,
was widely considered to be the most poorly treated under this fiscal
arrangement because its share of total revenue was the lowest among the
three municipalities: while Beijing and Tianjin were allowed to keep about
30% of their revenue for local spending, Shanghai was only able to retain a
little over 10% of its revenue.[6] More revenue was decentralized to Shanghai, first in 1985 and latter in 1988. These measures were given a further
boost by the decision of the central government to develop Pudong 浦東
which amounts to no less than a strategic shift in the emphasis of national
development.[7]

Policy development and élite changes in Shanghai have been closely
followed by China scholars. Lynn White, for example, has examined in
great depth the degree of exploitation in Shanghai by the Centre in the
1980s, and he discusses how such exploitation has affected the city's
economic and social development.[8] Zhimin Lin has traced the development and changes in central–Shanghai fiscal relations in the decade of the
1980s.[9] However, the processes and the underlying factors leading to such
changes have remained largely unexamined. For example, Zhimin Lin's
analysis purports to examine "the importance of local strategy in helping to
convert economic reform programmes to local advantages,"[10] but his article says very little about such issues as *whether* and *how* policy changes
were shaped by local struggles and bargaining in Shanghai.

I would like to thank Peter N. S. Lee and Keith Forster for their comments on
earlier drafts of this chapter. Keith Forster's assistance in editing is also gratefully
acknowledged.

This chapter examines the articulation of local interest in Shanghai over central–Shanghai relations in the 1980s. Section 1 seeks to place Shanghai's interest articulation in theoretical perspectives by discussing how it differs from bureaucratic bargaining and clientalism. Section 2 examines the ambivalent roles of the municipal leadership in Shanghai's struggle for greater local control of finance and for greater autonomy. It is suggested that to understand the politics of central–Shanghai relations, it is necessary to move beyond the municipal leaders to look at the actors and their actions. Section 3 details the rich variety of interest articulation activities in Shanghai in the 1980s, discussing in particular the arenas in which views and arguments challenging prevailing central policy have appeared, and the limitations of these efforts. The concluding section discusses the importance of Shanghai's assertion of its interest by placing it in historical context.

Local Interest Articulation in Theoretical Perspectives

Two theoretical models, bureaucratic bargaining and clientalism, have dominated the study of Chinese politics in recent years. The bureaucratic bargaining model argues that policy making and resource allocation are determined by a complex process of negotiation among interdependent bureaucratic actors.[11] Central–local relations have also been analyzed in the bureaucratic framework because, as Lieberthal and Oksenberg argue, "interdependence characterizes the relationship [between the Centre and the provinces]" and "the leaders of [both the Centre and provinces are] capable of extracting resources or other values they seek in exchange for goods at their command."[12] In this model, localist interests are presented, negotiated and accommodated within the bureaucracy. As a result, the policy-making process in China is highly fragmented and disjointed, but the political regime continues to prohibit political participation from outside the bureaucracy. Lieberthal coins the term "fragmented authoritarianism" to characterize the coexistence of the fragmentation of power and its authoritarian character.[13]

The clientalist model of politics proposes that political demands and needs work through a rich network of informal relationships.[14] People seek to achieve their interests and objectives through particularistic actions by building patron–client relations or other forms of informal relationships broadly labelled as *guanxi* 關係 in Chinese. Because political organization and collective political action are severely prohibited, particularistic actions through informal networks is often the only and most effective means available to ordinary Chinese to obtain political and economic benefits. Rarely do Chinese people try to accomplish their objectives or to meet their ends by openly seeking the support of other people or by openly imposing pressure on the policy makers. Moreover, as Walder argues, "the network of clientalist ties ... provides a structural barrier to concerted worker resistance. ... This complex web of personal loyalty, mutual support and material interest creates a stable pattern of tacit acceptance and active co-operation for the regime ...."[15]

While politics under Communist China, particularly under Mao, does largely fit with the arguments of these two models, there are some "unconventional" types of politics that can hardly be explained by these theoretical perspectives. Examples include the scathing criticism of the Chinese Communist Party (CCP) by the intellectuals and members of the democratic parties during the Hundred Flowers Campaign,[16] the strike wave in Shanghai in 1957[17] and, of course, the Cultural Revolution.[18] In the post-Mao era, "unconventional" types of politics have also occurred occasionally, the most important of which is the 1989 pro-democracy movement.[19] While these political events are important in their own right, they also provide valuable opportunities for probing important political issues that are suppressed and obscured by the authoritarian political regime.[20]

The focus of this chapter, articulation of local interest in Shanghai in the 1980s, does not fit comfortably with either the bureaucratic or the clientelist frameworks. The people in Shanghai not only harboured strong resentment and grievances against the "exploitation" of their city by the Centre. They had also tried, over a period of several years, to articulate their interests and to press for change in central–Shanghai relations within the limited political space. Open interest articulation differs from bureaucratic bargaining: the issue of central–Shanghai relations was not left to the bureaucratic actors and, therefore, not confined to the bureaucracy. Another difference is that bureaucratic bargaining, as Lieberthal and Oksenberg and others demonstrate, has become a legitimate form of political activity, while open articulation of interest is still treated with strong suspicion. In reality, of course, the distinction between bureaucratic bargaining and open interest articulation is blurred, as shall be evident below. The clientelist framework does not envision this mode of political activity, nor struggle for greater local autonomy.

Open articulation of interest, to be sure, has been constrained in important ways in China even when it did have a chance to surface. Therefore, a number of limitations are inevitable. Here the main features and the limitations of interest articulation in Shanghai in the 1980s are examined. However, the political import of open interest articulation goes beyond the direct and immediate impact on policy making. Moreover, like previous political events which shed light on important political issues in contemporary China, this case also provides a window to examine the complicated yet uneasy relationship between the people (and cadres) of Shanghai, the municipal leadership and the central government.

The emergence of interest articulation in Shanghai in the 1980s is especially important when placed in historical perspective. It contrasts sharply with the sheer neglect of the interests of the people of Shanghai by Shanghai's radical leaders during the Cultural Revolution.[21] Viewed from a historical perspective, this perhaps represents a return to the long-standing antipathy between the political power in Beijing and this "other China."[22] It also suggests that the conflict between the Centre and Shanghai will probably not end with the belated decisions to allow the city to keep more locally generated revenue and to make Shanghai the "dragon head" of China's economic modernization. In view of the complicated role played by the municipal leaders, it may be premature to expect such antipathy to evaporate despite the fact that a growing number of Shanghai leaders have been incorporated into the national leadership, or even dominate the national government.

Municipal Leadership and Local Interest Articulation

A common focus in studies of central–provincial relations in China is provincial leadership. However, controversies about the role and behaviour of local cadres have bedevilled the study of Chinese politics.[23] David Goodman regards provincial leaders as "political middlemen" facing cross pressures from both the central government and their localities and, there-fore, as central agents and local representatives at the same time.[24] Lieber-thal and Oksenberg suggest that apart from these two conflicting roles, the behaviour of provincial leaders is also governed by a third objective: to survive.[25] The conflicts embedded in these roles and objectives provide the dynamics and complexities of central–provincial politics in China. Precise-ly which of these roles and objectives are emphasized in particular cases is determined by a range of variables, such as leadership personality, the characteristics of the policies at stake and other circumstances pertaining to the provinces in question. Because these factors vary from one case to another, as well as over different periods of time, it is very difficult to generalize about the role of provincial leadership.

Generally speaking, Shanghai's municipal leaders, like leaders in other provinces, are both central agents and local representatives at the same time. And they also are seeking to survive in the dangerous political environment of Chinese politics. A closer examination of Shanghai's municipal leadership, however, suggests two further points: first, the municipal leadership should not be viewed as a united group holding similar views on central–Shanghai relations; second, the most important political figures (party secretary and mayor) in Shanghai should probably be viewed more as "central agents" rather than as "local representatives."

The most important figures in the municipal leadership are, of course, the municipal party secretary (before June 1985, first party secretary) and the mayor.[26] Between January 1979 and Jiang Zemin's 江澤民 elevation to Beijing in August 1989, there were four party secretaries in Shanghai: Peng Chong 彭冲 was the first party secretary between January 1979 and March 1980, followed by Chen Guodong 陳國棟, who stayed in the position for more than five years (March 1980–June 1985). Chen Guodong was succeeded by Rui Xingwen 芮杏文. After Rui's move to Beijing to become a central secretariat member in late 1987, Jiang Zemin was sent to take up the position. Changes in mayorship largely corresponded to changes in the party secretary during the same period. Peng Chong was concurrently the mayor and the first party secretary. Although he continued to be mayor until April 1981, after moving to Beijing in March 1980, he passed the responsibility to Wang Daohan 汪道涵, who became acting mayor in October 1980 and mayor in April 1981. Wang Daohan stepped down from the mayorship in July 1985 and was succeeded by Jiang Zemin. Then Zhu Rongji 朱鎔基 took up the mayorship in April 1984 when Jiang Zemin succeeded Rui Xingwen as party secretary.[27]

An examination of the background of these key figures generates useful information relevant to arguments concerning their roles and behaviour in central–Shanghai relations. With few exceptions, all these figures were sent from the central government to Shanghai when they were appointed to these key positions in the city.[28] Peng Chong had been the third party secretary since 1976 prior to becoming first party secretary in 1979. However, before 1976, Peng Chong's career did not have a close connection with Shanghai. His main career after 1949 was in Shanghai's neighbouring province, Jiangsu 江蘇, first as Nanjing's 南京 party secretary and mayor, and later as Jiangsu's provincial governor and party secretary before being transferred to Shanghai.

The career path of Chen Guodong is similar. He was first appointed the second party secretary in January 1980 and succeeded Peng Chong as first party secretary two months later. Although Chen worked in various capacities in the East China Administrative Region in the 1950s and 1960s, his main career path before his appointment to Shanghai was in the central government. Wang Daohan had a strong background in engineering and economic management, but his direct association with Shanghai was in the early 1950s when he was with the East China Military and Administrative Council. In the post-Mao period, Wang first worked as first vice-minister for economic relations with foreign countries, and then as vice-director of the State Foreign Investment Management Commission led by Gu Mu 谷牧.

The key municipal leaders succeeding Chen Guodong and Wang Daohan in 1985 also had roughly similar career backgrounds. Rui Xingwen's entire career after 1949 had been in the central government and in the Beijing municipal government. He was deputy director of Beijing's national defence industry in 1977–1978. Between 1978 and his appointment as Shanghai's party secretary in 1985, he served as vice-minister of the Seventh Ministry of Machine Building and of Astronautics Industry, and later as vice-commissioner of the State Planning Commission. Immediately before being sent to Shanghai, he was minister of Urban and Rural Construction and Environmental Protection.

Although Jiang Zemin and Zhu Rongji are presently viewed as leaders of the so-called "Shanghai Faction," they also did not have particularly strong linkages with Shanghai before being sent there in 1985 and 1988, respectively. Jiang Zemin was educated at the famous Jiaotong University (交通大學) in Shanghai and worked in the city until 1954. He returned to work in Shanghai for several years in the early 1960s. After the fall of the "Gang of Four," Jiang was sent to Shanghai again as a member of the work team (*gongzuozu* 工作組) to put things in the municipality back on the right track.[29] In the early 1980s, however, Jiang's major experiences were with various central ministries and functional areas. Zhu Rongji was educated in Tsinghua University (清華大學) and spent his entire career in the central government before being appointed mayor of Shanghai in 1988.

Admittedly, there are serious problems in interpreting élite positions and behaviour merely from information about their socioeconomic and career backgrounds.[30] However, because élite behaviour and activities are kept behind the bureaucratic curtain, élite background remains an important way to ascertain the views and policy positions of the political élite in Chinese politics. This analysis of the career backgrounds of Shanghai's party secretaries and mayors in the 1980s provides a starting point for interpreting their roles in the politics of central–Shanghai relations in the 1980s.

Considering Shanghai's strategic importance in China's economy, it is reasonable to assume that these leaders were dispatched to Shanghai mainly to fulfil the purposes of the Centre.[31] This argument may perhaps be supported by the careers of some of these leaders after they left Shanghai. Peng Chong became a central secretariat member when the secretariat was re-established in early 1980, and he continued his political career on the Standing Committee of the National People's Congress. Wang Daohan has continued his association with Shanghai after stepping down from the mayorship in 1985, in his capacity as advisor to the municipal government. Wang now plays a prominent role in China's united front affairs as president of Association for Relations across the Taiwan Straits. Rui Xingwen relinquished the position of party secretary to become a central secretariat member in 1987. Jiang Zemin, as is well known, became general secretary of the CCP after the fall of Zhao Ziyang 趙紫陽 in 1989. After acting as Shanghai's party secretary and mayor for three years, Zhu Rongji went back to Beijing to become vice-premier and later a member of the Standing Committee of the Politburo. After stepping down as first party secretary in 1985, Chen Guodong continued to exercise considerable political influence in Shanghai as chairman of the Municipal Party Advisory Committee. However, Chen is widely considered to have consistently stood for the Centre's interests on the issue of central–Shanghai relations.[32]

While it is possible to interpret the particularly prominent rise of these figures as evidence of the growing influence of Shanghai in national politics, a reverse interpretation is probably closer to the truth. The case of Jiang Zemin is particularly illuminating. Shanghai's economy during Jiang Zemin's mayorship performed poorly as a result of many unanticipated factors, resulting in a sharp decline in revenue. Against this background, it is hard to think that Jiang's later promotion was due to his contribution to improving Shanghai's economic performance when he was mayor and party secretary. These circumstances suggest that as a result of Shanghai's economic importance, the Centre imposed tighter control by appointing officials who enjoyed greater central trust and support, and probably had a strong central orientation. On the other hand, it should also be noted that even among this group of municipal leaders, there might be some disagreement. Wang Daohan seems to have been more sympathetic to Shanghai's difficulties than Chen Guodong. In interviews with outsiders, Wang did not hide his view that Shanghai should be given more autonomy in steering its economic development.[33]

An examination of the career backgrounds of the deputy party secretaries and mayors yields somewhat different results. Most of these leaders spent all or most of their careers in Shanghai before being promoted to the municipal level. The best example of this is the new group of deputy mayors elected in April 1983. Ruan Chongwu 阮崇武 (executive deputy mayor) was the only deputy mayor transferred from outside Shanghai. However, most of Ruan's career before 1978 was also in Shanghai. All other deputy mayors, Zhu Zhongbao 朱宗葆 , Li Zhaoji 李肇基 , Liu Zhenyuan 劉振元 , Ni Tianzeng 倪天增 and Ye Gongqi 葉公琦 , all worked in the municipal government bureaucracy immediately prior to assuming the new positions.[34] This group of deputy mayors was replaced by another group in April 1988.[35] Like the one before it, this new group was also entirely drawn from Shanghai.[36] The backgrounds of the deputy party secretaries after 1985, not surprisingly, also had similar characteristics.

In view of the sharp contrast in the backgrounds of the first and second tiers of the municipal leadership, it may be reasonable to think that they had different views regarding central–Shanghai relations and, therefore, played different roles in Shanghai's struggle for greater autonomy. However, this proposition should be qualified by two caveats. First and foremost, career background is only one of the many variables affecting the positions and behaviour of provincial leaders. Second, whether these Shanghai officials were more localist than the party secretaries and mayors remains a question for further research. Open articulation of local interests, be it by Chen Guodong or Jiang Zemin, or by their deputies, was similarly rare.

Important differences within the leadership sometimes did surface. When Shanghai's revenue did not grow at the same rate as output value (*zengchan yu zengshou butongbu* 增產與增收不同步) in the early 1980s, Chen Guodong stressed that this should not be blamed entirely on objective factors. He pointed out that Shanghai's advanced economic indicators were largely a result of the transfer of value from other localities through the supply of raw materials at cheaper prices. Countering the widespread sense of dissatisfaction among Shanghainese over "exploitation" by the central government, Chen Guodong warned against a sense of complacency and arrogance, stressing that Shanghai's cadres should have a clear head.[37] Chen's view differed noticeably from that of Wang Daohan and deputy mayor Zhu Zhongbao; they attributed the slow growth of Shanghai's revenue to objective difficulties that Shanghai could not control.[38] Chen Guodong also reportedly refused to support Shanghai in playing a more pioneering role in China's economic reform and opening to the outside world.[39] Rui Xingwen, likewise, viewed Shanghai's problems more from the central perspective than from Shanghai's. In 1987, when Shanghai's economy was in great trouble, Rui Xingwen pointed out that Shanghai's economy had grown because of the support of the whole country and the central government. Rui emphasized that the central government had always given special attention and care to Shanghai's needs (*kai xiaozao* 開小灶), such as guaranteeing the supply of coal and electricity for Shanghai, and that it was not too much to ask Shanghai to make greater contributions [to the Centre and the country]. Most importantly, Rui seemed reluctant to press the central government to decentralize further control over locally generated revenue to Shanghai, saying that the Centre had given more revenue to Shanghai in 1985 and it was not appropriate to ask for more money again after just one year.[40]

Meanwhile, although Shanghai's municipal leaders rarely articulated localist interests openly, Municipal Party Committee newspapers (i.e., *Jiefang ribao* and *Wen hui bao* 文匯報) published numerous articles on the central–Shanghai relationship, and on the need to alleviate Shanghai's financial burden. The frequent appearance of these articles in the mouthpieces of the Municipal Party Committee indicates that at least some municipal leaders supported these views and their open expression.

Not surprisingly, in the 1980s localist interests were articulated more often and more explicitly by Shanghai's quasi-officials, intellectuals and even by officials who held less formal positions in the party–state bureaucracy. Enterprise managers were also seen actively complaining about the pressure of high — and increasing — production quotas and about their increasingly obsolete production facilities.[41] Two groups of people were particularly active and outspoken in articulating on behalf of Shanghai's interests. One of them included the intellectuals associated with Shanghai Academy of Social Sciences (SASS). The other was former municipal officials who were then affiliated with the special committees of the Municipal People's Congress and the Political Consultative Conference.

Where and How Were Local Interests Articulated?

Unlike the Soviet Union where the National Party Congress had become a major arena for local interest articulation,[42] both the National Party Congress and the National People's Congress in China have been marked by an absence of open political debate.[43] Shanghai's intellectuals and government officials sought to press their arguments in a number of national arenas. For example, in 1980, the head of Shanghai's Financial Bureau argued at a national conference on city finance that three sets of relationships — revenue remittance and retention, extraction and investment, and production and livelihood — should be properly handled.[44] On the whole, however, the major arenas of interest articulation were at the local level. Arguments and views challenging central policy appeared in different arenas of varying political importance: seminars and conferences, academic journals and local newspapers, and the Municipal People's Congress and the Political Consultative Conference.

Seminars and Conferences

Initially, the seminars organized by Shanghai's academic associations and government agencies provided opportunities for intellectuals and government officials in the city to exchange views and articulate common interests and values. The seminar series, held once every two weeks, was initially organized by the Municipal Planning Commission and SASS in July 1979. Later, the Municipal Economic Commission, the Shanghai Economic Research Centre (SERC), the Finance and Economic Committee of the Municipal People's Congress, and the Economic Committee of the Municipal People's Political Consultative Conference joined to sponsor the seminar series. From July 1979 to early 1982, about 60 seminars were held.[45] While a wide range of issues pertaining to Shanghai's short-term and long-term development were discussed, the focus was on central–Shanghai relations. The organizers selected the theme of "what kind of Shanghai we should seek to build" (*jianshe yige zenmeyang de Shanghai* 建設一個怎麼樣的上海). Issues such as how to develop Shanghai's comparative advantage, whether Shanghai could become a national economic centre, the long-term objectives of Shanghai's economic development, the livelihood of the people, and whether the central government should fully or scientifically utilize Shanghai's contributions were heatedly discussed.[46]

The seminar series continued well into 1982. In 1982, the focus was linked to the drafting of Shanghai's Sixth Five-year Plan, as indicated by

Ma Yihang 馬一行 , then head of the Municipal Planning Commission.[47] In late September 1982, the seminars considered the question of how Shanghai should respond to the national objective of quadrupling (*fanliangfan* 翻兩翻) total output value by the end of the century. Instead of taking the national target as that of Shanghai, Shanghainese asked: If the whole country seeks to quadruple output value, what should Shanghai do? The proposal that Shanghai should follow the national objective of seeking to quadruple total output value was questioned. Instead, it was suggested that Shanghai should aim at making a greater contribution to China's modernization.[48]

SERC and the Institute of Departmental Economics (IDE) of SASS were two important institutional bases for articulating local interests in Shanghai in the 1980s. The former, established in 1980, played a key role in co-ordinating and conducting research on issues of Shanghai's economic development.[49] The role of the latter was especially pronounced in the articulation of local interest. In the early 1980s, a research group on Shanghai's economic development strategy was formed at the IDE, and it played an active and influential role.

Two linked conferences held in 1984 also became important arenas for Shanghai's intellectuals and officials to articulate their views and arguments. In April 1984, the Municipal Planning Commission, SERC and SASS organized a conference to formulate a strategy for Shanghai's economic development. The IDE's research group presented a series of reports and systematic arguments at the meeting, demanding a fundamental change in Shanghai's development strategy. This conference and the arguments made by the research group played an important role in Shanghai's bargaining with the Centre for more autonomy during the rest of the year. In August 1984, the municipal leaders reported to the Central Finance and Economic Small Leading Group and the State Council on Shanghai's economic situation.[50]

Another conference on Shanghai's development strategy was convened by the Municipal Party Committee and government in September 1984.[51] This conference had the same focus as the one held in April, but many national figures (including Xu Dixin 許滌新 , Xue Muqiao 薛暮橋 , Tong Dalin 童大林) and officials from the State Council attended. The conference also played an important role in the policy-making process. It was held just before the central government and Shanghai were about to work out the terms of fiscal decentralization and local autonomy.[52]

Academic Journals and Local Media

Because intellectuals were vocal actors in the articulation of Shanghai's interests, academic journals and publications for economic officials naturally became important forums for arguments and analyses supporting Shanghai's interests. Such publications included *Shanghai qiye* 上海企業 (Shanghai Enterprise), *Shanghai jingji* 上海經濟 (Shanghai Economy), *Caijing yanjiu* 財經研究 (Financial and Economic Research), and *Shanghai shehuikexueyuan xueshu jikan* 上海社會科學院學術季刊 (SASS Academic Journal) which published a large number of similar articles. The monthly published by SASS, *Shehui kexue* 社會科學 (Social Sciences), was especially important as an arena for local interest articulation. The journal created two forums in the period between mid-1979 and 1980, the first entitled "The state and problems of Shanghai's economy," and the second "What kind of Shanghai should we seek to build?" Nearly one hundred articles, research papers and policy recommendations were published at part of these two forums. Although some of these articles sought to offer objective analyses, most explicitly demanded more favourable policies for Shanghai. A majority of these articles were authored by the research staff of the IDE, but some were written by people from other institutions. *Shehui kexue* continued to publish many articles on these themes after the forums were formally closed. Nearly every issue contained articles analysing the problems of Shanghai's economy, and advancing policy recommendations.

The most important of such articles published in *Shehui kexue* was probably the one authored by Chen Minzhi 陳敏之 , deputy head of the IDE in the early 1980s and later its advisor.[53] He was also a key member of the IDE's research group on Shanghai's economic development strategy. An expanded version of the article was published in *Shanghai jingji yanjiu* 上海經濟研究 (Research on Shanghai Economy), a journal published for internal circulation by SERC. In this article, Chen directly addresses the issue of whether Shanghai should seek to quadruple its output value, arguing that criteria other than output value should be adopted to measure Shanghai's contribution to China's modernization.

This view differed markedly from the position of the municipal government. In his work report to the 8th Municipal People's Congress in April 1983, Wang Daohan continued to argue that Shanghai should seek to quadruple its total output value by the end of the century.[54] Chen Minzhi's article anticipated the more systematic and vigorous arguments about

Shanghai's economic development strategy articulated by the research group he led. As outlined above, at the April and September 1984 conferences, the IDE's research group developed systematic arguments calling for a fundamental change in Shanghai's economic development strategy. Later, the research group's main report was also published in *Shehui kexue*.[55]

The mouthpiece of the Municipal Party Committee, *Jiefang ribao* 解放日報, also was an arena for the articulation of local interests from time to time. However, the role of *Jiefang ribao* was more ambivalent. Its ambivalence stemmed from the conflict and tension built in the role and objectives of the municipal leadership. At most times, *Jiefang ribao* was used to propagate and justify the status quo, and even the central government's continuing "exploitation." However, there were moments when views and arguments sympathetic to Shanghai's interests managed to appear in this newspaper, sometimes in vocal ways.

As early as 1979, several *Jiefang ribao* commentator articles raised the problem of the relationship between production and consumption. These articles likened the central government's policy to "draining the pond to get all the fish" (*jieze eryu* 竭澤而漁) and demanded that the relationship between bone (*gutou* 骨頭) and meat (*rou* 肉) be improved.[56] Another report pressed that Shanghai, being a tree that sheds coins when shaken, i.e., a ready source of money (*yaoqianshu* 搖錢樹), needed to be nourished and cultivated.[57]

On 3 October 1980, *Jiefang ribao* published a long article on its front page written by Shen Junbo 沈峻坡, an IDE member.[58] Shen's article had an eye-catching and sensational title: Ten Firsts and Five Lasts (*Shige diyi he wuge daoshu diyi* 十個第一和五個倒數第一). The article skilfully presents Shanghai's enormous contribution to the entire country and the central government (by saying that Shanghai's revenue was one-sixth of the national total, and that one-third of the central government's expenditures came from Shanghai) and lists those aspects of its livelihood and infrastructure construction which lag far behind other cities in China. Shen's arguments found immediate and widespread echoes among the people of Shanghai. *Jiefang ribao* created a column on its front page called "What is meant by ten firsts and five lasts?" (*shige diyi he wuge daoshu diyi shuoming shenme* 十個第一和五個倒數第一說明甚麼), which lasted for about one month. This provided a rare opportunity for the people of Shanghai to communicate their views and grievances to their fellow citizens. Both the publication of Shen's article and the following column should not be seen merely as the simple expression of individual view-points. Because *Jiefang ribao* is the mouthpiece of the Municipal Party Committee, it is hard to imagine that these views could appear on its front pages without the support of certain key leaders in the municipal leadership.

Jiefang ribao also occasionally published in its columns academic discussion-type articles articulating Shanghai's interests. Typical examples included Wang Zhukang's 王竹康 articles demanding a reduction of pressures on Shanghai's finance and production capacity;[59] Ni Yiping's article complaining of the dispersed use of limited funds and raw materials in the nation-wide bicycle industry;[60] Shen Junbo and his colleagues' articles on problems in economic co-operation between Shanghai and other regions;[61] and Shen's article calling for putting more emphasis on fully developing Shanghai's role as a core city.[62]

The role of *Jiefang ribao* as an arena for local interest articulation varied from time to time. In 1979 and 1980, as shown above, many views and arguments which deviated from the central government's policy managed to appear in prominent positions in this party newspaper. However, the open and explicit articulation of local interests as those that were published in October 1980 was very rare. *Jiefang ribao* was reportedly criticized by central planners for publishing Shen Junbo's article.[63] From early 1981 onwards, it turned to criticizing the views and arguments advanced in Shen's article and those who supported him. This change corresponded with the central government's desperate emphasis on collecting more revenue from Shanghai amidst the fiscal crisis at the Centre.

Therefore, in 1981, numerous articles in *Jiefang ribao* stressed that Shanghai's production capacities were far from fully exploited, and there was room for economizing in the use of raw materials and fuel, and for increasing production. New production and revenue targets were imposed on the city's industrial enterprises.[64] Ideological appeals such as "making greater contributions to the state is Shanghai's glory" and "seeking to share the heavy burden of the state" were stressed.[65] In response to the grievances and the resistance to the central demand to increase production and revenue in the early 1980s, a *Jiefang ribao* commentator criticized the complacency of Shanghainese, claiming that they had a parochial arrogance (*yelang zida* 夜郎自大). The commentator also challenged the view that Shanghai's economic performance had reached its maximum. Seeking to dispel Shanghai's "parochial arrogance," the commentator contended that its better economic performance was not entirely a result of its own efforts, but was largely the result of support from other localities.[66]

Besides *Jiefang ribao*, another arena for local interest articulation was *Shijie jingji daobao* 世界經濟導報 . *SJD*, a national weekly published in Shanghai, was widely regarded as having a strong reformist orientation.[67] Until its forced closure in May 1989, *SJD* served as an outlet for unconventional ideas and arguments. Each issue of *SJD* usually had two pages devoted to discussion of Shanghai's economic development. In 1982, *SJD* served as an outlet for the ideas expressed in the seminar series held in Shanghai. The role of *SJD* was especially important in the mid-1980s. Many views and arguments, directly or indirectly challenging prevailing central–Shanghai relations, appeared frequently.[68] When the linked conferences on Shanghai's economic development strategy were convened in 1984, *SJD* published a number of articles calling for a fundamental change of strategy.[69]

While these views demanded greater autonomy for Shanghai, they also proposed concentrating greater authority at the municipal government level. Several articles pointed out that while Shanghai's economic structure needed to be fundamentally transformed from resource and labour intensive to knowledge and technology intensive, the investment pattern in the early 1980s had not been in this direction. Because each industry and enterprise behaved according to its own narrow interests, these articles argued, there was a lack of concentration in the use of Shanghai's limited resources.[70] A researcher from the IDE, for example, compared the ability of the state to develop key industries through control of capital investment in the pre-reform period and Shanghai's dispersed investment pattern in the previous several years, implying that more resources needed to be concentrated at the municipal level.[71]

SJD also published a large number of reports and analyses on various aspects of Shanghai's economy. Most were related in one way or another to central–Shanghai relations. These included the slow development of new products in Shanghai's enterprises, and the weak linkage between scientific research and the development of new products.[72] Shen Junbo and Zhu Zhengyi 朱正頤 penned a column called "Ways of doing business in old Shanghai" (*jiu Shanghai shengyijing* 舊上海生意經) in *SJD*, advocating that Shanghai should learn from its past and reinvent the old entrepreneurial spirit that it had lost under communist rule.[73] It was very common for Shanghai intellectuals and officials to contrast Shanghai's contemporary miserable situation with the city's prosperous past before the communist take-over. For example, a deputy to the Municipal People's Congress lamented the deterioration of Shanghai's role as an international business and finance centre.[74] They considered that the future of Shanghai lie in turning it from an industrial city to what it used to be before 1949. Systematic research on Shanghai's history, and a relatively positive evaluation of it, began to flourish in Shanghai in the 1980s.[75]

Shanghai's intellectuals not only looked back to its pre-1949 tradition and status with nostalgia, but also to the early 1960s. An engineer from the Municipal Construction Commission, in an interview with a *SJD* reporter, highly praised the ability of the municipal government to concentrate authority in the early 1960s, and its achievements in developing new and advanced industries under tight resource constraints. The title of the interview, "Dangshi xinxing gongye shi zenyang gan qilai de? 當時新興工業是怎樣幹起來的？" (How did we build up the new industries at that time [in the early 1960s]?) clearly revealed a longing for the past and a dissatisfaction with the present.[76]

Similar comparisons were drawn with respect to the piecemeal progress of the construction of Shanghai's subway. Before 1966, a report stated, the municipal government, under the direct leadership of a deputy mayor, extended strong authority to overcome the difficulties encountered by the subway's pilot scheme. This was contrasted with the lack of authority in the construction of the subway at the present.[77] When the Municipal People's Congress and the Political Consultative Conference were in session in April 1984, many deputies compared Shanghai's plight in the 1980s to how the city fared in the 1950s, leading to a dive in the morale among the Shanghainese.[78]

Municipal People's Congress and Political Consultative Conference Meetings

The Municipal People's Congress and Political Consultative Conference meetings sometimes were also arenas for articulating local interests. This was particularly evident during the meetings in April 1988, when the political atmosphere was unprecedentedly liberal, thanks to the political structural reform endorsed by the CCP's 13th National Congress in October 1987. Before the Municipal People's Congress and the Political Consultative Conference were convened, Shen Junbo urged greater transparency and participation, complaining that in the past the municipal leaders evaded, or did not let the people of Shanghai know, the crux of the difficulties and problems in Shanghai's development. He also argued that the people should be allowed to "release" (*fang* 放) their demands at these meetings.[79] Deputies to these two meetings did not let Shen Junbo down when they were given the opportunity. They poured severe criticism on Jiang Zemin, the chief agent of the Centre in Shanghai.[80] They raised many problems about Jiang's Work Report and seemed to have a very negative evaluation of the performance of the government led by Jiang.

For example, a member of the Political Consultative Conference said that while Jiang's report covered every issue, it did not give adequate attention to problems of great concern to the people or requiring serious thought. Another member stated that while there were some achievements in the past five years, *there were no major achievements*. Still another member criticized Jiang Zemin for failing to address the real problems facing Shanghai.[81] The criticisms of Jiang Zemin were so numerous and severe that Zhu Rongji, who had just arrived in Shanghai to become the new mayor, found it necessary to come to his defence. He urged a more objective evaluation of the performance of Jiang's municipal government, and stressed that many problems of the past several years were caused by objective factors.[82]

Apart from directing their criticism towards the municipal government, the deputies, of course, also focused on the root cause of the problems confronting Shanghai — central–Shanghai relations. Zhu Xingqing 朱杏清 , a deputy to the Municipal People's Congress and also deputy director of *SJD*, argued that Shanghai's problems, such as policy rigidity and low morale, should not be viewed at face value. Rather, they should be traced to the existing institutions, which lay at the root of these phenomena. Li Wuhui 厲無畏 , another deputy and deputy director of the IDE, complained that Shanghai, as a "price basin" (*wujia pandi* 物價盤地), had been squeezed to the limit. On the one hand, the prices of the raw materials used by Shanghai's industrial enterprises had increased substantially but, on the other hand, the prices of Shanghai's industrial products had not risen at the same rate, costing Shanghai, Li suggested, to lose about RMB0.8 to 1.3 billion in income annually.[83]

The deputies' dissatisfaction with the municipal leadership was reflected directly in the election of the deputy mayors. The deputies nominated a large number of candidates to compete with the officially nominated candidates. Initially, a total of 24 candidates were nominated, either by the deputies or by the municipal leadership. After considerable manoeuvring, the list was narrowed down to 10, only 2 of them being directly nominated by the deputies. Of these 10 candidates, 6 were incumbent deputy mayors, and it is reasonable to think that they were among the

8 candidates put forward by the municipal leadership. While it is not clear whether the 2 candidates nominated by the deputies were elected, only 4 of the incumbent deputy mayors were returned, suggesting that the deputies had strong reservations about the performance of the municipal government.[84]

Weapon of the Weak: Passive Resistance and Discontent

Apart from making their voices heard in different arenas, the people of Shanghai also had some impact on the municipal leadership and the central government through passive resistance. In the early 1980s, when Shanghai was asked to make greater contributions to the country, there were extensive complaints and grievances in Shanghai. This led the municipal leadership to invoke ideological appeals, the effectiveness of which, however, was doubtful.[85] Mayor Wang Daohan urged that it was necessary to boost the morale of the people. In particular, he suggested that the cadres' state of mind would determine whether Shanghai could meet the targets set by the central government. This indicated that there was also some resistance among the cadres in Shanghai.[86]

On another occasion, Wang Daohan admitted that many people did not have enough understanding of the central government's desperate expectation for Shanghai in a time of financial difficulty.[87] The widespread existence of grievances and resistance probably helps explain that, for instance, for the first seven months of 1981, Shanghai's total industrial output value, instead of growing at a faster rate as demanded, was down from the level of the previous year.[88]

The problem of morale was a chronic issue in Shanghai in the 1980s. One only has to recall Shen Junbo's article in *Jiefang ribao* and the echoes it had drawn to appreciate how extensive such grievances and grumbling were among the Shanghainese and what they were about. This state of mind was also noted by journalists reporting about Shanghai. A report in *Far Eastern Economic Review*, for example, quoted a Shanghai official as saying: "The average Shanghainese is not happy. He works hard to contribute one out of every six *yuan* the country spends, but he cannot even get a decent place to live."[89] Similarly, a reporter for *Time* cited the following complaint from a Shanghai journalist: "Shanghai leaders and ordinary citizens are aghast when they visit Beijing or Shenzhen 深圳 and see all the wide highways and high-rise buildings. They cry, 'This is where all our money went!'"[90]

A perceptive Chinese writer has defined such feelings and sentiment as the heart of the so-called "Shanghai complex."[91] It was common for the Shanghainese to think that their city could certainly catch up with Guangdong 廣東 , and even Hong Kong and Singapore, if it were to be allowed to go about its own business.[92] Mayor Wang Daohan seemed also to share this feeling. When interviewed by Susan Shirk, he said, "Of course, we're behind Guangdong on reform. If the Centre gave us the same financial deal they gave Guangdong, we would be moving faster on reform."[93]

The problem of morale and frustration came to a peak in 1987 and 1988 when Shanghai was hit by a hepatitis A wave,[94] and its economic superiority was doubly challenged by the rise of the economy in such localities as Guangdong and Jiangsu 江蘇 , and by a substantial rise in the prices of raw materials and fuel.[95] A vivid indicator of how Shanghai lost ground to Guangdong in the new era was that Jiang Zemin led a group of high-level Shanghai officials to Guangdong to learn from its experience.[96] The problem of low morale became the main issue at the Municipal People's Congress and the Political Consultative Conference meetings held in April 1988.[97]

At that time, the morale of Shanghainese also seemed to be related to the negative effects of some reform measures (such as the relaxation of price controls) on the people's livelihood.[98] A deputy to the people's congress complained that the living standard of many citizens had already gone down 31%.[99] In response to the depression and grievances reflected in the April meetings, in the following month *Jiefang ribao* carried a number of articles trying to inspire morale (*zhenfen shiqi* 振奮士氣).[100] A commentator criticized Shanghainese for having too many grievances, and said that they should find the causes for the problems in themselves instead of blaming others.[101] At a cadre meeting in May 1988, Jiang Zemin said that the sense of depression and dissatisfaction should be "properly guided." And it should not be allowed to spread uncontrolled.[102]

Limitations of Local Interest Articulation under an Authoritarian Regime

This detailed examination of interest articulation activities in Shanghai suggests that the political regime had set stringent limits on how, and the extent to which, local people could articulate their interests and could influence policy making. A main weakness was the lack of organization and co-ordination, which limited its political impact. The seminar series on Shanghai's economic problems organized regularly in the early 1980s did constitute some co-ordinated effort among Shanghai's intellectuals and organizations, but these ended in 1982. Moreover, the degree of co-ordination among the organizations which sponsored the seminar series was not high; there were few activities other than the seminar series itself. The lack of co-ordination and organization is particularly evident in the emergence of strong resentment against setting higher production and revenue targets in the early 1980s, and the eruption of discontent and grumbling during the meetings of the Municipal People's Congress and the Political Consultative Conference in April 1984.

Institutions such as the IDE of SASS and SERC, and to a lesser extent, the municipal economic co-ordinating agencies, provided the institutional bases for efforts to press for a more favourable central–Shanghai relationship. In particular, under the leadership of Chen Minzhi and Yao Xitang 姚錫棠, the IDE hosted a number of researchers who were particularly active in articulating Shanghai's interests. The role of the IDE's research is especially important, as suggested above. The committees under the Standing Committee of the Municipal People's Congress and the Political Consultative Conference, led by former economic officials (for example, Li Jiagao 李家鎬, a former director of the Municipal Planning Committee) in the municipal government, also served, to a certain extent, as an institutional basis.

There are limits, however, to treating these institutions as independent of the party–state bureaucracy. Although this chapter insists that open interest articulation should be viewed as a different kind of politics from bargaining within the bureaucracy, in China it is very difficult to draw the boundary clearly. SERC was officially an advisory body to the Municipal Party Committee and government. The Municipal Party Committee and government economic agencies[103] joined with other less-official bodies to organize the seminar series in the early 1980s. The conference organized by the Planning Commission, SERC and SASS in April 1988 obviously had the support of the Municipal Party Committee and the government. Viewed together with the conference convened by the Municipal Party Committee and the government the following September, this conference was obviously an integral part of the bargaining process between Shanghai and the Centre.

This aspect of interest articulation was a double-edged sword: it was a source not only of strength but also of weakness. On the one hand, proximity and access to the policy-making process gave the intellectuals from the IDE considerable influence in shaping the formulation of Shanghai's new economic development strategy. The arguments of the IDE's research group seemed to have a direct impact on policy making, leading to fiscal decentralization in 1985. However, dependence on the party–state bureaucracy also allowed the municipal party–state bureaucracy to control societal initiatives and efforts. Throughout the 1980s, although the Municipal Party Committee and government did sometimes encourage the rank and file Shanghainese to express openly their grievances and discontent, as in 1980 and during the meetings of the Municipal People's Congress and the Political Consultative Conference in April 1988, at most other times, they sought to control local sentiment and suppress initiatives from below in 1981–1982 and later in May 1988.

The absence of co-ordination and organization, and the dependence on the party–state bureaucracy, account for the greatest weakness of Shanghai's interest articulation efforts in the 1980s: there was no vehicle to communicate and articulate the views and interests of a large number of people. In late 1980, such a vehicle was provided by *Jiefang ribao*. Shen Junbo's dramatic presentation of Shanghai's asymmetrical position in the balance of contribution to the national economy and local development touched the hearts of hundreds of thousands of Shanghainese. However, as a propaganda instrument of the Municipal Party Committee, *Jiefang ribao* could not help but become an instrument of control and containment. This resulted in a great distance between those who were best capable of articulating and expressing local demands, and the bulk of the population who had great objections to the Centre's "exploitation" of Shanghai.[104]

From the "Absence of Local Interest" to Local Interest Articulation

Shanghai, by virtue of its economic strength and political radicalism, has played a unique role in contemporary Chinese politics. Shanghai's eminence in national politics is fully evident in the rise of three Shanghai-based radicals to the pinnacle of national power during the Cultural Revolution.[105] The singular importance of the so-called "Shanghai Faction" in national politics, however, was accompanied by policies and measures that worked to the city's disadvantage. Lucian Pye notes,

"Shanghai's political leaders have consistently failed to assert the special economic and cultural interests of their city. Indeed, quite to the contrary, they have over considerable periods advocated policies and programmes diametrically opposed to the interests and the welfare of the people they presumably represented."[106]

Regardless of the many limitations suggested above, the importance of Shanghai's local interest articulation in the 1980s is perhaps best appreciated in this historical context of an "absence of local interest" along with Shanghai's influence in national politics. The 1980s witnessed the growing recognition of local interests in Shanghai, and also their increasing legitimacy. By 1988, the notion of local interest had become so firmly established that a commentator for *Jiefang ribao* urged Shanghai to press the Centre to give it more autonomy. He pointed out that Shanghai was not treated favourably because it had not fought fiercely enough with the Centre for its own interests.[107] The strong demands for pragmatic interests in Shanghai in the 1980s may also suggest that Shanghai has changed from being a base for radical politics to one supporting political conservatism.[108] Zhu Rongji, while mayor at the time of Tiananmen (天安門) crackdown, was able to rely on the support of the workers to suppress the radical students, therefore forestalling the need to call in the army as was done in Beijing.[109]

At the same time, Shanghai's struggle for more local autonomy in the 1980s finds rich precedents in its political history in the early twentieth century. In this regard, the strong nostalgia for Shanghai's pre-1949 history, evidenced in the views and arguments in the 1980s, is a phenomenon of considerable significance. In the early twentieth century, Shanghai developed a unique and strong tradition of struggle for local autonomy, resulting in constant conflict between the political power of the state and the economic power represented by Shanghai.[110] To what extent Shanghai's present struggle for more autonomy is supported by its rich history of struggle for local power is unclear, but an interesting parallel can be drawn.[111]

Shanghainese have well recognized that, as Bergere says about pre-1949 Shanghai, the city's prosperity and well-being thrives on a relative independence from the bureaucratic national government.[112] Of course, along with this observation, we have to note also that since the late 1980s, there seems to have been a coincidence of interests between Shanghai and the Centre. This perhaps helps account for the relatively harmonious central–Shanghai relations in recent years. How long this harmony will continue, however, is still an open question.

This examination of interest articulation in Shanghai in the 1980s also illuminates the complex relationship between the central government, Shanghai's leaders and the local people and cadres. The discontent of Shanghainese was not only directed at the central government, but also at the municipal leaders who were viewed as agents of the Centre. Two party secretaries, Chen Guodong and Jiang Zemin, particularly did not enjoy much support among the Shanghainese, as reflected in the negative response to Jiang Zemin's Work Report in April 1988 by the deputies to the Municipal People's Congress.

Leadership changes since the early 1990s might lead one to think that this tripartite relationship may have tipped in favour of local interests. After Zhu Rongji's return to Beijing in 1991, Wu Bangguo and Huang Ju were appointed municipal party secretary and mayor, respectively. Both have spent their entire careers in Shanghai. While this is an important variable in predicting élite behaviour, the structural parameters conditioning the political behaviour of provincial leaders in China, as Goodman argues, have remained basically unchanged. Therefore, the tension between the Centre, the municipal leadership and local society will not disappear easily.

Notes

1. Jia Hao and Lin Zhimin (eds.), *Changing Central–local Relations in China: Reform and State Capacity* (Boulder: Westview Press, 1994); Elizabeth Perry and Christine Wong (eds.), *The Political Economy of Reform in Post-Mao China* (Cambridge, Mass.: The Council on East Asian Studies, Harvard University, 1985).

2. David Goodman stresses the "inherent variability of the relationship between the centre and each province." See David Goodman, "Provinces Confronting the State?" in *China Review 1992*, edited by Kuan Hsin-chi and Maurice Brosseau (Hong Kong: The Chinese University Press, 1992), pp. 3.9–3.11. On similar argument, see Kenneth G. Lieberthal and Michel Oksenberg, *Policy Making in China: Leaders, Structures, and Processes* (Princeton, New Jersey: Princeton University Press, 1988), p. 341.

3. Lin Zhimin, "Reform and Shanghai: Changing Central–local Fiscal Relations," in *Changing Central–local Relations in China* (see note 1), p. 239.

4. For variations within the scheme of "eating in separate kitchens," see Michel Oksenberg and James Tong, "The Evolution of Central–provincial Fiscal Relations in China, 1971–1984: The Formal System," *The China Quarterly*,

No. 125 (March 1991), pp. 18–22.

5. *Shanghai jingji 1949–1982* (neibu ben) 上海經濟 1949–1982 (內部本) (Shanghai Economy 1949–1982 [internal circulation copy]) (Shanghai: Shanghai renmin chubanshe 上海人民出版社, 1984), p. 888; Oksenberg and Tong, "The Evolution of Central–provincial Fiscal Relations in China, 1971–1984" (see note 4), p. 21; Lin, "Reform and Shanghai" (see note 3), p. 244.

6. Lin, "Reform and Shanghai" (see note 3), p. 245; Oksenberg and Tong, "The Evolution of Central–provincial Fiscal Relations in China, 1971–1984" (see note 4), p. 21.

7. *Time*, 5 October 1992, pp. 25–31.

8. Lynn T. White III, *Shanghai Shanghaied? Uneven Taxes in Reform China* (Hong Kong: Centre of Asian Studies, University of Hong Kong, 1989).

9. Lin, "Reform and Shanghai" (see note 3), pp. 239–60.

10. Ibid., p. 240.

11. Lieberthal and Oksenberg, *Policy Making in China* (see note 2), Kenneth G. Lieberthal, "Introduction: The 'Fragmented Authoritarianism' Model and Its Limitations," and David Lampton, "A Plum for a Peach: Bargaining, Interest, and Bureaucratic Politics in China," in *Bureaucracy, Politics, and Decision Making in Post-Mao China*, edited by Kenneth G. Lieberthal and David Lampton (Berkeley, Los Angeles: University of California Press, 1992), pp. 1–30, 33–58 respectively.

12. Lieberthal and Oksenberg, *Policy Making in China* (see note 2), pp. 352–53.

13. Lieberthal, "Introduction: The 'Fragmented Authoritarianism' Model and Its Limitations" (see note 11).

14. Andrew Walder, *Communist Neo-traditionalism: Work and Authority in Chinese Industry* (Berkeley and Los Angeles: University of California Press, 1986); Jean Oi, *The State and Peasants in Contemporary China: The Political Economy of Village Government* (Berkeley and Los Angeles: University of California Press, 1989).

15. Walder, *Communist Neo-traditionalism* (see note 14), pp. 246, 249.

16. Roderick MacFarquhar, *The Origins of the Cultural Revolution*, vol. 1 (New York: Columbia University Press, 1974).

17. Elizabeth Perry, "Shanghai's Strike Wave of 1957," *The China Quarterly*, No. 137 (March 1994), pp. 1–27.

18. Hong Yung Lee, *The Politics of the Chinese Cultural Revolution*, (Berkeley and Los Angeles: University of California Press, 1978); Lynn T. White III, *Policies of Chaos: The Organizational Causes of Violence in China's Cultural Revolution* (Princeton, New Jersey: Princeton University Press, 1989).

19. Tony Saich (ed.), *The Chinese People's Movement: Perspective on Spring 1989* (Armonk: M. E. Sharpe, 1990); Jonathan Unger (ed.), *The Pro-democracy Protests in China*, (Armonk: M. E. Sharpe, 1991); Andrew

Walder and Gong Xiaoxia, "Workers in the Tiananmen Protests: The Politics of the Beijing Workers' Autonomous Federation," *The Australian Journal of Chinese Affairs*, No. 29 (January 1993), pp. 1–29.

20. For example, see Perry, "Shanghai's Strike Wave of 1957" (see note 17); Walder and Gong, "Workers in the Tiananmen Protests" (see note 19).

21. Lucian Pye, "Forward" and David Goodman, "The Shanghai Connection: Shanghai's Role in National Politics during the 1970s," in *Shanghai: Revolution and Development in an Asian Metropolis*, edited by Christopher Howe (Cambridge: Cambridge University Press, 1981), pp. xi–xvi, and pp. 125–52 respectively.

22. Maria-Claire Bergere, "'The Other China': Shanghai from 1919 to 1949," in *Shanghai: Revolution and Development in an Asian Metropolis* (see note 21), pp. 1–34.

23. Vivienne Shue, *The Reach of the State: Sketches of the Chinese Body Politics* (Stanford, California: Stanford University Press, 1988); Jean Oi, *The State and Peasants in Contemporary China* (see note 14); David Goodman, *Centre and Province in the People's Republic of China: Sichuan and Guizhou 1955– 1965* (Cambridge and London: Cambridge University Press, 1986); David Goodman, "The Shanghai Connection" (see note 21), pp. 125–52; Lieberthal and Oksenberg, *Policy Making in China* (see note 2).

24. Goodman, *Centre and Province in the People's Republic of China* (see note 23), pp. 12–19.

25. Lieberthal and Oksenberg, *Policy Making in China* (see note 2), pp. 344–47.

26. Ibid, pp. 341–44.

27. He Husheng 何虎生, Li Yaodong 李耀東 and Xiang Changfu 向常福 (eds.), *Zhonghua renmin gongheguo zhiguan zhi* 中華人民共和國職官誌 (Positions and Officials of the People's Republic of China) (Beijing: Zhongguo shehui chubanshe 中國社會出版社, 1993), pp. 624–28.

28. The following information is drawn from *Who's Who in China: Current Leaders* (中國人名大詞典，現任黨政軍領導人物卷) (1st edition, 1989, Beijing: Foreign Languages Press, 1994).

29. *Jiefang ribao* 解放日報 (Liberation Daily) (hereafter cited as *JFRB*), 7 August 1989, p. 2.

30. For an analysis of this problem, see Robert Scalapino (eds.), *Élite in the People's Republic of China* (Seattle: University of Washington Press, 1972).

31. Lieberthal and Oksenberg, *Policy Making in China* (see note 2), p. 345.

32. Hong Wu 宏悟, "Shanghai yu diyige shinian gaige" 上海與第一個十年改革 (Shanghai and the First Ten Years of Reform), *Minzhu Zhongguo* 民主中國 (Democratic China), No. 11 (August 1992), p. 18. See also Ruan Ming 阮銘, "Lun Shanghaipai" 論上海派 (On the Shanghai Faction), *Minzhu Zhongguo*, No. 11 (August 1992), p. 14. Ruan Ming suggested that both Huang Ju 黃菊 and Wu Bangguo 吳邦國 were initially promoted by Chen Guodong 陳國棟.

Although Huang and Wu did not come to prominence until they were promoted to deputy party secretaries in 1985, they were elevated to members of Standing Committee of Shanghai's Party Committee in 1983 when Chen was still first party secretary. See *Shanghai quanshu* 上海全書 (Shanghai Encyclopaedia) (Shanghai: Xuelin chubanshe 學林出版社, 1989), p. 24; *Who's Who in China: Current Leaders* (1st edition) (see note 28), pp. 247-48.

33. Susan Shirk, *The Political Logic of Economic Reform in China* (Berkeley and Los Angeles: University of California Press, 1993), p. 141.

34. *JFRB*, 28 April 1983, p. 2.

35. In October 1986, Huang Ju, Xie Lijuan 謝麗娟 and Qian Xuezhong 錢學中 were appointed new deputy mayors.

36. *Who's Who in China* (1st edition) (see note 28), pp. 168, 247-48, 447, 512-13, 786, 1028.

37. *JFRB*, 13 January 1984, p. 1.

38. *JFRB*, 19 November 1983, p. 1; and 13 January 1984, p. 3. Zhu Zhongbao's view differed in a subtle way from a series of *JFRB* reports prompting enterprises in Shanghai to further exploit their potentials. See *JFRB*, 12 May 1982, p. 1; 22 July 1983, p. 1; and 29 October 1983, p. 1.

39. Ruan Ming, "Lun Shanghaipai," (see note 32) p. 15. Chen reportedly said that "Shanghai bu wei tianxia xian" 上海不爲天下先 (Shanghai Cannot Be the First under the Heaven). This thinking was severely criticized in Shanghai in 1988. See *Shijie jingji daobao* 世界經濟導報 (World Economic Herald) (hereafter cited as *SJD*), 4 July 1988, p. 9; and 17 April 1989, p. 13; *JFRB*, 1 February 1988, p. 4; 9 May 1988, p. 2; and 30 May 1988, p. 2. On Hu Yaobang's 胡耀邦 support for Shanghai to play a pioneering role, see Shen Shiwei 沈世緯, "Zhenxing Shanghai de hongwei lantu" 振興上海的宏偉藍圖 (The Grand Blueprint for Developing Shanghai), *Liaowang* 瞭望 (Outlook), 18 March 1985, p. 20.

40. *SJD*, 21 September 1987, p. 7.

41. *JFRB*, 21 July 1979, p. 4. The factory manager of Shanghai No. 3 Bicycle Factory, Ni Yiping 倪一平, was quoted as complaining that the surplus of his enterprise had been extracted to such an extent that the factory could not maintain its current level of production. See also Ni Yiping's interview with a *Renmin ribao* 人民日報 (People's Daily) reporter, *JFRB*, 19 November 1979, p. 1.

42. Howard Biddulph, "Local Interest Articulation in CPSU," *World Politics*, Vol. 36, No. 1 (October 1983), pp. 28-52.

43. Things have started to change in late 1980s. See Kelvin J. O'Brien, *Reform without Liberalization: China's National People's Congress and the Politics of Institutional Change* (Cambridge and New York: Cambridge University Press, 1990).

44. *JFRB*, 12 October 1980, p. 1.

45. *SJD*, 15 February 1982, p. 11; *JFRB*, 1 March 1980, p. 3.

46. *JFRB*, 20 August 1980, p. 4.

47. *SJD*, 22 March 1982, p. 10.

48. *SJD*, 27 September 1982, pp. 1-2.

49. *SJD*, 22 March 1982, p. 11; 19 April 1982, p. 10; and 27 September 1982, p.2.

50. *Wen hui bao* 文匯報 (Shanghai), 16 January 1985, p. 1.

51. Shanghai shehuikexueyuan *Shanghai jingji nianjian* bianjibu 上海社會科學院《上海經濟年鑑》編輯部 (ed.), *Shanghai jingji 1983-1985* 上海經濟 1983-1985 (Shanghai Economy 1983-1985) (Shanghai: Shanghai renmin chubanshe, 1985), p. 946. These reports were published in Chen Minzhi 陳敏之 (ed.), *Shanghai jingji fazhan zhanlüe yanjiu* 上海經濟發展戰略研究 (A Research on Shanghai's Economic Development Strategy) (Shanghai: Shanghai renmin chubanshe, 1985).

52. *Wen hui bao* (see note 50), 16 January 1985, p. 1.

53. Chen Minzhi, "Shanghai jingji fazhan zhanlüe chutan" 上海經濟發展戰略初探 (A Preliminary Analysis of Shanghai's Economic Development Strategy), *Shehui kexue* 社會科學 (Social Science) (Shanghai), No. 6 (1983), pp. 2-4.

54. *JFRB*, 30 April 1983.

55. "Shanghai jingji fazhan zhanlüe mubiao jueze" 上海經濟發展戰略目標抉擇 (Choosing the Strategic Goals of Shanghai's Economic Development), *Shehui kexue*, No. 10 (1984), pp. 8-13.

56. *JFRB*, 29 March 1979, p. 1; 15 July 1979, p. 1; and 3 August 1979, p.1.

57. *JFRB*, 11 July 1979, p. 1.

58. *JFRB*, 3 October 1980, p. 1.

59. *JFRB*, 11 June 1981, p. 3; and 26 November 1981, p. 4.

60. *JFRB*, 21 July 1979, p. 4.

61. *JFRB*, 13 August 1981, p. 3; and 15 July 1982, p. 4.

62. *JFRB*, 1 October 1984, p. 4.

63. Hong Wu, "Shanghai yu diyige shinian gaige" (see note 32), p. 17.

64. For example, an industrial company's production targets were revised twice in 1981. See *JFRB*, 6 October 1981, p. 1. Shanghai's industrial bureaux were asked to "share" increased output value targets. See *JFRB*, 15 December 1980, p. 1; and 10 December 1980, p. 1.

65. *JFRB*, 6 March 1981, p. 1; and 4 April 1981, p. 1.

66. *JFRB*, 12 May 1982, p. 1.

67. Cheng Li and Lynn White, "China's Technocratic Movement and the World Economic Herald," *Modern China*, Vol. 17, No. 3 (July 1991), pp. 342-88. Li and White focus on *SJD*'s pseudo-democratic, technocratic orientation.

68. For examples, see *SJD*, 4 August 1986, p. 14; 16 February 1987, p. 2; 21 December 1987, p. 14; 4 July 1988, p. 7; and 17 April 1989, p. 13.

69. *SJD*, 16 April 1984, p. 5; 24 September 1984, p. 5; 15 October 1984, pp. 5-6; and 26 November 1984, p. 2

70. *SJD*, 2 January 1984, p. 4; 23 January 1984, p. 5; and 16 April 1984, p. 5.

71. 16 April 1984, p. 5. Sun Hengzhi 孫恒志, the author, later became deputy head of the Research Office of the Municipal Party Committee. See *Zhongguo gongchandang Shanghaishi zhuzhishi ziliao, 1920.8-1987.10* 中國共產黨上海市組織史資料, 1920.8-1987.10 (Material on the History of CCP Organization in Shanghai, 1920.8-1987.10) (Shanghai: Shanghai renmin chubanshe, 1991), p. 568.

72. *SJD*, 15 February 1982, p. 10; and 19 April 1982, p. 11.

73. For examples, see *SJD*, 5 April 1982, p. 12; and 20 September 1982, p. 10; See also the report in *Time*, 5 October 1992, pp. 25-28.

74. *JFRB*, 28 April 1988, p. 1.

75. Edmond Lee, "A Bourgeois Alternative? The Shanghai Arguments for a Chinese Capitalism: The 1920s and the 1980s," in *Contemporary Chinese Politics in Historical Perspective*, edited by Brantly Womack (Cambridge and London: Cambridge University Press, 1991), p. 91.

76. *SJD*, 2 January 1984, p. 2.

77. *SJD*, 11 June 1984, p. 5.

78. *JFRB*, 28 April 1988, p. 3.

79. *JFRB*, 18 April 1985, p. 1.

80. Rui Xingwen had quit the position of municipal party secretary in November 1987. Jiang was concurrently party secretary and mayor, before vacating the mayorship to Zhu Rongji in April 1988. Later, a commentator suggested that the sentiment went out of control. See *JFRB*, 19 May 1988, p. 2.

81. *JFRB*, 25 April 1988, p. 2.

82. *JFRB*, 24 April 1988, p. 1.

83. *JFRB*, 28 April 1988, p. 1.

84. *JFRB*, 28 April 1988, pp. 1-2; and 29 April 1988, p. 1.

85. *JFRB*, 10 December 1980, p. 1; 6 March 1981, p. 1; 4 April, 1981, p. 1; and 15 February 1982, p. 1.

86. *JFRB*, 21 June 1981, p. 1

87. *JFRB*, 4 April 1981, p. 1.

88. *JFRB*, 21 June 1981, p. 1. See also *JFRB*, 3 August 1981, p. 1.

89. *Far Eastern Economic Review*, 12 December 1985, p. 28.

90. *Time*, 5 October 1992, p. 28.

91. *Minzhu Zhongguo* 民主中國 (Democratic China), No. 11 (August 1992), p. 9.

92. Ibid; *Zhongguo qingnianbao* 中國青年報 (Chinese Youth Daily), 20 September 1988, quoted in Lynn T. White III, *Shanghai Shanghaied* (see note 8), p. 101.

93. Shirk, *The Political Logic of Economic Reform in China* (see note 33), p. 141.

94. *JFRB*, 31 March 1988, p. 1.

95. Lynn T. White III, *Shanghai Shanghaied* (see note 8), pp. 58–86.

96. *JFRB*, 23 January 1988, pp. 1–2; and 24 January 1988, p. 1.

97. *JFRB*, 23 April 1988, p. 1; and 25 April 1988, p. 1.

98. *JFRB*, 10 May 1988, p. 1.

99. *JFRB*, 25 April 1988, p. 2; and 28 April 1988, pp. 1–2.

100. *JFRB*, 24 April 1988, p.1; 19 May 1988, p. 2; and 26 May 1988, p. 1.

101. *JFRB*, 27 April 1988, p. 1.

102. *JFRB*, 26 May 1988, p. 1.

103. It is interesting to point out that in Shanghai, the Planning Commission (jiwei 計委) was under the municipal government, but the Economic Commission (jingwei 經委) was under the Municipal Party Committee. See *Zhongguo gongchandang Shanghaishi zhuzhishi ziliao, 1920.8–1987.10* (see note 71), pp. 573–74, 598.

104. The gap between intellectuals and workers during Shanghai's strike wave of 1957, and its political implication are discussed in Perry, "Shanghai's Strike Wave of 1957" (see note 17).

105. Parris Chang, "Shanghai and Chinese Politics: Before and after the Cultural Revolution," in *Shanghai: Revolution and Development in an Asian Metropolis*, edited by Christopher Howe (see note 21), pp. 66–90.

106. Pye, "Forward" (see note 21), p. xiv.

107. *JFRB*, 30 May 1988, p. 2.

108. Chang, "Shanghai and Chinese Politics: Before and after the Cultural Revolution" (see note 105).

109. *Time*, 5 October 1992, p. 31.

110. Marie-Claire Bergère, "'The Other China': Shanghai from 1919 to 1949" (see note 22).

111. Edmond Lee, "A Bourgeois Alternative?" (see note 75), pp. 90–126.

112. Marie-Claire Bergère, "'The Other China': Shanghai from 1919 to 1949" (see note 22) pp. 1–2, 14.

6

Fiscal Relations between Shanghai and the Central Government

Ho Lok-sang and Tsui Kai-yuen

Compared with other provinces and municipalities, Shanghai's fiscal remittances to the coffers of the central government have always been substantial. It is estimated that as much as one-sixth of total central government revenue used to originate from Shanghai.[1] Some have attributed the relative economic decline of Shanghai during the 1980s to the excessive fiscal contribution of the municipality.[2] Ironically, while Shanghai suffered a fiscal squeeze in the 1980s, it is also believed that Shanghai's contribution to the central government declined rather rapidly during the 1980s. Did Shanghai decline economically, therefore leading to a shrunken contribution to the central government; or did the onerous tax burden on Shanghai imposed by the central government lead to Shanghai's relative economic decline? Did Shanghai's revenue contribution to Beijing 北京 in fact decline? It is the purpose of this chapter to demonstrate the complicated nature of intergovernmental fiscal relations in a planned economy, which certainly cannot be easily summarized by one or two statistics like remissions to the central government. We shall argue that Shanghai's apparent fiscal contribution to the central government in the pre-reform era was achieved with a great loss of efficiency. Economic reforms which apparently led to Shanghai's loss of fiscal prowess actually offered the first opportunity for Shanghai to contribute positively to the development of the rest of the country.

The next section will provide a historical review of Shanghai's fiscal relations with Beijing. It will be followed by a discussion of the impact of the economic reforms on Shanghai's fiscal relations with the central government and how this has affected Shanghai's economic development. Then, Shanghai's fiscal crisis and fiscal relations during the reform era will be traced. Finally, the chapter will conclude with a favourable preview of the prospects confronting the country in the second half of the 1990s.

The Role of Shanghai in China's Intergovernmental Finance: A Historical Perspective

In order to make sense of the central–local fiscal problems confronting Shanghai in the reform era, it is important to comprehend the role of Shanghai in the pre-reform fiscal system. Not unlike other countries, there are two dimensions to intergovernmental fiscal relations in China, namely, the vertical balance dimension and the horizontal balance dimension. The former relates to the sharing of taxes and spending responsibilities between the central and the local governments. The latter pertains to the redistribution of resources among local governments.[3] The peculiar features of the Chinese socialist system and its institutions affects the way in which China has tackled these issues. In particular, the following background information should be noted:

1. Unlike market economies and similar to many former socialist countries, profits from state-owned enterprises (SOEs) prior to the opening up of the country in 1978 were the major source of central and local budgetary revenue. In the 1970s, revenue from state-owned enterprises made up more than 50% of the state budget.[4]

2. China is a big country with significant interregional disparities. For instance, in 1992 the per capita gross domestic product (GDP) of Shanghai was RMB8,726 as compared with RMB1,009 for Guizhou.[5] There is considerable pressure on the central government to redistribute resources from the richer to the poorer provinces.

As the industrial powerhouse of China, Shanghai was natural candidate to shoulder a disproportionately large share of the country's fiscal responsibility. As shown in Table 6.1, the fiscal revenue of Shanghai is made up of two major components: central and "local" revenue. The former consists of incomes and taxes of those enterprises and administrative units under the direct control of the central government, all of which is remitted to the central government. The latter consists of incomes generated by local SOEs and the shares and types of taxes accruing to the city. Though designated "local," this has to be shared with the central government. On the eve of the reform era, some 60% to 70% of "local fiscal revenue" was derived from the profits of enterprises under the control of the Shanghai government.

The local-to-central transfer is determined by the current fiscal arrangement between Shanghai and Beijing. Over the years, the fiscal system has undergone a number of changes. Different formulae have been determined the share of retained local revenue. The formulae used over time are shown in Table 6.2.

Two partial indicators may be employed to shed light on the magnitude of the resource outflow over the years. One indicator is the ratio of local fiscal revenue remitted to total local fiscal revenue. Local fiscal revenue remitted may be approximated by the difference between local fiscal revenue and local fiscal expenditures.[6] As indicated in Table 6.1,

Table 6.1 Shanghai's Fiscal Revenue and Expenditure

(Unit: RMB100 million)

	(1) Total revenue	(2) Central revenue	(3) Local revenue	(4) Local expenditure	Estimate of remission (3) – (4) (% of local revenue)
1952	19.30	16.75	2.55	2.10	0.45 (17.6)
1957	45.77	41.15	4.62	3.75	0.87 (18.8)
1962	61.70	17.34	44.37	3.87	40.50 (91.3)
1965	83.18	20.28	62.90	7.59	55.31 (87.9)
1970	114.02	14.12	99.90	12.88	87.02 (87.1)
1975	147.11	10.92	136.18	26.53	109.65 (80.5)
1978	190.67	21.45	169.22	26.01	143.21 (84.6)
1980	198.85	24.12	174.73	19.18	155.55 (89.0)
1981	204.52	30.17	174.35	19.06	155.29 (89.1)
1982	200.69	32.70	167.99	20.68	147.31 (87.7)
1983	204.34	47.95	156.39	22.39	134.00 (85.7)
1984	215.79	51.83	163.96	30.32	133.64 (81.5)
1985	263.86	79.63	184.23	46.07	138.16 (75.0)
1986	257.72	78.26	179.46	59.08	120.38 (67.1)
1987	241.36	72.39	168.97	53.85	115.12 (68.1)
1988	261.69	100.07	161.62	65.88	95.74 (59.2)
1989	297.25	130.37	166.88	73.31	93.57 (56.1)
1990	284.36	114.33	170.03	75.56	94.47 (55.6)
1991	324.66	149.13	175.53	86.05	89.48 (51.0)
1992	340.13	154.57	185.56	94.99	90.57 (48.8)

Source: Shanghaishi tongjiju (ed.), *Shanghai tongji nianjian 1993* (see note 21 below).

Table 6.2 Shanghai–central Fiscal Systems

Period	Revenue retention formula
1976–1984	Total revenue (R_f) and expenditure (E_f) were fixed by the state plan. The share of revenue actually retained by Shanghai is equal to $(E_f/R_f) \times R + (R - R_f) \times 0.03 + F$, where R is the actual local revenue and F is a fixed sum for urban construction
1985–1987	$23.54\% \times R$
1988–1993	$R - RMB10.5$ billion
1994–	*Fenshuizhi* (Tax sharing)

Source: Information before 1988 is from Sun Huairen (ed.), *Shanghai shehuizhuyi jingji jianshe fazhan jianshi* (see note 6 below); for details of the tax-sharing system, see Tsang Shu-ki and Cheng Y. S., "China's Tax Reforms of 1994: Breakthrough or Compromise?" (see note 10 below); the figure for the period 1988–1993 is from interviews with Shanghai officials.

over an extended period, 80% to 90% of local fiscal revenue was remitted. The second indicator provides a more comprehensive picture of the net resource outflow. Under the socialist national accounting framework, Shanghai's net material product (*guomin shouru* 國民收入 ; NMP) is the net output of Shanghai's material production sectors.[7] Shanghai's national income utilized (*guomin shouru shiyong'e* 國民收入使用額 ; NIU), consisting of consumption and investment expenditures, is the amount of NMP retained in Shanghai. The difference between NMP and NIU then is equal to the net transfer of resources out of Shanghai. In general, this would indicate net tax remissions and other transfers out of the province minus net inward investment (from out of the region and out of the country) in Shanghai.[8] As shown in Figure 6.1, the share of net transfers to NMP hovers around 50% and 60%. Compared with other provinces, the share of net transfer is very high (see Table 6.3). The resources from Shanghai were then transferred to the poor provinces. Interprovincial transfers play a very important role in the reduction of interprovincial disparities.[9]

Starting in 1994, China adopted a "tax-sharing system" (*fenshuizhi* 分稅制) in place of the earlier fiscal contract system. Whereas the old fiscal contract system provided differential treatment for the various provinces and major cities based on bilateral bargaining, the tax-sharing system provides, for the first time, a uniform formula to be applied across the nation. Under the tax-sharing system, taxes are divided into three categories: central taxes (*zhongyangshui* 中央稅), local taxes (*difangshui* 地方稅) and shared taxes (*gongxiangshui* 共享稅). Central taxes include tariffs which are collected by customs, value-added taxes, consumption taxes, profit taxes and profit remissions from SOEs under the central government, taxes on railways, general offices of banks and insurance companies, as well as profit taxes on financial institutions. Local taxes include business taxes other than those paid by railways and the general offices of banks and insurance companies, profit taxes on local SOEs other than those levied on financial institutions, personal income taxes, land-use taxes, investment-related adjustment taxes, surtaxes for city maintenance and construction, property taxes, taxes on the use of vehicles and ships, stamp duties, butcher taxes, taxes on agriculture and farming, special farm product taxes, taxes on the use of farmland, contract taxes, estate and gift taxes, land appreciation taxes, levies on the use of state-owned land, etc. Shared taxes include the value-added tax, resource taxes and securities trading (stamp duties) taxes. Local governments collect 25% of value-added taxes and 50% of stamp duties on securities trading, and different

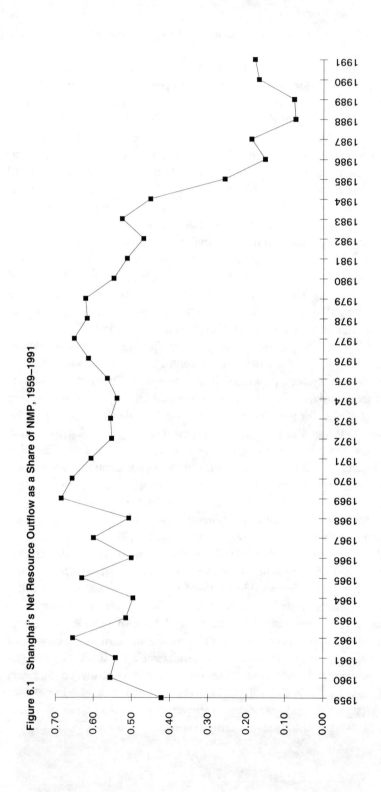

Figure 6.1 Shanghai's Net Resource Outflow as a Share of NMP, 1959–1991

percentages of resource taxes depending on the resource concerned. The major factors leading to an expected improvement in central government finances under the tax-sharing system include: (1) that all consumption taxes accrue to the central government, (2) that 75% of value-added taxes accrue to the central government, and (3) that remissions on various indirect taxes on petroleum, electricity, petrochemical products, non-ferrous metals, etc., are revised. Budgetary revenue at the disposal of local governments will then include: income from local taxes, local share of shared taxes, income from fixed shares of local revenue, tax rebates from the central government, special allocations from the central government and general transfers, and remissions from lower levels of government. Budgetary expenditures include: direct expenditures, remissions to the central government, rebates, transfers, and subsidies to local governments. Direct expenditures include all operational expenditures pertaining to the local government and developmental expenditures. Examples are infrastructure investment, expenditures in support of local SOEs for research and development, agricultural support, city maintenance and construction, education, health, price subsidies, cultural activities, etc.[10]

Given the favourable fiscal contract for Shanghai prior to 1994, in principle the tax-sharing system will reduce the revenue at Shanghai's direct disposal. China, however, has adopted a rebate system that ensures that each local government will not, nominally at least, fare any worse than it did in 1993.

Was Shanghai's Fiscal Contribution Really Substantial?

On the surface, then, up to the eve of the economic reform, Shanghai was playing a pivotal role in the fiscal arena. More than any other province, Shanghai was the money-making machine of the central government. It is not surprising that the central government kept a tight rein on Shanghai and tried to ensure that the metropolis secured the resources needed to fulfill the plan targets assigned to her. There is, however, another side of the story.

The significant fiscal contributions of Shanghai were sustained by the high returns of investment in Shanghai's SOEs. As shown in Table 6.4, some 68% of all local revenue was derived from enterprise income. It is illuminating to compare Shanghai's ratio of profit and tax to capital (*zijin lishuilu* 資金利稅率) reported in Table 6.5. The rate for Shanghai before the reform era was routinely more than three times the national rate. The

Table 6.3   Absorption as a Percentage of Regional Output in China

(Unit: %)

Region	1st Five-year Plan	5th Five-year Plan	6th Five-year Plan	1986–1989	Total 1950–1989
Beijing	201.1	73.6	92.3	114.0	98.1
Tianjin	65.2	68.5	76.1	96.2	76.9
Hebei	99.1	86.7	90.5	95.4	93.2
Shanxi	99.3	97.1	99.9	112.2	102.4
Inner Mongolia	80.9	129.4	127.3	121.9	115.5
Liaoning	82.3	73.4	81.9	91.9	81.9
Jilin	102.1	106.9	107.4	106.3	103.5
Heilongjiang	93.0	80.0	89.6	97.8	89.8
Shanghai	58.1	39.3	57.0	25.6	35.2
Jiangsu	89.1	85.8	86.5	67.2	77.1
Zhejiang	90.7	91.4	91.5	98.0	94.4
Anhui	100.2	96.5	99.5	100.3	99.5
Fujian	102.6	107.9	105.1	106.1	106.8
Jiangxi	94.2	106.4	106.1	104.6	104.7
Shandong	98.4	92.5	90.3	95.4	93.1
Henan	103.0	99.2	97.1	96.6	98.6
Hubei	108.2	96.7	91.3	n.a.	n.a.
Hunan	96.5	91.3	97.7	98.8	95.8
Guangdong	103.0	91.7	99.7	100.8	98.6
Guangxi	109.9	110.6	110.5	107.9	109.4
Sichuan	99.9	104.5	102.5	104.4	105.0
Guizhou	108.9	124.6	114.4	109.9	117.8
Yunnan	103.0	122.9	117.1	108.0	114.2
Shaanxi	111.4	104.0	118.7	119.3	118.2
Gansu	141.1	90.8	100.6	117.5	108.4
Qinghai	n.a.	128.6	160.4	150.7	104.3
Ningxia	112.7	125.8	131.4	136.9	131.4
Xinjiang	105.4	136.8	134.0	128.5	128.9
Nation	84.1	99.4	102.8	104.7	102.2

Source: Jiang Yue 蔣岳 and Liu Yin 劉垠 (eds.), *Zhongguo diqu jingji zengzhang bijiao yanjiu* 中國地區經濟增長比較研究 (A Comparative Study of Regional Economic Growth in China) (Shenyang 沈陽 : Liaoning renmin chubanshe 遼寧人民出版社, 1991). The editors quote these statistics drawn from Guojia tongjiju (ed.), *Quanguo ge sheng, zizhiqu, zhixiashi, lishi tongji ziliao huibian, 1949–1989* 全國各省、自治區、直轄市、歷史統計資料匯編 1949–1989 (A Collection of Historical Statistical Materials of Provinces, Autonomous Regions and Centrally Administered Municipalities of the Whole Country) (Beijing: Zhongguo tongji chubanshe, 1990); data for Hainan and Tibet are missing.

Table 6.4   Composition of Local Revenues for Shanghai, 1952–1978

(Unit: RMB100 million)

Year	(1) Local revenue	(2) Enterprise income	Tax	Other income	(2)/(1) (%)
1952	2.55	0.28	0.54	1.20	11.0
1957	4.62	3.15	0.70	0.67	68.2
1962	44.37	27.01	16.37	0.86	60.9
1965	62.90	39.87	21.71	1.15	63.4
1970	99.90	69.12	29.14	1.46	69.2
1975	136.18	93.41	40.65	2.01	68.6
1978	169.22	115.30	51.51	2.38	68.1

Source: Shanghaishi tongjiju, *Shanghai tongji nianjian 1993* (see note 21 below).

Table 6.5   Ratios of Profits and Taxes to Capital, 1970–1991

(Unit: %)

Year	National	Shanghai
1970	27.6	85.51
1971	26.3	84.27
1972	26.2	82.13
1973	25.3	82.37
1974	23.2	78.87
1975	22.8	74.07
1976	21.3	67.64
1977	22.3	70.69
1978	24.1	75.40
1979	24.2	78.20
1980	24.0	80.41
1981	23.9	76.86
1982	23.4	73.44
1983	22.8	65.65
1984	23.2	63.01
1985	23.6	58.53
1986	22.3	40.68
1987	22.6	34.11
1988	17.8	31.98
1989	14.9	27.58
1990	n.a.	21.40
1991	n.a.	20.14

Source: Guojia tongjiju, *Quanguo ge sheng, zizhiqu, zhixiashi, lishi tongji ziliao huibian, 1949–1989* (see Table 6.3, source); Shanghaishi tongjiju (ed.), *Shanghai tongji nianjian 1992* 上海統計年鑑 1992 (Statistical Yearbook of Shanghai 1992) (Beijing: Zhongguo tongji chubanshe, 1992).

high returns of enterprises were the direct consequence of artificially low input prices and of the monopolistic position enjoyed by the state enterprises prior to the economic reforms.[11] The low input prices and the high output prices on account of the lack of competition entailed an implicit transfer from other provinces to Shanghai. However, with the introduction of competition and the liberalization of input prices, Shanghai's return to capital ratio has quickly converged towards the national rate.

More formally, we can write P^* and W^* to be the notional efficient output and input prices applicable to Shanghai. Because of the monopoly position that Shanghai enjoyed, the actual prices P are higher than P^*. Because of artificially depressed input prices, the actual input prices W are lower than W^*. Let e % stand for the percentage of total Shanghai output exported to the rest of the country. Let n % stand for the percentage of total Shanghai-consumed input originating from outside Shanghai. Then, there is a net transfer, resulting from these distorted output and input prices, to Shanghai from the rest of the country equal to:

$$Q\ (P - P^*)\ e\ \% + F\ (W^* - W)\ n\ \%$$

where Q is the total output of Shanghai and F is the total amount of input used.

Assuming that remissions to Beijing ultimately benefit the rest of the country, the net and true contribution of Shanghai to the rest of the country can then be written:

$$\text{Net contribution} = t\ (PQ - FW) - Q\ (P - P^*)\ e\ \% \\ - F\ (W^* - W)\ n\ \% - G$$

where t is the ratio of *tax* plus *profit remitted* to *total nominal profit* while $PQ - FW$ is the nominal profit generated in Shanghai; G is net transfers from the central government and includes any direct investment in infrastructure funded by the central government minus non-profit related taxes remitted. It is unfortunate that a lack of information has prevented us from estimating the net contribution. It is, however, certain that the net contribution is definitely less than local-to-central fiscal remittances, i.e., $t\ (PQ - FW)$. It is by no means certain that the net contribution is positive.

Fiscal Crisis and Fiscal Relations During the Reform Era

Shanghai–central fiscal relations detailed in the previous section could no longer be sustained as the economic reforms brought with them a rapid deterioration of central and local finance. While economic reforms are needed to revitalize China's economy in the long run, the fiscal crisis has become an unintended outcome in the short term.

In order to understand better the causes of the fiscal crisis in the 1980s, some background information is in order. The vastness of China and the regional disparities have rendered fiscal decentralization inevitable in order to ensure a more efficient use of public funds. Beginning with a highly centralized fiscal system in the early 1950s, China experienced two waves of fiscal decentralization, during the Great Leap Forward and during the early 1970s.[12] The history of fiscal decentralization in the last four decades is a case of searching and experimenting with various revenue-sharing arrangements.

The third wave of fiscal decentralization started in 1980 and may be viewed as a continuation of China's long-term search for an optimal local–central fiscal arrangement. The fiscal decentralization which was introduced simultaneously with the economic reforms triggered the fiscal crisis confronting local and central governments. Many Chinese economists have argued that the fiscal decentralization accounted for the deteriorating balance sheet of the central government.[13] However, Christine Wong contends that this argument ignores the fact that along with the decentralization of revenue raising responsibilities, many important spending responsibilities were also decentralized.[14] There seems to be some support for this hypothesis. Local expenditures rose about 402% from 1981 to 1992 whereas total expenditures (inclusive of central and local) rose only 294% during the same period (see Table 6.6).[15] However, one should also be extremely careful in arriving at any conclusion based on budgetary revenue and expenditure data. As pointed out by those who argue that the central government's fiscal crisis has been triggered by fiscal decentralization, extrabudgetary funds accruing to local governments increased tremendously in the 1980s.[16]

Focusing on the more recent period between 1985 and 1992 is of interest partly because the budget deficit increased rapidly since 1985.[17] The year 1985 is also when China's urban reforms really commenced. With increasing competition and the liberalization of the prices of intermediate inputs, the profitability of SOEs drastically declined, adversely affecting state and local budgets. It is a natural consequence of the economic reforms that the growth of government revenue falls behind economic growth, as one major objective of the reforms is to allow the non-state sector to grow and prosper. However, in the transitional period

Table 6.6   Indices of GNP, Fiscal Revenue and Expenditure of China as a Whole and Shanghai, 1985–1992

Year	(1) GNP of China	(2) Total budgetary revenue of China	(3) Total budgetary expenditure of China	(4) Local budgetary expenditure	(5) Budgetary expenditure of Shanghai
1985	100.00	100.00	100.00	100.00	100.00
1986	113.31	121.10	126.34	135.75	128.24
1987	132.06	126.92	132.72	140.51	116.89
1988	164.39	140.81	146.72	163.28	143.00
1989	186.89	157.95	164.80	191.93	159.13
1990	206.76	177.49	187.13	206.25	164.01
1991	236.47	193.47	206.72	227.71	186.78
1992	280.88	222.52	237.95	255.09	206.19

Sources: Figures in columns (1) to (4) from Guojia tongjiju (ed.), *Zhongguo tongji nianjian 1993* (see note 4 below); Figures in column (5) from Shanghaishi tongjiju (ed.), *Shanghai tongji nianjian 1993* (see note 21 below).

when the various levels of government cannot shed many of their spending responsibilities inherited from the old system (e.g., food subsidies, subsidies to unprofitable enterprises, etc.), there is not much room in the short run to suppress budgetary spending considerably. Specifically, the growth rate of revenue stood at 123% compared with a growth rate of 138% for total central-plus-local expenditures and 181% for gross national product (*guomin shengchan zongzhi* 國民生產總值 ; GNP). In the case of Shanghai, local expenditures rose 106%. In the long run, urban reforms will boost the efficiency of China's industrial sector. However, the short-run impact is to generate unprecedented pressure on the state and local budgets.

In the case of Shanghai, economic reforms really forced the issue of fiscal reform. As pointed out before, a large share of Shanghai's local revenue is derived from the profits of enterprises. Price liberalization and increasing competition sharply reduced the profits of Shanghai's enterprises. Many SOEs were in the red. Furthermore, the sources of revenue controlled by Shanghai did not grow as fast as those under the central government. As shown in Table 6.7, the profits and taxes remitted by local industrial SOEs declined sharply in the 1980s. Economic reform also results in mounting price subsidies to urban residents. For example, in 1991, this amount was RMB11.9 billion or 15% of Shanghai's local expenditures.[18]

As Table 6.7 indicates, state enterprise profits and taxes used to account for 50% of Shanghai's national income prior to the economic

Table 6.7   Profits and Taxes of Local Industrial SOEs, 1978–1990

(Unit: RMB100 million)

Year	Total value of profits and taxes	Amount remitted	Enterprise profit and tax as % of national income
1978	136.83	136.37	50.2
1979	148.67	144.41	54.2
1980	152.41	142.68	47.7
1981	150.49	139.92	46.3
1982	150.34	135.05	44.6
1983	134.30	117.41	37.0
1984	130.75	110.84	33.5
1985	139.40	110.64	29.9
1986	130.73	100.63	26.6
1987	121.73	84.17	22.3
1988	124.21	74.12	19.2
1989	112.49	72.06	16.1
1990	88.45	65.93	11.9

Source: Shanghaishi tongjiju (ed.), *Shanghai tongji nianjian 1993* (see note 21 below).

reform. Since 1978, this percentage has been steadily declining, reaching 11.9% by 1990.

The Outlook for Shanghai–central Fiscal Relations

Looking into the future, the reliance of the central government on Shanghai for revenue is likely to continue its recent decline. From 1988 to 1993, a new fiscal arrangement allowed Shanghai to keep all the local revenue after remitting a fixed sum to the central government, thus giving Shanghai more breathing space to develop her economy. From 1994 onwards, a new tax-sharing system has been put in place throughout the country and new taxes have been introduced. The intention is not only to boost the share of fiscal revenue accruing to the central government, but also to standardize the treatment of all provinces and directly administered cities according to common criteria. To induce the provinces to accept this plan, a rebate scheme was introduced. The basic amount (*jishu* 基數) of the rebate system was equal to the extra revenue that would have been remitted to the central government in 1993 under the new formula. The principle was that the local governments would have no less revenue at their disposal in 1993 had the new system been implemented in that year. In 1994, the rebate was based on the basic amount (*jishu*) plus an additional factor reflecting the percentage increase of the sum of the value-added taxes and the consumption tax times 0.3. From 1995, the rebate has been updated to the actual rebate of the previous year, plus the same factor mentioned above. Economic reform has resulted in rapid growth in the tax base. Shanghai's economic growth exceeded 14% for three years in a row up to 1994, and tax payments by foreign-funded enterprises in 1994 hit a record high of over RMB4.5 billion, representing currently over 12% of total fiscal revenue. Shanghai's total fiscal revenue rose by more than 40% to RMB37.25 billion in 1994, while Shanghai's local tax revenue was RMB17.53 billion, also a record high.[19]

As pointed out by Chen Min 陳民 in a recent assessment of the possible impact of the new tax-sharing system, under the new arrangement the central government is entitled to all or a large share of the major taxes.[20] Chen conjectures that, of the taxes accruing to local governments, the business tax (*yingye shui* 營業稅) will emerge as the major source of local revenue in those localities where the service sector grows rapidly. Like many other coastal cities, Shanghai enjoys a comparative advantage in tertiary production as witnessed by the rapid growth of the service sector. On the eve of the economic reform in 1978, manufacturing accounted for 76.1% of GNP. By 1992, this percentage had fallen to 59.7%. The percentage of GNP due to the tertiary sector, however, rose from 18.6% to 33.2% during the same period.[21] The rapid expansion of the tertiary sector is closely related to the fact that Shanghai is rapidly emerging as a major consumption centre in China; retail sales for consumption goods in 1993 amounted to RMB65.351 billion, up 33.5% from 1992, with personal consumption outpacing "collective consumption" (*shehui jituan xiaofei* 社會集團消費).[22] The new tax system will further stimulate the Shanghai government to boost investment in the service sector and strengthen Shanghai's determination to be the financial centre of China.

During the 1980s, Shanghai's industrial position was on a decline. Some studies show that total factor productivity of Shanghai's SOEs did not improve as fast as that of other administered cities and provinces.[23] From a long-term perspective, all is not lost. It should be noted that while Shanghai's industrial position declined during the 1980s, the lack of genuine competitiveness of many of the earlier "profitable" enterprises was really nothing new. While Shanghai's direct fiscal remissions to Beijing languished during the 1980s, the removal of protection of Shanghai's SOEs actually improves the efficiency of resource allocation from the national perspective. By exposing the earlier-protected state enterprises to competition, economic reform also turned some of them into truly viable industries. The long-term outlook for Shanghai is likely to be better than during the 1990s.

Notes

1. A good general discussion of the early fiscal relation between Shanghai and the central government is provided in a special review in *Ming bao* 明報 (Ming Pao) (Hong Kong), 30 January 1989.
2. See, for example, Lynn T. White III, *Shanghai Shanghaied? Uneven Taxes in Reform China* (Hong Kong: Centre of Asian Studies, University of Hong Kong, 1989).
3. R. Bird, *Tax Policy and Economic Development* (Baltimore: The Johns Hopkins University Press, 1992).
4. Guojia tongjiju 國家統計局 (ed.), *Zhongguo tongji nianjian 1993* 中國統計年鑑 1993 (Statistical Yearbook of China 1993) (Beijing: Zhongguo tongji chubanshe 中國統計出版社, 1993).
5. Guojia tongjiju (ed.), *Zhongguo tongji nianjian 1994* 中國統計年鑑 1994 (Statistical Yearbook of China 1994) (Beijing: Zhongguo tongji chubanshe, 1994).
6. See Sun Huairen 孫懷仁 (ed.), *Shanghai shehuizhuyi jingji jianshe fazhan jianshi, 1949-1985* 上海社會主義經濟建設發展簡史, 1949-1985 (A Concise History of the Development of Shanghai's Socialist Economic Construction, 1949-1985) (Shanghai: Shanghai renmin chubanshe 上海人民出版社, 1990). Local revenue remitted does not include the remittances from enterprises and administrative units under the direct control of the central government.
7. NMP does not include most outputs of the service sector.
8. In general, we can write transfers out of the region as

$$NX = NMP - NIU = NMP - C - I,$$

where NX = the resource outflow or net exports, C = society's consumption, and I = society's capital formation in the period. NX is composed of the following items: (1) net fiscal transfer out of the region; (2) net interregional and international capital outflow. In the Mao era, NX was largely made up of (1).
9. See Tsui Kai-yuen, "China's Regional Inequality, 1952–1985," *Journal of Comparative Economics*, Vol. 15 (1991), pp. 1–21.
10. Tsang Shu-ki and Y. S. Cheng, "China's Tax Reforms of 1994: Breakthrough or Compromise?" *Asian Survey*, Vol. 34 (1994), pp. 769–88.
11. A referee correctly points out that low input prices and high output prices were

the result of the State Plan rather than market power as such. However, the absence of competition and the guarantee of supplies certainly gave the SOEs an enviable position of guaranteed profits.

12. For a history of fiscal decentralization, see Zuo Cuntai 左春台, *Zhonggou shehuizhuyi caizheng jianshi* 中國社會主義財政簡史 (A Concise History of Chinese Socialist Public Finance) (Beijing: Zhongguo caizheng chubanshe 中國財政出版社, 1990); Michel Oksenberg and James Tong, "The Evolution of Central-provincial Fiscal Relations in China, 1971-1984: The Formal System," *The China Quarterly*, No. 125 (1991), pp. 1-32; Nicholas Hardy, *Economic Growth and Distribution of Income* (New York: Cambridge University Press, 1978).

13. See, e.g., Wang Shaoguang 王兆光 and Hu Angang 胡鞍鋼, *Zhongguo guojia nengli baogao* 中國國家能力報告 (A Report on the National Capability of China) (Hong Kong: Oxford University Press, 1994).

14. Christine Wong, "Central-local Relations in an Era of Fiscal Decline: The Paradox of Fiscal Decentralization in Post-Mao China," *The China Quarterly*, No. 128 (1992), pp. 691-715.

15. It should, however, be pointed out that the above analysis is based on budgetary data. In recent years, extrabudgetary funds have increased rapidly.

16. See, e.g., Deng Yingtao 鄧英淘 et al., *Zhongguo yusuan wai zijin fenxi* 中國預算外資金分析 (Analysis of China's Extrabudgetary Funds) (Zhongguo renmin daxue chubanshe 中國人民大學出版社, 1990); Wang Shaoguang and Hu Angang, *Zhongguo guojia nengli baogao* (see note 13).

17. Prior to 1985, price subsidies were reported as an offset against revenue while after 1985, price subsidies were reported as an expenditure. This would lead to a jump in the reported rate of revenue growth in 1985 if a time series spans both the pre-1985 and post-1985 periods.

18. Zhonghua renmin gongheguo caizhengbu *Zhongguo caizheng nianjian* bianji weiyuanhui 中華人民共和國財政部《中國財政年鑑》編輯委員會 (ed.), *Zhongguo caizheng nianjian* 1992 中國財政年鑑 1992 (Finance Yearbook of China 1992) (Beijing: Zhongguo caizheng zazhishe 中國財政雜誌社, 1992).

19. *Lianhe bao* 聯合報 (United Daily News), 2 January 1995.

20. Chen Min 陳民, "Caizheng xin tizhi yunxing zhong liyi geju di biandong yingxiang ji duice" 財政新體制運行中利益格局的變動影響及對策 (The Distributional Changes, Impact of the New Fiscal System and Policy Proposals), *Jingji yanjiu cankao* 經濟研究參考 (References on Economic Research), No. 134 (September 1994), pp. 2-21.

21. See Shanghaishi tongjiju 上海市統計局 (ed.), *Shanghai tongji nianjian 1993* 上海統計年鑑 1993 (Statistical Yearbook of Shanghai 1993) (Beijing: Zhongguo tongji chubanshe, 1993).

22. *Lianhe bao*, 26 January 1994.

23. Cui Qiyuan 崔啓源 (Tsui Kai-yuen), T. Rawski and Xue Tiandong 薛天棟 (T.

T. Hsueh) (1993), "Jingji tizhi gaige dui guomin yongyouzhi gongye de yingxiang — diqu poushi" 經濟體制改革對國民擁有制工業的影響 — 地區剖釋 (The Impact of Economic Reform on the State-owned Industry — A Regional Analysis), in *Zhongguo shengchanli biandong qushi zhi yanjiu* 中國生產力變動趨勢之研究 (Studies on China's Productivity Trends), edited by Li Jinwen 李京文, Zheng Yuxin 鄭玉歆 and Xue Tiandong (Shehui kexue wenxian chubanshe 社會科學文獻出版社, 1993).

7

"Dragon Head" of China's Economy?

Sung Yun-wing

Since the opening of Pudong 浦東 in 1990, Shanghai's official mission has been to become the "dragon head" (龍頭) of the Chinese economy. Shanghai is to become "three centres," namely, a financial centre, a trading centre and an economic centre. Due to Shanghai's strategic location, its abundance of skilled manpower and national policies highly favourable to Shanghai, few doubt that Shanghai will soon recover its pre-war dominance as the centre of China's economy. This chapter, however, takes a sceptical view. Though Shanghai has tremendous economic potential, Shanghai is far from the "dragon head" of China's economy. Shanghai's strategic location has been grossly overstated, and China's special policies for Shanghai may do it more harm than good.

Shanghai: "Dragon Head" of the Yangzi?

Shanghai is often referred to as the "dragon head" of the Yangzi River Basin. Though the Yangzi River Basin has a third of China's population and 40% of China's gross domestic product (GDP), it must be remembered that the Yangzi River Basin is not an integrated economic region. By modern standards, river transportation is inefficient and many provinces along the Yangzi are better linked to other cities than to Shanghai. For instance, it is known that around 90% of Sichuan's 四川 foreign trade goes through Hong Kong instead of Shanghai, though Sichuan is on the upper reaches of the Yangzi and ships of 1,500 dwt can reach Sichuan from Shanghai. Similarly, the bulk of Wuhan's 武漢 foreign trade goes through Hong Kong,[1] though ships of 5,000 dwt can reach Wuhan from Shanghai.

By modern standards, river transportation is slow and inefficient. For instance, travel between Wuhan and Shanghai usually takes 45 hours downstream and 60 hours upstream, while travel between Wuhan and Guangzhou by rail only takes 17 hours. As China's economy develops, China's industries will shift towards higher-grade manufactures with smaller production runs, and the slowness of river transport will be more and more a negative factor.

_____

Research for this chapter was supported by two research grants: one from the South China Programme of The Chinese University of Hong Kong, and the other from the Research Grants Council of Hong Kong. The financial help enabled the author to take three field trips to conduct in-depth interviews with scholars and officials in Shanghai.

Besides the inherent weakness of river transport, transportation along the Yangzi is doubly inefficient due to institutional constraints and planning mistakes. Water transport from Sichuan to Shanghai goes through many provinces, and co-ordination of river transport among different provinces is poor because river transport is provincially owned and operated rather than nationally owned and operated (as in the case of railway transport). Co-ordination between piers and river vessels is also poor.[2] Furthermore, transportation west of Nanjing 南京 is hampered by the Nanjing Changjiang Bridge (南京長江大橋) which is not tall enough to allow the passage of ships of over 10,000 dwt.[3] While the construction of the Three-Gorges Dam (三峽大壩) will enable ships of 10,000 dwt to navigate along the flooded channel, the gain is merely theoretical as the Wuhan Changjiang Bridge (武漢長江大橋) can only allow the passage of ships smaller than 5,000 dwt. Moreover, ships will have to wait in line to pass through the locks after the completion of the Three-Gorges Dam, and as a result river transport may be less even attractive due to an increase in turnaround time.

The inefficiency of transportation along the Yangzi is compounded by the lack of an east–west railway or superhighway. Though there is presently a plan to connect Shanghai and Wuhan by railway, the plan is still on the drawing board and one cannot be optimistic that the railway will be built within this century. The geographic reality is such that the construction of an east–west railway or motorway will be very expensive due to the mountainous terrain and the sharp drop in elevation from the west to the east. It is no accident that most of China's land transport links go north–south instead of east–west. Besides the traditional north-south trunk routes, the newly built Beijing–Jiujiang–Kowloon railway (京—九—九鐵路) and Beijing–Shenzhen motorway (北京—深圳公路) also go north–south, enhancing Hong Kong's pre-eminence as a transport hub. The completion of the Beijing–Jiujiang–Kowloon railway will divert some of the cargo of China's eastern provinces (Anhui 安徽 and Jiangxi 江西) to Hong Kong.

Shanghai's Inadequate Port Facilities

Though the Yangzi River Basin is not an integrated economic region, the Yangzi River Delta comprising southern Jiangsu 江蘇, northern Zhejiang 浙江, and Shanghai is well integrated. Shanghai, Nanjing, and Hangzhou 杭州 are connected by railways and in 1997 will be connected by superhighways. The Yangzi River Delta has a population of 80 million and is a rich and industrialized region. Unfortunately, Shanghai's position as the hub of the Yangzi River Delta is not undisputed. Though Shanghai is certainly the largest city in the Delta, it does not have the best port. Due to sandbars at the mouth of the Yangzi, ships of 25,000 dwt can only enter the Yangzi at high tide. Presently, Beilun 北侖 near Ningbo 寧波 in Zhejiang province has the best port in the Delta, and ships up to 100,000 dwt can dock there. However, Beilun is not centrally located in the Delta. When the cities of the Delta are better linked by motorways, more cargo will be diverted from Shanghai to Beilun and other ports.

As large ships cannot enter Shanghai, Shanghai is more of a river port than a sea port. In 1994, Shanghai handled 166 million tonnes of cargo, or 22.7% of the total cargo tonnage of all major seaports in China. Although Shanghai was the largest port in China, only 15.7% of Shanghai's cargo was ocean-going. In 1994, Shanghai's ocean-going cargo of 26 million tonnes was only 23.5% that of Hong Kong. Medium-sized ships at Shanghai sail to Tokyo or Hong Kong, where cargo is loaded onto large vessels for onward shipment. Shanghai is thus only a feeder port of Hong Kong. In fact, Hong Kong is by far the dominant ocean-going port of the whole of China. Hong Kong handles a large and growing volume of China's international trade, and Hong Kong's 1992 ocean-going cargo of 83.5 million tonnes was 75% of China's total (data after 1992 are not available for China).

There is no lack of proposals to deal with the inadequacy of Shanghai's port. One proposal calls for dredging the sandbars at the mouth of the Yangzi to allow the passage of large ships. This plan will cost over RMB10 billion. Another group of proposals calls for the expansion of deep-water ports away from the mouth of the Yangzi, e.g. at Beilun, the Zhoushan Islands (舟山羣島), or in northern Jiangsu. At the time of this writing, the pros and cons of these proposals are still being debated and construction work has not yet begun. This implies that the development of the Yangzi River Delta will continue to be hampered by inadequate port facilities well into the early years of the next century. Moreover, after the completion of the proposal(s), Shanghai's position as the hub of the Yangzi River Delta is likely to be weakened due to the competing ports in the Delta. If the sandbars at the mouth of the Yangzi are successfully dredged, large ships will be able to visit all the deep-water ports in southern Jiangsu, and Shanghai will continue to be hampered by the shallow Huangpu River (黃浦江). Dredging the Huangpu River is not only expensive but also an unattractive option in view of the availability of other ports in southern

Jiangsu. If China chooses to develop deep-water ports away from the mouth of the Yangzi, e.g., the Beilun port in Zhejiang, Shanghai's position will also be undermined. The Shanghai municipal government is thus neither enthusiastic about dredging the sandbars at the mouth of the Yangzi, nor is it keen to develop ports away from Shanghai. Its favourite plan, recently revealed in 1995, is to develop a port on two small islands (Da Yang 大洋 and Xiao Yang 小洋) some 30 km from Shanghai.[4] The islands, previously under Shanghai's jurisdiction, are presently administered by Zhejiang. The logic of the plan is that it does not involve the dredging of the sandbars at the mouth of the Yangzi as the islands are outside of the sandbars, and it will not strengthen rival ports in Jiangsu and Zhejiang. The plan has yet to receive central approval, and it is by no means certain that Zhejiang will return the islands. Aside from the political hurdles, the plan is economically dubious as it involves the costly transfer of cargo from big ships to small vessels some 30 km from the coast. The fact that Shanghai's embracing such a dubious plan further underlines its dilemma. Despite the many discussions and plans to develop a seaport in or near Shanghai, there are no easy or speedy solutions to the problems.

Table 7.1 shows the volume of cargo carried by ocean-going vessels in Shanghai, with the figures for Hong Kong included for comparison. From 1978 to 1992, though Shanghai's volume of cargo increased from 9 million tonnes to 25 million tonnes, its share of the national total declined from 25.7% to 22.6%. Comparable figures for Hong Kong are only available from 1983 onwards. Shanghai's volume of cargo in 1983 was 38.3% that of Hong Kong, and it declined to only 23.5% that of Hong Kong in 1994. This shows that Shanghai's position as a port is increasingly being eclipsed by Hong Kong. It should be noted that Hong Kong's volume of cargo relative to that of China rose from 66.3% in 1983 to 74.6% in 1992. In 1994, around 70% of the value of Hong Kong's trade was China related. This percentage is large and increasing. Hong Kong appears to be destined to be China's dominant ocean-going port well into the early years of the next century.

The shares of Shanghai in China's rail, road and water freight are shown in Table 7.2. Figures for Guangdong 廣東 are shown for comparison. From 1981 to 1984, Shanghai's share of China's rail and water freight declined slightly, and Shanghai's share of China's road freight declined drastically. This can be attributed to the dramatic increase in road freight in other parts of the country, especially in Guangdong. Shanghai's share of China's total freight fluctuated around 5% from 1981 to 1988,

Table 7.1   Cargo Carried by Ocean-going Vessels: Shanghai versus Hong Kong, 1978–1994

| | Shanghai's ocean-going vessels | | | Hong Kong's ocean-going vessels | |
| | | Percent of | | | Percent of |
Year	mn tonnes	China's	Hong Kong's	mn tonnes	China's
1978	9.39	25.7	—	—	—
1979	—	—	—	—	—
1980	10.98	25.6	—	—	—
1981	11.18	24.7	—	—	—
1982	10.97	23.8	—	—	—
1983	12.09	25.4	38.3	31.57	66.3
1984	13.70	24.7	38.8	35.29	63.6
1985	14.02	21.2	35.3	39.69	59.9
1986	16.34	22.6	34.4	47.47	65.7
1987	18.47	23.1	34.5	53.56	67.1
1988	20.32	23.8	33.1	61.32	71.9
1989	20.66	22.9	32.0	64.65	71.6
1990	22.46	23.9	34.0	66.01	70.2
1991	24.91	23.6	32.6	76.45	72.3
1992	25.25	22.6	30.3	83.45	74.6
1993	25.29	—	26.3	96.10	—
1994	26.05	—	23.5	110.95	—

Sources: Shanghaishi tongjiju 上海市統計局 (ed.), *Shanghai tongji nianjian*, 1983–
            1987 上海統計年鑑, 1983–1987 (Statistical Yearbook of Shanghai, 1983–
            1987) (Shanghai: Shanghai renmin chubanshe 上海人民出版社, 1983–
            1987); Shanghaishi tongjiju (ed.), *Shanghai tongji nianjian*, 1988–1995 (Bei-
            jing: Zhongguo tongji chubanshe 中國統計出版社, 1988–1995); Guojia
            tongjiju 國家統計局 (ed.), *Zhongguo tongji nianjian* 中國統計年鑑, 1981–
            1984, (Statistical Yearbook of China, 1981–1984) (Hong Kong: Xianggang
            jingji daobao she 香港經濟導報社, 1982–1984); Guojia tongjiju (ed.),
            Zhongguo tongji nianjian, 1985–1995 (Beijing: Zhongguo tongji chubanshe,
            1985–1995); Hong Kong Government (ed.), *Hong Kong Annual Digest of
            Statistics*, 1983–1994 (Hong Kong: The Government Printer, 1983–1994).

dropping sharply to around 3% from 1989 to 1993, and further falling to 2.6% in 1994. Guangdong's share also fluctuated around 5% from 1981 to 1988, but jumped to 8% in 1988, rising further to 9% in 1991 to 1993. Guangdong's freight surpassed that of Shanghai from 1988 onwards.

Table 7.2 also shows the shares of Shanghai and Guangdong in the volume of cargo handled at China's ports. From 1980 to 1994, Shanghai's share declined substantially from 39% to 22.3%, while Guangdong's share declined moderately from 32.5% to 24.5%. Guangdong's decline can be attributed to its reliance on roads to deliver goods through the port of Hong

(Unit: %)

Table 7.2   Share of Shanghai and Guangdong in China's Transportation, 1978–1994

Year	Share of Shanghai in China's					Share of Guangdong in China's				
	Cargo transported				Cargo handled at seaports	Cargo transported				Cargo handled at seaports
	TOTAL	Rail	Road	Waterway		TOTAL	Rail	Road	Waterway	
1978	—	—	—	—	40.1	—	—	—	—	—
1979	—	—	—	—	—	—	—	—	—	—
1980	—	—	—	—	39.0	—	—	—	—	32.5
1981	4.8	1.1	10.4	4.8	38.0	4.9	2.7	3.9	12.3	—
1982	4.8	1.1	9.9	4.9	37.8	4.5	2.4	3.4	11.9	—
1983	4.8	1.1	10.2	4.9	36.8	4.3	2.4	3.2	11.4	—
1984	9.8	1.1	11.0	5.1	36.5	8.5	2.9	2.9	10.1	—
1985	5.1	1.0	12.0	5.0	36.2	3.2	2.9	2.9	4.1	28.3
1986	5.2	1.0	12.8	4.9	36.6	4.6	3.1	2.6	11.2	—
1987	5.1	1.0	12.7	4.5	35.1	4.9	3.3	2.6	12.2	—
1988	4.9	0.8	13.6	4.6	29.2	5.0	3.0	2.7	13.3	—
1989	2.7	0.8	2.9	4.2	29.8	8.2	3.0	8.6	13.3	24.1
1990	3.0	0.8	3.3	3.9	28.9	8.4	2.9	8.8	14.8	24.6
1991	3.0	0.9	3.4	3.9	27.6	9.0	3.1	9.5	15.2	24.8
1992	3.0	0.9	3.4	3.6	27.0	9.3	3.1	9.8	15.6	24.7
1993	3.1	0.9	3.4	4.2	26.0	9.0	3.2	9.4	15.7	24.8
1994	2.6	0.9	2.7	4.2	22.3	8.3	3.3	8.5	14.9	24.5

Source: *Shanghai tongji nianjian*, 1983–1995 (see Table 7.1, Sources); Guangdongsheng tongjiu 廣東省統計局 (ed.), *Guangdong tongji nianjian* 廣東統計年鑑, 1984–1985 (Statistical Yearbook of Guangdong, 1984–1985) (Hong Kong: Xianggang jingji daobao she, 1984–1985); Guangdongsheng tongjiu (ed.), *Guangdong tongji nianjian*, 1986–1995 (Beijing: Zhongguo tongji chubanshe, 1986–1995); *Zhongguo tongji nianjian*, 1981–1995 (see Table 7.1, Sources).

Kong. It should be noted that the volume of cargo handled at Guangdong ports surpassed that of Shanghai ports for the first time in 1994.

In 1994, Shanghai's freight and cargo handled at seaports fell not only relatively but also absolutely, the first absolute decline since 1978: Shanghai's cargo handled at seaports fell by 5.9%, and the volume of its land, water, and air freight fell by 12%. It should be noted that this fall took place while cargo handled by the major ports in China grew by 7.6% and Hong Kong's volume of ocean-going cargo expanded by 15.5%, showing that Shanghai's long and steady decline as a transport hub accelerated markedly in 1994.

Skilled Manpower and Special Policies: Blessing or Curse?

It is true that Shanghai is well-endowed with skills. In 1990, Shanghai had 638 tertiary/university graduates per 10,000 population, much higher than Guangdong's ratio of 133.[5] However, it should be noted that an abundance of skilled manpower is a mixed blessing for economic development. Many developing countries, including the Philippines and India, have an abundance of university graduates who are frustrated and unemployed. Shanghai's pre-eminence as China's centre of radical politics in the Maoist era can be partly attributed to its abundance of university graduates. Moreover, Shanghai's well-trained bureaucrats have been known for their strict adherence to central directives. This may not be conducive to economic development.

China's special policies favouring Pudong and Shanghai may be a curse instead of a blessing for Shanghai. As a special zone Pudong may suffer from too much central attention. There have long been mumblings that Pudong's leadership does not want to subordinate itself to the Shanghai municipal government. Pudong's leadership can afford to stand up to its immediate boss, the Shanghai municipal government, partly because Pudong is well connected to the central government. This conflict was revealed in 1995 when the Shanghai mayor did not attend the fifth anniversary celebrations of the formation of the Pudong New Area.[6] Moreover, instead of concentrating on Pudong, the Shanghai municipal government is redeveloping the Bund as Shanghai's financial district, in direct competition with Pudong.

The heavy involvement of the state in Pudong may lead to the development of bureaucratic state capitalism which tends to ignore market forces and risks. For instance, the simultaneous construction of up to one hundred skyscrapers in Pudong's financial district has led to a chronic excess supply of office space. Most of these high rises were built by central ministries and provincial or city governments without a proper assessment of future demand and risks. In 1995, utilized office space in Shanghai was around 11 million sq m, and the land leased in 1994 alone will give rise to 20 million sq m of new office space after the completion of construction. Due to the chronic oversupply, the cost of office rentals in Shanghai is forecasted to fall from US$4 per sq m per day in 1995 to US$1 per sq m per day in 1997.[7] The policy of Shanghai municipal government to redevelop the Bund as Shanghai's financial district has made things worse for Pudong. It has been reported that foreign investors are holding back investment in the financial district of Pudong precisely because the Shanghai government is redeveloping the Bund as a financial district.[8]

The heavy involvement of the state has already led to very costly mistakes in infrastructural construction. It is well known that Shanghai's urban planners overwhelmingly favoured building tunnels instead of bridges across the Huangpu River. Tunnels only have to be built 15 m down as the Huangpu River is 8 m deep, while bridges have to be built as high as 55 m to allow the passage of ships.[9] Zhu Rongji 朱鎔基, however, chose to build the Nanpu Bridge (南浦大橋) simply because a bridge is a highly visible monument while a tunnel is not. Trucks have to climb 55 m on long elevated roads to lead up to the bridge, and the elevated roads take up vast tracts of land. In arguing for the bridge, Zhu apparently ignored the costs of the vast amounts of land that would be taken up by the elevated roads, and he also ignored the additional expenses in terms of time and auto-mobile fuel to climb 55 m instead of 15 m.

The bureaucrats' preoccupation with bridges continued unabated for a while, and the Shanghai municipal government started the Yangpu Bridge (楊浦大橋) soon after the completion of the Nanpu Bridge. It seems that every mayor wants to have his own monument.

The bureaucrats' preoccupation with bridges was dampened by Shanghai's wintry sleet, which closed the Nanpu Bridge in early 1993, leaving the old Yenan 延安 tunnel as the only link connecting Pudong and Puxi 浦西. After building two bridges across the Huangpu, the bureaucrats have been forced by Shanghai's weather to enlarge the Yenan tunnel. The bureaucrats' mistake in choosing bridges implies that Puxi's link with Pudong will remain vulnerable to the vagaries of the weather and the Yenan tunnel will have to take up the burden of both the Yangpu and Nanpu bridges during unfavourable weather.

The choice of Pudong as the site for the new international airport is another ghastly planning mistake. Nanjing is only 270 km from Shanghai, and Wuxi 無錫 is the centre of the Shanghai–Nanjing megalopolis. A modern airport located in Wuxi, or at most two airports spaced along the Shanghai–Nanjing superhighway, could have easily served the whole of the Shanghai–Nanjing megalopolis. Pudong, off from the centre, is on the extreme east of the Shanghai–Nanjing axis. Moreover, traffic from Pudong to Puxi and westward is constricted by two bridges and one tunnel, and the two bridges may be closed during wintry sleet! The choice of Pudong as the site for the new airport implies that the whole Yangzi River Delta will be subject to the vagaries of Shanghai's vulnerable bridges. However, in the debates on the site of the airport in the Yangzi River Delta, Pudong had the upper hand because of its connections to Beijing.

Presently, traffic conditions across the Huangpu are not bad because people do not want to settle in Pudong and Pudong has the appearance of a dead city at night. However, if Pudong were really to develop, traffic over the Huangpu would be a planner's nightmare. Even in good weather, the long climbs of 55 m up the two bridges can easily cause endless congestion.

Shanghai's Position as an Economic Centre

Shanghai's official mission is to become China's economic, trading centre and financial centre. While the official slogan is quite vague, it is possible to operationalize the concept of the "three centres" and gauge Shanghai's performance. Shanghai's position as an economic centre will be examined first.

Table 7.3 shows Shanghai's share of China's GDP, industrial output, and value-added of the tertiary sector. Guangdong's corresponding shares are shown for comparison.

Share of China's GDP

Shanghai's share of China's GDP declined continuously from 7.5% in 1978 to a record low of 4.1% in 1990, recovering to 4.4% in 1994. Shanghai's 4.4% share in 1994 was still far below its 1978 share of 7.5%.

Guangdong's GDP surpassed that of Shanghai in 1983. Despite the opening of Pudong in 1990, the gap in GDP between Guangdong and Shanghai has continued to widen. Guangdong's 9.4% share of China's GDP in 1994 was more than twice that of Shanghai.

Table 7.3   Share of Shanghai and Guangdong in China's GDP,
            Industrial Output and Value-added of the Tertiary Sector, 1978–1994

Year	Share of Shanghai in China's			Share of Guangdong in China's		
	GDP	Industrial output	Value-added of the tertiary sector	GDP	Industrial output	Value-added of the tertiary sector
1978	7.5	12.1	5.9	5.1	4.7	5.1
1979	6.7	11.9	6.2	5.0	4.6	5.8
1980	6.9	11.6	6.8	5.4	4.3	6.4
1981	6.7	11.5	6.7	5.9	5.0	6.8
1982	6.4	10.9	6.5	6.3	5.1	7.0
1983	6.0	10.3	6.3	6.1	5.1	6.5
1984	5.4	9.6	5.6	6.1	5.3	6.4
1985	5.2	8.9	4.8	6.2	5.5	6.1
1986	4.8	8.5	4.6	6.3	5.6	6.8
1987	4.6	7.8	4.6	6.8	6.4	7.3
1988	4.3	7.2	4.2	7.4	7.2	7.7
1989	4.1	6.9	3.7	7.8	7.5	8.0
1990	4.1	6.9	4.2	7.9	8.0	8.6
1991	4.1	6.9	4.3	8.2	8.9	8.5
1992	4.2	6.6	4.4	8.6	9.4	8.5
1993	4.4	6.3	5.1	9.4	9.9	9.3
1994	4.4	5.5	5.5	9.4	9.4	9.8

Sources: *Shanghai tongji nianjian*, 1983–1995 (see Table 7.1, Sources); *Guangdong tongji nianjian*, 1984–1995 (see Table 7.2, Sources); *Zhongguo tongji nianjian*, 1981–1995 (see Table 7.1, Sources).

Share of China's Industrial Output

Shanghai's share of China's industrial output declined continuously from 12.1% in 1978 to 5.5% in 1994. Guangdong's industrial output surpassed that of Shanghai in 1988. Despite the opening of Pudong in 1990, the gap between Shanghai and Guangdong in industrial output has continued to widen. In 1994, Guangdong's industrial output was nearly 1.7 times that of Shanghai.

Shanghai's lacklustre performance in industrial output is perhaps not surprising. Unlike Guangdong and other provinces, Shanghai has limited supplies of labour and land and its industrial output cannot expand as rapidly as that of other provinces. The important question is whether Shanghai can be the service hub of China or even of the Yangzi River Delta. To gauge the growth of Shanghai as a service hub, Table 7.3 shows the share of Shanghai in China's output of services (value-added of the tertiary sector).

Share of China's Services Output

Shanghai's share of China's output of services declined from a record high of 6.8% in 1980 to a low of 3.7% in 1989, rebounding to 5.5% in 1994. The rapid rise in Shanghai's share of China's output of services from 3.7% in 1989 to 5.5% in 1994 reflects the rapid expansion of Shanghai's tertiary sector. However, Guangdong's services output surpassed that of Shanghai in 1980 and the gap between Shanghai and Guangdong in services output continued to be large despite the opening of Pudong. In 1994, Guang- dong's services output was 1.8 times that of Shanghai. Moreover, the growth of Shanghai's service sector suffered a sharp setback in the first half of 1995 due to the macrostabilization in China which hit the financial and real estate sectors in Shanghai. The real estate sector also suffered from a correction after the frantic speculation in 1994. In the first half of 1995, Shanghai's financial sector experienced a negative growth of 3.4%, partly a result of the closing down of Shanghai's future markets in govern- ment bonds, and Shanghai's real estate sector contracted by 17%![10]

As China's financial and banking system is only partially marketized, the central government has to resort to administrative controls to tame inflation, and such controls will severely hamper the development of finan- cial markets in Shanghai. Given the partially reformed economic system of China which is highly vulnerable to inflationary pressures, such controls will be imposed quite often. The experience of economic reforms in Com- munist or former-Communist countries shows that the reform of the bank- ing and financial system is one of the most difficult parts of the reform process and it usually takes a long time to complete. Until such reforms are completed, Shanghai will not be able to realize fully its potential as the financial centre of China.

Shanghai's weakness as a port will also have an adverse effect on its development as a services hub. Shanghai's total freight declined by 12% in 1994 and declined by another 6.7% in the first half of 1995.

In a nutshell, Shanghai's position in the national economy has declined sharply from 1978 to 1990. Guangdong surpassed Shanghai in economic strength in the 1980s. Though Shanghai's position rebounded somewhat from 1990 to 1994 with the opening of Pudong, Shanghai failed to regain its dominant position of the late 1970s and early 1980s.

Moreover, the gap between Guangdong and Shanghai remains quite large. Shanghai is clearly a long way from becoming China's economic centre.

Share of China's Foreign Trade

Shanghai's position in foreign trade is shown in Table 7.4, and figures from Guangdong are shown for comparison. As shown in Table 7.4, Shanghai's exports are only available in the statistics of the Ministry of Foreign Economic Relations and Trade (MOFERT),[11] but Guangdong's exports are available both from MOFERT statistics and from China customs statistics. The main difference between MOFERT statistics and China customs statistics is the valuation of exports from processing operations. In MOFERT statistics, exports from processing operations are valued according to the generated processing fees, whereas China customs statistics value exports according to the value of goods exported, which is the international practice. As processing fees usually only constitute around 10% of the value of the goods exported, MOFERT statistics are biased downwards. This downward bias is significant for Guangdong, as export processing is important in Guangdong. Since 1993, however, Guangdong's MOFERT statistics value all exports according to the value of output, eliminating the downward bias of the MOFERT statistics. As export processing is not important in Shanghai, the unavailability of China customs statistics for Shanghai is of no great concern. Guangdong's exports as given by the China's customs statistics exceeded that of the MOFERT statistics largely because of the downward bias of the MOFERT statistics.

Shanghai's exports include a substantial portion of non-Shanghainese products (products produced elsewhere and purchased by Shanghainese foreign trade companies for export). Table 7.4 thus distinguishes between Shanghai's exports (column 1), including the exports of non-Shanghainese products, and exports of Shanghai's products (column 2). Such a distinction cannot be made for Guangdong due to the lack of statistics. However, it is known that the bulk of Guangdong's exports are products made in Guangdong.

The share of Shanghainese products in China's exports declined sharply throughout the 1980s and 1990s, falling from 17.7% in 1978 to 6.1% in 1992. Data after 1992 for exports of Shanghainese products are unfortunately not available. The share of Guangdong's products in China's exports declined moderately from 14.2% in 1978 to 10.2% in 1984. In fact,

Table 7.4   Exports of Shanghai and Guangdong, 1978–1994

(Unit: US$ mn)

Year	Shanghai's exports MOFERT statistics		Guangdong's exports	
	TOTAL	Shanghai's products	MOFERT statistics	China customs statistics
1978	2,893	1,725	1,388	—
	(29.7)	(17.7)	(14.2)	—
1979	3,675	2,220	1,702	—
	(26.9)	(16.3)	(12.5)	—
1980	4,266	2,777	2,195	—
	(23.3)	(15.2)	(12.0)	—
1981	3,807	2,950	2,373	—
	(18.2)	(14.1)	(11.4)	—
1982	3,605	2,737	2,256	—
	(16.5)	(12.5)	(10.3)	—
1983	3,648	2,689	2,385	—
	(16.4)	(12.1)	(10.7)	—
1984	3,587	2,762	2,487	—
	(14.7)	(11.3)	(10.2)	—
1985	3,361	2,619	2,953	—
	(13.0)	(9.6)	(11.4)	—
1986	3,582	2,590	4,251	—
	(13.3)	(9.6)	(15.7)	—
1987	4,160	2,924	5,444	10,140
	(12.0)	(8.4)	(15.7)	(25.7)
1988	4,605	3,142	7,484	14,817
	(11.3)	(7.7)	(18.4)	(31.2)
1989	5,032	3,491	8,168	18,113
	(11.6)	(8.0)	(18.8)	(34.5)
1990	5,317	3,712	10,560	22,221
	(10.2)	(7.1)	(20.3)	(35.8)
1991	5,740	4,086	13,688	27,073
	(9.4)	(6.7)	(22.5)	(37.7)
1992	6,555	4,616	18,440	33,458
	(8.6)	(6.1)	(24.3)	(39.4)
1993	7,382	—	27,027	37,394
	(8.0)*	—	(29.5)*	(40.8)
1994	9,077	—	46,993	50,211
	(7.5)*	—	(38.8)*	(41.5)

Notes: Figures in brackets represent percentage share of the national total.

* Since 1993, the figures in brackets represent the percentage of the exports of Guangdong and Shanghai (in MOFERT statistics) as a share of China's total exports, measured by China customs statistics because the figure for China's total exports in MOFERT statistics is no longer available.

Sources: Data on exports of Shanghai's and Guangdong's products (MOFERT statistics) are obtained from *Shanghai tongji nianjian*, 1983–1995 (see Table 7.1, Sources) and *Guangdong tongji nianjian*, 1984–1995 (see Table 7.2, Sources); data on export of Shanghai's products (MOFERT statistics) are obtained from Shanghai municipal government; data on Guangdong's exports (China customs statistics) are obtained from Guangdongsheng tongjiju (ed.), *Guangdongsheng duiwai jingji maoyi lüyou tongji ziliao*, 1990, 1991, 1992 廣東省對外經濟貿易旅遊統計資料, 1990, 1991, 1992 (The Statistics of the External Economy, Trade and Tourism of Guangdong Province, 1990–1992) (Guangdongsheng tongjiju, 1991, 1992, 1993), and *Guangdong tongji nianjian*, 1994–1995 (see Table 7.2, Sources).

both Shanghai and Guangdong performed well in exports from 1978 to 1981. The decline in their export shares was mainly due to the sharp rise in world oil prices in 1979 and 1981, which rapidly boosted China's total exports because China was an oil exporter. From 1981 to 1986, Shanghai's exports declined absolutely because Shanghai's industries failed to bid for raw materials as economic reforms began. Guangdong, however, benefited from economic reforms and Guangdong's exports took off in 1985, mainly as a result of the relocation of Hong Kong's labour intensive export-oriented industries to Guangdong. The share of Guangdong products in China's exports jumped from 10.2% in 1984 to 24.3% in 1992. Guangdong surpassed Shanghai to become China's foremost province in exports in 1985, and the gap between Guangdong and Shanghai continued to widen. By 1994, according to MOFERT statistics, Guangdong's exports were over five times that of Shanghai. However, the gap is overstated as Guangdong's exports from processing operations have a low value-added content.

Share of China's Foreign Investment

Table 7.5 shows the shares of Shanghai and Guangdong in China's utilized foreign capital, including loans and foreign investment. As a substantial amount of loans borrowed by China consists of soft loans, foreign investment is a better indicator of the investment environment. In the fifteen years from 1979 to 1994, cumulative utilized foreign investment in Guangdong was 4.1 times that in Shanghai.[12] What is even more striking is that the foreign investment in Shanghai appears to be predominantly inward oriented rather than outward oriented. This is the major explanation for Shanghai's weak export performance. The most outward-oriented type of foreign investment is investment in processing operations, and there was

Table 7.5   Utilized Foreign Capital in Shanghai and Guangdong, 1979–1994

(Unit: US$ mn)

Year	TOTAL	Loans	Foreign investment			
			Subtotal	Direct foreign investment	Other investment	
					Subtotal	Processing
Shanghai						
1979–1985	170	70	100	58	43	—
	(0.8)	(0.4)	(1.6)	(1.2)	(3.2)	
1986	281	132	149	148	1	—
	(3.9)	(2.6)	(6.6)	(7.9)	(0.3)	
1987	576	362	214	214	0.4	—
	(6.8)	(6.2)	(8.1)	(9.2)	(0.1)	
1988	440	207	233	233	—	—
	(4.3)	(3.2)	(6.2)	(7.3)		
1989	466	44	422	422	—	—
	(4.6)	(0.7)	(11.2)	(12.4)		
1990	321	147	174	174	—	—
	(3.1)	(2.3)	(4.6)	(5.0)		
1991	330	185	145	145	—	—
	(2.9)	(2.7)	(3.1)	(3.3)		
1992	899	406	494	481	13	—
	(4.7)	(5.1)	(4.4)	(4.4)	(4.4)	
1993	3,178	18	3,160	3,160	—	—
	(8.1)	(0.2)	(11.4)	(11.5)		
1994	2,582	109	2,473	—	—	—
	(6.0)	(1.0)	(7.3)			
1979–1994	9,243	1,680	7,564	—	—	—
	(5.1)	(2.1)	(7.9)	(8.1)*	(1.4)*	
Guangdong						
1979–1985	2,845	345	2,500	1,801	699	457
	(13.1)	(2.2)	(41.2)	(38.1)	(52.2)	(100)
1986	1,404	541	863	723	140	104
	(19.3)	(10.8)	(38.4)	(38.6)	(37.8)	(74.2)
1987	1,167	430	737	603	134	76
	(13.8)	(7.4)	(27.8)	(26.1)	(40.2)	(85.5)
1988	2,415	1,164	1,251	958	293	51
	(23.6)	(17.9)	(33.5)	(30.0)	(53.8)	(74.2)
1989	2,390	1,067	1,323	1,156	167	39
	(23.8)	(17.0)	(35.1)	(34.1)	(43.8)	(70.0)
1990	2,015	433	1,582	1,460	122	43
	(19.6)	(6.6)	(42.1)	(41.9)	(45.6)	(54.7)
1991	2,584	641	1,943	1,823	120	61
	(22.4)	(9.3)	(41.6)	(41.8)	(40.0)	(71.7)
1992	4,746	1,045	3,701	3,552	150	42
	(24.7)	(13.2)	(32.8)	(32.3)	(52.7)	(62.5)
1993	9,843	2,287	7,556	7,498	58	22
	(25.3)	(20.4)	(27.2)	(27.3)	(22.7)	(18.0)
1994	10,928	1,464	9,463	9,397	66	22
	(25.3)	(15.8)	(27.9)	(27.8)	(25.9)	—
1979–1994	40,337	9,417	30,919	28,970	1,949	917
	(22.3)	(13.1)	(31.0)	(30.3)	(45.8)	(77.0)*

Notes: Figures in brackets represent percentage shares of the national total.
          * Data for 1979–1993.

Sources: *Zhongguo duiwai jingji maoyi nianjian* bianjiweiyuanhui《中國對外經濟貿易
          年鑑》編輯委員會 (ed.), *Zhongguo duiwai jingji maoyi nianjian,* 1984–1986
          中國對外經濟貿易年鑑, 1984–1986 (Almanac of China's Foreign Relations
          and Trade, 1984–1986) (Beijing: Huarun maoyi zixun youxian gongsi 華潤貿
          易諮詢有限公司, 1984, 1985, 1986); *Zhongguo duiwai jingji maoyi nianjian*
          bianjiweiyuanhui (ed.), *Zhongguo duiwai jingji maoyi nianjian 1987* (Hong
          Kong: Zhongguo guanggao youxian gongsi 中國廣告有限公司, 1987);
          Zhongguo duiwai jingji maoyi nianjian, 1988–1989 (Beijing: Zhongguo zhan-
          wang chubanshe 中國展望出版社, 1988–1989); *Zhongguo duiwai jingji
          maoyi nianjian* bianjiweiyuanhui (ed.), *Zhongguo duiwai jingji maoyi nianjian
          1990* (Beijing: Zhongguo caizheng jingji chubanshe 中國財政經濟出版社,
          1989); *Zhongguo duiwai jingji maoyi nianjian,* 1991–1992 (Beijing: Zhongguo
          shehui chubanshe 中國社會出版社, 1991–1992); *Zhongguo duiwai jingji
          maoyi nianjian* bianjiweiyuanhui (ed.), *Zhongguo duiwai jingji maoyi nianjian
          1993–1994, 1994–1995, 1995–1996* (Beijing: Zhongguo shehui chubanshe,
          1993, 1994, 1995).

negligible foreign investment in processing operations in Shanghai. The cumulative amount of foreign investment in processing operations in Guangdong is over a hundred times that in Shanghai. It should be noted that the Shanghai municipality includes a substantial amount of rural areas which could provide suitable sites for processing/assembling operations. The Shanghai municipality has an area of 6,340 sq km, of which only 800 sq km are urbanized. The area of Shanghai substantially exceeds the combined total area of Hong Kong, Shenzhen and Dongguan 東莞. Just Hong Kong industries have largely relocated to Shenzhen and Dongguan due to rising costs, industries in Shanghai's urban areas should relocate to the rural areas of the Shanghai municipality. However, the Shanghai government wants to maintain the rural areas as bases of food supply. The development of industry in the rural areas is not encouraged. Moreover, the Shanghai government wants to attract foreign investment with advanced technology and shuns processing operations, with the result that foreign investment in processing operations go to neighbouring Jiangsu and Zhejiang.

Moreover, foreign-funded enterprises in Shanghai are much more inward oriented than those in Guangdong. In the fourteen years from 1979 to 1993, cumulative direct foreign investment in Guangdong was US$19,573 million, with Guangdong's foreign-funded enterprises generating a total of US$32,329 million of exports, or an average of US$ 1.65 worth of exports per US dollar of investment. Over the same period, cumulative direct foreign investment in Shanghai was US$5,091 million, generating a total of US$3,885 million in exports, or an average of US$0.76 worth of exports per US dollar of investment.[13] Shanghai's foreign-funded enterprises were substantially less outward oriented than those of Guangdong. It is known that Shanghai's foreign-funded enterprises exported less than 30% of their output in 1990.

In a nutshell, Shanghai is far from China's foremost economic centre in terms of most of the major economic indicators, including GDP, industrial output, size of the services sector, exports, and foreign investment.

The Inward-oriented Nature of Shanghai Industries

Shanghai is much more inward-oriented than Guangdong. In 1994, the exports to GDP ratio of Guangdong was 95.4%, while that of Shanghai was 39.6%. The inward-oriented nature of Shanghai's foreign investment was just noted. The inward-oriented nature of Shanghai's industries can be attributed to China's policy of import-substitution. This policy has led to its building up of a massive and sophisticated industrial base behind high tariffs in the three decades preceding China's open policy. However, this industrial base was inefficient by international standards and could not easily survive under international competition. Since the open policy, China has introduced selective policies of export-promotion within its overall regime of import-substitution. However, unlike Guangdong, Shanghai has largely failed to capitalize on the selective policies of export-promotion as it is burdened by the traditional structure and practices fostered from import-substitution. Even in the era of the open policy, Shanghai has attracted import-substituting foreign investment rather than outward-oriented foreign investment. Shanghai takes pride in attracting foreign investment with advanced technology. However, it must be emphasized that China presently does not have a comparative advantage in producing high-tech products, and attracting inward-oriented foreign investment through the protection of the domestic market is highly dangerous because it may lead to the development of inefficient industries that cannot survive under international competition. For instance, Shanghai often boasts of the joint-venture with Volkswagen to produce automobiles. However, the cost of this automobile is twice the international price and the joint-venture is profitable only because of heavy protection. In fact, protected industries may be so inefficient that China's GNP, evaluated at international prices, may decrease with more foreign investment (though such industries still appear to be profitable because domestic prices under protection are much higher than international prices).[14]

Under the guise of fostering high-tech industries, Shanghai's industrial policy continues to support inward-oriented industries, such as automobiles, chemicals, and power generators and equipment. Shanghai certainly has some comparative advantage in higher technology due to its skill endowment, but high-tech industries do not have to be inward-oriented. Truly efficient high-tech industries should be able to compete in the international market. Shanghai's policy of supporting inward-oriented and heavily-protected industries can be disastrous. China will have to slash its tariffs to enter the World Trade Organization (WTO) and thus many of Shanghai's industries may go bankrupt once China enters the WTO.

Shanghai's Position as a Trading Centre

To gauge Shanghai's position as a trading centre, statistics on internal trade such as retail sales are not very useful. Retail sales are highly correlated with GDP, and Shanghai's share of China's retail sales moves in unison with its share of China's GDP. It is more instructive to look at data on foreign trade as they are less correlated with GDP.

Table 7.6 compares the position of Shanghai and Guangdong in foreign trade. Table 7.6 is different from Table 7.4 in two ways. First, both imports and exports are included. Second, Table 7.6 refers to trade via Shanghai's or Guangdong's customs. It thus includes the exports of non-local products via Shanghai by firms not located in Shanghai, and imports via Shanghai by firms not located in Shanghai. To gauge the position of Shanghai as a trading centre, such trade should, of course, be included.

Table 7.6 shows that, from 1985 to 1990, the share of trade via Shanghai's customs in the national total declined sharply from 21.4% to 15%. Since 1990, the share has stabilized at 15%. This is perhaps related to the opening of Pudong in that year. However, Shanghai is way behind Guangdong in foreign trade. Trade via Guangdong's customs was more than three times as large as that via Shanghai's customs.

However, the comparison in Table 7.6 is stacked against Shanghai. Due to lower costs of labour and land, Guangdong is a larger manufacturing centre in comparison with Shanghai, and Guangdong tends to export more, regardless of its efficiency as a trading centre. To gauge the efficiency of a trading centre, it is better to concentrate on the export of non-local products, by excluding the export of local products.

Table 7.6   Trade of Shanghai and Guangdong, 1985–1994   (Unit: US$ mn)

Year	Via Shanghai's customs			Via Guangdong's customs			Guangdong's trade		
	TOTAL	Export	Import	TOTAL	Export	Import	TOTAL	Export	Import
1985	14,873	4,908	9,965	—	—	—	—	—	—
	(21.4)	(18.0)	(23.6)						
1986	16,066	5,476	10,590	—	—	—	—	—	—
	(21.8)	(17.7)	(24.7)						
1987	15,635	6,601	9,034	—	—	—	21,037	10,140	10,897
	(18.9)	(16.7)	(20.9)				(25.5)	(25.7)	(25.2)
1988	18,654	7,324	11,330	—	—	—	31,019	14,817	16,202
	(18.2)	(15.4)	(20.5)				(30.2)	(31.2)	(29.3)
1989	19,437	7,711	11,726	—	—	—	35,578	18,113	17,465
	(17.4)	(14.7)	(19.8)				(31.9)	(34.5)	(29.5)
1990	17,289	8,662	8,627	—	—	—	41,898	22,221	19,677
	(15.0)	(14.0)	(16.2)				(36.3)	(35.8)	(36.9)
1991	20,409	10,151	10,258	—	—	—	52,521	27,073	25,448
	(15.1)	(14.1)	(16.1)				(38.7)	(37.7)	(40.0)
1992	25,145	11,964	13,181	77,662	41,322	36,340	65,748	33,458	32,290
	(15.2)	(14.1)	(16.4)	(46.9)	(48.7)	(45.1)	(39.7)	(39.4)	(40.1)
1993	30,931	13,977	16,954	88,519	43,472	45,046	78,344	37,394	40,950
	(15.8)	(15.2)	(16.3)	(45.2)	(47.4)	(43.3)	(40.0)	(40.8)	(39.4)
1994	36,246	18,938	17,308	110,775	60,140	50,635	96,663	50,211	46,452
	(15.3)	(15.7)	(15.0)	(46.8)	(49.7)	(43.8)	(40.9)	(41.5)	(40.2)

Notes: Figures in brackets represent percentage share of China's national total.

Sources: [a] Trade via Shanghai's customs: data since 1993 are obtained from *Shanghai tongji nianjian,* 1994–1995 (see Table 7.1, Sources); data before 1993 are obtained from Shanghaishi tongjiju (ed.), *Shanghaishi duiwai jingji tongji nianjian 1985–1990* 上海市對外經濟統計年鑑 1985–1990 (The Foreign Economic Statistical Yearbook of Shanghai 1985–1990) (Shanghai: Shanghai kexue jishu chubanshe 上海科學技術出版社 , 1991); Shanghaishi tongjiju (ed.), *Shanghaishi duiwai jingji tongji nianjian 1993* (Shanghai: Shanghaishi tongjiju, 1993).

[b] Trade via Guangdong's customs: data are obtained from Zhonghua renmin gongheguo haiguan zongshu 中華人民共和國海關總署 (ed.), *Zhongguo haiguan tongji zhaiyao* 中國海關統計摘要, 1987–1988 (Summary Surveys of China's Customs Statistics, 1987–1988) (Beijing: Zhishi chubanshe 知識 出版社 , 1987–1988); Zhonghua renmin gongheguo haiguan zongshu (ed.), *Zhongguo haiguan tongji nianjian 1990* 中國海關統計年鑑 1990 (China Customs Statistics 1990) (Beijing: Xiandai chubanshe 現代出版社 , 1991); Zhonghua renmin gongheguo haiguan zongshu (ed.), *Zhongguo haiguan tongji nianjian,* 1991–1995;

[c] Guangdong trade: data since 1993 are obtained from Guangdongsheng tongjiju (ed.), *Guangdong tongji nianjian,* 1983–1995 (see Table 7.2, Sources); data before 1993 are obtained from Guangdongsheng tongjiju (ed.), *Guangdongsheng duiwai jingji maoyi lüyou tongji ziliao,* 1990–1992 (see Table 7.4, Sources).

A trading centre is well endowed with skills and facilities in trade, finance, insurance, storage, communications and transportation. Enterprises elsewhere rely on its facilities for exports. A trading centre thus tends to export substantial amounts of non-local products. For instance, Hong Kong has been active in the trading of huge and increasing amounts of non-Hong Kong products.

Shanghai's exports of non-local products can be estimated from Table 7.4 and Table 7.6, and the results are presented in Table 7.7. Shanghai's exports of non-local products can be disaggregated into two different categories: (1) non-local products exported via Shanghai by firms elsewhere, and (2) non-local products exported by Shanghai firms. The former is equal to the difference between exports via Shanghai (column 2 in Table 7.6) and Shanghai's exports (column 1 of Table 7.4). The latter is equal to the difference between Shanghai's exports and exports of Shanghai's products (columns 1 and 2 in Table 7.4).

The economics of the two categories are different. The first category involves only transportation via Shanghai, while the second category involves intermediation by Shanghai firms as well. The first category is determined purely by transport costs, while the second category involves also costs of intermediation, which are determined by trading skills and efficiency in intermediation. The first category can be used to gauge Shanghai's efficiency in transportation, while the second category can be used to gauge Shanghai's efficiency as a middleman. The second category involves more value-added activities than the first.

As mentioned above, the bulk of Guangdong's exports are Guangdong products and Guangdong's statistics do not distinguish between the two concepts. It is, however, possible to estimate non-local products exported via Guangdong by firms elsewhere by subtracting Guangdong's exports (column 4 in Table 7.4) from exports via Guangdong's customs (column 5 in Table 7.6).

Chinese products exported via Hong Kong are also shown in Table 7.7 for comparison. Chinese products exported via Hong Kong are equal to Hong Kong's re-exports of products of Chinese origin less Hong Kong's re-export margin.[15] Unfortunately, Chinese products exported via Hong Kong cannot be disaggregated into two categories as in the case of Shanghai due to lack of data.

In 1978, non-local products exported via Shanghai by Shanghai firms were as much as 12% of China's exports. However, this was not due to the efficiency of Shanghai as a middleman, as non-Shanghainese firms had to

Table 7.7   Exports of Non-local Chinese Products: Shanghai, Guangdong, and Hong Kong, 1978–1994

	Non-local Chinese products exported via				
	Shanghai			Guangdong	Hong Kong
Year	by Shanghai's firms	by firms elsewhere	TOTAL	by firms elsewhere	
1978	1,168 (12.0)	—	—	—	625 (6.4)
1979	1,455 (10.7)	—	—	—	905 (6.6)
1980	1,489 (8.1)	—	—	—	1,350 (7.5)
1981	857 (3.9)	—	—	—	1,836 (8.3)
1982	868 (3.9)	—	—	—	1,936 (8.7)
1983	959 (4.3)	—	—	—	2,165 (9.7)
1984	915 (3.5)	—	—	—	2,876 (11.0)
1985	742 (2.7)	1,547 (5.7)	2,289 (8.4)	—	3,556 (13.6)
1986	992 (3.2)	1,894 (6.1)	2,886 (9.3)	—	5,289 (17.1)
1987	1,236 (3.1)	3,677 (9.3)	4,913 (12.5)	—	8,645 (21.9)
1988	1,463 (3.1)	2,719 (5.7)	4,182 (8.8)	—	13,480 (28.4)
1989	1,541 (2.9)	2,679 (5.1)	4,220 (8.0)	—	19,310 (36.7)
1990	1,605 (2.6)	3,345 (5.4)	4,950 (8.0)	—	24,496 (39.5)
1991	1,654 (2.3)	4,411 (6.1)	6,065 (8.4)	—	31,987 (44.5)
1992	1,939 (2.2)	5,409 (6.5)	7,348 (8.7)	7,864 (9.3)	40,751 (48.0)
1993	—	6,595 (7.2)	—	6,087 (6.6)	47,498 (51.8)
1994	—	9,861 (8.1)	—	9,929 (8.2)	54,331 (44.9)

Notes: Figures in brackets represent percentage share of China's exports (China Custom Statistics).

Sources: Chinese products re-exported via Hong Kong: Hong Kong Census and Statistics Department, *Review of Overseas Trade* (Hong Kong: The Government Printer, 1979–1995); other statistics are obtained from Table 7.4 and Table 7.6.

follow the plan and sell their output to the foreign trade corporations in Shanghai. With economic reforms and the decentralization of powers to export, enterprises have the freedom to choose among different foreign trade corporations. The export of non-local products by Shanghai firms fell rapidly in the early 1980s. Though such exports rebounded after 1985, their share of China's exports continued to decline slowly. In 1992, the latest year when data are available, such exports were only 2.2% of China's exports, showing that Shanghai is a very small trading centre for China's exports.

Data on the export of non-local products via Shanghai by firms else-where are only available since 1985. Such exports were around 5% to 6% of China's exports until 1991. The share of these exports in the national total has risen since 1991, reaching 8.1% in 1994. Data on the export of non-local products via Guangdong by firms elsewhere are only available since 1992. Such exports via Guangdong are slightly larger than those via Shanghai. This confirms that Guangdong's much larger share in foreign trade was mainly due to the export of its own products and not due to its greater efficiency as a trading centre.

Both Shanghai and Guangdong are far behind Hong Kong in the exporting non-local Chinese products. In 1978, Chinese products exported via Hong Kong was only 6.4% of the national total, and Hong Kong was far behind Shanghai in the exporting of Chinese products. However, with the decentralization of the trading system in China, Chinese enterprises have more freedom to choose among different exporters, and an increasing share of China's exports have been channelled to Hong Kong for re-export due to Hong Kong's efficiency as a trading centre.[16] By 1993, 51.8% of China's exports were re-exported via Hong Kong.

In 1994, the share of China's exports re-exported via Hong Kong declined to 44.9%, the first decline in the reform era. The decline is perhaps misleading because the transshipment of Chinese products via Hong Kong is not regarded as part of Hong Kong's trade and is not included in the figures shown in Table 7.5. It is known that lately there has been a substitution of transshipment for entrepôt trade in the flow of goods between China and Hong Kong because shipping companies have recently established offices in China and transshipment services have become more available. As a result, transshipment of Chinese products via Hong Kong increased rapidly in 1994.

In any case, Hong Kong's share of China's trade and ocean-going cargo is so large that Hong Kong will continue to be China's foremost port and centre of foreign trade for a long time to come. Given Shanghai's severe natural limitations as a port, the gulf between Hong Kong and Shanghai as centres of foreign trade is likely to continue even in the long run.

Shanghai's Position as a Financial Centre

Shanghai has had some success in developing its financial services. The capitalization of Shanghai's stock market surpassed that of Shenzhen in early 1992 and the size of the Shanghai stock market was around three times that of Shenzhen in 1995. With the 1994 reform of the foreign exchange regime and the unification of China's exchange rate, Shanghai has become the centre of foreign exchange transactions in China, with the volume of transactions projected to reach US$60 billion in 1995. Shanghai also has the largest number of foreign banks in China.

The greatest disappointment in Shanghai's development as a financial centre is that the specialized banks of China have refused to move their headquarters from Beijing to Shanghai. Zhu Rongji has tried to pressure the Bank of China to move its headquarters to Shanghai, but to no avail. Given China's system of planned allocation of bank credit, banks naturally prefer to stay in Beijing, where decisions on the planned allocation of bank loans are made. The Bank of Communications, which traditionally had its headquarters in Shanghai, found itself at a great disadvantage as its managers often had to fly to Beijing to attend meetings on short notice, and they failed to attend some meetings because planes were fully booked. The specialized banks of China will prefer to stay in Beijing unless China thoroughly reforms its system of administrative allocation of bank credit. East European experience has shown that the reform of the banking system in a Communist economy is a long and tortuous process, and China will be no exception. Though China is well into the eighteenth year of its reform era, its banking system is largely unreformed.

It must be emphasized that, in comparison with the stock market, banks play a much more important role in financing in any country. In countries such as the United States, the United Kingdom, Germany, Japan and France, over 80% of the capital investments of firms are raised from internal funds, 15% from bank borrowing, and less than 5% through the issue of shares and bonds.[17] The relative unimportance of direct financing can be attributed to inherent difficulties for shareholders to monitor effectively the performance of publicly-listed firms. Despite Shanghai's active stock market, the growth of China's financial system will be severely stunted unless China thoroughly reforms its banking system. Until then, Shanghai will not be able to realize its potential as a financial centre.

As mentioned above, the recent use of administrative controls to tame inflation has set back both banking reforms in China and also the development of Shanghai's financial sector. Shanghai's financial sector shrank by 3.4% in the first half of 1995. Given the partially reformed economic system of China which is highly vulnerable to inflationary pressures, controls to tame inflation have to be imposed periodically, and such controls will make banking reforms doubly difficult. The growth of financial services in Shanghai is constrained by the reform and development of the national financial system.

Conclusion

Despite Shanghai's strategic location, its abundance of skilled manpower, and national policies highly favourable to Shanghai, there are still many obstacles to Shanghai becoming the "dragon head" of China's economy. Though Shanghai is the largest city in the Yangzi River Delta, it does not have the best port. In recent years, Shanghai's position as a port has increasingly been eclipsed by Hong Kong and Shanghai has been operating as a feeder port for Hong Kong. There is no easy solution to the severe inadequacy of Shanghai's port.

China's special policies for Pudong may be more of a curse than a blessing as Shanghai may suffer from too much central attention. The heavy involvement of the state in Shanghai has already led to ghastly mistakes in infrastructural construction. It has also led to a chronic excess supply of real estate in Pudong.

Despite the opening of Pudong in 1990, Shanghai's shares in China's exports, sea cargo, and industrial output have continued to fall. Since 1990, Shanghai's shares in China's GDP, services output, and foreign investment have rebounded, but Shanghai failed to regain her dominant position of the late 1970s and early 1980s. Moreover, the gap between Shanghai and Guangdong remained large and sometimes even increasingly large, as is the case in GDP, industrial output, exports, and cargo handled at seaports. Shanghai managed to narrow the gaps somewhat with Guangdong in services output and in foreign investment, but these gaps remained quite large. In 1994, services output and utilized foreign investment in Guangdong were respectively 1.8 times and 3.8 times those of Shanghai.

Shanghai's weak performance in sea cargo is largely the result of its inadequate port facilities. In 1994, for the first time in many years, Shanghai's volume of sea cargo and volume of freight fell absolutely, revealing severe weaknesses in transportation. Such weaknesses have no easy solution.

Shanghai's weak performance in industrial output is mostly the result of policy mistakes. Shanghai failed to devolve power to its rural areas and to let them attract and develop dynamic township and village enterprises. The rural areas were chained to Shanghai's policy of attracting high-tech industries, with the result that both foreign investment and Shanghai's own industries moved to neighbouring Jiangsu and Zhejiang. Shanghai's industrial output was surpassed by Jiangsu in 1984, by both Guangdong and Shandong 山東 in 1988, and by Zhejiang in 1994.

Shanghai's weak performance in exports is again mostly the result of policy mistakes. Shanghai's weak position in industrial output is bad for exports. Moreover, the industries that Shanghai has managed to develop are largely inward-oriented industries thriving behind high tariffs. Shanghai has largely failed to develop export-oriented industries that can compete in the world market.

Shanghai has performed better in the services industries and in attracting foreign investment. However, Shanghai's services sector, including financial services, suffered sharp setbacks in 1995 due to China's macro-stablization and the real estate slump in Shanghai. As the reform of China's banking and financial sector is going to be a long and tortuous process, one cannot be overly optimistic about the development of Shanghai as a financial centre.

Even if Shanghai were to rectify all of its policy mistakes, and even if China were to reform its banking and financial sector thoroughly, there is very little hope that Shanghai will regain its dominant position of the late 1970s, not to mention its pre-eminent position of the 1920s. Unlike the 1920s, when Shanghai was the only major industrial city in China, in the 1990s Shanghai has to contend with strong rivals. In the 1990's, three prosperous regional economies have emerged along China's coast, namely, the Pearl River Delta with Hong Kong as the hub, the Yangzi River Delta with Shanghai as the hub, and the Bohai 渤海 littoral with Beijing–Tianjin as the hub.

In the long run, if Shanghai rectifies its policy mistakes and China successfully reforms its financial sector, Shanghai will be the domestic financial centre of China, while Hong Kong will continue to be a regional and international financial centre. Guangdong will excel in light industries geared for export, while the Yangzi River Delta and the Bohai littoral will excel in heavy industries geared for the domestic market. Hong Kong will have the best port, and it is likely to be the centre of communications, information, and popular culture, while Beijing will be the political centre and also the centre of high culture. Shanghai will be a prosperous metropolis, but it may not be the first among equals.

Notes

1. Information obtained from interview with Chen Zilong 陳子龍, President, Shanghai Yangzi River International Economics Cooperation Research Centre (上海揚子江國際經濟合作中心) in September 1994.
2. Ibid.
3. *Xianggang jingji ribao* 香港經濟日報 (Hong Kong Economic Daily), 13 December 1994.
4. Information given by Li Wuwei 厲無畏 of the Shanghai Academy of Social Sciences (上海社會科學院) in a seminar at The Chinese University of Hong Kong held on 9 November 1995.
5. See Sung Yun-wing, Wong Yue-chim, Lau Pui-king and Liu Pak-wai (eds.), *The Fifth Dragon: The Emergence of the Pearl River Delta* (Singapore: Addison Wesley, 1995), p. 125.
6. *Xin bao* 信報 (Hong Kong Economic Journal), 6 June 1995.
7. Information obtained from Wang Xinkui 王新奎, vice-president, Shanghai Institute of Foreign Trade (上海對外貿易學院) in June 1995.
8. See note 3.
9. Information obtained from interview in January 1993 with a Shanghai town planner who preferred to remain anonymous.
10. See note 4.
11. MOFERT has changed its name to MOTECH (Ministry of Foreign Trade and Economic Cooperation) in 1994.
12. The figures in Table 7.5 are stacked against Shanghai because Shanghai has plenty of centrally run enterprises, and the utilized foreign capital of these enterprises are credited to the central ministries rather than to Shanghai in China's national statistics on foreign investment in Shanghai. Shanghai's own local statistics on foreign investment include the investment of such enterprises, thereby giving a larger figure for Shanghai. According to Shanghai's statistics, utilized foreign investment in 1994 should be US$3,231 million instead of the US$2,473 million shown in national statistics on Shanghai, and cumulative utilized foreign investment should be US$8,885 million instead of US$7,564 million. Guangdong's local statistics on foreign

investment do not differ greatly from the national statistics because there are few centrally run enterprises in Guangdong. According to local statistics, Guangdong's 1994 utilized investment is 2.9 times that of Shanghai instead of the 3.8 times shown in national statistics, and Guangdong's cumulative utilized foreign investment from 1979–1994 is 3.5 times that of Shanghai instead of the 4.1 times shown in national statistics. This chapter sticks to national statistics because there are indications that the definition of foreign investment in local statistics may be quite different from that in national statistics, and there is no guarantee that the definition of foreign investment in Shanghai's statistics is the same as that in Guangdong's statistics. The use of national statistics on foreign investment in Shanghai and in Guangdong should give greater comparability. Regardless of whether local or national statistics are used, it remains true that foreign investment in Guangdong is much greater than that in Shanghai.

13. See Song Enrong 宋恩榮 (Sung Yun-wing), "Shanghai yu Guangdong waimao he touzi de bijiao yanjiu" 上海與廣東外貿和投資的比較研究 (A Comparative Study of Foreign Trade and Investment in Shanghai and Guangdong), in *Hu Jing Gang zhuanjia zonglun Shanghai fazhan* 滬京港專家縱論上海發展 (Shanghai's Development: Views of Experts from Shanghai, Beijing and Hong Kong), edited by Pan Mingshan 潘名山, Sung Enrong, Dong Xinbao 董新保 and Yu Zhonggen 俞仲根 (Shanghai: Shanghai renmin chubanshe 上海人民出版社, 1995), pp. 21–33.

14. The phenomenon is known as "immiserizing foreign investment" in economics literature.

15. The re-export margin is not known with great precision, though survey data and common sense point to a substantial re-export margin of around 25% to 30%, and it is also known that the margin has risen in the 1990s. In this chapter, Hong Kong's re-export margin is taken to be 25% before 1990. From 1990 onwards, the re-export margin is assumed to increase by one percentage point every year, reaching 30% in 1994. For a more detailed account of the re-export margin, see Sung Yun-wing, "The Economic Value of Hong Kong to China," in *The Other Hong Kong Report 1991*, edited by Sung Yun-wing and Lee Ming-kwan (Hong Kong: The Chinese University Press, 1991), p. 481.

16. For a detailed theoretical and empirical analysis of Hong Kong's role in China's trade, see Sung Yun-wing, *China–Hong Kong Connection: The Key to China's Open Door Policy* (Cambridge: Cambridge University Press, 1991).

17. See J. Stiglitz, "The Role of the State in Financial Markets," Chung-Hua Series of Lectures, No. 21 (Taipei: Institute of Economics, Academia Sinica [中央研究院經濟研究所], 1993).

8

Industrial Development

Victor Mok

Shanghai as an Industrial City

As a municipality directly under the central government, Shanghai encompasses the city and six neighbouring *xian*'s 縣, with an area of 6,340.5 sq km and a total population of around 13 million. Despite its size, a high concentration of economic activities enables Shanghai to rival some of China's large provinces in productive capacity. In 1994, it accounted for 4.5% of China's gross domestic product (GDP), 12.5% of fiscal revenue, 7.1% of gross value of industrial output, 16.7% of total merchandise exports and it handled 20% of China's total port cargoes. Its GDP per capita was 5 times higher than the national average.[1]

The old Shanghai city is well-known. It was the undisputed economic centre of China with thriving industrial, commercial and financial activities. After 1949, while its commercial and financial sectors suffered in the process of China's socialist transformation, the gross value of its industrial output increased 50 times from 1952 to 1993.

Two trends are clearly discernible in Table 8.1. First is the nature of Shanghai's industries. In 1952, the year before China embarked upon her First Five-year Plan, close to 80% of the gross value of Shanghai's industrial output was from light industries, nearly a quarter of all of China. In

Table 8.1   Gross Value of Industrial Output, 1952–1994
(value at current prices)

Year	Value: RMB100 million	Share of light industries (%)	Share of heavy industries (%)	Share in China (%) TOTAL	Light industries	Heavy industries
1952	66.00	79.3	20.7	19.1	23.6	11.1
1955	91.42	75.5	24.5	17.1	21.8	10.3
1960	298.97	45.0	55.0	18.3	24.6	15.1
1965	230.77	56.1	43.9	16.5	17.9	14.9
1970	312.18	51.9	48.1	15.0	16.6	13.2
1975	420.37	48.5	51.5	13.1	14.1	12.1
1980	598.75	55.3	44.7	11.6	13.6	9.8
1985	862.73	52.9	47.1	8.9	9.9	8.0
1990	1,642.75	51.5	48.5	6.9	7.2	6.6
1994	4,255.19	44.4	55.6	7.1	—	—

Sources: *Xin Shanghai gongye tongji ziliao 1949–1990* 新上海工業統計資料 1949–1990 (New Shanghai Industrial Statistical Data 1949–1990) (Shanghai: Shanghaishi tongjiju 上海市統計局 , 1992), table 1.1 to table 1.3; *Shanghai tongji nianjian 1993* (see note 6), table 1.2; and *Shanghai tongji nianjian 1995* (see note 1), p. 15 and pp. 146–47, table 10.1.

those days, major products were textiles, flour, cigarettes, leather and rubber goods, matches and soap, while the machinery, metallurgy, chemical, electricity and shipbuilding industries were still at an early stage of development. Since then, however, the bulk of industrial investment has been in heavy industries due to China's drive to build up an independent industrial structure. The gross value output of heavy industries soon caught up with that of light industries.[2]

The second trend is the gradual decline in the relative importance of Shanghai in China's industrial output. Overall, Shanghai's share dropped from a high of 19.1% in 1952 to only around 7% in the 1990s. Even in heavy industries, its share increased for a while but later also started to decline. One reason is the overall industrialization of China; another is China's efforts to decentralize her industries for economic and strategic reasons, especially during the late 1950s and 1960s when some of Shanghai's industries were moved inland. But what has become worrisome for Shanghai in more recent years is the newly emerging industrial capabilities of some provinces, notably Guangdong 廣東 and Jiangsu 江蘇 , which pose a threat to its industrial superiority.

This, however, should not be interpreted as a weakening of Shanghai's industrial might. Over the years, it has built up a broad industrial base with a wide range of products for both domestic and export markets. Its shares in many major industrial products in China, as shown in Table 8.2, suggest that its position remains solid.

What Shanghai faces now is the challenge of China's reform and open policy. As many of its industrial enterprises are state-owned large and medium-sized ones, built in the days of a command economy, their

Table 8.2   Shanghai's Share in China's Major Industrial Products, 1994

(Unit: %)

Product	Share	Product	Share
Sewing machines	45.9	Domestic refrigerators	14.5
Synthetic cleansing materials	10.1	Television sets	15.7
Civilian steel vessels	21.4	Plastic materials	15.4
Bicycles	20.5	Steel	14.5
Electricity generating equipment	20.6	Finished steel materials	14.4
		Domestic washing machines	16.6
Ethylene	19.3	Chemical fibres	12.1
Woollens	15.0	Pig iron	9.8

Source: *Shanghai tongji nianjian 1995* (see note 1), p. 150, table 10.3.

equipment and mode of operation are outdated. A pressing problem is to
revitalize these enterprises and acclimatize them to the new environment of
a market economy. Indeed, the present task for Shanghai well exemplifies
China's current efforts to change the operating mechanisms of her vast
sector of state enterprises.

Economic Transformation since 1949

The economy of Shanghai has undergone substantial changes since 1949.
It has grown into a great industrial city and, at the same time, there have
been significant structural changes. Its transformation was first a major
task in China's programme of socialist construction and now again it is a
focal point in China's policy of reform and openness.

Changes in Economic Structure

In terms of GDP, growth in Shanghai's economic sectors has been highly
uneven. As seen in Table 8.3, growth in the primary sector was painfully
slow and suffered periodic setbacks. The tertiary sector was even worse for
a while, but it has bounced back significantly since the late 1970s. A
continuous and high rate of growth is found in the secondary sector,
especially industry.

These differential growth rates clearly indicate China's development
strategy. While we cannot say the primary sector has been ignored, relatively little investment has gone into it. It largely had to work under
existing conditions and make improvements therein. Industry was considered to be the key to modernization, especially heavy industries where a

Table 8.3   Indices of GDP, 1952–1992

Year	Gross domestic product (GDP)	Primary sector	Secondary sector	Industry	Tertiary sector
1952	100.0	100.0	100.0	100.0	100.0
1962	206.2	175.6	277.5	287.9	127.2
1970	501.3	205.5	770.6	805.7	197.4
1975	690.8	189.2	1,078.1	1,119.8	266.4
1980	1,035.1	198.1	1,623.9	1,683.8	402.4
1985	1,598.6	244.2	2,405.8	2,471.5	717.9
1990	2,105.9	259.6	3,069.4	3,136.8	1,052.4
1992	2,591.5	261.6	3,841.9	4,013.2	1,277.7

Source: *Shanghai tongji nianjian 1993* (see note 6), p. 36, table 1.9.

tremendous amount of capital was directed. The tertiary sector is always in an awkward position in socialist countries, because some services are considered "unproductive." As a commercial and financial centre, old Shanghai had a large tertiary sector which since 1953 has been reorganized according to socialist principles: basic services were put under state control and community services were collectivized, while personal services were all but abolished. It was not until the 1980s that the tertiary sector was allowed to revive, and Shanghai once again has been able to reveal its ability in providing commercial and financial services, in addition to manufacturing.

This pattern of development led to basic changes in Shanghai's economic structure, as seen in Table 8.4 and Table 8.5. In 1952, the secondary sector was already dominant, with a 52.4% share of GDP, which grew well into the late 1970s. Its relative importance started to decline after China adopted her reform and open policy but, by 1993, it still had about a 60% share of GDP, with industry alone accounting for almost

Table 8.4 Sectoral Composition of GDP, 1952–1993

(Unit: %)

Sector	1952	1962	1970	1975	1980	1985	1990	1993
Primary	5.9	5.3	4.7	4.0	3.2	4.2	4.4	2.5
Secondary	52.4	69.4	77.1	77.2	75.7	69.7	64.8	59.6
Industry	49.7	68.5	76.5	76.1	74.0	66.7	60.0	55.9
Tertiary	41.7	25.3	18.2	18.8	21.1	26.1	30.8	37.9

Note: GNP for 1952–1975 and GDP for 1980–1993.
Sources: *Shanghai tongji nianjian 1993* (see note 6), p. 35, table 1.8; and *Shanghai tongji nianjian 1994* (see note 12), pp. 28–29, table 1.4 and p. 34, table 1.7.

Table 8.5 Sectoral Composition of Labour Force, 1952–1993

(Unit: %)

Sector	1952	1962	1970	1975	1980	1985	1990	1993
Primary	42.6	40.5	36.9	36.6	29.2	16.6	11.4	9.9
Secondary	29.6	35.2	42.5	42.9	48.7	57.9	60.2	58.7
Industry	—	—	—	—	43.6	51.4	53.9	—
Tertiary	27.8	24.3	20.6	20.5	22.1	25.5	28.4	31.4

Sources: Calculated from figures in *Shanghai tongji nianjian 1993* (see note 6), p. 74, table 2.14 and p. 75, table 2.15; and *Shanghai tongji nianjian 1994* (see note 12), pp. 28–29, table 1.4.

56%. The tertiary sector suffered heavily during the period of socialist economic planning but, since the 1980s, its comeback has been dramatic. The primary sector was small in terms of GNP early on, and its share has continued to decline.

The sectoral composition of Shanghai's workforce presents a similar picture. Initially, more than 40% of the labour force was engaged in primary production. By 1993, it dropped to below 10%. Despite Shanghai's industrial activities, only about 30% of the labour force was engaged in secondary production in 1952. This share doubled during the process of its further industrial development. The share of the tertiary sector dropped in the initial period but then recovered when Shanghai's position as a commercial and financial centre was revived.

It is quite interesting to note that, despite markedly different historical and institutional factors, the pattern of structural change during Shanghai's industrialization is not dissimilar to that of many other economies undergoing the same process — an upsurge in industrial activities which gradually peters out, an emergence of modern services, and a rapid decline in the relative importance of the primary sector.[3]

Changes in the relative importance of various sectors in the economy imply reallocation of resources, which is a source of economic growth. Comparing Table 8.4 and Table 8.5, we find that for the primary sector, shares of the labour force are much larger than shares of GDP. In 1952, 42.6% of the labour force was engaged in primary production, contributing only 5.9% of GDP. This is typical of the condition in developing economies where a high proportion of the rural population lives off the land in low productivity agriculture. Improvements began in the early 1980s but, by 1993, labour productivity was still below average, as around 10% of the labour force in primary production could only contribute 2.5% of GDP.

By contrast, labour productivity was relatively high in the secondary sector, as its shares in the labour force were all smaller than its shares in GDP. Differences were great for some three decades, until the 1980s when the shares in GDP started to decline but shares in the labour force continued to grow. By 1993, 58.7% of Shanghai's labour force was engaged in secondary production and accounted for 59.6% of its GDP. In other words, labour productivity was just about average.

As for the tertiary sector, its share in GDP was much larger than that in the labour force in 1952. That was a time when many service industries were still in private hands. Socialist transformation changed all that. The share of the tertiary sector, both in GDP and in the labour force, was kept low, especially the former. But both shares began to grow again in the early 1980s, with the share in GDP rising above the share in the labour force, which suggests a higher-than-average labour productivity.

These trends are again similar to those of other developing economies. More specifically, there has been a gradual reduction in sectoral disparities of labour productivity due to resource reallocation when labour leaves the low productivity sector, namely, agriculture, to join other high productivity sectors, namely, industry, trade and services, and results in a convergence of labour productivity among various sectors.[4]

In the case of Shanghai, however, such changes took place only after 1980 because there was little room for regional and occupational labour mobility in a command economy. Since the reform and opening, an increasing portion of the rural population has taken to manufacturing, trading and other activities. Witness the fast mushrooming of *xiangzhen qiye* 鄉鎮 企業 (township and village enterprises) which are definitely more profitable than farming.

Like so many big cities in developing countries, Shanghai is a centre of industrial, commercial and financial activities serving its vast hinterland. In the past, it broadened its industrial base under socialist transformation, so much so that other sectors were generally undernourished. Understandably, primary production should gradually give way to other activities in growing metropolitan areas, but an undeveloped tertiary sector will eventually hamper the proper functioning of a central city. Under the policy of reform and opening, Shanghai is finally on its way back to building an economic structure more becoming of its role as a regional economic centre.

Changes in Industrial Ownership

In 1952, most industrial and commercial enterprises in China were still in private hands. The state had under its control only some large enterprises which had been taken over from the former Kuomintang (Guomindang 國民黨) government or confisticated from the capitalists. Then in a wave of socialist transformation during the First Five-year Plan, all private enterprises were converted to state–private joint enterprises and later taken over by the state. Small individual enterprises were grouped into collectives and put under state control. As a result, as seen in Table 8.6, private ownership of industrial enterprises virtually disappeared in Shanghai for more than two decades.[5]

After the reform and opening, the category of "others" began to re-emerge and their number increased at high speed. In 1993, about half were joint ventures among local and out-of-city enterprises resulting from the development of "horizontal linkages." The rest were mostly *sanzi qiye* 三資企業 (three types of foreign-funded enterprises, namely, Sino–foreign joint ventures, Sino–foreign co-operatives and wholly-owned foreign enterprises) and some private enterprises.

Table 8.6 is, in fact, far from comprehensive because it only includes industrial enterprises at the *xiang* 鄉 level and above. When the communes were dissolved, local governments in rural areas were restored at the *zhen* 鎮 (township), *xiang* (village) and *cun* 村 (small village) levels below the *xian* (county) level. The *cun* authorities also began to operate their own collective industrial enterprises which easily flourished due to more flexible local policies. Equally thriving are industrial enterprises operated by private individuals and units operated by *getihu* 個體戶 (individual households) in townships and rural areas. Table 8.7 shows the recent development of these industrial enterprises in Shanghai.

Table 8.6   Number of Industrial Enterprises by Ownership Sector, 1952–1993[a]

Year	State enterprise	Collective enterprise	Others[b]	TOTAL
1952	228	37	25,613	25,878
1962	3,529	5,280	0	8,809
1970	3,253	6,581	0	9,834
1975	3,374	5,369	0	8,743
1980	3,164	3,914	71	7,149
1985	4,176	6,141	339	10,656
1990	4,517	7,122	1,581	13,220
1993	4,270	6,762	2,656	13,688

Notes: [a] Includes all enterprises operating at the *xiang* level and above. Excluded are those operating at the *cun* level and the *chengxiang geti gongyehu* 城鄉個體工業戶 (township and village industrial units operated by individual households).

[b] Others include private and state–private joint enterprises for 1952; state–collective, state–private, collective–private, local–foreign joint enterprises and enterprises operated by overseas Chinese and Hong Kong/Macau industrialists for 1980–1993.

Sources: *Shanghai tongji nianjian 1993* (see note 6), p. 96, table 3.1; and *Shanghai tongji nianjian 1994* (see note 12), pp. 134–35, table 9.1.

Table 8.7 Number of *Cun*-operated and Other Industrial Enterprises, 1985–1992

Nature	1985	1990	1992
Cun-operated enterprises	5,796	9,376	10,212
Rural co-operative enterprises	3,703	3,200	2,700
Private enterprises	—	1,356	3,192
Rural *geti* enterprises*	6,217	7,638	8,105
Township *geti* enterprises*	2,468	1,467	1,510

Notes: * *Geti* enterprises are those operated by individual households.
Source: *Shanghai tongji nianjian 1993* (see note 6), p. 96, table 3.2.

These various forms of lower-level industrial enterprises have overtaken the state and collective enterprises at the *xiang* level in sheer number. They are, of course, smaller in scale, but not necessarily backward in technology because they are relatively new. The *cun*-operated enterprises play a dominant role in this sector. In 1993, they accounted for around 10% of Shanghai's gross value of industrial output, suggesting that they increasingly constitute a sector to be reckoned with.[6] Presumably some of the *cun*-operated enterprises are, in fact, private or joint private–collective enterprises. They are registered as collective enterprises only because it is more convenient and appealing to local authorities for favourable treatment.[7]

To summarize, the reform and opening has changed the simple ownership structure of Shanghai's industrial sector of the 1960s and 1970s. In addition to the re-emergence of private and foreign enterprises, various types of joint, co-operative and collective enterprises have given rise to a complicated pattern of ownership. In more recent years, some of the state enterprises have become joint-stock companies and have made shares available to the public and overseas investors.

Industrial Structure

Shanghai built up a relatively complete structure of basic industries in the 1960s. New industries like metallurgy, electronics, petrochemicals and precision instruments emerged in the 1970s. Typical of a planned economy, the heavy industries were emphasized.[8] Changes were made when the current economic reforms began.

Industrial Structure since 1979

The gradual development of a market economy implies that heavy industries must be reoriented. They have to serve light industries which cater to the needs of consumers, instead of feeding upon themselves. In the face of an upsurge in demand for consumer durables, light industries require new machinery and input materials both to upgrade traditional products and to provide new ones. Increasing competition is on its way, notably from Guangdong. Shanghai's industries have to redress their production to meet this challenge.

There is an additional reason for this change, which is the profitable export market afforded by the open policy, and this again requires substantial industrial restructuring. With low labour costs, surely China's international comparative advantage is in her labour-intensive manufactures. Shanghai's traditional industries, e.g. textiles, are in an advantageous position to exploit this, but they urgently need renovation. Hard pressed are the heavy industries. Expectations of China's resumption of General Agreement on Tariffs and Trade (GATT) status has actually caused worries among these industries as they will no longer be able to enjoy protection.

Shanghai's industrial structure is shown in Table 8.8. The range and balance of its major industries bear ample witness to its broad base. Generally speaking, the textile, clothing and machinery industries are labour-intensive in that their shares of employment are much higher than their shares of output, while it is the reverse for the metal, chemical and transport equipment industries which are capital-intensive.

The restructuring of Shanghai's industrial sector since the economic reform is seen in Table 8.9. Production of some major traditional goods, such as textiles and radios, has actually decreased. There have been moderate increases in the output of a number of industries, such as machinery, steel, shipbuilding, bicycles and some other consumer goods. But the rise of a new generation of consumer durables, such as video recorders, colour televisions, air-conditioners, washing machines and refrigerators, is simply phenomenal.

Industrial restructuring is necessarily a continuous and long process. It means not only the introduction of new products and industries, but also the removal and phasing out of old ones. As the majority of Shanghai's large and medium-sized industrial enterprises are state-owned, institutional rigidities inherited from the past have created many problems for restructuring. Adjustment to a market economy is slow and sometimes painful. Some gigantic enterprises, such as Shanghai Petro-chemical (上海石化, with a workforce of 61,000 in 1992), Shanghai Automobile (上海汽車, 58,000) and Baoshan Iron and Steel Complex (寶山鋼鐵, around 32,000),

Table 8.8 Employment and Output of Major Manufacturing Industries, 1993[a]

Industry	Employment (year end)		Value of output[b]	
	10 thousand	%	RMB100 million	%
Food & beverages	13.30	3.5	135.20	4.2
Textiles	50.85	13.2	275.10	8.5
Clothing & manufactures of fibres	47.61	12.4	113.58	3.5
Chemicals & chemical products	18.10	4.7	194.04	6.0
Chemical fibres	6.70	1.7	95.94	3.0
Non-metallic mineral products	13.63	3.5	80.32	2.5
Ferrous metals	18.99	4.9	545.48	16.8
Non-ferrous metals	4.62	1.2	83.91	2.6
Metal products	21.56	5.6	150.51	4.6
Machinery	29.77	7.7	191.02	5.9
Specialized equipment	23.76	6.2	160.38	5.0
Transport equipment	26.72	6.9	289.80	9.0
Electrical machinery & equipment	24.27	6.3	220.68	6.8
Electronic & communication equipment	14.12	3.7	130.27	4.0
Instruments & office machinery	13.01	3.4	57.11	1.8
Others	58.10	15.1	512.97	15.8
TOTAL	385.11	100.0	3,236.31	100.0

Notes: [a] Include all industrial enteprises.
              [b] Gross value of industrial output at current prices.

Source: Calculated from figures in *Shanghai tongji nianjian 1994* (see note 12), pp. 134–35, table 9.1.

have little to fear because they enjoy certain monopolistic power and protection. Some others can take advantage of the upsurge in the demand for consumer durables and shift their product lines. But many others are not so fortunate. They are hard pressed by competition and find restructuring tough going.

As a result, the general estimation is that one-third of Shanghai's industrial enterprises are actually incurring losses. Yet, they can neither close down nor lay off workers. They have to be bailed out by government subsidies year after year. In so doing, industrial restructuring has been slowed down because resources are prevented from flowing to uses where they can be better employed.

In July 1992, the State Council promulgated regulations[9] to separate state and enterprise functions. Enterprises are to be *zizhu jingying* 自主經營 (operated autonomously) and *zifu yingkui* 自負盈虧 (responsible for their own profit and loss). There are provisions for *guan* 關 (closure), *ting* 停 (stoppage), *bing* 併 (merger), *zhuan* 轉 (transformation) as well as division,

Table 8.9   Growth of Major Industrial Products, 1980 and 1994

Product	Unit	1980	1994	1994/1980 (%)
Yarn	10,000 tonnes	38.13	30.36	80
Cloth	100 million m	16.14	9.50	59
Electric fans	10,000	109.48	176.06	161
Radios	10,000	414.75	173.67	42
Sewing machines	10,000	226.49	369.40	163
Woollens	10,000 m	3,024.00	4,400.00	146
Cameras	10,000	20.69	189.90	918
Steel	10,000 tonnes	521.61	1,326.77	254
Finished steel products	10,000 tonnes	412.63	1,149.26	279
Civilian steel vessels	10,000 tonnes	17.26	64.87	376
Bicycles	10,000	376.06	829.47	221
Elec. generating equipment	10,000 kw	58.20	350.95	603
Automobiles	unit	14,675.00	117,600.00	801
Video recorders	unit	880.00[a]	574,000.00	65,227
Televisions	10,000 sets	75.24	499.97	665
colour	10,000 sets	0.55	132.99	24,180
Air-conditioners	unit	958.00	500,200.00	55,213
Domestic refrigerators	10,000	0.42	110.90	26,405
Domestic washing machines	10,000	0.81	182.04	22,474

Note: [a] 1990 figure.
Sources: *Shanghai tongji nianjian 1993* (see note 6), pp. 18–21, table 1.2, pp. 22–25, table 1.3 and pp. 119–22, table 3.14; and *Shanghai tongji nianjian 1995* (see note 1), p. 150, table 10.3.

dissolution and bankruptcy of enterprises in order to improve efficiency and to facilitate industrial restructuring. To be politically and socially feasible, however, these will have to be accompanied by other measures, such as a social security system. But progress so far has been slow.

Ownership Structure since 1979

If it is not easy to change existing enterprises in the state sector, industrial restructuring can be achieved by expanding the non-state sector, provided that it is allowed and the economy is buoyant enough. This is exactly what has been happening in Shanghai since the economic reform.

In Table 8.10, the dominance of the state sector is all too clear, except in its share of number of enterprises, which only means that state enterprises are relatively large. They are also relatively capital-intensive as seen in their high shares in fixed assets. More significant is their rapidly

Table 8.10 Comparison of Industrial Enterprises by Ownership Sector, 1980–1992[a]

Sector	1980	1985	1990	1992
	\% share in number of enterprises			
State	39.8	32.1	26.1	23.5
Collective	59.1	64.0	58.8	57.8
Others	1.1	3.9	15.1	18.7
State-collective	1.0	3.1	12.0	—
Sanzi qiye[b]		0.1	2.9	5.8
	\% share in number of workers (year-end)			
State	69.8	64.4	60.4	56.3
Collective	28.9	32.2	28.3	26.5
Others	1.3	3.4	11.3	17.2
State-collective	1.2	3.1	9.3	—
Sanzi qiye	0.1	0.2	1.7	3.9
	\% share in gross value of industrial output			
State	89.6	81.8	73.9	62.8
Collective	9.3	15.5	13.6	13.6
Others	1.1	2.7	12.5	23.6
State-collective	1.0	2.2	6.9	—
Sanzi qiye	0.1	0.4	5.5	11.8
	\% share in original value of fixed assets (year-end)			
State	91.6	87.7	80.4	77.5
Collective	7.9	10.4	9.5	7.8
Others	0.5	1.9	10.1	14.7
State-collective	0.4	1.5	4.8	—
Sanzi qiye	0.1	0.3	5.2	6.3
	\% share in total profits-tax[c]			
State	91.6	85.6	78.6	63.7
Collective	7.6	12.3	10.0	9.0
Others	0.8	2.1	11.4	27.3
State-collective	0.7	1.8	5.4	—
Sanzi qiye	0.1	0.3	5.9	15.7

Notes: [a] Includes all independent accounting industrial enterprises at the *xiang* level and above.

[b] *Sanzi qiye* are wholly foreign-owned enterprises, Sino–foreign joint ventures and Sino–foreign co-operative enterprises.

[c] *Lishui zong'e* 利稅總額 is the sum of profits and sales tax.

Sources: Calculated from figures in *Xin Shanghai gongye tongji ziliao 1949–1990* (see Table 8.1, source), table 6.2, table 6.3, table 6.6, table 6.8, table 6.11 to table 6.13; and *Shanghai tongji nianjian 1993* (see note 6), pp. 127–30, table 3.18 and p. 156, table 3.32.

declining share in all aspects. By contrast, collective enterprises have much lower shares of workers, output and fixed assets than of numbers of enterprises, suggesting that they are relatively small and labour-intensive. But they show no sign of losing ground.

The "others" category was insignificant at first but soon expanded at the expense of the state sector. By the early 1990s, it has become an important component in Shanghai's industrial sector. It is composed mainly of state–collective enterprises and *sanzi qiye*. The state–collective enterprises are joint ventures set up by state and collective enterprises as a result of the development of "horizontal linkages" in the 1980s to profit from Shanghai's new opportunities. Some are entirely local, while others have partners from other provinces, cities and *xian*'s. They are larger than collective enterprises but also relatively labour-intensive.

Sanzi qiye are enterprises in which foreign (including Hong Kong, Macau and Taiwan) investments are involved. They are new-comers in Shanghai, mainly in light industries, somewhat capital-intensive, but definitely much smaller than enterprises in the state sector.[10] In 1992, they had a 6.3% share in the original value of fixed assets, 5.8% share in number of enterprises, 3.9% share in number of workers, but 11.8% share in gross value of industrial output and 15.7% share in total profits-tax.

Prompted by changes in enterprise ownership structure, a finer classification is provided in recent Chinese statistics as shown in Table 8.11. The state and (formerly state) joint-stock enterprises have much higher shares of persons engaged than number of enterprises, suggesting that they are large in size. By comparison, the collective enterprises are the smallest, while joint enterprises and *sanzi qiye* (foreign, Hong Kong, Macau and Taiwan enterprises) are somewhat below average. But in terms of output per person, foreign and joint-stock enterprises are the highest, with output shares much higher than shares of persons engaged. They are followed by Hong Kong, Macau, Taiwan and state enterprises. Joint and collective enterprises are at the bottom, with shares of persons engaged higher than shares in output.

In all, as China's modernization programme unfolds, some of Shanghai's large state and collective enterprises might have become a liability. There are many system rigidities resistant to structural change. But the market economy also affords new opportunities in which new enterprises and modes of operation can flourish. New capital, business connections, technical and management know-how are brought in. They move into new areas, supply new products, help reform obsolete enterprises and thus

Table 8.11   Ownership Structure of Industrial Enterprises, 1993[a]

Sector	Enterprise		Persons engaged		Output[b]	
	Number	%	10 thousand	%	RMB100 million	%
State enterprises	4,270	31.2	189.82	52.5	1,629.66	54.5
Collective enterprises	6,762	49.4	89.21	24.7	384.65	12.9
Joint enterprises[c]	1,331	9.7	32.32	8.9	196.95	6.6
Joint-stock enterprises[d]	44	0.3	24.80	6.9	300.51	10.0
Foreign enterprises	625	4.6	13.36	3.7	346.77	11.6
Hong Kong, Macau & Taiwan enterprises	622	4.5	11.01	3.0	116.41	3.9
Others	45	0.3	0.85	0.3	14.83	0.5
TOTAL	13,699	100.0	361.37	100.0	2,989.78	100.0

Notes: [a] Include all enterprises operating at the *xiang* level and above. Percentages here are not comparable to those in Table 8.10 above because only "independent accounting" enterprises are included in Table 8.10.
   [b] Gross value of industrial output.
   [c] Joint ventures of state, collective and private enterprises.
   [d] Some of these joint-stock enterprises have investors overseas and, therefore, enjoy preferential treatments.
Source: *Shanghai tongji nianjian 1994* (see note 12), p. 134, table 9.1.

facilitate industrial restructuring as the traditional state sector retreats in their advance.

Sanzi qiye

Shanghai's *sanzi qiye* need more elaboration. In fact, its first Sino–foreign joint venture came into being as early as 1980, followed by some joint ventures and co-operative enterprises as well as compensation trade agreements with foreign businesses. Shanghai became an open coastal city in 1984. Despite these features as well as its industrial base, foreign capital has been slow to come to Shanghai for manufacturing in comparison with Guangdong.

For one reason, of course, Shanghai is not as close to Hong Kong as Guangdong. As China opened up to foreign investors, Hong Kong's industrialists looked northwards for investment opportunities. Geographic proximity, low land and labour costs, kinship relations and more flexible policies made Guangdong, particularly the Pearl River Delta, a fertile hinterland for their manufacturing activities under all sorts of arrangements. This is something Shanghai could hardly rival.

There is also a more subtle reason. Unlike Guangdong, Shanghai, with its broad industrial base, is more interested in attracting modern technology to renovate its industries than in bringing in labour-intensive industries or in doing export processing for Hong Kong. Shanghai's policy towards *sanzi qiye* is also more rigid in its insistence on local participation. As a result, a great deal of foreign investment has instead gone to neighbouring cities and *xian*'s which offer much more flexibility. It was not until the late 1980s that Shanghai set up Economic and Technological Development Zones in Minhang 閔行 , Hongqiao 虹橋 and Caohejing 漕河涇 to attract more foreign investment in manufacturing.

For these reasons, only 36.3% of Shanghai's direct foreign investment was from Hong Kong, whereas it was 62.2% in Guangdong; 57.9% of its foreign investment was in manufacturing, compared to 77.5% in Guangdong. While Guangdong had 52.5% of direct foreign investments in equity joint ventures and almost 10% wholly owned by foreign investors, Shanghai had 70.2% and less than 5% respectively.[11]

Table 8.12 shows the development of *sanzi qiye* in Shanghai since the reform and opening. As pointed out earlier, it was slow in the first part of the 1980s, but the pace accelerated remarkably thereafter. The opening up of the Pudong New Area (浦東新區) will no doubt attract more foreign investments.

It is interesting to compare how *sanzi qiye* are doing *vis-à-vis* their local counterparts. Some efficiency indicators are given in Table 8.13. The overall picture is that they are doing well in terms of comparative efficiency. Among the local counterparts, only the joint-stock enterprises come close to their performance. This is hardly unexpected because *sanzi qiye* are relatively new enterprises, modern in management and technology, and they also enjoy certain preferential treatments. They have little of the nagging problems which plague enterprises in local sectors. It is not surprising that many Shanghai enterprises are eager to attract foreign investments so as to get *sanzi qiye* status.

There are still areas reserved for state enterprises. But that does not prevent *sanzi qiye* from exploiting many opportunities. Being market oriented, they can cater to emerging local demands for materials and consumer durables, and to export demands for labour-intensive manufactures. Though they are somewhat late-starters compared to those in Guangdong, they are in time to fill in the gap in Shanghai as state enterprises are still groping their way around to restructure themselves.

Table 8.12   Growth of *Sanzi qiye*, 1980–1993[a]

Characteristics	1980	1985	1990	1993
Number of establishments	1	14	289	1,247
Persons employed: 10,000 at year-end	0.13	0.73	6.68	24.37
Value of direct exports: RMB100 million	0.04	0.13	18.12	—
Gross value of industrial output: RMB100 million	0.29	3.04	81.86	463.18
Net value of industrial output: RMB100 million	0.13	0.91	23.89	—
Revenue from sales: RMB100 million	0.27	3.11	81.77	454.15
Total profits: RMB100 million	0.09	0.37	8.85	54.34
Total profits-tax: RMB100 million	0.10	0.55	12.02	43.56*
Original value of fixed assets: RMB100 million at year-end	0.11	1.18	40.65	139.08
Total capital: RMB100 million	0.19	1.34	54.23	185.37*

Notes: [a] Includes all independent accounting *sanzi qiye* in operation at the *xiang* level and above. Value at current prices.
　　　　 * 1992 figure.
Sources: *Xin Shanghai gongye tongji ziliao 1949–1990* (see Table 8.1, source), p. 190, table 8.7; *Shanghai tongji nianjian 1993* (see note 6), p. 156, table 3.32; and *Shanghai tongji nianjian 1994* (see note 12), pp. 140–43, table 9.5 and p. 154, table 9.11.

Management and Organization

There are more than ten thousand independent accounting industrial enterprises in Shanghai at the *xiang* level and above. By jurisdiction, some of them are under the central government and others are under the local government (or different levels of the local government); by ownership, they belong to different sectors, as shown in Table 8.11.[12] This complicated pattern has made government management of enterprises exceedingly intricate. It has also certain implications for Shanghai's industrial restructuring.

Management of Enterprises

With the completion of socialist transformation in the mid-1950s, all local industrial enterprises in Shanghai were grouped under 83 specialized

Table 8.13 Efficiency Indicators of Industrial Enterprises by Ownership Sector, 1993[a]

Sector	Capital profits-tax ratio (%)	Cost profits ratio (%)	Value-added ratio (%)	Labour productivity (RMB)	Liquid asset turnover (times)
State enterprises	12.71	6.74	29.07	26,010	1.71
Collective enterprises	11.13	4.38	30.98	13,651	1.85
Joint enterprises	12.96	6.32	29.76	18,319	2.15
Joint-stock enterprises	16.29	14.55	34.15	40,747	1.44
Foreign enterprises	26.81	15.71	32.26	87,919	2.08
Hong Kong, Macau and Taiwan enterprises	12.96	9.71	34.79	38,484	1.59
Others	15.39	10.08	36.54	19,706	2.04

Note: [a] Includes all independent accounting industrial enterprises. The efficiency indicators are defined as:
  1. Capital profits-tax ratio: total realized profits-tax/average liquid assets + average balance of net fixed assets.
  2. Cost profits ratio: total realized profits/total costs.
  3. Value-added ratio: value-added/gross value of output.
  4. Labour productivity: value-added/average number of all persons engaged.
  5. Liquid asset turnover: revenue from sales/average liquid assets.

Source: *Shanghai tongji nianjian 1994* (see note 12), pp. 144–45, table 9.6 and pp. 267–68.

corporations along industrial lines. Some corporations and enterprises were consolidated later, resulting in the formation of some large enterprises which became the backbone of Shanghai's industrial sector.

The primary function of these specialized corporations was administrative. They supervised, co-ordinated and, when deemed necessary, reorganized enterprises which were run by appointed managers. The development of the respective industries was also their responsibility. During the early 1960s, some enterprises were put directly under the respective ministries of the central government but later, during the Cultural Revolution, most were decentralized back to Shanghai's jurisdiction under the specialized corporations. Inside the municipality of Shanghai, however, various city districts and *xian*'s retained certain powers over the industrial enterprises within their own territories. This resulted in a very complex network of *tiao kuai guanxi* 條塊關係 (vertical and horizontal relations), which was further strengthened by the system of contracted taxation.

Enterprise Reforms

Like elsewhere in China, reform of Shanghai's industrial sector started at the enterprise level. During the first few years, enterprises were given more autonomy to manage their daily operation. An economic responsibility system was put in place where benefits and perfomance were linked together. The profit retainment scheme allowed enterprises to keep a certain percentage of their profits in funds for factory improvement, welfare and bonuses for workers. Up-delivery of profits was gradually replaced by tax payments. But these were still all within the parameters of an essentially command economy.

It was around the mid-1980s that enterprises were urged to assume the role of an "independent commodity producer." That is to say, they had to be run like business concerns and deal in the market for inputs and outputs. With the introduction of the contract system, essentially all enterprises were contracted out by the late 1980s.

For some enterprises, this new "freedom" was not all that welcome. In the past, they operated like factories that just filled orders with assigned inputs from the Plan. They did not have to worry about sales because they would be taken care of by the commercial units of the state. Now they are being exposed to the vicissitudes of a market economy to which they are not accustomed. But as long as they are in the public sector, the government has to bail them out when they are incurring losses. Moreover, a state enterprise is also like a "society" in that it is obliged to take care of the housing, medical and retirement needs of its workers and their families. This constitutes a heavy drain on the resources of the enterprises, especially the larger and older ones.

Just like industrial restructuring, enterprise reforms through changes in the internal operation mechanism have to be accompanied by corresponding changes in the external environment. The concentration of state enterprises as well as the huge population of Shanghai have certainly made enterprise reform very complicated, especially when China has repeatedly reconfirmed the importance of large and medium-sized state enterprises in her socialist economy.

Horizontal Economic Linkages

As a legacy of the days of the Cultural Revolution, many enterprises in Shanghai were self-sufficient regardless of their sizes, known as *da er quan, xiao er quan* 大而全，小而全 (large and complete, small and complete), which is contrary to the principle of specialization. In July 1980, the State Council passed a resolution[13] to promote *jingji lianhe* 經濟聯合 (economic linkages) among enterprises in order to break down regional and industrial segmentation. It was aimed at industrial restructuring through better co-ordination and specialization. Linkages were to be voluntary and mutually beneficial, established not by administrative orders, and not subject to industrial, regional, ownership and jurisdictional restrictions. But the "ownership, jurisdictional and fiscal relations" of the parties involved were not to be changed at will. This has come to be known as the policy of *san bu bian* 三不變 (no change in three aspects).

In March 1986, the State Council promulgated regulations on further promoting *hengxiang lianhe* 橫向聯合 (horizontal linkages) so as to break down *tiao kuai fenge* 條塊分割 (vertical and horizontal segmentation) and to separate state and enterprise functions.[14] By the end of 1986, more than two thousand horizontal linkages involving Shanghai's industrial enterprises, under a great variety of arrangements ranging from simple technical co-operations, joint productions to joint ventures and mergers were reported.[15] Although in theory enterprises should act on their own, many linkages were in fact arranged. The Shanghai government took to rationalize its industries by administrative match-making. But under the *san bu bian* policy, cross-regional and cross-industrial linkages were loose and temporary, since close and permanent linkages could only involve enterprises within the same industry in Shanghai. This has actually strengthened the existing *tiao kuai guanxi* and the hold of the administrative corporations on its enterprises.

In a move to separate business operations from ownership, the State Council ordered the abolition of the administrative corporations and allowed large industrial combinations *dan lie* 單列 (treated as one single enterprise) in the state plan. Shanghai reorganized its administrative corporations into business corporations along industry lines. Some of them were called *jituan* 集團 (groups). These corporations are supervised by the State Property Management Bureau and the Industry Bureau, both under the Shanghai municipal government. Local control is as strong as ever.

Enterprise Groups

In December 1987, the State System Reform Commission and the State Economic Commission expressed their opinions on the formation of *qiye jituan* 企業集團 (enterprise groups). The voluntary principle was re-asserted. In addition, enterprise groups were to enhance competition, prevent monopoly and break down vertical and horizontal segmentation. A group was to be a multi-level organization, its core having legal person status with autonomous operation and independent accounting, and was to be responsible for its own profit and loss. It was also allowed to experiment with the joint-stock system.[16] Further provisions were announced in the following years.[17]

The central government's repeated concern over economic segmentation reveals the fact that in China's current economic reform, legislation is falling behind actual developments. In some ways, the formation of cross-region and cross-industry enterprise groups should loosen the grip of the *tiao kuai* authorities over their enterprises, but decentralized power has furnished local authorities with ample counter-measures to protect their own interests. The issue of enterprise groups is just one aspect in this power game.

There are more than 130 enterprise groups in Shanghai, and many of its industrial corporations are so named. Three basic types of organizational structure can be identified. First is the *jinmi xing* 緊密型 (closed type) which has legal person status with assets consisting of all assets of the participating enterprises. In the extreme case, it is a merger, but this occurs only rarely. Planning, management and operation are unified, and there is *dan lie*. But very often participating enterprises retain their legal person status and maintain only contract relations with the group in operation.

Second is the *ban jinmi xing* 半緊密型 (semi-closed type) in which all enterprises keep their legal person status and assets. Usually the "group" only refers to new joint ventures which make investments, co-ordinate plans and render services to its member enterprises.

Third is the *songsan xing* 鬆散型 (loose type) in which all enterprises maintain their independence. Transactions between enterprises and the group are by agreement, meaning that linkage is only a longer term and more stable business connection.[18]

In fact, most enterprise groups have all the ingredients of the three types, with a core of enterprises in the inner circle and numerous enterprises in the outer layers. The core is made up of local enterprises in the same industry. Since enterprises are linked together mainly by business connections rather than by asset control and, in some cases, groups can even overlap, operation of the group is more like a Japanese *keiretsu* than like a Western-style holding company.

As Shanghai's enterprise groups are locally based and formed along industry lines, needless to say, there is strong regionalism and self-centredness. They help industrial rationalization, restructuring and the building up of monopolistic power locally, yet much is to be desired in promoting cross-regional and cross-industry integration within the broader context of China. But this problem is not limited to Shanghai. As long as there are *tiao tiao kuai kuai* 條條塊塊 , the formation of enterprise groups will have to obtain the approval of a complex network of local authorities. Since every unit tends to take steps to safeguard its own interests, hard bargaining and drawn-out negotiations are inevitable. This explains why the integration of enterprises is much more difficult than the expansion of existing enterprises or the setting up of new ones.

The development of enterprise groups has inevitably caused concern about the concentration of economic power, especially when some gigantic industrial enterprises are moving into such areas as finance, trading, real estate development, and so on. By international standards, however, Shanghai's enterprise groups are still very small. Their healthy development depends very much on further reforms and the opening up of markets for more national and international competition.

Concluding Remarks

In China, Shanghai has every reason to be proud of its industrial tradition which dates back to early this century. With further developments after 1949, it has a high concentration of industries, research facilities, technical personnel and skilled workers. However, many of its industrial enterprises were built under a command economy and some have become obsolete. They must be renovated and restructured to meet the challenges of the new environment of a socialist market economy. But many accompanying reforms are needed to overcome wider system constraints for a smooth transition.

In the longer run, there is a more basic consideration for Shanghai's future industrial development. Traditionally, Shanghai was not only renowned for its industries, it was also a commercial and financial centre. Under the current policy of reform and opening, Shanghai is making every effort to resume its glamour as an all-round economic centre. Indeed, it has all the qualifications to be successful. But in so doing, Shanghai must consider its comparative advantage in balancing its various sectors and charting the future course of its industrial development.

Notes

1. See Shanghaishi tongjiju 上海市統計局 (ed.), *Shanghai tongji nianjian 1995* 上海統計年鑑 1995 (Statistical Yearbook of Shanghai 1995) (Beijing: Zhongguo tongji chubanshe 中國統計出版社, 1995), pp. 13, 15.

2. Generally speaking, light industries are those producing consumer goods and heavy industries are those producing capital goods. Since the 1960s, there has been considerable year-to-year fluctuation in the ratio between light and heavy industrial output. Adjustments are usually made to correct the imbalance caused by over-investment in one way or the other.

3. This process is called "the movement away from agriculture" by Simon Kuznets which is widely observed in the process of industrialization. For the general pattern of relationship between economic development and structural change, see his *Modern Economic Growth: Rate, Structure and Spread* (New Haven: Yale University Press, 1966), especially chapter 6.

4. This is also discussed in Simon Kuznets's *Modern Economic Growth* (see note 3).

5. There have been several reorganizations (mergers) in the ensuing years leading to fluctuations in the number of state enterprises. See Shanghaishi jingji weiyuanhui 上海市經濟委員會 (ed.), *Shanghai gongye sishi nian 1949–1989* 上海工業四十年 1949–1989 (Shanghai Industries in Forty Years 1949–1989) (Shanghai: Sanlian shudian 三聯書店, 1990).

6. Amazingly, almost half of these *cun*-operated enterprises are classified under "heavy industries," and their major manufactures are fabricated metal products, electrical machinery, machinery, chemicals, textiles and clothing. In 1993, their gross value of industrial output amounted to RMB321 hundred million, compared to RMB435 hundred million of all *xiang*-operated enterprises, and RMB473 hundred million of all *sanzi qiye*. See Shanghaishi tongjiju (ed.), *Shanghai tongji nianjian 1993* 上海統計年鑑 1993 (Statistical Yearbook of Shanghai 1993) (Beijing: Zhongguo tongji chubanshe, 1993), p. 306, table 9.10.

7. This is a common phenomenon in Guangdong. See Lau Pui-king, "Industry and Trade" in *Guangdong: Survey of a Province Undergoing Rapid Change* edited by Y. M. Yeung and David K. Y. Chu (Hong Kong: The Chinese University Press, 1994), pp. 116–36.

8. For a detailed description of Shanghai's industrial policy from 1949 to 1978, see, for instance, Shanghaishi jingji xuehui 上海市經濟學會 (ed.), *Kaifa, kaibu, kaifang ── Shanghai jingji fazhan zonglun* 開發，開埠，開放 ── 上海經濟發展縱論 (Development, Treaty Port and Openness ── A Historical Account of Shanghai's Economic Development) (Beijing: Zhongguo guangbo dianshi chubanshe 中國廣播電視出版社, 1992), part 2.

9. Quanmin suoyouzhi gongye qiye zhuanhuan jingying jizhi tiaoli 全民所有制

工業企業轉換經營機制條例 (Regulations on Changing the Operation Mechanism of the State-owned Industrial Enterprises). Details of these regulations can be found in Zhonggong zhongyang xuanchuanbu 中共中央宣傳部 (Propaganda Department of the Chinese Communist Party Central Committee), Guojia jingji tizhi gaige weiyuanhui 國家經濟體制改革委員會 (State Commission for Restructuring Economy) and Sifabu 司法部 (Ministry of Justice) (eds.), *Quanmin suoyouzhi gongye qiye zhuanhuan jingying jizhi tiaoli jianghua*《〈全民所有制工業企業轉換經營機制條例〉講話》 (Talks on Regulations on Changing the Operation Mechanism of the State-owned Industrial Enterprises) (Beijing: Gaige chubanshe 改革出版社, 1992), pp. 172–97.

10. In 1992, the average size of enterprises in the state sector was 836 persons, the collective sector was 160 and the *sanzi qiye* sector was 232 (calculated from figures in *Shanghai tongji nianjian 1993*), pp. 127–30, table 3.18 and p. 156, table 3.32.

11. Shanghai figures are for 1992, see *Shanghai tongji nianjian 1993* (see note 6), table 9.11. Guangdong figures are for 1990, see Lau Pui-king, "Industry and Trade" (see note 7), pp. 131–34.

12. Of the 10,254 independent accounting industrial enterprises in 1993, 2,173 were *guoyou* 國有 (state-owned). The rest were *jiti suoyou* 集體所有 (collectively owned), *sanzi qiye*, joint-stock, etc. But according to jurisdiction, there were only 157 *zhongyang qiye* 中央企業 (central enterprises) and the rest were all *difang qiye* 地方企業 (local enterprises). See Shanghaishi tongjiju (ed.), *Shanghai tongji nianjian 1994* 上海統計年鑑 1994 (Statistical Yearbook of Shanghai 1994) (Beijing: Zhongguo tongji chubanshe, 1994), table 9.5. This means in addition to collective and other enterprises, the municipal government has jurisdiction over the bulk of state-owned enterprises as a result of decentralization.

13. Guanyu tuidong jingji lianhe de zanxing guiding 關於推動經濟聯合的暫行規定 (Tentative Regulations on Promoting Economic Linkages). Details of these regulations can be found in Shanghaishi qiye guanli xiehui 上海市企業管理協會 (ed.) *Qiye jituan wenti yu shijian* 企業集團問題與實踐 (Problems and Practice of Enterprise Groups) (Shanghai: Shanghaishi qiye guanli xiehui, 1987), pp. 239–42.

14. Guanyu jinyibu tuidong hengxiang jingji lianhe ruogan wenti de guiding 關於進一步推動橫向經濟聯合若干問題的規定 (Regulations on Some Issues in Further Promoting Horizontal Economic Linkages). Details of these regulations can be found in *Qiye jituan wenti yu shijian* (see note 13), pp. 256–64.

15. See Fudan daxue jingji yanjiu zhongxin 復旦大學經濟研究中心, *Qiye gaige yu fazhan xinlu — Shanghai gongye qiye hengxiang lianhe diaocha baogao ji* 企業改革與發展新路 —— 上海工業企業橫向聯合調查報告集 (New Road to

Enterprise Reform and Development — Survey Reports on the Horizontal Linkage of Shanghai's Industrial Enterprises) (Shanghai: Fudan daxue chubanshe 復旦大學出版社, 1988). This book is based on a survey of Shanghai's industrial enterprises with discussions on various issues relating to horizontal linkages and some case studies.

16. Guanyu zujian he fazhan qiye jituan de jidian yijian 關於組建和發展企業集團的幾點意見 (Some Opinions on Establishing and Developing Enterprise Groups). Details can be found in Guojia jihua weiyuanhui diqu jingji si 國家計劃委員會地區經濟司 and Zhongguo qiye guanli peixun zhongxin 中國企業管理培訓中心 (eds.), *Qiye jituan de zuji yu fazhan* 企業集團的組織與發展 (Organization and Development of Enterprise Groups) (Beijing: Kexue jishu wenxian chubanshe 科學技術文獻出版社, 1990), pp. 388-92.

17. For instance, Guanyu qiye jianbing de zanxing banfa 關於企業兼併的暫行辦法 in 1989 (details in *Qiye jituan de zuji yu fazhan*, see note 16), pp. 393-97; and Qiye jituan zujian yu guanli zanxing banfa 企業集團組建與管理暫行辦法 in 1993, see Jin Quanxiang 金銓香, *Woguo qiye jituan de xianzhuang ji chulu* 我國企業集團的現狀及出路 (The Present and Future of Our Country's Enterprise Groups), mimeo., 1993.

18. See Dai Jinde 戴金德 and Li Gengchun 李更春, Shanghaishi qiye guanli xuehui 上海市企業管理學會 (eds.), *Shanghai qiye jituan — jianli yu fazhan* 上海企業集團 — 建立與發展 (Shanghai Enterprise Groups — Establishment and Development) (Shanghai: Kexue puji chubanshe 科學普及出版社, 1988), pp. 45-58.

9

Industrial Location

Rupert Hodder

The Pattern of Industrial Location

Many commentators have noted the chaotic and fragmented distribution of industrial land use in Shanghai.[1] At a descriptive, impressionistic level, there is a general lack of distinctiveness between one part of the city and another. This is not to suggest that distinctive areas cannot be identified. Parts of Huangpu 黃浦 clearly exhibit administrative, financial and commercial functions; parts of Wusong 吳淞 are dominated by iron and steel works; and parts of Xuhui 徐匯 seem to contain nothing but residential estates. In general, however, the mixture of houses, apartment buildings, offices, factories and shops appears to have been thrown down almost at random. One part of the city merges with another, and the city with the suburbs, creating a landscape of monotonous confusion.

Huangpu, for instance, contains over 500 industrial enterprises — mostly handicraft and light industrial neighbourhood enterprises — packed in among office buildings, houses, factories and shops. To the north, Huangpu merges with Hongkou 虹口 and Yangpu 楊浦 where, to the east of the latter district, factories and workers' estates and even farmers' houses are jumbled together. Just to the south of Wujiaochang 五角場 in northern Yangpu, workers' estates predominate, interspersed with an occasional factory. Closer to Baoshan 寶山 county, fields of vegetables begin to appear in between the factories and residential estates; and in the tongue of Baoshan county lying between the main body of the city proper and Wusong, the landscape is the same jumble of estates, factories, houses and vegetable fields. A little to the south of Wusong, steel works and a large railway complex rise out of patches of wheat and vegetables dotted with the familiar clusters of farmers' houses. In Wusong district, there are scattered fields of wheat and vegetables among workers' estates, a variety of factories, and an import–export complex. All this only gradually merges into an area dominated by steel-smelting and workers' estates. But even this district is quickly replaced by a confusion of factories and residential estates which, in turn, merge into the Baoshan industrial quarter — itself just a continuation of all that has gone before.

The same functional confusion is found in every direction. The first impression of Minhang 閔行 , if approached from the south across the Huangpu River, is that of a large industrial settlement. Yet the district also comprises large expanses of vegetable fields, dotted with farmers' houses and islands of factories and workers' estates. North-east of Minhang lies Wujing 吳涇 which, like Minhang, is little more than a collection of fields, workers' estates, factories and farmers' houses. To the north of Wujing, towards Gangkou 港口 , the factories and houses gradually become more numerous and closely grouped so that Gangkou merges imperceptibly with the city proper. Even after entering the main body of the city, there are large expanses of vegetable fields dotted with clusters of houses and apartment blocks. It is not before another 2–3 km, after having entered Xuhui and still heading north, that the narrow streets make it clear that the city proper has at last been reached.

Although Xuhui may be characterized as a high-grade residential area, where most of the city's leading politicians and administrators live, there are many factories mixed in among the residential estates; and, lying on the south–western edge of Xuhui, is the Caohejing 漕河涇 industrial quarter. Once part of Shanghai county, this industrial quarter, like most of the industrial districts established after 1949 around what was then the outskirts of the city proper, was gradually absorbed into the main body of the city, and was later incorporated into the urban districts. Approaching this quarter, the plan of the buildings and roads becomes more expansive. Caohejing itself is a mixture of houses, apartment buildings and factories, some still surrounded by large vegetable plots.[2]

These impressionistic observations indicate that the chaotic and fragmented use of land in and around the city proper is not simply an occasional, local aberration, but rather is a general feature of the city's past and present development. The chaotic use of land applies not just to those areas already described, but to all parts of the city; and this impression is confirmed by the still rather limited cartographic information available on the overall pattern of land use in the main body of the city. Figure 9.1 is a simplified version of the official map, but it clearly indicates the fragmented pattern of land used for industrial purposes in the city proper. Figure 9.2, which shows details of the location of specific industries in the city proper, provides further evidence of their chaotic distribution.

More specific and detailed evidence of this phenomenon may also be found in the literature which examines the logistical problems faced by Shanghai's industries. The shortage of space and the fragmentation of industrial land use are said to have made the co-ordinated and ordered planning of industry, housing, commerce and transport all but impossible. And certainly, whatever the difficulties in separating cause from effect, the shortage of land and its fragmentation, combined with congestion, multi-occupancy, the duplication of activities, and the high cost and inefficiency of transport impose severe constraints on industrial performance, and

Figure 9.1   Land Use in Shanghai

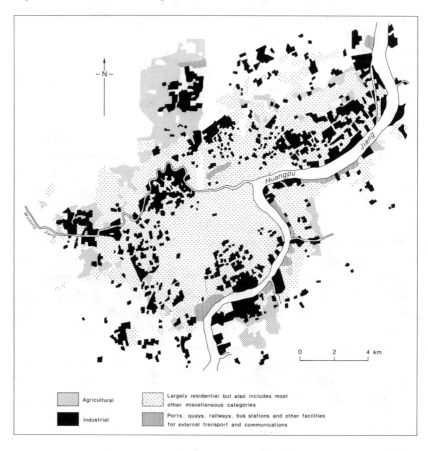

Source: Adapted from R.N.W. Hodder, "China's Industry — Horizontal Linkages in
            Shanghai" (see note 27).

illustrate only too clearly the urgent need for a policy directed at a more
rational pattern of industrial location. Fragmentation may be of little consequence for some industries, such as handicrafts; but for others it has
created a severe disjunction between production activities.

A good example of this is the iron and steel industry. The Metallurgical Bureau of Shanghai has a total of 28 steel works and mills. But if 19
separate branch factories and workshops, 45 storehouses, and numerous
hired lots are included, then there are more than 110 sites scattered
throughout the city. Similar descriptions can even be made of individual

Figure 9.2 The Location of Specific Industries in the City Proper

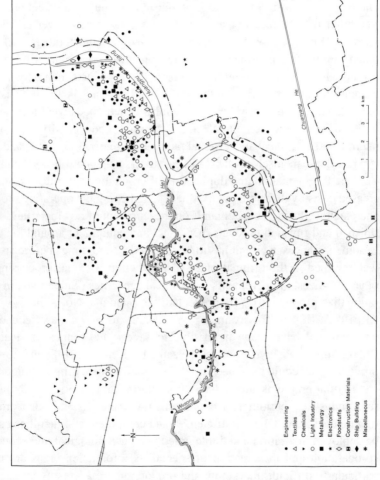

Engineering •
Textiles △
Chemicals ▶
Light Industry ○
Metallurgy ■
Electronics ✳
Foodstuffs ◇
Construction Materials ⊞
Ship Building ◆
Miscellaneous ✴

Source: Adapted from R.N.W. Hodder, "The Shanghai Municipality, 1978–1987" (see note 1).

plants. The Shanghai Eighth Steel Works has its 4 workshops in 4 separate locations in 2 urban districts; and another 3 storehouses are situated in 3 different locations in 2 suburban counties. So, too, the workshops and storehouses of the Xinhu Steel Works are located in 6 separate locations.[3] And of the three main steel-producing works (Factories 1, 3 and 5), only Factory Number 3 reportedly had a high processing rate (just over 86%) — that is, it used most of the steel it produced to manufacture steel products. The other two Factories (1 and 5), however, had much lower processing rates — 21.6% and 39.5% respectively — as did most other steel pro-ducing units. The intermediate and technical factories, which were con-cerned with processing steel into semi-finished products, had only a small capacity for steel smelting and manufactured only a very limited share of the final steel products. Most of the semi-finished goods were then sent to terminal factories which manufactured the final products. Moreover, these intermediate, technical and terminal factories were generally small and scat-tered and were themselves often physically broken up into still smaller units.[4]

The fragmentation and duplication of production activities greatly in-creased costs by disrupting work flows, lengthening the operating process, and placing considerable demands on the shipment of raw materials, semi-finished and finished products, personnel and equipment around the city.[5] In some instances, a circuit has to be repeated several times before an item was returned to the original place of production for final processing. In other instances, improvements in technical capacities (which may, in turn, rationalize production) were prevented: the Shanghai No. 2 Steel Factory (上海第二鋼鐵廠), for example, was unable to adopt new technology which would have made it possible to save 4,000 tonnes of steel and RMB2 million each year and, at the same time, manufacture an improved product which could have been used for superior processing techniques.

Similar problems attend the wide scattering and chaotic distribution of rural industries: buildings, access roads, raw materials and other produc-tion inputs cannot be used efficiently, and equipment and facilities cannot be deployed in a rational and integrated way; technological and economic co-operation and the creation of specialized production areas are made particularly difficult; marketing and production are adversely affected by an inadequate flow of information; and the delivery of electricty, water and communications is made both difficult and expensive. *Xiangzhen* 鄉鎮 (township and village) industries must also face direct competition for land with the agricultural sector and, predictably, have frequently been charged with encroaching upon too much cultivable land. By 1990, they occupied around 100,000 *mu*, and were absorbing more sites at a rate of around 6,200 *mu* each year — figures which reflect their growing importance in the local economy, for by 1990, they produced some 10% of the municipality's total industrial output value.[6] At the same time, the demand for land for all types of construction has increased rapidly: urban districts have been expanding, suburban settlements have been growing, and farmers, though dwindling in number, have been spending more of their growing wealth on the construction of new houses.

Certainly there have been attempts to bring a more rational pattern and structure to Shanghai's industries. Indeed, since 1949, there has been a gradual outward expansion of industries into satellite towns and some specialization has occurred. Nevertheless, there has been a tendency for Shanghai's industries to concentrate in, or close to, those industrial areas established between 1846 and 1949. In the late 1980s Nanshi 南市 , Huangpu, Luwan 盧灣 , Jing'an 靜安 and Yangpu all of which correspond roughly with territorial expansion before 1949 — contained just over 30% of all industrial enterprises operating within the municipality and accounted for nearly 50% of the municipality's total industrial output value; and many of Shanghai's industrial enterprises were said to be using old equipment and operating in buildings constructed before 1949.[7]

One writer, elaborating on these observations, identifies four major zones: the central core, the inner ring, the outer ring and the satellite industrial centres (Figure 9.3). The relative industrial significance of the first three zones in the City Area is given in Table 9.1. As expected, the core area is now the least important and the inner ring is easily the most important in terms of the various criteria set out in the table, resulting in what has been described as the "hole in the doughnut" pattern. The core area is a lively commercial centre, but it also contains over 1,000 industrial enterprises. Most of these are small-scale "flatted factories" and "neighbourhood workshops"; they may also be found in the same buildings as business, commercial and office units; and many are split among different locations. Just outside this commercial centre lie 70 industrial blocks and some 3,000 other individual industrial sites which, taken together, form a ring with a radius of 6–10 km encircling the core area (Figure 9.3). This inner ring contains well over three times as many industrial enterprises, most of which are large or middle-scale engineering, chemical, textile and metallurgical industries, so that the contribution of this ring to total industrial output value is some ten times that of the core area. There is also little multi-occupancy and a much greater concentration of industries:

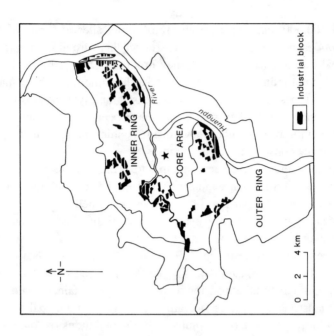

Figure 9.3   Four Major Industrial Zones in Shanghai

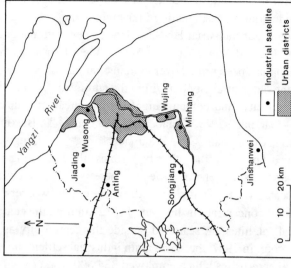

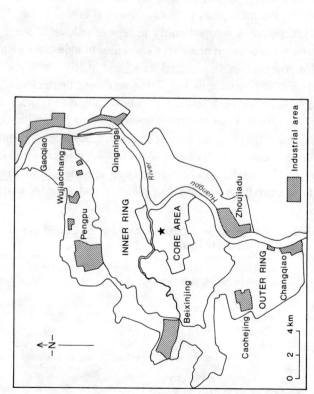

Source: Adapted from Shen Yufang, "Industrial Development in Shanghai Municipality since 1978" (see note 1), and R.N.W. Hodder, "The Shanghai Municipality, 1978–1987" (see note 1).

about one-fifth of the industrial enterprises in this inner ring are located
within the industrial blocks, creating four highly compact industrial areas
coincident with four industrial land-use density peaks in Yangpu, Zhabei
閘北 , Putuo 普陀 and Xuhui–Luwan.[8] Within these four areas, more than
30% of the land has been turned over to industrial purposes. The outer ring
lies outside the old central city but within the administrative jurisdiction of
the new central city, and contains eight distinct areas of industrial concentration — Gaoqiao 高橋 , Wujiaochang, Pengpu 彭浦 , Beixinjing 北新
涇 , Caohejing, Changqiao 長橋 , Zhoujiadu 周家渡 and Qingningsi 慶寧
寺 . Developed later than the other two zones, the outer ring has rather
different characteristics. The main feature here is that all eight industrial
zones are located on selected sites with purpose-built workers' villages.
These industrial concentrations lie some 11–12 km from the central core.

Industrial satellites are scattered outside the central city as far as 70
km from the core. In 1987, the seven main industrial settlements contained
555 industrial enterprises which employed 334,000 workers and produced
around 12% of the municipality's total industrial output value. These industrial centres were developed partly to relieve industrial congestion in
the centre, partly to develop or attract those kinds of industry which are not
suitable for location in the central city, and partly to allow for the
specialization of industrial activities. To some extent, these objectives may
have been realized, for each settlement is now said to be characterized by
particular industries: Gaoqiao is characterized by petrochemicals industries, Taopu 桃浦 by chemical industries, Caohejing by enterprises
manufacturing measuring devices and other electronic equipment, and
Changqiao by the production of construction materials.[9] New industrial
satellites have since been developed or planned, and these include Pudong

Table 9.1   **Industrial Distribution in Different Areas of the Central City of
Shanghai Municipality, 1987**

	Industrial enterprises	Labour & staff (thousand)	Industrial output (RMB billion)	Area covered (km^2)	Industrial land-use (km^2)
Core area	1,059	217.00	4.68	16.50	3.65
Inner ring	3,366	1,423.70	41.81	118.00	27.44
Outer ring	1,178	521.70	14.44	126.00	22.41
Total central	5,603	2,162.40	60.93	260.50	53.50

Source: Adapted from Shen Yufang, "Industrial Development in Shanghai
Municipality since 1978" (see note 1).

浦東, the development of a huge modern steel manufacturing industry at Baoshan, and the Jiefang Cotton Textile Mill.[10]

Explanations

Historical and environmental factors are clearly important considerations in any explanation of the pattern of industrial location in Shanghai. Created a treaty port in 1842 and subsequently divided into a number of concessions, Shanghai rapidly developed an important cotton textile industry, together with shipbuilding, flour milling and the manufacture of silk. Dependent as they were so largely on trade and imported raw materials, these industries were port-oriented and tended to grow up along the waterways. This pattern continued into the present century; and even after 1949, when heavy industry was developed under the new communist government, these new basic industries were still located mainly along the banks of the two main rivers, where water supply and cheap transport were available.[11] Industrial inertia, then, resulting in part from administrative divisions, has certainly played a significant role in the location of industry, and to this extent the industrial location history of Shanghai is little different from that of most large industrial centres throughout the world. The natural environment has also had a strong influence. Textile mills and related operations such as printing and dyeing factories tend to be concentrated along waterways; chemical industries and factories producing dangerous materials have been set up outside the city proper; and many iron and steel factories have been built in the north-east of the municipality away from the city proper to allow the prevailing winds to carry emissions away from the major population concentrations. Similar considerations have been important in the planning and location of the Jinshan Petrochemical Complex.

After 1949, however, the communist government exerted a very powerful and distinctive influence on industrial location. Indeed, it may be suggested that in both the urban and rural areas in Shanghai municipality, the fragmented and chaotic distribution of industry derives primarily from the legacy of the government's policies on self-sufficiency and from the administrative apportionment of land. In its turn, self-sufficiency reflected wider strategic considerations and attempts nationally to reduce the burden on the state system of procurement and distribution; but it was also a natural accompaniment to, and was reinforced by, the organization of the economy into areal administrative units. The concentration of industry in the city proper of Shanghai, then, is in part a consequence of history, but it is also partly a consequence of the function of the municipality as it was conceived in China after 1949. Although the establishment of Shanghai municipality in the late 1950s and the formalization and strengthening of administrative divisions alleviated food shortages and allowed a broad selection of locations for industrial development and new satellite towns, it also restricted the absolute amount of land available to the new municipal authorities. And the emphasis upon self-sufficiency (at both municipal and at lower administrative levels) in food supplies and industrial goods, and upon the creation of self-contained urban settlements, restricted the proportion of land available for different economic activities, creating severe competition for land for agriculture, industry and residential purposes. This tended to lead naturally to a chaotic pattern of land use — a tendency which was reinforced still further by the apportionment of land without the agency of rent or price.[12]

The fragmentation of industrial land use in Shanghai may also derive from vertically structured administrative divisions between economic sectors, bureaux, companies, enterprises and factories. The materials from which Figure 9.1 and Figure 9.2 have been adapted were drawn up at a time (the early 1980s) when most industrial factories and enterprises fell under the administration of companies which were themselves administered by an industrial bureau. The production and manufacture of all other goods were arranged in a similar fashion. In Figure 9.2, it is possible to identify scattered clusters of factories — including a wide range of activities from the manufacture of cotton, wool and chemical fibres to the production of textile goods, the printing and dyeing of textiles, and the manufacture of equipment for the production of textiles — which fell under the textile industrial bureau and its companies. There is, of course, no reason why clusters should not be expected as a matter of chance. However, within the restrictions imposed by such determinants as administrative areal limits, available space, the pattern of industrial activities laid down before 1949, and by certain special requirements such as a good supply of water and transport, each administrative unit has attempted to organize its constituent activities in as compact a manner as possible. The result has been a mosaic of cells of industrial activities, overlapping and fusing together.[13]

Continuing Problems

In the era of reform, although there has been a devolution of authority to lower administrative levels, a weakening of state procurement and distribution, a retraction of planned output, competition for domestic and foreign investment, the ownership system and, therefore, the fundamentals of administrative organization (both areal and vertical) have remained in place, thereby strengthening localism. In other words, the framework of self-sufficiency and the cellular administrative structure have been adopted by competing administrative units: single-minded attention is given to short-term economic targets as a means of protecting or advancing the interests of managers and bureaucrats; and industrial development tends to be focused on existing factories or industrial areas, perpetuating and intensifying existing patterns of land use.[14]

A frequent criticism of recent efforts to bring new life to Shanghai's industries is that bureaucrats and managers have concentrated only on immediate economic goals without taking into account planning difficulties. During the Sixth Five-year Plan (1981–1985), for example, 1,300 new industrial projects and 250 technology-importing projects were implemented within the municipality, most of which were located in the central city. The Planning Commission and the Bureau of Urban Planning — the main bodies responsible for planning in the municipality — attempted to rationalize industrial land use by locating new projects in the suburbs and by gradually moving unsuitable factories out of the central city. For the most part, however, these attempts were unsuccessful for the simple reason that economic development (the "solid" or "first" task) was regarded by the administration as more important than planning (the "soft" or "second" task). Factory managers found it easy to protect their interests by manipulating political contacts against the planning authorities, even if this meant building new projects in unsuitable and overcrowded sites.[15] One example is the Second Shanghai Iron and Steel Works (a plant specializing in the production of wire rods) which applied through the Iron and Steel Industrial Bureau to the Planning Commission for permission to import new equipment from the United States in order to modernize production. The Planning Commission refused to allow the works to develop this new capacity at the old site which was, in the view of the Commission, already too congested: the new plant would have to be set up in Baoshan, closer to its main supplier. The plant managers and their administrative overseers, however, would not accept the decision, preferring instead to double capacity on the existing premises. The Industrial Bureau managed to drum up support within the Municipal People's Congress, and then accused the Planning Commission of "bureaucracy" which had "obstructed" the reforms and had "incurred loss through delay." The Congress decided in favour of the Industrial Bureau and instructed the Planning Commission to be more self-critical. Not surprisingly, more new factories and upgraded plants have been developed in the central city of the municipality. Within the four core districts of Huangpu, Nanshi, Luwan and Jing'an, the number of industrial enterprises increased from 1,506 to 1,943 between 1980 and 1984.[16] And during the Seventh Five-year Plan, the agglomeration of industry accelerated: of the 1,520 technology-importing projects completed in the municipality by the late 1980s, the vast majority were sited in, or near, existing enterprises in the central city.[17]

Additional impetus has been given to competition between competing administrative units (and therefore to the intensification of localism) by the introduction of the management responsibility contract system which link workers and staff interests to the success of a factory. Managers have come under increasing pressure to attract more investment and to increase production on existing premises (and thereby raise not only their income but also their own political and social prestige), and to resist attempts to move their factories to new sites, regardless of environmental consequences. New projects have been approved under the guise of "technology transfers," enabling enterprises to replace old equipment in existing sites with new, imported technology. Although many factories have doubled or even trebled output, they have done so without regard to planning or other controls.[18]

In the suburbs, the fragmented and chaotic distribution of rural industrial enterprises has also been exacerbated by shortages of funds and land, forcing rural industrial enterprises to use old and scattered buildings previously used for livestock, crop drying and storage. Here, too, the legacy of self-sufficiency and the cellular administrative structure are key considerations. Although restrictions on *xiangzhen* developments were loosened, the municipal authorities required such industries to "localize" raw materials, production, marketing and sales as part of an attempt to prevent peasants from migrating to urban areas.[19] Moreover, land "ownership" — or, more accurately, administrative jurisdiction — has been apportioned on the basis of areal administrative divisions, such as *xiang* 鄉 or *cun* 村, making it difficult for a *xiangzhen* enterprise to set up operations outside its own areal division.[20]

Solutions

In attempting to solve these problems associated with the characteristics of industrial location in Shanghai, a number of approaches have been adopted since the reforms of 1978. The present discussion emphasizes just four of these.

The first approach has been to increase the area legitimately available for industrial expansion. After 1978, two new urban districts were established — Wusong in 1980 and Minhang in 1982 — bringing the total number of urban districts to twelve, and increasing the total area of the urban districts from 141 sq km to just over 230 sq km. This was later followed by the further expansion of the administrative area of the urban districts to almost 350 sq km. But the municipal area remained the same, so that the area of the suburbs was correspondingly reduced. In these suburbs, existing satellite towns and industrial districts were expanded, and new satellite towns and industrial districts were created or planned.[21] It was suggested that these new satellite towns should be formed by the concentration of *xiangzhen* industries, and by the relocation of industrial enterprises from the urban districts of the city proper. The resulting focal points would comprise groups of related industries — rural and urban — working together in specialized or semi-specialized areas.[22]

It was hoped, then, that the expansion of industrial areas outside the city proper would allow the growth of industries located there and, at the same time, would encourage industries sited inside the city proper to move out. Commercial enterprises and services could be given more room for development, although certain types of industrial enterprises — notably those producing high-grade precision instruments and other advanced industrial goods — could be permitted to remain in the city, but only in specialized industrial areas separated from residential estates. The main centres for the absorption of those industrial enterprises moving out of the city proper would include Wusong and Minhang, the counties of Shanghai, Chuansha 川沙 and Baoshan, and in particular, the outer suburbs and the southern coastal areas.[23]

But perhaps the most striking contemporary example of the extension of industrial land is to be found in Pudong (Figure 9.4). This industrial satellite, which covers some 350 sq km on the east side of the Huangpu River, is explicitly intended to serve as a release valve for the congestion in the city proper and has been designed as a major industrial zone for manufacture of vehicles, vehicle parts and computer components.[24] As Figure 9.4 illustrates, four development zones are being created within Pudong: the Waigaoqiao Free Trade Zone (外高橋保稅區), the Jinqiao Export-processing Zone (金橋出口加工區), the Zhangjiang High-tech Park (張江高科技園區) and the Lujiazui Financial and Trade Zone (陸家嘴金融貿易區).

Figure 9.4   Pudong Development Area

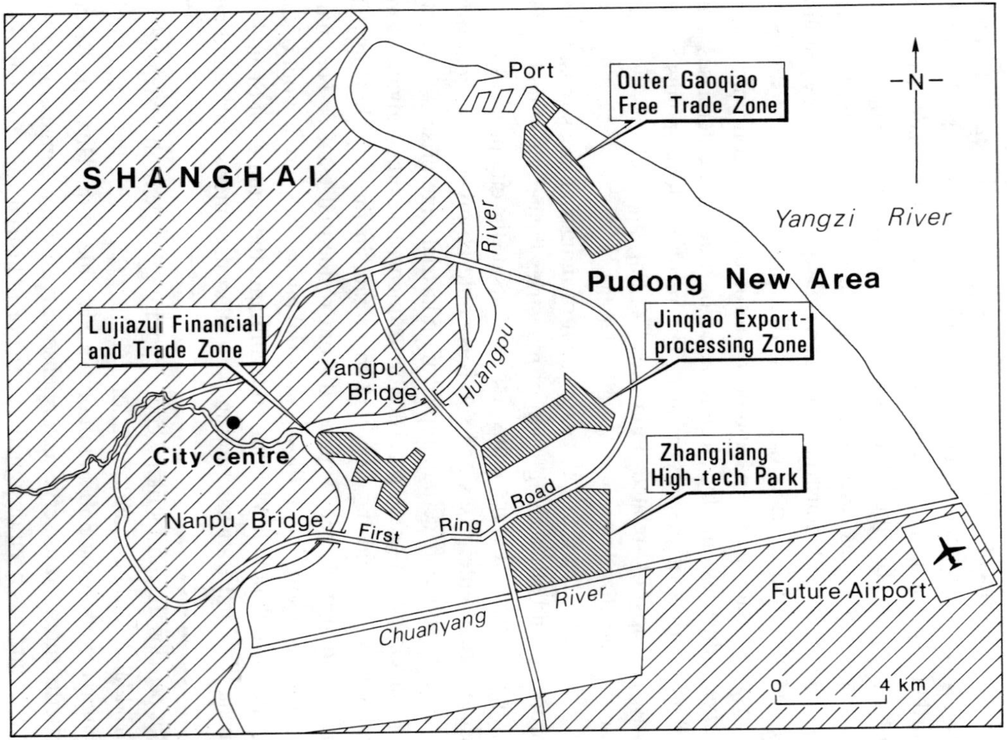

Source: Adapted from H. Sender "Passion for Profit" (see note 23).

Pudong's integration into Shanghai's transport system and the construction or modernization of air and sea ports, combined with the development and construction of export-processing and high-technology industries, is intended, at least in part, to upgrade the quality of Shanghai's industries as a whole, and to alter both the industrial structure and the pattern of industrial location. But there are also, perhaps more important, political and strategic considerations at work. It is significant that the model of Hong Kong is very much in evidence in the building of Pudong. Indeed, it is explicitly claimed that Pudong will become "a socialist Hong Kong," and it is hoped that the benefits flowing from Pudong's development will trickle down throughout the Yangzi River Delta. More widely, the Pudong development programme is a clear signal that China means to continue with its open policy and with the economic reforms, though the strength of southern China and the consolidation of the Shanghai clique in Beijing may strongly influence the emphasis and pace of change. For Shanghai, all this presents a clear opportunity to secure its future as China's major industrial city.

Even so, the present development of Pudong also shows that however logical a development programme to extend industrial development into new land may be, and however admirable the location, this by itself does not guarantee success. Location is clearly not everything. It was anticipated that Pudong would provide low-cost sites in an ideal location for low-cost industrial development. In practice, however, land prices have soared to such an extent that they are already beginning to threaten industrial development there. As one report puts it, "charges to use industrial land have soared to the point where they are equivalent to the fees on prime commercial land ownership in the United States."[25] Land costs in Pudong are already five times higher than in areas to the west of Shanghai and eight times higher than in Tianjin's 天津 Special Economic Zone (SEZ). Inevitably, industry is being drawn away from Pudong to those areas, such as Minhang, where land is cheaper.[26]

The second approach has been to encourage and facilitate the formation of horizontal linkages. The need for horizontal linkages arose partly from changes in the philosophy guiding local and national development, and partly from the shortage of land and its chaotic apportionment — two logistical problems which have imposed severe constraints on the efficiency, growth and rational distribution of industry in China's urban-industrial settlements.

The reform of industry was initially concerned with devolving authority to make decisions to individual enterprises, and thereby with drawing a distinction between the state's administrative organs and industrial enterprises as a precondition for the formation of horizontal linkages among those enterprises. Vertical channels of command through which production was coordinated were to be replaced by linkages between enterprises and factories and between these production units and research institutes and marketing organizations, allowing industrial enterprises to mimic a system of private ownership.[27] In theory, a company was no longer to be thought of as an administrative organ, but rather as a collection of enterprises bound together and into the rest of the economy by horizontal linkages. It was hoped that through these linkages, some cohesion would be brought to fragmented areal administrative units and that the regional specialization of industrial activities would be effected. More specifically, it was argued in Shanghai that the development of horizontal linkages would facilitate the spread of industry from the narrow corridor which centres on a few major urban settlements and transport routes through Ningbo 寧波 and Hangzhou 杭州 to Shanghai and thence to Nanjing 南京 , and that it would then be possible to put an end to the wasteful duplication of industrial activities in separate areal administrative units (both provincial and sub-provincial).[28]

If there can be no integrated transport system without a more rational distribution of land, then there can be no rationalization of the present chaotic and fragmented pattern of industries without a more efficient, integrated and substantial transport system in the municipality: the two are clearly complementary. However, the fact remains that providing adequate transport where industry is widely scattered and where so many activities are duplicated is particularly difficult. And as with the rationalization of industrial activities, difficulties in realizing the development of a transport sector that is integrated, efficient and self-sustaining are rooted in the unitary nature of the economy. Until China is prepared to privatize, material improvements in any sector will have to be investment-led, and an increase in any one sector will mean that another sector is likely to be constrained. Transport in China is inadequate today because for much of the time since 1949 investment has been concentrated in other sectors of the economy. Moreover, the policy of self-sufficiency meant that China could afford to restrict the integration of its transport system. The attempt to create a national, commercially integrated market economy dominated by trade means that a transport system with much greater capacity and flexibility is needed, especially in a great metropolis like Shanghai. The response, however, has been predictable: to demand increases in investment in transport at the expense of other sectors, while paying only lip-service to privatization.

Although the transport system in Shanghai is probably better than in most other parts of China,[29] peripheral roads as well as major thoroughfares frequently experience bottlenecks, and the proportion of sub-standard and antiquated road vehicles is steadily increasing. The railway system is inadequate, the capacity of marshalling yards and stations is unable to meet demand, and engines are dated (20% of the locomotives are steam trains). Airports and port facilities also need improving: docks and berths, for example, are believed to be overloaded by about 40%; and most ocean-going and river vessels are both old and inefficient. According to one authority, both the quantity of freight and number of passengers carried within the municipality will need to increase around threefold by the year 2000 — targets which, if they are to be met, will require a massive programme of investment and marked improvements in the quality and training of personnel. More specifically, the same author argues that the existing airport at Hongqiao 虹橋 must be expanded while another at Pudong is completed; a new railway through Pudong must be constructed; a high speed rail line should be built to Nanjing; the old port must be improved and new port facilities provided; inland waterways will have to be dredged and kept in a better state of repair; and road networks will have to be extended.[30]

As already noted, a number of projects are being implemented. Bridges, tunnels, roads, a metro, a new airport and port are being developed in connection with Pudong. A new railway station at Shanghai East Station has recently opened and a new international port is to be built near Wusong on the lower course of the Huangpu. The outer ring road of Shanghai to Hangzhou is now open for traffic; the new expressway now under construction, linking Hangzhou, Nanjing and Shanghai, is scheduled to be finished next year; and there is a direct expressway from Wusong through the central city to Minhang and Jinshanwei 金山衞.[31] But there is as yet no sense of an effective integrated transport policy; nor does it appear that transport has yet been given a sufficiently high priority. Investment is still both piecemeal and inadequate.

The financial implications of infrastructure development are, of course, immense, and several ways of improving the amount and quality of investment have been suggested.[32] Central and local governments are urged to make more funds available: investment in transport as a proportion of total municipal investment in fixed assets must be raised from current levels of around 5% to more than 25%. Other administrative units, state, collective and private enterprises in other sectors of the economy should be encouraged to invest in transport projects; alternatively a Municipal Construction Fund could be established which could sell shares and bonds to administrative units, enterprises and the general public.[33] More vigorous attempts should be made to attract foreign investment. Banks should be persuaded to give preferential interest rates to units involved in transport projects, and the state should set up a special fund to subsidize interest payments on credit. New fees and taxes could be levied by the municipal government, and the revenues channelled into the development of Shanghai's transport infrastructure. Significantly, it is also suggested that if direct subsidies made by the state to transport units are to be eliminated finally, rates of depreciation should be raised and transport units should be allowed greater freedom to set prices and to establish alternative sources of funding.[34] Most interestingly, however, is the suggestion that even though the opening up of Pudong provides Shanghai with the opportunity to turn itself into China's largest economic and trade centre, and one of Asia's largest international trade and financial centres, the basic goals of Pudong will be difficult to achieve unless the "enterprise management system" is fundamentally changed to allow enterprises to become truly independent market entities[35] — in other words, until industrial enterprises are privatized.

And, indeed, a fourth strategy which remains for the moment largely speculative, but which is nevertheless openly discussed in the literature, is privatization. Arguably, attempts to push enterprises into planned specialized areas, and calls for the reform of the land administration system, for land pricing, and for a more advanced and integrated transport system, are little more than weak palliatives. Moreover, horizontal linkages are in practice a way of asking enterprises to co-operate and yet at the same time to compete with each other, and may thereby only serve to perpetuate elements of China's cellular economy. As one author suggests, it may be that the only effective remedy is to begin by tackling the "circulation system" — that is, the flow and exchange of goods, materials, information and services.[36] Problems with the circulation system find expression in the continuation of areal administrative divisions, including regional blockades; in the sectoral and vertical administrative divisions of economic units, each of which is intent on pursuing its own interests; and in the blurring of a distinction between administration and economic units, and between profits, taxes and investment. While this author does not go so far as to suggest the complete privatization of state and collective enterprises, it is suggested that the growth of private traders must be facilitated, and that administrative interference must be prevented in order to allow enterprises greater freedom to move goods, materials and personnel, to obtain equipment, and to purchase their own buildings and land from which to operate.[37]

Conclusion

Since the reforms of 1978, the more open and liberal attitude of the municipal government to economic growth and industrial development has failed to produce any dramatic change in industrial location of the kind envisaged by the authorities.[38] It is true that a pattern of suburban industrial satellite towns has developed, and that changes in administrative boundaries have, to some extent, helped rationalize the distribution of industry. It is also important to emphasize that the haphazard apportionment of land is not unique to Shanghai nor to other cities in China. Nor should Shanghai be regarded as a special case in the literature on urban industrial growth, in spite of the rather special factors (most especially self-sufficiency and administrative compartmentalization) introduced or institutionalized by the communist government after 1949. But the fragmented and chaotic distribution of industry is a characteristic which has obvious implications for planning, for the efficiency of industry, and for the environment. Perhaps more importantly, it is a characteristic which is symptomatic of fundamental weaknesses in China's industry — weaknesses which must be tackled directly if the goal of rapid and sustained material progress is to be realized.

The central problem is whether or not the authorities in Shanghai municipality, and in Beijing 北京 , are prepared to allow a further and more rapid privatization of industry. If they are not willing to make this leap, then industrial development is likely to remain inhibited by state interference and control and by imbalances.[39] In Shanghai, private industry's share of industrial output by value rose from zero in 1978 to about 9% in 1986, and the collectives' share (largely rural industries) rose from just over 8% to over 23%. Over the same period, the state sector's share fell from over 91% to under 68%.[40] But this is little enough, and within the current ownership structure a more rational locational pattern of industry demands more consideration — and effective government control — of the environment, pollution, residential development, transport, agriculture, commerce and services as well as aggregate industrial production. The essence of planning is balance, and yet this is only rarely of interest to industrialists determined to maximize production. It is within this political framework, then, that the conflict arises most starkly between policies for industrial growth and for the location and relocation of industry. For the time being, the task facing the authorities in Shanghai is how to allow greater economic freedoms to industrial enterprises, while at the same time controlling and directing the location of industry in such a way that the government fulfils its wider environmental, economic and social responsibilities without restricting the city's future industrial growth.

Notes

1. R.N.W. Hodder, "The Shanghai Municipality, 1978–1987: A Study of Commercial, Agricultural and Industrial Change" (Ph.D. dissertation in Geography, University of Leeds, 1989); Christopher Howe (ed.), *Shanghai: Revolution and Development in an Asian Metropolis* (Cambridge: Cambridge University Press, 1981); Shen Yufang, "Industrial Development in Shanghai Municipality since 1978" (Ph.D. dissertation in Geography, University of London, 1995).

2. Hodder, "The Shanghai Municipality, 1978–1987" (see note 1), p. 245.

3. Guo Bailin 郭柏林, "Shanghai jiaoqu xiangzhen gongye jiju buju tantao" 上海郊區鄉鎮工業集聚布局探討 (An Inquiry into the Location of *Xiangzhen* Industry in the Suburbs of Shanghai), *Jingji dili* 經濟地理 (Economic Geography), No. 4, Vol. 13 (1993), pp. 58–63.

4. Hodder, "The Shanghai Municipality, 1978–1987" (see note 1), p. 249.

5. Guo, "Shanghai jiaoqu xiangzhen gongye jiju buju tantao" (see note 3).

6. Ibid.

7. Wei Xinzhen 魏心鎮, *Gongye dili xue* 工業地理學 (Industrial Geography) (Beijing: Beijing daxue chubanshe 北京大學出版社, 1982), pp. 245–46.

8. Shen, "Industrial Development in Shanghai Municipality since 1978" (see note 1), p. 28.

9. Ka-iu Fung, Zhong-min Yan and Yue-min Ning, "Shanghai: China's World City," in *China's Coastal Cities: Catalysts for Modernization*, edited by Yueman Yeung and Xu-wei Hu (Honolulu: University of Hawaii Press, 1992), p. 137.

10. Ibid., p. 131.

11. Yan Zhongmin, "Shanghai: The Growth and Shifting Emphasis of China's Largest City," in *Chinese Cities: The Growth of the Metropolis since 1949*, edited by V.F.C. Sit (Hong Kong: Oxford University Press, 1985), pp. 94–

127.

12. Hodder, "The Shanghai Municipality, 1978–1987" (see note 1), p. 247.

13. Ibid., p. 246.

14. Ibid., p. 247.

15. Shen, "Industrial Development in Shanghai Municipality since 1978" (see note 1), p. 37.

16. Ibid.

17. Ibid.

18. Ibid.

19. Guo, "Shanghai jiaoqu xiangzhen gongye jiju buju tantao" (see note 3).

20. Ibid.

21. Hodder, "The Shanghai Municipality, 1978–1987" (see note 1).

22. Wan Zengwei 萬曾煒, "Chanye da qianyi yu Shanghai chengshi geju de sheji" 產業大遷移與上海城市格局的設計 (Industrial Migration and the Design of Shanghai's Urban Pattern), *Shanghai gaige* 上海改革 (Shanghai Reforms), 5 (1992), p. 14.

23. H. Sender, "Passion for Profit," *Far Eastern Economic Review*, 23 June 1994, pp. 54–58.

24. Ibid.

25. Ibid.

26. Hodder, "The Shanghai Municipality, 1978–1987" (see note 1), p. 251.

27. R.N.W. Hodder, "China's Industry — Horizontal Linkages in Shanghai," *Transactions* (Institute of British Geographers), 15 (1990), pp. 487–503.

28. Ibid.

29. Liu Zhiyuan 劉志遠, "Guanyu Shanghai keji yu jiaotong de tantao" 關於上海科技與交通的探討 (An Inquiry into the Scientific and Technical Rise of Transport in Shanghai), *Jiaotong yunshu jingji, youdian jingji* 交通運輸經濟、郵電經濟 (Transport and Communications Economics), 3 (1994), pp. 6–11. See also Zhao Qingyi 趙青弋, "Shanghai liutong tizhi shuaixian gaige de ruogan sikao" 上海流通體制率先改革的若干思考 (Some Reflections on Shanghai's Circulation System Taking the Lead in Reform), *Chengshi jingji yanjiu* 城市經濟研究 (Urban Economic Research), 3 (1994), p. 79.

30. Ibid.

31. Sender, "Passion for Profit" (see note 23).

32. Liu, "Guanyu Shanghai keji yu jiaotong de tantao" (see note 29); and Zhao, "Shanghai liutong tizhi shuaixian gaige de ruogan sikao" (see note 29).

33. Ibid.

34. Ibid.

35. Ibid.

36. Ibid.

37. Ibid.

38. Guo, "Shanghai jiaoqu xiangzhen gongye jiju buju tantao" (see note 3).

39. R.N.W. Hodder, "State, Collective and Private Industry in China's Evolving Economy," in *China: The Next Decades*, edited by Denis Dwyer (London: Longman, 1994), pp. 116–27; "Exchange and Reform in the Economy of Shanghai Municipality: Socialist Geography under Reform," *Annals of the Association of American Geographers*, 83 (1993), pp. 303–19; and *The Creation of Wealth in China: Domestic Trade and Material Progress in a Communist State* (London: Belhaven, 1993).

40. Shen, "Industrial Development in Shanghai Municipality since 1978" (see note 1); and *Zhonghua gongshang shibao* 中華工商時報, 20 September 1994, p. 5.

10

Investment Environment
Perceptions of Overseas Investors of Foreign-funded Industrial Firms

Nyaw Mee-kau

In China's quest for economic modernization, it has suffered from two severe bottlenecks, namely, the lack of savings for capital formation and foreign exchange constraints. Consequently, China has sought an inflow of foreign capital to increase its capital formation, and to increase its foreign exchange earnings by attracting export-oriented industries to the country, thereby alleviating the two constraints. In addition, foreign investment has facilitated the transfer of technology and management techniques, both badly needed by China in its modernization drive. These have been the main objectives behind China's open policy since 1979.

The success of attracting foreign investment to a country depends to a large extent on the attractiveness of its investment environment. China's open policy has been successful, as evidenced by the large amount of foreign direct investment (FDI)[1] which it has attracted to the country since 1979. The contractual values of FDI amount to about US$302 billion, whereas the realized values were approximately US$99 billion during the 1979–1994 period (Table 10.1). China has become one of the major recipients of FDI in the world. In 1994, it received 17% of the global FDI

Table 10.1   Total Foreign Direct Investment in the PRC, 1979–1994

(Unit: US$ million)

Year	Projects	Contractual values	Realized values
1979–1982	922	4,608	1,771
1983	470	1,731	916
1984	1,856	2,650	1,419
1985	3,073	5,931	1,956
1986	1,498	2,834	2,245
1987	2,233	3,709	2,647
1988	5,945	5,297	3,740
1989	5,779	5,600	3,774
1990	7,273	6,596	3,410
1991	12,978	11,980	4,366
1992	48,764	58,122	11,008
1993	83,437	111,436	27,515
1994	47,549	82,680	33,767
TOTAL	221,777	303,174	98,534

Source: Zhongguo duiwai jingji maoyi hezuobu, *Zhongguo duiwai jingji maoyi nian-jian* bianji weiyuanhui 中國對外經濟貿易合作部《中國對外經濟貿易年鑑》編輯委員會 (ed.), *Zhongguo   duiwai   jingji   maoyi   nianjian* 中國對外經濟貿易年鑑 (Almanac of China's Foreign Economic Relations and Trade) (Beijing: Zhongguo shehui chubanshe 中國社會出版社, various years).

and accounted for one-third of the total FDI in developing countries.[2] From a zero base with no FDI in the country in 1978, this is a truly remarkable record by any standard.

Several special investment areas with different names were established by the Chinese government to attract foreign investment. They include: (1) Special Economic Zones (SEZs): Four SEZs were formally established in 1980, i.e., Shenzhen 深圳, Zhuhai 珠海, Shantou 汕頭 and Xiamen 厦門. Hainan Island (海南島) was designated the fifth SEZ after its elevation to provincial status in 1988. (2) Open Coastal Cities: 14 coastal cities including Shanghai were designated as open coastal cities in 1984.[3] (3) Open Coastal Economic Areas: Pearl River Delta (珠江三角洲), Yangzi River Delta (長江三角洲), Min River Delta (閩江三角洲) were established in 1985. Shandong 山東 and Liaoning 遼寧 were added in 1988 as the fourth Open Coastal Economic Area. (4) Pudong New Area (浦東新區) was established in 1990. (5) Free Trade (or Bonded) Zones: Free trade zones were established in the coastal cities after 1990. As of June 1994, there were 14 such bonded zones.[4] The above-mentioned investment areas offer various investment incentives to attract foreign investment.[5]

Shanghai has been the best-known industrial city in China since the 1930s. In fact, industry is part of the city's culture. After the founding of the PRC in 1949, Shanghai's industrial development accelerated. However, for a long period of time, the city's resources were mobilized to support national economic development which was at a high cost to the city. Most notably, its housing and other infrastructural construction was kept at a low level which was out of step with the city's population and industrial growth. This imbalance gradually changed after Pudong and the Yangzi River Delta (of which Shanghai is a core area) were targeted to attract FDI in recent years. In the initial years of China's open policy, Shanghai lagged behind Guangzhou and Shenzhen in attracting FDI. However, due to the new initiatives to develop Shanghai by the Chinese government, the amount of FDI increased very rapidly in the 1990s in terms of both contractual and realized values (Table 10.2). Shanghai's relative shares of FDI in terms of realized value increased *vis-à-vis* the SEZs and Beijing 北京 in the 1990s (Table 10.3). Contractual foreign investment in Shanghai reached a record of US$10 billion in 1994, surpassing Guangzhou and Shenzhen.[6]

The main objective of this chapter is to investigate how overseas investors in foreign-invested industrial firms perceive the investment environment in Shanghai. Factors affecting their investment decisions will

Table 10.2   Foreign Direct Investment in Shanghai, 1985–1994

(Unit: US$10,000)

Year	Contractual		Realized	
	Project (no.)	Year value	Year value	Accumulated value (year ending)
1985	94	71,080	6,242	10,769
1986	62	29,714	9,750	20,519
1987	26	24,658	21,196	41,715
1988	219	33,328	36,415	78,130
1989	199	35,900	42,212	120,342
1990	203	37,463	17,719	138,061
1991	365	45,001	17,527	155,588
1992	2,012	335,725	125,894	281,482
1993	3,650	701,614	231,762	513,244
1994	547	688,630	—	—

Sources: Shanghaishi duiwai jingji maoyi weiyuanhui, Shanghai *Zhongguo duiwai*
jingji maoyi congshu bianzuan weiyuanhui 上海市對外經濟貿易委員會、上
海《中國對外經濟貿易叢書》編纂委員會 (ed.), *Shanghaishi duiwai jingji*
maoyi nianjian 1994 上海市對外經濟貿易年鑑1994 (Yearbook of Shanghai
Foreign Economic Relations and Trade Statistics 1994) (Shanghai: Sanlian
shudian 三聯書店, 1994); Shanghaishi tongjiju 上海市統計局 (ed.), *Shang-*
hai tongji nianjian 1995 上海統計年鑑 1995 (Statistical Yearbook of Shanghai 1995) (Beijing: Zhongguo tongji chubanshe 中國統計出版社, 1995).

Table 10.3   Shares of Foreign Direct Investment in the PRC by Region, 1979–1993
            (Realized values)

Year	Guangdong %	SEZs %	Shanghai %	Beijing %	China (US$ million)
1979–1989	42.2	20.5	8.1	9.8	15,495
1990	45.0	20.2	5.5	8.5	3,487
1991	44.9	23.9	4.1	7.0	4,366
1992	31.6	10.8	7.0	3.1	11,007
1993	28.7	9.8	8.9	2.6	27,515

Sources: Computed from *Zhongguo duiwai jingji maoyi nianjian*, (see Table 10.1,
            Source), various years.

first be examined, followed by an analysis of how they assess the "hard"
and "soft" investment climate in Shanghai. It will also evaluate various
aspects of the investment climate which need improvement in Shanghai.
The chapter will conclude with a brief discussion of the prospects for
foreign investment in Shanghai.

Methodology and Profile of Sample Firms

The survey method was employed to collect the data needed for analysis. A five-page questionnaire written in Chinese was developed. To ensure that the terminologies and concepts used in the questionnaire were understood by overseas investors, a pilot test was first administered to two overseas investors and a management scholar teaching at Fudan University (復旦大學), Shanghai. A refined questionnaire was prepared after incorporating their comments.

Two hundred foreign-invested industrial firms were selected randomly from the list of firms compiled by the Shanghai Foreign Investment Commission. The survey area covers Pudong New Area, Minhang 閔行, Caohejing 漕河涇 and Hongqiao 虹橋 Development Areas. The author solicited the help of two management scholars at Shanghai's Fudan University who in turn recruited several research assistants to conduct the survey. As Chinese are usually not in the habit of filling out questionnaires, the response rate to mailed questionnaire surveys is usually very low in China. In order to maximize the response rate, face-to-face interviews were conducted at firms close to the city after confirmation of the factory visit by telephone. Firms located in far-away areas, such as the Minhang Development Area, were sent questionnaires by mail. The field and mail surveys were conducted in the last five months of 1994.

A total of 81 firms either agreed to the interview or returned their completed questionnaires by mail. As all 81 completed questionnaires were found to be usable, it represented a response rate of 40.5%, which is considered to be a good response for researchers who are familiar with questionnaire surveys of enterprises, either state-owned or foreign-invested. Those who filled out the questionnaires were mainly the overseas investors themselves or senior managers from the foreign-side who represented the foreign views.

A profile of the 81 sample industrial firms is presented in Table 10.4. The sample comes from a large variety of industry groups, with electronics/electrical products, textiles, garments, building materials and machinery industries accounting for 57.7% of the total sample. As far as modes of foreign investment are concerned, joint ventures were dominant (84.0%) in the sample industries. In our sample data, the capital for the foreign-invested firms came mainly from Hong Kong, the United States, Japan and Taiwan. This mirrors the actual accumulated value of FDI in Shanghai during 1979–1993 as shown in Table 10.5. Thus, the sample firms are quite representative as far as sources of capital are concerned.

As shown in Table 10.4, most of the sample firms started their operations after 1989, notably during the 1992–1994 period. Most large-scale foreign-invested firms in China are not very receptive to requests from questionnaire-type surveys. This is reflected in our sample data where respondents are mainly medium or small in scale, employing less than 500 workers and staff. Only 6.2% of the sample firms (5 in total) were large in size, employing over 500 persons.

Table 10.4   Profile of Sample Industrial Firms (n = 81)

	No. of firms	%
Industry groups		
Electronics/electrical products	20	24.7
Machinery	7	8.6
Chemical	5	6.2
Textiles	10	12.4
Garments	8	9.9
Building & building materials	8	9.9
Food	4	4.9
Printing	2	2.5
Leather products	2	2.5
Others (including watches, telecommunications, plastics, pharmaceuticals, shoes, energy, etc.)	15	18.5
TOTAL	81	100.0
Types of foreign investment		
Wholly foreign-owned	6	7.4
Joint ventures	68	84.0
Co-operative ventures	7	8.6
TOTAL	81	100.0
Source of foreign capital by country of origin		
United States	22	27.2
Japan	14	17.3
Hong Kong	25	30.9
Taiwan	11	13.6
Singapore	2	2.5
Germany	3	3.7
Others	4	4.9
TOTAL	81	100.0
Period operations started		
1984–1988	9	11.1
1989–1991	21	25.9
1992–1994	51	63.0
TOTAL	81	100.0

Table 10.4 *(Cont'd)*

	No. of firms	%
Shares of foreign investors		
< 40%	29	35.8
40% ≤ 50%	26	32.1
50% ≤ 60%	16	19.8
60% ≤ 70%	4	4.9
≥ 70%	6	7.4
TOTAL	81	100.0
Size of firms in terms of no. of employees		
< 50	25	30.9
50 ≤ 100	26	32.1
100 ≤ 500	25	30.9
500 ≤ 1,000	3	3.7
≥ 1,000	2	2.5
TOTAL	81	100.0

Note: Figures may not add to 100% due to rounding.

Table 10.5   Accumulated Value of Foreign Direct Investment in Shanghai (Classified by Country/Area of Origin), 1979–1993

(Unit: US$ million)

	Contractual				Realized	
	Projects	%	Value	%	Value	%
Hong Kong	3,375	48.6	7,002	51.1	2,051	40.0
Macau	85	1.2	237	1.7	50	1.0
Taiwan	1,002	14.4	917	6.7	125	2.5
Japan	637	9.2	1,190	8.7	557	10.9
Thailand	56	0.8	189	1.4	71	1.4
Singapore	182	2.6	371	2.7	111	2.2
Germany	43	0.6	236	1.7	236	4.6
France	34	0.5	54	0.4	31	0.6
Italy	19	0.3	65	0.5	55	1.1
The Netherlands	17	0.3	60	0.4	74	1.5
U.K.	76	1.1	331	2.4	96	1.9
Switzerland	14	0.2	140	1.0	173	3.4
Canada	134	1.9	272	2.0	50	1.0
U.S.A.	865	12.5	1,666	12.2	936	18.3
Australia	82	1.2	53	0.4	14	0.3
Others	318	4.6	922	6.7	505	9.8
TOTAL	6,939	100.0	13,705	100.0	5,135	100.0

Source: *Shanghaishi duiwai jingji maoyi nianjian 1994* (see Table 10.2, Sources).

Motives for Investment in Shanghai

Motives for investment are the reasons given for the investor's behaviour prior to an investment actually takes place. The survey results in Table 10.6 indicate that the top five motivating factors for investment are in the following descending order of rank in terms of frequency mentioned by overseas investors: huge market potential in China, lower wage levels of Shanghai workers, high technical skills of workers, high technological capabilities and low recoupment period of investment. It seems that the huge market potential of China was always in the minds of many overseas investors. Shanghai is strategically located at the mouth of the Yangzi River Delta. In addition, it is the gateway to the East China region. Overseas investors use Shanghai as a springboard to tap the vast market of eastern China.

The wage level for workers and staff is lower in Shanghai than it is in Shenzhen, Guangzhou and other cities in southern China. It is even more attractive when it is compared to the wage levels of Hong Kong, Japan, the United States and Taiwan, the place of origin of most foreign investments in Shanghai. Take Hong Kong as an example. An average worker in Hong Kong could earn about HK$8,000 per month in 1995, which is at least 10 times more than the wage level of his/her counterparts in foreign-invested

Table 10.6 Motives for Investment in Shanghai (n = 81)

Motives/reasons	Frequencies*	Ranking
Huge market potential in China	51	1
Lower wage levels of Shanghai workers	30	2
High technical skills of workers	25	3=
High technological capabilities	25	3=
Low recoupment period of investment	20	5
Being a Shanghainese	17	6
Convenience of transportation	16	7
Low price of raw materials	16	7
Quick access to information	16	7
Sound investment laws and regulations	15	8
Help in developing Shanghai	13	9
High efficiency of administrative bureau	13	9
Good factory facilities	11	10
Good infrastructure	8	11
Ease of raising funds	3	12
Low investment fees	2	13

Note: * Respondents may choose more than one reason.

enterprises in Shanghai. The pay for professional staff in Shanghai's state-owned enterprises is even lower. "Reverse hang of mental workers *vis-à-vis* blue-collar workers" is a common phenomenon in China whereby mental workers (professional staff) generally earn less than skilled workers. This lower pay, coupled with the generally high level of skilled workers in Shanghai, is another major motivating factor for overseas investors to invest in Shanghai. The skilfullness of Shanghai workers can be demonstrated by the fact that although industrial equipment was older in Shanghai than in inland areas in the past, industrial productivity in Shanghai was higher because of its higher labour productivity. The older industrial equipment in Shanghai can be attributed to the low level of reinvestment in the city because China adopted a low depreciation rate policy. Moreover, the nation's industrial policy, in general, favoured lesser developed regions.

Shanghai's technological capability is second only to Beijing in terms of the number of institutes of higher learning and scientific research as well as the actual number of technical personnel, engineers and scientists engaged in research and development. In addition, Shanghai always scores well in the nation-wide competition for scientific and research and development awards organized by the State Science Commission. This factor is conducive to attracting high-tech industries to Shanghai.

It is also interesting to note that another major motive for investing in Shanghai is the low recoupment period of investment. This finding is consistent with a recent survey result which reveals that, among the various locations for joint ventures in China, those in Shanghai scored the highest average rate of return on investment (ROI) (16.2%) over a five-year period (1985–1989). Shenzhen was second at 13.6%.[7]

Other more important motives for investment were as follows: being a Shanghainese, convenience of transportation, quick access to information, sound investment laws and regulations, and help in developing Shanghai. Many pioneer investors in Shanghai are ethnic Shanghainese industrialists from Hong Kong. Like other Chinese, many maintain strong sentimental attachments to their area of origin. In addition, as personal relations are an important element in Chinese culture, Shanghainese investors from overseas can tap their past relationships and familiarity with the area. Their linguistic skills in Shanghainese also help. Their ethnic background may also prompt their desire to help develop Shanghai, although that may not be as strong as the profit motive.

In the 1930s and 1940s, Shanghai was an important financial and trading centre on the western Pacific coast. After 1949, Shanghai's overseas connections were curtailed for many years due to China's self-imposed isolation. Following China's economic reforms and open policy after 1979, Shanghai strengthened its relationships with the rest of the world. Its connections with the outside world, such as transportation links and access to information, are among the best in the country. When overseas investors consider investment in China, convenience in transportation and quick access to information will play a role.

Based on our survey, "sound investment laws and regulations" is another motive for investing in Shanghai, although not as important as other motives. When Zhu Rongji 朱鎔基 was the mayor of Shanghai, he introduced the "one window, one office and one stamp" procedure to simplify the cumbersome bureaucratic red-tape for the approval of overseas investments. Coupled with other economic incentives provided to overseas investors, the city's investment climate has improved. But there are other issues in the "laws and regulations for investment in Shanghai" which remained to be solved. These will be discussed later.

Other motives for investment which are down the list are "good factory facilities," "good infrastructure," "ease of raising funds" and "low investment fees." In view of the low frequencies of these factors, they are not considered to be important motives for investment by overseas investors.

Importance of Environmental Factors for Investment

Table 10.7 presents the survey results as to how overseas investors in Shanghai view the importance of various environmental factors for investment. This portion of the questionnaire was couched in general terms without specifically referring to the situation in Shanghai. However, the results provide useful insights into our assessment of "hard" and "soft" environmental factors for investment in Shanghai which will be discussed later.

The following environmental factors have a mean score of 3.80 or above using a 5-point Likert scale, ranging from 5 (very important) to 1 (unimportant): "good prospects for development," "various incentive policies," "convenience in transportation," "goodwill of collaborative partners," "quick and easy access to information," "efficiency of administrative bureau," "sound business laws and regulations," "access to huge market," "law and order" and "support of government." The factor of

Table 10.7   Importance of Various Environmental Factors for Investment (n = 81)

Environmental factors	Mean score[a]	Standard deviation
Good prospects for development	4.31	0.81
Various incentive policies	4.07	0.95
Convenience in transportation	4.00	0.93
Goodwill of collaborative partners	4.00	1.12
Quick and easy access to information	3.94	1.14
Efficiency of administrative bureau	3.90	0.88
Sound business laws and regulations	3.85	1.09
Access to huge market	3.84	1.02
Law and order	3.83	1.00
Support of government	3.79	1.12
Visibility (known or unknown) of locality	3.72	1.28
Supply of electricity	3.64	1.17
Quality of workers and staff	3.57	1.05
Workers' pay	3.57	1.02
Service of foreign exchange management	3.52	1.07
Strong industrial base	3.47	1.13
Easy access to raw materials	3.42	1.06
Consumption levels of local residents	3.36	1.02
Ease of raising funds	3.11	1.04
Ease of complementarities of industries	3.10	1.07

Note: [a] Respondents were asked to rate on a 5-point scale ranging from 1 to 5:
5 = very important, 4 = important, 3 = neither important nor unimportant, 2 = somewhat unimportant, and 1 = unimportant.

"good prospects for development" has the highest score of 4.31. It seems that overseas investors are looking for long-term prospects in China. This is also consistent with the survey result that "huge market potential" is the most important motive for investment as perceived by overseas investors in Shanghai, given in Table 10.6.

It is also noteworthy that of all the environmental factors for investment as presented in Table 10.7, none has a mean score of less than 3.10 (3.00 being neither important nor unimportant). "Ease of raising funds" and "ease of complementarities of industries" have the lowest mean scores. Given a sample size of 81, the standard deviation as shown in Table 10.7 is considered acceptable.

Assessment of "Hard" Environmental Factors

The survey results of the assessment of "hard" environmental factors for investment as perceived by overseas investors in Shanghai are presented in

Table 10.8, using a 5-point Likert scale, ranging from 5 (highly satisfied) to 1 (highly dissatisfied). The mean score for the overall satisfaction level was 3.52, which indicates that overseas investors are generally satisfied with the "hard" environmental factors in Shanghai. In an earlier survey of the perceptions of Hong Kong investors on the "hard" investment climate in Shanghai conducted by the Shanghai Academy of Social Sciences (SASS) in early 1989, it was found that the overall satisfaction level was rather low. About one-third (31.2%) of the sample firms were "dissatisfied" and 4.5% were "very dissatisfied" based on a sample size of 47 firms.[8] As the SASS survey was conducted in early 1989, our survey results may indicate that there has been a recent improvement in the "hard" investment climate as perceived by overseas investors. The municipal government of Shanghai increased infrastructure investment beginning in the Seventh Five-year Plan (1986–1990).[9]

As far as specific factors are concerned, our survey results show that overseas investors are in general satisfied with the following "hard" environmental factors in Shanghai: human resources, international postal and communication services, transportation links with overseas cities and purchase of necessities. This is consistent with the findings in a survey conducted by Li and Xiao in 1989.[10] In the latter survey, it was found that

Table 10.8   Assessment of "Hard" Environmental Factors for Investment in Shanghai (n = 81)

Environmental factors	Mean score of satisfaction[a]	Standard deviation
Adequacy of human resources	3.91	0.83
International postal and communication services	3.69	0.86
Transportation links with overseas cities	3.59	0.89
Purchase of necessities	3.49	0.70
Supplies of water, electricity and other utilities	3.37	1.00
Urban transportation and communication services	3.35	1.01
Health care conditions	3.30	0.79
Cultural and recreational facilities	3.22	0.86
Development of a raw material market	3.17	0.81
Apartment and housing services	3.05	0.80
Education facilities for children	3.00	0.79
Price of real estate	2.90	0.87
Overall satisfaction level	3.52	0.63

Note: [a] Respondents were asked to rate on a 5-point scale ranging from 1 to 5: 5 = highly satisfied, 4 = satisfied, 3 = neither satisfied nor dissatisfied, 2 = dissatisfied, 1 = highly dissatisfied.

Hong Kong investors were very frustrated with Shanghai's urban transport problem, with 79% rated "dissatisfied" or "very dissatisfied". Our results indicate, however, that some improvements in urban transportation have been made over the last few years. This is also true of cultural and recreational facilities in Shanghai (Table 10.8). But the problems of educational facilities for overseas investors' children in Shanghai remain to be solved.[11] In addition, overseas investors are critical of the high property prices in Shanghai. This has increased their operating costs of investment substantially.

Assessment of "Soft" Environmental Factors for Investment

The substance of "soft" environmental factors for investment is more diversified than that of "hard" environmental factors. The survey results will be analyzed under the following four sub-headings. (1) policy aspects; (2) legal environment aspects; (3) human relations and manpower aspects; and (4) market conditions, administration and other aspects. The survey results show that, on a whole, overseas investors are generally satisfied with the "soft" environmental factors, with a mean score of 3.56 based on a 5-point Likert scale ranging from 1 (highly dissatisfied) to 5 (highly satisfied) (Table 10.9). The overall satisfaction level is slightly higher than that of the "hard" environment.

Policy Aspects

China's foreign investment policy is multi-faceted and relates to various laws, regulations and provisions which have been formulated to change the industrial mix of the country, to effect investment flows to certain designated geographical areas, to target particular forms of investment and to protect the interests of foreign investors. Since 1979, there have been more than 200 laws and regulations introduced which, today, constitute a complex web of regulating mechanisms. Some laws and regulations are applied to the nation as a whole, whereas some cities or areas may formulate supplementary investment policies of their own in conjunction with the laws and regulations at the national level.

The first piece of legislation on foreign investment in China was the law of the PRC on Chinese–Foreign Joint Ventures (hereafter referred to as the "Joint Ventures Law") promulgated by the State Council in July 1979. It is very brief with only 15 articles, and thus lacks substance.

Table 10.9 Assessment of "Soft" Environmental Factors for Investment in Shanghai (n = 81)

Environmental factors	Mean score of satisfaction[a]	Standard deviation
Policy aspects		
Policies on tax incentive schemes	3.51	0.72
Policies on technology transfer	3.46	0.86
Policies on labour wages	3.44	0.77
Policies on customs incentives	3.43	0.59
Continuity of policies and regulations	3.41	0.77
Policies on foreign exchange management	3.37	0.64
Policies on product pricing	3.31	0.62
Purchasing and pricing policies of raw materials	3.30	0.69
Land-leasing policies	3.20	0.60
Legal environmental aspects		
Law and order	3.83	0.72
Protection of investors' interests	3.57	0.87
Comprehensiveness of laws and regulations	3.33	0.77
Execution of laws and regulations by government	3.33	0.75
Human relations and manpower aspects		
Relationships among investment partners	3.99	0.84
Assessment of PRC employees	3.86	0.62
Skill levels of professional/technical staff	3.81	0.69
Level of concern and support by municipal government	3.77	0.74
Skill levels of managerial staff	3.69	0.75
Educational quality of existing workers and staff	3.57	0.70
Appraisal of lower-ranking government officials	3.20	0.79
Market conditions, administration and others		
Conditions of custom services	3.43	0.70
Efficiency of administrative bureaux	3.40	0.75
Development of a labour market for skilled personnel	3.36	0.73
Conditions for fund-raising and loans	3.33	0.70
Interconnectedness of local purchasing organizations	3.20	0.51
Rationality of various fee charging	3.06	0.82
Level of inflation rates	2.68	0.95
Overall satisfaction level	3.56	0.59

Note: [a] Respondents were asked to rate on a 5-point scale ranging from 1 to 5: 5 = highly satisfied, 4 = satisfied, 3 = neither satisfied nor dissatisfied, 2 = dissatisfied, 1 = highly dissatisfied.

Subsequent laws and regulations were passed on income taxes, company registration, labour management, trade-marks, contracts, advertising and various other matters relating to foreign-invested firms. Then, in September 1983, the Chinese government adopted the Regulations for the Implementation of the Law of the PRC on Chinese–Foreign Joint Ventures. This came more than four years after the promulgation of the Joint Ventures Law, but it contained 118 articles which codified and elaborated the 1979 Joint Ventures Law and other laws and regulations that had been issued since 1979. Essentially, the Joint Ventures Law spelled out the following key preferential treatments for EJVs (equity joint ventures): (a) an EJV in SEZs, economic and technological development zones, and Hainan, pays an income tax of only 15%; a new joint venture may be exempt from the income tax in its first two years and allowed a 50% reduction in taxes for the third to fifth years; (b) it is exempt from import duties on imported advanced equipment; (c) it can repatriate abroad all its profits as well as funds it receives upon expiration or early termination of the venture; and (d) its foreign employees can remit all after-tax income abroad.

Although the above investment incentives seemed attractive, foreign investors later found that they ran into a host of problems with the Chinese bureaucracy. It was widely reported in the Hong Kong and overseas media that overseas investors were dismayed by the practice of Chinese officials to levy fees indiscriminately or to make up arbitrary rules. The influential magazine, *Time*, reported that Chinese cadres "often made up taxes, rules and regulations as they went along, rather than following any written policy."[12] These criticisms certainly applied to Shanghai as well. As a result, foreign-invested firms in China found that their profits were eroded by hundreds of unforeseen expenses.

In view of the very negative responses from overseas investors, China acted swiftly to enact the "Provisions of the State Council for the Encouragement of Foreign Investment" (22-article provisions) in October 1986. This was intended to rectify the inadequacies or limitations of past laws and regulations on foreign investment. Furthermore, it provided additional incentives to foreign-invested firms. The "22-article provisions" is definitely one of the most important documents on foreign investment in China. Essentially, the provisions grant strong incentives to both "export-oriented enterprises" and "technology-intensive enterprises" which have priority in allocations for water supply, electricity, transportation and communication equipment. If a "technology-intensive enterprise" is an EJV, the pre-existing tax holiday is extended by an additional three years at half the tax rate.

In addition to the various laws and regulations enacted at the national level, there are at least 35 other laws and regulations that have been adopted by Shanghai Municipality and Pudong New Area at the time of this writing.[13] Usually, additional economic incentives are given to foreign-invested enterprises in Shanghai and the Pudong New Development Area. For example, it is stipulated that the newly-emerging technology-intensive enterprises located in Caohejing High-tech Park "shall be exempt, for five years beginning with 1990, from a construction tax on its new production and business buildings which are built with its own funds for the purpose of technical research and development."[14]

Our survey results in Table 10.9 indicate that overseas investors in Shanghai are more satisfied with policies for tax incentive schemes, technology transfer and customs incentives than purchasing and pricing policies of raw materials and land-leasing policies. Because of the dual-price system currently practised in China, foreign-invested firms have difficulties obtaining certain materials or resources which are still under central allocation. For a few scarce resources such as iron and steel, coal and cement, the gap between the administered price and the free market price is quite wide. Foreign-invested enterprises have to purchase these products in the open domestic market at much higher market prices which, in their view, puts them at a disadvantaged competitive position *vis-à-vis* the state-owned enterprises. One positive note is that there is little intervention by the state bureaucracy as far as the pricing of products produced by foreign-invested enterprise is concerned.

The land-leasing policies have the lowest satisfaction score among the various policy environmental factors. Land costs in Shanghai are much higher than other cities. The land costs in Pudong, for example, are "five times higher than in areas to the west of Shanghai and eight times higher than in Tianjin."[15] In addition, how land is allocated for industrial use is sometimes ambiguous under the decentralized system where conflicts between the district councils and the municipality can mean long delays or the scraping of projects.

Legal Environment Aspects

One aspect which overseas investors often criticize is the weak legal framework pertaining to foreign investment in China. Although there are over 200 such rules and regulations, oftentimes they are not fully enforced. Most Chinese cadres cannot grasp the true meaning of the law as they were not exposed to the business legal environment prevailing in the outside world prior to 1979. They are learning, but their behaviour is conditioned by their socialist background. Therefore, it is not totally surprising to find that "execution of laws and regulations" has the lowest score (3.33) among the four legal environmental factors in our survey results.

Overseas investors are most satisfied with the "law and order" in Shanghai, with an average score of 3.83. This may be due to the tough penalty (usually a death sentence) imposed on those who commit serious crimes. In the last few years, reports of serious crimes in the Pearl River Delta and certain parts of Fujian 福建 province have made headline stories in newspapers in Hong Kong. Given the rather high mean score of "law and order" in Shanghai, it seems that "law and order" is better in Shanghai than southern China.

Protection of investment is a major concern of foreigners investing in China and this is due to two obvious reasons. First, the PRC is a socialist country, and when the Communist Party took power in 1949, it confiscated properties of both the so-called Chinese bureaucratic capitalists and the Western companies. The nationalization of foreign investors' properties also has occurred in Third World and "socialist" countries, resulting in tremendous losses. These recollections are very much in the minds of foreign capitalists or multinational managers when they consider invest- ment in China. Second, foreign investors are fearful of drastic political changes that can affect the existing open policy. This is understandable, as in the past PRC policies have oscillated between radicalism and prag- matism. In order to allay these fears, Article 2 of the PRC Joint Ventures Law in 1979 states that "The Chinese Government protects, in accordance with the law, the investment of foreign joint ventures, the profits due them and their other lawful rights and interests in a joint venture." Unfortunate- ly, there are no clear provisions or mechanisms stipulated. In enforcing the law, other Asian countries have more specific laws and provisions for protecting the interests of foreign investors. To strengthen the confidence of foreign investors, China moved one step forward to legitimize foreign investment in the country by including a new article in the revised Con- stitution of the PRC, adopted at the Fifth Session of the 5th National People's Congress in December 1982. Article 18 of the revised Constitu- tion stipulates that "The PRC permits foreign enterprises, other foreign economic organizations and individual foreigners to invest in China and to enter into various forms of economic co-operation with Chinese economic organizations in accordance with the law of the PRC." The article further stresses that the "lawful rights and interests of all foreign-invested enterprises are protected by the laws of the PRC." Obviously, such recog- nition of the legitimate rights of foreign investors has great symbolic value.

China has taken concrete actions to sign bilateral agreements on investment protection with a number of countries since 1982. First, two bilateral investment protection pacts were signed in 1982. More pacts were signed in subsequent years. In 1992, China signed a record number of 17 protection pacts with other countries. During the 1982–1992 period, it signed a total of 47 pacts with 48 countries (Belgium and Luxembourg shared one pact with China), including the United States, Canada, Japan, Australia, European Economic Community (EEC) members, and countries in Latin America, the Middle East, Eastern Europe, Africa, Southeast Asia and the Commonwealth of Independent States. Another 13 agreements are now under negotiation or in the planning stage.[16] The signing of bilateral agreements on investment insurance and protection with other countries implies that China is willing to adopt international rules to deal with flows of FDI between countries. Admittedly, this should boost the confidence of foreign investors.

Our survey results show that overseas investors in Shanghai are quite satisfied with the "protection of investors' interests" (the mean score of satisfaction is 3.57). At present, there is no agreement on protection of investment between Taiwan and PRC due to political reasons. As most Taiwanese firms in the PRC are registered in a third country/area such as Singapore, they are not overtly concerned with this particular issue. The sovereignty of Hong Kong will be reverted to China after 1 July 1997. According to the Basic Law of the future Hong Kong Special Administrative Region, it will adopt the so-called "one country, two systems." Whether or not special protection will be given to Hong Kong investors in the PRC remains to be seen. At present, overseas investors are more concerned with the profitability of their investments than with the protection of investors' interests *per se.*

Human Relations and Manpower Aspects

As shown in Table 10.9, among all the "soft" environmental factors for investment in Shanghai, the mean scores of satisfaction of various factors in the "human relations and manpower aspects" are high as compared to the policy, legal and market condition environments. There is, however, one exception. The mean score of satisfaction for "appraisal of lower-ranking government officials" as perceived by overseas investors is relatively low (3.20). Overseas investors in Shanghai are satisfied in particular with "relationships among investment partners." This factor enjoys the highest mean score of satisfaction (3.99). Investors are also happy with the "skill levels of professional/technical and managerial staff," "support by the municipal government" and the "educational quality of existing workers and staff." These results are consistent with the overseas investors' motives for investing in Shanghai as discussed earlier. As far as the low score of lower-ranking government officials in Shanghai is concerned, this may be a reflection of their lower level of education and poor work attitudes. Overseas investors are particularly displeased with the interventionist posture of some Chinese lower-ranking cadres. This was one of the major findings gathered by the author from several field trips to Shanghai which spanned over several years from 1985 to 1994.

Market Conditions, Administration and Others

China is now in the process of transforming its Stalinist, centrally planned economy to a "socialist market economy," a term formally adopted at the 14th Party Congress held in October 1992. The transition from socialism to a market economy in China first began in the early 1980s, even though the sensitive term "market economy," which was at one time considered equivalent to capitalism, was not used in official documents prior to 1992. At present, the market mechanism coexists with planned elements in the economy. Labour reform of state enterprises in China has been in progress since 1979 to break the "iron rice bowl" system of guaranteeing lifetime employment to workers and staff. This has now been replaced by a new labour contract system with specified terms. It also allows for labour mobility under certain circumstances. Labour reform has a positive impact on foreign-invested enterprises which can now recruit their staff under a more competitive labour market.

In Shanghai, the pace of reform lagged behind the provinces in southern China, such as Guangdong 廣東 and Fujian, during the 1979–1991 period. In 1992, the central government decided to loosen its grip on this metropolis. Labour and financial markets have gradually been developed. Our survey results show that overseas investors are, in general, satisfied with the "development of a labour market for skilled personnel" and "conditions for fund-raising and loans" with mean scores of 3.36 and 3.33 respectively (Table 10.9). The mean score for "interconnectedness of local purchasing organizations" is slightly lower (3.20).

Overseas investors are more satisfied with the administrative bureaux in Shanghai, with higher mean scores for both "conditions of customs services" and "efficiencies of administrative bureaux." However, they are less satisfied with the "rationality of various fee charging" and, in particular, the "level of inflation." The level of inflation in China in the early 1990s was high, with an average rate of 18% for the nation as a whole. Inflation rates in urban areas including Shanghai were higher than inland areas. Overseas investors are certainly not happy with the high costs of office buildings and industrial land in Shanghai in general and in the Pudong New Area in particular.[17] High inflation rates and high land costs will be detrimental to the "soft" investment environment in Shanghai unless they are checked.

Environmental Factors which Need Improvement

Although overseas investors are, in general, satisfied with both the "hard" and "soft" environmental factors, with the exception of a few sub-factors, there are bound to be some aspects which can be improved. An instrument was designed to measure the urgency of various environmental factors for investment which need improvement based on a 10-point scale ranging from 1 (least urgent) to 10 (most urgent). The survey results are presented in Table 10.10.

Using the mean score of 8 as a base-line, the following four sub-environmental factors for investment are considered to be the spheres which need the most urgent improvement, as perceived by overseas investors in Shanghai: "improvement of local transportation," "bogus and inferior products," "corruption and malpractices" and "improving the efficiency of administrative bureaux." Although local transport has improved somewhat lately with the completion of a rapid transit system (1st phase), Yangpu Bridge 楊浦大橋 and the First Ring Road, it is far from solving the long-standing local transport problem. Apparently, more infrastructural investment is needed.

Laws have been enacted for patent/trade mark protection in China. Unfortunately, state, collective and private enterprises usually do not give due respect to intellectual property rights acquired by overseas investors. Bogus and inferior products produced by these enterprises are widespread in the domestic markets. This has resulted in considerable economic losses for foreign-invested firms. The recent row between the US and Chinese governments was also due to the lack of protection for intellectual property rights in China. Therefore, it is not surprising to find that "bogus and inferior products," together with "improvement of local transportation,"

Table 10.10   Urgency of Environmental Factors for Investment Which Need Improvement (n = 81)

Environmental factors	Mean score[a]	Standard deviation
Improvement of local transportation	8.58	2.09
Bogus and inferior products	8.56	1.98
Corruption and malpractices	8.32	1.86
Improving the efficiency of administrative bureaux	8.30	1.59
Further opening up of the labour market	7.85	1.86
Streamlining the market competition mechanism	7.70	1.63
Introducing modern management skills practised in other advanced countries	7.62	1.90
Enhancing regulations which govern business operations	7.54	1.96
Revising the unreasonable payment system imposed on enterprises	7.53	2.30
Improving financial discipline	7.48	1.92
Strengthening foreign exchange services	7.41	1.58
Reducing government intervention in enterprises	7.40	2.22
Upgrading the quality of workers and staff	7.32	1.71
Guaranteeing supplies of water, electricity and gas	7.01	2.54
Strengthening macro management of real estate industry	6.99	1.91
Forging closer relationships between administrative bureaux and enterprises	6.98	2.04
Improving law and order	6.80	2.30
Improving co-operative spirit of partners	6.78	2.39
Strengthening government control mechanisms over enterprises	5.94	2.77
Increasing cultural and recreational facilities	5.78	2.04

Note: [a] Respondents were asked to rate the urgency of various environmental factors which need improvement on a 10-point scale ranging from 1 to 10, i.e., 10 = most urgent, 9 = next to most urgent, ... , 1 = least urgent.

are the two major factors which need most urgent improvement. The mean scores for both factors are very close at 8.56 and 8.58 respectively.

Corruption is rampant throughout China. News of corruption and the prosecution of cadres who commit economic crimes appears almost daily in the overseas media. Corruption by government officials increases the costs of doing business in China. According to some businessmen and China traders, bribes paid to Chinese cadres may account for as high as 15% of their operating costs in some instances. It is, therefore, understandable that "corruption and malpractices" is perceived by overseas investors as the third most urgent factor that needs improvement.

Efficiency of administrative bureaux in Shanghai is not totally negative, as discussed earlier. But there is certainly much room for improvement. This is shown in our survey results where "improving the efficiency
of administrative bureaux" is rated as the fourth most important environmental factor which urgently needs improvement.

The survey results of other environmental factors which need improvement, according to various degrees of urgency, are presented in
Table 10.10. This shows that overseas investors would like to see the
labour market in Shanghai further developed and the competitive market
mechanism streamlined and strengthened. The least urgent among the
various factors are "strengthening government control mechanisms over
enterprises" and "increasing cultural and recreational facilities." Apparently, the latter might suggest that the government's control of foreign-
invested enterprises is adequate and there are already enough cultural and
recreational facilities in Shanghai. Therefore, there is less urgency to improve them as compared to other environmental factors for investment.

Conclusion and Prospects

Without question, China has made great strides in attracting foreign investment since 1979 (Table 10.1). In the initial years, Shanghai lagged behind
Shenzhen, Guangzhou and Beijing in terms of both foreign-funded
projects and in attracting investment. However, its share of foreign investment has been increasing very significantly in the last few years. In 1993,
it accounted for 9% of China's total foreign investment, surpassing all
other coastal cities (Table 10.3). Shanghai has now emerged as the leading
investment centre in China. As discussed in the preceding sections, this is
mainly attributable to the shift of the central government's policy to
develop this traditional industrial city as well as to its strategic location as a
gateway to vast eastern China.

The prospects for Shanghai as a leading centre to attract foreign investment hinges upon the macroeconomic environment of the country as a
whole as well as on the investment climate of Shanghai itself. China is
increasingly moving towards economic liberalization. The most important
change since the adoption of the open policy is perhaps a "market mentality" which now deeply imbues Chinese cadres. Ideological conflicts
between Chinese officials and overseas investors seem to be fading as
dogma is replaced by a sense of pragmatic "economism." These will
facilitate the rooting of "marketization" in China. Clearly the current trend

is in this direction, and this development is conducive to attracting foreign investment. In addition, China's impending membership in the World Trade Organization will provide a further impetus to liberalize the domestic economy. This will appeal to more and more overseas investors, given the sheer size of the country and the improved income level of the Chinese people.

As far as Shanghai's investment climate is concerned, our survey results show that both "hard" and "soft" sides of the environmental factors are generally satisfactory. There has been a marked improvement as compared to the early periods.[18] However, more needs to be done. On the "hard" side, the infrastructure has been a bottleneck in dampening foreign investment. A positive note is the Shanghai municipal government attaches high priority to improving its physical infrastructure. On the "soft" side of the investment climate, the rules and regulations for investment in Shanghai need to be made more transparent. Although laws governing foreign investment are important, attitudes towards the rule of law are even more crucial. In the past, the grievances of many overseas investors often fell on the deaf ears of the bureaucracy. According to Xu Kuangdi 徐匡迪 , the present mayor, Shanghai will soon establish a "Complaints Unit" for overseas investors directly under the mayor's office to deal with any grievances which overseas investors may have.[19] This policy adjustment is another positive and direct way to address the problems and obstacles in attracting foreign investment to the city.

Notes

1. Foreign direct investment (FDI) in China includes "equity joint ventures," "contractual joint ventures," "wholly foreign-owned enterprises" and "joint development ventures" which the latter relates mainly to oil exploration. It excludes compensation trade, export processing and international leasing which are grouped under the "other foreign investment" category in Chinese official statistics.
2. Quoted in "Feeling Upbeat" (no author), *The China Business Review*, May–June (1995), p. 39.
3. Other 13 open coastal cities are Beihai 北海, Dalian 大連, Fuzhou 福州, Guangzhou 廣州, Lianyungang 連雲港, Nantong 南通, Ningbo 寧波, Qingdao 青島, Qinhuangdao 秦皇島, Tianjin 天津, Wenzhou 溫州, Yantai 煙台 and Zhanjiang 湛江.
4. The 14 free trade zones are Dalian, Futian 福田, Fuzhou, Guangzhou, Haikou 海口, Ningbo, Qingdao, Shantou, Shatoujiao 沙頭角, Tianjin, Xiamen,

Waigaoqiao 外高橋 and Zhangjiagang 張家港.

5. See Mee-kau Nyaw, "Direct Foreign Investment in China: Trends, Performance, Policies and Prospects," in *China Review 1993*, edited by Joseph Y. S. Cheng and Maurice Brosseau (Hong Kong: The Chinese University Press, 1993), pp. 16.1–16.38.

6. See *Hong Kong Standard*, 3 July 1995. Data was from *Shanghai Security News*.

7. Leigh Stelzer, Ma Chunguang et al., "Gauging Investor Satisfaction," *The China Business Review*, November–December (1992), p. 55.

8. Li Douyuan 李斗垣 and Xiao Keyong 蕭克榮, "Shanghai touzi huanjing de pingjia yu fenxi," 上海投資環境的評價與分析 (Appraisal and Analysis of Investment Environment in Shanghai) (Unpublished manuscript, Shanghai Academy of Social Sciences, December 1990). This survey covered firms in both industrial and service sectors. It is part of the project on "Inter-city Business Cooperation under Two Different Socioeconomic Systems: The Case of Hong Kong and Shanghai" jointly conducted by Shanghai Academy of Social Sciences and Faculty of Business Administration, The Chinese University of Hong Kong. The author of this chapter was a team member from Hong Kong.

9. The infrastructure in Shanghai was severely underinvested prior to 1979. It had gradually increased to about RMB11 billions during 1986–1990. In The Eighth Five-year Plan period (1991–1995), it will further increase to RMB30 billions. See Li and Xiao, "Shanghai touzi huanjing de pingjia yu fenxi" (see note 8).

10. Li and Xiao, "Shanghai touzi huanjing de pingjia yu fenxi" (see note 8), p. 5.

11. Ibid, p. 5.

12. See *Time*, 2 June 1986, p. 46.

13. See *Shanghai Overseas Investment Manual* (Shanghai: Shanghai yuandong chubanshe 上海遠東出版社, 1993), enlarged edition.

14. See article 27, "Interim Regulations on Shanghai Caohejing High-tech Park" adopted on 1 May 1990.

15. See *Far Eastern Economic Review*, 23 June 1995, p. 55.

16. *China Daily* (Beijing), *Business Weekly*, 10–16 January 1993.

17. H. Sender, "Passion for Profit," *Far Eastern Economic Review*, 23 June 1994, p. 55.

18. Li and Xiao, "Shanghai touzi huanjing de pingjia yu fenxi" (see note 8).

19. *Wen hui bao* 文匯報 (Wen Wei Pao) (Hong Kong), 24 February 1995.

11

Pudong
Remaking Shanghai as a World City

Anthony G. O. Yeh

Development Background

Shanghai has been China's business and industrial centre since the 1930s. Its enormous wealth and importance as China's financial centre can be reflected by the office buildings which were built in its prime time before World War II but still stand elegantly along the Bund (*wei tan* 外灘). Hong Kong, which now outshines Shanghai as a financial and industrial centre in the world, was a small entrepôt port when Shanghai was a world city. Although Shanghai still remains as China's most important financial and industrial centre after 1949, its importance as a world financial and industrial centre has declined. In particular, there was not much development in the financial sector. The official announcement by Premier Li Peng 李鵬 on 18 April 1990 on the development of Pudong 浦東 marked an important era for Shanghai, giving hope that it will be developed into a world city again.

There was not much development in Shanghai after 1949, especially in the city centre. This was mainly because cities in China were considered to be consumptive. The national policy was to transform them from consumer cities to production cities. Emphasis was given to industrial development and to control the growth of large cities. Much investment was given to the development of industries outside the city centre. Satellite towns were developed to decentralize the population of the city centre.[1] Shanghai was designated as one of the fourteen open coastal cities in 1984 after the adoption of the economic reforms and the open policy in China in 1978.[2] Similar to other open coastal cities which designated some of their areas as economic and technological development zones to attract foreign investment, Shanghai designated the Hongqiao Economic and Technological Development Zone (ETDZ) (虹橋經濟技術開發區), Minhang ETDZ (閔行經濟技術開發區) and Caohejing High-tech Park (漕河涇新興技術開發區) at the peripheral areas of the city as special development zones, each with its own area of specialization. There has been some success in attracting foreign investment. The most notable example of this is the Volkswagen joint venture motor car factory in Anting satellite town (安亭衛星城) in Jiading 嘉定 county. Although there was an increase in economic development in Shanghai after the economic reforms in 1978, it was slow as compared with that in the Pearl River Delta, especially the Shenzhen Special Economic Zone (SEZ) (深圳經濟特區). One of the reasons for this was the lack of preferential treatments similar to those adopted in the Shenzhen SEZ. Another reason was the lack of space for expansion. The city centre at Puxi 浦西 was very dense and there was little room for further development without massive urban renewal which would have been very difficult and expensive. The development of the Pudong New Area (浦東新區) was considered to be the only possible direction for the further development and urban growth of Shanghai.[3]

The concept of the development of Pudong is not new. It had been in the minds of planners in Shanghai and China since the early twentieth century. Dr. Sun Yatsen (孫逸仙), the founding father of modern China, declared his programme of developing the "Great Port of Pudong" (浦東大港) as one of the national reconstruction projects after the Revolution in 1911. This plan was not carried out, partly because of the civil war and World War II and partly because of the huge investment involved in infrastructure development and problems in dealing with entrenched domestic and foreign interests. The "Master Plan for Shanghai," prepared in 1946 by the Shanghai City Planning Board, included the development of Pudong as its final development goal.[4] This master plan did not have a chance to be implemented after the downfall of the Kuomintang (Guomindang 國民黨) in 1949 in mainland China. Shanghai was heavily involved in satellite town development and the *xiafang* 下放 campaign of sending urban youths and cadres to the countryside and did not have time or resources to think about the development of Pudong. The adoption of the economic reforms in China in 1978, especially the land reform in 1987, gave city officials and planners in China a new opportunity to rethink the development of Pudong.

Economic reforms and the open policy adopted in 1978 have had a significant impact on urban development in China, especially on the internal structure of cities.[5] The economic reforms have freed the economy from the total reliance on state investment and planning. The open policy enables the use of foreign investment for economic development. Housing reform has created a property market which attaches value to land. The most important reform that affects urban development in China has been the 1987 land reform which allows the paid transfer of land-use rights (*tudi shiyongquan youchang zhuanrang* 土地使用權有償轉讓) or land leasing. This creates a land market which enables the city to capture revenue from land which, in turn, can be used to develop infrastructure to enhance land value. The use of land leasing has been an increasingly common method of land development in Chinese cities and in the financing of large infrastructure projects, such as the construction of highways and underground railways. Such urban development is known as using land to further develop land (*yi di yang di* 以地養地). City governments do not have to rely too much on state investment to develop their cities. The development of Pudong has always been considered to be very expensive because of the construction of bridges and transport networks to link Pudong with Puxi.[6] The economic and land reform provided a good opportunity to overcome these financial problems by using foreign investment and by the sale of land to finance the necessary infrastructure to develop Pudong. Special preferential treatment would enhance its ability to attract foreign invest-ments in developing Pudong. Such preferential treatments were finally given when the State Council approved the plan for the development of Pudong in 1990.

As early as 1984, in considering the overall economic development strategy of Shanghai, the Shanghai municipal government proposed the development of Pudong. In the following year, this proposal was con-sidered by the State Council. In October 1986, when commenting on the Overall Shanghai Development Plan, the State Council again pointed out that "at present, special attention should be paid to the planned develop-ment and renewal of Pudong," and "to develop Pudong into a modern district." In 1987, the Pudong Consultative Group headed by a vice-mayor was formed by the Shanghai government. In 1988, the Shanghai govern-ment organized an international symposium on the development of Pudong. Jiang Zemin 江澤民, the party secretary of Shanghai municipality at that time, emphasized the need to develop Pudong. He said:

> Shanghai as a well-known metropolis had by the 1930s developed into one of the most important international trading and financial centres in Asia. Since 1949, much emphasis has been put on economic development, in particular industrial development. However, due to various reasons, the development and renewal of our city have lagged behind, thereby weakening the function of Shanghai as an economic centre and as a hub for other parts of the country. This situation obviously cannot be allowed to continue. Various means were adopted in the past to renew old city areas, but results have not been cost-effective. A new direction, therefore, has been taken which comprises two parts: namely, the renewal of old districts and the simultaneous development of new districts. As the biggest city in the country and occupying the most important position, it is totally in line with party policy to further reform, open up and develop Pudong, and to expedite the development of Shanghai's economy into one that is externally-oriented, and to build a new district that is international and that performs the function of a nerve-centre. This plan must, therefore, be properly implemented.[7]

In 1988, a leading group for the development of Pudong was formed to plan for the development of Pudong. On 18 April 1990, the State Council endorsed the report submitted by the Shanghai government on Pudong's Development Plan. A new Pudong Development Leading Group (浦東開發領導小組) and the Pudong Development Office (浦東開發辦公室) were formed.

Ten preferential policies for the development of Pudong were announced when Pudong was declared a special development area on 30 April 1990. The ten preferential policies are related to:[8]

1. Income tax of foreign investors.
2. Custom duties and tax for equipment, vehicles and building materials related to foreign investment.
3. Foreign investment should be export oriented.
4. Foreign investors are allowed to invest in infrastructure projects.
5. Foreign investors are allowed to operate tertiary industries.
6. Foreign banks are allowed to open foreign branches in Shanghai, including the Pudong New Area.
7. There will be a free trade zone in Pudong New Area.
8. Preferential treatment in terms of income tax reduction will be given to enterprises conforming with the industrial policies and beneficial to Pudong development.
9. Land leasing for 50–70 years will be used in Pudong. Foreign investors may contract large tracts of land for development.
10. Pudong New Area can keep the revenue for further development.

Most of the ten preferential policies are similar to the preferential policies in the other economic zones. But several preferential policies, such as the setting up of foreign banks, the operation of tertiary industries and a free trade zone, are limited to Pudong, the SEZs, and a few open coastal cities. Financial and retailing activities from which foreign enterprises were previously totally prohibited or partly restricted, may be carried out with prior approval from the State Council. The Shanghai Stock Exchange will also be established in Pudong. Within the free trade zone and with the approval of the relevant departments of the State Council, foreign trading companies may be allowed to carry out entrepôt activities.

After the announcement by the State Council, on 10 September 1990 the Shanghai municipal government promulgated nine sets of regulations and guidelines based on the ten preferential policies granted by the State Council for encouraging foreign businessmen to invest in Pudong New Area:[9]

1. Regulations for the Administration of Financial Institutions with Foreign Capital and Financial Institutions with Chinese and Foreign Joint Capital in Shanghai
2. Regulations on Reduction and Exemption of Enterprise Income Tax and Industrial and Commercial Consolidated Tax to Encourage Foreign Investment in Shanghai Pudong New Area
3. Customs Regulations of the People's Republic of China concerning Control Over the Goods, Means of Transport and Personal Articles Entering or Leaving the Waigaoqiao Free Trade Zone of Shanghai
4. Regulations of the Shanghai Municipality for the Encouragement of Foreign Investment in the Pudong New Area
5. Measures on Administration of the Waigaoqiao Free Trade Zone of Shanghai
6. Provisions of Land Administration in Shanghai Pudong New Area
7. Provisional Measures on the Administration of Planning and Construction in Shanghai Pudong New Area
8. Examination and Approval Measures for Foreign-invested Enterprises in Shanghai Pudong New Area
9. Guidelines for Industries and Investment in Shanghai Pudong New Area

These regulations and guidelines formed the basis for the implementation of the plan for the development of Pudong. The Pudong Development Office of the Shanghai municipal government was set up for developing Pudong. Three development companies were set up for developing the three priority development zones in Pudong — the Waigaoqiao Free Trade Zone (外高橋保稅區), the Lujiazui Financial and Trade Zone (陸家嘴金融貿易區), and the Jinqiao Export-processing Zone (金橋出口加工區). Each development company has a registered capital of RMB100 million.

Planning and Strategies of Development

Pudong is located opposite the Shanghai city centre at Puxi on the eastern side of the Huangpu River (黃浦江) (Figure 11.1). It is immediately opposite the Bund, the central business district (CBD) of Shanghai. It is a triangular area of 350 sq km. It is not a greenfield site. Although before 1990 most of the land was cultivated, there was also some industry, such as petrochemical, shipbuilding, steel and building materials. In 1990, the agricultural and industrial output of Pudong accounted for about 10% of that of Shanghai. It had a built-up area of 38 sq km and a population of 1.33 million (Table 11.1). There were 1,930 industrial enterprises, including 47 joint ventures and three wholly foreign-owned enterprises operating in Pudong. The planning objective of Pudong is to develop it into a well-integrated district with an advanced communication network, complete infrastructure and convenient communication and information systems so as to enable Shanghai to become one of the major economic and trading centres in the western Pacific Rim in the next century. After 2000, although the proportion of the population of Pudong in the total population of Shanghai is not expected to increase much, it will be an important financial and industrial area in Shanghai with a significant increase in its proportion of gross national product (GNP) and retailing. Its share of GNP in Shanghai will increase from 8.1% in 1990 to 25% in 2000, and retailing will increase from 4.0% to 30%.

The overall plan for Pudong consists of five relatively independent complex subareas — Waigaoqiao–Gaoqiao Subarea (外高橋一高橋分區), Qingningsi–Jinqiao Subarea (慶寧寺一金橋分區), Lujiazui–Huamu Subarea (陸家嘴一花木分區), Beicai–Zhangjiang Subarea (北蔡一張江分區) and Zhoujiadu–Liuli Subarea (周家渡一六里分區) (Figure 11.2). The total planned area is 177 sq km with a target population of 1.7 million. Priority is given to develop four special development zones in the subareas. They are the Waigaoqiao Free Trade Zone, the Jinqiao Export-processing Zone, the Lujiazui Financial and Trade Zone, and the Zhangjiang High-tech Park (張江高科技園區) (Table 11.2). The Lujiazui Financial and Trade Zone, which is immediately opposite the Bund in the Puxi city centre, is the focal point of development. It will be the CBD of Pudong, as well as the new CBD of Shanghai. It is intended to be developed as the Manhattan of Shanghai. The characteristics of the four priority zones for development are described as follows:[10]

Lujiazui Financial and Trade Zone

The Lujiazui area faces the central business district of the Bund at Puxi on the other side of the Huangpu River. It is the golden area of Pudong. It will be developed mainly as a centre for finance, trade, commerce, service for foreign businessmen, real estate, information, consultancy and other modern service industries as an extension of the functions of the Bund.

Figure 11.1   The Location of Pudong in Shanghai

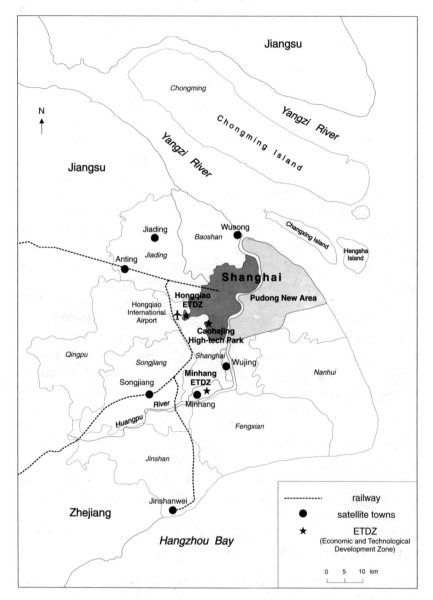

Table 11.1 Existing Conditions and Planned Development for Pudong, 1990, 1993 and 2000

| | 1990 | | | 1993 | | | 2000 | | |
	Pudong	Shanghai	%	Pudong	Shanghai	%	Pudong	Shanghai	%
GNP (RMB million)	6,000	74,470	8.1	16,400	151,173	10.8	50,000	200,000	25.0
Retailing (RMB million)	1,400	35,310	4.0	4,743	57,307	8.3	30,000	100,000	30.0
Commercial floor space (sq m)	50,000	n.a.	—	80,000	n.a.	—	2,300,000	9,000,000	25.5
Built-up area (sq km)	38	n.a.	—	45	n.a.	—	100	400	25.0
Population (million)	1.33	12.83	10.4	1.44	12.94	11.1	2.00	13.50	14.8

Note:　Percentages refer to Pudong in relation to Shanghai.

Sources:　Shanghaishi Pudong xinqu guanli weiyuanhui (ed.), *Shanghaishi Pudong xinqu shouce* (see note 10), p. 2.
　　　　Shanghaishi tongjiju (ed.), *Shanghai tongji nianjian 1994* (see note 15), p. 238.

Figure 11.2 Planned Areas of Pudong

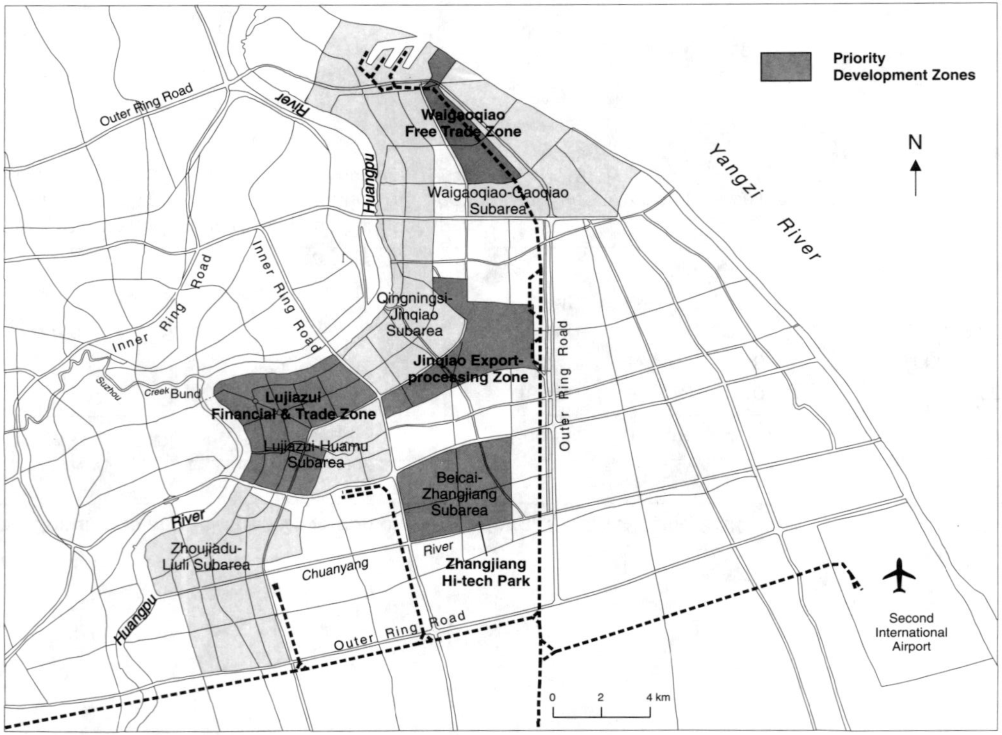

Source: Master Plan of Pudong New Area, Shanghai Urban Planning and Design Institute, 1991.

Table 11.2 Planning Subareas and Special Development Zones of Pudong

	Waigaoqiao–Gaoqiao Subarea	Qingningsi–Jinqiao Subarea	Lujiazui–Huamu Subarea	Beicai–Zhangjiang Subarea	Zhoujiadu–Liuli Subarea	TOTAL
Planned area (sq km)	75	21	28	19	34	177
Target population	260,000	340,000	350,000	350,000	400,000	1,700,000
Special development zone	Waigaoqiao Free Trade Zone	Jinqiao Export-processing Zone	Lujiazui Financial and Trade Zone	Zhangjiang High-tech Park	—	—
Planned functions	Export-processing industries, warehouses, port	Export-processing industries	Finance, commerce, tertiary industries	High-tech industries	—	—
Planned area of special development zone	10	8.9	6.8	17	—	—
Area for 1st phase of development	4.0	4.0	1.5	4.0	—	—

Source: Pudong Development Office of Shanghai Municipality and People's Construction Bank of China, Shanghai Branch (eds.), *The Investment Guide in Pudong New Area of Shanghai*, No. 1 (see note 8).

Jinqiao Export-processing Zone

It is planned that export-processing industries will be developed in this zone. Areas will be reserved for industries relocated from the city.

Waigaoqiao Free Trade Zone

The construction of a large modern port and the Waigaoqiao Power Plant began in 1991. In connection with the port development, a 5–10 sq km export-processing and foreign investment zone will be developed. Sino–foreign joint ventures, and solely foreign-funded ventures, especially investment from multinational corporations, will be invited to develop high-value export products with advanced technologies. To co-ordinate the construction of export-processing zones, a free trade area will be set up where bonded warehouses and related public service facilities will be developed so as to create a transit, storage and transportation centre. In the free trade area, trade agencies owned by foreign businessmen will be allowed to engage in transit trade and imports and exports for the enterprises operating in the area. Entrepôt trade and export-processing zones will be established to form an international free trade port. Along the east bank of Waigaoqiao, a 1.7 sq km area will be used for building shipways for 10,000 ton-class ships, making it a new base for shipbuilding and repairing.

Zhangjiang High-tech Park

Located in the eastern part of the Pudong New Area, it is to be built into a science and education zone. Emphasis will be placed on high technologies and newly developed industries, such as precision medical apparatus and computer software.

Apart from preferential policies, the importance of infrastructure provision to attract foreign investment has long been recognized since the development of the special economic zones in the early 1980s. Site formation and infrastructure provision, the so-called "four linkages and one levelling" (*si tong yi ping* 四通一平), were emphasized in the development of Shenzhen 深圳, the most successful special economic zone in China.[11] Such an approach which has been followed in the development of Pudong, has been widely adopted for urban development in China. Ten major infrastructure projects for Pudong New Area are to be constructed to improve the transport, communication and facilities of the area for attracting foreign investment. The ten major infrastructure projects are:[12]

1. Waigaoqiao Power Station (外高橋電廠)
   To supply 1.2 million KW of electricity in 1996
2. Lingqiao Water Works (凌橋水廠)
   An increase of 200,000 tonnes in the daily water supply
3. Second Phase of Pudong Gas Works
   An increase of 1,000,000 cu m of the daily gas supply
4. Nanpu Bridge (南浦大橋)
   With six lanes
5. Yangpu Bridge (楊浦大橋)
   8,354 m long, with six lanes
6. Inner Ring Road (內環路)
   Connecting the Nanpu Bridge and the Yangpu Bridge
7. Road Widening and Rerouting of Yanggao Road (楊高路)
8. Waigaoqiao Deep Water Berths (外高橋深水港)
   Four 10,000 ton-class deepwater berths with an annual handling capacity of 2.4 million tons along the bank of Waigaoqiao
9. Telecommunication Project
   A net increase of 100,000 telephone lines. The total number of lines will be increased to 120,000
10. Sewage Treatment and Discharge Project

Projects in the next ten years include a second subway line from Puxi to Pudong, Pudong international airport, and 10,000 ton-class berths in Waigaoqiao.

Pudong is a big project which will require many years of effort before it can become the symbol of a modern Shanghai in the twenty-first century. The general development principles are:

1. Overall planning and phased implementation;
2. Emphasis on higher technology, although general industries and labour-intensive enterprises may be allowed at the initial stage of development;
3. Mainly externally oriented. Foreign capital will be attracted by various measures; and
4. Co-ordination between the development of Pudong and that of the existing urban areas in Puxi. By removing some of the existing enterprises in the city areas, rationalizing the existing economic

Figure 11.3   Ten Key Infrastructure Projects of Pudong

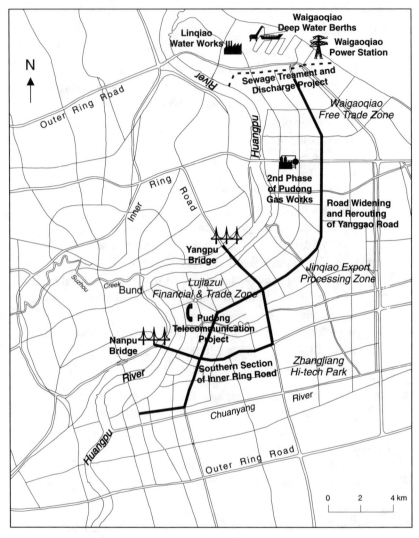

Source: *Shanghai Pudong New Area Administration, 1991*

structure and distributing economic activities in the whole of
Shanghai, some of the problems associated with over-crowded-
ness and the shortage of public utilities in the old urban areas will
thereby be relieved.

The development of Pudong will be implemented in the following phases:[13]

1. In the Eighth Five-year Plan (八五計劃) (1990–1995) period, emphasis was given to infrastructure development and resolving traffic problems to create the necessary conditions for attracting foreign investment. This involved the construction of river crossings, trunk roads and other public utilities, together with port facilities in Waigaoqiao, power stations, and the export-processing zone. Beginning in 1990, development concentrated on the creation of a good environment for attracting foreign investment through plan making, infrastructure and transport projects, and site formation. Cross-river projects to link the city proper with the Pudong area, major roads and other infrastructures were constructed. The Waigaoqiao Port and Waigaoqiao Power Plant were built. Export-processing zones and a bonded area for transit trade with a total area of 5–10 sq km are to be developed in phases.

2. In the Ninth Five-year Plan (九五計劃) (1996–2000) period, development will be selectively carried out. Trunk roads and public utilities will continue to be built, giving Pudong a comparatively complete set of infrastructural facilities to provide a solid base for further growth. Beginning in 1996, there will be a five-year stage of key development. Key roads, public utilities and other infrastructures will continue to be built, creating co-ordination of the infrastructure in the area.

3. In the next two to three decades after the year 2000, development will be on a fuller scale. Through the development of Pudong and renewal of parts of the existing city areas, Shanghai will be transformed into a financial, trade, technological and communication centre with a modern industrial base and with an externally oriented economy. Spanning 20–30 years or longer after the year 2000 will be a stage of overall construction. The Pudong New Area will be developed into a rational development and layout structure with advanced and comprehensive traffic networks, good city facilities, fast and convenient communications and information systems and a modernized new area with an excellent natural and ecological environment.

In the first phase of the development of Pudong, the four slogans of development are "Financial and business sector comes first, commerce and trade will boom the market, infrastructure paves the way for development, and industries will come jointly." The development of Pudong is a grand project and will be developed in stages according to the overall plan. Emphasis will be placed on the construction of a basic infrastructure and transportation network. Development will concentrate mainly in the development of Lujiazui Financial and Trade Zone, Jinqiao Export-processing Zone, and Waigaoqiao Free Trade Zone.

Socioeconomic Planning and Development

Pudong is different from the existing ETDZs in China. A new free trade zone (bonded area or *bao shui qu* 保稅區) will be established in Waigaoqiao to guarantee the free movement of commodities, personnel and capital, so that it will eventually become a "free port." Entrepôt and wholesale business will be allowed in this zone. Pudong is among the first zones in China to introduce foreign banks and thereafter, gradually allow and develop other associated services such as financial, insurance, consultancy and accountancy services. Measures for attracting foreign investment will be improved. For example, investment on a share-holding basis. New avenues will be explored in the sale of land-use rights and the development of the property market to help the development of Pudong.

A huge amount of investment is needed for the development of Pudong. The Shanghai authorities estimate that more than US$10 billion will be required by the end of the 1990s for infrastructure development. Domestic funds will be supported first by the central government. The State Council has decided that RMB6.5 billion will be provided to Shanghai (mainly in the form of loans). Second, funding will be from local revenue accumulation in Shanghai. In the past, over RMB10 billion was accumulated in ten years. Foreign funds are expected to come from the World Bank, the Asian Development Bank, and international financial organizations. Foreign governments are expected to offer, as in the past, long-term low-interest loans for infrastructure construction. Foreign investors are expected to invest directly in the area. The free trade zone and export-processing zone will be opened to attract foreign investment. At the same time, policies for the paid-transfer of land-use rights will be adopted to raise funds for development. It has been estimated that the annual sources of funding for Pudong will comprise US$100 million from commercial foreign loans, RMB200 million in allocations from the Shanghai municipal government, RMB300 million in allocations from the central government for technological renovation, and RMB400 million in allocations from the central government for infrastructure construction. Another important source of funding will be the purchase of bonds by Shanghai residents.

Similar to other special investment zones in China, preferential tax treatment, land-leasing and other policies are offered to foreign investors. Particularly favourable terms are being offered to investors in infrastructure projects.

The central government has clearly indicated that the main sources of finance must come from overseas. Various incentives, including reduced profits taxes, tax holidays and exemptions from customs duties are available to foreign investors. With prior approval, some manufactured products may be marketed locally, and partly for foreign exchange. Financial and retailing activities for which foreign enterprises have hitherto been totally prohibited or partly restricted may be carried out with prior approval from the State Council. Within the free trade zone, and with the approval of the relevant departments of the State Council, foreign trading companies may be allowed to carry out entrepôt activities.

Pudong is not an economic and technological development zone. In China, the (ETDZs) are normally around 1.2 sq km in area. Pudong has an area of 350 sq km.

The period 1990–1995 marks the first phase of development of Pudong. It is expected that the major development will be in the secondary and tertiary sectors with an average annual growth rate of 22.5% and 42% respectively (Table 11.3). The economic structure will be dominated slightly by the secondary sector. But by 2000, the tertiary sector is expected to be similar in size to the secondary sector, transforming Pudong into a financial and industrial area of Shanghai. It is expected that there will not be a major increase in population from migration like that which occurred in Shenzhen SEZ. The net migration for 1990–1995 was 250,000 and for 1995–2000 it is estimated to be 430,000. About 76% of the target population of 1.8 million in 2000 will be from the existing population.[14] A large proportion of the net migration will be from other areas of Shanghai, particular from Puxi; Pudong will serve as a decanting site for urban renewal of the highly dense old areas of Puxi. Migrants from other areas will be screened and selected for their skills.

Development of Pudong since Its Designation in 1990

Pudong has been rapidly developing according to the master plan and the socioeconomic development plan since it was first designated in 1990. It was able to attract US$1,757 million of agreed foreign investment in 1993 which was 25.1% of that of Shanghai (Table 11.4).[15] Most of the foreign investment was in industry, real estate and services. Compared to the sectoral distribution of foreign investment in other parts of Shanghai, it has a relatively higher proportion of investment in transport and communication. About 79% of the foreign investment in transport and communcation of Shanghai went to Pudong. The sources of investment in Pudong are similar to those of Shanghai, with Hong Kong, the United States, Japan and Taiwan constituting 73.6% of the foreign investment. The contribution of Hong Kong's foreign investment, although less than that in the Pearl River Delta because of the distance from Hong Kong, still constitutes over 50% of the foreign investment.[16] Apart from attracting foreign investment, Pudong was able to attract an equal amount of domestic investment. In 1993, it attracted US$1,742 million (RMB13,590 million) domestic investment.[17] The overwhelming majority (96%) of the domestic investment was from areas outside of Shanghai.

Land leasing is one of the most dominant features of development in Pudong. In 1993, 224 land parcels were leased in Shanghai, with a total of 49.3 sq km. Of these, a dominant majority of 93% was in Pudong, with a total of 45.9 sq km.[18] The majority of the land leasing in Pudong was in the form of leasing of large tracts of land to developers to be subdivided and developed. About 89.7% of the land leased in Pudong are of this type.

There were 59,214 persons who migrated to Pudong in 1993.[19] The decentralization function of Pudong was beginning to be observed. Only 17.7% of these persons (10,469) were from areas outside of Shanghai; the other 82.3% were relocated from other parts of Shanghai.

Prospects for Development

The development plan for Pudong is very ambitious. It is as ambitious as when Shenzhen was developed in 1981. Pudong is larger than other SEZs and ETDZs in China. Its total area of 350 sq km, with 177 sq km of planned built-up areas is larger than that of Shenzhen, the largest SEZ with an area of 327.5 sq km; with 98 sq km of planned built-up areas. Unlike Shenzhen, which was basically a green field site, Pudong already had 1.33 million inhabitants before the 1990 announcement of the Pudong New Area development. As its development started more or less ten years later than Shenzhen, it has the advantage of learning from the development

Table 11.3 Socioeconomic Development Plan of Pudong, 1990–2000

| (In 1990 constant prices) | 1990 | 8th Five-year Plan 1990–1995 | | 2000 | 9th Five-year Plan 1995–2000 | 1990–2000 |
		1995	Average annual growth rate		Average annual growth rate	Average annual growth rate
GNP (RMB million)	6,020	20,000	27.2%	50,000	20.1%	23.6%
Primary sector (RMB million)	220 (3.7%)	330 (1.7%)	8.5%	500 (1.0%)	8.5%	8.5%
Secondary sector (RMB million)	4,590 (76.2%)	12,670 (63.4%)	22.5%	24,500 (49.0%)	14.1%	18.2%
Tertiary sector (RMB million)	1,210 (20.1%)	7,000 (35.0%)	42.0%	25,000 (50.0%)	29.0%	35.3%
Retailing (RMB million)	1,440	6,000	33.0%	18,300	25.0%	28.9%
Export (US$ million)	570	2,000	28.5%	6,100	25.0%	26.8%
Investment in fixed assets (RMB million)	—	45,500*	—	100,000*	—	—
Population (million)	1.34	1.60	3.6%	1.80	2.4%	3.0%
from natural increase	1.34	1.35	0.2%	1.37	0.2%	0.2%
from net migration	—	0.25	—	0.43	—	—
Per capita GNP (RMB)	4,498	12,500	22.6%	27,777	17.3%	20.0%
Housing floor area (million sq m)	—	10*	—	10*	—	—

Note: * 5-year cumulative total.
Source: Shanghaishi Pudong xinqu guanli weiyuanhui (ed.), *Shanghaishi Pudong xinqu shouce* (see note 10), p. 16.

Table 11.4   Comparison between Foreign Investment in Pudong and Shanghai in 1993

Agreed foreign investment in US$1,000	Pudong		Shanghai		% of Pudong in Shanghai
By methods of investment:					
Equity joint venture	1,308,490	74.5%	4,451,360	63.6%	29.4%
Joint co-operative venture	153,370	8.7%	1,331,860	19.0%	11.5%
Wholly foreign-owned venture	277,530	15.8%	1,215,140	17.4%	22.8%
B-stock	17,280	1.0%	—	—	—
TOTAL	1,756,670	100.0%	6,998,360	100.0%	25.1%
By sectors:					
Industry	533,020	30.3%	2,387,120	34.1%	22.3%
Construction	24,580	1.4%	104,160	1.5%	23.6%
Transport and communication	33,770	1.9%	42,740	0.6%	79.0%
Real estate and services	654,540	37.3%	3,210,250	45.9%	20.4%
Others	510,760	29.1%	1,254,090	17.9%	40.7%
TOTAL	1,756,670	100.0%	6,998,360	100.0%	25.1%
By major countries and areas:					
Hong Kong	887,000	50.5%	4,337,760	62.0%	20.4%
Taiwan	92,000	5.2%	530,000	7.6%	17.4%
Japan	134,000	7.6%	370,150	5.3%	36.2%
United States	180,000	10.2%	598,580	8.6%	30.1%
TOTAL	1,293,000	73.6%	5,836,490	83.4%	22.2%

Sources: Shanghaishi tongjiju (ed.), *Shanghai tongji nianjian 1995* 上海統計年鑑1995 (Statistical Yearbook of Shanghai 1995) (Beijing: Zhongguo tongji chuban-she, 1995); Shanghaishi Pudong xinqu tongjiju (ed.), *Shanghai Pudong xinqu tongji nianjian 1994* (see note 15).

experience of Shenzhen and other SEZs in urban planning and in attracting foreign investment. Many of the development strategies, such as the importance given to infrastructure development and preferential policies to foreign investment, had been experimented with and used quite successfully in Shenzhen.

Although it is hoped that much of the funding for developing Pudong will come from foreign investment, there is scepticism over whether this can be achieved at the early stage of development.[20] First, at the time that Shenzhen was developed, China was just opening up to the outside world. Apart from being located right at the border of Hong Kong, which is one of the largest sources of foreign investment in China, it was much easier for Shenzhen to attract foreign investment because there were few competitors in China. But, after more than ten years of economic reform and opening of China to foreign investment, there are more competitors now. Pudong even has to compete with Puxi for foreign investments. Second, the ten preferential policies given by the State Council to Pudong for attracting foreign investment are not unique in China. Most of them can be found in other parts of China, directly competing with Pudong. Some foreign investments may even prefer to stay in Puxi rather than moving to Pudong because of office and industrial linkages. Third, because of the tight control by the central government in the past, Shanghai is less flexible in dealing with foreign investment compared with Shenzhen and cities in the Pearl River Delta. Some systems and methods of economic management currently practised in Shanghai are still incompatible with the requirements for attracting foreign capital. For example, the procedures for approving a foreign investment enterprise in Shanghai municipality are far more complicated than in the Pearl River Delta. In Shanghai, three different approval procedures are required: identifying the project, conducting a feasibility study, and drafting contracts and regulations. Regardless of the size of the project or the degree of difficulty, these three procedures have to be followed. In the Pearl River Delta, the approval of small or medium-sized investments has been made much more simple by combining the three procedures into one. Fourth, the world economy is not as robust as when Shenzhen and the Pearl River Delta were developed in the 1980s. In addition, there is more competition in Asia for attracting foreign investment. The land and labour costs in China are no longer as attractive as in the past. Vietnam and other countries in Indochina are able to provide cheaper land and labour to attract foreign investments.

Despite the above scepticism, Pudong has favourable factors to attract development. Unlike Shenzhen SEZ, which started more or less from scratch and with a poor base for economic development, Shanghai has a long history and strong base of development. Shanghai people are enterprising. The Shanghai industrialists who migrated to Hong Kong contributed greatly to the early days of its industrial development after World War II.[21] They laid the foundation for Hong Kong's development into a world city. It also has good industrial support in the surrounding region. The labour in Shanghai is highly trained. It is an important base for scientific research. There are 52 colleges and universities, 8 of which, such as Tongji University (同濟大學), Fudan University (復旦大學), and Jiaotong University (交通大學), are China's top universities. It has a more solid base of development than Shenzhen or the Pearl River Delta had when they were developed in the 1980s. The only disadvantage is its distance from Hong Kong which is the most dominant source of foreign investment in China. However, it is closer to Japan, Korea, Taiwan and the United States, which are also major foreign investors in Asia.

In the development history of Shenzhen, although foreign investment did play a catalytic role in promoting development, domestic firms and investors from other parts of China also played a significant role. With the large hinterland of the Yangzi River Economic Region (長江經濟區), Pudong can be developed as the financial centre of this important and prosperous economic region in China. The future development prospects for Pudong may not rely too heavily on foreign investment but more on the economic development of the Yangzi River Economic Region.

One of the objectives of the development of Pudong is to use it to help to redevelop Puxi. But, this objective is limited. It can only accommodate a limited amount of population from Puxi. Many industries in Puxi which need to be relocated are polluting industries which are incompatible with the industries that Pudong intends to attract. Pudong is also in direct competition with Puxi for attracting the much-needed foreign investment for the redevelopment of Puxi, especially in office and real estate development.

The five planned subareas only occupy 177 sq km of the 350 sq km of Pudong. Much of the land outside these planned subareas is made up of old industries and dense housing that are not compatible with the modern development in these subareas. Much redevelopment and planning is needed to make these areas compatible and integrated with the development of the five planned subareas in the future.

Conclusion

The development of Pudong is a major step in revitalizing Shanghai into a world city. Faced with severe competition in the international and domestic markets and the transformation from the old to the new system, Shanghai will have to face the choice between decline or prosperity. Shanghai, as the biggest economic centre of China and an important international city on the west coast of the Pacific and, with its historical development advantages, geographical location and industrial and technological knowhow, should be able to advance itself further. The development of Pudong will provide invaluable space for Shanghai to develop its financial districts, to develop export-processing and high-tech industries and decanting areas for population and economic activities that are affected by urban renewal in the heavily congested areas in Puxi. Apart from contributing significantly to the development of Shanghai, the development of Pudong is also a key measure to foster the development of the Yangzi River region. It is considered to be the "dragon head" of the Yangzi River development. The development of Pudong, therefore, is also of national strategic importance.

The development of Pudong has attracted the world's attention. Given the scale and importance that has been accorded by the central and Shanghai governments, the 1980s may be considered the era of Shenzhen's development, whilst the 1990s and, possibly, 2000s may be considered the era of Pudong's development. The development of Pudong represents a major shift in central government policy of the 1980s which favoured the development of the southern provinces, especially the SEZs. The development of Pudong also represents a new experiment in using foreign investment and the development of special areas to revitalize and redevelop old large cities.

High priority is given to attracting foreign investment to develop Pudong. Infrastructure and preferential policies for foreign investments are not adequate to attract foreign investment. A more efficient and flexible system to deal with foreign investment is needed. It is also necessary to create an economic environment favourable for foreign investment, especially an economic system which operates according to the principles of a market economy. Foreign investors must be given sufficient guarantees for their investments if they observe Chinese laws and regulations. All related laws and regulations should be implemented so that foreign investors will have confidence in the system and can effectively assess the risks and returns of their investments. At present, the land, capital, and labour markets are still at their early stages of development. The central government must formulate laws and regulations to protect the legal rights and interests of various economic entities, to ensure the execution of contracts, and to protect intellectual property (such as company law, banking ordinances, and bankruptcy laws).

The master plan of Shenzhen has changed many times since the first plan was prepared in the early 1980s. It will not surprise anyone if the master plan of Pudong will change many times, too. Indeed, there is already some discussion about rethinking the development strategy and the master plan of Pudong. For example, in its role to help Puxi's redevelopment, should Pudong be developed as a separate city district rather than as part of the existing city district in Puxi? Also, the desirability of locating the CBD of Shanghai in Lujiazui has been debated.[22]

Despite some scepticism about the success of Pudong in attracting foreign investment, it still may succeed in becoming the largest financial centre in China based on the resources and support from the central government and the hinterland of the Yangzi River region. But the fact that it is a large city does not mean that it can become a world city.[23] Population size is one of the less important criteria in becoming a world city. Integration with the world economy, such as being a major financial centre, headquarters for transnational corporations (TNCs), international institutions, rapid growth of a business services sector, and a centre for the dissemination of information, are more important criteria. Pudong is only at its early stage of development. The major results of the efforts that Shanghai has put into developing Pudong will not be seen before the year 2000. One has to wait to see whether Pudong will become a world city like Hong Kong after 2000. With the rapid growth of the Chinese economy and with the determination of the central government to develop Pudong, Shanghai may have an opportunity to redevelop itself as a world city, even surpassing Hong Kong, in the not-too-distant future.

Notes

1. R.J.R. Kirkby, "A Review of Satellite Town Policies in the People's Republic of China: The Experience of Shanghai," in *New Towns in East and Southeast Asia: Planning and Development*, edited by D. R. Phillips and A.G.O. Yeh (Hong Kong: Oxford University Press, 1987), pp. 205–30; and Anthony Gar-on Yeh and Hua-qi Yuan, "Satellite Town Development in China: Problems and Prospects," *Tijdschrift voor Economische en Sociale Geografie*, Vol. 78, No. 3 (1987), pp. 190–200.

2. Ka-iu Fung, Zhong-min Yan and Yue-min Ning, "Shanghai: China's World City," in *China's Coastal Cities: Catalysts for Modernization*, edited by Yue-man Yeung and Xu-wei Hu (Honolulu: University of Hawaii Press, 1992), pp. 124–52.

3. Fu-xiang Huang, "Planning in Shanghai," *Habitat International*, Vol. 15, No. 3 (1992), pp. 87–97.

4. Kerrie L. MacPherson, "The Head of the Dragon: The Pudong New Area and Shanghai's Urban Development," *Planning Perspective*, Vol. 9 (1994), pp. 61–85.

5. Anthony Gar-on Yeh and Wu Fulong, "Internal Structure of Chinese Cities in the Midst of Economic Reform," *Urban Geography*, Vol. 16, No. 6 (1995), pp. 521–54.

6. MacPherson, "The Head of the Dragon" (see note 4).

7. Zhao Qizheng 趙啓正 (ed.), *Xin shiji, xin Pudong* 新世紀、新浦東 (New Century, New Pudong) (Shanghai: Fudan daxue chubanshe 復旦大學出版社, 1994), p. 17.

8. On 30 April 1990, the State Council approved ten preferential policies for Pudong development. For details, see Pudong Development Office of Shanghai Municipality (上海市人民政府浦東開發辦公室) and People's Construction Bank of China, Shanghai Branch (中國人民建設銀行，上海市分行) (eds.), *The Investment Guide in Pudong New Area of Shanghai*, No. 1 (上海浦東新區投資指南，第一冊) (Shanghai: Pudong Development Office of Shanghai Municipality and People's Construction Bank of China, Shanghai Branch, 1990); and Shanghai Pudong New Area Administration (上海市浦東新區管理委員會) (ed.), *Policies and Regulations of Shanghai Pudong New Area 1990.9-1992.6* (Shanghai: Pudong Development Office of Shanghai Municipality and People's Construction Bank of China, Shanghai Branch, 1992). See also Pudong Development Office of Shanghai Municipality (ed.), *Pudong Development of Shanghai* (Shanghai: Pudong Development Office of Shanghai Municipality, 1990).

9. Pudong Development Office of Shanghai Municipality and People's Construction Bank of China, Shanghai Branch (eds.), *The Investment Guide in Pudong New Area of Shanghai*, No. 1 (Ibid.), and *The Investment Guide in Pudong New Area of Shanghai*, No. 2 (Shanghai: Pudong Development Office of Shanghai Municipality and People's Construction Bank of China, Shanghai Branch, 1990) (in English, Chinese and Japanese).

10. Shanghaishi Pudong xinqu guanli weiyuanhui 上海市浦東新區管理委員會 (Shanghai Pudong New Area Administration) (ed.), *Shanghaishi Pudong xinqu shouce* 上海市浦東新區手冊 (Shanghai Pudong New Area Handbook) (Shanghai: Shanghai yuandong chubanshe 上海遠東出版社, 1993) (in Chinese, English and Japanese).

11. Anthony Gar-on Yeh, "Physical Planning of Shenzhen Special Economic Zone," in *Modernization in China: The Case of the Shenzhen Special Economic Zone*, edited by K. Y. Wong and D.K.Y. Chu (Hong Kong: Oxford University Press, 1985), pp. 108-30.

12. Shanghaishi Pudong xinqu guanli weiyuanhui (ed.), *Shanghai Pudong xinqu: Touzi huanjing yu fazhan qianjing* 上海浦東新區：投資環境與發展前景 (Shanghai Pudong New Area: Investment Environment and Development Prospect) (Shanghai: Shanghaishi renmin zhengfu Pudong kaifa bangongshi and Zhongguo renmin jianshe yinhang, Shanghaishi fenhang, 1991).

13. Shanghaishi Pudong xinqu guanli weiyuanhui (ed.), *Shanghaishi Pudong xinqu shouce* (see note 10).

14. Ibid.

15. Shanghaishi Pudong xinqu tongjiju 上海市浦東新區統計局 (ed.), *Shanghai Pudong xinqu tongji nianjian 1994* 上海浦東新區統計年鑑 1994 (Statistical

Yearbook of Shanghai Pudong New Area 1994) (Beijing: Zhongguo tongji chubanshe 中國統計出版社, 1994); and Shanghaishi tongjiju 上海市統計局 (ed.), *Shanghai tongji nianjian 1994* 上海統計年鑑 1994 (Statistical Yearbook of Shanghai 1994) (Beijing: Zhongguo tongji chubanshe, 1994).

16. Anthony Gar-on Yeh and Xueqiang Xu, "Globalization and the Urban System in China," in *Emerging World Cities in Pacific Asia*, edited by Fu-chen Lo and Yue-man Yeung (Tokyo: United Nations University Press, 1996), pp. 219–67.

17. Shanghaishi tongjiju (ed.), *Shanghai tongji nianjian 1994* (see note 15), p. 255.

18. Shanghaishi tudi shiyong zhidu gaige lingdao xiaozu bangongshi 上海市土地 使用制度改革領導小組辦公室, Shanghaishi tongjiju (ed.), *Shanghaishi fangdichan shichang 1994* 上海市房地產市場 1994 (Shanghai Real Estate Market 1994) (Beijing: Zhongguo tongji chubanshe, 1994).

19. Shanghaishi tongjiju (ed.), *Shanghai tongji nianjian 1994* (see note 15), p. 241.

20. *Ming bao* 明報 (Ming Pao) (Hong Kong), 5 December 1991.

21. Wong Siu-lun, *Emigrant Entrepreneurs: Shanghai Industrialists in Hong Kong* (Hong Kong: Oxford University Press, 1988).

22. Sun Shiwen, "Some Thoughts on the Development Strategy of Shanghai's Pudong District," *China City Planning Review*, Vol. 10, No. 4 (1994), pp. 21–25.

23. Peter Geoffrey Hall, *The World Cities* (New York: St. Martin's Press, 1984). Also Fu-chen Lo and Yue-man Yeung (eds.), *Emerging World Cities in Pacific Asia* (Tokyo: United Nations University Press, 1996).

12

Urban Development and Redevelopment

Roger C. K. Chan

Urban development and redevelopment can be regarded as cyclical patterns of change and transformation of industrial societies. Obsolete and dilapidated areas within the city are often abandoned whereas prime sites in the city centre are subject to continuous pressure of having to tear down existing buildings to make room for more ambitious undertakings.[1]

In the case of China, the efforts since 1949 have been on modernization, namely, to transform the semi-colonial and semi-feudalist and war-torn national economy, with a view to making the country one of the leading economic powers in the world. As socialist construction is synonymous with rapid industrialization, an area in which China had hitherto little experience, she had to look to the former Soviet Union for initial inspiration and assistance. China was left at the crossroads of development after 1960 when Sino-Soviet relations turned sour. A self-reliance development strategy was then formulated. In his work "On the Ten Major Relationships" (25 April 1956), Mao Zedong 毛澤東 reflected on the course China should take on the road to nation-building. The emphasis was on industrial development, with a preference for heavy industry.[2] Not much was achieved as national economic construction was made to play second fiddle during the Cultural Revolution when politics were in command. The return of Deng Xiaoping 鄧小平 and the introduction of the open policy since December 1978 has opened up a new chapter in socialist development in China. Since 1980, market forces have formed part of the planned strategy and have also played a significant role in reshaping urban land use and the landscape of the big Chinese metropolises. In the course of these changes, the urban configuration of the major cities evolved and changed to accommodate an industrial development plan under national and regional development strategies.

As one of the important and major Chinese cities, Shanghai's growth and development have been unparalleled to other cities and metropolitan regions. Industrial development during Mao's time prompted the expansion of the city fringes and the setting up of industrial satellite towns (see Chapter 13). In the Deng era, the process of urban development has proven to be economically viable because of the potential material gains. In the last two decades, land reform and the leasing of land have been considered

I wish to thank Ning Yuemin 寧越敏 of East China Normal University (華東師範大學) for sharing information and for assistance on a field trip in Shanghai.

a means to achieve more cost-effective land-use planning; hence land plots in the city centre are closely sought after by both domestic developers and overseas investors. The direction of urban development and redevelopment in Shanghai is mainly affected by the increase in population caused by rural in-migration and the return of former city dwellers who were "sent down" to the countryside during the Mao period.

This chapter first reviews the development of Shanghai and her visions for the twenty-first century. It seeks to demonstrate that the factors leading to urban degradation are political, economic and historical. It then proceeds to examine the urban renewal mechanism of using economic and administrative means and the social repercussions and implications of the redevelopment process. It concludes that a successful redevelopment scheme will have to take into account not only the economic calculus, but also the social and cultural aspects of urbanism.

Post-1949 Development in Shanghai

Shanghai was initially a small river-port township along the mouth of the Huangpu River 黃浦江 which joins the Yangzi River. Under the Treaty of Nanking in 1842, the city became one of the five treaty ports to be opened for foreign trade. The first foreign settlement was established in 1848. Henceforth, the city was transformed from a walled-city to a city with a built-up area of 82.4 sq km in 1949.[3] By 1957, the size of the city was further expanded to 116 sq km. After a series of administrative changes and expansion, the spatial coverage of the city region of Shanghai in late 1958 was 6,340.5 sq km.[4] The quest for big and comprehensiveness was commonplace, whereby industrial development and urbanization were the order of the day. Big squares and main streets were constructed by tearing down the existing city fabric. According to Fung, "In 1954 city officials were criticized for indulging in the preparation of plans for million-person cities occupying areas of several hundred square kilometres, and for being overzealous in implementing prematurely long-term plans to create the spacious appearance of large cities."[5] Although the promotion of small and medium-sized cities was also advocated, it remained a discussion on paper and was never faithfully practised.

A new urban development strategy was introduced in the mid-1950s which tried, on the one hand, to contain the rapid development of large industrial cities and on the other hand, to promote small and medium-sized cities by decanting population and industrial development from the city core. The debate over city size and urban development reappeared on the planning agenda as recently as the 1980s.

In the early days of socialist construction, Shanghai was not among the designated key point cities. The geopolitical location of the municipality renders her too vulnerable to foreign attack in the event of warfare. Development was focused on the interior and the northeast region of the country during the First Five-year Plan. In the meantime, there was a conscious effort to relocate the working population from the city centre to the suburbs. New worker communities were built with a comprehensive range of facilities. New quarters were built near factories and industrial districts so as to reduce the cost and time involved in commuting to work. A large-scale housing development for Shanghai was launched. More than 20,000 housing units were earmarked in nine different locations.[6]

In brief, throughout the thirty years of construction and development in Shanghai, a series of issues presented themselves on the urban scene and stood in the way of the subsequent planning and development for the metropolis. In spite of the various master plans, there was a lack of impetus for urban construction. Plans were either implemented half-heartedly or not carried out at all.

The situation was particularly acute during the Cultural Revolution period when all was at a standstill. The situation regarding the population distribution and industrial location is a case in point. With more than 41,000 persons per sq km in the main urban area, there were over 10,000 production sites. The interface between residential and industrial areas is a serious issue confronting urban planners, particularly when people begin to aspire to a better living environment as their living standard improves. The new satellite towns were unable to attract voluntary migration out of the old urban areas where services and other amenities were concentrated. Investment in housing stock as well as in infrastructure, such as roads and other means of transport, was evidently lacking. These inadequacies, however, tended to be universal rather than unique to Shanghai. People chose to stay in the city core in spite of a deteriorating standard of living. In the 1980s, about 27% of the city dwellers were regarded as "households with a poor living standard" while some 3 million sq m of slum areas were identified. More than 0.8 million households used coking coal briquettes as a source of fuel. Industrial development took place at the expense of the environment so that the once prided Suzhou Creek (蘇州河) degenerated into the dirty and smelly nullah of Shanghai.

Urban Development in Shanghai since the 1980s

The 1984 Master Plan is probably the first comprehensive plan for Shanghai since the 1960s. Spatially speaking, it aims to renew and reinforce the urban centre with parallel development of the north (Baoshan–Wusong 寶山一吳淞 area)–south (Jinshanwei–Caohejing 金山衛一漕河涇 area) axis of Shanghai. The population of central Shanghai is earmarked at 6.5 million. The central city is divided into 11 zones, all of which are independent commercial centres. The central city and its outer zones are separated by green belts comprised of agricultural land, parks, botanical gardens and zoos. About 30–40 km from the central city is a set of satellite towns, including Minhang 閔行 , Jiading 嘉定 , Songjiang 淞江 , Wujing 吳涇 and Anting 安亭. The estimated population of the satellite towns is 1.5 million, the majority of which are to be resettled from the central area. Urban sprawl has been a noted feature of the rapid urban development since the 1980s. Four of the ten counties have been upgraded to districts, making a total of 14 districts. Second-level cities are planned in the suburban areas, too.[7]

In February 1985, the State Council approved the *General Report on the Strategy to Develop Shanghai's Economy*. In order to realize the objectives of the *Report*, a General Development Plan, representing a long-term effort on the part of the municipality towards a new development strategy, was introduced in 1986. The Plan consists of three sections: (1) guiding principles for Shanghai's economic development; (2) the policies and tasks for Shanghai's economic development strategies; and (3) measures for reforming the urban economic system. Five measures are suggested to achieve the objectives: (1) to promote the "opening to the outside world" policy; (2) to remodel traditional industry; (3) to develop new industries such as high-tech and bio-tech; (4) to develop the tertiary sector, from 30% of the gross domestic product (GDP) to 60% by the year 2000; and (5) to renew the old urban districts and to construct new urban areas.[8]

The opening of Pudong 浦東 provided the impetus for improving overall transport in Shanghai. The city's inner ring road (a highway constructed above the existing one along Zhongshan Road 中山路) opened in late 1994. In April 1995, the first line of the Metro began to serve commuters. The ring road, an elevated orbital, except for the section in Pudong, together with an underground railway system, changed the transport geography of the city. By the early 1990s, the road and bridge networks in Shanghai were improved significantly as a result of intensive planning and development since 1978. A total of RMB17.25 billion was spent on urban infrastructural projects in 1993 alone, as compared to RMB1.75 billion in 1985.

At the end of 1993, the total road length was 3,677 km, with a road surface of 28.29 million sq km. The Nanpu Bridge (南浦大橋) and Yangpu Bridge (楊浦大橋), which span the Huangpu River, were constructed and began operating within a short space of five years (see Figure 12.1). The 47.66 km-long inner ring road and the Chengdu north–south highway are now open. The road project along the Bund comprises three components: the extension of the embankment of the Huangpu River; the conversion and expansion of the land strip along the Bund into a 6 to 10-lane boulevard; and the construction of an underground car park with a sitting-out area above it.[9] Traffic conditions on the Bund to the northeast have improved significantly. The landscape and the outlook along the Bund have been radically transformed. The scale and the magnitude of these road improvement projects have immense implications for the urban landscape of Shanghai as a whole. In order to make way for the project work, tens of thousands of households have been resettled to the suburban districts and counties of the city, making the commuting to work a lengthy one for some and uprooting many from their neighbourhoods. These issues will be examined later in the section on urban renewal.

Visions for the Twenty-first Century

On 11 November 1994, the municipal government of Shanghai sponsored an international conference on the development strategy of Shanghai towards the twenty-first century. The objective of developing the metropolis into an international economic and financial centre of China in the next century was discussed and a report under the same title was published.[10] The promotion of the urban spatial location and sectoral restructuring are regarded as a means to achieve the targets of economic development.

The report highlights the advantages that the city stands to gain from the increased manufacturing activities in the Asia–Pacific region and the rapid economic growth in East Asia. China, during the current reform and open era, will complement and fit into the development trends of the region. At the same time, Shanghai, with the Pudong development plan, will become the focal point of development for both the region and China as a whole by virtue of its strategic location. To that end, Shanghai will

Figure 12.1   Shanghai: Infrastructure Development

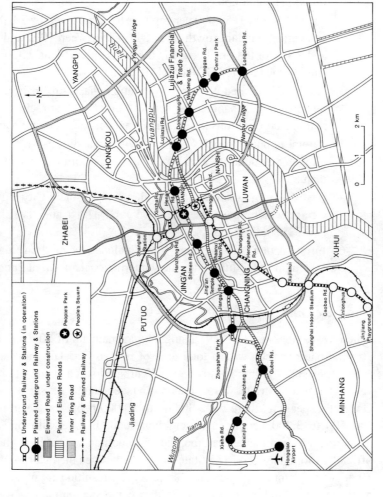

Source: Modified from Brooke Hillier Parker, October 1994.

have to catch up with other international metropolitan cities in East and Southeast Asia in the coming decade in a number of ways. The strategic development objectives to be attained by the municipality by the year 2010 are:

1. A total urban area of 6,300 sq km with a multiple-centre, multiple-function megalopolis.
2. A GDP of RMB150,000 per capita is to be achieved by 2010, with an average annual growth rate of 11.4% between 1995 and 2000, and 9.8% for the first decade in the next century. This will bring to fruition the targeted GDP of RMB2,000 billion.
3. A tertiary-oriented economy with an emphasis on finance, trade, information exchange, the service sector and attracting multi-national corporations to set up regional headquarters in Shanghai.
4. A total population of 14 million (with an additional 4–5 million "floating population"), meaning an urbanization level of more than 80%.
5. Restructuring urban land use with a 5 sq km new City Business Centre which spans the Bund (in Puxi 浦西) and the Lujiazui 陸家嘴 area (in Pudong).
6. Infrastructure development that includes a modern highway system, port facilities and a new international airport at Pudong.[11]

Land Resources

When it was liberated in 1949, Shanghai was made up of 20 districts and 10 suburban districts, with a total area of 636 sq km. The built-up area amounted to 82.4 sq km. In July 1950, 20 urban districts were set up. One year later, sub-districts were created to take charge of social affairs. Generally speaking, there were 30,000 to 50,000 people in a sub-district and 500 to 3,000 people in a neighbourhood. In line with the socio-economic development at the time, the metropolitan area of Shanghai was officially formed in 1958. The State Council approved the incorporation of 10 adjacent counties of Jiangsu 江蘇 province, resulting in an additional 5,500 sq km of land. In the same year, the people's communes were set up to replace the townships at the sub-district level. The districts of Wusong and Minhang were established in 1980 and 1982, respectively. Shanghai ended up in 1982 with an administrative set-up of 12 urban districts, 120 sub-districts, 10 counties, 33 designated towns and 206 people's communes.[12]

Population density is high in Shanghai. The average is 25,104 persons per sq km and 42,900 persons per sq km in the old urban areas. Urban amenities are not well provided for in these districts and buildings exhibit signs of dilapidation. This is the result of poor planning at the earlier stages of development. As Shanghai was one of the treaty ports in pre-liberation China, development along the Bund — the old city core — was not co-ordinated and took place haphazardly. Within the international concession districts, different planning standards were applied. Road networks were designed only to facilitate communication within the respective zones, leaving a legacy of east–west rather than north–south routing. The old city soon proved to be out of tune and incompatible with the development in other parts of the metropolis.

Since 1949, few resources have been committed to urban development. Industrial development went side by side with a minimum amount of capital input. Street factories were squeezed into the residential areas because of the low set-up costs there. It also reduced the distances to work and alleviated the burden on the transport authorities. Since the 1960s, the street-level dwellings on Huaihai Road (淮海路) were converted into shop fronts. Land-use patterns were mixed and incompatible. Land development lacked a plan and was out of control. Surrounding the heart of the city were eight key industrial zones, 70 industrial streets and more than 1,000 industrial plants.[13]

The initial idea of cost-saving industrial and commercial development generated a vast array of urban problems which still exist. The over-concentration of industrial activities has led to all sorts of pollution, hence to the degradation of the environmental quality of the city (see Chapter 18). The situation is aggravated by the highly concentrated population and the under supply of transport and other infrastructural facilities.[14] Urban redevelopment is necessary and essential to transform Shanghai into a Chinese metropolis in the coming millennium.

It was contemplated to use the price differential between urban industrial land and urban commercial land as an incentive to encourage the relocation of industrial enterprises. The implementation was disappointing. During the Seventh Five-year Plan and the Eighth Five-year Plan, only 103 and 131 factories respectively were relocated from the urban core to the suburban districts. The key factor was a monetary one. The cost of land acquisition, amounting to some 40% of the total relocation costs, was of great concern to the enterprises. Until 1992, firms did not benefit directly from the price differential of the land they vacated, yet they had to find resources to foot the bill for relocation. Few firms were financially sound and had the required funds.[15] To get round this problem, the price differential was put into practice, while land valuation and leasing constituted a second option.

Land valuation is one of the changes accompanying the open policy. The administrative size of Shanghai stands at 6,340.5 sq km. Under the land-use grading method, a classification scheme of 10 grades has been devised for land in Puxi and of eight grades in Pudong. In Puxi, sites ranked between grades 1–4 are regarded as prosperous sites (*fanhua diduan* 繁華地段), with the remaining areas belonging to non-prosperous sites (*feifanhua diduan* 非繁華地段).[16] In August 1988, the first land lot to be leased out since 1949 was lot No. 26 at Hongqiao 虹橋 new development zone. This marked the advent of a new phase in urban land reform in Shanghai.

In 1992 and 1993, more than 450 land plots covering a total land area of 6,977 ha, were leased. Of the newly leased land, 0.52% was in old districts where obsolete buildings were torn down to make room for new ones.[17]

Factors Leading to Urban Degradation

Shanghai was founded as a treaty port but underwent rapid urban development in the early decades of this century. Development prior to 1949, despite the fact that the city was a global metropolis, was piecemeal in nature and haphazard in form. The Cultural Revolution, when "politics took command," left no room for urban planning. A host of planning problems beset the city such that much effort was needed to improve the obsolete urban system.[18] These problems ranged from high density and concentration of buildings, poor urban facilities, lack of urban housing space to pollution of various kinds. These "urban ills" were further aggravated by an "ideological bias."[19]

A metropolitan plan for Shanghai was formed in 1927, with a view to converting Wujiaochang 五角場 in the northeastern part of the city into the new city centre. A municipal government building, a library and a museum were included in the blueprint. The plan was shelved in 1937 with the outbreak of the anti-Japanese war. The concessions made for foreign settlements in the early decade of this century had facilitated urban development of the city. The old walled-city jointly shared between the French, the Japanese and the International settlements, laid down the urban fabric of

Shanghai before the communists took over. Due to the resulting divergent outlooks and city lights, Shanghai earned the nickname of "a paradise for risk-takers." Between 1946 and 1949, the municipal city planning commission prepared three master plans, the first of their kind in China. These plans aimed at containing the urban sprawl of Shanghai by creating a green belt with new satellite towns 20–40 km from the city. New quays and elevated expressways were also conceived for the new urban districts that were to be constructed. Most of these plans were formulated under the influence of the then prevailing planning ideologies in Western countries.

The initial plan for the city after 1949 was devised with the assistance of Soviet planners. It envisaged the formation of a single-centre metropolitan region with 5.5 million people. Extensive renovation of the old urban districts was also planned. As this did not fit into the national plan and the then economic situation of Shanghai, it was aborted. Towards the end of the First Five-year Plan, proposals were made for merging existing factories into medium and large ones. Ten industrial districts with specialized production functions were conceived: the Taopu 桃浦 and Beixinjing 北新涇 for chemical production; Pengpu 彭浦 , Caohejing 漕河涇 , Wujiaochang 五角場 for mechanical industry; Zhoujiadu 周家渡 and Wusong 吳淞 for iron and steel; Changqiao 長橋 for building materials, Qingningsi 慶寧寺 for ship building and Gaoqiao 高橋 for chemical and oil refineries.[20] The increasing scale of production brought about a new level of conflict to the fore between production and environmental protection. In order to resolve the growing tension, the dispersion of industrial activities to satellite towns began in 1958. Minhang, Wujing, Jiading, Anting and Songjiang were chosen as sites for satellite towns. The primary objective of these new towns was industrial production rather than decanting the population within the urban districts, a planning ethos which is rather unique in the socialist planning strategy.

The series of political campaigns which took place from the late fifties to the early seventies stalled further capital construction in the urban areas. In 1978, the municipal government rehabilitated the Urban Planning and Management Bureau and the Urban Planning and Design Institute and they were to look after the urban planning and development of Shanghai. It was against this background that municipal Shanghai underwent a long period of unplanned and unco-ordinated growth and expansion, with little attention paid to its physical planning and environment. The importance of urban infrastructural planning and development was also overlooked under the development concepts of anti-urbanism and industrial-led development.[21] The need to improve conditions in Shanghai was evident at the beginning of the current opening and reform era.

The Mechanism of Urban Renewal[22]

One of the limitations on efficient planning prior to the reform era was the complicated web of decision-making circuits within the bureaucracy. Apart from a top-down planning framework, various levels of government were involved in the operation and management of industrial enterprises, which affected the spatial arrangement of activities. This huge and complicated set of relations suffocated the initiative of redevelopment and renewal, especially in areas of rapid development. Since the 1980s, the decision-making power devolved to the district and county levels and other lower authorities. The district authorities may approve development projects up to RMB5 million. The scope of activities of the district authorities has been augmented to invite initiatives in the realm of urban construction as well as land-use management.[23]

The impact of an uneven taxation system upon Shanghai is illustrated by Lynn T. White III.[24] The amount of money going to the central authorities far exceeds that retained by the municipal government. The resources available for government disposal and for capital construction tend, therefore, to be meagre. It is estimated that between 1949 and 1989, Shanghai was "taxed" by the central government an amount of RMB411.7 billion against a total revenue of RMB476.9 billion, leaving the government with only RMB65.2 billion for local expenditures.[25] The central government, which was responsible for large-scale projects in Shanghai, received the bulk of the revenue. For the remaining revenue, as much as 50% went to local capital construction in the fields of education, health, housing, and the like. Subsidies for wages and bonuses accounted for a significant portion of the local expenditures. About 7.3% went to rural development projects to support rural industry, as relief funds and for irrigation projects. In 1982, only about 4% went to urban construction and maintenance which explains in part why urban facilities in most cities are poorly maintained and an overhaul is urgently required. One of the solutions to the problems is financial reform.

Financial reforms were introduced in 1985. Although the share of the local government in terms of percentage was increased, there was no significant improvement in real terms. The disposable income of the municipal government remained low due to a general decline in revenue.

The amount stood at RMB18.16 billion in 1985 and RMB15.35 billion in 1988. The situation was going from bad to worse. In 1988, greater financial autonomy was granted to the municipal government with a favourable policy in the form of the contract responsibility system which was similar to that adopted in Guangdong province. In essence, the system took the revenue of 1987 as the base year, so with a revenue of RMB16.5 billion, RMB10.5 billion was remitted to the central government, leaving the balance at the disposal of the municipal government of Shanghai. This "contract" lasted from 1988 to 1990. From 1991 onwards, any "surplus" had to be equally divided between the central and the local government.[26]

Since the introduction of land and housing reforms in China, the stimulus for urban renewal has been on the increase. It is believed that land leasing can help raise funds for urban renewal.[27] The Pudong development plan, which sets out to transform Shanghai into the key economic hub of China in the next century, heightens the demand for prime-site land in the Puxi region. The pace of demolition is in full swing and the area around Huaihai Road resembles the booming sites during World War II. The forces which work to tear down the existing urban fabric in old Shanghai are the infrastructural projects initiated by the municipal government and the demand generated by private developers. The system of urban management in Shanghai is shown in Figure 12.2.

In order to improve the investment environment of Shanghai, the government has worked zealously on elevated highways, bridges and motor roads in the city. A commanding office is to be set up under the mayor's office, the terms of reference of which include the resumption of land plots and the resettlement of residents affected by the project. Resettlement is carried out by neighbourhood committees at the local level. Since it is a municipal project, and the local committees have for long been liaising with the residents, land resumption and resettlement are carried out effectively. There are reported cases of residents resenting being "sent down" to the peripheral districts because of problems in commuting to work and in gaining access to amenities, but they were appeased either by persuasion or by monetary compensation.

Generally speaking, housing shortages and the ageing of the building stock are two key issues preventing a quicker pace of urban redevelopment. Since 1978, the government has spent RMB13.24 billion to improve housing conditions in Shanghai. Between 1949 and 1978, the amount of construction in terms of gross floor area was 71%.[28] While housing remains in acute demand in Shanghai, new buildings have been erected,

**Figure 12.2   Government Structure and Land Management Institutions in
Shanghai Municipality**

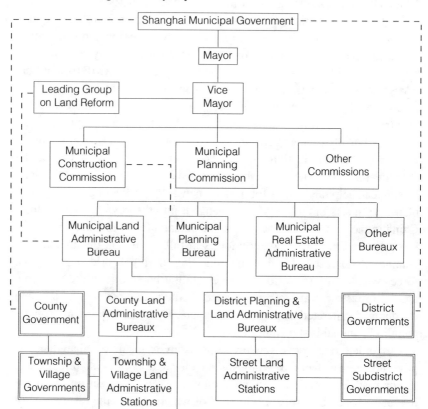

Note: The subordination of the Land Bureau to the Construction Commission is
           atypical, though the same arrangement exists in Guangzhou. In most cities,
           the Land Bureau reports directly to the relevant vice-mayor or indirectly
           through other commissions.

Source: World Bank, *China: Urban Land Management in an Emerging Market
           Economy* (see note 15), p. 213.

existing alongside the dilapidated ones on the main streets of the city.

State enterprises at times removed the existing factories to make way
for a better utilization of the land. Development companies, usually
formed jointly by the enterprises and the local neighbourhood committees,
take the issues of resumption and resettlement into their own hands. The
tension tends to be weak for projects involving only residents of a few

blocks in a district. Foreign developers also participate in the redevelopment and renewal activities in Shanghai, in which case, the job of land resumption and arranging compensation is mostly left to the Chinese partner or agent.

The land leasing records of 1993 show that some US$1.8 billion was raised from the leasing of land. The money was spent on compensating the residents and improving the existing urban infrastructure. As the leasing system necessitates contributions by foreign developers for the actual building construction, this strategy also alleviates pressures on the municipal government to raise funds for construction and redevelopment. In recent years, the average price for office buildings, residential blocks and mixed buildings is US$600 per sq m, with some fetching as much as US$888 per sq m. In Huangpu district, buildings of about 3,520,000 sq m in area are branded as "ailing and dangerous." An example of urban renewal in Shanghai occurred in April 1992, when land plot No. 71 along Beijing East Road (北京東路) was leased at US$4.6 million for the development of two buildings. By the end of 1993, more than 10 ha of land had been leased out, with a projected build-up space of 640,000 sq m. The leased land fetched a total income of US$283 million. About 30% of it went to urban facilities and infrastructural development and the remaining 70% was spent on compensation and resettlement of the tenants. The total number of affected households was 5,380.[29]

Another dimension of urban renewal is the squatter areas (*penghu* 棚戶) in the city. The reasons for demolishing the squatter areas are many. It can be for overall neighbourhood improvement, for making way for urban infrastructural projects, or because of the development plans initiated by foreign investors as mentioned earlier. In 1985, the total squatter area was 4 million sq m. The figure decreased to 1 million in 1995. It is expected that by 1997 the issue of squatter housing will be resolved.[30] For a long time, the guiding principle for squatter redevelopment was "to rebuild on demolished sites, resettle on original sites and to benefit the neighbourhood." As reflected in Table 12.1, the differences between living area allocations to the fringe areas or to nearby sites are compensated for by accessibility to social and other amenities within the urban area for near site allocation. This policy resulted in concentration and high-density redevelopment. This is contrary to the objective of renewal by thinning out the over-crowded settlements.

In practice, there are three methods to redevelop the *penghu*. The first concerns those located in prime sites in the city centre. The dwellers

Table 12.1   Shanghai Standards for the Replacement of Demolished Housing

(Unit: m^2/person)

Original living area	Living area allocation in the same or near site	Living area allocation to fringe area
under 4	maintain previous amount	4
4–7	4–5	5–6
7–10	5–6	6–7
10–13	6–7	7–8
13–16	7–8	8–9
16–19	8–9	9–10
19–22	9–10	10–11
22–25	10–11	11–12
25–30	11–12	12
30+	12	12

Source: Shanghai City Building Demolition and Relocation Administration Detailed Implementation Regulation, 19 July 1991, quoted in World Bank, China: Urban *Land Management in an Emerging Market Economy* (see note 15), p. 233.

should be resettled to make room for commercial and more profitable undertakings in order that the latent value of the plots can be realized. The second one affects ordinary land sites, whereby new dwellings based on planning standards and regulations are constructed (see Table 12.1). The third method of development involves the resettlement of existing dwellers and the freeing up of land for recreational, infrastructural facilities and communal activities, so that the overall planning of the city can be carried out.[31] Effective and fair development policies are introduced for monitoring the redevelopment of the squatter areas. It includes legislations to facilitate squatter removal, reasonable pricing for development, tax reductions and rebates, value-added and appreciation taxes, housing loans for disadvantaged groups, regulations governing development companies and so on. Diversity is vital to a successful renewal strategy, for the concept of uniformity is at variance with what the residents can afford and with the aspirations of the dwellers and will lead to a poor response to redevelopment proposals. The financial arrangements originating from different sources and from diversity in housing standards for different groups will, on the other hand, attract greater support for redevelopment proposals. It is important that the needs of those affected are noted and accommodated in a flexible manner. The setting up of a specialized department to deal with *penghu* renewal and reconstruction of old houses is desired and is being planned to reduce the red-tape and to expedite the process of renewal and redevelopment.[32]

The Dilemma of Urban Renewal

During the interwar period, the transformation of Shanghai into a modern metropolis was fuelled by both indigenous and international forces. Hence, the rate of development was uneven and planning standards varied. These were manifested in, for instance, bottlenecks for passenger flow as well as for resource flow. Underground piping of varying standards was laid at different times, making it more difficult to achieve standardization and uniformity.[33] In the post-liberation era, attempts to reduce the demands for urban land were made with the development of satellite towns surrounding the city. During the 1960s and 1970s, open space and parks were eliminated in the downtown areas. Some street-level dwellings were converted into commercial and retailing outlets. A sizable number of mansions were demolished, thereby undermining the architectural legacy of the city. The controversy between preservation and development is now a moot point among the country's planners. With land available for development fetching a higher price than ever, the options available for resettlement are correspondingly limited. As long as job opportunities and other amenities stay within the main urban area, any solution will only generate greater demands for commuting to and from the urban area. The pressures are the same on infrastructural development. The Shanghainese are reluctant to move across to the east bank of the Huangpu River, despite the promotion of Pudong by the government.[34]

The distaste for resettlement by the residents affected by the construction of the city metro (subway) system, the ring road and others stems not only from their being physically uprooted, but also from the feeling of losing a community or being moved out of a familiar setting. A sense of community, which has a profound meaning among the Chinese, takes generations to cultivate. Yet, together with the old buildings, it is being devastated by the sledge hammer overnight. In some circumstances, the new resettlement areas are not ready, in terms of infrastructure and amenities, to take in new residents. Some of these areas are, for instance, far away from the city centre, but the major traffic link is still rather basic so that congestion and bottlenecks are common. Safety and security are additional concerns of the newcomers. Thefts, petty crimes and even blackmail have been reported in the new areas. The apprehension felt by the dwellers is evident. The response of the authorities to all these problems is, almost unequivocally, that sacrifice is inevitable for the city as a whole to benefit in the long run.[35]

Redevelopment in the urban core often generates problems because of the piecemeal nature of development. Due to the high population density and fragmentary land plots, land resumption and subsequent development are often carried out without systematic and long-term planning. In some instances, zoning plans contradict the proposed land-use for leasing sites. The principle of "planning comes before leasing" is unlikely to be adhered to nor effectively implemented. Some 600 land parcels were released between 1992 and 1995, aimed at providing Grade A office space for international investors. In this regard, the total office space produced is equivalent to what Hong Kong produced in the last three-and-a-half decades. The rapid pace of development is considered counter-productive by some experts on real estate development.[36]

The above serves as an illustration of some aspects of the "redevelopment syndrome" in Shanghai and other big metropolises in China. In order to make more room for commercial and office development in prime city sites and to ease traffic congestion, the population in the densely inhabited districts has to be resettled to the peripheral areas. Some of the affected residents, dissatisfied with the amount of compensation offered, have taken their frustrations to the street by organizing demonstrations.[37] While the principle remains that sacrifice is needed for the sake of the city and the common good, there is an increasing concern that the economic gains may be outweighed by the social costs.[38]

Conclusion

In this chapter we have reviewed the processes and impetus for urban development and redevelopment in Shanghai during the reform era and the historical legacy leading thereto. Many of the problems facing city planners in Shanghai today can be attributed to the early development under Mao when new directions for growth were contemplated. A high population density, an unbalanced economic structure, an inefficient transport system and an obsolete mode of social production all make current reform attempts and measures arduous tasks. Instead of resorting to administrative directives and mass mobilization, market value is regarded as the panacea to the city's urban problems. Shanghai is one of the metropolises in China where a significant portion of the working population relies on the state and quasi-state enterprises for a living. In the early 1990s, state industry accounted for 65% of industrial output as compared to 40% in Guangdong. Overstaffing is ubiquitous.[39] The elimination of redundancy is perhaps economically viable, but since state employments is tied to a string of benefits-in-kind, such as housing and other social welfare benefits, a rapid introduction of the market mechanism will invite systemic instability.

The foregoing account shows that the urban renewal mechanism, although capable of addressing the issue of the "freeing up" of land for high-value development, has left many stones in the social domain unturned. Behind the wrecker's ball hammering at the city's architectural fabric, new and old, an entire tier of cultural heritage is also being erased. It could well be true that demolishing dilapidated buildings is less expensive than rehabilitating them, but the fact remains that too little concern has been given to cultural aspects and preservation in the process of redevelopment. The city hosts 25 of the total 90-odd national buildings, mostly located along the Bund. The buildings are preserved by the Law on Preserving Excellent Historic Buildings. They are unfailing tourist attractions and landmarks in Shanghai. At the street level, the *lilong* 里弄 type of settlement, which is representative of a unique Chinese architectural design and also a form of neighbourhood planning, is under a less than caring hand. The cultural supremacy Shanghai enjoyed in the 1930s is the reason the city was once the Mecca of Chinese performing artists and literature writers. It used to be not only the financial centre, but also the cultural centre of the country. Under the freewheeling capitalistic mentality of the current reform, it could perhaps recapture its fame as the Manhattan of the Orient, but less of the glitter of its Parisian heritage. The dilemma of urban renewal described in this chapter will express itself in an array of costly and thorny issues straddling the development plan of Shanghai in the next century.

The expansion of Pudong finally completes the "big-pie" development for Shanghai and the former two-pronged development plans (Baoshan in the north and Jinshanwei in the south) have become history. Under the new blueprint for Shanghai, spatial coverage and population size are unprecedented in the Chinese development experience. The ability to deal with the problems in this metropolis presents a serious challenge to the authorities. The plans which have been tabled tend to paint an optimistic picture, although it remains to be seen as to what the actual outcome of these strategies might be.

To arrest the social consequences of urban renewal demands a new thinking and arrangement of societal resource allocation. This is a process which will put pressures on the existing social welfare and benefit framework of Chinese society — a framework which is under evaluation and is, in fact, under constant erosion. Although we are not prophesying a doomsday scenario, the reality is that under the current reform, social securities such as housing and other welfare provisions, are crumbling. There appear to be few signs of a new and dynamic framework within sight. Until a parallel institutional reform is carried out, the prospects for development appear bleak, despite the seeming accomplishments of the initial stage.

Notes

1. This phenomenon is particularly prevalent in big American cities. Urban sprawl or expansion is an ongoing process. The process is related also to "the graying of suburbia" which represents a decline of population in the inner city area with increasing people living in the suburbs. See *The Economist*, 15 October 1994, p. 41.

2. See, for instance, the discussion by Chan Kam Wing, *Cities with Invisible Walls* (Hong Kong: Oxford University Press, 1994), pp. 59–72.

3. For a review of the pre-1949 development of Shanghai, see Ka-iu Fung, Zhong-min Yan and Yue-min Ning, "Shanghai: China's World City," in *China's Coastal Cities: Catalysts for Modernization*, edited by Yue-man Yeung and Xu-wei Hu (Honolulu: University of Hawaii Press, 1992), pp. 124–52.

4. Fung, Yan and Ning, "Shanghai: China's World City" (see note 3), p. 135. Ka-iu Fung, "The Spatial Development of Shanghai," in *Shanghai: Revolution and Development in an Asian Metropolis*, edited by Christopher Howe (Cambridge: Cambridge University Press, 1981), pp. 271–72.

5. Fung, "The Spatial Development of Shanghai" (see note 4), p. 276.

6. Ibid., p. 282.

7. See *Touzi Zhongguo da shichang —— Shanghaishi zhuanji* 投資中國大市場 —— 上海市專輯 (*A Guide to Investment in China: Shanghai Municipality Section*) (Hong Kong: Ta Kung Pao Press Ltd., 1994), p. 15.

8. Chen Minzhi 陳敏之, "Lun Shanghai chengshi fazhan zhanlüe" 論上海城市發展戰略 (Development Strategy of Shanghai City), *Chengshi guihua* 城市規劃 (City Planning Review), Vol. 10, No. 6 (1986), pp. 21–24.

9. *Touzi Zhongguo da shichang —— Shanghaishi zhuanji* (see note 7), p. 28.

10. See Cai Laixing 蔡來興, "Maixiang 21 shijie de Shanghai" 邁向21世紀的上海 (Shanghai: Striding towards the 21st Century), in *Maixiang 21 shijie de Shanghai* (Shanghai: Striding towards the 21st Century) (Shanghai: Shanghai renmin chubanshe 上海人民出版社, 1995), pp. 15–46. The volume is the latest collection of reports illustrating the current leading thinking on the

development strategies commissioned by the Shanghai municipal government.

11. *Hua qiao ribao* 華僑日報 (Overseas Chinese Daily News), 23 November 1994, p. 24.

12. Information supplied by Ning Yuemin of East China Normal University in 1995.

13. Liu Ta, "Urban Renewal and Development of Shanghai City," *Chinese Geographical Science*, Vol. 4, No. 3 (1994), p. 224.

14. According to Fung, Yan and Ning, "Shanghai: China's World City" (see note 3), p. 128, Shanghai used to boast of the wealth of surface and underground water resources her estuary topography had to offer. Exploration in 1860 found the natural resources to be of good quality. Exploitation of water resources in an uncaring manner began to take its toll in current decades. The aquifers have lowered to an alarming level whereas the Suzhou Creek and other water networks are grossly polluted by industrial and residential discharges. The costs for resurrection is enormous. In the 1980s, appeals had been made to The World Bank and the Australian International Development Assistance Bureau for feasibility study and loans to deal with the liquid waste management problems of the Huangpu River. Reported in J. Hyslop "The Spatial Structure of Shanghai City Proper" in *China's Spatial Economy*, edited by G.J.R. Linge and D. K. Forbes (Hong Kong: Oxford University Press, 1990), p. 148.

15. World Bank, *China: Urban Land Management in an Emerging Market Economy* (Washington, D.C.: World Bank, 1993), pp. 18–19.

16. *Touzi Zhongguo da shichang —— Shanghaishi zhuanji* (see note 7), pp. 29–30.

17. Wang Tongdan 王同旦, "Yi di chouzi gaizao chengshi" 以地籌資改造城市 (Raise Funds by the Land to Deal with Urban Reform), *Chengshi yanjiu* 城市研究 (Urban Research), No. 1 (1995), p. 30.

18. Fung, Yan and Ning, "Shanghai: China's World City" (see note 3), pp. 147–49.

19. See Kam-wing Chan, "The Distinguishing Features of Urbanization in Socialist Countries," *Chinese Journal of Population Science*, Vol. 3, No. 3 (1991), pp. 165–78; Yue-man Yeung, *Changing Cities of Pacific Asia: A Scholarly Interpretation* (Hong Kong: The Chinese University Press, 1990), pp. 35–36.

20. According to Fung, Yan and Ning, "Shanghai: China's World City" (see note 3), "These industrial districts and settlements, with a total area of 56 sq km, have 440 industrial plants and 380,000 employees" (p. 137). It also reflects the directions of spatial expansion of the city during the early phase of industrial development.

21. Won Bae Kim, "The Role and Structure of Metropolises in China's Urban

Economy," *Third World Planning Review*, Vol. 13, No. 2 (1991), pp. 155–77.

22. World Bank, *China: Urban Land Management in an Emerging Market Economy* (see note 15), discusses the procedures and costs of urban resettlement in selected cities in China, including case studies from Shanghai, pp. 228–33.

23. Information supplied by Ning Yuemin of East China Normal University in 1995.

24. Lynn T. White III, *Shanghai Shanghaied? Uneven Taxes in Reform China* (Hong Kong: Centre of Asian Studies, University of Hong Kong, 1989).

25. Complied from Shanghaishi tongjiju 上海市統計局 (ed.), *Xin Shanghai sishi nian* 新上海四十年 (New Shanghai in Forty Years) (Beijing: Zhongguo tongji chubanshe 中國統計出版社, 1989), pp. 61, 77.

26. Data collected during an interview conducted in Shanghai in 1995.

27. Wang, "Yi di chouzi gaizao chengshi" (see note 17), pp. 29–31.

28. Liu, "Urban Renewal and Development of Shanghai City" (see note 13).

29. Wang, "Yi di chouzi gaizao chengshi" (see note 17).

30. Personal communication with a city planner from Shanghai.

31. Chen Yewei 陳業偉, "Shanghai jiuqu zhuzhai gaizao de xin zhengce" 上海舊 區住宅改造的新政策 (New Strategy for Old Residential Redevelopment in Shanghai), *City Planning Review*, Vol. 15, No. 6 (1991), pp. 26–30.

32. Ibid., pp. 29–30.

33. Liu, "Urban Renewal and Development of Shanghai City" (see note 13), pp. 219–31.

34. There was the saying amongst the Shanghainese that "Ning yao Puxi yi zhang chuang, bu yao Pudong yi jian fang" 寧要浦西一張床，不要浦東一間房 (They prefer a bed in Puxi to a flat in Pudong).

35. "Shanghai in Moving Plea," *South China Morning Post*, 14 August 1995, p. 8.

36. Kari Huus, "Boom and Busted, Shanghai Construction Takes off, but Profits May Fizzle," *Far Eastern Economic Review*, 13 April 1995, pp. 48–49.

37. It was reported that a few hundred residents demonstrated in the street to voice out their dissatisfaction regarding resettlement arrangement. The authorities, however, were quick to deny such incident. See *Ming bao* 明報 (Ming Pao) (Hong Kong), 11 March 1995, p. B1.

38. For a critical discussion on the relations between state intervention and industrial development, see Allen Scott, "The Meaning and Social Origins of Discourse on the Spatial Foundations of Society," in *A Search for Common Ground*, edited by Peter Gould and Gunnar Olsson (London: Pion Press, 1982), pp. 141–56.

39. "Giant Emerges from Dark Years," *South China Morning Post*, China Business Review, 26 July 1992, p. 5; "China: Big City Blues," *The Economist*, 11 April 1992, p. 26.

13

Satellite Towns
Development and Contributions

K. I. Fung

In his *Grand Scheme of Nation Building* (*Jianguo dagang* 建國大綱), Dr. Sun Yat-sen (孫逸仙) first propounded the idea of building satellite towns in China. He suggested the development of this type of settlement for the city of Chongqing 重慶 in Sichuan.[1] Like his other idealized plans for national construction, such as the building of a national railway network, water conservancy projects, deep sea port construction, and the development of modern industry and mining, the building of satellite towns never materialized due to the Sino–Japanese War and the ensuing open conflicts between the Communists and the Nationalists.

The satellite town programme was not actively implemented until the late 1950s, almost a decade after the ascendancy to power of the Chinese Communist Party. The introduction of the programme was designed to curb fast metropolitan growth during the First Five-year Plan period (1953–1957), when China emulated the Soviet development model of concentrating on large-scale industrial projects in major urban centres. Since the early 1980s, several articles have appeared, discussing the planning and development of Shanghai's satellite towns. Articles in the late 1980s and early 1990s also evaluate the success of the satellite town programme in this world city.[2] This chapter discusses the development of satellite towns in Shanghai, and the contributions of these suburban communities to the city region and, in particular, to the central city.

Background of Satellite Town Development in Shanghai

Before 1949, Shanghai had already attained prominence as China's most important industrial city, with about 1.1% of the nation's population.[3] The metropolis was the creation of several foreign powers during the treaty port era. For almost a century, the city grew of its own accord without any co-ordinated planning. Much of this haphazard growth is evident from the randomly spaced, narrow and windy streets. A chaotic land-use pattern evolved from the unplanned growth of the city. Within the major industrial areas of Zhabei 閘北, Nandu 南渡 and Pudong 浦東, factories intermingled with high-density squalid dwellings. In 1951, the municipal government established the Urban Construction Committee which initiated the transformation of the existing intermixture of factories and dwellings into spatially distinct zones of industrial and residential land use.[4]

Because Shanghai's coastal location was vulnerable to the Nationalists' military attacks, the central authorities did not favour large-scale industrial and urban development in the city, while major industrial investments were made in key-point cities in the interior regions. Despite the lack of capital investments, the gross value of industrial production of the metropolis climbed steadily from RMB3.6 billion in 1949 to RMB9.1 billion in 1955. The coastal region, as a whole, also claimed a larger share of the total gross value of industrial output in China.[5] Subsequently, the regional development policy implemented by the central government in the early 1950s was revised in the spring of 1956 in order to utilize the old industrial bases of Shanghai and Tianjin 天津 to accelerate the process of national industrialization. Since the mid-1950s, an upsurge of state capital input in coastal manufacturing centres greatly stimulated the expansion of industries in Shanghai. It also acted as a catalyst for accelerating the transformation of the industrial land use in the city. The choice of suburban locations for Shanghai's rapidly growing heavy industries, such as iron and steel manufacturing, chemical works and oil refining, was primarily based on environmental factors. The availability of suburban land, as a result of land reform, at the disposal of Shanghai's city planners facilitated the rational dispersal of manufacturing activities from the extremely congested central city. By the end of 1957, a multi-nodal pattern of industrial land use emerged in Shanghai. The preliminary stage of socialist urban transformation of this largest foreigner-created city in contemporary China was accomplished by building all nine new workers' villages at the immediate periphery of the city's built-up areas.[6]

The year 1958 heralded the beginning of a new phase of planning and development of the metropolis. The rapid spatial growth and influx of peasants resulting from a substantial increase of state investments in industrial expansion in that year made it necessary to disperse both residents and economic activities from the central city.

The development of planned satellite settlements in the suburban areas of large urban centres was a ramification of central policy of building small and medium-sized cities to avoid the "urban gigantism" which was prevalent during the latter part of the First Five-year Plan period. Another state policy that contributed to Shanghai's satellite town programme was the institution of city regions at all major economic centres. Each city region included a central city and extensive suburban territories which were subdivided into the near-suburb (*jinjiao* 近郊), the outer limits of which were about 10 km from the edge of the central city, and the far-suburb (*yuanjiao* 遠郊) outside the near-suburb. The near-suburb was exclusively devoted to intensive market gardening, producing over 70% of the vegetable needs of the central city. The far-suburb, on the other hand, was generally a less intensively cultivated area, producing a staple food crop and other agricultural crops. Most of China's satellite towns were built within the far-suburb. The urban-centred administrative and planning unit allowed the municipal government to adopt a unitary planning approach for the entire area, facilitating decentralization of industrial activities from the urban core to the suburbs, demographic and labour planning, development of internal and external linkages, and organization of agricultural land use, with special emphasis on achieving self-sufficiency in subsidiary food supply for the central city population. During the 1958 to 1960 period, the city regions that vigorously pursued the satellite town programme included Beijing 北京 , Tianjin, Shanghai, Guangzhou 廣州 , Nanjing 南京 , Hefei 合肥 , Zhengzhou 鄭州 , Ji'nan 濟南 , Hantan 邯鄲 , Changchun 長春 , Changsha 長沙 and the oil city of Daqing 大慶 .[7]

In Shanghai, the initial spatial reorganization took place early in 1958 when the city gained administrative control over three adjacent counties — Baoshan 寶山 to the north, Jiading 嘉定 to the northwest and Shanghai to the south. In December of the same year, the total area placed under the direct control of the Shanghai People's municipal government increased to 5,908.42 sq km as a result of the further annexation of the surrounding counties of Chuansha 川沙 , Nanhui 南匯 , Fengxian 奉賢 , Jinshan 金山 , Songjiang 松江 , Qingpu 青浦 and Chongming 崇明 .[8] Such a vast territory allowed the planners to locate the city's satellite towns within a radius of up to 70 km from the city limits.

Satellite Town Planning

Concurrent with the institution of the city region, a General Development Plan for the city's suburban areas was drawn up. The Plan included the preliminary design for Minhang 閔行 , Shanghai's first satellite town, and a survey of other existing suburban settlements of Wujing 吳涇 , Anting 安亭 , Beiyangqiao 北洋橋 , Huangdu 黃渡 and Nanchang 南場 for future satellite town development. It also involved detailed transportation planning for the entire municipality and development of subsidiary food supplies to the urban population in the central city and to the satellite communities. Based on a number of planning guidelines and economic principles, Shanghai's planners proposed that all satellite towns be located at existing industrial districts, and settlements in the city region be located at or near existing major transportation lines. In order to minimize capital investment for "non-productive" construction, special preference for satellite town selection was to be given to suburban settlements with all the basic urban infrastructures. The planners also adopted the central guidelines of limiting the population of all satellite communities to within the range of 50,000 to 200,000, to avoid excessive concentration of industrial activities at one locality and to ensure provision of all basic public amenities and facilities. All the satellite towns were to accommodate industries and population dispersed from Shanghai and were not to be developed into dormitory towns or health resorts.[9] To shorten the travel distance of industrial workers between place of work and residence, all future satellites were to be designed to consist of a number of independent neighbourhoods, with workers' apartments located close to factories or commercial nodes, schools, medical clinics, markets and public amenities. To provide a pleasant and clean environment in these balanced and self-contained communities, all manufacturing plants were to be separated from residential areas by a green belt or parks. The optimal location of the satellite towns, as conceived by Shanghai's city planners, was to be in the far-suburbs, at least 20 km from the city limits. Such a distance would secure a symbiotic relationship in industrial production between the satellites and Shanghai, and prevent the satellite towns from being absorbed, thereby aggravating the problem of rapid spatial expansion of the metropolis.

After careful consideration of a preliminary survey of a total of twelve county towns and industrial districts, the planners selected five settlements, including Minhang, Wujing, Anting, Jiading and Songjiang, to be designed as Shanghai's satellite towns.[10] With the exception of Jiading, which served mainly as a science and research centre, all the other satellites specialized in specific types of industrial activities. Another important development during this initial stage was the construction of an improved road system, supplemented by branch lines of railways within the city region, which provided good overland linkages between the proposed satellite towns and various parts of Shanghai's urban core.[11]

Evaluation of the Satellite Town Programme

For the first time, China adopted Howard Ebenezer's innovative idea of building satellite communities to disperse population and industrial activities from heavily congested metropolises. However, the satellite town programme achieved various degrees of success. In Nanjing, for example, 52,000 or 44% of the industrial workers in the satellite communities came from the central city. At present, 75% of these workers live in the vicinity of their workplaces, and only 25% commute daily from Nanjing. It has been claimed that these suburban satellite towns have reduced the pressure on the central city for housing, transportation facilities and water supply.[12] Shanghai's satellite town programme, though the most vigorous among all major urban centres in China, has been relatively less successful. The amount of land for industrial uses reached 8% of the total area of the city's central district, the highest among all world cities.[13] The total population of the seven satellites of Minhang, Wujing, Wusong 吳淞 , Jiading, Anting, Songjiang and Jinshanwei 金山衛 was only 679,857 (1990 Population Census), which was only 9.1% of the central city's population of 7.5 million (Table 13.1).

Table 13.1   Shanghai Satellite Towns' Population, 1990

Satellite town	Population
Wusong	242,269
Minhang	125,215
Songjiang	91,381
Jinshanwei	78,219
Jiading	77,616
Wujing	33,571
Anting	31,586
TOTAL	679,857

Source: Personal communication, Ning Yuemin 寧越敏 , Department of Geography, East China Normal University (華東師範大學), 1996.

In early 1990, the average population density in Shanghai was over 45,000 persons per sq km — the highest in the nation. In some of the urban districts, it was as high as 80,000 persons per sq km; the neighbourhood of Xiaobeimen 小北門 in the urban district of Nanshi 南市 recorded the highest density of 230,000 persons per sq km.[14] Although the city has an excellent record on birth control and family planning, its population has been increasing steadily, due mainly to the return flow of former residents sent out of the city to the countryside or remote regions during the 1956–1977 period. The extremely low gross residential space of only 2.47 sq m per capita is a major indicator of serious population congestion in the central city. The amount of urban green space and road surface per capita was only 0.47 sq m and 1.6 sq m, respectively,[15] the lowest among China's million cities.

While the urban districts of this huge city are bulging with ever swelling populations, the size of the population in its satellite towns, on the other hand, has been far below what the city planners had anticipated when the programme was first launched in the late 1950s. A substantial number of workers commute daily to work from Shanghai, as more than half of the 440,000 workers in these towns still have their household registrations in the parent city. The satellite town of Minhang, Shanghai's largest, has over 80,000 commuters daily.[16] Although Jinshanwei, a satellite located 70 km south of the city, has been regarded as relatively successful, only 15% of the workers brought their families and settled in the community. Another example is Songjiang, where only 3% of the workforce of 10,000 settled permanently in the town.[17] All this evidence strongly suggests that Shanghai's satellite town programme has not been very successful since its inception in achieving the goal of relieving the high level of congestion in the central city.

When the programme was first launched, every effort was made to attract central city industrial workers and their families to relocate in the suburban communities. Shanghai's newspapers frequently publicized the benefits of living in the suburban towns, including their pleasant and unpolluted environment, the new and relatively spacious apartments with an average residential space of over 9 sq m per person (compared to under 4 sq m per person in Shanghai) and excellent availability of subsidiary foods from the surrounding countryside.[18] Despite the campaign, population growth in most satellites has been very slow, as the majority of the workers who moved out with their factories or work units were unwilling to resettle their families in the satellite towns. Only 47,000, or 28% of the total 167,000 workers and their families, settled permanently in the satellites.[19] Also, a substantial number of these workers still retain their household registration (*hukou* 戶口) in Shanghai. Consequently, even after more than three decades, the total permanent population of Minhang, the most well-developed satellite town in the Shanghai City Region, is still far short of the original planned population size of 500,000. Instead of releasing population pressure in Shanghai, the satellites have attracted immigration from the surrounding regions and provinces. In the recently expanded satellite town of Wusong, since the construction of the integrated iron and steel complex, as much as 70% of the permanent population immigrated from the provinces of Jiangsu 江蘇 and Zhejiang 浙江 .[20]

Several major factors which have retarded the development of suburban satellites in Shanghai may be identified. Because of the special emphasis of central policy on developing industries during the First

Five-year Plan period, industrial construction, as a rule, received the lion's share of capital allocation. The consequence was a slow pace of "non-productive" construction in towns and cities, which could not keep up with the increasing demands for urban facilities, public amenities and services. On average, only 11.4% of all the capital investment was assigned to urban infrastructures and amenities in cities during the First Five-year Plan period. During the 1960s and 1970s, this proportion was reduced to a mere 6%. To make things worse for the satellite towns, a very small proportion of the limited financial resources was provided for the construction of their urban infrastructures, due to entrenched interests favouring the parent city.[21] Therefore, construction of many "non-productive" urban projects was not undertaken as originally planned. In the satellite town of Anting, where Shanghai's largest motor vehicle assembly plant was located, there were no sports facilities, cinemas and other essential amenities for its over 13,000 employees and their family members. The residents complained that they lived in a desert.[22] It was a common belief among central city residents that schools in the suburban towns were not as good as those in the central city. Without a good eduction, their children might have lesser opportunities for more advanced education or for employment.[23] This was another major reason for their unwillingness to relocate their family in the suburban satellites.

Several central policies actually have hindered the development of small towns like satellite settlements in the city region of China's major cities. Both the urban rationing system and the wage system, which are primarily based on the differential costs of living among settlements in the various urban hierachies, actually encourage small-town residents to move to larger urban centres. Workers in large cities generally receive higher wages and larger rations of grain and edible oil than their counterparts in smaller urban places. Quite often, although the cost of living in small towns may be higher than that in large cities, those moving from a large city to a county town, for example, will be placed in a lower wage category and, at the same time, receive a smaller ration of staples. Furthermore, those who live in a settlement with a population of less than 500,000 are not eligible for the monthly bicycle subsidy, according to the regulations of the Ministry of Finance.[24]

During the 1960s and 1970s, because of the low wage system, most families depended on household incomes rather than the sole income of the head of the family. In large cities, family members of employable age would have a good chance of finding employment because of the diversity of economic activities there. By contrast, because of the high degree of specialization in manufacturing in the satellite towns, such as electrical machinery manufacturing in Minhang, motor vehicle assembly in Anting, and production of chemicals in Wujing, the range of employment opportunities in those settlements was relatively limited. When workers resettled with their families in those satellites, many of their spouses and other family members would become unemployed. Besides these material disincentives for factory workers who resettled in suburban satellites, which remained a major factor causing the slow population growth of Shanghai's satellite towns in the last three decades, the general shortages of expertise in satellite-town design and construction among China's urban planners partly contributed to the failure of the programme.

Post-1980 Development

Since the 1980s, the Chinese leadership has been seriously adopting the large city-based urbanization strategy, as the manufacturing industries of the large urban centres have been the backbone of the nation's economy. Further, the prevailing economic climate in China tends to favour active agglomeration and strong economic linkages and, as a result, the "key-point city" (*zhongdian chengshi* 重點城市) system of the 1950s has been restored. The fact that all of these large cities are major industrial centres as well as "million cities" reflects both their importance in the national economy and official determination to use their scale of economy to the fullest advantage. All these factors explain the recent growth of large cities in China and the concentration of the urban population in metropolitan centres. By the mid-1980s, those urban places classified as super-large cities with a population of over 1 million contained over 40% of China's total urban population.[25]

The open policy implemented by the central government has revitalized the development of Shanghai's satellite towns. The metallurgy of Wusong near the huge Baoshan Iron and Steel Complex (寶山鋼鐵) is located to the north of Shanghai. Since the early 1980s, construction of housing, urban infrastructures and public amenities has been actively pursued. By 1990, the town's population reached almost 250,000, the largest among all Shanghai's satellites. After the opening of a large motor vehicle assembly plant, a Sino–German joint venture, at Anting, a satellite town located to the northwest of Shanghai, other related industries have relocated there recently from the central city. More urban infrastructures have been constructed to meet the needs of the growing population. At present, Anting is the smallest among all Shanghai's satellite towns, with a total population of slightly over 30,000. It is anticipated the town's population will reach 100,000 when the final phase of the motorworks is completed at the end of the century.[26]

In April 1984, Shanghai was selected as one of 14 coastal cities opened to foreign investments. It has become a recipient point for foreign advanced technology, capital and management skills. The municipal authorities established an Economic and Technological Development Zone (ETDZ) at Minhang to divert the growth of the central city to the satellites. Within the 230 ha industrial site located to the northwest of the existing industrial area of the town, there are more than 70 foreign-funded manufacturing industries, including pharmaceuticals, aerospace engineering, electronics, toys, synthetic rubber, gauges and meters, medical equipment and modern construction materials. In the first half of 1990, the total industrial output of RMB464 million of Minhang ETDZ accounted for 26% of the total of the 14 coastal development areas, and 27% in export earnings of foreign exchange.[27] Foreign investments also provided capital for the construction of a road system and other urban infrastructures, as well as multistoreyed workers' housing within the ETDZ. As much as 40% of the district has been designated for green space which provides a much more pleasant environment, a sharp contrast to the acute shortage of green space in the parent city. A number of incentives have been introduced to attract Shanghai workers to settle in the ETDZ. Workers' lodgings are more spacious, averaging more than 7 sq m per person, and the rents are subsidized by the enterprises. Furthermore, the wages of the workers in the district are 25% higher than those of their counterparts in Shanghai city and other industrial satellites.[28] By 1990, the population of Minhang had climbed steadily to over 125,000. To diversify the functions of the satellite town, part of the renowned Jiaotong University (交通大學), the School of Electrical Energy (電力學校) and the Shanghai Institute of Electrical Energy (上海電力學院) have established branch campuses in the specially designated post-secondary education and research district located in the eastern part of Minhang. Since the early 1990s, the town has developed relatively complete urban infrastructures, with over 82 km of roads, waterworks, power plants, telephone exchanges, sewage treatment plants and coal gas supplies. The town is also conveniently linked by several highways with the central city and the surrounding counties. In fact, Minhang, together with Caohejing High-tech Park (漕河涇新興技術開發區) and

Hongqiao ETDZ (虹橋經濟技術開發區), has been designated as a pilot zone in Shanghai's effort to resume its position as a major economic centre of the nation.[29]

The development of Pudong since 1990 has opened a new chapter in Shanghai's economic and urban growth. Pudong lies to the east of Shanghai city, the designated area of development is bordered by the Huangpu River to the west, the Yangzi River to the north and the east, and the Chuanyang River(川楊河)to the south (see Fig. 13.1). In April 1990, Premier Li Peng 李鵬 announced the decision of the central government to open Pudong to the outside world,[30] a key move which not only transforms Shanghai into an epicentre of China's modernization, but also exerts the city's potential to promote its export-oriented economy and its status as a world city. The planned development scale of Pudong will be much larger than that of any other existing economic development areas in the nation. The total area of development in Pudong is larger than the size of the city proper (Puxi 浦西). It has been anticipated that the Pudong project will stimulate the rapid economic development of Shanghai, and in time will integrate the entire Yangzi River Delta and the nine provinces in the Yangzi Valley into an active and prosperous economic network.

In the last several years, the majority of the capital projects undertaken in the city have been related directly to the development of this new economic zone, including construction of the Yangpu Bridge(楊浦大橋)and the Nanpu Bridge(南浦大橋), and several tunnels crossing the Huangpu River (黃浦江) to provide an efficient linkage between Pudong and Puxi.[31] Intensive land development and construction of urban infrastructure are currently underway at the Waigaoqiao Free Trade Zone (外高橋保稅區), the Jinqiao Export-processing Zone (金橋出口加工區), and the Lujiazui Financial and Trade Zone (陸家嘴金融貿易區).[32] These large construction projects include a 12 million kw power station and a new harbour with four deep-water berths at Waigaoqiao, the second phase of the Pudong Gas Plant with a production capacity of 2 million cu m per day and the Linqiao Waterworks (凌橋水廠), with a daily capacity of 200,000 tonnes.[33] Completion of these projects will help to solve Shanghai's bottleneck problems in energy and external linkage, and create favourable conditions for further development of the metropolis.

As part of the scheme to optimize Shanghai's urban spatial structure, the city's new business, trade and financial centre will be relocated in Lujiazui Financial and Trade Zone, at the western fringe of Pudong and on

Figure 13.1   The Satellite Towns of Shanghai

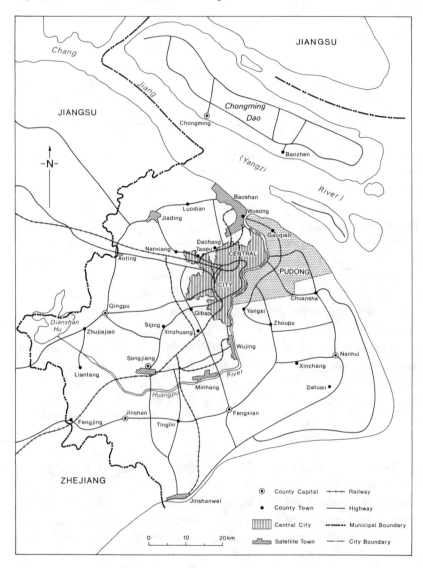

the eastern bank of the Huangpu River. Because of its close proximity to Puxi, Pudong is regarded as a favourable destination for both population and industry away from the congested inner city. The 10-year development plan of the Pudong New Area (浦東新區) sets the population limit of the area at 1.8 million. At present, Pudong has a population of 1.44 million, 11.1% of Shanghai's total.[34] It can absorb a population of only about 400,000 from the central city. It is not likely that Pudong will help to ease the problem of overcrowding of polluting industries in the central city. A variety of industries already exist in Pudong: petrochemical, shipbuilding, machinery, steel, building materials, textile and other light industries. These industries have been sources of both air and water pollution in Pudong. The new industrial area of Jinqiao specializes in electronics, computer hardware and software, and information transfer technology,[35] all of which are non-polluting industries.

Contributions of Shanghai's Satellite Towns to the Central City and the City Region

A general evaluation of the contributions of the satellite towns to the central city and to the entire Shanghai City Region as a whole will recognize that these communities have promoted both the economic and social development of Shanghai. Their contributions to the parent city's economic growth are by far the most significant. Although the dispersal of the population from Shanghai to its satellite settlements cannot be considered satisfactory, these suburban towns have at least slowed down the population growth in the central city. The siting and relocation of large-scale heavy industries in the satellites also have alleviated the problem of the fast areal expansion of the metropolis.

Since the First Five-year Plan period, the rapid development of heavy industries in Shanghai has drastically transformed the city's industrial structure. At present, Shanghai has six "pillar" industries: iron and steel, petrochemical, motor vehicles, equipment for nuclear power stations, aircrafts and electronics. The first four industries are located in the satellite towns. Development of the iron and steel industry is centred at the Baoshan Iron and Steel Complex of Wusong. The output of steel will reach 10 million tonnes when production enters its third phase. At that time, together with the existing steel production facilities in the city, total steel production in Shanghai will reach 15 million tonnes. The petrochemical industry is located at Gaoqiao 高橋 and the satellite towns of Wujing and Jinshanwei.

Every year, these facilities produce a total amount of 1.8 million tonnes of raw materials for the chemical, plastics, synthetic fibres and synthetic rubber industries.[36] The Anting Motor Vehicle Assembly Plant, a Sino–German joint venture, was established in Anting after implementation of the open policy. Its production reached 100,000 units in 1993.[37] Nuclear power plant equipment is produced in Minhang. The 300,000 kw generating equipment was produced for the Jinshan Nuclear Power Station. It has been anticipated that systems generating 600,000 kw and 900,000 kw will soon be manufactured. By then, China will be one of the top-ranking countries producing nuclear power generating equipment in the world.[38]

The development of the above-mentioned industries not only exerts an important influence on the development of Shanghai's satellite towns, but also has significant impacts on the growth of the economy of the entire city region, such as promotion of transformation and development of industrial technology and enhancement of the ability to manufacture large and complete sets of industrial equipment. For example, part of the equipment for the second and the third phases of construction at the Baoshan Iron and Steel Complex will be manufactured in China, including the 4,000 cu m furnace and other large-sized equipment. It has been proposed that 83% of the parts required for the assembly of the Santana sedan at Anting will be manufactured domestically, and 82 of the 181 major items will be produced in Shanghai.[39] Such an arrangement will stimulate the growth of a large number of related industries in the city and the city region.

Cities and towns are the nuclei of a region. When the development of the satellite towns reaches a certain scale, these settlements will exert influences radially towards the surrounding regions. In this respect, Shanghai's satellite towns perform two major functions: to stimulate the economic development of the surrounding regions, and to provide services to neighbouring areas.

A relatively large number of large and medium-sized industries, with a high level of technological strength, are located in Shanghai's satellite towns. Through the contracting out of production of parts, supply of industrial raw materials, transfer of technology and purchase of industrial products, these satellites promote the economic development of the surrounding areas within the city region. For example, the camera manufacturing plant at Songjiang assisted Songjiang county (*xian* —) in setting up ten factories to manufacture camera parts. Before 1983, there were only cottage industries in the village of Anting. Since the late 1980s, with the help of the municipal factories in the satellite town of Anting, over 20 factories were established in the village. The gross value of industrial production in 1990, when compared to that in 1988, increased by 172%, which greatly exceeded the rate of development of rural industries in the entire county. At least 40% of the gross value of industrial production was related to the motor vehicle industry. Recently, the village of Anting established a joint venture with the Shanghai motor vehicle plant at Anting.[40] These new developments have stimulated the development of the rural economy in the city region.

The structure of the agricultural production of the rural villages around the satellite towns has been transformed through supplying agricultural and subsidiary products to the suburban towns. Such changes often brought about an increase in the incomes of the peasants of these rural villages. Because of the need to supply vegetables to the residents of Jinshanwei, the rural villages around the satellite increased their vegetable fields to 3,000 *mu* 畝 a radical change from its traditional grain and cotton production.[41]

Shanghai's satellite towns also function as service centres for their surrounding areas. The commercial and medical service areas of Jinshanwei, for example, include six counties in the Shanghai City Region and the adjacent province of Zhejiang. The counties of Jinshan and Fengxian in the Shanghai City Region, and the county of Pinghu 平湖 in Zhejiang, are the primary service area, while the secondary service area embraces Songjiang county of the Shanghai City Region and the counties of Haien 海恩 and Jiaxian 嘉縣 in Zhejiang. Jinshanwei is often known to the residents of these neighbouring counties as "Little Shanghai" (*xiao* Shanghai) because of their close relationships with the satellite town. According to a recent survey, the peasants of the above-mentioned six counties purchased from Jinshanwei as much as 70% of the consumer goods, 50% of the restaurant foods, and 30% of the tobacco and sugar. Furthermore, 50% of the out-patients and in-patients in the general hospital of Jinshanwei came from the surrounding villages. According to a recent survey in Minhang, about 40% of its hospital's patients were county residents.[42]

Although Shanghai's satellite towns provide sites for new industries, relocation of some of the industries and dispersal of part of the population from the central city have, to some extent, restrained its fast rate of growth and have been beneficial to the protection of its environment. As noted earlier, the total satellite town population in the city region reached 679,857 in 1992, representing over 9% of the central city population.

Spatially, the total area of Shanghai's satellite towns reached 75.22 sq km; the total area designated for industrial use was 32.6 sq km.[43] If satellite towns had not been developed, and all the post-1949 industries had been built within the central city or its peripheral areas, the severe congestion and environmental pollution of urban Shanghai, without a doubt, would have been far more serious. Although Shanghai's satellite town programme has not achieved the planned objectives of dispersing the central city's population and industry, it has contributed to restraining the rapid expansion of Shanghai city.

Before the development of the satellite towns, the spatial structure of the Shanghai City Region consisted of one mononuclear city. Most of the population and industries were concentrated within the urban core and its peripheral areas. All the rural villages in the surrounding counties were organized within an agro-economic structure. After more than thirty years of satellite-town development, Shanghai has been transformed into a multi-hierarchical urban system that consists of a central city, satellite towns, county towns, small towns under the administration of counties and market towns. Although there are only seven in number, these satellite towns play an important role in the development of the urban system, as they provide linkages between the central city and towns of lower rank-ings. The establishment of satellites and other smaller urban places has changed the urban map of Shanghai. In addition, the distribution of Shanghai's population and economic activities has been substantially im-proved, which lays a strong foundation for the future development of the metropolis in an era of fast economic growth.

Conclusion

The creation of the city regions in China in the 1950s and the development of satellite towns within the administrative-cum-planning unit initiated a process of dispersal of large urban agglomerations. Basically, the programme implemented in Shanghai aimed at dispersing the population and relocating industries from the highly congested inner city in order to rectify the chaotic pattern of land use created by the colonial powers during the treaty port era.

The development of these suburban industrial communities was inter-rupted by the Great Leap Forward (1959–1961) and the Cultural Revolu-tion (1966–1976). Since the early 1980s, the state government's policy favouring strong centrality and concentration as the basic precondition for rapid national economic growth, together with the implementation of its open policy, revitalized Shanghai's satellite town programme. The increase in population in both Wusong and Minhang to their present size was the direct result of a significant increase in capital investments, from both state and foreign sources, for the development of housing and urban infrastructures. This approach has been adopted in Huangcun 黃村 , a satellite town located about 15 km to the south of Beijing. Private developers have been building low density residential units, with small front gardens.[44] The better quality and relatively low-cost housing, a cleaner environment, and close proximity to the national capital certainly provide strong incentives to Beijing's residents to move to the satellite. If the Shanghai municipal government opens all the satellite towns to foreign investment, as in the case of Minhang, private capital from overseas could be utilized to improve both the quantity and quality of housing stocks and urban amenities in all the satellite towns, and to make these communities more attractive to the residents of the central city.

Reform of the existing household registration system can contribute to the success of the satellite-town programme. Relaxation of restrictions on population movement and place of residence will eliminate the worries of settlers from the central city that they will not be able to return — an important psychological barrier to relocation. Surplus rural labour from within the city region and the surrounding provinces should be allowed to settle in the satellite towns. This is consistent with the state policy of encouraging the growth of towns and small cities.

The problems of a chronic shortage of services and the poor quality of existing services in satellite communities, in general, may be addressed by the opening up of the satellite towns and the central city, as is the case of the Pudong New Area, to foreign and domestic investments to improve the tertiary sector in the suburban satellites. An increase in the number of businesses in those towns will also increase employment opportunities for the spouses of industrial workers relocated from the inner city.

Despite a decline in the natural increase rate of 1.8 per thousand in Shanghai, it has been anticipated that at least 100,000 residents will have to move out every year until the end of the century for the population of central Shanghai to remain at its present level.[45] It seems necessary to increase the planned population density in Pudong and, at the same time, revitalize the satellite-town programme which has been neglected since the beginning of the development of Pudong.

Notes

1. Sun Zhongshan wenji 孫中山文集 (Selection from the Writings, Letters and Speeches of Sun Yat-sen) (Shanghai: Shangwu yinshuguan 商務印書館 [The Commercial Press], 1935), p. 186.
2. K. I. Fung, "Satellite Town Development in the Shanghai City Region," *Town Planning Review*, Vol. 52, No. 1 (January 1981), pp. 26–46; R.J.R. Kirkby, "A Review of Satellite Town Policies in the People's Republic of China: The Experience of Shanghai," in *New Towns in East and Southeast Asia: Planning and Development*, edited by D. R. Phillips and A.G.O. Yeh (Hong Kong: Oxford University Press, 1987), pp. 205–30; Atash Farbad and Xinhao Wang, "Satellite Town Development in Shanghai, China: An Overview," *The Journal of Architecture and Planning Research*, Vol. 7, No. 3 (1990), pp. 245–57.
3. L. A. Orleans, *Every Fifth Child* (London: Methuen, 1972), p. 175.
4. *Xinwen ribao* 新聞日報 (News Daily) (Shanghai), 20 September 1951.
5. *Tongji gongzuo tongxun* ziliaoshi《統計工作通訊》資料室, "Guanyu woguo shehuizhuyi gongyehua de jige wenti" 關於我國社會主義工業化的幾個問題 (Several Problems of China's Socialist Industrialization), *Xinhua banyuekan* 新華半月刊 (New China Semi-monthly), No. 1 (January 1957), p. 68.
6. *Xinwen ribao*, 29 October 1952.
7. Development of satellite towns in the city regions of China was cited in Chinese publications appeared in 1958–1960, and in western sources in later dates. These city regions included Hefei, Zhengzhou, Tianjin, Nanjing, Ji'nan, Hantan, Changchun, Beijing, Guangzhou, Changsha and Daqing. These sources include: *Jianzhu xuebao* 建築學報 (Journal of Architecture), No. 11 (1959), p. 20; *Peking Review*, 16 February 1960, p. 17; *Chengshi jianshe* 城市建設 (Urban Construction), No. 10 (1959), p. 11; *Dili zhishi* 地理知識 (Geographical Knowledge), No. 11 (1959), p. 538; A. W. Galston et al., *Daily Life in People's China* (New York: Thomas Y. Crowell, 1973), p. 133; R. Thompson, "Containing the City," *Architectural Design*, (March 1974), p. 152; R. Murphy, "Chinese Urbanization under Mao," in *Urbanization and Counterurbanization*, vol. 11 of *Urban Affairs Annual Reviews*, edited by B.J.L. Berry (London, Beverly Hills: Sage Publications, 1976), p. 324.
8. *Jiefang ribao* 解放日報 (Liberation Daily) (Shanghai), 20 December 1958.
9. Interview with Gu Ming 顧明, deputy director, Bureau of Urban Construction and Administration of Shanghai, 26 June 1977.
10. *Wen hui bao* 文匯報 (Cultural Contact Daily) (Shanghai), 10 January 1959.
11. *Xinwen ribao*, 17 April 1959.
12. Shen Daoqi and Yao Shimu, "Nanjing: Evolution and Development," in *Chinese Cities: The Growth of the Metropolis since 1949*, edited by Victor F. S. Sit (Hong Kong: Oxford University Press, 1985), p. 145.

13. Guo Bolin 郭柏林, "Shanghaishi zhongxin qu gongye shusan di tantao" 上海市中心區工業疏散的探討 (On the Dispersion of Industries in the Central District of Shanghai City), *Jingji dili* 經濟地理 (Economic Geography), Vol. 12, No. 2 (1992), p. 77.

14. Interview with a Shanghai planner, 5 November 1992.

15. *Zhongguo tongji nianjian 1992* 中國統計年鑑 1992 (Statistical Yearbook of China 1992) (Beijing: Zhongguo tongji chubanshe 中國統計出版社, 1992), p. 92.

16. Interview of a Minhang town official, 22 November 1992.

17. Zhang Fubao 張福保, "Guanyu Shanghai jingji qu shi guan xuan di yixie wenti" 關於上海經濟區市管縣的一些問題 (Some Problems about Counties Managed by the Economic Region of Shanghai City), *Jingji dili*, Vol. 8, No. 4 (1984), pp. 299–303.

18. *Xinwen ribao*, 11 November 1958.

19. Wang Guixin 王桂新, "Jiakuai Shanghai jiaoqu chengzhenhua fazhan zhi wo jian" 加快上海郊區城鎮化發展之我見 (My View on Speeding up Shanghai Suburbs' Urbanization), *Renkou yanjiu* 人口研究 (Population Research), No. 2 (1986), p. 27.

20. Author's field work, 12 November 1990.

21. Conversation with Wu Chuanjun 吳傳鈞 at the Institute of Geography, Beijing, 15 May 1992.

22. *Dazhong ribao* 大眾日報 (Public Daily) (Shanghai), 15 September 1979.

23. Bai Demao 白德懋, "Weixing cheng neng qi kongzhi di zuoyong ma?" 衛星城能起控制的作用嗎？(Can Satellite Towns Control Urban Scale?), *Jianzhu xuebao*, No. 4 (1981), p. 27.

24. *Dazhong ribao*, 6 September 1979, quoted in R.J.R. Kirkby, *Urbanization in China: Town and Country in a Developing Economy 1949–2000 AD* (Kent: Croom Helm, 1985), p. 158.

25. Fang Lei 方磊 and Lui Hong 劉宏, "Woguo chengshi fenlei he chengshi fazhan wenti di chubu yanjiu" 我國城市分類和城市發展問題的初步研究 (A Preliminary Study on the Problems of Chinese Urban Classification and Urban Development), *Acta Geographical Sinica* (地理學報), Vol. 43, No. 1 (1988), p. 2.

26. Interview with a Shanghai planner, 16 November 1992.

27. Zhou Zhengping, "Fourteen Coastal Development Areas Thriving," *New China Quarterly*, No. 20 (May 1991), p. 47.

28. Interview with a Minhang town official, 16 November 1992.

29. Wu Fumin and Lu Guoyuan, "Shanghai's Strategy for Economic Development in the 1990s," *New China Quarterly*, No. 23 (February 1992), p. 23.

30. "Li Peng zongli xuanbu kafa Pudong, Pudong kafa" 李鵬總理宣布開發浦東，浦東開發 (Premier Li Peng: To Announce the Opening and Developing of

Pudong), *Pudong kaifa* 浦東開發 (Developing Pudong), No. 1 (January 1992), p. 2.

31. Xiao Hang 曉航, "'siyan' zhanlüe quan fangwei fazhan Zhonghua dadi yongdong kaifang relang" "四沿" 戰略全方位發展中華大地湧動開放熱浪, *Jingji daobao* 經濟導報 (Economic Reporter), 28 September 1992, p. 35.

32. Author's field work, 22 November 1992.

33. Shao Yang, "One Year of Development in Pudong," *New China Quarterly*, No. 23 (February 1992), p. 54.

34. *Shanghai tongji nianjian 1994* 上海統計年鑑 1994 (Statistical Yearbook of Shanghai 1994) (Beijing: Zhongguo tongji chubanshe, 1994), p. 237.

35. *Time*, 5 October 1992, p. 64.

36. *Shanghai quanshu 1992* 上海全書 1992 (Shanghai Encyclopaedia 1992) (Shanghai: Xuelin chubanshe 學林出版社, 1993), p. 128.

37. Correspondence with Ning Yuemin 寧越敏, Department of Geography, East China Normal University (華東師範大學), Shanghai.

38. Inteview with a Shanghai planner, 16 November 1992.

39. See note 38.

40. See note 38.

41. *Shanghai quanshu 1992* (see note 36), p. 225.

42. See note 38.

43. See note 38.

44. Author's field work in Beijing, 8 May 1992.

45. He Xinggang, "Development of Pudong and Optimization of Urban Area Structure in Shanghai," in *Chinese Environment and Development*, edited by Luk Shiu-hung and Joseph Whitney (New York: M. E. Sharpe, 1993), p. 87.

14

Housing

Rebecca L. H. Chiu

Shanghai is known to have a wide variety of architectural styles. The opening up of Shanghai to the foreign powers for trade in 1843 and the subsequent establishment of concession areas by these countries engendered enclaves of buildings and urban forms of various national styles, including that of Britain, France, Germany and Japan. The city also inherited local housing styles originating from the Ming dynasty. The lane houses (*lilongfang* 里弄房), a hybrid form of the exotic and the indigenous housing designs, adds further character to the city. Thus, Shanghai has the most diversified architectural types among Chinese cities. But regardless how fascinating the city is to visitors, housing shortages seem to be a perennial problem for local residents. Squatter huts, dangerous buildings and shanties dot the city.

Efforts by the communist government to solve the housing problems[1] began in 1950–1952. The conditions of some 300 squatter and shanty areas were improved and nine new housing districts (21,830 housing units) were constructed. The average floor area of the new housing units was 30 sq m, and communal kitchens and toilets were provided. The living area[2] per capita in the city was 3.4 sq m. Improvements in the squatter and shanty areas continued in the period between 1953 and 1965. In addition, satellite towns and new industrial areas were constructed at the urban fringe, providing new housing stock. A total of 8.05 million sq m of residential floor area was constructed and the average per capita living area increased slightly to 3.6 sq m. Although housing standards higher than those of the urban area were intended for the new towns, financial constraints impeded the provision of sufficient community facilities to meet the needs of the residents. The satellite towns, therefore, did not successfully decentralize the population. Housing investment almost came to a halt during the early years of the Cultural Revolution. The resumption of housing production in the 1970s was, nevertheless, able to raise the average living area per capita to 4.5 sq m in 1978. Multi-storey residential buildings were also introduced

This chapter presents some of the findings of the research project "Managing Municipal Change in Reform China Programme," funded by the Research Grants Council of the University Grants Committee, Hong Kong. The author also wishes to thank Wu Zhengtong (胡政同) of the Office of Shanghai Housing Authority (上海市住房委員會辦公室) for his valuable assistance and useful insights in the preparation of this chapter.

into the city. But the return of hundreds of thousands of intellectual youth to the city in the wake of the Cultural Revolution as the bulk of the population reached marriageable age aggravated the housing shortage.[3]

Following the adoption of liberal economic policies by Deng Xiaoping's 鄧小平 government in 1979, and its deliberate efforts to improve the living standards of the populace, unprecedented measures and policies were devised and implemented in Shanghai to improve markedly housing standards. Unlike the previous measures which were physically oriented, the new policies developed in the 1980s and 1990s fundamentally shifted the nature of Shanghai's housing system, and the improvements in housing conditions have been phenomenal. Therefore, this chapter aims to explore and analyze housing developments which have taken place in Shanghai since 1980, and the reform measures that have propelled the development.

Accordingly, this chapter initially discusses changes in Shanghai's housing conditions since 1980 as reflected by a range of housing indicators. Subsequently, it analyzes the housing reform measures introduced to the city since 1980, noting in particular the newly developed housing market. Finally, the conclusion reflects upon the direction of housing development in Shanghai.

Housing Conditions since 1980

Municipal Level

Improvements in housing conditions were made possible by increases in housing investment. As shown in Table 14.1, with the exception of 1983 and 1989,[4] the gross annual increase in housing investment since 1980 generally has been higher than 20%. The peak was 59% in 1980 and the average annual growth rate was 28%. Similar growth was not found in the annual production of floor area, however. The average rate of increase was only 7%. This discrepancy might be due to exponential rises in production costs. While the average official inflation rate over the same period was 9%, available data show that the prices of building materials rose by 17.4% and 12.3% in 1990 and 1992 respectively.[5] Further, despite a continuous increase in investment, production in fact dropped in 1981, 1987, 1988 and 1989 compared to that of the previous years. The sharp decrease in 1989 can be a corollary of the outbreak of the disruptive social movements in that year.

Table 14.1   Housing Investment and Production in Shanghai, 1980–1993

Year	Housing investment (RMB million)	Growth rate (%)	Floor area completed (1,000 m²)	Growth rate (%)
1980	434	59	3,043	41
1981	570	31	2,976	-2
1982	634	11	3,946	33
1983	643	1	4,059	3
1984	820	27	4,382	8
1985	1,300	58	4,886	12
1986	1,756	35	4,910	1
1987	2,259	29	4,863	-1
1988	2,717	20	4,749	-2
1989	1,973	-27	3,710	-22
1990	2,626	33	4,220	13
1991	3,567	36	4,777	13
1992	4,470	25	5,437	14
1993	6,670	49	6,165	13

Sources: *Shanghai zhuzhai 1949–1990* (see note 3 below), p. 145; Shanghaishi tongjiju (ed.), *Shanghai tongji nianjian 1993* 上海統計年鑑 1993 (Statistical Yearbook of Shanghai 1993) (Beijing: Zhongguo tongji chubanshe, 1993), p. 381; *Shanghai tongji nianjian 1994* (see note 5 below), p. 88.

The aggregate space standard has been raised as a result of the expansion in the housing stock. Between 1980 and 1993, the housing stock more than doubled from 41,170,000 sq m to 105,640,000 sq m.[6] Table 14.2 shows that the average per capita living area almost doubled from 4.4 sq m in 1980 to 7.3 sq m in 1993. In fact, the housing shortage was reduced. Ignoring the phenomenal increase in the number of "hardship households" due to a changed definition in 1985, a general downward trend occurred for all types of "hardship households" (Table 14.3). On average, there was a decrease of 34% in the number of these households from 1985 to 1990. While overcrowded households were reduced by 39% in that period, households with less than 2 sq m per capita had all been rehoused by 1988. By the end of 1993, the total number of all types of "hardship households" with less than 4 sq m per capita had been reduced to 246,000, accounting for 9% of the households in Shanghai.[7]

The changing composition of the housing stock also reflects improvements in housing conditions (Table 14.4). Despite an absolute increase in old lane houses[8] in the same period,[9] its proportion in the total housing stock decreased from 41% in 1980 to 31% in 1993. Instead, staff quarters[10] became the major type of housing. Its proportion increased from 32% in

Table 14.2 Average Per Capita Living Area, 1980–1993

(Unit: sq m)

Year	1980	1981	1982	1983	1984	1985	1986	1987	1988	1989	1990	1991	1992	1993
Average per capita living area	4.4	4.5	4.7	4.9	4.7	5.4	6.0	6.2	6.3	6.4	6.6	6.7	6.9	7.3

Sources: *Shanghai zhuzhai (1949–1990)* (see note 3 below), p. 152; *Shanghai tongji nianjian*, various issues.

Table 14.3   Households with Housing Hardships, 1981–1990

Year	Homeless households	Inconvenient households	Overcrowded households	Households with 2–4 m²/ capita	Households with less than 2 m²/ capita	TOTAL[c]
1981	5,621	66,795	28,652	n.a.	15,259	116,327
1982	4,929	68,756	24,261	n.a.	12,025	109,971
1983	4,198	67,532	21,793	n.a.	10,596	104,119
1984	3,356	59,385	18,609	n.a.	11,761	93,111
1985[a]	9,800[b]	243,000	216,600	199,900	16,700	686,000
1986	9,800	243,000	216,600	199,900	16,700	686,000
1987	9,800	243,000	204,000	199,900	4,100	660,800
1988	9,800	243,000	199,900	199,900	0	652,600
1989	7,070	175,296	144,204	144,204	0	470,774
1990	6,681	169,511	132,523	132,523	0	441,238

Note: [a] The expansion in 1985 was due to the re-definition of "hardship household," raising the criterion from less than 3 sq m per capita to less than 4 sq m per capita.

[b] It is noted that the identical figures between 1985–1988 could have been erroneous. However, there is no authoritative source for verifying the possible mistakes.

[c] Figures in this column are calculated by the author. The original figures are discarded because they are inaccurate.

Source: *Shanghai zhuzhai 1949–1990* (see note 3 below), p. 166.

1980 to 60% in 1993. Moreover, shanties and housing converted from non-residential buildings had decreased from 4.4 million sq m to 1 million sq m and from 822,000 sq m to 780,000 sq m respectively, in the same period. Thus, housing conditions as a whole improved as staff quarters, especially those built after 1980, were generally better equipped than the lane houses. However, it has been pointed out that only 41.8% of the housing stock was self-contained in 1993, and that only 70% was equipped with toilets and gas supplies. Further, 15 million sq m of dilapidated housing awaited redevelopment.[11]

District Level

1985

Housing conditions at the district level also changed over time. A comparison of the living environment of various districts in 1985[12] with that of 1993 shows the spatial differences in improvement. As illustrated in Table 14.5 and Figure 14.1, the outer districts of Yangpu 楊浦 and Xuhui 徐匯

Table 14.4 Housing Types in Urban Shanghai, 1980–1993

(Unit: 1,000 sq m)

Year	Apartments	Single houses	Staff quarters	New style lane houses	Old style lane houses	Shanties	Conversion from non-residential buildings	TOTAL
1980	916	1,341	14,013	4,338	18,222	4,373	822	44,025
1981	912	1,346	15,919	4,342	18,536	4,188	831	46,074
1982	897	1,345	17,932	4,343	21,186	2,912	840	49,455
1983	923	1,353	20,225	4,368	21,492	2,964	954	52,279
1984	921	1,356	22,832	4,387	21,723	2,874	996	55,089
1985	946	1,363	27,301	4,649	26,421	2,807	956	64,443
1986	1,045	1,521	32,621	4,758	31,216	1,345	919	73,425
1987	1,030	1,530	36,800	4,760	30,750	1,290	930	77,090
1988	1,040	1,520	40,850	4,750	30,580	1,290	790	80,820
1989	1,110	1,580	44,910	4,760	30,950	1,240	800	85,350
1990	1,180	1,580	48,840	4,740	30,670	1,230	770	89,010
1991	1,120	1,550	52,480	4,740	30,000	1,190	770	91,850
1992	1,110	1,640	55,750	4,730	29,350	1,120	770	94,470
1993	1,150	1,590	63,580	4,730	32,810	1,000	780	105,640

Sources: *Shanghai zhuzhai 1949–1990* (see note 3 below), p. 147; *Shanghai tongji nianjian 1993* (see Table 14.1, sources), p. 383; *Shanghai tongji nianjian 1994* (see note 5 below), p. 89.

Table 14.5 Distribution of Housing Types by District, 1985

(Unit: 1,000 sq m)

Districts	Single houses		Apartments		Staff quarters		Lane houses		Shanties & conversions		District total	Total urban housing stock
	Floor area	%	Floor area	%	Floor area	%	Floor area	%	Floor area	%	Floor area	%
Huangpu	23	0.4	26	0.4	1,944	33.5	3,278	56.5	535	9.2	5,806	9.0
Nanshi	15	0.2	1	0.0	2,244	34.6	3,552	54.8	666	10.3	6,478	10.1
Luwan	122	3.2	187	4.9	783	20.4	2,648	69.0	99	2.6	3,839	6.0
Xuhui	435	5.8	301	4.0	3,072	41.1	3,511	47.0	153	2.0	7,472	11.6
Changning	304	5.9	40	0.8	2,317	44.9	2,270	44.0	232	4.5	5,163	8.0
Jing'an	270	6.5	213	5.1	521	12.6	2,936	70.8	207	5.0	4,147	6.4
Putuo	0	0.0	0	0.0	3,600	55.5	2,758	42.6	123	1.9	6,481	10.1
Zhabei	10	0.2	1	0.0	2,439	44.4	2,271	41.4	768	14.0	5,489	8.5
Hongkou	141	2.0	167	2.4	2,516	36.1	3,646	52.4	492	7.1	6,962	10.8
Yangpu	43	0.5	10	0.1	4,940	57.3	3,156	36.6	474	5.5	8,623	13.4
Wusong	0	0.0	0	0.0	1,737	63.9	972	35.7	11	0.4	2,720	4.2
Minhang	0	0.0	0	0.0	1,188	94.1	72	5.7	3	0.2	1,263	2.0
TOTAL	1,363	2.1	946	1.5	27,301	42.4	31,070	48.2	3,763	5.8	64,443	100.0

Source: *Shanghai tongji nianjian 1986* (see note 15 below), p. 417.

held the largest shares of the housing stock in 1985, whereas the inner district of Nanshi 南市 , together with Putuo 普陀 and Hongkou 虹口 in the outer ring, contained the second largest shares. Jing'an 靜安 and Luwan 盧灣 occupied relatively small proportions despite their central locations. The size of the housing stock of the districts might, of course, be contingent upon the area of the respective districts. Parameters of housing density, defined as 1,000 sq m of residential floor area per km of district area, are, therefore, derived to indicate the intensity of housing development in each district.

It is found that the inner districts of Jing'an and Luwan, despite their small shares in the housing stock, have the highest housing density, 548 and 511 respectively (Table 14.6 and Figure 14.2). In contrast, Yangpu and Xuhui which possess the largest share of housing stock have the lowest density, 163 and 171 respectively, if the outmost districts of Minhang 閔行 and Wusong 吳淞 are excluded. It can be seen from Figure 14.2 that if Jing'an and Luwan are taken as the apex, with the highest residential density, the intensity tapers off in a northward direction. Apart from Hongkou and Huangpu 黃浦 , the housing density of Zhabei 閘北 (198) and Putuo (221) are also moderately higher than that of Changning 長寧 (181) and Xuhui (171). The quality of housing and the effect of other land uses (such as industrial and commercial land uses) aside, lower housing density in the southern districts implies a better living environment there.

While housing density provides a better understanding of the spread of

Table 14.6   Housing Characteristics by District, 1985

Districts	% in total urban housing stock	Housing density $(1,000 \text{ m}^2/\text{km}^2)$	Occupancy rate $(\text{m}^2/\text{person})$
Huangpu	9.0	310	8.4
Nanshi	10.1	287	8.5
Luwan	6.0	511	8.0
Xuhui	11.6	171	11.4
Changning	8.0	181	10.5
Jing'an	6.4	548	8.4
Putuo	10.1	221	9.8
Zhabei	8.5	198	8.2
Hongkou	10.8	305	8.5
Yangpu	13.4	163	8.8
Wusong	4.2	52	15.1
Minhang	2.0	34	10.7

Source: *Shanghai tongji nianjian 1986* (see note 15 below), pp. 58, 417.

Figure 14.1   Spatial Pattern of Housing Distribution in Urban Shanghai, 1985

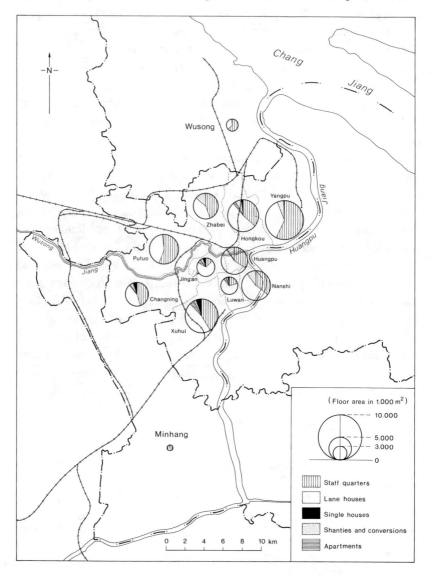

Figure 14.2   Spatial Pattern of Housing Density in Urban Shanghai, 1985

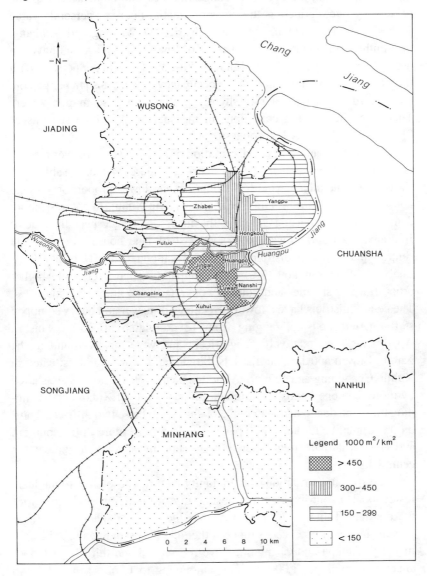

the housing stock, the degree of congestion needs to be measured by the occupancy rate, defined as the gross residential floor per person.[13] Table 14.6 shows that excluding the outer districts of Wusong and Minhang, the southern and southwestern districts of Changning and Xuhui have the highest occupancy rates, with Xuhui peaking at 11.4 sq m per person. With the exception of Putuo which has an occupancy rate of 9.8 sq m per person, all other districts have a rate slightly higher than 8 sq m per person. Therefore, the housing conditions in the south and southwest areas of Shanghai are generally less congested.

The spatial pattern of the distribution of housing types further reflects the living environment of various districts. Figure 14.1 and Table 14.5 show that generally the outer districts have a lower proportion of lane houses, ranging from 37% in Yangpu to 47% in Xuhui. In contrast, more than half of the housing stock in the inner districts, especially that of Jing'an (71%) and Luwan (69%), consist of lane houses. Further, the central and northern districts, namely, Huangpu (9%), Nanshi (10%), Zhabei (14%), Hongkou (7%) and Yangpu (6%) have relatively higher proportions of shanties and housing converted from non-residential uses. The central districts have a lower percentage of newer and better equipped staff quarters housing, ranging from 13% (Jing'an) to 35% (Nanshi). Apartments[14] are relatively insignificant and were mostly found in the Xuhui, Luwan and Jing'an districts. Single houses are mainly situated in Xuhui, Changning and Jing'an. Although some of these houses are shared by more than one family, the higher occupancy rate of Xuhui and Chang-ning might be due to a lower degree of sharing in these two districts. Thus, on the whole, better housing types are concentrated more in the southern and southwestern districts, whereas poorer housing stock is clustered in the central districts.

The spatial distribution of community facilities accessible to the local residents also contributes to the desirability of the living environment of the districts. Table 14.7 shows that the floor area of schools per 1,000 persons in Xuhui far exceeds that of other districts, standing at 2,052 sq m in 1985. Yangpu and Changning have the second and third largest floor areas of schools per 1,000 persons, amounting to 1,268 sq m and 1,146 sq m respectively. Further, the other outer districts, Hongkou, Putuo, Zhabei and Minhang have higher school areas relative to population size than the inner districts. The location of retail services show a different pattern. The central district of Huangpu has the largest retail service space per 1,000 population (809 sq m). Surprisingly, the outer districts of Minhang (441

Table 14.7   Distribution of Housing-related Services by District, 1985

(Unit: m^2/1,000 persons)

Districts	Schools	Retail services	Hospitals	Theatres & cinemas	% of green area
Huangpu	702	809	194	119	5.5
Nanshi	516	381	110	12	4.7
Luwan	670	367	338	102	11.5
Xuhui	2,052	289	360	12	9.6
Changning	1,146	386	293	12	13.9
Jing'an	751	356	334	41	15.1
Putuo	983	390	116	23	10.4
Zhabei	900	417	244	18	6.2
Hongkou	861	344	249	24	8.9
Yangpu	1,268	350	176	14	14.6
Wusong	322	1,039	178	33	5.4
Minhang	958	441	271	51	5.4

Source: *Shanghai tongji nianjian 1986* (see note 15 below), pp. 58, 418, 429.

sq m), Zhabei (417 sq m) and Putuo (390 sq m) have larger retail space per 1,000 population than the other inner districts. It is noteworthy that Xuhui has the lowest retail service area per 1,000 persons.

However, the highest hospital floor area is found in Xuhui (360 sq m per 1,000 persons). Luwan (338 sq m per 1,000 persons), Jing'an (334 sq m per 1,000 persons) and Changning (293 sq m per 1,000 persons) also have higher hospital floor areas. Therefore, apart from Nanshi (110 sq m per 1,000 persons) which has the lowest hospital floor area, the southern districts are more generously provided with hospitals than the northern districts. Logically, the central district of Huangpu has the highest provision of theatre and cinema space (119 sq m per 1,000 persons). Luwan, which is situated south of Huangpu, is also well served with entertainment facilities (102 sq m per 1,000 persons). But Nanshi, Changning and Xuhui each only has 12 sq m of theatres and cinemas for 1,000 persons. The percentage of green areas in the districts shows an irregular pattern. Jing'an in the central–west and Yangpu in the north have the highest percentages, 15.1 and 14.6 respectively. The lowest are found in Nanshi (4.7%) near to the city centre, Minhang (5.4%) in the far south, and Huangpu in the centre (5.5%). The proportions of green area in other districts do not differ significantly.

Thus, on the whole, it seems that while housing development was more intense in the northern and central districts by 1985, the living

Table 14.8 Distribution of Housing Types by District, 1993

Districts	Single houses		Apartments		Staff quarters		Lane houses		Shanties & conversions		District total	Total urban housing stock
	Floor area	%	Floor area	%	Floor area	%	Floor area	%	Floor area	%	Floor area	%
Huangpu	10	0.3	30	1.0	250	8.7	2,300	79.9	290	10.1	2,880	2.7
Nanshi	10	0.2	0	0.0	1,240	27.0	3,020	65.7	330	7.2	4,600	4.4
Luwan	120	2.6	200	4.4	1,510	33.0	2,690	58.7	60	1.3	4,580	4.3
Xuhui	670	5.6	370	3.1	7,060	59.0	3,780	31.6	80	0.7	11,960	11.3
Changning	290	3.5	110	1.3	5,720	69.6	2,050	24.9	59	0.7	8,229	7.8
Jing'an	330	6.5	270	5.3	1,180	23.2	3,210	63.1	100	2.0	5,090	4.8
Putuo	0	0.0	0	0.0	7,380	76.7	2,080	21.6	160	1.7	9,620	9.1
Zhabei	10	0.1	0	0.0	4,810	60.2	3,130	39.2	40	0.5	7,990	7.6
Hongkou	100	1.0	160	1.6	5,490	55.3	3,940	39.7	230	2.3	9,920	9.4
Yangpu	40	0.3	10	0.1	8,710	72.6	2,930	24.4	300	2.5	11,990	11.3
Minhang	0	0.0	0	0.0	3,140	71.4	1,260	28.6	0	0.0	4,400	4.2
Baoshan	0	0.0	0	0.0	4,880	75.8	1,560	24.2	0	0.0	6,440	6.1
Jiading	10	0.3	0	0.0	2,150	71.4	840	27.9	10	0.3	3,010	2.8
Pudong	0	0.0	0	0.0	10,060	67.2	4,790	32.0	130	0.9	14,980	14.2
TOTAL	1,590	1.5	1,150	1.1	63,580	60.2	37,580	35.6	1,789	1.7	105,689	100.0

Source: *Shanghai tongji nianjian 1994* (see note 5 below), p. 89.

environment in the south and southwest districts was more favourable. This is reflected by the lower housing density, higher occupancy rate and smaller proportions of poor quality housing types in the south and southwest, especially Xuhui. Education and medical facilities in these districts were also more generously provided for, but there were fewer retail and entertainment facilities than in the inner districts. Typical of districts situated at or close to the city centre, Shanghai's inner districts are characterized by more slum areas and higher congestion, but more retail and entertainment facilities than the other districts.

1993

Conditions in 1993 were different. By contrasting Table 14.5 and Figure 14.1 with Table 14.8 and Figure 14.3, it is obvious that the housing stock of the inner districts of Huangpu and Nanshi diminished substantially, by 50% and 29% respectively. This was partly due to a reduction of the districts when the boundaries were redefined in 1986 (only Huangpu, Nanshi and Yangpu were reduced; all others were expanded, especially Minhang) and partly due to redevelopment. Correspondingly, the housing stock of all other districts increased, with the highest growth rates found in Xuhui (60%) and Changning (59%). Although Xuhui and Yangpu still held substantial shares of the aggregate housing stock, each amounting to

Table 14.9 Housing Characteristics by District, 1993

Districts	% in total urban housing stock	Housing density $(1,000m^2/km^2)$	Occupancy rate $(m^2/person)$
Huangpu	2.7	634	9.0
Nanshi	4.4	584	9.2
Luwan	4.3	569	10.9
Xuhui	11.3	218	15.6
Changning	7.8	215	13.7
Jing'an	4.8	668	11.7
Putuo	9.1	175	11.9
Zhabei	7.6	280	11.8
Hongkou	9.4	422	11.8
Yangpu	11.4	230	11.5
Minhang	4.2	119	8.6
Baoshan	6.1	15	9.9
Jiading	2.9	7	6.3
Pudong	14.2	29	10.4

Source: *Shanghai tongji nianjian 1994* (see note 5 below), pp. 42, 89.

Figure 14.3   Spatial Pattern of Housing Distribution in Urban Shanghai, 1993

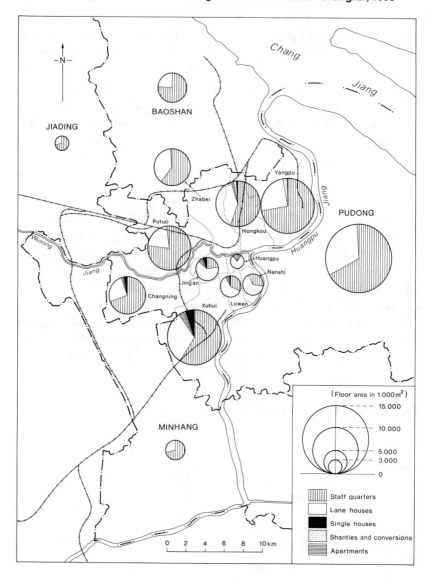

Figure 14.4   Spatial Pattern of Housing Density in Urban Shanghai, 1993

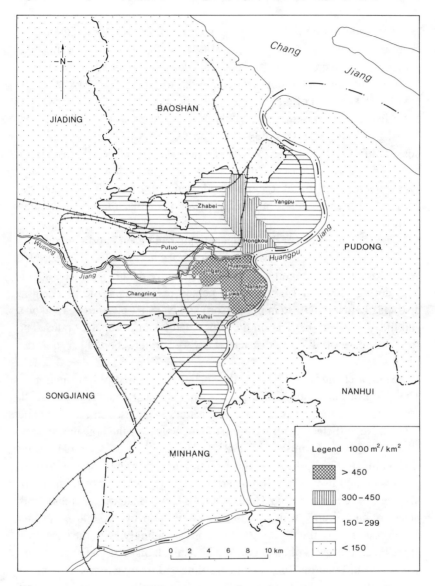

11%, the 14% share of the newly developed urban centre of Pudong was the largest.

The redefinition of district boundaries produced some interesting changes in housing density (Table 14.9 and Figure 14.4). Despite the decrease in housing stock, the housing density of Huangpu (634) and Nanshi (584) more than doubled from 1985 to 1993. This may be due to the loss of 14 sq km of the less congested peripheral area to neighbours in both districts.[15] Consequently, while Jing'an (668) still had the highest housing density, Huangpu (634) replaced Luwan with the second highest density. Further, the difference between the northern and southern districts had been blurred, with only Hongkou having an exceedingly high density. The housing density of the newly designated urban districts on the periphery was, of course, markedly lower than that of the established districts.

The spatial pattern of the occupancy rate had become more diversified despite a general growth for all districts (Table 14.5 and Table 14.9). While Xuhui and Changning continued to achieve the highest space standard, scoring 15.6 and 13.7 sq m per person respectively, the two central districts of Huangpu (9 sq m per person) and Nanshi (9.2 sq m per person), and the new urban districts on the fringe had lower occupancy rates. The space standard of all other districts was very similar, about 11.6 sq m per person.

Similar changes are found in the spatial distribution of housing types. The share of lane houses in the inner districts' aggregate housing stock remained high, and this proportion had actually increased in Huangpu and Nanshi. Nevertheless, the proportion of lane houses in the housing stock of all other districts diminished by 1993, the largest drop in Putuo (21%) and Changning (19%). Likewise, the shanties and housing converted from non-residential uses were eliminated in absolute and relative terms in all districts, except Putuo and Huangpu. The most dramatic decrease took place in Zhabei and Nanshi, with the demolition of 720,000 sq m and 330,000 sq m floor area, respectively. Correspondingly, with the exception of the central districts of Huangpu and Nanshi, all districts had experienced growth in staff quarter floor area in absolute and relative terms. Except for Zhabei, all outer districts produced more than 3 million sq m of new staff quarters between 1985 and 1993, and staff quarters became the dominant housing type in all these districts. The stock of apartments generally only grew mildly and it remains a minor housing type. While single houses were also insignificant, 235,000 sq m of new stock was built in Xuhui.

Thus, the four inner districts, especially Huangpu and Nanshi, had become less important as residential areas by 1993, due to their diminished sizes and their increasing role as central business districts. Only 2.7% and 4.4% of the city's housing stock was located in Huangpu and Nanshi respectively, the majority of which was lane houses and shanties. Their housing stock remained of the poorest quality. Nonetheless, the southern and southwestern districts ceased to be the concentrations of better housing. This diffusion was due to the massive construction of staff quarters in other districts, especially in the newly designated urban districts of Pudong (67%), Baoshan (76%) and Jiading (71%). It should, however, be noted that Jing'an, Xuhui and Changning in the west and southwest continued to have the highest proportion of apartments and single houses in their housing stock.

There was also less spatial disparities in the distribution of community facilities in 1993 than in 1985, and the provision of such facilities generally increased in quantitative terms (Table 14.7 and Table 14.10). Regarding the provision of school space per 1,000 persons, although Xuhui (2,659 sq m), Yangpu (1,941 sq m) and Jiading (1,170 sq m) remained the best, the difference between the inner and outer districts had been reduced. It is, however, noteworthy that the central districts of Huangpu (627 sq m) and Nanshi (620 sq m), and the two new peripheral districts of Baoshan (512

Table 14.10   Distribution of Housing-related Services by District, 1993

(Unit: m^2/1,000 persons)

Districts	Schools	Retail services	Hospitals	Theatres & cinemas	% of green area
Huangpu	627	1,974	313	251	7.9
Nanshi	620	400	200	20	7.3
Luwan	1,023	666	452	119	11.0
Xuhui	2,659	378	404	39	11.3
Changning	1,579	549	349	33	15.3
Jing'an	962	641	550	69	15.5
Putuo	1,137	482	148	37	13.5
Zhabei	1,053	430	222	15	10.5
Hongkou	991	454	275	24	14.0
Yangpu	1,941	404	202	38	21.9
Minhang	956	332	98	39	9.1
Baoshan	512	496	155	47	19.1
Jiading	1,170	710	230	42	15.0
Pudong	591	369	125	21	8.4

Source: *Shanghai tongji nianjian 1994* (see note 5 below), pp. 90, 92.

sq m per 1,000 persons) and Pudong (591 sq m per 1,000 persons), provided the least. With regard to space provision for retail services, while the inner districts had experienced sharp increases, notably the 144% growth in Huangpu, retail space provision was rather even among other districts. Jiading was the only exception.

The spatial discrepancies in provision of hospitals was basically unchanged between 1985 and 1993. The southern districts continued to have a higher provision of hospitals than the northern districts, and their provision also surpassed that of the new districts. However, Luwan (452 sq m per 1,000 persons) replaced Xuhui (404 sq m per 1,000 persons) as the best provided district. In contrast, Huangpu (251 sq m per 1,000 persons) and Luwan (119 sq m per 1,000 persons) continued to provide the most theatres and cinemas. The fewest, however, were found in Zhabei (15 sq m per 1,000 persons), replacing Nanshi, Changning and Xuhui. It is surprising to find that the provision of entertainment facilities in the new districts was generally higher than the average space standard. Despite general improvements in expanding the green area, Yangpu (22%) and Jing'an (16%) remained districts with high rates of plantation. The 1985 irregular spatial pattern of green area prevailed to 1993. Whereas Jing'an had a high rate, the other two central districts of Huangpu and Nanshi had low rates, 8% and 7% respectively. Similarly, while 19% and 15% of the two peripheral districts of Baoshan and Jiading were respectively covered with green area, only 9% and 8% of Minhang and Pudong were covered with green area.

Thus, a more balanced spatial pattern of housing conditions developed in Shanghai between 1985 and 1993. More housing development took place in the south and the southwest, thus raising the housing density closer to that of the northern districts. However, the demolition of poor quality housing stock and the massive growth of staff quarters all over Shanghai, especially in the new peripheral districts, diluted the southern and southwestern districts as concentrations of better housing stock. Nonetheless, Xuhui and Changning still had the highest occupancy rates and higher proportions of apartments and single houses. They continued to be served with more education and medical facilities, and the provision of retail and entertainment facilities improved.

In contrast, the residential function of the central districts of Huangpu and Nanshi diminished and the quality of housing conditions deteriorated in relative terms. They had the highest housing density and the lowest occupancy rates. All these point to the fact that living conditions in these districts were the most congested. They also possessed the highest proportion of poor quality housing stock. Further, although there was ample supply of retail services and entertainment facilities, the provision of hospitals and schools was meagre. In contrast, the new peripheral districts had low housing density since they had not yet matured. As new urban centres, the proportions of staff quarters as part of the housing stock was high and the provision of community facilities was generally the least.

Undeniably, housing development in Shanghai since 1980 has been phenomenal both in quantitative and qualitative terms. The rapid pace of development is not without cause. It is the corollary of heightened investment and of the introduction of unprecedented changes to the housing system, the most dramatic being implemented in the production sector. The next section examines housing reform measures launched in the city since 1980.

Housing System Reform

Since the Communist government came to power in 1949, housing provision in Chinese cities had been, until recently, regarded as a state responsibility. Shanghai was no exception. Although in the early 1950s some enterprises did build quarters for their staff or assist their employees in rehabilitating their homes, housing was in the main provided by the government almost free of charge. Rent was, therefore, very low and housing production costs were non-recoverable, creating a heavy financial burden on the government. The financial strain was acutely felt in the late 1970s when hundreds and thousands of intellectual youths returned to the city in the wake of the Cultural Revolution. The average annual production of housing before 1980 was only 650,000 sq m (compared to the 1993 production of 6,165,000 sq m).[16] There was a strong need for housing reform. It was gradually recognized that the low-rental policy not only created endless housing spending, it also fuelled inflation, dampened the residents' incentives to buy their own housing, caused over-consumption of housing and lowered the efficiency of the housing system.[17] Housing system reform was, therefore, one of the initial issues which Deng Xiaoping addressed in 1980 as he began to introduce liberal economic policies to the country.

Initial Reform Measures

Reform measures introduced in the 1980s were threefold: to require work units to maximize the use of internal resources for housing construction; to encourage overseas Chinese to participate in housing construction; and to experiment on housing commodification by selling housing to enterprises, organizations and individuals at prices set according to the quality of the units. As a result, the capital invested in housing between 1980 and 1990 was 90% (RMB15.5 billion) of the total amount invested between 1949 and 1990. The share of the work units' contribution (including funding allocated by the government and their own resources) in the total investment increased from 54.8% to a peak of 86.3%, averaging 75.7% between 1980 to 1990. Total floor area produced was 45,630,000 sq m, accounting for 69% of the total production between 1949 and 1990.[18]

The sale of homes was regarded as a means to commodify the housing sector. The initial step was to build housing for sale to friends and relatives of overseas Chinese residing in Shanghai. Later, state housing was sold at concessionary prices (one-third of the production costs) to enterprise employees. Moreover, development companies were established to produce and provide housing at market prices to enterprises and individuals, leading to the emergence of a housing market[19] (see details in the next section).

Apart from the above three foci of the new policy, two supplementary measures were introduced. One was the provision of transient housing to the newly-wedded at rents (RMB1.1 per sq m) four times the normal rate. This was known as "couple housing" which consisted of one-room flats. The units were leased for a fixed term of one to two years and management services were provided. This type of housing provided a solution for young couples who had had to defer marriage because of the unavailability of housing. It also constituted a first step by the government to provide housing for fixed terms and at higher rents. The other measure was the trial formation of housing co-operatives. Members bore one-third of the construction costs, the rest of which were borne by the members' work units and loans borrowed from relevant government organizations. The co-operatives were in charge of the construction, allocation and management of the housing stock.[20]

Thus, the initial measures were heavily geared towards the diversification of the sources and capital for production. Commodification was rudimentary in that operations were confined to the sale of homes and the scale was limited to relatives of overseas Chinese and enterprise employees. Further, although home ownership was advanced, enterprises rather than the end-users, i.e., the households, paid the full market price for housing consumption. As the housing funds of the enterprises dissipated, the above measures were less effective in relieving the problems of housing shortages. Therefore, a more radical and comprehensive reform blueprint was considered in the late 1980s.

The 1991 Reform Programme

From 1988 to 1990, a housing reform leading group and a housing reform office were set up in the government to carry out extensive housing surveys and accordingly to propose reform packages for the government's detailed discussion and consideration. A more radical and comprehensive reform programme was finally proposed and was approved by the State Council and the Ninth Standing Committee Meeting of the Shanghai People's Congress in February 1991.[21] The new reform programme, which has been in operation until the present day, reaffirms the commodification principle. However, for the first time it advocates the principle of "housing according to one's ability" (*zizhuqili* 自住其力). Accordingly, the low-rental and free housing services policy was redressed and individuals are now expected to contribute to housing construction. A new organization has also been set up to rectify abuses in housing allocation. The reform targets for the end of this century are to raise the average per capita living space to 8 sq m, to boost the proportion of self-contained units to 60% of the total housing stock, to rehouse all those whose living space is less than 3.5 sq m per capita and the majority of those whose living space is between 3.5–4 sq m, and to redevelop the bulk of dangerous buildings, squatter huts and dilapidated buildings.

To complement reform measures already in operation, four of the five new measures announced in the reform programme pertain to consumption. These are, namely, the establishment of a housing superannuation scheme, concurrent rent increases and the granting of housing allowances, the compulsory purchase of housing bonds by new tenants and the extension of home purchase concessions to all employees. The remaining measure concerns an organizational change in housing policy formulation and implementation. It involves the setting up of a housing authority comprised of leaders of relevant government departments, renowned social figures and citizen representatives to study, administer and supervise Shanghai's housing system reform and its policies. The consumption reform measures deserve further discussion.[22]

The housing superannuation scheme is an obligatory savings scheme aimed at accruing funds for employees' future housing expenditures. All local employees (except temporary workers) are required to contribute a certain proportion of their monthly salaries to the scheme, and employers deposit an equal amount from the work unit budgets (specifically from the budgets of housing depreciation, maintenance and management, if any). The deposits are kept in the employees' individual accounts. They can withdraw the deposits for purchase, construction or major renovation of their homes. The contribution rate in 1993 was 5% of the monthly salary. The interest rates for the deposits follow that of the savings deposits in banks.

Rents were doubled, increasing from RMB0.25 per sq m to RMB0.5 per sq m. Based on the principle of balancing the total payment of the housing allowance with the aggregate rental increase, the housing allowance is fixed at 2% of the monthly salary or retirement payments. As there are households exempt from the rental increase on humanitarian grounds, it has yet to be ascertained whether this new rental policy creates financial benefits or deficits to the government or the enterprises.

The on-off purchase of housing bonds is compulsory for all new tenants. Tenants with real financial difficulties are permitted to buy bonds by instalments. The sum of the bonds to be purchased is determined by the gross area of the leased unit, the basic rate per sq m of gross area (subject to revision) and the location factor. The average price in 1993 was RMB50 per sq m. The bond is recoverable after five years and a simple interest rate of 3.6% per annum is applied. The bond capital is earmarked for housing construction and work units with staff who purchase bonds enjoy borrowing priorities. A total value of RMB200 million in bonds had been sold by the end of 1993.

Home purchases at concessionary prices have been extended to staff and workers of state organizations and institutions patronized by the government. The housing price consists of two components and a depreciation factor if the sale unit is not newly completed. One of the price components is the full housing construction costs, which is about one-third of the total production costs (i.e., construction costs, land costs and rehousing costs) or the building replacement costs. The other component is the quality factor, including location, orientation, height and amenities. A 20% discount is rewarded to purchasers who pay the price outright. For those who pay by instalments, a 2.5% discount is granted for every 10% of the housing price paid at transaction in addition to the minimum 30% downpayment. Tax concessions are also provided to the sellers and purchasers.

The sale proceeds are, nonetheless, confined to reinvestments for further housing construction. By the end of 1993, a total of 120,000 units were sold at concessionary prices.

By the mid-1990s, the implementation of the 1991 reform programme, coupled with the continuation of the pre-1991 reform measures, had created a hybrid housing system in Shanghai. The production of housing is no longer the sole responsibility of the government. While the pre-1991 reform measures diversified and multiplied the construction resources, the implementation of the 1991 blueprint intensified the trend through the consumption reforms. The aggregate deposits of the housing superannuation scheme, the compulsory purchase of housing bonds and proceeds from home sales fostered new channels of non-government construction funds, basically sourcing from individual households. The consumption reforms have, of course, transformed housing consumption itself.

Housing service is no longer costless, although it is not priced at full cost yet. As demonstrated by Table 14.11, the rent payment was still among the smallest spending item of households in 1993, although in absolute terms, it had increased fourfold compared with that of 1982. Nonetheless, the cost of renting has been made closer to that of home ownership as housing bonds have to be purchased by tenants on one hand,

Table 14.11 Consumption Pattern of Urban Households in 1982 and 1993

		(Unit: RMB)
Consumption items	1982	1993
Food	339	1,868
Clothing	81	414
Household appliances, goods and services	49	307
Medical and health expenditures	7	68
Transport	18	199
Recreation, education and cultural activities	33	301
Rent	10	41
Water and electricity	9	71
Fuel	9	60
Other related housing expenditures	5	23
Miscellaneous goods and services	16	177
TOTAL	576	3,529

Note: The figures do not add up to the total because of rounding of figures.
Sources: *Shanghai tongji nianjian 1983* 上海統計年鑑 1983 (Statistical Yearbook of Shanghai 1983) (Shanghai: Shanghai renmin chubanshe, 1983), p. 338; *Shanghai tongji nianjian 1994* (see note 5 below), p. 60.

and considerable concessions are granted to home purchasers on the other. Although the provision of a housing allowance negated the impact of the rental increases on affordability, the policy has, nevertheless, amplified the cost consciousness of housing consumption. The allocation of housing in Shanghai today still largely operates through administrative means, but market elements have been introduced. This is evident in the inclusion of locational factors in determining housing price and the sum of the housing bonds to be purchased by new tenants. The most conspicuous shift to the market principle is inevitably the emergence of the housing market.

Housing Market

As mentioned above, development companies have been set up to build housing for sale to enterprises and individuals at market prices. In addition, other housing providers, including the government itself, also produce housing for sale at market rates, although in most cases discounts are applied. The development companies are not privately-owned, but are subsidiaries of state-owned enterprises or government organizations. However, they operate on commercial principles. Their establishment relieves work units from the burden of having to build housing directly for their staff. Work units purchase market housing and rent it to their staff at heavily subsidized rates. Since the inauguration of the first development company in 1979, a total of 1,788 development companies producing residential, commercial and industrial properties had been set up by October 1994. A majority of these were formed after 1992.[23] Properties are not exclusively for domestic buyers and some are specifically provided to relatives of overseas Chinese. However, for the purpose of this chapter, only conditions of the internal market catering for the average citizens are explored.

Table 14.12 shows the supply and demand conditions of the market for ordinary housing. It can be seen that the market took off in 1988 when a sizable amount of housing (1,018,000 sq m, approximately 18,000 units) was built in that year. New supplies in the subsequent four years never reached the same level, possibly due to inadequate demand. The take up rates only ranged between 50% to 74%. However, both supply and demand escalated by more than onefold in 1993. The growth in supply continued to 1994 but the increase in effective demand flattened. Hence the take up rate dropped to a record low of 47%, creating an over-supply market situation.

Table 14.13 shows the demands of various buyers between 1983 and

Table 14.12 Supply^a and Demand of Ordinary Market Housing^b (Internal Market), 1979–1994

(Unit: 1,000 sq m)

Year	Surplus from last year	New supply	Total supply	Effective demand	Take up rate (%)
1979–1987	—	1,036	1,036	1,036	100
1988	0	1,018	1,018	679	67
1989	272	764	1,036	517	50
1990	452	729	1,181	872	74
1991	304	716	1,020	640	63
1992	380	646	1,026	558	54
1993	390	1,559	1,949	1,449	74
1994	500	2,343	2,843	1,334	47

Note: ^a The supply included the production of market housing by development companies, work units, the government and housing co-operatives.

   ^b Ordinary market housing (*yiban neixiao shangpinfang* 一般內銷商品房) refers to housing consumed by average local households, as opposed to high quality housing (*gaobiaozhun neixiao shangpinfang* 高標準內銷商品房) mainly purchased by households with overseas connections and by foreign-related enterprises.

Source: *'95 Shanghaishi fangdichan shichang* (Beijing: Zhongguo tongji chubanshe, 1995), p. 77.

1994. It is obvious that a majority of the individual buyers purchased market housing at discounted prices from their employers — in other words, market rates were not applied. In fact, this type of buyer dominated the "market" between 1984 and 1986. It was not until 1988 that real individual market buyers began to appear. Their share in the market was neither dominant nor steady by 1993. Nonetheless, the proportion increased to 50% in 1994, significantly transforming the nature of housing demand. Assuming that the average size of a housing unit is 55 sq m, only 2,345 and 1,473 individuals would have bought market housing in 1991 and 1992 respectively. In 1993 and 1994, however, the number of buyers reached 7,454 and 12,218 respectively. Regarding purchases by work units, the number of flats purchased in 1992, 1993 and 1994 was 8,673, 19,090 and 12,036 respectively. The scale of the housing market was therefore rather limited up to 1992, but the growth in 1993 and 1994 was remarkable.

In terms of price movements, a generally upward trend can be traced, although the extent of the increase fluctuated over the years (Table 14.14). Comparing the prices in 1985 and 1992, the extent of the increase in walk-up apartments doubled that of high rises. Prices dropped in 1991, but

Table 14.13   Purchasers of Ordinary Commodity Housing (Internal Market), 1983–1994

(Unit: 1,000 sq m)

Year	Individuals at discounted price	Individuals at market price	Work units at market price	TOTAL
1983	4	—	39	44
	(9)		(89)	
1984	83	—	—	83
	(100)			
1985	74	—	38	111
	(67)		(34)	
1986	173	—	110	283
	(61)		(39)	
1987	168	—	269	438
	(38)		(61)	
1988	158	38	483	680
	(28)	(6)	(71)	
1989	46	50	422	518
	(9)	(10)	(81)	
1990	47	80	745	872
	(5)	(9)	(85)	
1991	—	129	512	641
		(20)	(80)	
1992	—	81	477	559
		(15)	(85)	
1993	—	360	1,090	1,450
		(25)	(75)	
1994	—	672	662	1,334
		(50)	(50)	

Notes: [a] In 1991 and 1992, housing produced by work units, the government and housing co-operatives and sold at discounted prices were excluded from market housing. Buyers of these types of housing are, therefore, not tabulated.

[b] Numbers in brackets are percentages calculated by the author.

[c] The figures do not add up to the total and percentages do not add up to 100 because of rounding of figures from the original source of data.

Sources: *'93 Shanghaishi fangdichan shichang* (see note 23 below), p. 49; *'95 Shanghaishi fangdichan shichang* (see Table 14.12, source), p. 79.

1992 witnessed a onefold and twofold increase for high-rise and walk-up apartments respectively. Although statistics on price movements in 1993 and 1994 are not available, it is believed that the upward trend continued into 1993 and levelled off in 1994, resembling the pattern of high quality market housing.[24] This skyrocketing could have been due to Deng Xiaoping's visit to the South in that year, which affirmed the continuation

Table 14.14 Price Indices[a] of Ordinary Commodity Housing in Urban Areas, 1985–1992[b]

Year	High rises		Walk-up apartments	
	Index	Growth rate (%)	Index	Growth rate (%)
1985	100	—	100	—
1986	100	—	118	18
1987	100	—	244	106
1988	144	44	299	22
1989	167	15	328	10
1990	176	5	335	2
1991	157	–10	313	–7
1992	277	102	518	205

Notes: [a] Although unspecified, the indices are believed to be those of newly produced units.

[b] It is unfortunate that the 1994 and 1995 issues of *Shanghaishi fangdichan shichang* do not contain statistics on the price indices of ordinary market housing. Updating is, therefore, impossible.

Source: *'93 Shanghaishi fangdichan shichang* (see note 23 below), p. 51.

of the liberal economic policies. On the whole, however, the price movements between 1985 and 1992 do not seem to correspond with the supply and demand conditions as shown in Table 14.12.

A secondary housing market has also been in operation, although the scale is rather modest (Table 14.15). The number of transactions reached a

Table 14.15 Transactions in the Secondary Housing Market[a] in Urban Areas, 1986–1994

Year	No. of transactions	Gross floor area (m^2)	Transaction amount (RMB 1,000)	Price (per m^2)
1986	3,136	102,322	11,061	108
1987	3,778	93,562	11,862	126
1988	3,841	97,200	19,876	204
1989	3,657	92,000	23,201	252
1990	3,373	88,000	43,323	492
1991	3,340	89,982	63,013	700
1992	6,325	201,399	129,934	645
1993	4,922	166,123	154,317	929
1994	2,597	105,896	223,911	2,114

Note: [a] This includes both the high-quality housing market and the ordinary housing market. No separate statistics on the ordinary housing market segment are available.

Source: *'95 Shanghaishi fangdichan shichang* (see Table 14.12, source), p. 107.

peak in 1992, totalling 6,325. The transaction amount was highest in 1994 due to the sharp rise in prices.[25] The gross floor space transacted was also the greatest in 1992, reaching 201,399 sq m, which was equivalent to 31% of the new supply in the same year. The ratio nevertheless diminished to 11% and 5% in 1993 and 1994 respectively, showing that the secondary market did not grow in tandem with the primary market.

Thus, Shanghai's housing market underwent rapid development in the early 1990s. In 1992, the new supply of ordinary commodity housing was only 12% of total housing production, but it increased to 25% in 1993 (Table 14.1 and Table 14.12). Further, the proportion of individual home buyers also expanded rapidly. Other positive signs have emerged since 1992. First, a secondary market has begun operation. Second, there have been phenomenal increases in housing prices, despite robust supply, signalling strong market demand. Third, and perhaps the most important, the superstructure of the housing market has rapidly developed. The Shanghai government has enacted a series of ordinances and regulations governing property development, transactions, exchange, mortgage, registration and management. Other legislation related to urban planning and land development have also been promulgated.[26] Thus, it seems that the housing market should continue to make good progress in the second half of the 1990s.

Conclusion

This chapter initially traced the changes in the housing conditions of Shanghai since 1980. It was found that the living environment of the northern and central districts was markedly inferior to that of the south and southwestern districts before 1985. However, this disparity diminished thereafter as the old housing stock was demolished and new staff quarters and community facilities were built on a large scale all over the city. While new urban districts have been established in the fringe areas, the residential functions of the inner districts has been dwarfed. Although the problems of housing shortages and of low quality still persist in the 1990s, it is undeniable that improvements in housing have been phenomenal.

The housing system reform programs were mainly responsible for the improvement. Whereas the preliminary reform measures concentrated on the diversification and expansion of production resources, the 1991 program emphasized consumption reforms, extending the scope of commodification. In the context of Shanghai, commodification seems to refer to a long process by which residents who can afford it are incrementally required to pay the full costs of housing based on the principle of the consumption of housing according to one's ability. The resultant measures thus far implemented include the promotion of home sales at subsidized and market price levels, the raising of rents (but without conspicuously linking the rent with production and operating costs), mandating the purchase of housing bonds by new tenants and the establishment of an obligatory housing superannuation scheme. By the mid-1990s, although housing services are not yet priced at full costs, and the government, mediated through the work units, still bears much of the housing costs, more non-government resources have been tapped into the housing sector. The increasing number of individual home buyers in the housing market and the emergence of a secondary market are strong evidence of this. Indeed, the housing market has developed quickly and there are signs of its continued growth.

Thus, it can be quite certain that the commodification process will be intensified in the future. Its velocity may, however, be modified. Institutional constraints, external non-housing factors and residents' responses all will affect the pace and the direction of the housing reform process. The Shanghai government, as a response to the "State Council's Decision on the Deepening of Urban Housing System Reform" promulgated in July 1994, formulated a package to intensify housing reforms in 1995.[27] Although the details have not yet been announced at the time of this writing, it is obvious that the principle of *zizhuqili* will be further realized in the coming years.

Notes

1. Since the provision of state housing has only been confined to the urban sector, and rural residents are to cater for their own housing needs, the scope of this chapter only covers the urban housing sector.
2. "Living area" is conventionally used in China as the parameter for measuring housing area. It is defined as the internal floor area of bedrooms and sitting rooms inside a dwelling unit. Kitchens, toilets and corridors are excluded. When included, it is termed usage area.
3. *Shanghai zhuzhai (1949–1990)* 上海住宅 (1949–1990) (Shanghai Housing [1949–1990]) (Shanghai: Shanghai kexue puji chubanshe 上海科學普及出版社, 1993), pp. 1–16; Wu Zhengtong 吳政同, "The Rising of Shanghai's Real Estate Industry," *China Mail*, Vol. 6, No. 5 (1993), pp. 50–52; Wu Zhengtong, "Shanghai guomin zhuzhai jianshe he fangdichan shichang" 上海國民住宅建設和房地產市場 (State Housing and Real Estate Market in Shanghai),

Kongjian zazhi 空間雜誌, Vol. 7, No. 60 (1994), pp. 45–50.

4. According to the Office of Shanghai Housing Authority, the drop in the growth rate in 1983 was due to the depletion of enterprises funds for housing investment. Prior to 1980, all housing investment was sourced from the government only. Since that year, enterprises were also asked to contribute to housing production. This explains for the high increase rate in 1980. The rate, nevertheless, tapered off as enterprise funds dissipated. The negative growth rate in 1989 was attributed to the macroeconomic adjustment policy.

5. Shanghaishi tongjiju 上海市統計局 (ed.), *Shanghai tongji nianjian 1994* 上海統計年鑑 1994 (Statistical Yearbook of Shanghai 1994) (Beijing: Zhongguo tongji chubanshe 中國統計出版社, 1994), p. 65; *Shanghai tongji nianjian*, various issues; *Shanghai jingji nianjian 1991* 上海經濟年鑑 1991 (Shanghai Economy Yearbook 1991) (Shanghai: Sanlian shudian Shanghai fendian 三聯書店上海分店, 1991), p. 105; *Shanghai jingji nianjian 1993* (Shanghai: Shanghai shehuikexueyuan *Shanghai jingji nianjian* she 上海社會科學院《上海經濟年鑑》社, 1993), p. 69.

6. *Shanghai zhuzhai (1949–1990)* (see note 3), p. 147; and *Shanghai tongji nianjian 1994* (see note 5), p. 89.

7. Wu Zhengtong, "Shanghai guomin zhuzhai jianshe he fangdichan shichang" (see note 3).

8. The lane houses are two- or three-storey row houses built of a mix of local and foreign housing design. The Office of Shanghai Housing Authority classified them into two types: the old style lane house and the new style lane house. The former type was built in the years between 1870 and 1930. The structure is simple and are built of brick and wood. Usually there are no toilet and bath facilities and courtyards are very small. The latter type was built after 1930. The structure is better and toilet and bath facilities are installed. Some are provided with a small garden, fence and balconies.

9. The increase in old style lane houses was due to the rectification of housing statistics at the wake of the 1982 and 1986 general housing surveys (Information provided by the Office of Shanghai Housing Authority).

10. Staff quarters have been built after 1949. The more recent quarters are generally higher than eight storeys whereas the older ones are generally lower than seven storeys. Those which were built in or before the 1970s are of a poorer structure but all are equipped with toilet and kitchen facilities although some are communal. Quarters built in the 1980s and afterwards are all equipped with independent toilet and kitchen facilities and balconies. The high-rise apartments are also served with lifts (Information provided by the Office of Shanghai Housing Authority).

11. Wu Zhengtong, "Shanghai guomin zhuzhai jianshe he fangdichan shichang" (see note 3), p. 46.

12. The year 1985 has been chosen because published data on the distribution of housing characteristics by districts can only be traced to that year. It is noted that in the process of comparison district boundaries have changed over time.

13. Planning Department of Hong Kong Government, *Hong Kong Planning Standards and Guidelines*, chapter 2: Residential Densities (Hong Kong: The Government Printer, 1991), p. 2.

14. Apartments comprise the best housing type in the city. Each unit in the apartment is self-contained, endowed with a proper lounge room and balcony. Each is also installed with a cooling and heating system, and fittings and finish are of a high quality. Although single houses have more facilities such as gardens and garages, they are normally shared by more than one family. Therefore, the housing conditions of house dwellers are normally inferior to those of apartment dwellers.

15. Shanghaishi tongjiju (ed.), *Shanghai tongji nianjian 1986* (Statistical Yearbook of Shanghai 1986) (Shanghai: Shanghai renmin chubanshe 上海人民出版社, 1986), p. 58; and *Shanghai tongji nianjian 1994* (see note 5), p. 42.

16. Wu Zhengtong, "Shanghai guomin zhuzhai jianshe he fangdichan shichang" (see note 3), p. 47.

17. For detailed discussion, please see Rebecca L. H. Chiu, "Housing," in *Guangdong: Survey of a Province Undergoing Rapid Change*, edited by Y. M. Yeung and David K. Y. Chu (Hong Kong: The Chinese University Press, 1994), pp. 286–87.

18. Wu Zhengtong, "Shanghai guomin zhuzhai jianshe he fangdichan shichang" (see note 3), pp. 47–48.

19. Ibid.

20. Ibid.

21. Ibid.; Shanghaishi zhufang zhidu gaige bangongshi 上海市住房制度改革辦公室 (ed.), *Shanghai zhufang zhidu gaige* 上海住房制度改革 (Housing System Reform of Shanghai) (Shanghai: Shanghai renmin chubanshe, 1992).

22. For details of the reform schemes, see *Shanghai zhufang zhidu gaige* (see note 21).

23. Shanghaishi tudi shiyong zhidu gaige lingdao xiaozu bangongshi 上海市土地使用制度改革領導小組辦公室 and Shanghaishi tongjiju 上海市統計局 (eds.), *'93 Shanghaishi fangdichan shichang* '93上海市房地產市場 ('93 Shanghai Real Estate Market) (Beijing: Zhongguo tongji chubanshe, 1993), p. 51; *Ming bao* 明報 (Ming Pao) (Hong Kong), 24 November 1994.

24. For details of the price indices of high quality market housing, please refer to *'94 Shanghaishi fangdichan shichang* '94 上海市房地產市場 ('94 Shanghai Real Estate Market) (Beijing: Zhongguo tongji chubanshe, 1994), p. 86.

25. The stark price increase contrasted with the levelling off pattern in the primary market. No official explanation is offered for the sharp rise.

26. *'93 Shanghaishi fangdichan shichang* (see note 23); and *Ming bao*, 24 November 1994.

27. *Ming bao*, 5 May 1995.

15

Education

Grace C. L. Mak and Leslie N. K. Lo

The recent situation in education in Shanghai is a test case of just how many roles education can serve and how well it can play them. Education in modern Shanghai, as in China, has been charged with the goals of national development. In the current reform era, stress is laid on the economic aspects of national development. The education system is modified all too frequently to prepare more and better workers. Optimism regarding education's contribution to greater prosperity in Shanghai is evident in both policy formulation and daily practice. On the other hand, there are constant reminders of education's role to inculcate in the young values and attitudes deemed desirable. Are the economic and moral roles as defined in Shanghai compatible?

Schools in capitalist democracies are sites of inherent conflict and contradiction because they carry the twin responsibilities of preparing both workers and citizens. They must impart skills to students to fit the hierarchical corporate work structure as well as knowledge about equal rights for all under the law. These economic and political goals are antithetical. The success of one undermines that of the other.[1] Schools in socialist China have similar goals, which also appear to be at odds with one another. One of the direct consequences of the stormy politics in China since 1949 has been corresponding swings in the use of schools either as sources of skilled labour or of properly behaved citizens. The economic reform since 1978 represents the latest move in this perpetual dilemma. More than ever before, education is explicitly made a vehicle to accomplish the transition to a market economy. While this is true in all China, the transition has been most remarkable in advanced regions like Shanghai and Guangdong. However, the spirit of the market economy — to pursue the greatest profit in the least amount time for the benefit of the individual and subsequently of the collective — does not accommodate China's official moral stance — to subsume one's interests under those of the nation. Potentially, the more successful economic reform, the more elusive the moral goal. Shanghai is moving full steam ahead into the market mode, and so it may be more acutely torn than elsewhere in China. Can it do an equally good job in teaching both skills and values?

Following the framework employed in a similar study on education in Guangdong,[2] this chapter examines the nature of educational change in Shanghai since 1978. It is argued that an interactive relationship exists between education and the economy. Although economic aspirations have lent wings to educational reform, it is Shanghai's lead in education in the many decades preceding 1978 that has made this interaction feasible. This suggests that given similar policy encouragement, Shanghai will be able to fulfill such aspirations better than the rest of China. Our discussion begins with a historical account. It captures some traits of Shanghai education which have survived over the decades. Our main discussion is education's adjustment to the new market situation, and how strains that were exposed in the process have been relieved to make the system more efficient and to make learning a more bearable experience for students. Then, Shanghai's anxiety in promoting moral education is examined. Finally, it is argued that the current social and economic context renders it unrealistic that the two fundamentally contradictory goals can become a coherent whole.

Shanghai Education in Historical Perspective

Shanghai's modern economic and educational development emerged from a frail China in the mid-nineteenth century. Its central location on China's coastline and its proximity to a fertile hinterland made it an ideal choice for a trading port. Nascent industrialization, modern schooling and a new middle class created a need; they were mutually supporting. This setting favoured developments which subsequently contributed to Shanghai becoming number one in China in both education and in the economy.

Shanghai was home to a diversity of schools. While traditional indigenous schools (*sishu* 私塾) remained, modern schools began to sprout. They were run by often competing forces: Chinese schools supported by the government or private individuals, and quasi-colonial schools supported by Western missionaries. These schools varied in purpose. Some were in the mainstream of Chinese culture, others taught patriotism, and others taught Western values. From the 1920s on, some Chinese schools followed Kuomintang (Guomindang 國民黨) ideology and others followed that of Communism. A similar diversity was reflected in educational thought and methods. During the Republican period (1911–1949), great educators, such as Cai Yuanpei 蔡元培, Shu Xincheng 舒新城, Tao Xingzhi 陶行知, Yan Yangchu 晏陽初 (James Yan) and Liang Shuming 梁漱溟; the visits of Dewey and Monroe; the setting up of the first modern vocational school by Huang Yanpei 黃炎培, and a host of other innovations inspired the nation's intelligentsia. New methods of teaching and learning, IQ testing and other standardized forms of assessment, and coeducation were introduced. A thriving publishing industry helped propel new ideas. It was a time of "cultural awakening" in China, and Shanghai was at the forefront of this change.

Education in Shanghai was widespread by Chinese standards. According to one survey, the enrolment rate of school-aged children in urban Shanghai reached 59% in 1936; of which 33% were girls.[3] This achievement was due in part to the introduction of school districts in the late Qing. Shanghai was divided into a number of school districts, each of which was to oversee its subsystem of schools. Autonomy was thus ensured, allowing districts to compete and for each district to meet its own needs more effectively.[4] In higher education, Shanghai also excelled. Of 205 institutions of higher learning in China in 1949, Shanghai had 41 (20%), while it accounted for only 1.43% of the nation's population.[5] It had some of the best universities in China, including Fudan University (復旦大學), Tongji University (同濟大學), Jiaotong University (交通大學) and St. John's University (聖約翰大學).[6]

Schools attempted to fit into the economy through utilitarianism. Job opportunities lured primary school dropouts into the labour market or on to vocational or teacher training schools at the secondary level. Vocational schools taught knowledge that reflected the nature of Shanghai's economy, such as manufacturing, commerce and the English language. The attraction of grammar schools paled in comparison. This emphasis continued in higher learning and overseas education. In addition, students opted for knowledge that would lead to senior positions in employment, namely, law, medicine, political and military studies, and so on. Shanghai's relative ease in the acquisition of modern knowledge was matched by its readiness to abandon traditional knowledge, such as the Chinese classics and knowledge which carried a lower commerical value, such as history and geography.[7]

A distinct Shanghai identity was taking shape. In education, Shanghai was as a pioneer in taking new initiatives and in its flexibility to adapt to new environments. Shanghai's development as an economic centre and as a meeting point of Chinese and foreign influences made this possible.[8] Shanghai's pride in its identity has been a source of psychological drive in its pursuit for excellence.

In 1949, Shanghai inherited an education system which, though weak by today's standards, was way ahead the rest of China. The headstart paved the way for expansion, as Table 15.1 shows. Enrolment registered a rising trend over the years. The fluctuations in numbers reflect changes in politics, fertility rates and population migration into Shanghai. The achievement is better articulated by the fact that by 1958 urban Shanghai, and by 1983 rural Shanghai, had attained universal primary education,[9]

while many poor regions in China are still struggling towards this goal today. Greater access to education has raised the quality of Shanghai's
population. In 1964, about 20% of Shanghai's population had received at
least a lower secondary education, and by 1982, 51%.[10]

In the three decades since 1949, a number of themes persisted which
are of relevance here. The first was a continual swing between the prior
function of schools as disseminators of knowledge versus their role as
disseminators of moral values. In the first few years of new China, schools
were preoccupied with the inculcation of patriotism and the shaping of the
new socialist citizen. At the outset of the First Five-year Plan in 1953,
the goal of which was economic progress, schools stressed the cognitive
aspect of teaching. This trend changed in 1958, when politics reigned,
only to be reverted back to a cognitive emphasis again in 1961. During
the Cultural Revolution, conventional school knowledge was yet again
frowned upon.[11] The experience in this period shows that although schools
never performed one role only to the exclusion of the other, they failed to
strike a balance. Which role came to the fore depended heavily on the
forces in power at a given period of time. When academic knowledge came

Table 15.1   Enrolment Trends in Education by Level, 1949–1994

(Unit: 10,000)

Year	Tertiary	Secondary	Primary
1949	2.02	10.45	48.17
1952	2.23	18.90	91.17
1957	3.87	39.09	124.48
1962	5.86	51.03	175.94
1965	5.20	72.63	207.92
1970	0.38	71.60	164.59
1975	3.13	111.81	123.93
1978	5.06	101.81	87.06
1980	7.67	71.68	85.47
1985	10.79	63.50	84.18
1990	12.13	62.59	110.19
1993	13.10	76.54	116.70
1994	14.04	87.24	113.98

Sources: Shanghaishi tongjiju (ed.), *Shanghai tongji nianjian 1993* 上海統計年鑑 1993
(Statistical Yearbook of Shanghai 1993) (Beijing: Zhongguo tongji chubanshe, 1993), p. 53; Shanghaishi tongjiju (ed.), *Shanghai tongji nianjian 1994*
上海統計年鑑 1994 (Statistical Yearbook of Shanghai 1994) (Beijing:
Zhongguo tongji chubanshe, 1994), p. 216; and *Shanghai tongji nianjian*
1995 (see note 20 below), p. 228.

to the fore, competition for promotion to higher levels of education became keen. To tackle this negative effect, educationalists attempted to devise innovations to make learning a more pleasant activity.[12] The organization of the system witnessed similar hesitation. Between 1949 and 1966, primary education lasted six years. In the first three years of the Cultural Revolution, primary and secondary education operated on a 5 + 4 model; in 1970 6 + 4, and in 1976 5 + 5. The 6 + 3 + 3 model is the mainstay now, although there are also advocates for a 5 + 4 combination of compulsory education. Vocational education, which flourished in Kuomintang Shanghai, took on a new slant. In 1953, Soviet-style specialized technical schools were introduced. They aimed at preparing semi-professionals for teaching, industry, agriculture, medicine and other fields which were in great demand. These schools swelled in number during the Great Leap Forward campaign in the late 1950s, only to be trimmed down again a few years later, and to come to a complete halt during the Cultural Revolution.[13]

Developments since 1978

China's economic reform set the stage for subsequent educational responses. Under this national policy, however, each region is to develop according to its own characteristics. The new development strategy favours such a city as Shanghai with a historical legacy, and the ways education can serve the economy depend also on the type of city Shanghai aspires to be. With major cities in newly industrializing Asia as models, in particular Hong Kong and Singapore, Shanghai in the 1980s sought to grow into a burgeoning economic centre supported by experts in science and technology, and with labour, food and other materials from its surrounding rural areas. A strong education system must contribute to the realization of this goal. By the early 1990s, Shanghai had refined and expanded this goal: to become a centre of international finance and economy by the year 2010. It envisages a drop in its proportion of value of total output in the primary sector from 2.3% in 1993 to 1% in 2010, and in the secondary sector from 59.8% to 34%, and a corresponding rise in the tertiary sector from 37.8% to 65%.[14] The central government's endorsement to develop Pudong 浦東, hitherto with 50% of the population rural, into an advanced industrial and financial centre boosts the goals. Education carries an unambiguous mandate: to reform in such a way as to fit the "socialist market economy" and its accompanying political characteristics, and to ensure an abundant supply of quality workers.[15] Changes have taken place to fulfill this mandate.

Changes in the content, quantity and quality of education are examined below.

The Call from Economic Shanghai

Content of Education

One of the most drastic changes in education in China since 1978 has been the vocationalization of education. It has affected the upper secondary level the most, but also the tertiary level.

At the secondary level, two factors have prompted the change, the first being the bottleneck from upper secondary to tertiary education. A place in university was the sole ambition of most upper secondary students. In 1979, the grammar stream[16] accounted for 95%, and the vocational stream only 5% of the enrolment at the upper secondary school. Each year, about 200,000 upper secondary graduates competed for 20,000 university places.[17] To ease this tension, students are channelled to the vocational stream. Just as important, the new economy has an urgent need for a large number of semi-skilled workers at the middle stratum, which hitherto were in short supply. The education system responded by increasing the proportion of vocational education at the expense of grammar education at the post-compulsory level. China has a complicated system of vocational education, comprising specialized secondary schools, workers' schools and vocational schools. Specialized secondary schools, under the joint responsibility of the education ministry and the relevant ministry, prepare semi-professionals in the fields of engineering, agriculture and forestry, teacher education, medicine, economics and finance, politics and law, physical education and art. Workers' schools, run by business departments, train apprentices. Vocational schools, virtually non-existent before the reform era,[18] which are under the auspices of the education department and focus on skills needed in the new service industries, such as tourism, fashion and commerce. Traditionally, specialized schools constituted the bulk of vocational education. They were reinstituted in 1978. However, in spite of more than a twofold increase in enrolment between 1980 and 1994, they are losing their dominance as a result of the spectacular growth of vocational schools.[19] Although specialized schools still lead in enrolment (92,300 in 1994), vocational schools have been catching up (75,413). If enrolment in workers' schools (49,005) is included, specialized secondary schools have already been overtaken in enrolment.[20] The types of skills specialized schools teach no longer satisfy the labour market. Skills associated with new light industries and commerce are in demand. In 1979, the nation called for a restructuring of secondary education, the goal being to raise the weight of vocational education to grammar education at the upper secondary level from 4:6 to 6:4. Shanghai was among the first to move in this direction, and it proved to be the most successful. By 1984, the ratio reached 5:5, and by 1988, 6:4.[21] Significantly, the composition of knowledge has also shifted. In recent years, tourism, commerce, finance, transportation and communication account for 81% of the courses offered in vocational schools.[22] The popularity of vocational education and the pattern of courses mirror the direction of the development of Shanghai's economy.

The glamour of vocational education dims in rural Shanghai, however. As in so many other rural areas in China and in other developing societies, there is tension between the needs of the rural economy and those of the students. Providers of vocational education aim at rural development, whereas students seize upon education as a way out of life in the sticks. Agricultural courses, which befit rural Shanghai, attract few students. The differential reaction to the vocational drive shows how the economy is a crucial context for vocational education. Even in urban Shanghai, when the labour market shrinks, vocational education subsides. For example, when enterprises downsized for efficiency in 1989, they recruited fewer graduates from vocational schools which, in turn, attracted fewer entrants.

Prosperity in urban vocational education has not obscured some of its problems. Most schools are poorly equipped and what they teach lags behind the state-of-the-art trades. Course offerings reflect an unco-ordinated, rash reaction to the market situation, resulting in an oversupply of courses like clothing and hotel services, often with small enrolments in each, and little attention devoted to necessary but neglected trades like hot-working and foundry. Whereas the schools will adjust themselves in a mature market economy, Shanghai has not reached that stage, and intervention from the departments that oversee them is necessary. This problem is aggravated by complications in the sponsorship of vocational education. Specialized secondary schools have the additional problem of job placement. Traditionally, their graduates were assigned jobs at the rank of technical cadres. Now enterprises cannot absorb all graduates, and so the schools fail to attract students. This stalemate is caused in part by inflexible course offerings. Because of fragmented sponsorship, schools are typically undersized and suffer from diseconomies of scale. For example, in 1990 each vocational school enrolled an average of 244 students, and each specialized secondary school enrolled 500. To overcome the problem, schools in each category were reorganized or merged to acceptable sizes. The number of specialized secondary schools shrunk by 18%, from 110 in 1985 to 90 in 1994, while the number of new entrants soared by 62%, from 13,000 in 1990 to 21,000 in 1993.[23] Another perennial limitation of vocational education is whether it meets labour market needs. To address this issue, vocational schools have experimented with different patterns of sponsorship, such as sponsorship by the education department, business units, or both. The last model proved the most desirable. Schools in this model draw on the expertise of both education departments and business units, and are more sensitive to market needs.[24] Critics also point out that skills learned in vocational schools quickly become obsolete, as do their graduates. Besides schools in the vocational stream, grammar schools also offer some vocational classes.

In line with national changes, higher education in Shanghai is also characterized by a new version of utilitarianism. In the 1950s, higher education devoted most of its resources to producing engineers, doctors and teachers who were most needed for national reconstruction. The accent on utilitarianism continues today, but the focus has been diverted to other badly needed skills. Since the 1980s, new programmes have been established, and more are being added, as the economy articulates newer needs. The change is illustrated in the distribution of graduates by field of study over the years (Table 15.2). There has been a decline in the proportion of what used to be priority fields (e.g., medicine and teacher education) and fields with low utilitarian value (e.g., humanities and natural sciences), but a rise in fields with a high demand in the market economy (e.g., finance and economics, and political science and law). Engineering begs further investigation. In China, it is a conglomerate of subjects comprised of applied geology, mining, power engineering, metallurgy, mechanical engineering, electrical mechanics and instruments, radio and electronics, chemical engineering, grain processing and food industry, light industry, surveying and hydrology, civil engineering and architecture, transportation, telecommunications, and others. With the changes over the years, there was a high priority attached to technology in heavy industry or national infrastructure.[25] The internal proportion now has changed, especially in Shanghai. The new priority specialties in Shanghai are automobile production, telecommunications, biological engineering, computer engineering, and the like. Enrolment in these fields is expected to double between 1995 and 2000.[26] To speed up the process, some universities have set up branch

Table 15.2   Percentage Composition of Graduates by Field of Study, 1950–1983 and 1993

Field of study	1950–1983	1993
Engineering	46	50
Agriculture & forestry	1	2
Medicine	11	9
Teacher education	17	12
Humanities	8	5
Natural sciences	8	5
Finance & economics	6	11
Political science & law	2	4
Physical education	1	1
Art	1	2

Note: The totals do not add up to 100 due to rounding.
Source: *Shanghai tongji nianjian 1983* (see note 5), p. 279; *Shanghai tongji nianjian 1994* (see Table 15.1, Sources), p. 218.

campuses, which focus on fields for which there is a short supply of manpower.[27] Amidst the boom, however, the problem of uneven course offerings, such as that in secondary vocational education, has also emerged. There is an oversupply of popular courses, resulting in dis-economies of scale for each course. In contrast, the humanities and the natural sciences are underenrolled.[28]

Adjustment in the content of basic education takes a different bent. As long as the students' destination is the university, the content of education is dictated by an academic emphasis and by an assessment mechanism based on public examinations, the irrelevance of which was concealed as long as the economy and job placements were planned. But this changed once the two opened up. More seriously, a uniform curriculum had been used for the entire nation, thus ignoring local needs in a land of vast disparities. The state realizes this problem and now promotes curriculum diversity to suit uneven levels of development.

In 1988, a committee was set up in Shanghai to develop a curriculum for primary and secondary schools in economically developed coastal areas. In 1990, a draft curriculum was in place and, in 1991 it was tried out in pilot schools. In 1993, the new curriculum was formally adopted. It has ambitious objectives: to ensure effective learning of cultural and scientific knowledge; to integrate learning and application; to introduce or increase the proportion of elective courses, extracurricular activities and vocational education; to make schooling a pleasant experience for students by re-ducing pressures on them and by making it more sensitive to individual differences.[29] The problems of the old curriculum and the needs of the new situation have been accurately identified. The questions are: Can schools teach more and better while simultaneously making children happier? Are the teachers sufficiently equipped for this new mandate?

Our data reveal a gap between aspirations and ability. Teachers were trained in an age when all they had to do was to teach conventional school knowledge according to rigid guidelines. Now they are expected to teach creatively and effectively in shorter curricular time, and to take up a multitude of new courses and activities, in the classroom, where the students, who are members of the generation of the one-child per couple policy, present a challenge in management.[30] Not surprisingly, some teachers are guided by the old spirit in new forms, and most are still trying to grapple with the new curriculum.

Shanghai's adaptation to the content of knowledge accentuates the question of the relevance of education so prevalent in developing and rapidly changing societies. Unlike many developing regions, Shanghai has a history of sophistication and receptiveness to education. It has the wisdom to identify its needs and the ability to act accordingly, and a thriving economy to absorb school dropouts readily. However, the articulation between the schools and the workplace is too complex to be resolved in a relatively short time. Age-old traditions die hard. Shanghai has taken bold strides in the right direction. Even so, it should heed the fact that while administrative measures are fairly feasible, it takes much longer for change to settle and to be meaningful.

Quantity

The overwhelming concern in China is to universalize nine-year basic education. Shanghai has already passed this point. In 1988, the enrolment rate in primary and lower secondary education reached 82%; by 1993, 99.7%.[31] The rates are higher in urban Shanghai. Attention is now focused on expanding post-compulsory education. A survey of human power supply was conducted in the 1980s to provide data for subsequent educational planning. One of the goals that emerged was to seek to double the enrolment rate in upper secondary education between 1983 and 1990. This has been accomplished. The enrolment rate rose from 37.5% to 75% in the target period, and to 80% in 1993, and it is now catching up with that of developed societies.[32] The supply of professionals has been less straightforward. The survey revealed, much to the alarm of Shanghai and the nation, a severe shortage of skilled personnel, especially those in the 25 to 35 age bracket.[33] Some statistics will illustrate the problem. In 1993, Shanghai needed 25,000 graduates from tertiary institutions, but the supply was only 17,000. The discrepancy was especially acute among those with such skills as foreign languages, computer science, finance, trading, accounting, machinery building, shipbuilding and pharmaceuticals. An intense drive ensued. Between 1991 and 1993, the number of new entrants to tertiary institutions soared by 34% (from 32,609 to 43,643). By 1993, 21% of the 18–21 age cohort were enrolled in tertiary education; the target is to raise this figure to 30% by 2000.[34] To accelerate the supply of educated manpower, there is a focus on non-degree higher education, which takes two or three years to complete, as compared to four years for a typical degree course. The proportion of entrants to non-degree courses in higher education has varied over the years. It was low in the early phase of new China (30% in 1952 and 25% in 1960), and extremely low during the Cultural Revolution (less than 1% in 1974). The urgent need for national rehabilitation thereafter raised it to 88% (1978), but it then decreased to 28% in 1980 and 29% in 1983.[35] Shanghai University (上海大學, founded in 1983) reflected the policy change. Enrolment in non-degree courses there accounts for half of its total enrolment.[36]

Quality

Ambitions for educational expansion may yield negative side effects, and Shanghai is well aware of this. Delegations have been sent abroad to learn from other education systems and identify possible pitfalls. The measures adopted to ensure the smooth operation of the system result from both wisdom acquired from such visits and efforts to overcome structural shortcomings peculiar to China. These measures focus on individual students and the system respectively.

A major effort to lighten the burden of studying is by reforming the selection system. The revival of the national entrance examination to tertiary institutions in 1977 underscored the importance of intellectual education. How can stresses on students be reduced? Shanghai attempted to reduce the number of public examinations. Previously, each level of education concluded with a public examination and promotion to the next level was based on a public entrance examination. Since the mid-1980s, the examination system has been revised. The graduation examination serves both as an indicator of attainment and as a selection mechanism. At the compulsory level, individual schools and the district in which they are located have more autonomy. In compliance with a directive from the State Education Commission in 1986, primary schools set their own graduation examination questions. Children enter primary and lower secondary schools in the district in which they reside. Scaling down the size of the administrative unit aims to reduce competition among children. The examinations at the end of lower secondary education and upper secondary education are administered by the municipality.[37] In the same spirit, the key school system at the compulsory level was abolished in 1981; by 1986, there were no longer any key compulsory schools.[38] But key schools at the upper secondary level remain. They recruit students from across Shanghai. They are divided into district keys and municipal keys. The former recruit the best students from the entire district and the latter the best from the entire municipality, based on a public examination at the corresponding level. The goal of examination reform and key school system reform is to reduce student stress while maintaining the cultivation of élites. Delegating autonomy to the district is also intended to assure quality. As in pre-Communist China, each district tries to outperform the others.

The effectiveness of reform in this respect has thus far been mixed. The results of Shanghai's efforts to have the best of both worlds are unclear. One set of measures (upper secondary key schools and university entrance examinations) undermines the other (deemphasis on élitism in compulsory education). The social behaviour in the response illustrates the uncomfortable relationship between the two. As long as scarcities remain, so will competition. The aspirations of students, parents and teachers have only been postponed to key upper secondary schools, but preparation starts at primary school.[39] Similarly, against the government's better judgment, public demand for higher education persists. For one to achieve in a developed society, a secondary education no longer suffices.[40]

Efforts to reduce student stress also unfurl inside the schools. Teachers are encouraged to diversify from the use of conventional tests and examinations to other assessment and evaluation mechanisms. They are reminded of the importance of fostering students' analytical and creative capacities. Again, the goal is lofty, but the teachers may not be able to attain it. The results may be more of a change in form than in essence.[41] Moreover, as long as entrance to key upper secondary schools and to tertiary institutions continue to rely on examination scores, the majority of teachers will avoid risking innovations.

There is a new recognition of student experience as a legitimate focus of concern in schooling. This is a fundamental change in Chinese views on teaching and learning. Chinese education has been heavily teacher-centred, and students rather than the system have been blamed for failure. Now Chinese educationalists have begun to subscribe to a student-centred approach. They try livelier means with more activities. The innovations in some schools have attracted interest and are being extended to other schools. Notable among these are the efforts to make learning an enjoyable experience which was first promoted at the primary school affiliated with Shanghai No. 1 Teachers College (上海第一師範學院) and the project led by Gu Lingyuan 顧泠沅 to enhance effective teaching and learning. Schools are encouraged to experiment on their own. However, success has not reached all schools in Shanghai. In most schools, teaching and learning continue to operate more or less in the same mode. In sessions on how to teach that we observed, the change tends to be in behaviouristic techniques rather than in the spirit of heuristic education.

The tradition of treating students as a uniform mass is also fading. Individual difference are tolerated and accommodated in a culture that normally disapproves of individuality. Western theories of child psychology have made a comeback. In 1980, the municipal education bureau formulated a less demanding syllabus for students of lower ability at the upper secondary level.[42] Schools offer remedial classes after hours to help slow learners. Parallel measures, such as promoting extracurricular activities and elective courses at upper secondary schools, aim at increasing options to suit differences in student aptitudes. This open-mindedness in the search for alternatives is reminiscent of a similar vitality in pre-Communist Shanghai. Although the tension between educators' good intentions and the competition engendered by the system is unlikely to be resolved in the foreseeable future, the move towards student-centred education is applaudible.

The quality of the system merits as much attention. In the planned system, schools, like other institutions in China, grew out of control in number, with little concern for efficiency. The obvious task for Shanghai has been to streamline its school system. Schools have been reorganized based on economies of scale. They have decreased in number while maintaining the same total enrolments. Tertiary institutions are being merged, with the target of bringing down their number from 47 in 1994 to 40 by 2000, and of increasing the average enrolment of each institution from 2,980 to 5,000.[43] While the strategy has been approved, its results have yet to be seen. At this stage, mergers have not demonstrated a significant improvement in efficiency.[44]

Another dimension of efficiency focuses on the sponsorship of schools. The predominant mode of government sponsorship, complemented by government-assisted people-run schools (*minban gongzhu* 民辦公助) in cases of deprivation, is giving way to increased participation from non-government forces. While government sponsorship continues to be the mainstream, private schools and joint sponsorship of schools by the education department and enterprises represent a point of departure.

In spite of a history as long as that of the PRC, *minban* schools are going through a change in nature. From a makeshift, typically inferior system for which the government failed to provide sufficient schools, some *minban* schools which appeared after 1978 have tended to increase in prestige. Yet they are not quite the exclusive private schools that people outside of China understand them to be. At the current stage, they are a hybrid. There are two types of new *minban* schools: those run by private groups or individuals, much like private schools outside of China; and those managed by private groups or individuals but under the direction of a government department. In 1992, Shanghai had five *minban* primary and secondary schools, all of which belonged to the latter mode. They had been set up by the district education bureau. More than financial considerations, these schools carry a mandate to experiment with education reform. Within the boundaries of curriculum guidelines, they have greater freedom than typical schools to innovate. They are staffed by some of the best teachers and administrators, who thus ensure high quality. However, their prestige is possible only as long as they remain small in number, for good teachers are in short supply.[45] The significance of *minban* schools, Shanghai style, thus lies in their potential in breaking new ground rather than in their numbers.

There has been a new pattern of financing among government schools, reflecting changing central and local economic relations. Decentralization in the post-Mao era allows for greater provincial financial autonomy, after submitting an agreed upon sum to the state. The formula is negotiable. For example, Shanghai deemed the 1980 sum to be unfavourable and in 1988 bargained for a better deal which allowed it to retain a larger proportion of its revenues.[46] This has had a direct impact on schools in Shanghai. Of the 50 tertiary institutions in 1993, 28 are under the jurisdiction of central ministries, 21 under the municipal government, and one is *minban*. As Shanghai becomes wealthier and the state is more financially scrapped, municipal institutions are better off. So are primary and secondary schools, which enjoy annual increases in educational expenditures of 30% to 40%.

Here the district government again plays a crucial role. To excel, they are willing to invest in education.[47]

However, prosperity in Shanghai is relative. After long years of lean budgets, school needs are not all met. The increase mentioned above is not spectacular in real terms when inflation rates are taken into account. Yet another means to improve quality is to broaden the sources of income. An education tax is now levied. Also, primary and secondary schools are allowed to charge some fees. To prevent abuse, schools must not charge more than the categories and amount of fees set by the Shanghai Education Bureau.[48] In addition, schools can seek additional income from small enterprises, from the community, as well as from profit-generating activities such as the lease of school property for commercial purposes. The necessity to raise funds, which used to be government responsibility, has in effect extended school responsibilities to the non-educational sphere. This competes for the time of educationalists who should spend their time on professional work. Tertiary institutions tackle this problem by cost-sharing devices. Free higher education is on the wane. Since 1980, Shanghai has experimented with fee-charging universities which do not provide dormitory facilities.[49] In the last few years, a considerable number of students have been admitted on a fee-paying basis, in contrast to those recruited under the state quota and who do not pay fees. From 1995, this difference has been eliminated. All students have to pay tuition fees, the amount of which varies according to the field of study. The fees thus collected should constitute 30% to 40% of budgetary expenditures. Students in less sought after fields needed for national construction, namely, teacher education, agriculture and forestry, continue to enjoy free tuition.

However, the tuition fee will impose a heavy burden on parents. A student loan system is being devised to absorb the shock from this abrupt change. Its feasibility is uncertain, however, for there are a great deal of complications, such as meagre funds for loans, resistance from students and parents, and lack of support from banks. It is too early to review the tuition fee policy. However, Shanghai appears to be in a haste to implement the policy without adequate preparation for its obvious drawbacks. Nor has it addressed the issue of equality. The rationale behind the policy is that higher education yields high economic returns to individuals who should, therefore, contribute to its costs. The validity of this argument notwithstanding, opportunities will likely be skewed in favour of students from better-off families.

Increased autonomy at the local government level also takes hold in individual schools. The dominance of the party secretary has been eclipsed, resulting in a separation of professional leadership from party leadership. With variations in the division of labour between party secretary and school principal, in general the latter has regained authority over educational matters. To increase the efficiency and accountability of the staff, the "iron bowl" system is giving way to recruitment based on performance. A complex salary structure has appeared, comprised of one's basic salary, which is uniform across the board, and of pay for additional hours of teaching, performance, seniority, and the like.[50]

The intensity in the above drive has been prompted by Shanghai's high self-esteem. Indeed, greater autonomy and wealth in the post-Mao period have accelerated the resurgence of Shanghai as a leader in China. Many in Shanghai share the goal of "first-rate education for a first-rate city" and are proud of Shanghai's worth as a role model for China.[51] Shanghai's planning has been informed by its own experience as well as by lessons from advanced societies. In spite of contradictions within, the high quality of its planners is reflected in its policies and the ways they are implemented.

Competition from Moral Shanghai

The teaching of values deemed appropriate to society has been a major function of education in China. In traditional China, ethics was taught through the Confucian classics; teachers were bearers of both knowledge and morality. In the PRC, this function took up a new content — the nurturing of communist citizenship. The erosion of moral China began in the chaos of the Cultural Revolution. However, the current economic preoccupation has drawn attention further away from moral education. In the market economy, rewards are based more on ability than on moral virtue, efficiency leads to competition among individuals, and self-interest provides the motivating force for hard work. By implication, the more successful the market economy, the heavier the blow on moral education. As values and attitudes which are undesirable in the eyes of the political leaders spread, it will be all the more urgent to fend them off with moral education. So the vicious cycle continues. The problem boils down to the dilemma of an open economy and a closed political system. The ideal of the political leaders is for moral education to mend the holes caused by the economic reform. In other words, it is a re-emergence of the dilemma between "Western learning for practical use and Chinese culture for essence," which has puzzled China since the decline of the Qing dynasty.

To tackle the problem, three strategies are discernible. The first is repeated political rhetoric. The press and periodicals often carry speeches from political and educational leaders on the importance of moral education. These leaders fail to admit that the context of moral education has changed. In the beginning of the PRC's rule, the people's faith in the brave new world was fresh, and there were role models to support their faith. During the later periods, correct political performance, or virtuocracy,[52] was a major criterion for the distribution of rewards. However, the context today encourages people to pursue material gains, and the moral call no longer carries the same meaning. The rhetoric is, therefore, only rhetoric.

The second strategy to boost moral education is to "modernize" its content. The shifting emphasis in content in the reform years reflects the various phases or crises in which China found herself.[53] The overall pattern can be summed up in three themes: patriotism, collectivism and good character formation. Students are told time and again of the importance of putting the interests of the nation and the collective above those of the individual. For example, prospective university students are advised to choose fields of study which are unpopular but which are crucial to the long-term well-being of the nation, and that rather than clinging to prosperous Shanghai, they should try universities elsewhere in China, and by implication, stay there after graduation. The question is: Who will listen? The theme of good character formation has met with similar frustrations. There is an additional obstacle due to the one-child policy. Children today are so used to being spoiled that they have little consideration for others, and even less for the collective. Indeed, the family's ineffectiveness in character formation has shifted the weight of this responsibility to the schools. How can these themes be fulfilled when they are so divorced from today's reality? Can schools counter the influence of society at large? Is moral education, therefore, an exercise in futility?

In line with innovations in teaching, schools are trying to make the teaching of morals more interesting.[54] The success of this strategy will be limited, for it identifies the solution in techniques, when the fundamental problem lies elsewhere. As the society industrializes, the schools have replaced the family and the church as agents of socialization. Scholars in mainstream sociology of education tend to be optimistic about the schools' ability to transmit moral messages to the young. An alternative view has been gaining ground in the last two decades or so. Scholars working from a critical perspective have examined student resistance to establishment ideology. We concur with the argument that rather than a one-way street, socialization is negotiated. Some messages get across, others are refuted. Even where socialization succeeds, it is possible as a process in its entirety, which lasts at least nine years, but more often not until the end of secondary education. The teaching of morals is a different thing. In Shanghai, it is contrived — in the form of a subject, a specific activity, or a campaign. There have been few, if any, examples of success in specific moral education programmes.

Conclusion

In this chapter, we examine the ways the education system has adapted to new social demands in Shanghai. We focus on pursuits on the economic front, which can be summed up in the word "efficiency." This refers to preparing many quality workers with relevant skills in a short time. However, this ideal has encountered disruption from the very measures employed to attain it. The motives behind the measures may contravene one another; or different components may proceed on their own without sufficient inter co-ordination; or actors in the system (teachers, administrators and policy makers) may not be adequately prepared in their mindset and ability for innovations. These obstacles exist in many societies, but especially in Shanghai, which is undergoing a tough transition, both in terms of the economy and in terms of the orientation of its work force. Even so, we believe that because of its historical assets, Shanghai is better equipped than most cities in China in the search for an education system that works well.

We are more doubtful about Shanghai's goal of moral perfection. The tension between economic and moral demands is pervasive and few societies have come up with a satisfactory balance between the two. At the beginning of this chapter, we looked at the situation in Western democracies. Some eastern societies approach this problem differently. In Japan, economic and moral needs are met by a deliberately stratified system. Compulsory schooling is charged with a heavy moral responsibility and aims at producing a mass of workers who comply with behavioural norms within the bounds of the establishment. Post-compulsory education takes on a different nature. Economic advancement needs creative and able individuals. Higher education, as a source of supply of such individuals, embraces élitism, at the risk of ideological dissent. Societies like Hong Kong and Singapore primarily stress the skills component, resulting in a competitive, cognitive system. If it is difficult for these societies to resolve the tension, it may be twice as difficult for Shanghai to solve it. As long as the political and market spirits in Shanghai are antithetical, it will be unlikely for economic Shanghai and moral Shanghai to integrate readily.

Notes

1. Martin Carnoy and Henry Levin, *Schooling and Work in the Democratic State* (Stanford: Stanford University Press, 1985).
2. Grace C. L. Mak, "Education," in *Guangdong: Survey of a Province Undergoing Rapid Change*, edited by Y. M. Yeung and David K. Y. Chu (Hong Kong: The Chinese University Press, 1994), pp. 207–32.
3. Shanghaishi tongzhiguan 上海市通志館 (ed.), *Shanghaishi nianjian minguo nianliu nian* 上海市年鑑民國廿六年 (Shanghai Yearbook 1937) (Shanghai: Shanghaishi tongzhiguan, 1937), p. L3. The range of "school-age" was not specified, the figures nevertheless gave an idea of the spread of education in Shanghai then.
4. Shi Kouzhu 施扣柱, "Qing mo Shanghai jiaoyu gaige zhi yanjiu" 清末上海教育改革之研究 (A Study of Educational Reform in Late Qing China), in *Shanghai yanjiu luncong*, vol. 7 上海研究論叢，第七輯 (Shanghai Study Series, vol. 7), edited by Shanghai shehuikexueyuan 上海社會科學院 (Shanghai: Shanghai shehuikexueyuan, n.d.), pp. 173–76.
5. *Zhongguo jiaoyu nianjian* bianjibu《中國教育年鑑》編輯部 (ed.), *Zhongguo jiaoyu nianjian 1949–1984 (difang jiaoyu)* 中國教育年鑑 1949–1984 (地方教育) (China Education Yearbook 1949–1984 [Regional Education]) (Changsha 長沙: Hunan jiaoyu chubanshe 湖南教育出版社, 1986), p. 433; Shanghaishi tongjiju 上海市統計局 (ed.), *Shanghai tongji nianjian 1983* 上海統計年鑑 1983 (Statistical Yearbook of Shanghai 1983) (Shanghai: Shanghai renmin chubanshe 上海人民出版社, 1984), p. 49; Guojia tongjiju renkou tongjisi 國家統計局人口統計司 (ed.), *Zhongguo renkou tongji nianjian 1992* 中國人口統計年鑑 1992 (China Population Statistics Yearbook 1992) (Beijing: Zhongguo tongji chubanshe 中國統計出版社, 1993), p. 450.
6. Zhongguo renmin zhengzhi xieshang huiyi Shanghaishi weiyuanhui wenshi ziliao gongzuo weiyuanhui 中國人民政治協商會議上海市委員會文史資料工作委員會 (ed.), *Jiefang qian de Shanghai xuexiao* 解放前的上海學校 (Schools in Pre-Liberation Shanghai) (Shanghai: Shanghai renmin chubanshe, 1988).
7. Shi, "Qing mo Shanghai jiaoyu gaige zhi yanjiu" (see note 4), pp. 182–200.
8. Wang Juexuan 王厥軒, "Haipai jiaoyu yanjiu zatan" 海派教育研究雜談 (Random Thoughts on Shanghai Identity in Education), *Shanghai jiaoyu* 上海教育 (Shanghai Education), No. 11 (1990), pp. 5–7.
9. *Zhongguo jiaoyu nianjian 1949–1984 (difang jiaoyu)* (see note 5), pp. 399, 401.
10. Shanghai shehuikexueyuan 上海社會科學院 (ed.), *Shanghai jingji 1949–1982*

上海經濟 1949–1982 (Shanghai's Economy 1949–1982) (Shanghai: Shanghai renmin chubanshe, 1983), p. 1238.

11. *Zhongguo jiaoyu nianjian 1949–1984 (difang jiaoyu)* (see note 5), pp. 399, 410.

12. Ibid., p. 410.

13. Ibid., p. 420.

14. Shanghai zhili kaifa yanjiusuo 上海智力開發研究所, *Shanghai gaodeng jiaoyu: Xianzhuang, xuqiu yu fazhan qianjing* 上海高等教育：現狀、需求與發展前景 (Higher Education in Shanghai: Current State, Needs and Future Outlook) (Shanghai: Shanghai zhili kaifa yanjiusuo, 1994), pp. 1, 3.

15. *Zhongguo jiaoyu bao* 中國教育報, 7 September 1994, p. 1.

16. This refers to the mainstream of secondary education whose schools in China are known as "general secondary schools." They are comparable to grammar schools in the British Commonwealth, hence the term "grammar schools" will be used below.

17. Lü Xingwei 呂型偉, "Zhongdeng jiaoyu de jiegou fei gai bu ke" 中等教育的結構非改不可 (Secondary Education must be Restructured), *Shanghai jiaoyu*, No. 4 (1979), pp. 16–17, 36.

18. The first agricultural vocational school appeared in 1958, but the number of vocational schools since then was negligible.

19. Guojia tongjiju 國家統計局 (ed.), *Zhongguo tongji nianjian 1995* 中國統計年鑑 1995 (Statistical Yearbook of China 1995) (Beijing: Zhongguo tongji chubanshe, 1995), p. 587.

20. Shanghaishi tongjiju (ed.), *Shanghai tongji nianjian 1995* 上海統計年鑑 1995 (Statistical Yearbook of Shanghai 1995) (Beijing: Zhongguo tongj chubanshe, 1995), p. 228.

21. Shanghaishi jiaoyu kexue yanjiusuo jiaoyu shi zhi yanjiushi 上海市教育科學研究所教育史誌研究室, *Shanghai xuexiao gailan* 上海學校概覽 (Directory of Schools in Shanghai) (Shanghai: Shanghai shehuikexueyuan chubanshe 上海社會科學院出版社, 1990), p. 9.

22. Fei Ailun 費愛倫 and Wang Xiangqun 王向群, "Shentou, yanshen, tuozhan, lianshou — Jinri Shanghai de zhongdeng zhiye xuexiao" 滲透、延伸、拓展、聯手 —— 今日上海的中等職業學校 (Penetration, Extension and Collaboration: Vocational Secondary Schools in Shanghai Today), *Shanghai jiaoyu*, Nos. 7–8 (1994), pp. 38–40.

23. Ma Genrong 馬根榮, "Dui zhiye jishu jiaoyu tiaozheng zhengdun de yixie sikao" 對職業技術教育調整整頓的一些思考 (Some Thoughts on the Reorganization of Vocational Education), *Shanghai jiaoyu*, No. 5 (1990), pp. 31–32; Huang Xiangkui 黃向葵 and Zhuang Ruqian 莊如倩, "Shanghai zhongzhuan jiaoyu de xianzhuang, kunhuo yu duice chutan" 上海中專教育的現狀、困惑與對策初探 (A Preliminary Study of the Current Situation, Difficulties and Solutions in Specialized Secondary Education in Shanghai),

Shanghai jiaoyu, No. 4 (1991), pp. 35–37; Fei and Wang, "Jinri Shanghai de zhongdeng zhiye xuexiao," (see note 22).

24. *Zhongguo jiaoyu nianjian 1949–1984 (difang jiaoyu)* (see note 5), p. 422.

25. Department of Planning, Ministry of Education, PRC, *Achievement of Education in China 1949–1983* (Beijing: People's Education Press, 1984), p. 78.

26. Shanghai zhili kaifa yanjiusuo, *Shanghai gaodeng jiaoyu* (see note 14), p. 7.

27. *Zhongguo jiaoyu nianjian 1949–1984 (difang jiaoyu)* (see note 5), p. 438.

28. Zheng Lingde 鄭令德, "Shanghai gaoxiao zonghe gaige de huigu yu zhanwang" 上海高校綜合改革的回顧與展望 (Review and Future Prospect of Comprehensive Higher Education Reform in Shanghai), *Shanghai gaoxiao yanjiu* 上海高校研究 (Shanghai Research in Higher Education), No. 2 (1994), pp. 1–6.

29. Yuan Hu 袁乎, "Yi tigao xuesheng suzhi wei hexin gaige zhongxiaoxue kecheng jiaocai —— Shanghaishi zhongxiaoxue kecheng jiaocai gaige de jiben silu" 以提高學生素質爲核心改革中小學課程教材 —— 上海市中小學課程教材改革的基本思路 (With Raising Student Quality as Focus of Curricular and Textbook Reform for Primary and Secondary Education —— Basic Thinking in Curricular and Textbook Reform for Primary and Secondary Education in Shanghai), *Shanghai jiaoyu*, No. 5 (1990), pp. 2–4.

30. Interview with an academic on 18 November 1994 in Shanghai.

31. Shanghai jiaoyu bianxiezu 上海教育編寫組 (ed.), *Shanghai jiaoyu 1988* 上海教育 1988 (Shanghai Education 1988) (Shanghai: Tongji daxue chubanshe 同濟大學出版社, 1989), p. 4; Shanghaishi renmin zhengfu jiaoyu weisheng bangongshi 上海市人民政府教育衛生辦公室 (ed.), *Shanghai jiaoyu 1993* 上海教育 1993 (Shanghai Education 1993) (Shanghai: Shanghai jiaoyu chubanshe 上海教育出版社, 1994), p. 4.

32. Shanghai zhili kaifa yanjiusuo, "Shanghai gaodeng jiaoyu" (see note 14), p. 4, and *Shanghai jiaoyu 1993* (see note 31), p. 4.

33. *Zhongguo jiaoyu nianjian 1949–1984 (difang jiaoyu)* (see note 5), p. 439.

34. Shanghai zhili kaifa yanjiusuo, *Shanghai gaodeng jiaoyu* (see note 14), pp. 6–7.

35. Calculated from Shanghaishi gaodeng jiaoyu yanjiusuo 上海市高等教育研究所 (ed.), *Shanghai gaodeng jiaoyu nianjian 1949–1983* 上海高等教育年鑑 1949–1983 (Yearbook on Higher Education in Shanghai 1949–1983) (Shanghai: Shanghai waiyu jiaoyu chubanshe 上海外語教育出版社, 1989), pp. 253–54.

36. Ibid., p. 30.

37. Interview with an academic on 18 November 1994 in Shanghai.

38. *Zhongguo jiaoyu nianjian 1949–1984 (difang jiaoyu)* (see note 5), p. 407.

39. Interview with an academic (see note 30).

40. Interview with a researcher on 19 November 1994 in Shanghai.

41. Hu Xuezeng 胡學增, "Guanjian zaiyu jianli xinying de kecheng he rencai pingjia de kexue tizhi" 關鍵在於建立新穎的課程和人才評價的科學體制 (The Key Lies in Establishing an Innovative Curriculum and a Scientific Appraisal System), *Shanghai jiaoyu*, No. 1 (1989), pp. 2–4.

42. *Zhongguo jiaoyu nianjian 1949–1984 (difang jiaoyu)* (see note 5), p. 400.

43. Shanghai zhili kaifa yanjiusuo, *Shanghai gaodeng jiaoyu* (see note 14), p. 8.

44. The limited success in increasing efficiency can be attributed in part to the motivation behind the merger. The State Education Commission (國家教育委員會) is in the process of selecting 100 key universities for development in the twenty-first century (the "21.1 project"). One of the criteria of selection is size. This has sent tertiary institutions in a rush to merge. For example, in 1994, Shanghai University, Shanghai University of Science and Technology, Shanghai Industrial University, Shanghai Technological College were merged into a new comprehensive university called the new Shanghai University. It boasts an enrolment of 25,000, and because of its size is dubbed "Shanghai No. 2 Higher Education Bureau". Size, more than efficiency, being the goal, the limited success in efficiency is understandable. See Shanghai zhili kaifa yanjiusuo, *Shanghai gaodeng jiaoyu*, p. 8, and interview with a researcher (see note 40).

45. Zhu Yiming 朱益明, "Zhongguo minban xuexiao toushi" 中國民辦學校透視 (Perspectives on *Minban* Schools in China), *Jiaoyu cankao* 教育參考 (Shanghai), Nos. 4–5 (1994), p. 38; interview with a researcher (see note 40).

46. Suizheng Zhao, "From Coercion to Negotiation: The Changing Central–local Economic Relations in Mainland China," *Issues and Studies*, Vol. 28, No. 10 (1992), p. 19.

47. Shanghai zhili kaifa yanjiusuo, *Shanghai gaodeng jiaoyu* (see note 14), p. 10; interview with a researcher (see note 40).

48. *Zhongguo jiaoyu bao*, 25 August 1994, p. 1.

49. *Shanghai gaodeng jiaoyu nianjian 1949–1983* (see note 35), pp. 28–29.

50. Jia Zhenxin 賈振欣 and Yang Guoshun 楊國順, "Benshi zhongxiaoxue neibu guanli gaige de jiben silu" 本市中小學內部管理改革的基本思路 (Basic Thoughts on Management Reform in Primary and Secondary Schools), *Shanghai jiaoyu*, No. 11 (1991), pp. 5–7; Quandi 泉笛, "Shanghai zhixiao shixing 'xiaozhang fuze zhi,' 'quanyuan pinren zhi,' 'jiegou gongzi zhi' de chubu diaocha" "上海職校實行'校長負責制'、'全員聘任制'、'結構工資制'的初步調查" (A Preliminary Survey on the Implementation of the Systems of School Principal Responsibility, Recruitment of All Staff and Salary Structure in Vocational Schools in Shanghai), *Shanghai jiaoyu*, No. 9 (1992), pp. 4–5.

51. See, e.g., *Zhongguo jiaoyu bao*, 9 September 1994, p. 1; Shanghai zhili kaifa yanjiusuo, *Shanghai gaodeng jiaoyu* (see note 14).

52. Susan Shirk, *Competitive Comrades* (Berkeley: University of California Press, 1982).

53. W. O. Lee, "Changing Ideopolitical Emphases in Moral Education in China: A Documentary Analysis." Paper presented at the International Symposium on Education and Socio-political Transitions in Asia, 29–31 May 1995, University of Hong Kong.

54. See, e.g., the special issue on how to conduct moral education. *Shanghai jiaoyu*, Nos. 7–8 (1993).

16

Changing Health Needs and Emerging Health Problems

Wong Tze-wai, Gu Xingyuan and Suzanne C. Ho

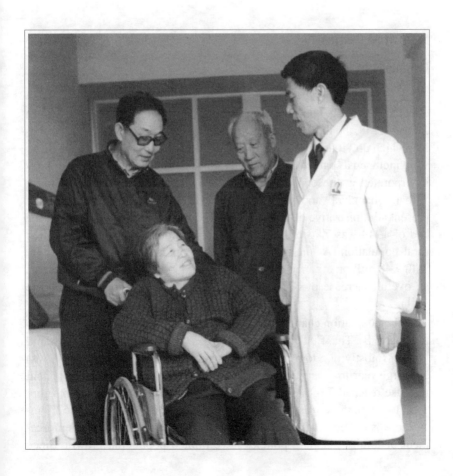

This chapter is divided into three sections. Section One describes the health status of the population in Shanghai in the past fifty years. The improvement in health indices is a reflection of socioeconomic development in general and also of the efforts by the authorities to develop health services and manpower. It deals with population changes, health indices and disease patterns. Section Two focuses on a description of the health care system, with special reference to the development of health services and human resources. Important issues facing the health care system, such as the escalation of health care cost and the inadequacies of the market system in health care, are also discussed. Section Three deals specifically with the problem of the rapidly expanding elderly population, their health needs, measures taken by the authorities to meet these needs and new challenges for the twenty-first century.

Health Statistics

Demography

Since 1950, the population of Shanghai and its urban–rural ratio have been affected by changes in the demarcation of its administrative districts. In January 1958, the three counties of Jiading 嘉定 , Baoshan 寶山 and Shanghai, which previously were under the jurisdiction of Jiangsu 江蘇 province, were included as part of Shanghai city. Seven more counties were similarly incorporated at the end of the same year, transforming the city into an "urban Shanghai" and ten neighbouring rural counties. Based on the present administrative districts, the total population of Shanghai city at the end of 1949 was 7.73 million, with 4.52 million urban and 3.21 million rural population. At the end of 1993, the population was 12.95 million, with 9.48 million urban and 3.47 million rural inhabitants.[1] This represents an overall increase of 67% and an annual growth rate of 1.18% (Table 16.1).

The population changes during the past forty years can be divided into two periods. The first period (1950–1977) was characterized by rapid growth (mostly due to a high rate of natural increase in the early 1950s) and large year-to-year fluctuations. From 1951 to 1954, the average annual increase reached 7.69%, half of which was attributed to migration. From 1955 to 1956, there was a net emigration of 650,000. In 1957, a 8.62% increase was recorded. Thereafter, immigration restrictions and the enforcement of family planning policies have limited population growth. Since

Table 16.1　Population of Shanghai, 1949–1993

(Unit: million)

Year	Population		
	Urban	Rural	TOTAL
1949	4.52	3.21	7.73
1950	4.53	3.15	7.68
1955	5.72	3.53	9.25
1960	6.45	4.09	10.54
1965	6.43	4.51	10.94
1970	5.80	4.92	10.72
1975	5.57	5.20	10.77
1980	6.01	5.45	11.46
1985	6.98	5.18	12.16
1990	7.83	5.00	12.83
1993	9.48	3.47	12.95

Sources:　Hu Huanyong 胡煥庸 (ed.), *Zhongguo renkou (Shanghai fence)* 中國人口（上海分冊）(China Population [Shanghai]) (Beijing: Zhongguo caizheng Jingji chubanshe 中國財政經濟出版社, 1987), p. 66; Shanghai renkou qingbao zhongxin 上海人口情報中心 (ed.), *Renkou xinxi* 人口信息 (Population Information), February 1993, p. 28.

1970, the pattern has changed to one of a low birth rate, a low death rate and a low growth rate. In the second period (from 1978 to the present), the population has steadily increased from 10.86 million to 12.95 million in 1993. This represents an increase of 2.09 million in 16 years, or an annual increase of 1.11%. This increase is mostly due to an excess of immigration over emigration, with a minimal natural increase. In the 1990s, the rate of natural increase fell to a low level (0.351% in 1990, 0.118% in 1991 and 0.021% in 1992). In 1993, a decline (–0.077%) was recorded for the first time.[2]

The mean household size has been declining steadily, from 4.6 persons per household in 1950 to 4.5 in 1960, 4.2 in 1970, 3.8 in 1980 and 3.1 in 1990. The above population statistics refer to the population of residents. The *de facto* population (including the transient, mobile population, estimated to be around 3 million in 1992) was much higher. The population sex ratio has been affected mostly by migration, with a higher proportion of males emigrating in the 1950s and 1960s and immigrating since 1980. The proportion of the population aged 0–14 years was 33.03% in 1954, rising to 42.31% in 1964, a result of high birth rates, thereafter falling with declining birth rate to 18.15% in 1982 and 18.23% in 1990 — years of the Population Census. With the decline in the birth rate, the death rate and an increase in life expectancy, the proportion of population aged 65 and above rose steadily, from 1.97% in 1953 (first census) to 3.60% in 1964 (second census), 7.60% in 1982 (third census) and 9.38% in 1990 (fourth census). Shanghai has become the first "ageing city" in China as defined by one whose elderly population exceeding 7%. The median age of its residents has also been rising steadily (Table 16.2). The population above 80 years increased dramatically over the years, from 6,994 in 1954 to 29,200 in 1964, 111,300 in 1982 and 170,400 in 1990. The problem of ageing population in Shanghai is expected to worsen, with significant socioeconomic ramifications in the twenty-first century.

Table 16.2   Sex Ratio, Age Distribution and Median Age in Shanghai, 1953–1990

(Unit: years)

Year	Sex ratio	Age groups			Median age
	%	0–14	15–64	>65	
1953	115.1	33.03	65.00	1.97	22.10
1964	98.6	42.31	54.09	3.60	18.10
1982	99.3	18.15	74.25	7.60	29.37
1990	104.1	18.23	72.39	9.38	33.91

Source: Unpublished data, Shanghaishi tongjiju 上海市統計局, Shanghaishi di si ci renkou pucha 上海市第四次人口普查, (The Fourth Population Census).

The proportion of the economically active population (aged 15–64) was 74.25% in 1982 and 72.39% in 1990. Shanghai experienced high birth rates (above 4%) from 1951–1957, reaching a peak of 5.27% in 1954. Since 1958, birth rates have fallen, except in the mid-1960s and the early 1980s. The implementation of the family planning programme and the "one-child policy" resulted in a remarkable decline in birth rates, to 1.03% in 1990, 0.77% in 1991, 0.73% in 1992 and 0.65% in 1993. An urban–rural difference in birth rates exists. The total fertility rate (TFR) of women of reproductive age in Shanghai is the lowest of all major cities in China. From a high level of 5.60 in 1950, the decline in TFR paralleled that of birth rates, to 2.6–2.9 in the 1960s and reached replacement level by the early 1970s. Since 1975, TFR has stayed below replacement level (Table 16.3).

Table 16.3   **Urban and Rural Crude Birth Rates and Total Fertility Rates in Shanghai, 1950–1993**

(Unit: per 1,000)

Year	Crude birth rate		Total fertility rate
	Urban	Rural	
1950	22.1	26.4	5.60
1955	41.1	48.9	5.59
1960	27.4	28.2	2.90
1965	10.4	26.5	2.55
1970	8.1	21.0	2.28
1975	6.6	12.5	1.12
1980	8.9	14.9	0.87
1985	14.2	10.8	1.00
1990	9.9	10.8	1.23
1991	6.8	9.5	—
1992	6.2	9.0	—
1993	5.7	8.7	—

Sources: Gu Xingyuan 顧杏元 et al., "Shanghai renkou fu zengchang de chengyin 上海人口負增長的成因 (Reasons for Shanghai's Negative Population Growth), *Renkou* 人口 (Population), No. 3 (1994), pp. 34; Zuo Xuejin 左學金, "Shanghai renkou fu zengchang de beijing" 上海人口負增長的背景 (Background to Shanghai's Negative Population Growth), *Renkou*, No. 3 (1994), p. 21.

Mortality Rates[3]

The crude death rate declined by 70% from 1951 to 1958, largely a result of improvement in living conditions and health care facilities. A brisk increase was recorded during the period of economic hardship from 1959 to 1961, falling thereafter and reaching the lowest level in the 1960s. From 1966 onwards for urban districts and from 1970 onwards for rural districts, the crude death rate gradually rose, commensurate with changes in the population structure (Table 16.4). The age-standardized death rate, however, continued to fall. The standardized death rate (urban) per 1,000 was 18.9 in 1951, 7.13 in 1960, 4.31 in 1970 and 3.73 in 1980. Higher crude death rates were observed in rural compared to urban districts of Shanghai in the years before 1965. In the 1990s, the trend was reversed. The age-standardized death rates per 1,000 (in 1980) were 3.73 in urban and 4.35 in rural districts, indicating that the urban–rural difference was due to differences in the age structure.

Using the age structure of the whole nation as the reference, Shanghai

Table 16.4   Urban and Rural Crude Death Rates in Shanghai, 1950–1993

(Unit: per 1,000)

Year	Crude death rate	
	Urban	Rural
1950	13.3	19.7
1955	8.0	9.2
1960	6.1	7.9
1965	4.3	7.7
1970	5.3	4.6
1975	6.2	5.8
1980	6.8	6.1
1985	6.8	6.5
1990	7.0	6.4
1991	6.9	6.3
1992	7.3	6.6
1993	7.5	6.6

Sources: Gu Xingyuan et al., "Shanghai renkou fu zengchang de chengyin" (see Table 16.3, Sources); Shanghaishi weisheng fangyi zhan 上海市衛生防疫站, *Shanghaishi weisheng fangyi zhan shengming tongji ziliao* 上海市衛生防疫站生命統計資料 (unpublished data).

has the lowest standardized death rates among all major cities and the longest life expectancy. The death rates in females were higher than in males in the 1950s but this has been reversed since the 1960s. The male:female ratio ranged from 94 to 95 in the 1950s and from 100 to 105 since the 1960s, with a higher sex ratio in death rates in rural districts compared to urban districts. Like other cities in China, the age-specific death rates in Shanghai are V-shaped, with the highest death rate in infants, falling to a trough in the 10–14 years age group, thereafter rising with age. The age group with the lowest age-specific death rate in 1990 was much younger than that in the 1950s. A significant decrease was observed for all age-specific death rates, notably among infants, children and young adults. The decline was less remarkable among the middle aged and the elderly (Table 16.5). Age-specific death rates for all age groups among rural residents were higher than among urban residents, indicating poorer health status and health services in the former.

The age distribution of mortality in 1951 is as follows: 52% were infants/children aged 0–14 years (46% were among those aged 0–4 years); 23% were aged 15–49, and 24% were aged 50 and above. In 1990, the majority of deaths occurred among the elderly, the corresponding percentages within the urban community in Shanghai being: 3.6% (0–14 years),

Table 16.5   Age-specific Death Rates in Shanghai, 1951 and 1990

(Unit: per 1,000)

Age group	1951 (Urban)		1990 (Urban)		1990 (Rural)	
	Male	Female	Male	Female	Male	Female
0–	82.4	77.2	12.65	10.82	18.71	12.94
1–4	53.8	57.0	0.59	0.52	1.90	1.29
5–9	9.9	9.8	0.31	0.24	0.53	0.33
10–19	2.7	3.5	0.34	0.24	0.58	0.40
20–29	3.7	4.1	0.64	0.41	0.77	0.65
30–39	4.4	5.2	0.93	0.69	1.44	1.04
40–49	7.3	5.9	1.83	1.32	2.76	1.85
50–59	14.2	8.7	6.54	4.45	8.90	4.58
60–69	27.5	15.6	18.20	11.79	23.28	11.09
70–79	133.4	92.1	53.74	37.38	62.23	36.56
80–	133.4	92.1	144.59	121.81	163.82	120.87

Sources: Shanghai renkou qingbao zhongxin (ed.), *Renkou xinxi*, February 1993, p. 31.

3.1% (0–4 years), 8.8% (15–49 years), 87.6% (50 and above) and 57.4% (70 and above).

The infant mortality rate (IMR) is a useful indicator of the health status of a country, being affected by environmental hygiene, water supply, food supply and the level of health care provision. The fall in the IMR has been dramatic, from a high of 82 per 1,000 in 1951 to 10 per 1,000 in 1993. Three periods can be discerned: a rapid fall in the 1950s, a transient rise followed by a continuous but slower decrease in the 1960s, and insignificant changes in the 1980s and 1990s. The exceptionally low IMR in 1970 is a result of under-reporting deaths during the Cultural Revolution. Throughout the four decades, IMRs among male babies were generally higher than among female babies. The decline in IMRs was similar in both sexes (Table 16.6). The neonatal mortality rate (NMR), an index of maternal and child health care provision, also declined steadily from a high level of 15.48 per 1,000 in 1955 to 7–9 per 1,000 in recent years. The NMR in rural communities was higher than that in urban areas. Neonatal deaths contributed to 40% of the infant mortality in the urban population in the 1950s. This rose to 70% in recent years, indicating a significant improvement in maternal and neonatal health care. A survey of urban neonatal deaths in 1981 to 1984 showed that early neonatal deaths (deaths during the first week of life) accounted for 77% of all neonatal deaths. About 64% of the deaths occurred during the first two days. Similar observations were

Table 16.6   Infant Mortality Rates in Shanghai, 1951–1993

(Unit: per 1,000 live births)

Year	Infant mortality rate		
	Male	Female	TOTAL
1951	82.41	77.21	79.92
1955	42.13	44.85	43.46
1960	29.94	33.14	31.48
1965	13.36	12.62	13.00
1970[a]	9.81	7.64	8.77
1975	11.88	11.33	11.62
1980	11.50	10.13	10.84
1985	14.84	12.66	13.78
1990	12.18	9.67	10.95
1991	11.55	11.18	11.37
1992	11.52	11.31	11.42
1993	9.90	10.06	9.98

Note: [a] The low figures were due to incomplete reporting of mortality.
Source: *Shanghaishi weisheng fangyi zhan shengming tongji ziliao* (see Table 16.4, Sources).

made among the rural population. Improvement in maternal health care and neonatal medical service are, therefore, key areas for a further reduction in infant mortality in Shanghai. A distinct seasonal pattern was observed in the IMR in the 1950s and 1960s, with peaks in winter and spring, and troughs in summer and autumn. With the implementation of childhood immunization programmes, and the consequent successful control of measles, and with improvement in perinatal health care, the seasonal fluctuations in IMRs became inconspicuous.

The life expectancy at birth is another important indicator of health. In 1951, the life expectancy at birth was 42 years for males and 45.6 years for females in urban Shanghai. A significant improvement was noted in the 1950s, being 61.22 years for males and 63.36 years in 1954. In the 10-year period from 1951 to 1960, the average life expectancy for males increased by 23.9 years, while that for females increased by 22.6 years, representing an average annual increase of 2.3 to 2.4 years (Table 16.7). Since 1960, the increase in life expectancy has slowed down. In 1970, the figures for males and females were 70.2 years and 73.9 years respectively, a modest increase of 5.1 and 6.3 years respectively, for the decade. The life expectancies in 1992 were 74.4 years for males and 77.9 years for females. Calculations of life expectancy among the rural population were not available until 1970. For the past 20 years, the average life expectancy for rural

Table 16.7 Life Expectancy at Birth among Urban and Rural Residents of Shanghai, 1951–1992

(Unit: years)

| Year | Life expectancy at birth | | | | | |
| | Urban | | Rural[a] | | TOTAL | |
	Male	Female	Male	Female	Male	Female
1951	42.0	45.6	—	—	—	—
1955	61.6	63.8	—	—	—	—
1960	65.1	67.5	—	—	—	—
1965	69.6	73.2	—	—	—	—
1970	70.2	73.9	—	—	—	—
1975	70.6	73.9	68.2	73.9	69.4	73.8
1980	72.6	75.3	69.7	75.8	71.3	75.4
1985	73.4	76.7	70.3	76.0	72.1	76.4
1990	73.8	77.8	72.1	77.7	73.2	77.7
1992	74.4	77.9	72.9	78.2	74.0	77.9

Note: [a] Information on life expectancy at birth in rural areas and all areas were not available from 1950–1970.

Source: *Shanghaishi weisheng fangyi zhan shengming tongji ziliao* (see Table 16.4, Sources).

males was slightly shorter than their urban counterparts, while the life expectancies for rural and urban females were similar (Table 16.7). A comparison across the provinces based on data from the Third Population Census shows that the average life expectancy for the Shanghai population was 73.01 years (70.71 for males and 75.23 for females) in 1982, the highest of all provinces and cities.

Major Causes of Death

In the 1950s, the major causes of death among the Shanghai population were, in descending order, infectious diseases (which, including tuberculosis, accounted for 30% of all deaths), cardiovascular diseases, diseases of the respiratory system, diseases of the digestive system and malignant neoplasm. This pattern has changed significantly since the 1960s, with a dramatic decline in mortality due to infectious diseases, and a progressive increase in death rates due to cardiovascular and neoplastic diseases. From 1980 onwards, cardiovascular diseases have constituted about one-third of all deaths. Malignant neoplasm, the second most common cause of death has contributed one quarter, while "diseases of the respiratory system" (mainly chronic obstructive pulmonary diseases) and "injuries and poisoning" have

Table 16.8 Major Causes of Death as Percentages of all Deaths, 1953–1993

(Unit: %)

1953		1963		1973		1983		1993	
Cause of death		Cause of death		Cause of death		Cause of death		Cause of death	
Infectious diseases	29.9	Cardiovascular diseases	18.8	Cardiovascular diseases	28.5	Cardiovascular diseases	32.7	Cardiovascular diseases	31.2
Cardiovascular diseases	10.9	Malignant neoplasm	18.0	Malignant neoplasm	23.8	Malignant neoplasm	25.3	Malignant neoplasm	24.8
Diseases of the respiratory tract	9.1	Infectious diseases	13.3	Diseases of the respiratory tract	12.3	Diseases of the respiratory tract	11.6	Diseases of the respiratory tract	19.7
Diseases of the digestive system	8.6	Diseases of the respiratory tract	9.8	Accidents	8.6	Accidents	6.1	Accidents	6.9
Malignant neoplasm	4.1	Diseases of the digestive system	6.8	Infectious diseases	6.4	Diseases of the digestive system	4.4	Diseases of the digestive system	3.4

Source: Shanghaishi weisheng fangyi zhan, *Shanghaishi weisheng fangyi zhan si yin tongji ziliao* 上海市衛生防疫站死因統計資料 (unpublished data).

occupied the third and fourth places respectively. Infectious diseases, by contrast, have lost its predominance as a major cause of death (Table 16.8).

In 1993, the top cause of death for the Shanghai population was cardiovascular diseases accounting for 31% of all deaths, with cerebrovascular diseases contributing 21% and heart diseases contributing 10%. This was followed by malignant neoplasm, constituting 25% of the total deaths. The major cancers in the males, in descending order of magnitude, were: lung cancer, stomach cancer, liver cancer, oesophageal cancer and colorectal cancer; whereas in the females, these were: stomach cancer, lung cancer, liver cancer, colorectal cancer and breast cancer. Among the rural population, the major causes of death were essentially similar. These were, in descending order, diseases of the respiratory system, cardiovascular diseases, malignant neoplasm, injuries and poisoning, and diseases of the digestive system. The mortality rate for respiratory diseases among the rural population (186 per 100,000) was significantly higher than that in the urban population (127 per 100,000), while the mortality rate for cardiovascular diseases among the rural population (161 per 100,000) was much lower than that for their urban counterparts (251 per 100,000) (Table 16.9).

Health Care System

Medical and Health Services in Shanghai

Since the 1950s, a three-tier network of medical and health services has been developed to cover the entire city. These include medical services,

Table 16.9 Death Rates by Major Causes among Urban and Rural Populations, 1993

(Unit: per 100,000)

Urban			Rural		
Cause of death	Death rate	%	Cause of death	Death rate	%
Cardiovascular diseases	251	33.32	Diseases of the respiratory tract	186	28.37
Malignant neoplasm	193	25.59	Cardiovascular diseases	161	24.49
Diseases of the respiratory tract	127	16.91	Malignant neoplasm	147	22.36
Injury and poisoning	49	6.48	Injury and poisoning	55	8.39
Diseases of the digestive system	24	3.20	Diseases of the digestive system	27	4.08

Source: Shanghai renkou qingbao zhongxin (ed.), *Renkou xinxi*, July 1994.

maternal and child health services, and public health services. The three tiers of medical services are: "city level" institutions, which include city general and specialist hospitals, and teaching hospitals of medical universities, "district (county) level" institutions, which include district (county) general and special hospitals, and "primary health care level institutions," which include "community hospitals" and "neighbourhood health centres" in urban areas and "township health centres" in towns and "village health stations" in rural areas. Many state-owned industrial enterprises have their own hospitals and worksite health centres. Hospitals at various levels offer out-patient clinics, in-patient services and preventive health services for residents and staff of industrial enterprises. Urban and rural health centres and health stations represent the basic units of primary health care, providing essential preventive, promotive and rehabilitative health services and treatment of minor illnesses for residents and staff of industrial enterprises. Maternal and child health services are provided at "city level" maternal and child health centres, obstetric and gynaecology hospitals, children's hospitals and the maternal and child health section of urban and rural health centres. The first three types of institutions, besides the provision of services, also act as consultative centres of maternal and child health services. Urban and rural health centres, on the other hand, are the major providers of maternal and child health services, with an emphasis on family planning, antenatal and perinatal care, infant and child health, health promotion in women in general, and working women in particular. Public health services serve to monitor and improve the health conditions in the community, and to provide for a healthy and safe environment for the general public and the working population. Anti-epidemic stations as specialist institutions for preventive medicine have been established at "city" and "county" levels since the 1950s. Their tasks include childhood immunization, the prevention and control of communicable (including parasitic) diseases, surveillance of environmental health, occupational health and food hygiene, and the promotion of health through health education. Health education centres have been established since the 1980s. A number of "disease-specific" health centres for infectious diseases, occupational diseases, mental illnesses, eye and skin diseases and dental health problems have also been established.

From 1950 to 1992, there was a seven-fold increase in the total number of health institutions (Table 16.10). The number of hospitals (at all levels) increased from 140 to 207. There are now more than 6,000 health centres for industrial enterprises. Anti-epidemic stations and maternal and child health centres are present in every district/county. The development in health manpower has increased seven-fold, from 19,200 in 1950 to 156,700 in 1992. The number of physicians (including traditional) rose from about 6,000 to over 40,000. The number of nurses increased from 2,480 to 33,680. In addition to graduates from medical colleges, a large number of health care workers in Shanghai have been trained among workers and peasants, constituting a strong force in the development of urban and rural health. From 1952 to 1992, the number of hospital beds per 1,000 of the population increased from 2 to 3.5, while the number of physicians rose from 1.27 per 1,000 to 3.51 per 1,000 (Tables 16.11).

Table 16.10   Distribution of Health Institutions in Shanghai, 1950–1992

	1950	1960	1970	1980	1990	1992
Teaching hospitals	5	12	14	14	14	16
General hospitals	88	79	84	109	110	108
Specialist hospitals	47	30	29	44	68	83
Community hospitals	—	112	102	109	109	109
Country/township health centres	—	147	195	201	209	209
Outpatient clinics	297	2,606[a]	1,362	5,397	6,947	6,644
Anti-epidemic stations	30	20	23	35	33	31
Centre/clinics for special diseases	5	45	20	49	41	34
Maternal and child health centres	12	40	1	21	37	34
TOTAL	484	3,091	1,830	5,979	7,568	7,268

Note: [a] Including "village production team" health clinics.
Source: Shanghai renkou qingbao zhongxin (ed.), *Renkou xinxi*, July 1994.

Table 16.11   Health Care Personnel and Hospital Beds in Shanghai, 1950–1992

	1950	1960	1970	1980	1990	1992
Health personnel (× 1,000):						
Traditional Chinese physicians	2.75	4.94	3.77	6.35	6.62	6.42
Physicians	3.57	6.59	10.15	17.64	36.82	39.10
Physician assistants	0.06	1.97	4.95	15.26	14.65	11.94
Nurses	2.48	9.59	15.55	22.35	32.70	33.68
Pharmacists	0.43	2.05	2.46	5.26	6.32	7.37
Laboratory technicians	0.30	1.87	1.94	4.63	5.20	5.33
TOTAL	19.20	53.47	68.13	131.94	158.54	156.70
Hospital beds (× 1,000):	10.89	41.30	43.87	57.99	69.64	71.21

Source: Unpublished data, Shanghai Bureau of Health.

Current Problems in Health Care

Comparing the health indices of the 1950s to those of the 1990s, one can conclude that in the past four decades, the health status of the people of Shanghai and its health services have undergone remarkable improvement. However, with rapid socioeconomic development and significant changes in health care financing policies, many new problems have emerged. To further improve the health and health care of the people, these problems, which will be discussed below, need urgent attention and solution. With the economic reforms, several changes in the pattern of health services utilization have been observed. There has been a shift in patient demand for health services from primary health care levels to hospital care. Village health stations, traditionally staffed by low-level health care providers, cannot meet the higher expectations of an increasingly affluent rural population. This, together with improved transportation, diverts the health care demand of the rural population to county and city hospitals. The escalation of health care cost, in particular, hospital cost, is a major problem. A six-fold increase in health spending from 1978 to 1988 was estimated.[4] It poses a heavy burden on the patients and their families, and exaggerates the difference between the rich and the poor.

Compared with past generations, Shanghai has a more educated population with higher expectations and ever increasing demands for better quality health care. The urban–rural differences in income and in the level of health care provision and utilization, exacerbate urban–rural inequalities in the health status which were previously mentioned. Major causes for the escalation in health care costs are inflation, demographic changes which result in a rapidly increasing proportion of elderly population, and changes in hospital financing and payment policies. The latter have resulted in abuse of high technology procedures and expensive drugs. It has been observed that the "demand strategy" involving co-payment by patients for medical costs has had very little impact on cost containment.[5] Another problem encountered in today's health care system is the waste of health resources which leads to inefficiencies. In China, the average length of hospital stay according to Diagnostic Related Grouping is about three times that in the United States. Also, pre-operative stays are often unduly prolonged, owing to poor scheduling and little sharing of major laboratory equipment.[6] Factors contributing to this phenomenon include the organizational structure and the pricing policies. In general, there is inadequate quality assurance for health services delivered. The problems encountered in the health care system are common to many Chinese cities and regions undergoing rapid economic reforms and where the price of commodities has been left to free market forces. But there are a number of intrinsic characteristics of health care (public health needs, provider-induced demands, external effects, etc.). Appropriate central and local health policies, co-ordinated health planning, regulations and a system of evaluation including economic appraisal are essential for the provision of an equitable, efficient and effective health care system to meet the challenges of modernization.

Health of the Elderly Population in Shanghai

Ageing Population

With the decline in the birth rate, the infant as well as the overall mortality rate, the population in China is ageing. The increase in the elderly population has been especially fast during the recent decades.[7] By the year 2050, it is projected that 21% of the population in China will be aged 60 and above.[8] It is projected that the proportion of the aged (65) will double from 7% to 14% within the first three decades of the twenty-first century.[9] There will also be a fast increase of the very old population aged 80 and above. In 1990, the population aged 80–89 was 9.3% of the total elderly population and it is expected to increase to 12.8% in the year 2000.[10]

The distribution of the elderly population in China is uneven, with a higher concentration in the big coastal cities as compared to the inland and western parts of China. In 1990, the proportion of those aged 65 years and above accounted for 5.6% of the whole of China. However, the proportion was 9.2% in Shanghai, 6.4% in Beijing, 6.0% in Guangdong and 4.9% in Yunnan.[11] Thus, Shanghai faces tremendous challenges to meet the health care and social needs of a growing elderly population.

Needs for Health Care Services

Cancer, strokes and chronic bronchitis have been the three major causes of death in the elderly population.[12] It was estimated that in 1986 one-third of the health expenditures in Shanghai were spent on elderly patients.[13] Three separate surveys on health care services, the handicapped and the health status of the elderly population in Shanghai were carried out respectively, in 1986, 1987 and 1988.[14] The surveys found that 74% of the elderly population were affected by chronic diseases and 1.5% had difficulties in activities of daily living. About 53.7% of the handicapped were elderly, and 85% of the family clinic beds were occupied by elderly patients. A breakdown on the reasons for bed occupancy shows that cerebrovascular diseases accounted for 33%, cardiovascular diseases 12.5%, terminal cancer 12%, chronic bronchitis 9.3% and fractures 5.9%. A more recent survey found that during May to August 1993, 29% of the patients seeking medical consultations were aged 60 or over.[15]

The 1989 data also reveal that of the 41,712 family clinic beds among the 201 community based clinics, 86% were occupied by elderly patients. Three-quarters of the health consultations took place in community based settings, such as clinics and district hospitals.

With the prolongation of life expectancy, an increasing proportion of the work force will be retired workers. A survey carried out during 1988–1989 among retired workers reveals that 56% felt that medical fees were too high. They also expressed the desire for improvement in the attitudes of health care personnel, and for an increase in the number of hospital and family clinic beds.[16] The survey results reflect the needs to improve economic and physical accessibility to health care services for the elderly, a desire to increase services in the medical network to register complaints about difficulties in seeking medical consultations and hospitalization. Since the 1980s, Shanghai has gradually implemented a policy of privileged access for the elderly, aged 70 and above, for registration, medical consultations and for the dispensary. In 1989, the Protection for the Elderly Legislation was passed in Shanghai, specifying the provision of medical and health care conveniences for the elderly in medical and health care units.[17]

It is estimated that 55% of the medical coverage for the elderly in Shanghai was covered by full public (labour) insurance, 13% by partial insurance and 24% by village cooperative health insurance at the village level, while the remaining 8% was covered by means of self-support.[18] In 1986, only two-thirds of the elderly subjects living in the rural areas had pensions. It is estimated that 92% of the elderly population in urban Shanghai had full or partial medical coverage by public sources.[19] Since 1 August 1992, readjustments were made on charges for medical services for elderly subjects aged 60 and above. Medical fees for those with no fixed income were reduced to half that of the regular fees.[20]

Basic geriatric services are available in the general hospitals. Since 1986, there has been a gradual conversion of some district hospitals into geriatric hospitals (e.g., Ching-on, Chuai Whai). Also, geriatric medical clinics, care and attention homes, and health clinics for the elderly have also been gradually established in the various districts in Shanghai.[21] Together with the Red-Cross, nine care and attention homes were opened by 1993.[22] Periodic medical and health services are rendered for non-ambulatory elderly subjects who are unable to attend to self-care.

Difficulties

The provision of medical and rehabilitation services for the elderly is based on the three-tier health care system. Until recently, there has not been much emphasis on preventive health care for the elderly in China. Half of the cities or districts have preventive health care for the elderly, but they are included in their overall Health Care Work Plans. Elderly patients have generally complained of problems in the accessibility of medical consultations, hospitalization and rehabilitation.[23] Many difficulties are encountered by the health authorities in trying to meet the health care demands of the fast growing elderly population. Such difficulties include inflation and the escalating costs of health care. There is also inadequate manpower and knowledge about the aged at various levels of the health care services — including the primary, secondary and tertiary levels. Not all medical schools yet offer the discipline of geriatric medicine.

In order to improve on the overall health status of the elderly population in Shanghai and to meet the health needs of the elderly population, targets have been set by the Shanghai Department of Health.[24] These targets are:

1. to lengthen the active life expectancy by 0.5 to 1 year
2. to decrease the proportion of dependent elderly by 5% to 10%
3. to decrease the mortality and morbidity of preventable causes including
   - decrease deaths caused by injury by 10% to 30%
   - decrease side effects of medication by 10%

The strategies to achieve these targets are:

1. to improve the leadership in preventive health care services
2. to include care of the elderly in the Overall Management Plan in Health Care Services
3. to improve the three-tier system in the provision of health services
4. to develop geriatric hospitals in districts and counties where more than 20% of the population belongs to the elderly age group

5. to improve manpower training through the development of training materials and the provision of in-service training, with the
aim of at least 30% of the health care personnel having received
training in the health care of the elderly
6. to increase emphasis on caring for common health problems encountered by the elderly
7. to emphasize health education of the elderly, especially on
lifestyle, hypertension, cardiovascular diseases and psychological
aspects of the aged
8. to increase the availability of beds in family clinics
9. to conduct research on the care and prevention of common diseases in the elderly population

Development of Research in Geriatrics and Gerontology

The discipline of geriatric medicine began in the 1950s. The Chinese
Medical Association incorporated the specialty of geriatric medicine in
1960. The Shanghai Geriatric Society was formed in 1984. The discipline
grew fast and by the 1990s there were already about 25 academic associations to carry out academic and research activities. However, there seems
to have been a lack of research focus and a need for more focused research
directions to meet health care needs and to catering to the common health
and disease problems of the elderly population in Shanghai.

With the escalating costs of medical and health care services and with
the increasing size of the elderly population who are and will need such
services, there is an urgent need to research the economies of health care,
the marketing system and organization and structure of health care services. There is also a need to study ways and means of maintaining healthy
ageing and quality of life in the elderly population.

The health care providers in Shanghai are already facing tremendous
tasks to meet the needs of the existing elderly population. It will be a
challenge to plan and develop strategies and a system to cater to the fast
escalating demands of the growing elderly population in Shanghai.

Notes

1. *Zhongguo weisheng nianjian* bianji weiyuanhui《中國衛生年鑑》編輯委員會
(ed.), *Zhongguo weisheng nianjian*, 1988–1994 中國衛生年鑑, 1988–1994
(China Yearbook of Health, 1988–1994) (Beijing: Renmin weisheng

chubanshe 人民衛生出版社, 1988-1994).

2. See Table 17.2 in Chapter 17 for recent historical population statistics of Shanghai.

3. *Zhongguo weisheng nianjian, 1988-1994* (see note 1).

4. Lü Du et al., *Strategic Studies of the Health Care Financing and Resource Allocation in China.* (Monograph) (Beijing: Ministry of Public Health, 1991).

5. X. Z. Liu and W.C.L. Hsiao, "The Cost Escalation of Social Health Insurance Plans in China: Its Implication for Public Policy," *Social Science and Medicine*, Vol. 41, No. 8, (1995), pp. 1095-1101.

6. W.C.L. Hsiao, "The Chinese Health Care System: Lessons for Other Nations," *Social Science and Medicine*, Vol. 48, No. 48, (1995), pp. 1047-55.

7. He Huide 何慧德, Zeng Erhang 曾爾元 and Cui Dongming 崔東明, "Woguo laonian renkou xianzhuang ji qi fenbu de chubu fenxi" 我國老年人口現狀及其分布的初步分析 (A Preliminary Analysis of the Demography of the Elderly Population and Their Distribution), *Zhonghua yixue zazhi* 中華醫學雜誌 (Chinese Medical Journal), No. 7 (1988), pp. 162-65.

8. Lü Weishan 呂維善, "Woguo xiandai shehui laolinghua de yanjiu" 我國現代社會老齡化的研究 (Research into the Ageing of the Modern Society in China), *Zhongguo shehui yixue* 中國社會醫學, No. 1 (1993), pp. 10-12.

9. Yuan Jihui 袁緝輝 and Zhang Zhongru 張鍾汝, *Shehui laonianxue jiaocheng* 社會老年學教程 (Teaching in Community Gerontology) (Shanghai: Fandan daxue chubanshe 復旦大學出版社, 1992); and Feng Xueshan 馮學山 and Gu Xingyuan 顧杏元, "Shanghaishi 'lao you suo yi' wenti yanjiu" 上海市'老有所醫'問題研究 (A Study of Medical Care for the Elderly), *Zhongguo weisheng zhengce* 中國衛生政策 (China Health Policy), No. 5 (1991), pp. 10-11.

10. Wang Zanshun 王贊舜, "Shanghaishi de laonian yiliao baojian" 上海市的老年醫療保健 (Health Care for the Elderly in Shanghai), *Zhongguo laonian yixue zazhi* 中國老年醫學雜誌 (Journal of Chinese Gerontology), No. 14 (1994), pp. 73-75.

11. Lü Weishan, "Woguo xiandai shehui laolinghua de yanjiu" (see note 8).

12. Yang Ruimin 楊蕊敏 et al., "Shanghai Xuhui qu laonian ren 6,860 fen siwang zhengshu tongji fenxi" 上海徐匯區老年人6,860分死亡證書統計分析 (An Analysis of Causes of Death from 6,860 Elderly Death Certificates in Xuhui District in Shanghai), *Laonianxue zazhi* 老年學雜誌 (Journal of Gerontology), No. 10 (1990), pp. 143-44.

13. Wang Zanshun, "Shanghaishi de laonian yiliao baojian" (see note 10).

14. Ibid.

15. Zhang Jianzhong 張建中, "Shanghaishi weisheng gaige yu fazhan cuishi" 上海市衛生改革與發展趨勢 (Reform and Development Trends of Health Care in Shanghai), *Zhongguo weisheng zhengce* 中國衛生政策 (Health Policy in China), No. 11 (1992), pp. 9-10.

16. Feng Xueshan 馮學山, "Shanghai Wanhang diduan li tuixiu renyuan yiliao

fuwu xuqiuliang fenxi" 上海萬航地段離退休人員醫療服務需求量分析 (An Analysis of the Health Care Service Needs of the Retired Elderly Workers in Wanhang District in Shanghai), *Weisheng fuwu yanjiu* 衛生服務研究 (Research in Health Care Services), No. 50 (1992), pp. 504-506.

17. Wang Zanshun, "Shanghaishi de laonian yiliao baojian" (see note 10).

18. Zhang Wang 張網, "Shanghai bingren jiuyi xuqiu tezheng yanjiu" 上海病人就醫需求特徵研究 (A Study of the Characteristics of Medical Needs of Patients in Shanghai), No. 6 (1994), pp. 316-18.

19. Zhou Guanhong 周冠虹, Jiang Xiongwan 蔣雄萬 and Ye Zhenda 葉振達, "Shanghaishi 'lao you suo yi' duice xintan" 上海市 "老有所醫" 對策新探 (A New Look into the Policy of Health Care for the Elderly in Shanghai) (Discussion paper for the Seminar on Strategies towards an Ageing Population in Shanghai, Shanghai, 1990).

20. Zhang Jianzhong, "Shanghaishi weisheng gaige yu fazhan cuishi" (see note 15).

21. Shanghaishi weishengju 上海市衛生局, "Shanghaishi laonian yiliao baojian 'ba wu' quihua" 上海市老年醫療保健 "八五" 規劃 ("85"Health Plan for Medical Care of the Elderly in Shanghai), *Hu wei yi zheng* 滬衛醫政 (Shanghai Health Policy), No. 36 (1992), pp. 1-7.

22. *Zhongguo weisheng nianjian*, 1988-1994 (see note 1).

23. Shanghaishi weishengju, "Shanghaishi laonian yiliao baojian 'ba wu' guihua" (see note 21).

24. Ibid.

17

Shanghai's "Horizontal Liaisons" and Population Control

Lynn T. White III

Debates about China's population policies have focused mainly on fertility. Alternative methods for reducing birth rates have been at the centre of public attention. Academic discourse has also tended to stress fertility policy, giving short shrift to the larger contexts in which population measures arise, find political support, or are effective for human ends. Birth control has too often been conceived as if it could be isolated from internal migration, demands for labour, parents' life expectancies, household registration, financial interests for birth planning, differences between localities, and the rise and fall of China's revolution.

Shanghai and its delta provide a fine place to explore a range of questions that are not usually conceived as demographic but that deserve to be asked about population policy. How do fertility control policies link with more general policies for controlling people? Whom in China do such policies most immediately serve, and what groups are most interested in them? Has the recent industrial boom, for example, in Shanghai's suburbs and nearby cities of Jiangsu 江蘇 and Zhejiang 浙江 , reduced state control not just of fertility but also of other human activities that affect the number of people there? "Population control" is a term that can be given a wide meaning.

Demographic patterns in and near Shanghai have been driven by several forces besides government policy. Important among these factors are:

1. pre-existing historical links between people in China's largest metropolis and places outside that central place, especially elsewhere on the Shanghai delta,

2. unintended effects after the Maoist policies that sent youths and cadres to rural areas,

3. technological and cultural changes in media that make rural people aware of urban life, and

The author is grateful to Princeton University and to the Chiang Ching-kuo Foundation (蔣經國基金) for research support. For logistics, he thanks all hands at Edward Chen's Centre of Asian Studies at The University of Hong Kong, notably Coonoor Kripalani-Thadani and Carol Chan. Jean Hung of Universities Service Centre, and many at The Chinese University of Hong Kong whose names appear elsewhere in this book, have also helped the project — as has Kevin M. White. But all views in this chapter are solely the author's responsibility.

4. booming suburban and rural industrialization since the early 1970s, which has allowed the Chinese Communist Party (CCP) to reign over, but not effectively to tax, an economic structure that encourages a quickening of labour mobility.

Each of these topics is large. Each requires a broader search for facts than is usual in discussions of demography. This chapter presents data on Shanghai population trends, but it mainly attempts to supplement the existing large literature about the appropriateness of various fertility control policies by stressing other factors that impinge on their meaning.

How should such a study be organized? Population increases can be most neatly conceived under the usual two broad categories: births minus deaths, plus immigration minus emigration. This is admittedly the most comprehensive analytical approach to the problem. Net increase and net migration fully determine Shanghai's size. But to repeat this kind of analysis would hardly be novel; it would be to show readers general relationships they already know. Migration and increase are often studied separately from each other, but institutional factors (such as the effectiveness of household registration) influence both net natural increase and net immigration. Since the present study seeks to supplement the two usual approaches, whose effects on population size are not wholly separable, this chapter is organized along dimensions different from these two. Such a purview may not cover the whole topic with total analytic exhaustiveness (as the increase and migration approaches surely do), but there is a trade-off benefit. This institutional approach points to practical considerations that can improve the realism of thinking about population policy.[1] To begin, Shanghai's population controls may be explored in terms of their political history, which tells more about their present status than the government advertises.

Traditions in Shanghai Population Control

When the People's Liberation Army marched into Shanghai, the population there was abnormally high. People who had fled their homes in the city were outnumbered by refugees from the civil war elsewhere. Shanghai's population had fluctuated sharply in the city's recent history,[2] and the new Mayor Chen Yi 陳毅 in August 1949 took a decisive attitude towards the influx: "We must evacuate the population of the city systematically and transfer factories to the interior whenever possible."[3]

Despite such clear intentions, during the economic boom from 1950 to 1953, the number of factory jobs in Shanghai rose by 29%, from 434,000 to 558,000.[4] Yet the gap between urban and rural incomes in this part of China, as elsewhere, also rose throughout the early communist years. Officials at many levels of administration, often urban immigrants themselves who had arrived with the Red Army, had major interests in securing their own posts by designating their subordinates. Shanghai's proletariat became a specially favoured urban class, to which access was restricted. During the "transition to socialism," culminating in 1956, new socialist business cadres mainly wanted their minions to work, not to raise costs for welfare — and specifically, not to raise babies.

Serious local attempts at birth control in Shanghai first became important by 1956, regardless of the much-reported ideological debates on national birth policies. Nationalization put socialist business cadres in charge. One of their first goals was to reduce the money their firms paid into welfare budgets for people outside their own businesses. By the mid-1950s, Shanghai's household registration system had more effective police enforcement than ever before, and it was used to evict many from the metropolis. The quickest forced emigration from the city occurred in 1955 (as Table 17.1 shows), although this fact has not received much attention because few intellectuals were involved.[5] Mass deportation, not fertility control, was the main official means to control Shanghai's size during the 1950s and 1960s.

In 1955, the Zhabei 閘北 and Penglai 蓬萊 district governments, for example, sent cadres to "interview peasants" in the city and move them elsewhere. North Jiangsu and Anhui 安徽 were, at this time and since, the origins of many poor immigrants, against whom Jiangnan 江南 Shanghai people tend freely to admit their prejudice.[6] Demographers such as Douglas Massey have shown that individuals' decisions to migrate, although influenced initially by wage differentials, depend to a great extent on personal connections between people in target locales and people who might go there. Early Shanghai CCP policy was simply to reverse this flow back to the rural places. Transport companies expanded their schedules to haul people out of Shanghai. Police sent groups of "vagabonds" to the Zhabei train station and to piers beside the Huangpu River (黃浦江), all to board transport inland.[7]

The population turnover from slum areas at this time was very quick. A survey of three residential regions shows that, during 1955 in one of them, 74% of the people had to leave. Turnover in most areas was much

Table 17.1 Shanghai Population: Inflow, Outflow, Net Immigration

Year	Pop.	Pop. in	% in	Pop. out	% out	Net in	% net
1950	4,978,213	566,951	11.4	623,342	12.5	−56,391	−1.1
1951	5,224,621	1,004,032	19.2	566,208	10.8	437,824	8.4
1952	5,624,141	430,039	7.6	352,117	6.3	77,922	1.4
1953	5,939,367	487,806	8.2	255,492	4.3	232,314	3.9
1954	6,339,740	457,576	7.2	296,712	4.7	160,864	2.5
1955	6,429,039	260,430	4.1	847,293	13.2	−586,863	−9.1
1956	6,290,196	382,551	6.1	443,326	7.0	−60,775	−1.0
1957	6,623,157	418,474	6.3	134,833	2.0	283,641	4.3
1958	7,202,492	193,728	2.7	513,432	7.1	−319,704	−4.4
1959	8,895,972	323,163	3.6	322,050	3.6	1,113	0.0
1960	10,423,439	237,697	2.3	265,903	2.6	−28,206	−0.3
1961	10,576,449	192,723	1.8	335,522	3.2	−142,799	−1.4
1962	10,584,286	213,809	2.0	375,867	3.6	−162,058	−1.5
1963	10,657,542	152,565	1.4	238,262	2.2	−85,697	−0.8
1964	10,799,301	154,140	1.4	200,999	1.9	−46,859	−0.4
1965	10,900,050	161,679	1.5	206,458	1.9	−44,779	−0.4
1966	10,948,123	101,005	0.9	178,724	1.6	−77,719	−0.7
1967	11,007,744	39,983	0.4	73,385	0.7	−33,402	−0.3
1968	11,073,463	94,274	0.9	172,413	1.6	−78,139	−0.7
1969	11,014,847	77,488	0.7	352,535	3.2	−275,047	−2.5
1970	10,832,725	58,527	0.5	370,955	3.4	−312,428	−2.9
1971	10,698,848	126,392	1.2	253,829	2.4	−127,437	−1.2
1972	10,654,624	128,718	1.2	188,503	1.8	−59,785	−0.6
1973	10,670,592	171,298	1.6	158,909	1.5	12,389	0.1
1974	10,718,962	166,509	1.6	161,670	1.5	4,839	0.0
1975	10,752,502	212,096	2.0	217,199	2.0	−5,103	0.0
1976	10,790,117	200,180	1.9	202,068	1.9	−1,888	0.0
1977	10,838,868	196,291	1.8	188,350	1.7	7,941	0.1
1978	10,923,759	248,335	2.3	181,288	1.7	67,047	0.6
1979	11,152,094	598,260	5.4	333,390	3.0	264,870	2.4
1980	11,465,200	287,559	2.5	210,834	1.8	76,725	0.7
1981	11,628,400	236,223	2.0	192,127	1.7	44,096	0.4
1982	11,805,100	234,601	2.0	196,557	1.7	38,044	0.3
1983	11,940,100	226,773	1.9	190,821	1.6	35,952	0.3
1984	12,047,800	196,551	1.6	174,842	1.5	21,709	0.2
1985	12,166,900	182,904	1.5	129,873	1.1	53,031	0.4
1986	12,323,300	197,700	1.6	135,000	1.1	62,700	0.5
1987	12,495,100	221,700	1.8	154,000	1.2	67,700	0.5
1988	12,624,200	221,100	1.8	170,200	1.3	50,900	0.4
1989	12,764,500	210,900	1.7	169,500	1.3	41,400	0.3
1990	12,833,500	188,700	1.5	174,100	1.4	14,600	0.1
1991	12,872,000	167,000	1.3	145,400	1.1	21,600	0.2
1992	12,893,700	175,300	1.4	149,200	1.2	26,100	0.2
1993	12,947,400	185,500	1.5	118,600	0.9	66,900	0.5
1994	12,988,100	199,600	1.5	125,400	1.0	74,200	0.6

Notes: [a] Migrants in and out, counting no births or deaths; and percentage ratios to total population in the whole municipality are shown on this table.

Notes: ^b Percentages are calculated. Most figures after 1979 are rounded in the
            sources, as prior ones surely should have been. The basis for data collection
            has changed somewhat in certain years, as noted below. Migrants to and
            from Shanghai have generally been registered; but increasingly after the
            mid-1980s, arrivals not counted here became numerous. Most migration has
            involved urban districts, although this also became less pronounced after
            the mid-1980s, when many migrants lived in suburban counties.
            ^c Administrative changes compromise the comparability of figures between
            specifiable periods. The population of the ten counties incorporated into
            Shanghai from Jiangsu in the late 1950s (by different decrees) was a
            noticeable fraction of the municipality's total at that time. This jurisdiction
            change, which mainly affects the first column, means that 1950–1959 figures
            are not quite comparable to later ones. The reliability of reporting also varied
            over time: The 1958 and 1967–1970 migration figures may be wrong by
            especially sizeable margins, overstating the net outflow; they are repub-
            lished here from the source only to provide the reader a sense of critical
            humour about such things. Also, the first-column figures through 1987 are
            average populations during those years; but the best source found for
            1988–1990 does not specify this, and the increment rate of the total popula-
            tion for the last two years may thus be slightly understated. But none of these
            problems affect the most important trends the table shows.

Sources: The raw data begin in *Zhongguo renkou: Shanghai fence*中國人口：上海分
            冊 (China's Population: Shanghai Volume), edited by Hu Huanyong et al.
            (Beijing: Zhongguo caizheng jingji chubanshe中國財政經濟出版社 , 1987),
            p. 77. Slightly different figures are in *Shanghai tongji nianjian 1988* (see note
            31), pp. 92, 76. The last years' data are on pp. 60, 67 of the *Shanghai tongji
            nianjian 1990*, pp. 60, 68 of the 1991 edition, pp. 60, 82 of the 1992 edition,
            pp. 64, 70 of the 1993 edition, pp. 41, 44 of the 1994 edition, and the latest
            source, pp. 47, 50 of the 1995 edition. Some of the figures are separately
            confirmed (with slight differences) in Lin You Su, "Urban Migration in China:
            A Case Study of Three Urban Areas" (Ph.D. dissertation, Department of
            Geography, Australian National University, 1992), p. 72. The first source
            makes clear that these numbers come from police records on legal per-
            manent and temporary residents. Illegal migrants are thus not counted; and
            their number was sometimes substantial even before the last years reported
            above.

less, but on 30 July, the *Liberation Daily* reported that the city council
"discussed and adopted" a resolution for the shipment of "peasants" elsewhere. The official news agency claimed that the September–October,
1955, influx of peasants to Shanghai was only 81% that of the same period
a year earlier.[8] Many later returned to the city, after visiting relatives at
their rural homes.

The system of careful urban registrations — and the threat of
deregistrations — became useful to a revolutionary state trying to guide
the careers of urban people who might threaten its rule.[9] But poor and
recent migrants, in China as in other developing countries, were unlikely to

cause such threats.[10] Shanghai leaders launched major campaigns to evict them in any case. The deputy mayor with special responsibility for this programme, Xu Jianguo 許建國 , declared that, "As for those who have come to the city recently and have no one to support their living, they are going to be cared for by the government. They will be sent back to their villages in batches."[11] In a later speech, however, he mentioned that of the people who registered legally in Shanghai between June 1956 and January 1958, more than 40% were dependents of cadres or government employees.[12] Officials did not throw their own relatives or followers out of Shanghai.

Emigration campaigns were locally very political. The first fertility control campaigns were no less political — or local. National debates are easy to overemphasize, despite the fame of controversies between Chairman Mao (who then opposed birth control) and economist Ma Yinchu 馬寅初 (President of Peking University [北京大學], who typified Chinese intellectuals by favouring very strong control). Shanghai business cadres, e.g. in the huge textile industry whose employees were 70% women, had more concrete interests. Pregnancies cost them money. For example, the annual birth rate from all workers in the No. 9 Shenxin Cotton Textile Mill in 1958 was running at the extremely high rate of 249 per thousand.[13] Because of the woman-days lost each year due to preliminary leaves only, in effect 5% of the work force at this mill was permanently idle on the payroll. Light industrial cadres might not be enthusiastic about birth control in the abstract, but cost margins stir them. They prefer their workers to tend bobbins, not babies.

Contraception could solve this problem, and business managers had financial incentives to fund it. CCP Puritan ideology notwithstanding, as early as 1957, the Shanghai Public Health Bureau fielded sex education and slide shows with titles like "Before and After Contraception" to discourage fertility.[14] National intellectuals and politicians often call birth control programmes, even when mandatory, by the rationalist euphemism "birth planning" (*shengyu jihua* 生育計劃); but local business cadres, having a lower profile but more specific interest in it, could more frankly call it "contraception propaganda" (*biyun xuanchuan* 避孕宣傳).

Economic depression and political turmoil in the 1960s tended to overwhelm both birth control and migration control. In periods such as 1959–1961, when food was scarce and new jobs even more so, population control was officially unintended more than intended. When the economy revived by 1963–1964, rustication campaigns resumed under military auspices. Urban residence controls through neighbourhood committees became more effective.[15] By the middle of the decade, administrative controls collapsed, along with the administrators, into the Cultural Revolution. But decentralized moralizing by neighbourhood leaders was at an all-time high then, and the birth rate remained low (Table 17.2).

Table 17.2   Births, Deaths and Natural Increase Rates in Shanghai[a]

Year	Births	Deaths	Increase
1952	39	9	30
1957	46	6	40
1962	26	7	19
1965	17	6	11
1970	14	5	9
1971	12	5	7
1972	11	5	6
1973	10	5	5
1974	9	6	4
1975	9	6	3
1976	10	6	4
1977	10	6	5
1978	11	6	5
1979	11	6	6
1980	12	7	5
1981	17	7	10
1982	19	6	12
1983	15	7	9
1984	14	7	7
1985	13	7	6
1986	15	7	8
1987	15	7	8
1988	15	7	9
1989	13	7	6
1990	10	7	4
1991	8	7	1
1992	7	7	0
1993	7	7	−1
1994	6	7	−1

Note: [a] Rates per thousand population, whole municipality.

Source: *Shanghai tongji nianjian 1993* (see note 44), p. 67 has a table for some years, as well as a chart for which the rates had to be visually and roughly estimated for other years. This has been supplemented with *Shanghai tongji nianjian 1994*, p. 43, and *Shanghai tongji nianjian 1995*, p. 49; but by the 1990s, birth reporting was apparently less complete because of migrations and political-administrative changes. Concerning changes in jurisdictional area and other minor anomalies, see the source note attached to Table 17.1. Figures may not add because of rounding.

Available statistics on Shanghai's births, deaths and natural increase show that the birth rate was low (9 per thousand) by 1974–1975. It did not fall below these mid-1970s levels after 1978, when high state politicos announced reforms (until, by the 1990s, illegal migrants made current statistics incomplete). Effective birth control is often conceived as a reform programme — one of the most important applications of post-revolution-ary or enlightened rationality in economic policy. At least in Shanghai, however, low fertility predated public reforms. Shanghai's yearly birth rate in 1972–1977 averaged less than 10 per thousand. But in 1978–1989, it averaged above 14 per thousand.[16]

Shanghai's death rates have been fairly stable since the mid-1950s (the slight upward trend since the early 1970s was probably caused by many factors, including more complete reporting of deaths in suburban areas). The birth rate has a far greater impact on natural increase — and fertility has shifted rather sharply, for a mix of reasons on which this chapter presents preliminary hypotheses. Vagaries of underreporting in the years when the rate was officially lowest (1974–1975 and after 1990) may well be important.[17] Immigration of relatively fertile youths, notably at the end of the 1970s but also in other years, also increased the local birth rate.[18]

Shanghai grows from immigrants, not just births. Data on the two tables suggest that the gross influx from elsewhere was roughly 1.6 times as important as Shanghai fertility, as in-migrants increased pressure on the city's population from 1972 to 1992. Net migration was less important than natural increase (local births minus deaths) over the whole two decades, because state pressure for emigration and for non-reporting of immigrants was less coherent than for preventing births or certification of them. Many local cadres, especially those needing cheap labour, benefited from having migrants in the city.[19] The published statistics may stray from reality slightly; but it is clear that immigration — not just fertility — was a very significant factor increasing Shanghai's size.

Sojourners, Send-Downs, and Sunday Engineers

"Horizontal liaisons" (*hengxiang lianxi* 橫向聯繫) with specific inland places have guided the immigration historically. It is debatable whether Shanghai people should mainly be called "sojourners."[20] But most of them have both strong local ties to the metropolis in which they live, as well as family linkages to places elsewhere on the Shanghai delta. This tradition was hindered during the first two decades of the Communist era, when the state's vertical command structures reorganized Shanghai's economy to maximize state revenues. But since the early 1970s, after the Cultural Revolution of the late 1960s weakened bureaucratic regulators, many Shanghai groups and individuals were again able to profit from the economic potential of their traditional links either to their family homes or to other similar places on the delta.[21]

The early 1970s saw a major revival of horizontal relations between rural enterprises and urban experts. "May 7 cadre schools" (*wuqi ganxiao* 五七幹校) were, at least in theory supposed to host cadres who still had reputable posts. Many of these temporary rusticates did little but read newspapers and drink tea, but some helped local peasants run new rural industries. The "May 7" cadres were the first "Sunday engineers" (*xingqitian gongchengshi* 星期天工程師) of the reform period — except that they stayed for the whole week. This Maoist policy had major un-intended (and proto-capitalist) results — and radicals during the early 1970s criticized such activities, arguing that the cadre schools were sup-posed to teach city people about agriculture, not to teach peasants about industry and marketing.

Cadre schools were just a late and high-profile example of a kind of revolutionary policy that had previously linked urban technicians to rural leaders. In the thirty years after the mid-1950s, 1,400,000 Shanghai people — *not* counting rusticated youths — went to help other places in China. Of these, three-tenths were technicians.[22] Of all personnel specifically seconded from Shanghai jobs to help other places during these three decades, a majority were workers. All of them together accounted for about one-sixth the total registered emigration from Shanghai over the three decades after 1949. This was a larger send-down than that of edu-cated youths. It has received less scholarly attention because many workers went earlier and more gradually, and because the programme's coercive aspects involved fewer writers.

State planners wrongly assumed they could always control such links. Rustication policies inadvertently created a staff to connect nonstate rural firms with consumer markets. They also brought new techniques to non-state factories. "Many people sent to rural areas from city offices, research agencies and universities, as well as young intellectuals, brought science and technology, culture, knowledge and economic information to the countryside. They linked city and countryside more closely. And because urban firms could not operate well to serve urban citizens' needs, rural industry found a market for its products."[23]

In the decade after 1978, this outflow of technicians continued. About 800,000 Shanghai personnel were seconded permanently or temporarily to other provinces for work. Most of the jobs were nearby, in Zhejiang or Jiangsu; but some specialists went further. By July 1980, in China as a whole, 3,400 joint enterprises across jurisdictions had been established, and these often justified personnel transfers between cities and new rural factories.[24] Urban consultants were colloquially called "high-priced old men," or "Sunday engineers," because they could earn RMB200 or RMB300 for just a few days of work each month — far more than their ordinary pay then — often on weekends by advising rural co-operatives or small-town factories.[25] They were employed to solve technical problems, help maintain machines, give technical lectures, and raise the quality of management. Often they kept such activities secret from their Shanghai units, so that no one would become jealous of the extra money they earned. But the extra work was not always a secret. It might either be approved by the Shanghai employers as a possible means of extending their own connections to rural sources of labour and materials, or it might be disapproved because it drained the energies of technical employees within Shanghai and created market competition elsewhere. In either case, the trend was not effectively stopped.

Rustication policies thus had the unintended effect of strengthening nonstate Shanghai connections with other places. This affected migration patterns in both directions — and reduced official controls. A journal reported that Jiaxing 嘉興 , a major delta city in Zhejiang, "has attracted many technicians and managers, especially those able to use its proximity to Shanghai … their role in the development of Jiaxing's economy, through their personal (*siren* 私人) connections, has led many Jiaxing enterprises to establish links with relevant units in Shanghai."[26]

Retired technicians and cadres from Shanghai often went to Jiangsu or Zhejiang to live, and others remained in Shanghai but went to other delta cities for several days each month. Inland firms kept records, usually in card files, of contacts in Shanghai — including relatives and anyone else who might prove to be of use to the business.[27] Such files recorded the address, specialization, telephone, work unit and other information about each possible consultant. At lunar New Year, and occasionally at other times, a Shanghai contact would often receive a cordial letter from the company, sending respects and sometimes asking specific market information about selling products or obtaining materials, or asking whether the consultant might supply introductions or come visit. Municipal authorities in Jiangsu or Zhejiang did not oppose links of this sort with Shanghai, when they benefited from any trade that developed.

Businessmen in the metropolis might try to establish links with their families' old home towns; but often it was economically more rational to make liaisons with other places more appropriate for their businesses. Local cadres in the hometowns of Shanghai entrepreneurs had their own networks that could help make such linkages with other localities. When such businesses prospered, money would frequently be donated to the towns of cadres who had aided such connections. East China is now sprinkled with schools, clinics and other institutions that have benefited from funds earned locally or elsewhere through the good offices of rural cadres who helped businessmen in Shanghai.

"Horizontal liaisons" became very common within the East China region, and these mutually reinforced old cultural ties. They arose because the old market for trade was also a cultural region.[28] Beijing politicians tried to weaken these connections from 1949 onwards, for the sake of administrative centralization and state revenues. Recent local gains from Shanghai links to nearby places have conflicted with the bureaucratic culture.[29] Quick economic growth throughout the delta has, at the same time, refinanced the regional culture of Jiangnan and has reduced state control of the population. But migration on this basis is just one of the contextual factors important in determining Shanghai's size. Other situational factors can be found entirely inside the city, and they are also useful to "complicate the story" of Shanghai's growth and to make it more realistic.

Urban and Suburban Population Control within Shanghai

The housing crunch may have been as effective in depressing Shanghai's birth rate as was the late-marriage-and-then-one-child policy. In July 1982, 129,000 nuclear families had legal registrations in Shanghai, but without any rooms. In addition, it was estimated that 408,000 people could not be married for lack of housing — even though all the grooms were above the recommended marriage age of 27, and all the brides were over the officially ideal minimum of 25.[30] In the eyes of the law, these couples were married; they had certificates. But many had not yet held the celebratory party that gives informal social recognition to marriage — because they had no housing in which to live together.

The 1987 residential population density in Jing'an 靜安 district was

64,000 people per km², the highest in the PRC.[31] In commercial areas, especially those around Nanjing 南京 and Huaihai 淮海 roads, the ratio could rise at least to 170,000 per km².[32] These places compare with the most densely populated areas of the world in terms of ground space, of which the extreme case is apparently in Mongkok, Hong Kong, a high-rise area in a much higher-per-capita income city, with more floor space (though less land space) per person.

Residential crowding in Shanghai is hardly a state plan. In practice, it strengthens Chinese kinship traditions because it forces members of more than two generations to live together. They cannot get enough housing to live apart. Nuclear households in separate residences remain the ideal of most, as a survey in Shanghai shows; but the housing crunch makes this impracticable. "Strong obligations to newly married children and to frail elderly parents repeatedly overrode the desire to have each married couple maintain its own home." Filial duties (combined with the state's long-term unwillingness to expand or even maintain most buildings it said it owned) created many three-generation households in China's most urban environment. Among a sample of Shanghai households, nuclear-family residence was less common in 1990 than it had been in 1987.[33] Shanghai young people were quoted as saying, "Here it is harder to find an apartment than to find a spouse."[34]

In the suburbs, prosperity encouraged marriages, although quick in-dustrialization and state policy discouraged the bearing of children.[35] The Shanghai suburban population size was almost totally stable from 1976 to 1988 in the best-studied village there — even though from 1976 to 1980 alone, the number of households increased by almost one-fifth.[36] The urban districts, on the other hand, saw a quick population rise — at first mostly registered because of legally returned ex-rusticate "educated youths," and then in the 1990s, perhaps more than half unregistered.

Rural wealth soon correlated with family size. The main reason was an ironic and unintended result of the equalization of rural land plots in the early 1950s under Mao. When plots for cultivation were assigned in the 1970s to many households on responsibility contracts, the amounts of contracted land were at first roughly equal. These plots were much closer to each other in size, for example, than had been typical of landholdings before the early 1950s Land Reform. So in this first stage of agricultural contracting, which involved many households, the amount of labour each contract plot demanded of its peasant family was also roughly equal. Thus, the amount of extra labour any household could devote to industrial work depended on how much labour remained, i.e., on family size. Figures on rural families in Shanghai's suburbs show that incomes depended strongly on family size, especially when families still tilled some land.[37] This policy was in effect pro-natalist. Also, relatively even post-1978 land redistributions, designed to equalize household prosperities, produced precisely the opposite effect: measures for equalization led to inequality.

Industrialization soon led to smaller households, for other reasons that were also not fully under the purview of the state. Birth control and departures of family members to even higher-paying jobs in the urban area of Shanghai combined to make average Shanghai suburban household size drop from 4.26 to 4.09 persons between 1980 and 1984.[38] The average number of industrial workers remaining per rural household, nevertheless, rose by 40%. More labour for all purposes was mobilized per family (from 1.02 workers at the beginning of the period, up to 1.43 at the end). The portion of suburban labourers working in industry rose from 36% to 52%, a very sharp change for only five years.

Some general relaxation of state controls in the mid-1980s led to family decisions that affected birth rates. In the new environment, more people got married. Shanghai's marriage rate topped that of all Chinese provinces by 1985, at 3.0% of the population (compared to the next-highest Beijing at 2.7, and Tianjin at 2.4).[39] Shanghai was the sole province in China where more than half of all married women of reproductive age had obtained "one child certificates." Shanghai was the only province in which that portion was over 60% among women living in urban districts. Fully 56% of fertile-age women in city and suburbs had one child certificates. (By contrast, the poorer provinces of Guangxi 廣西, Guizhou 貴州 and Jiangxi 江西 reported just 4% or 5%.)[40] For their own reasons or to accommodate the state, registered Shanghai families had few children.

It was difficult for neighbourhood committee cadres not to take an avuncular and welcoming attitude towards new babies, as is common in all societies including China. A late-1980s Shanghai regulation, which codified local practices common before then, provided that, "For babies born in violation of birth control policies, the Household Registration Office should approve to register them, but their parents should be given education about birth control policy."[41] Enforcement by that time was sensible enough not to punish children along with their parents after unauthorized births took place. But every effort was made to reduce births. After parents actually had their children, the policy had failed.

Official Mandates and Situational Causes

The Chinese government, backed by a majority of intellectuals but with less support from other groups, has claimed an economic need to have fewer people. For example, population control was the first-listed priority for social development in Shanghai's 1981–1985 plan.[42] Birth control policies are still moralistic and, in principle, the Constitution obligates citizens to follow birth plans. Individualism is certainly not an ideal of China's formal law. But was state policy the only cause of the reduced birth rates? A careful study tested the relative contributions to low fertility of two broad factors: general socioeconomic development and state birth planning. Did Chinese women have fewer children because they had more education? Or did they have lower fertility because of control policies? The conclusion of a complex correlation exercise, involving seventeen general development variables and eleven specific family planning variables, was that although the quick fertility transition in China has been partly induced by policy, the contribution to low fertility of fast socio-economic development is also great.[43]

The proportional contributions of state policy and economic growth are difficult to measure, because some economic expansion also results from state policy. Some also comes from unintended effects of government measures. A great deal comes from nonstate industries. In Shanghai, household size fell faster than birth rates. Average urban household size, surveyed in 1980 and again in 1992, plummeted from 4.06 to 3.11 people.[44] A continuous birth control campaign, based on fairly explicit collective coercion, was one factor contributing to this result. So were non-policy migration, largely of single-person "households," and other correlates of quick economic growth.

Another contextual factor that must be woven into this story involves the effects of medicine on specific kinds of mortality. Death rates had already dropped by the early 1970s, largely because of the success of Maoist communitarian campaigns against contagious "crowd" diseases that produce antibodies (e.g., cholera, yellow fever, rubella, measles, mumps and smallpox). Socialist campaigns had been less effective against chronic "individual" diseases that produce few or no antibodies (e.g., cancer, TB, snail fever, leprosy, stroke and heart disease). But control of the first set of illnesses, the contagions whose biological traits made them especially responsive to communitarian policies, had already reduced China's mortality by the early 1970s. Progress against individual or "modern" diseases has been harder to engineer, not just in China but worldwide. Communitarian education campaigns help prevent these maladies but do not eradicate them. China's death rate had already stabilized far below its pre-modern norm by the early 1970s. Irrespective of state policy, it was not going down much further very soon. So reducing births became the main task of national demographic planning. And China's population growth was halved between 1970 and 1977 (from 26 to 12 per thousand annually). This was the essence of reform in population policy.[45] Overall results in demographic reforms were faster in the early 1970s than after 1978.

Shanghai has long been the place in China with the highest per-capita expenditure on birth control. This contraception effort has, together with auxiliary factors, brought big results: In 1954, among all China's 29 provinces, Shanghai had both the highest rate of natural increase and the highest birth rate. But by 1981, Shanghai had the lowest rates both for natural increase and for births.[46] A sharp decrease of the local birth rate created this total reversal of Shanghai's rank among the provinces. Although Shanghai had the lowest death rate among China's provinces in 1954, by 1981, most other provinces reported lower mortality (apparently because relatively strict household registration in Shanghai made for many old people there). Several factors lowered Shanghai's birth rates, and not all depended on the main intended results of policies. Some came from the slow and bumpy growth of institutions to send youths out of Shanghai and reduce fertility.[47]

The rate of per-capita expenditure on birth control in 1974–1976 Shanghai was 15% lower than 1971–1973 spending for the same purpose earlier.[48] The reform process, in this and other fields, suffered one of its interruptions especially in 1975–1976. The official effort to control Shanghai's birth rate, while always strenuous, relaxed somewhat in the mid-1970s, during the temporary ebb of reforms after the first spurt of reforms in the early 1970s. This may seem ironic in light of the actually low Shanghai birth rate of those years. But campaigns may show what people are not doing or what they would do anyway, as much as they show effective state pressure to make them do it.

Parents with one child who promised to have no more could apply for a "one-child certificate." Officials might ask to see this on various occasions, but the extent to which this policy constrained behaviour varied by time and place. Technically, an urban couple could qualify to have a second child only under stringent conditions: if the first child was handicapped, if the wife in a couple that had adopted its first child became pregnant more than five years after the marriage, or if both the husband and wife were themselves only children. But peasant couples, even in Shanghai's suburbs, could have an authorized second child under these or any of eleven other conditions.[49] Applications had to be made through a work unit, which sent its "opinion" to higher levels for approval.

One child was the official norm for urban families during the reform period, but it was not uniformly applied. The procedures for arranging permission to have a second baby were complex. Letters of approval from both the husband's and wife's work units had to be brought to the local street committee (of the wife's residence, if work or housing forced them to live apart). These documents were supposed to be forwarded to the district or county birth planning committee, which was mandated to issue a certificate allowing two children (upon return of the one-child certificate that the family had previously received), presuming that any of the following conditions applied: if the first offspring was disabled, if the couple had adopted a foster child and five or more years after marriage the wife became pregnant, or if both the husband and wife were themselves single children.[50] Otherwise, the pregnancy was supposed to be aborted. But such rules in practice gave a great deal of power to local cadres.

What, over the years, was the effect of all these varied factors and rules on Shanghai's birth rate? Demography is a field in which long views are needed, because any human population is like a large ship; it does not change course quickly. During the early 1970s, Shanghai's natural birth rate reached an unprecedented low. From 1971 to 1977, it averaged 10 per thousand (as compared with an average of at least 13 per thousand from 1978 to 1992).[51] The early 1970s, while the pro-natalist Chairman Mao was still alive, apparently showed the greatest effectiveness of anti-natalist policy, which is often associated with rational "reforms" as planned by intellectuals. Shanghai's birth rate fell in the early 1970s. Then it rose irregularly — especially because of births in built-up areas, not just in the suburbs — until the late 1980s, when birth rates and registration rates both fell. Data from the 1990s may undercount immigrant babies.

The overall picture is that Shanghai fertility was low for many reasons. Government campaigns were significant but not exclusively so. In China as a whole, the pattern is similar. The main reform in birth planning was to reduce the rate, and this began for local reasons before reforms were announced. The early 1970s saw a very sharp national decline in comparison with births in the decade after 1978, when the rate fluctuated about a flat low level.[52] In 1969 and 1970, births were 34 and 33 per thousand people, respectively. By 1976 and 1977, they had fallen sharply to 20 and 19, respectively — a drop of 14 points in about 7 years. But after 1978, the figure varied only slightly: it was up to 21 in 1982 and 1987, down to a low of 17.5 in 1984. These post-1978 changes were far less than in the early 1970s. Since lowering the birth rate and keeping it down is the main reform, the early 1970s qualify as reform years at least as well as do the years after 1978. In the first period, natality dropped; in the second, it was held fairly stable.

Reforms have depressed the birth rate in cities because of campaigns and because some women have more diverse career possibilities, and especially more education, than in the past. A counterforce to these factors is the broader prosperity, which allows parents to support children more easily. Official demographic projections in 1985 "aimed at" a Shanghai population of 13 million by 2000 — but a total of 14 million had already been reached by 1990.[53] The extent to which planners affected the behaviour of Shanghai's legally resident population is moot, because these permanent Shanghailanders had many unofficial reasons to control their own fertility. And among others, especially the unregistered, cadres had less influence.

In particular, birth control became practically impossible to enforce among migrant workers, especially suburban farm workers:[54]

> Recently [1989], many people from Jiangsu, Anhui and Shandong have come to Shanghai seeking jobs because they were impoverished back home. After they got a female baby, they still wanted a male baby. Many had two children or more.... Some couples came to farm, so as to avoid the local urban government's birth control. Almost all these workers had one or more "black" children [unauthorized by the state]. Because the workers migrated, it was difficult for leaders on suburban farms to carry out the birth control policy among them. Some cadres were aware of this problem and wanted to adopt effective methods; but if so, the workers just floated to other places. Workers would move repeatedly until they had a male baby.

Women who migrated to Shanghai, especially those who came illegally, were difficult subjects for birth control campaigns. They "generally had little education; 13% were illiterate, although 47% had been to middle schools ... 40% had lived in the city for more than five months. They actually had become Shanghai 'residents'. About half of these women were engaged in economic activity. Many women thought that if they could make money and could pay their over-quota birth fines, they could have more children."[55] Monetary penalties for extra births unintentionally made wealth the new key to success for parents who wanted a traditionally large Chinese family. Illegal immigrants to Shanghai often made better incomes than state employees in the late 1980s and early 1990s. "The local [district and street] governments where they lived could not manage them because they were in Shanghai, and the offices had no information about them.... As a matter of fact, they were free to have more children."

Especially in rural areas, cadres put themselves in danger, if they tried to enforce the one-child policy without concern for the interests of very local networks. A survey of the causes of peasant attacks on local cadres during the late 1980s in twelve towns of Suining 睢寧 county, Jiangsu, showed that almost one-third were directly caused by contraception and abortion policies. Resentment about birth control was even more important, as a reason for these physical attacks against officials, than taxes and other imposts.[56] Reports of such violence come from rural areas, not cities, but they are sufficiently frequent to show that insensitive birth planning could threaten the very lives of the officials who tried to implement it. In some cases, cadres or their whole families (especially their sons) were murdered by peasants who were infuriated by this policy. A survey of Jiangsu, published in 1988, linked 32% of violent crime in one rural area to family planning.[57]

A more usual local response to unpopular birth control in both rural and urban areas was evasion. "Extra-birth guerrilla bands" (*chaosheng youjidui* 超生游擊隊), comprising both pregnant mothers and illegal midwives, often could "move to another town for births" (*yixiang shengyu* 異鄉生育). State cadres stood scant chance of catching up with this "underground railway." The availability of women's jobs in collective and private firms reduced the state's influence over them — while also reducing their motives to have children quickly. Many, nonetheless, resisted abortions, on their own or their husbands' wishes or both. As one official put it, "Few rural women agree to have abortions, and many who do first put up a strong fight." The reasons were apparently traditional or practical — invasive medical procedures are unpleasant and can be dangerous — but they were seldom religious in any other sense. A birth control cadre reported, "If women know we are coming, they frequently run away. Usually they come back at night. As a result, a lot of my visits take place after hours. Even then, they sometimes run away." Mothers-in-law tended to be strongly pro-natalist, telling officials to "mind their own business."[58]

Government pressure sometimes succeeded in rural areas, but ex-farm families whose incomes were rising had scant obvious interest in the official logic that birth control was needed for economic growth — even when, for their own reasons, they had fewer children. Some aspects of what they did clearly violated official policies, and it seems sensible to end this subsection with the most heinous of these: In China as a whole, birth planning and traditional prejudice clearly reduced the life expectancy of infant girls. Although almost identical infant mortalities were reported for boys and girls in 1978, the death rate for infant girls by 1984 was double that for boys. The mortality of Chinese boy babies in 1978 was 3.68%, and of girls, 3.77%; but by 1984, the male figure was 3.39%, and for female infants, 6.72%.[59] Less parental care for female than for male babies may have been more important than infanticide in producing this result, but girls perished nonetheless. This was a reform — a local one — and it shows an uncivil, unarticulated aspect of the process. Its causes, like those of the fertility decline, did not all come from the government.

Liaisons between Companies

The central state's interests and families' interests do not cover the whole political context of population change during China's reforms. Mid-level institutions, especially burgeoning rural nonstate firms, had strong financial stakes in patterns of both net population increase and net migration. They created whole new hierarchies of local political networks throughout China in the 1970s and 1980s. It may at first seem strange to consider these linkages alongside the more familiar demographic discourse about state intentions (which are propagated widely) and family intentions (which drive birth and residence decisions more obviously). A closer look will show that mid-level nonstate economic institutions constrained both the state and families during China's reforms.

By the early 1970s, rural communes and brigades in Shanghai's suburban Jiading 嘉定 county had already organized "trans-unit alliances" for economic co-operation.[60] This pattern spread, though in periods of supremacy for political radicals it was not reported, in later reform years too. For example, the Shanghai Industrial Consulting Service Company was set up by 1979 to help suburban plants co-operate with urban factories. Because it was subject to taxes and controls typical of all Shanghai companies, it soon ran into problems.[61] A sample survey of the company's transactions, nonetheless, determined that, "Every *yuan* spent in consulting fees by technology buyers enabled them to create 489 *yuan* worth of industrial output value per year. There were no specific rules, however, on the remuneration of the technicians who moonlighted and provided consulting services in their spare time." When the company clamped down for the moonlighters, "Many of them quit." The state could no longer control people as in the past — either where they lived or how they worked.

In 1984, 90% of the companies established jointly between Shanghai and suburban firms were producing light industrial products, especially textiles.[62] The greater availability of space in the suburbs was one reason why urban enterprises expanded there. But this was also a flight from the city's intensive bureaucratic monitoring — in particular, its control of wages. Most jobs in Shanghai suburban factories licensed at the village level and below, in the late 1980s, were held by unregistered and illegal immigrants. Village-run (*cunban* 村辦) Jiading firms so often hired outside workers that 90% of the labour force in some of their factories came from Anhui or Jiangxi.[63] Through out-contracting and other arrangements, this was a highly exploitive low-wage and low-tax environment, in which enterprises flourished. With nonstate agents creating so many new jobs, officials had less control of population size.

Suzhou 蘇州 leaders reported that 80% of the firms in their prefecture had Shanghai connections for raw materials or marketing. Three-quarters of the value of Suzhou's production by the late 1980s was made or sold under arrangements with firms in Shanghai.[64] The non-Suzhou capital that came to such projects was nearly half of their total assets.[65] In Wuxi 無錫 , one-third of the township enterprises were joint with Shanghai factories, schools, or research units. Nonetheless, competition was forcing even state firms to develop such ties. The number of large Shanghai firms with registered horizontal relations was 37% more in 1987 than in 1986. Joint registrations with other units inside the municipality were up 18%; and with other provinces, up 43%.[66] If medium-sized Shanghai industrial enterprises are counted along with large ones, more than 90% have subsidiaries or special relations with factories in other East China cities.[67] Personnel shifts between co-operating businesses were easy to justify.

Some such links were "arranged marriages," under which firms were "ordered to liaise."[68] A Shanghai vegetable market, for example, was mandated to join with an inland trading company in setting up a new hotel. But such negotiations were all between bureaucrats above the levels of these two units — and in such cases, the Shanghai partners were reported to disbelieve the link would be profitable. In this case, higher officials ordered them to accept the proposal anyway. Business proved to be bad, and the joint firm lost money. Local managers wanted more powers to shift their employees from place to place.

In other cases, such marriages were between eager partners — even when supervising bureaucrats disapproved. A Shanghai textile plant wanted to extend technical help to a shirt factory elsewhere, but the supervising garment company vetoed this proposal.[69] The liaison may have been realized quietly through trade anyway. Links were not publicized when they stirred opposition. So fully comprehensive statistics on Shanghai connections elsewhere are unavailable. No one could keep tabs on all the links in Jiangnan — presumably because so many managers of small communities had major interests in hiding these ties, which then could not be taxed. At least 800 specific connections between Shanghai and Hangzhou 杭州 firms in 1987 can be documented, nonetheless. Between Shanghai and Jiaxing in Zhejiang, at least 200 such links were registered; and many of these were not with Jiaxing city as a whole, but with counties or townships there.[70] Horizontal liaisons of this sort slowly restructured the labour market of East China.

This effect on population arose from state planners' decreasing ability to enforce socialism. When industrial bureaux in Shanghai found it difficult to deliver materials at low state prices, horizontal "enterprise groups" began to form. Shifting industries out of Shanghai helped to solve the problems of materials planners. This trend took jobs away from Shanghai workers, while providing jobs for suburban immigrants and others. There was resistance, and it was sometimes expressed:

> The effort has been merely confined to know-how transfer and granting use of [Shanghai] trade marks by local factories.... The factories in interior regions, which are supposed to be members of the Shanghai-based enterprise groups, actually work in the interest of the localities. In this way, Shanghai has only fostered competitors for its industry, contrary to the original intention of making the best use of raw materials locally.[71]

The economies of Shanghai and its delta became more intertwined. All major South Jiangsu cities had Shanghai connections at this time, and together they prospered. In the first nine months of 1986, Shanghai invested RMB850 million in 63 joint projects, to make a total by that time of 507 endeavours in "fraternal regions" (*xiongdi diqu* 兄弟地區). Many Shanghai factories developed profitable relations with similar plants in South Jiangsu.[72] North Zhejiang cities also had long-standing connections with prominent people in Shanghai. Business people from that province had enormous influence in pre-1949 Shanghai, and this situation did not change suddenly at mid-century.[73] In early 1989, nine "Shanghai people with Ningbo 寧波 origins" set up the Shanghai Association to Promote Ningbo Economic Construction, which was non-governmental.[74]

Local notables and centralist reformers alike found these traditional ties useful, but for very different reasons. Just as "administrative cities" were the reformers' recipe for circumventing old conflicts between geographical jurisdictions, "enterprise groups" became another way to change the structure of arthritic bureaucracies. Such change could at once weaken the autonomy both of the central state and of most individuals, while increasing the power of mid-level institutions. As with the "administrative cities" that centralized locally by taking over nearby geographical areas, "enterprise groups" assumed powers in fields that had once been subject to ministerial' plans. Reforms brought new revenues, but not for the central state. The coteries behind them were local leaders, who often had many kinds of affective ties to each other. These leaders were concerned with population issues, but they had post-revolutionary aims: to lower socialist welfare and tax costs their enterprises might have to pay, to assure that labour remained cheap, and to maintain whatever degree of broad political stability or instability to keep both high state bureaucrats and ordinary workers most malleable.

The new taipans did not mince words in presenting their demands. They wanted CCP regulators off their backs, and this required "opening the road of genuinely separating two powers," so as to clarify "the administrative subordination [*sic*] of Party and mass organizations in enterprises." They demanded the right to "participate in formulating plans." They wanted "to reduce the scope of mandatory planning and gradually to turn mandatory quotas into placing state orders." They claimed freedom from short-term checks by supervising cadres, so that they could "make independent decisions on investment." They further demanded rights to "establish connections directly with foreign counterparts" and with other parts of China.[75] They were interested in birth control among their own female employees, to reduce welfare costs. Hiring inexpensive and loyal labour was high among their priorities, no matter whether the workers were migrants.

The Shanghai Economic Zone

The central state attempted to organize, as a large unit, the main watershed whence this labour force came. The Shanghai Economic Zone had many precedents. Historically, during the 1950s, the East China Economic Co-ordination Zone (*Huadong jingji xiezuo qu* 華東經濟協作區) was one of several organizations that Chen Yi's field army bequeathed to the region. In July 1957, the Shanghai Party called a conference "on economic co-ordination for the provinces of Jiangsu, Zhejiang, Anhui, Fujian 福建, Jiangxi and Shanghai."[76] Already by 1970, the national planning system was decentralized, so that the civilian state plan was merely the sum of separate plans for "co-operation regions" (*xiezuo qu* 合作區). These worked inde-pendently of each other.[77] Interprovincial co-operation flourished in some fields during the early 1970s — even though it was often opposed by radicals in the central government. Eight counties around the geographical point joining Shanghai, Jiangsu and Zhejiang, for example, co-operated then in a local campaign against liver fluke. Radicals reportedly "struggled against" the regional anti-schistosomiasis campaign — which violated their stress on autarkic self-reliance. Regional cadres, nonetheless, called meetings even when higher authorities sent down directives to quash such activities, and they decided to continue the campaign anyway.[78]

Co-operation among local units, especially among these eight counties in the early 1970s, extended to many fields. Economic zones then became an official fad in China from the end of 1978, when the Third Plenum established three zones in Guangdong 廣東 and one in Fujian. But for Shanghai, the premier tax-paying city, Beijing's 北京 approval of such plans was delayed despite their local popularity. As two Shanghai econ-omists pointed out, the delta covers one of the richest and most densely populated parts of China. They called for something better than the old "co-operation zones" of the 1950s.[79] These reformers called for "breaking through provincial boundaries," so that areas could "both join together and compete."[80] From 1980, Shanghai Mayor Wang Daohan 汪道涵 began to hold regular joint meetings with the governors of Jiangsu and Zhejiang provinces and the mayors of Changzhou 常州, Hangzhou, Jiaxing, Ningbo, Shaoxing 紹興, Suzhou and Wuxi. An office for the Shanghai Economic Zone emerged as the secretariat of these sessions, although it never acquired the authority to countermand provincial or municipal cadres. It existed only to co-ordinate them, when they could agree.

By 1981, "more than one hundred experts" got together in Wuxi to confer on unified planning for the Shanghai delta. The Shanghai Social Sciences Academy established a research group to make a detailed report. On 19 May 1982, *Wenhui News* announced the founding of an organization to reconcile the economic plans of "the Yangzi River Delta, mainly in the Shanghai–Nanjing and Hangzhou areas." At this early date, North Jiangsu and South Zhejiang were already omitted. This initiative originated from Jiangnan leaders, even though Zhao Ziyang 趙紫陽 became interested in it.[81] On 7 October 1982, Zhao proposed a Shanghai economic area to overcome the "separation of horizontal from vertical management" (*tiaokuai fenge* 條塊分割). On 22 December, the Cabinet approved the Zone involving nine cities.[82] This regionalization did not increase the powers of the central state. It legitimized local power networks that took decisions about investment and jobs — and thus also about long-term migration and population change.

In January 1983, the Planning Office of the Shanghai Economic Zone formally announced the start of its work, which had actually begun before then. The Zone in this early, compact form consisted of ten cities (the Cabinet-approved nine — plus Shaoxing in Zhejiang, a quintessential Jiangnan place that the State Council had left out), along with all fifty-five counties that had been formally placed under their municipal administrations, covering the whole delta.[83] Although this zone comprised just 0.7% of China's land area and had only 2.7% of the country's arable land, its population (50 million then) was about 5% of the nation. These are small percentages; but the compact Shanghai Economic Zone in 1984 produced about one-third of China's textiles, one-fourth of its machines, and one-fifth of its chemicals. Rural industries already accounted for 16% of the zone's total output value and a much higher portion of the nation's total product from rural factories.[84] The whole delta became a magnet for immigration — i.e., for people who left poorer provinces that most Beijing conservatives still wanted Shanghai to support more directly.

Soon a central announcement of the Shanghai Economic Zone's "readjustment" (expansion) came, at a late 1984 symposium, to discuss strategy for the development of agriculture. A member of the Central Advisory Commission, Zhang Pinghua, said that Shanghai should "set an example in modernizing agriculture.... This is its bounden duty and is expected by the people."[85] One analysis distinguished Shanghai's relations to nearby areas (which involved extensive professional co-operation) and its links to more distant areas (which involved more extraction of raw materials and young people).[86] The newly enlarged Shanghai Economic Zone by 1985 was divided into first and second "layers" (*cengci* 層次). The "first layer" was Jiangnan (the Yangzi River Delta or *Changjiang sanjiaozhou* 長江三角洲), comprising Shanghai as well as Jiangsu's cities of

Changzhou, Nantong 南通, Suzhou and Wuxi (though not, in this case, the provincial capital of Nanjing) and Zhejiang's cities of Hangzhou, Huzhou 湖州, Jiaxing, Ningbo and Shaoxing. The "second layer" comprised the rest of Zhejiang and Jiangsu (including its relatively poor northern half) — and all of Anhui and Jiangxi provinces.[87] The two sub-zone "layers" within the expanded zone were evident to all, and the flat delta was the richer part.[88]

This expanded economic zone was much less coherent than the previous version. It had a population of 200 million, or 19% of China's people. At mid-decade, the large area's industrial and agricultural output value was 29% of China's total.[89] Especially in fields involving modern technology, competition between cities for investment was sharp. The viability of each Shanghai-inland connection depended on the particular proposal, whether individuals or large jurisdictions were more decisive in financing it, and the extent to which benefits would go to the active participants. Provincial governments, in particular, did not easily cooperate. "In terms of ecology, artificial boundaries within the delta have led to bad results, and these borders make it impossible to have a unified plan."[90] Specific evidence suggests that provincial authorities in Nanjing were less eager for close co-operation with Shanghai than were many entrepreneurs closer to the metropolis in southern Jiangsu. Province-level control of births or migration — or any other activity — became less effective than before. County and township controls became relatively more effective.

For example, by the early 1990s, a "Sunan development area" (蘇南發達地區) was defined by Nanjing provincial authorities as excluding (though bordered by) Shanghai.[91] But these boundaries ignored connections that Jiangnan people actually had. Local ties between individuals and networks spread readily across the Shanghai–Jiangsu border (whose current location is an administrative whim no more ancient than 1959). Like the Shanghai Economic Zone in its expanded form, this development area was officially declared — and then in practice mostly ignored.

High officials in provinces, as in Beijing, evinced fluctuating notions of what the Shanghai Economic Zone should be. What happened showed their considerable irrelevance. After 1984, especially in 1986, Shanghai's trade with Jiangsu and Zhejiang accelerated quickly — at 40% to 60% per year, according to the estimate of one economist interviewee. Business people could interpret official mandates in whatever ways would serve themselves, and they could get like-minded government offices to support them. Companies that stood to benefit were the main initiators of horizontal liaisons. The Shanghai Light Industrial Machines Corporation spurred links in particular with three counties of Jiangsu. Its "one city, three counties" committee in the mid-1980s involved this Shanghai corporation with counterparts in Wuxi, Shazhou 沙洲 and Wujin 武進 .[92] Such organization was novel, at least as a publicized model, because it was co-ordinated at the company and county levels. Each of the units was under a different mid-level jurisdiction, and horizontal links could be forged between them without regard to administrative boundaries. The plan for the Shanghai Economic Zone was reformulated in 1987, but it remained long-term and vague. Shanghai was designated in Cabinet documents as the centre of the region, and closer co-operation among all units was mandated "by 1990."[93] The central treasury wanted to protect an important tax base; but it had insufficient resources to assure this with a mandatory plan. "Harmonization" in East China, if centrally mandated, did not work well because that kind of harmony mainly meant taxes. Local harmonization, outside the central system, worked well because it was based on pre-existing connections between individual local élites throughout Jiangnan.

In several Chinese regions, areas centred around large cities were dubbed "comprehensive economic zones" (*zonghe jingji qu* 綜合經濟區), supposed to develop all kinds of goods and services. But the Guangdong and Fujian special areas were "sectoral economic zones" (*bumen jingji qu* 部門經濟區), in these cases specializing in foreign trade.[94] Beijing's concept of "comprehensive economic zones" had a great weakness. The head offices of "sectoral economic zones" were supposed to have powers to plan in a definitive, mandatory way for the production of the goods in which they specialized. But the head offices of comprehensive economic zones could only "harmonize (*xietiao* 協調) relations between other agencies," including provincial jurisdictions.[95] If one province leadership preferred not to co-operate, on any issue, the comprehensive zone could not easily bring it into line.

The Shanghai Economic Zone was very comprehensive, even though it was (unlike the comprehensive zones centred around Wuhan 武漢 or Chongqing 重慶) also coastal. It was supposed to attract foreign capital, but still had to pay higher remittances and taxes than places in sectoral zones further south, where foreigners could invest instead. Its office was established only in the weak, "comprehensive" mode. This zone survived formally, but its name was mainly raised at junkets and conferences. In April 1988, a delegation from the Shanghai Economic Zone visited Hong

Kong to strengthen co-operation in electronics, computers, textiles, toys, microwave ovens and sound equipment. By this time, Hong Kong had infused US$440,000 into Shanghai — a total that was second only to the American investment there, but which then remained quite small.[96] Shanghai soon attracted far more money, as Pudong 浦東 and other projects developed; but this was scarcely connected to the enlarged zone that central planners preferred.

Neither the Shanghai Economic Zone nor the Pudong Development Zone were ever dubbed "special" (*tebie* 特別) like Shenzhen 深圳, despite hopes among local entrepreneurs that they might become so. Shanghai firms received few import or export tariff preferences, few national subsidies to start new industries, and few lower taxes (these remained high) except when such benefits could be arranged on a project-by-project basis. If there had been anything "special" about the Shanghai Economic Zone, it might have lasted as an organization. After mid-1988, the Zone had no permanent organization. As a central project, it never got off the ground — but in the minds of many local entrepreneurs, its early compact form was a natural unit anyway. This zone did not die with fanfare; it simply faded away.[97] Yet interprovincial migration rose quickly with the economic boom. Local, not central, decisions quickened the creation of jobs. Linked industries on the whole Shanghai delta attracted labour of all kinds, both cheap and expensive.

Media Liaisons

Symbolic structures, not just economic structures, inform what people do. From the viewpoint of prospective emigrants from provinces like Anhui or Henan 河南, the attractions of the delta surely included hopes of higher income. International experience, based on ex-peasant urban immigration in other Third World nations, nonetheless suggests that the change to city lifestyles may not have been an independently crucial factor in decisions to migrate. Farmers leave fields throughout the world to make higher urban incomes; but they tend to replicate their rural environments in city slums, send remittances home, and retire back to the countryside as soon as possible.

The Chinese case may be somewhat atypical of this normal pattern, for two reasons: First, the portion of China's population in medium-sized cities is exceptionally great, as compared with other countries. Migrants to the metropolis and nearby places very often came from smaller cities, rather than directly from rural villages. Second, many immigrants during the reform period had been sent-down youths during the Cultural Revolution, or people who before migration had close contact with these previously urban people. They wanted life in larger settlements, and they heard about it largely through electronic media.

Extension of broadcasting affects individual and family migration decisions, although firm evidence to prove this link is less handy than for the migration effects of job creation. Media regionalization by itself is easy to show. Shanghai's direct television audience now extends throughout East China. That big city's broadcasting network had more radio frequencies, more television channels, more programmes, and more varieties of them than any other place in the country by the mid-1980s.[98] Programmes are transmitted from the metropolis directly to the city-run (as distinct from the central) stations of many provinces. This situation emerged rather quickly. By 1984, Shanghai's two city-run TV channels aired thirty hours of broadcasts daily; and Shanghai programmes were sent by microwave to stations covering all of Jiangsu and Zhejiang, as well as much of Anhui and Jiangxi.[99] With the leverage of microwave transmission and amplification through the broadcasting antennae of about thirty East China cities, these programmes spread very widely.

Provincial governments had been centrally mandated to invest in microwave equipment to connect all major cities in the region, originally with the aim of distributing programmes from Beijing. But according to Shanghai officials, central bureaucrats now regret having pressed for this, because the same equipment sends the livelier output of the Shanghai TV station. Local stations, administered by cities, can normally choose to broadcast what they wish. Many have close relations with the Shanghai city-run station, which provides many of their programmes.

In particular, Shanghai provides news items for other East China municipal stations. For example, when a story about police breaking a criminal case arose in Zhenjiang 鎮江 , Jiangsu, the local authorities telephoned Shanghai's TV station directly, asking it to send a crew for the scoop. Zhenjiang is much closer to Nanjing's provincial newscasters; Shanghai is about four times farther away. When Shanghai TV officials were asked whether this kind of incident made cadres at the Jiangsu Provincial Station angry, the answer was that it did. But even within Nanjing, the surveyed audience for Shanghai TV newscasts (carried over the city-run station there) is greater than that for the provincial station.[100] By 1988, extensive co-operation between Shanghai and other places in

East China was formalized for the purpose of sharing news stories. Thirty-one TV stations, all run by cities outside the central system, joined to form a "Shanghai News Centre" (*Shanghai xinwen zhongxin* 上海新聞中心) which covered all parts of the Shanghai Economic Zone. Officials of the Shanghai station said they were merely providing "what people want."

Reporting in the East China region is not split between provinces, so that people moving throughout this area have the same sources of information. For example, the Zhejiang provincial station produced a programme of "Economic News," which summarized highlights from about eight journals (not limited to those published in Zhejiang). The Shanghai station had a "Selections from Publications" programme that collected stories from any of 90 newspapers or 120 magazines, to disseminate not just economic information but also news of politics, culture and new techniques.[101] More evidence would be required to show that the changing cultural horizons of migrants was a "pull" factor in their decisions to move. Clearly the marketing of popular music in new styles, the quick expansion of advertising (which was inaugurated on PRC television in Shanghai in January 1979), and similar invasions of modern culture expanded very rapidly inland during reform.[102]

Immigrants and Birth Control

Many migrants to Shanghai had actually lived there before. In a large sample of people whose registrations between 1950 and 1985 had been moved out of Shanghai, 62% had returned by the mid-1980s. Fully 91% of those who left to join the Army were back in the metropolis. So were 69% of those who had gone for "adjusted" work assignments elsewhere. Among those who had left Shanghai "going up to the mountains and down to the villages," fully 66% had come back by the mid-1980s.[103]

Many immigrants in the 1980s were children of sent-down Shanghai parents — who, nonetheless, remained outside the metropolis. Three-generation families, in which the middle generation was absent and the youngest generation immigrant, were rather common. Two-thirds of permanently registered immigrants to Shanghai were aged 15 to 29, and three-quarters were unmarried.[104] Many obtaining legal registrations were of school age. Over three-fifths of all migrants registered as temporary in Shanghai in the mid-1980s were either children or, in even more cases, grandchildren of the household head.[105] The grandchildren were proportionally more than the children, especially among grandsons. Many of their parents had apparently been "educated youths," sent down in previous years. These ex-Shanghai parents remained away, but returned the youngest generation there in the 1980s to live in the grandparents' households and to attend urban schools.

Young legal migrants of this and other kinds were fertile or soon became so. When the immigrants were registered, however, they tended to be relatively vulnerable to the state's late-marriage and one-child policies — and legal residence in the city conferred some entitlement to regular careers, which may have delayed marriages and births. Many of the legal immigrants came from relatively educated backgrounds, so that social causes separate from state policy lowered their birth rates in comparison with others in young age cohorts. But legal immigration was, after the mid-1980s, not the only sort. Only registered arrivals are reported on Table 17.1. But after 1987–1988, unregistered migrants became a much larger portion of the total influx.

By 1987, migrants already comprised one-fifth of the population in China's twenty-four largest cities — and probably more than that in the built-up parts of Shanghai.[106] In the urban districts of that metropolis, according to an early 1989 estimate, one of every four persons lacked permanent household registration.[107] Towards the beginning of the 1990s, diverse reports from Shanghai suggest that one-fifth of the people were migrants; but these guesses may be somewhat low. Comprehensive and comparable figures from many cities have not yet been found for later years, but Shanghai sources indicate that, by 1994, the city's "floating population" was 3.3 million.[108] Over one-quarter of Shanghai's whole population were recent migrants by the mid-1990s.

The unregistered portion — i.e., those who had no employers to arrange documents — was quickly rising in most Shanghai delta cities.[109] Working-age persons (ages 15 to 59) in a 1988 census of migrants made up 81%. Three-fifths were males, if men were not more fully reported than women, who more often tended to work individually. More surprising, only a slight majority of the immigrants (52%) lived in designated urban districts. Almost half lived in the delta's green areas, which are called "rural" despite high population densities and newly booming industries. Household control in these places was less strict than in formally urban districts, where many of the migrants commuted for work.

These migrants tended to be young and fertile, and most had some previous schooling. Illiterates and semi-illiterates comprised only 15% of the incoming migrant total, while those with middle school educations were 45% (and with university educations, 2% higher than among legal permanent residents). These immigrants, self-reporting their former occupations, were 48% "farmers" probably including previous workers in factories run by rural units, 15% workers, 8% technicians, 4% businesspeople, 3% cadres and 20% unemployed. Many worked in construction and transport. Of the women, 51% were married. Fully 68% were of child-bearing ages; 24% had actually given birth to babies in Shanghai, and another 5% were pregnant during this 1988 survey. At least 14% of the total floating population worked as domestics, apparently full-time. One-third of the floaters came from Jiangsu, and over half hailed from either Jiangsu or Zhejiang.[110]

In the 1990s, immigration soared. A 1993 survey suggested that one of every six people in Shanghai had "recently arrived" from rural areas. This immigrant labour force was said to number 2.5 million, but only three-fifths had reliable jobs. On most days, one million had to look for new temporary jobs on most days. Immigrants with steady work tended to come from other places in the Shanghai delta. As a construction team chief from Jiangsu said, "We hire workers from our home town and from neighbouring towns, so that we can be sure of their credibility."[111] Apparently a majority of the others, coming largely from Anhui, Henan, Jiangxi and Sichuan 四川 , took Shanghai jobs without any kind of residence permit, not even temporary cards. They were breaking the law. More practically, they lacked any medical or injury benefits — and they often did dangerous construction or stevedoring work.

Women's Careers in Shanghai

Practically no immigrant women who became pregnant could hold jobs in large units. Many took up individual work, selling food on the streets, repairing clothes, or picking rubbish. Women domestic workers came especially from Anhui. Already in the 1970s, they had organized a house-maids' union informally called the "Anhui group." Inland authorities were so perturbed by the exodus, which reduced both economic production and political control in their areas, they prevailed on the Shanghai government to ship migrants back to Anhui by train.[112] Domestic helpers and family relatives, however, were generally welcomed by Shanghai residents, even if bureaucrats could not monitor their goings and comings. About three-fifths of Shanghai's temporary migrants, according to a mid-1980s study, lived in the households of permanent residents.[113] Without households of their own, their fertility may have been lower than average for their ages. But many raised Shanghai's population directly, by migrating there without state approval.

Some in the floating population gave birth illegally. Among those who did so in Shanghai, "13% had two children, and 4% had three or more." Despite this, the migrants were often seen as helping to construct a modern metropolis. "Without them, it would be difficult to imagine so many new buildings in today's Shanghai. A quarter million labourers from other places work in the textile industry and in environmental sanitation...."[114] Migrant proletarians, even if they lived under extraordinarily cramped conditions, were often in their own "communities outside the system" (*tizhi wai qunluo* 體制外群落). The central system did not control this population.

Shanghai contains a higher portion of women (49.68% by 1987) than any other Chinese province.[115] Women also comprise a greater portion of state workers in Shanghai than in any other Chinese province, as Table 17.3 indicates. Many of their jobs, e.g., in textile mills, are menial; but female participation in paid work correlates by province highly with

Table 17.3   Portions of Women among Employees in Chinese Provinces, 1985

(Unit: %)

Place	%	Place	%	Place	%
Shanghai	41.8	Heilong'g	37.6	Guizhou	33.9
Tianjin	41.8	Fujian	36.0	Yunnan	32.9
Liaoning	40.9	Hunan	35.7	Shaanxi	32.7
Beijing	40.7	Sichuan	35.6	Shandong	32.4
Xinjiang	39.7	In. Mong.	35.5	Henan	32.3
Jilin	39.1	Jiangxi	35.1	Qinghai	32.1
Zhejiang	38.8	Tibet	34.7	Hebei	32.0
Hubei	38.2	Guangxi	34.6	Gansu	31.1
Guangdong	37.8	Anhui	34.3	Shanxi	30.4
Jiangsu	37.7	Ningxia	34.2	Nat'l Av.	36.4

Source: "Employees" (*zhigong* 職工) refer mostly to staff and workers of enterprises; peasants and shepherds are not included. The index on this table correlates with many other indices of modernization, including urbanization and per-capita wealth. Put in order from data in Guojia tongjiju (ed.), *Zhongguo tongji nianjian 1986* (Statistical Yearbook of China 1986) (Beijing: Zhongguo tongji chubanshe, 1986), p. 135. The three East China provinces of major interest in this book are bold. Note that an ideal feminist rate, for this index, would be near 50%; but only the four most urbanized provinces registered over 40%.

per-capita wealth.[116] Shanghai, northern Zhejiang, and southern Jiangsu form the most populous region in China with high rates of working women.

Women workers had always been crucial in socialist mechanisms that accumulated capital for the state. Many women had jobs at low wages in state light-industrial and retail firms that generated revenue for Beijing's coffers. Although surprisingly little capital was put into such firms, these plants expanded on the basis of cheap urban labour (and mandated sales of low-priced agricultural inputs). Nationally, by the late 1980s there were almost fifty times as many woman workers in state industry as in 1949. Even after the nationalizations of the mid-fifties, the number of women in state industries went up eleven times by the late 1980s.[117] Having babies was not these women's main official job.

When they had offspring as well as official jobs, the state spent some money to free them from child care and keep them at work. Educational budgets were severely strained after the mid-1980s. Kindergartens, however, were supported by high-level budgets in the late 1980s, because state-owned enterprises needed the mothers' time for work. The Shanghai Education Bureau, with its local agencies, still ran institutions for 59% of the children aged 4 to 6. Of the others, 27% were cared for in collectives.[118] Reforms brought changes to Shanghai's large female work force, because nonstate factories elsewhere pre-empted raw materials Shanghai state light industries used to process. When the state sector slowed down, women were often the first to be laid off payrolls. "These women have to return from society to family, although they are reluctant to do so."

Many were well qualified to work. A 1989 survey in downtown Huangpu 黄浦 found that 87% of unemployed women were aged 40 or less, and 91% had at least middle school education. "They came home because there was not enough work to do.... Ms. Zhong was employed in a processing factory before she had a baby. Because she gave birth, she had to leave the plant temporarily and she received 80% of her wage. But after March [1989], she will only receive 60%." Short-term absences could thus turn into long-term unemployment. "The baby is growing up, and she wants to return to work. But she is not fortunate enough to go back, or even to get a temporary job. The living standard of this new generation of housewives is clearly decreasing." So many women,

> had to do other businesses without official registration.... Some sold every-
> day commodities in the streets. Most such women have a strong desire to go

back to work. But their old enterprises have no capacity to absorb them, for reasons such as insufficient tasks, financial losses and a surplus of labour. How should we deal with these unemployed women? Do they want to be housewives forever?[119]

Some women's rights that had been normalized in Maoist state plants became weaker during reforms because of state deficits. Pregnancy leave was controversial because of its cost to state enterprises. In 1981, under Shanghai's birth control regulations, pregnancy leave was just 15 days; and women's salaries even in rich plants were reduced by 20% during leaves.[120] Sometimes the arguments for pregnancy leave were justified by an idea that men and women have a social "division of labour."[121]

The portion of women among Shanghai's scientific workers decreased somewhat during reforms, from 36% in 1978 to 34% in 1983. This fall-off may not seem large, but the number of people involved (a total of 320,000 specialists by 1983) was great, and there was increasing competition for such jobs. The trend is especially surprising in light of high turnover rates among scientific professionals during the same years. So even in modern Shanghai, the PRC state tended to sponsor a Stalinist vision of womanhood for legally registered urban women whom it could no longer employ.

Production and reproduction were both honoured. Some Shanghai women who distinguished themselves in both professional and household work during the late 1980s received the title of "Three-Eight Red Flag Holder."[122] Reform deficits gave the state an interest in occupying women within families. This was not entirely consonant with ideas about low fertility. But ideas, even though intellectuals and officials stress them, have never been efficacious separate from practical constraints.

Conclusion: Population as People, Not Mainly Policy

Some achievements of Mao's communitarian policies were retained, as reform-era individualism swept the country. But these policies, and the controls that went with them, were gradually supplanted by markets. In important areas (including primary education and public health), they partially receded. State efforts at population planning showed the extent of what a late-revolutionary regime can do. Propaganda for birth control was partly effective as a response to extreme crowding over limited resources, but it was also an official excuse for bad economic management.[123] In Shanghai, it helped create many one-child families.

Since both urban parents often had jobs, their child would be left in a nursery or kindergarten, or with a grandmother or an amah (usually a peasant woman with far less education than the parents, sometimes in the city for long periods but without household registration). Child neglect was an occasional possibility under these circumstances. A much greater danger, given the strength of Chinese families, was that single children would be overindulged, treated like "little emperors" (*xiao huangdi* 小皇帝) or princesses. Chinese writers on this subject express a keen sense that today's children will become the adults who will decide the community's future. Not just lineages, but also the nation as a whole, depend on the quality of the upbringing that children have. Parents and officials alike during reform years have shown great concern that the "little emperor" phenomenon and the low moral tone set by the Cultural Revolution pose dangers to the future of China.

This concern was itself a reform. It made increasing numbers of middle-income urban parents demand a great deal from their children (at least after babyhood, when by tradition children are coddled unrelentingly). Grades in school became in many families the overwhelming micropolitical issue. Some factories and residence committees subsidize "schools for household heads" (*jiazhang xuexiao* 家長學校), which parents and grandparents attend to learn more about raising children and to discuss perennially difficult issues such as corporal punishment. This syndrome is not just a product of population policy, but it is a correlate of many elements that include the low birth rate. City population size is, to urban politicians, an abstraction. But Shanghai's leaders since 1949 have known that the general malleability or resistance of people to official mandates has been politically important. Intellectuals generally speak of population policy as if its centre were fertility control — rather than a combination of that factor with many others, including migration controls, job distribution, the availability of housing and of schools and hospitals, as well as the extent to which state funds go to general welfare rather than to politically exclusive groups. The relevant politics are now becoming more local, and the effects of official fertility campaigns are probably less than those of many other correlated factors in determining population size.

Pressures on individuals to succeed in densely populated, individually competitive environments, where resources are sparse relative to the number of claimants, cause most of China's politics now. People try to move to places where they can cope with these pressures. None of the problems in this huge country are completely new. Other nations as different as Japan and the United States continue to face many of the same issues. But extensive migration and the single-child policy have been major correlates of the "moral panic" in Chinese cities during reforms. Davin writes that, "China's obsessive search for the right way to educate her children reflects the much more general uncertainty with which she now faces the future."[124] This search is China's, only in the sense that many Chinese families and local networks share it at the same time as the centralist national revolution winds down. Population control as a state policy may be receding, but this does not free people from other constraints as the revolution ends.

Notes

1. Theoretical arguments for the method here can be found in Albert O. Hirschman, "Against Parsimony: Three Easy Ways of Complicating Some Categories of Economic Discourse," *Economics and Philosophy*, Vol. 1 (1985), pp. 7–21, which argues for explorations of the bases (not just the occurrence) of choice, for long-term (not short-term) analyses, and for relating explanatory logics to each other (rather than committing to just one). An earlier, similarly complicated access to another Shanghai problem is Lynn White, "The Road to Ürümchi: Approved Institutions in Search of Attainable Goals during Pre-1968 Rustication from Shanghai," *The China Quarterly*, 79 (September 1979), pp. 481–510.

2. Historical estimates vary considerably. Stanford University, China Project, *East Asia* (HRAF-29, Stanford 3) (New Haven: Human Relations Area Files, 1956), p. 91, gives Shanghai's population as follows: 1880, 129,000; 1900, 353,020; 1910, 1,185,000; 1920, 1,605,279; 1930, 3,023,111. It has estimates for 1950 and 1953 somewhat higher than those later published in the PRC. The precision of these figures is just one of their dubious points.

3. Quoted often, e.g., in Rhoads Murphey, *Shanghai: Key to Modern China* (Cambridge: Harvard University Press, 1953), pp. 27–28.

4. *Jiefang ribao* 解放日報 (Liberation Daily) (Shanghai) (hereafter cited as *JFRB*), editorial of 25 June 1954.

5. Table 17.1 shows that the 1955 removals from Shanghai were over 9% of the city's population at that time. The highest coerced evacuation rate during the Cultural Revolution was in 1970, when less than 3% had to leave. But these included more writers; so the later phenomenon is better known.

6. See Emily Honig, *Creating Chinese Ethnicity: Subei People in Shanghai, 1850–1980* (New Haven: Yale University Press, 1992).

7. *JFRB*, 24 May 1955.

8. See *New China News Agency* (Shanghai) (hereafter *NCNA*), 16 November

1955. More can be found in Christopher Howe, *Urban Employment and Economic Growth in Communist China, 1949–1957* (Cambridge: Cambridge University Press, 1971), p. 66.

9. See Lynn White, *Careers in Shanghai: The Social Guidance of Individual Energies in a Developing Chinese City* (Berkeley: University of California Press, 1978). A more recent work, taking a Foucauldian approach to household registration, is Michael Dutton, *Policing and Punishment in China: From Patriarchy to "The People"* (Cambridge: Cambridge University Press, 1992).

10. Latin Americanists reporting the lack of political demands from the slums of Lima and Mexico City have provided the best material. See works by anthropologist Oscar Lewis on Mexico and sociologist Françis Borricauld on Perú by political scientist Wayne Cornelius, "Urbanization and Political Demand Making," *American Political Science Review*, Vol. 9, No. 74 (1974), pp. 1125–46; and for theoretical background, by economist Albert Hirschmann, "Changing Tolerance for Income Inequality in the Course of Economic Development," *World Development*, Vol. 1, No. 12 (1973), pp. 24–36. Such extensive data about the political complacency of recent urban arrivals towards state officials in other developing countries should give analysts pause, before predicting quick political instability from these migrants.

11. *Xinwen ribao* 新聞日報 (News Daily) (Shanghai) (hereafter *XWRB*), 14 March 1957.

12. *XWRB*, 10 January 1958 and 18 January 1958.

13. This was 1,122 babies for 4,500 workers. See *Wen hui bao* 文匯報 (Shanghai) (hereafter *WHB*), 23 January 1958.

14. *Xinmin wanbao* 新民晚報 (New People's Evening News) (hereafter *XMWB*), 10 February 1957.

15. See Lynn White, *Careers in Shanghai* (see note 9), and for the sequel, *Policies of Chaos: The Organizational Causes of Violence in China's Cultural Revolution* (Princeton: Princeton University Press, 1989).

16. These are "crude birth rates." Demographers prefer to use "total fertility rate," which is a sum of prevailing age-specific fertilities for different cohorts of women who can bear children — but this rate has not been computed or found in publications from Shanghai. The current chapter does not pretend to be fully technical demography, although the considerations it raises about many factors that impinge on population increase should prove liable to statistical testing later.

17. Reporting is important. For example, demographers have extensive international data on a phenomenon they have not yet fully explained: Birth rates just prior to the demographic transitions in most countries seem to *rise* for a few years, just before they begin decisively to fall. Nutritional and

medical factors have not accounted for this, just as they also do not explain the later drop in fertility so well as does women's education. Schooling for females correlates with low fertility better than do occupational patterns or state birth policies, and much better than industrialization. (Some places, such as Kerala in India, are not industrialized but have much education for women —— and low birth rates.) Part of the fertility rise, before it plummets, may be a statistical mirage: The reporting of births, especially of infants who soon die, may become more reliable and comprehensive, in many countries, shortly before related factors make the birth rate drop.

18. It is tempting to think that demographic "ripples" from previous periods, notably the 1959–1961 famine, might also have effects on birth rates much later: On the usual premise that mothers' ages at first parity are in their middle or late twenties, part of the bulge in birth rates that peaked in 1982 might be ascribed to mid-1950's births of parents; and the downward trend of the late 1980s might be related to a shortage of parents born in the early 1960s. But the actual ages of birthing mothers cover periods much longer than the "ripples," so that such hypotheses are difficult to prove.

19. See Dorothy Solinger, "China's Transients and the State: A Form of Civil Society?" *Politics and Society*, Vol. 21, No. 1 (March 1993), pp. 91–107.

20. See Frederic Wakeman, Jr. and Wenhsin Yeh (eds.), *Shanghai Sojourners* (Berkeley: University of California Institute of Asian Studies, 1992), and a review that suggests Shanghai people were not just sojourners, by L. White in the *Australian Journal of Chinese Affairs*, No. 31 (January 1994), pp. 189–91.

21. Common verbiage reflects this contrast. Vertical "line" (*tiao tiao* 條條) hierarchies, organized by the state under functional ministries, tended in the 1970s to be replaced by geographic "piece" (*kuai kuai* 塊塊) arrangements that the high state controlled less fully. Shanghai technicians might go back to their families' rural "old homesteads" (*guxiang* 故鄉), or to similar places, and establish "horizontal liaisons" (*hengxiang lianxi* 橫向聯繫 or *hengxiang guanxi* 橫向關係; sometimes *hengxiang lianhe* 橫向聯合).

22. The number of technicians was specified as 410,000 in Shanghai shehuikexueyuan *Shanghai jingji nianjian* bianjibu 上海社會科學院《上海經濟年鑑》編輯部 (eds.), *Shanghai jingji nianjian 1988* 上海經濟年鑑 1988 (Shanghai Economic Yearbook 1988) (Shanghai: Sanlian shudian Shanghai fendian 三聯書店上海分店, 1988), p. 11.

23. Wang Haibo 汪海波 (ed.), *Xin Zhongguo gongye jingji shi* 新中國工業經濟史 (A History of New China's Industrial Economy) (Beijing: Jingji guanli chubanshe 經濟管理出版社, 1986), pp. 361–63.

24. Fang Weizhong 房維中 et al. (eds.), *Zhonghua renmin gongheguo jingji dashiji 1949–1980* 中華人民共和國經濟大事記 1949–1980 (Chronicle of Economic Events in the PRC 1949–1980) (Beijing: Zhongguo shehui kexue

chubanshe 中國社會科學出版社, 1984), p. 657.

25. *Gaojia laotou* 高價老頭 is a term sardonically based on *gaojia guniang* 高價姑娘 (high-priced girls). The information is from an interview with a researcher at the Shanghai Academy of Social Sciences.

26. *Chengshi wenti* 城市問題 (Urban Problems), January 1988, p. 25.

27. A Shanghai interviewee, whose hometown was in Zhejiang, had seen his own name in such a file, along with these items of information for many other contacts in the metropolis.

28. Debates rage in academe over the extent to which this correlation of economic with cultural activities takes a causal or comprehensible form in either direction. The most famous statement is by G. William Skinner, *Marketing and Social Structure in Rural China* (Ann Arbor: Association for Asian Studies, 1978, reprinted from the *Journal of Asian Studies*, 1964–1965). A comprehensive critique is by Rupert N. W. Hodder, *The Creation of Wealth in China* (London: Belhaven Press, 1992). The heart of the dispute is epistemological, about preferred kinds of evidence to confirm understandings. Since these analyses exclude each other only in logical form, the rest of us can be grateful for various insights both sides have unearthed about places like Shanghai.

29. See Rupert N. W. Hodder, "Exchange and Reform in the Economy of Shanghai Municipality: Socialist Geography under Reform," *Annals of the Association of American Geographers*, Vol. 83, No. 2 (1993), pp. 303–19; and especially the same author's "China's Industry — Horizontal Linkages in Shanghai," *Transactions* (Institute of British Geographers), 15 (1990), pp. 487–503. Page 487 offers a definition of horizontal liaisons that is usable in the current chapter: "linkages which enable economic organizations to interact freely and directly without having to operate through rigid, vertical channels of command."

30. Shanghai Economic Research Centre and Shanghai Science and Technology Committee (eds.), *Shijie xing jishu geming yu Shanghai de duice* 世界性技術革命與上海的對策 (The Global Revolution in New Technology and Shanghai's Policies in Response) (Shanghai: Shanghai shehuikexueyuan chubanshe 上海社會科學院出版社, 1986), p. 362. Although engagements (*dinghun* 訂婚) are not officially registered in China, these people had apparently asked for marriage certificates and were legally entitled to them.

31. In Luwan 盧灣 district, there were 59,000 people per km². Shanghaishi tongjiju 上海市統計局 (eds.), *Shanghai tongji nianjian 1988* 上海統計年鑑 1988 (Statistical Yearbook of Shanghai 1988) (Beijing: Zhongguo tongji chubanshe 中國統計出版社, 1988), p. 82.

32. *Far Eastern Economic Review*, 12 December 1985, p. 28.

33. Deborah Davis did interviews in Shanghai during separated years of the 1980s, reported in "Housing and Family Life in Shanghai," *China Update*,

Vol. 11, No. 3 (Fall 1991), p. 9.

34. *JFRB*, 20 January 1988.

35. To what extent did rural industrialization, rather than birth planning policies, account for the low natality on the Shanghai delta (even while the number of households and marriages rose)? To answer such a question, it would be useful to compare two kinds of rural places, with relatively high and low industrialization rates but with similar amounts of local birth planning effort. How well or badly would industrialization correlate with low natality? How much of the result of China's birth planning can actually be attributed to occupational changes?

36. These data come from Tangjiacun 唐家村, Fengxian 奉賢 county, a credibly typical place in suburban Shanghai. See Ishida Hiroshi, *Chûgoku nôson keizai no kiso kôzô: Shanhai kinkô nôson no kôgyôka to kindaika no ayumi* (Rural China in Transition: Experiences of Rural Shanghai towards Industrialization and Modernization) (Kyôto: Kôyô Shobô, 1991), pp. 94–95.

37. Zheng Gongliang et al. (eds.), *Shanghai shehui xiankuang he qushi 1980–1983* 上海社會現況和趨勢 1980–1983 (Situations and Trends in Shanghai Society 1980–1983) (Shanghai: Huadong shifan daxue chubanshe 華東師範大學出版社, 1988), p. 113.

38. Ibid., p. 114.

39. The lowest marriage rate, 0.5% of the population, was in Tibet; and the other low province was Guizhou 貴州. Shanghai's divorce rate, involving 0.11% of the population, was eighth among the provinces, far below divorce-prone Xinjiang 新疆 (0.83%), which was followed in order by Qinghai 青海 (only 0.15%), Heilongjiang 黑龍江, Jilin 吉林, Shanxi 山西, Beijing 北京 and Liaoning 遼寧. The reasons for Xinjiang's high divorce rate deserve research, partly because the Han population there is largely Shanghainese. Guojia tongjiju shehuitongjisi 國家統計局社會統計司 (ed.), *Zhongguo shehui tongji ziliao 1987* 中國社會統計資料 1987 (Chinese Social Statistics, 1987) (Beijing: Zhongguo tongji chubanshe, 1987), p. 28.

40. Peng Xizhe, *Demographic Transition in China: Fertility Trends since the 1950s* (Oxford: Oxford University Press, 1991), table 2.6 and table 2.7.

41. Shanghaishi xingzhengju 上海市行政局 (ed.), *Shanghai shimin banshi zhinan* 上海市民辦事指南 (Shanghai Citizens' Guide) (Shanghai: Shanghai renmin chubanshe 上海人民出版社, 1989), p. 1.

42. Shanghai shehuikexueyuan *Shanghai jingji* bianjibu 上海社會科學院《上海經濟》編輯部 (ed.), *Shanghai jingji (neibu ben) 1949–1982* 上海經濟 (內部本) 1949–1982 (Shanghai Economy 1949–1982 [Internal (i.e., classified) Volume]) (Shanghai: Shanghai shehuikexueyuan chubanshe, 1984), p. 14.

43. Path analysis, which is a kind of multiple regression, was used in this important study. It is difficult to assign a specific portion of the lowering of

fertility to either family planning behaviour or to general socioeconomic development, partly because these factors themselves are interrelated. But this massive number crunching exercise, in which 28 provinces were considered although the published article presented no geographically specific data below the national level, deftly corrects the usual public assumption that the only reason for China's low fertility is state policy. See Dudley L. Poston, Jr. and Saochang Gu, "Socioeconomic Development, Family Planning, and Fertility in China," *Demography*, Vol. 24, No. 4 (November 1987), pp. 531–49.

44. Shanghaishi tongjiju (ed.), *Shanghai tongji nianjian 1993* 上海統計年鑑 1993 (Statistical Yearbook of Shanghai 1993) (Beijing: Zhongguo tongji chubanshe, 1993), p. 408. Ibid., p. 414 shows that from 1980 to 1992, the average size of rural households in Shanghai's suburbs also decreased almost as sharply, from 4.28 to 3.43 people.

45. The policy also caused a rise of female infant mortality in 1979–1984. Guojia tongjiju 國家統計局 (ed.), *Zhongguo tongji nianjian 1988* 中國統計年鑑 1988 (Statistical Yearbook of China 1988) (Beijing: Zhongguo tongji chubanshe, 1988), p. 82. But also see J. Dreze and A. Sen, *Hunger and Public Action* (Oxford: Clarendon Press, 1989), table 11.2.

46. Other factors —— some growth of jobs for women in Shanghai's consumer product industries, for example, also contributed to this result. But it would take the usual argument of this book, against the full effectiveness of policies, too far to claim that "birth planning" had no link to these data on births. For the statistics, see Peng Xizhe, *Demographic Transition in China: Fertility Trends since the 1950s* (see note 40), table 1.1 and table 2.1. The 1954 figures for Shanghai crude births, deaths and natural increase per thousand are 52.74, 7.12 and 45.62, respectively. By 1981, these had declined to 16.14, 6.44 and 9.70. Similar figures are offered in the source for the other provinces.

47. See Lynn White, "The Road to Ürümchi: Approved Institutions in Search of Attainable Goals," *The China Quarterly*, 79 (October 1979), pp. 481–510; and by the same author, "A Political Demography of Shanghai after 1949," in *Proceedings of the Fifth Sino-American Conference on Mainland China* (Taipei: Guoji guanxi yanjiusuo 國際關係研究所, 1976), reprinted over several weeks in *Ming bao* 明報 (Ming Pao) (Hong Kong), November 1976.

48. Peng Xizhe, *Demographic Transition in China* (see note 40), table 2.2.

49. The main practical condition for peasant couples to have an authorized second child was probably that they got along with the local power network. Formally, the additional criteria may be worth describing because they exemplify the elaborations that are necessary so that the state can mobilize resources and save costs. Thus, in addition to the three standard criteria, peasants may also have a second child: (1) if the wife or husband is disabled; (2) if the couple lives with elderly parents who have no other child and need

support; (3) if, among more than two sisters or brothers, anyone has no possibility to be fertile and each of the others has no more than one child; (4) if the family has had its income from fishing for more than five years [although this is not presented as a concession to religious belief, it applies to many Catholic families in Shanghai's suburbs and must reduce resentment among them about the state's birth and abortion policies]; (5) if either spouse is an oceangoing sailor; (6) if either has been a miner in the pit for five years; (7) if either has Overseas Chinese status; (8) if either belongs to a national minority; (9) if either's parent was designated a martyr for the PRC; (10) if either is a disabled soldier of the official grade A or B; (11) if either married a second time and they together had fewer than two children before the second marriage. See *Shanghai shimin banshi zhinan* (see note 41), pp. 56–57.

50. *Shanghai shimin banshi zhinan* (see note 41), p. 57.

51. Partly estimated from a chart at the bottom of *Shanghai tongji nianjian 1993* (see note 44), p. 67. The next page shows an acceleration during the early 1980s in Shanghai's urban districts.

52. Ming Juzheng in Wu An-chia (ed.), *Zhonggong zhengquan sishi nian de huigu yu zhanwang* 中共政權四十年的回顧與展望 (Recollections and Prospects on the Forty Years of CCP Power) (Taipei: Guoji guanxi yanjiusuo, 1991), p. 358.

53. Gilles Antier, "New Planning Trends in Shanghai" (Paris: Institut d'Aménagement de d'Urbanisme de la Région d'Ile-de-France, 1993), p. 2.

54. *XMWB*, 7 April 1989.

55. Shanghaishi tongjiju (ed.), *Shanghai liudong renkou* 上海流動人口 (Shanghai's Floating Population) (Beijing: Zhongguo tongji chubanshe, 1989), pp. 162–64. Further material on this problem is presented in an article whose subtitle shows the viewpoint: Linda Wong, "China's Urban Migrants — The Public Policy Challenge," *Pacific Affairs*, Vol. 67, No. 3 (Fall 1994), esp. p. 341.

56. In addition, about one-eighth of the peasant reprisals can be traced to each of these three factors: cadres' insistence on cremations rather than burials, disputes over housing sites and "other" causes. The percentages add to 100 and are reported in Yang Dali, "Making Reform: The Great Leap Famine and Rural Change in China" (Ph.D. dissertation, Princeton University, Politics Department, December 1992, table 7, quoting *Nongmin ribao* 農民日報 [Farmers' Daily], 26 September 1988).

57. See *Federal Broadcast Information Service* [hereafter *FBIS*], 7 October 1988, p. 13, and Zhou Xiao, "How the Farmers Changed Communist China" (manuscript at Princeton University), chapter 8, p. 14.

58. *Asian Wall Street Journal*, 23 July 1988.

59. J. Dreze and A. Sen, *Hunger and Public Action* (Oxford: Clarendon Press 1989), table 11.3. The infant female deficit in 1978 was only 0.09% of births;

but by 1984, it was 3.33%.

60. Rupert N. W. Hodder, "China's Industry — Horizontal Linkages in Shanghai," *Transactions* (Institute of British Geographers), 15 (1990), p. 494.

61. *FBIS*, 20 November 1984, p. 3, reporting radio of 20 November.

62. Cao Linzhang 曹麟章, Gu Guangqing 顧光青 and Liu Jianhua 劉建華, *Shanghai shengchan ziliao suoyouzhi jiegou yanjiu* 上海生產資料所有制結構研究 (Studies of Shanghai Production and Ownership Structure) (Shanghai: Shanghai shehuikexueyuan chubanshe, 1987), p. 146.

63. Anthropologist Lu Feiyun 陸斐雲, a graduate student at The Chinese University of Hong Kong, has done field work in the Shanghai delta and kindly referred this author to 1989 data in Hua Daming 華大明, "Xiangban chang dui nonggong de guofen baoduo ying yinqi zhuyi" 鄉辦廠對農工的過份剝奪應引起注意 (The Overexploitation of Peasant Workers by Township-run Factories Calls for Attention), *Shehui* 社會 (Society) (Shanghai), No. 2 (1990), pp. 12–13.

64. Interview with a Shanghai economist who had personal experience with Suzhou leaders and Shanghai–Suzhou links.

65. The portion 44% is quoted in Shanghaishi jingji xuehui 上海市經濟學會 (ed.), *Hengxiang jingji lianhe de xin fazhan* 橫向經濟聯合的新發展 (The New Development of Horizontal Economic Links) (Shanghai: Shanghai shehuikexueyuan chubanshe, 1987), p. 96, which, however, carries the story only to 1986.

66. *Shanghai jingji* 上海經濟 (Shanghai Economy), April 1988, p. 63.

67. Interview with a Shanghai economist in 1989.

68. "*Baoban hunyin* 包辦婚姻", "*fengming lianhe* 奉命聯合." *Hengxiang jingji lianhe de xin fazhan* (see note 65), p. 243.

69. Ibid.

70. *Chengshi wenti* 城市問題 (Urban Problems), January 1988, p. 25.

71. *China Daily* [hereafter *CD*], 9 March 1988, quoting *World Economic Herald*.

72. Xu Yuanming 徐元明 and Ye Ding 葉鼎, *Tangqiao gongyehua zhi lu* 塘橋工業化之路 (The Way to Industrialization in Tangqiao) (Shanghai: Shanghai shehuikexueyuan chubanshe, 1987), pp. 40–41.

73. A 1920 survey of the most famous compradores in Shanghai showed almost half (43 out of 90) were from Zhejiang. See *Shehui kexue zhanxian* 社會科學戰線 (Social Science Front), 4 (1984), p. 7.

74. These *Shanghai de Ningbo ji renshi* 上海的寧波籍人士 set up the Shanghaishi Ningbo jingji jianshe cujin xiehui 上海市寧波經濟建設促進協會, which was a *qunzhong tuanti* 群眾團體 rather than a branch of the state. *XMWB*, 25 February 1989.

75. *FBIS*, 9 March 1988, p. 33–36, reporting a journal of 11 February. The chapter in this book by Lam Tao-chiu offers other examples of vocal

articulation in reform Shanghai.

76. The conference met on 19–25 July; see *NCNA*, 30 July 1957.

77. Shanghaishi bianzhi weiyuanhui bangongshi 上海市編制委員會辦公室 (ed.), *Shanghai dangzheng jigou yange* 上海黨政機構沿革 (The Transformation of Shanghai's Party and Administration) (Shanghai: Shanghai renmin chubanshe, 1988), p. 132.

78. The counties were Jiading 嘉定, Qingpu 青圃 and Jinshan 金山 in Shanghai; Taicang 太倉, Kunshan 昆山 and Wujiang 吳江 in Jiangsu; Jiashan 嘉善 and Pinghu 平湖 in Zhejiang. See *WHB*, 12 December 1977.

79. On these *"xiezuo qu,"* see *World Economic Herald* and Shanghai Economic Zone Research Society (世界經濟導報，上海經濟區研究會) (eds.), *Shanghai jingji qu fazhan zhanlüe chutan* 上海經濟區發展戰略初探 (Preliminary Research on the Development Strategy of the Shanghai Economic Zone) (Shanghai: Shanghai di ba renmin chubanshe Wuxi fanshe 上海第八人民出版社無錫分社, 1986), p. 213–14.

80. *"Dapo shengshi jiexian* 打破省市界限*",* and *"you lian you jing* 又聯又競*."*

81. Yao Shihuang 姚詩煌, *Jin sanjiao de tansuo* 金三角的探索 (Search for the Golden Delta) (Chongqing: Chongqing chubanshe 重慶出版社, 1988), pp. 82–88.

82. The cities, in addition to Shanghai, were Suzhou, Changzhou, Nantong 南通, Wuxi, Hangzhou, Ningbo, Huzhou 湖州 and Jiaxing. Shaoxing was left off the original list of cities but was included later. See *World Economic Herald* and Shanghai Economic Zone Research Society (eds.), *Shanghai jingji qu de jianli yu fazhan* 上海經濟區的建立與發展 (The Establishment and Development of the Shanghai Economic Zone) (Shanghai: Zhongguo zhanwang chubanshe 中國展望出版社, 1984), pp. 8–20.

83. The number of counties is in parentheses after each city name: Shanghai (10), Suzhou (6), Wuxi (3), Changzhou (3), Nantong (6), Hangzhou (7), Jiaxing (5), Huzhou (3), Ningbo (7), and Shaoxing (5).

84. *Shanghai jingji qu de jianli yu fazhan* (see note 82), pp. 1–2.

85. *FBIS*, 7 December 1984, p. 4, reporting radio of 5 December.

86. *Shanghai jingji nianjian 1988* (see note 22), p. 139.

87. *World Economic Herald* and Shanghai Economic Zone Research Society (eds.), *Shanghai jingji qu fazhan zhanlüe chutan* (see note 79), p. 32.

88. In Guangdong, the Pearl River's "small delta" *(xiao sanjiaozhou* 小三角洲) is contrasted with the "large delta" *(da sanjiaozhou* 大三角洲). See Ezra F. Vogel, *One Step Ahead in China: Guangdong under Reform* (Cambridge: Harvard University Press, 1989), chapter 5.

89. Chen Dongsheng 陳棟生 and Chen Jiyuan 陳吉元, *Zhongguo diqu jingji jiegou yanjiu* 中國地區經濟結構研究 (Studies on the Structure of China's Spatial Economy) (Taiyuan 太原: Shanxi renmin chubanshe 山西人民出版社, 1988), pp. 82–86.

90. Yao Shihuang, *Jin sanjiao de tansuo* (see note 81), pp. 67–74.

91. Task Force on the Environment for Educational Development Strategy in the Developed Region of Southern Jiangsu (ed.), *Sunan fada diqu jiaoyu fazhan zhanlüe huanjing yanjiu baogao* 蘇南發達地區教育發展戰略環境研究報告 (Research Report on the Environment for Educational Development Strategy in the Developed Region of Southern Jiangsu) and pub. Mimeographed "discussion draft" (*taolun gao* 討論稿), n.p., 1991, p. 3.

92. Wuxi county is subordinate to the city of the same name; Shazhou county is under Suzhou; and Wujin is under Changzhou. *Shanghai qiye* 上海企業 (Shanghai Enterprise), February 1985, p. 13.

93. *Shanghai jingji qu fazhan zhanlüe chutan* (see note 79), p. 26.

94. Other sectoral zones could be devoted to other sectors — and an economic zone was suggested for Northeast China, to specialize especially in coal and electricity. This "Dongbei de jingji qu 東北的經濟區" was not an institution's name, though it appears in *Shanghai jingji qu fazhan zhanlüe chutan* (see note 79), p. 94.

95. The Shanghai jingji qu guihua bangongshi 上海經濟區規劃辦公室 only had powers to "co-ordinate" such relations. Ibid.

96. Although there was a flow of people to Shenzhen from Shanghai, there was scant flow of information or projects. Even in Shenzhen, "a majority of Shanghai firms lacked rights" to import and export as freely as other companies there did, and they "were run only like administrative offices." They tended to be there less for business than as "travel reception stations" (*lüyou jiedai zhan* 旅遊接待站). The greater constraints on Shanghai business procedures were more obvious in Shenzhen than in other places, because companies from all over China were together for comparison there. See *JFRB*, 19 April 1988. The same paper, 27 April 1988 refers to deficient management autonomy (*jingying zizhu quan* 經營自主權) among Shanghai firms in Shenzhen.

97. Some other economic zones disappeared about the same time. *Ad hoc* regional revivals sometimes took place, the most famous of which was in aviation: Shanghai-based China Eastern Airlines. By 1990, this carrier flew to major PRC cities, Hong Kong and four different places in Japan. See *Shanghai Focus*, 21 May 1990.

98. This Shanghai boast comes from a national, not a local, source: *Dangdai Zhongguo* congshu bianjibu 《當代中國》叢書編輯部 (ed.), *Dangdai Zhongguo de guangbo dianshi* 當代中國的廣播電視 (Radio and Television in China Today) (Beijing: Zhongguo shehuikexue chubanshe 中國社會科學出版社, 1987), vol. 2, p. 405.

99. *Shanghai wenhua nianjian* bianjibu 《上海文化年鑑》編輯部 (ed.), *Shanghai wenhua nianjian 1987* 上海文化年鑑 1987 (Shanghai Culture Yearbook 1987) (Shanghai: Zhongguo da baikequanshu chubanshe 中國大百科全書出

版社, 1987), p. 134.

100. This information comes from interviews with Shanghai television officials, but also from watching the news coverage of local stories from all parts of East China on Shanghai stations in 1988.

101. The Zhejiang programme was "Jingji xinxi 經濟信息," and the Shanghai one, "Baokan wenxuan 報刊文選." *Dangdai Zhongguo* congshu bianjibu (ed.), *Dangdai Zhongguo de guangbo dianshi* (see note 98), vol. 1, p. 104.

102. On the start of TV advertising, see *Shanghai wenhua nianjian 1987* (see note 99), p. 133.

103. *Shangshan xiaxiang* 上山下鄉. Few people whose first regular work assignment was outside of Shanghai were allowed back, however. Among Shanghainese who married elsewhere, only one-quarter had returned. Zhongguo shehuikexueyuan renkou yanjiusuo 中國社會科學院人口研究所 (ed.), *Zhongguo renkou qianyi yu chengshihua yanjiu* 中國人口遷移與城市化研究 (Studies on Chinese Migration and Urbanization) (Beijing: Beijing jingji xueyuan chubanshe 北京經濟學院出版社, 1989), p. 296.

104. The first datum is based on a survey of long-term immigrants by the Population Research Institute of the Chinese Academy of Social Sciences, and the second reports 1977–1986 migrations. To the much smaller Shanghai delta city of Xiashi, fewer (just below half) of the 1977–1986 immigrants were unmarried. See Lin Yousu, "Urban Migration in China: A Case Study of Three Urban Areas," (Ph.D. dissertation, Australian National University, Department of Geography, 1992, pp. 111, 115).

105. See Alice Goldstein, Sidney Goldstein and Guo Shenyang, "Temporary Migrants in Shanghai Households, 1986," *Demography*, 28 (1991), p. 275.

106. *Chengshi wenti*, (March 1988), p. 64.

107. *Laodong bao* 勞動報 (Labour News) (Shanghai), 19 March 1989.

108. *Shanghai Star*, 22 March and 15 April 1994, suggested that about one-quarter of the migrants were in construction work, and another quarter were not working. Found by Li Cheng 李成.

109. For example, in Hangzhou, migrants were reportedly 11% of that city's population in 1985 and had already been 9% in 1975, but only 4% in both 1965 and 1955. See Li Mengbai 李夢白 et al. (eds.), *Liudong renkou dui da chengshi fazhan de yingxiang ji duice* 流動人口對大城市發展的影響及對策 (Policies on the Influence of Transient Population for the Development of Large Cities) (Beijing: *Jingji ribao* chubanshe 經濟日報出版社, 1991), p. 281.

110. Shanghaishi tongjiju (ed.), *Shanghai liudong renkou* (see note 55), pp. 11–16.

111. See the report by journalist T. S. Rousseau in *Eastern Express* (Hong Kong), 23 February 1994, p. 6.

112. This information on the Anhui *bang* 幫 comes from Zhou Xiao, who cites a

Shanghai 1991 book entitled "Food is the Basis of People: Report from Rural China."

113. Alice Goldstein, Sidney Goldstein and Guo Shenyang, "Temporary Migrants in Shanghai Households, 1986" (see note 105), p. 275, gives details on methods in the 1984 Shanghai Temporary Migration Survey.

114. The number of such labourers was specified at 240,000. See Shanghaishi tongjiju (ed.), *Shanghai liudong renkou* (see note 55), pp. 47–57.

115. Zhonghua quanguo funü lianhehui funü yanjiusuo 中華全國婦女聯合會婦女研究所 et al. (eds.), *Zhongguo funü tongji ziliao* 1949–1989 中國婦女統計資料 1949–1989 (Statistical Materials on Chinese Women, 1949–1989) (Beijing: Zhongguo tongji chubanshe, 1991), p. 25, shows Shanghai moving from one of China's least female populations to the highest portion (with the possible exception of Tibet, for which the relevant table apparently included a misprint).

116. The lowest provinces on this index include a populous, contiguous group in China proper: Henan 河南, Hebei 河北, Shandong 山東, Shaanxi 陝西 and Shanxi 山西 (north-central bedrock conservative territory for the most part). The overall index for Jiangsu is lowered by rates in Subei 蘇北. According to Jiangsu sheng tongjiju 江蘇省統計局, Jiangsu sheng renkou pucha bangongshi 江蘇省人口普查辦公室 (eds.), *Zhongguo 1987 nian 1% renkou chouyang diaocha ziliao: Jiangsu sheng fence* 中國1987年1%人口抽樣調查資料：江蘇省分冊 (Chinese 1987 1% Sample Survey: Jiangsu Province Volume) (Nanjing: Zhongguo tongji chubanshe, 1988), p. 165, women comprise much higher portions of the South Jiangsu industrial work force (Suzhou, 69%; or Wuxi, 64%) than they do in Subei (Xuzhou 徐州, 36%; or Lianyungang 連雲港, 25%).

117. Calculated from *Zhongguo funü tongji ziliao 1949–1989* (see note 115), pp. 241–42.

118. In addition, 11% were tended by factories; and 3% were under village and township auspices. Kang Yonghua, Liang Chenglin and Tan Songhua (eds.), *Shanghai jiaoyu fazhan zhanlüe yanjiu baogao* 上海教育發展戰略研究報告 (Research Report on the Strategy of Shanghai's Educational Development) (Shanghai: Huadong shifan daxue chubanshe 華東師範大學出版社, 1989), p. 228.

119. *XMWB*, 16 May 1989.

120. Shanghai shehuikexueyuan *Shanghai jingji* bianjibu (ed.), *Shanghai jingji (neibu ben) 1949–1982* (see note 42), p. 975.

121. *XMWB*, 22 November 1988.

122. *JFRB*, 1 March 1987.

123. A testy summary of this international controversy is Nick Eberstadt, "Population and Economic Growth," *Wilson Quarterly*, Vol. X, No. 5 (1986), pp. 95–127.

124. Delia Davin, "The Early Childhood Education of the Only Child Generation in Urban Areas of Mainland China," in *Education in Mainland China*, edited by Lin Bihjaw and Fan Limin (Taipei: Institute of International Relations, 1990), p. 326.

18

Environmental Quality and Pollution Control

Lam Kin-che and Tao Shu

Shanghai is the largest city in China, with a population of around 13 million. Its population density and concentration of economic and industrial activities are among the highest in the country. Shanghai's growth in the last few decades has been phenomenal; between 1949 and 1993, the population and gross industrial output increased by 2.6 and 36 folds respectively.

It is a challenge for such a city to maintain the environmental quality. This chapter describes the key environmental problems in Shanghai, outlines the efforts of the government in pollution control, the difficulties in environmental management and the way forward.

The experience of Shanghai has much to offer to environmental management in China and other developing economies. The problems found in Shanghai are reminiscent of development problems of rapidly developing areas. As will be exemplified in the rest of this chapter, the situation in Shanghai is the epitome of pollution problems found in other parts of China — an outdated industrial base, an inadequate municipal waste collection and treatment system, an energy structure that is based largely on coal, the quest for rapid economic growth and an environmental planning management system that is not yet capable of addressing these problems.

Shanghai, of course, has other qualities which distinguish it from other cities and Special Economic Zones in South China. Industries in Shanghai have been established for a long time; many were established before 1949 at a time when environmental planning and protection were not major considerations on the public agenda. Until recent times, investment has largely been from the state and most of the industrial products are for domestic consumption. In terms of decision making, Shanghai is a typical municipality in a centrally-planned economy, largely following the state's directives, policies and institutional arrangements. This is somewhat different from other open cities in China where there is a greater degree of autonomy and more local initiative in policy decision making.

State of the Environment

The overall environmental quality of Shanghai is best indicated by the composite score of a national comprehensive urban environmental quality and management assessment exercise undertaken for 37 cities.[1] First introduced in 1989 and undertaken annually since then, this assessment is based on 21 criteria which can be divided into three groups. The first group focuses on air, water and noise pollution. Out of a total of 37 cities subjected to the assessment, Shanghai ranked last in the 1993 exercise, indicating a pressing need for environmental improvement. The second group of criteria is based on the measures adopted to control pollution and the outcome of these efforts in terms of the extent of waste treatment and rate of compliance. Shanghai ranked admirably fifth in the nation. The third group refers to the provision of basic municipal infrastructure and waste treatment facilities, such as central heating and gas supply, refuse collection and treatment facilities for liquid and solid wastes. From this perspective, Shanghai ranked tenth out of the 24 southern cities.

The above assessment results bespeak the fact that, in spite of the strenuous efforts of the authorities to combat pollution, the results are still far from satisfactory. They bring out a paradox that needs to be unravelled — why does environmental quality remain poor despite commitment and effort? What adjustments are needed to achieve the desired environmental goals at a time when the economy is burgeoning and the growth incessant also calls for further scrutiny.

An examination of Shanghai's major environmental issues will give a proper understanding of the aforementioned paradox. Currently, Shanghai is beset by a multitude of problems; the air contains elevated levels of particulates and sulphur dioxide, the noise emanating from roadways and factories infiltrates most parts of the city, and deteriorating water pollution jeopardizes the city's potable water supply.

Figure 18.1 portrays the air quality in Shanghai since the late 1970s. The air pollutants of particular concern are total suspended particulates (TSP) and sulphur dioxide (SO_2), both of which are the products of coal combustion. The per unit area emission of TSP and SO_2 is in fact highest in the whole nation.[2] It can be seen that both TSP and SO_2 are in excess of the national secondary air quality standards for the long-term protection of human health. Of the two parameters, TSP is the more problematic, although the same diagram indicates that the amount of dust fall, which is an aggregate measure of settleable coarse materials, has been decreasing steadily. This suggests that while the settleable dust level is on the decline, the finer TSP fraction, which is suspended in the air and relates directly to human health, still remains at unacceptably high levels.

Similar conclusions were also obtained when the World Health Organization (WHO) initiated a global urban air quality monitoring programme.[3] Shanghai was one of the few Chinese cities included in this global monitoring network and the results obtained from 1981 to 1987

Figure 18.1   Air Pollution Trends in Shanghai

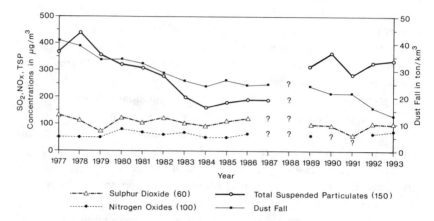

Note: * Figures in brackets indicate Chinese secondary air quality objectives for the
            protection of human health.

indicate that the daily TSP levels exceeded the WHO criterion for 80% to
90% of the time by as much as two to three folds. The studies also found
that TSP pollution was worst in industrial areas and sulphur dioxide pollution was worst in residential areas. These results are by no means encouraging because the WHO survey indicates that during the same period
of observation, the air quality of most other participating cities was ex-
hibiting varying degrees of improvement. Shanghai was one of the few
cities which did not show any appreciable improvement in air quality.

Water pollution is another problem that has long troubled Shanghai.
Located at the mouth of the Huangpu River (黃浦江), Shanghai is all
dependent on the river as a source of water supply and as a means of
transport. Millions of Shanghai's inhabitants live by the side of the river
and are in close contact with the water. The ecological state of the river is,
however, far from healthy. The lower 40 km of the river is grossly polluted; offensive smells were generated for 195 days in the year 1990 — an
increase of over 100% since 1980. The water quality is so poor that hardly
any fish or shrimp can be found and the city's potable water supply is in
jeopardy.

The causes of river pollution are not hard to discern, although rectify-
ing the roots of the problem is by no means an easy task. The lack of
adequate sewage collection and treatment facilities is the most notable
reason. The statistics show that in 1992, only 14% of the domestic sewage

produced by the 13 million inhabitants was treated prior to discharge.[4] Combined with those in the agricultural and industrial effluent, the organic pollutants in the sewage deplete the oxygen in the river water, bringing the level of dissolved oxygen to almost zero at those stretches close to the city centre and at the junction of the Suzhou Creek (蘇州河). Other studies[5] also indicate that the river water contains so many industrial pollutants, such as phenol and heavy metals, that the quality at some of the water intake points can no longer meet the relevant national standards. The continual abstraction of water from these locations will pose significant health risks to the inhabitants of Shanghai.

Shanghai is also a noisy city. With a total vehicle fleet of 320,000 in 1993, the traffic density on the roads is one of the highest in the country. According to a national noise survey undertaken in 1992,[6] the national traffic noise criterion of 70 dBA (Leq) was exceeded on 92% of the major roadways. Of even greater concern is the increase of night time traffic noise from 60 dBA in the early 1980s to 65 dBA in the 1990s, suggesting possibly a significant increase in sleep disturbances and interference with other human activities. The same survey also shows that the ambient noise criteria were exceeded in most of the land-use types in the city. The corresponding figures for the actual and target noise levels were 58.9 dBA vs. 50 dBA for residential areas, 59.3 dBA vs. 55 dBA for mixed residential areas, 62 dBA vs. 60 dBA for commercial areas and 64 dBA vs. 65 dBA for industrial areas. The high noise levels in Shanghai can be ascribed to many causes, the most significant being the intermingling of different land-use types, a large and escalating vehicle fleet, and the absence of buffer zones between noise sources and the sensitive receivers.

Disposal of solid wastes has become a more and more acute problem in Shanghai. Lacking a comprehensive waste disposal plan, most of the municipal and industrial waste is dumped at over three thousand large and small sites on the outskirts of the city,[7] most of which are temporary facilities with inadequate provisions to minimize nuisance to nearby residents and agricultural fields. Some are even located close to water intake points. There is as yet no special facility for the disposal of hazardous wastes generated by industry. The improper disposal of solid wastes has resulted in the loss of farmlands on the urban fringe, soil pollution around the dumping sites and possibly accumulation of heavy metals in the food chain. This will aggravate the soil pollution problem in parts of Shanghai where there was already evidence of heavy metal contamination due to sewage irrigation in the 1960s and 1970s.[8]

The Industrial Factor

Of the many factors affecting environmental quality in Shanghai, industry is the most significant. The 1993 figures indicate that industry was the major source of pollutants discharged into the environment (Table 18.1), accounting for over 90% of the gaseous emissions and 60% of the liquid discharges. The dominance of the industrial factor is not a recent phenomenon; industry has always been the most significant contributor to pollution in Shanghai, as shown in a national industrial pollution survey undertaken in 1985.[9]

Industrial pollution in Shanghai is due to a number of factors, the most notable being the lack of land-use planning. Scattered over the city core of about 147 sq km are tens of thousands of large and small factories, many

Table 18.1   **Environmental Quality in Shanghai: Basic Facts and Figures, 1980–1993**

Basic facts	Unit	1980	1985	1990	1993
Total population	million	11.46	12.05	12.83	12.95
Industrial output	RMB billion	599	863	1,643	3,272
Percent of national total	%	11.6	8.9	6.9	6.3
Wastewater generation					
Total discharge	$10^8 m^3$	16.50	19.60	19.99	20.32
Of industrial origin	$10^8 m^3$	13.15	14.99	13.32	12.80
Industrial effluent treated	$10^8 m^3$	1.66	3.79	7.91	10.99
Treatment compliance rate	$10^8 m^3$	0.96	3.07	6.24	9.10
Total gaseous emission	$10^8 m^3$	—	2,713	3,535	4,231
Of industrial origin	%	—	92.3	—	91.2
Industrial effluent treated	%	—	—	75.0	82.1
Sulphur dioxide					
Total emission	1,000 t	—	—	—	441.2
Of industrial origin	1,000 t	367.7	343.6	415.0	357.0
Particulates					
Total emission	1,000 t	—	—	—	189.3
Of industrial origin	1,000 t	312.6	200.0	189.3	148.0
Solid wastes					
Generation	1,000 t	5,824	7,221	11,070	11,980
Re-utilized	1,000 t	4,082	5,155	8,999	10,450
Air pollution					
TSP concentration	$\mu g/m^3$	320	180	358	337
SO_2 concentration	$\mu g/m^3$	120	110	95	98

Note: Figures compiled from a variety of official statistical sources. Gaps indicate data could not be found.

of which were established decades ago when environmental quality was not a major consideration. This has resulted in an undesirable mixing of residential and industrial land uses.[10] The problem is exacerbated by a high population density and the lack of open space in the old city core.

The reason why industry is the predominant source of air pollutants is obvious. Most of the industries in Shanghai are energy-intensive and air pollutants are derived from both energy consumption and industrial processes. The per unit area consumption of energy in Shanghai is, in fact, the highest in the whole nation and is almost double that of Beijing 北京, which is second on the list. Coal is the dominant industrial energy source in Shanghai and its consumption has been increasing at a rate of 10% per annum.[11] The industrial sector in Shanghai consumes 12 times as much coal as does the domestic sector (Table 18.2) and produces as the by-product of combustion as much sulphur dioxide and particulates. It is estimated that industries in Shanghai account for 81% and 78% of the total sulphur dioxide and particulates emission respectively. The major polluting sources are heavy industries, such as the power stations, iron and steel works, cement plants and the petrochemical industries.

Like air pollution, industry is the major source of water pollution in Shanghai. The major liquid effluent producers are the petrochemical, textile, metallurgical and machinery industries,[12] which are the backbone of Shanghai's industrial base. For various reasons, not all liquid effluent is

Table 18.2 Pattern of Energy Use in Shanghai, 1980–1993

Pattern of energy use		1980	1985	1990	1993
Total energy consumption	10^6t standard coal	—	20.49	—	38.08
Industrial	10^6t standard coal	16.45	18.78	23.70	30.27
Domestic	10^6t standard coal	—	—	—	2.50
Transport	10^6t standard coal	—	—	—	2.98
Commerce	10^6t standard coal	—	—	—	0.40
Industrial energy consumption					
Heavy industries	%	—	67.3	68.9	73.4
Light industries	%	—	32.7	31.1	26.6
Industrial raw coal	1,000 t	5,350	5,677	5,961	7,170
Industrial coke	1,000 t	2,115	2,586	4,192	6,172
Fuel oil	1,000 t	1,224	809	1,361	3,961
Electricity	10^9 KwH	13.69	17.13	20.92	26.28

Note: Figures compiled from a variety of official statistical sources. Gaps indicate data could not be found.

treated prior to discharge; in 1993, only 85% of industrial effluent was treated and the corresponding figure for domestic effluent was merely 14%. The relatively low figure for domestic sewage treatment is a reflection of inadequate sewerage, which covers less than 50% of the city area, and the lack of provisions for sewage sludge disposal.

In Shanghai, a substantial portion of solid wastes which require disposal are derived from industries, particularly from the power, metallurgical, paper and petrochemical industries.[13] About 2% of these industrial wastes are either toxic or hazardous in nature. Provisions for the collection, treatment and final disposal of wastes are as yet inadequate and hardly any of the toxic industrial wastes are currently properly disposed of.

This situation has generated itself from the existence of a large number of industries that are based on outdated and inefficient production processes. A survey of the light industries conducted in the early 1980s in Shanghai[14] reveals that half of the production lines employed technologies of the 1930s and 1940s, and the bulk of the remainder employed technologies of the 1950s and 1960s. Another study on the machinery industry similarly indicates that only less than 5% of the production lines used state-of-the-art technology at that time, while the majority of the others were based on technologies of the 1940s, 1950s and 1960s. The situation for many other industries, as shown in Table 18.3, is also similar.[15]

In other parts of the world, almost all industrial technologies, ranging from steel to fertilizer production, have undergone substantial technological transformation in the last few decades, resulting in considerable savings in raw material use and energy consumption.[16] In Shanghai, the over-reliance on outdated technology, either borrowed from the Soviet Union in the 1950s or developed in-house in the 1960s at a time when self-reliance was encouraged by the state, implies that more raw materials have to be used and more industrial wastes are produced per unit of output.

Table 18.3   Age of Production Technology Used in Shanghai Industry in 1980s [up to 1980s]

	Before 1950	1950s	1960s	1970s	1980s
Chemical industry	—	50%	25%	20%	5%
Pharmaceutical industry	—	21%	35%	32%	12%
Industrial steam boilers	3%	4%	29%	64%	—

Source: Note 13 and note 14.

The literature abounds with examples of industrial pollution linked to inefficient production technologies. It is believed that compared to advanced technologies, resource use and waste production can be two to three times higher.

Although there are thousands of factories in Shanghai, the majority of the pollution comes from a relatively small number of sources.[17] A survey undertaken in the 1980s found that less than a hundred factories of key industries were responsible for 60% of the industrial liquid effluent and 80% of the gaseous emission respectively. Other statistics also reveal that 51% of the gaseous emission was generated by 26 factories. Many of these major polluting sources are state enterprises supporting a large number of employees and their dependents. The above figures suggest that the pollution can be significantly reduced if waste generation at these major sources can be controlled.

Pollution Control Strategy

Shanghai's industrial pollution problems are not unique. Many Chinese cities are beset by similar problems and the difference lies probably only in terms of degree or intensity. The Chinese leadership is, of course, not unaware of the problems and has, indeed, devoted much time and effort to find remedies. Two national conferences have been held, first in 1982 and then in 1993.[18] A large-scale nationwide industrial pollution survey was undertaken in 1985 to ascertain the causes and the extent of the problem.[19] All these attest to the concern of the state regarding this matter and the determination of the leadership to rectify the problem. The choice of Shanghai as the venue of the Second National Conference on Industrial Pollution is also indicative of the immensity and complexity of the problem in Shanghai.

Shanghai has never been slow in responding to the state's initiatives to combat industrial pollution. The city was, in fact, one of the first in the country to try out and implement various industrial pollution control measures. The current state of the environment in Shanghai is not a fair reflection of the municipal government's efforts, but rather a reflection of the inherent difficulties in surmounting many of the ingrained obstacles.

Shanghai's industrial pollution control strategy has largely followed the state's initiatives, the emphasis of which has gone through several phases since the mid-1970s. In the 1970s, when the guiding paradigm of environmental management in China was focused on the "comprehensive use of resources" and "transformation of wastes," the people as well as the industrial enterprises were exhorted repeatedly to "turn wastes into treasure" and to resalvage and recycle wastes produced in industrial processes. This drive to reuse industrial wastes was seen not only as a means to generate revenue but also as a way to reduce the quantity of wastes discharged into the environment. While the approach was consonant with the nation's endeavour to become "self-sufficient," it was largely reactive in nature and was hardly capable of adequately managing the problems at hand.

It must be acknowledged that China achieved no mean results in eliminating various types of wastes and enhancing the environmental quality through simple and frugal recycling.[20] Nevertheless, the rapid pace of industrialization following the economic reform in the late 1970s generated wastes of such a quality and quantity that they were beyond the absorptive capacity of traditional ways of resource recovery. Pollution from oil refineries, power plants, metallurgical works, chemical plants and iron and steel works could only be handled by appropriate advanced technologies. Moreover, the nature of the wastes changes with time; while most of the organic wastes can be reused in a number of ways, not all of the industrial wastes can be resalvaged for beneficial use.

Realizing the inadequacy of the recycling approach, China's environmental programme took a turn in the early 1980s by placing a greater emphasis on pollution control through a number of regulatory, administrative and economic measures. A list of major polluting industries which required attention was drawn up and deadlines were set for the completion of remedial works (*xianqi zhili* 限期治理). For those industrial enterprises which could not comply with the requirements or the deadlines, there were provisions for closure (*guan* 關), stoppage (*ting* 停), merger (*bing* 併) and transformation (*zhuan* 轉).[21] In 1983, the State Council (*Guowuyuan* 國務院) promulgated a policy of integrating pollution control with industrial technological renovation.[22] It stipulated that, for existing industries, whenever technological renovation was to be undertaken, outstanding pollution problems had to be tackled at the same time. There were provisions for new industries to comply with the prevailing environmental standards and to adopt the best practical waste treatment and recycling technologies. This encouraged environmental considerations to be incorporated into various stages of the project cycle, covering the design, construction and operation stages of any development.[23]

The above regulatory measures were supplemented by the introduction of an effluent charge system on industrial emissions that exceed the discharge guidelines. The imposition of these charges not only helped generate the much needed revenue for pollution control, but also brought about some technological changes which might not have happened under the status quo of a centrally-planned economy. The reduced income, perhaps more than anything else, forced each and every one of the enterprises to reconsider their production processes and pollution control measures. Furthermore, refunds to the factories of up to 80% of the effluent charges paid and the subsequent use of these monies for pollution control measures as stipulated by the control authorities also brought about significant changes.[24]

The effectiveness of effluent charges has, however, been limited by a number of factors. Charges are usually too low to effect changes in the production system. Some enterprises prefer to pay the charges than to undertake pollution control measures. Furthermore, for state enterprises, these charges do not necessarily induce change because many of such enterprises are already in debt and funds have to be provided by the state.

Following the directives promulgated by the state, Shanghai has embarked on a rigorous programme of industrial pollution control since the 1980s. Abatement notices with deadlines were served on a large number of polluting enterprises. Arrangements were made for those that could not comply to stop, close, move or merge with others. Recognizing the relationship of air pollution to energy consumption, an ambitious programme was launched to renovate the industrial boilers and furnaces, and to extend the provision of gas and central heating to domestic areas so as to reduce coal consumption.[25] As the official statistics show (Table 18.4), Shanghai was clearly ahead of the nation in renovating industrial boilers, resulting in considerable savings in coal consumption and a reduction of waste generation.

The early 1990s marked the beginning of a new phase in China's environmental management. Unlike the previous emphasis on recycling and pollution control, the thrust of the new approach was on cleaner production technology.[26] In practical terms, industries were exhorted to infuse environmental considerations into every step of the production process, from the choice and efficient use of raw materials, to the adoption of clean manufacturing technologies and the treatment and re-utilization of wastes. This represents a response to the worldwide call for clean technology and the approach was affirmed at the Second National Conference on Industrial Pollution held in Shanghai in 1993.

Table 18.4 Renovation of Industrial Boilers and Furnaces in Shanghai, 1981–1993

Year	Industrial boilers renovated		Industrial furnaces renovated		Industrial ash recovered	
	Shanghai %	China %	Shanghai %	China %	Shanghai %	China %
1981	67.3	39.5	51.4	23.8	59.5	30.9
1982	67.5	49.0	71.2	30.0	67.7	40.7
1983	68.8	55.5	69.9	32.6	66.1	49.8
1984	70.2	60.6	69.0	35.3	77.8	52.3
1985	63.5	65.0	66.8	41.1	84.0	52.9
1986	71.7	—	69.2	—	88.4	—
1987	99.3	—	73.6	—	86.6	—
1988	99.7	—	73.7	—	91.0	—
1989	98.1	60.0	75.5	48.0	92.5	—
1990	—	—	—	—	93.3	71.8
1991	—	—	—	—	93.0	78.9
1992	—	—	—	—	94.5	81.0
1993	—	—	—	—	94.9	81.1

Source: Figures compiled from a variety of official statistical sources. Gaps indicate data could not be found.

Achievements and Problems

The achievements of Shanghai in environmental management are by no means insignificant. The 1980s was a decade of rapid development in Shanghai, as evidenced by a doubling of the gross national product (GNP) and a tripling of industrial output. This was parallelled by a four-fold increase in public spending on environmental protection. Results of these efforts are best exemplified in the official statistics on pollution control, both in terms of the proportion of industrial wastewater treated prior to discharge, the degree of compliance (Figures 18.2 and Figure 18.3), as well as the percentage of steam boilers and industrial furnaces renovated (Table 18.4). These data clearly indicate that throughout the 1980s, Shanghai was clearly ahead of the nation in terms of its efforts if not results.

The increase in public spending on environmental programmes also enabled some large capital intensive projects to be initiated, the most notable being the renovation of the Baoshan Iron and Steel Complex (寶山鋼鐵) and the Huangpu River Environmental Improvement Programme. All these industrial pollution control measures resulted in a reduction of toxic substances discharged into the environment (Fig. 18.4).

Figure 18.2 Wastewater Generation in Shanghai

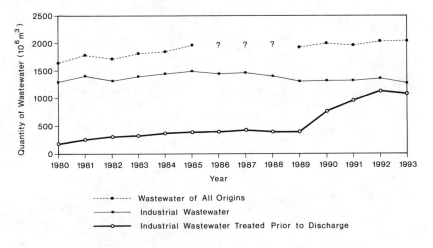

-----◆----- Wastewater of All Origins
——■—— Industrial Wastewater
——○—— Industrial Wastewater Treated Prior to Discharge

Figure 18.3 Industrial Wastewater Treatment and Compliance

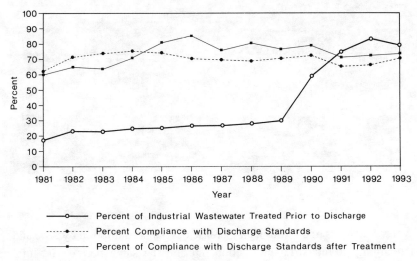

——○—— Percent of Industrial Wastewater Treated Prior to Discharge
-----◆----- Percent Compliance with Discharge Standards
——■—— Percent of Compliance with Discharge Standards after Treatment

Sources: Various sources

Since the early 1980s, almost the entire city was designated a smoke free zone and over 40% of the area gazetted quiet zones bringing relief to millions of people.

Some early signs of environmental improvement were noted in the latter half of the 1980s, in spite of a substantial increase in the population

Figure 18.4   Generation of Industrial Toxicants in Shanghai

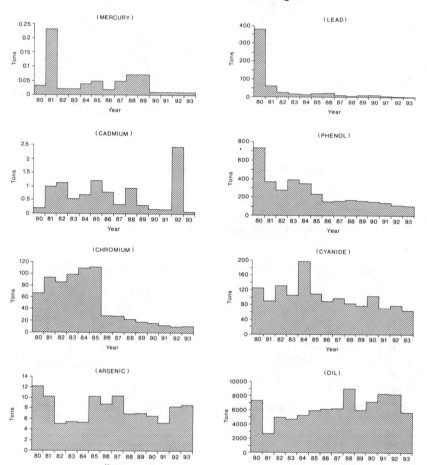

by three quarters of a million, an increase of coal consumption by 20% and a doubling of industrial production. During the same period, the total gaseous emission was cut by 14% and the dust fall by 17%.[27] The increase in wastewater generation had also been curbed so that the total quantity of liquid discharge could be contained at the early 1980s level. The number of days of offensive smell generated by the Huangpu River was also reduced from almost 200 to less than 50 in one year.

There is, however, little grounds for complacency. As highlighted at the beginning of this chapter, the general environmental quality in Shanghai still remains poor both in absolute terms and in comparison with other Chinese cities. The level of air particulates is high, sulphur dioxide levels are marginal and traffic noise is still very much a problem. None of these shows any sign of appreciable improvement. The disposal of industrial wastes has also emerged as a thorny issue. The 10% increase in waste re-utilization capability in the latter half of the 1980s was negated by a 46% jump in waste generation during the same period.

Looking into the future, rapid economic growth will continue to bring substantial pressure on the environment. In 1992, the rate of GNP and industrial output increase were 15% and 18% respectively. It is anticipated that this high rate of growth will result in a rapid increase in energy consumption, resource use and waste production. Coal consumption, for example, will increase at the rate of 10% per annum. By the year 2010, it has been projected that the total coal consumption will double that of the early 1990s, as will the generation of sulphur dioxide and atmospheric particulates.[28]

Table 18.5 shows the current environmental situation as compared with the targets for the years 2000 and 2010.[29] It can be seen that much has to be done to attain the targets, particularly in the areas of TSP, DO, domestic sewage treatment, traffic noise and the disposal of difficult and hazardous industrial wastes.

To attain the environmental targets, most would resort to the waste treatment approach by subjecting an increasing proportion of liquid and gaseous effluent to treatment and by enhancing the level of treatment. While this approach may help and is definitely needed for disposing of the domestic sewage, one should not be unaware of its limitations. Shanghai's rate of industrial wastewater and gaseous effluent treatment is already higher than the rest of the nation, and there is only a small gap between the existing treatment level and the target. Furthermore, virtually all of the industrial boilers and furnaces in Shanghai have been renovated (Table 18.4). It is likely that at the current technological levels, waste treatment has attained its probable achievable limits and not much further improvement can be expected from this approach. Other supplementary strategies thus must be explored if the environmental targets are to be attained.

The Way Forward

As Shanghai enters the next millennium with a rapid rate of growth, what then is the most appropriate environmental strategy?

Table 18.5　Environmental Targets of Shanghai for the 21st Century

Parameter	Unit	Situation in early 1990s	Target for 2000	Target for 2100
Air quality				
TSP	$\mu g/m^3$	350	100–200	90–180
SO$_2$	$\mu g/m^3$	95	30–60	20–40
Potable water supply				
DO	mg/l	7.50	6.00	6.00
Unionized ammonia	mg/l	0.85	0.05	0.05
Mercury	mg/l	0.07	0.05	0.05
Rural rivers				
DO	mg/l	4.80	5.00	6.00
Unionized ammonia	mg/l	2.00	0.02	0.02
Mercury	mg/l	0.07	0.10	0.05
Urban rivers				
DO	mg/l	1.00	2.00	5.00
Unionized ammonia	mg/l	0.70	0.20	0.20
Mercury	mg/l	0.15	0.10	0.10
Wastewater				
Industrial wastewater treatment	%	85	92	100
Domestic sewage treatment	%	15	70	85
Noise				
District noise	dBA	60	45–60	40–60
Traffic noise	dBA	73	55–70	50–65
Solid waste disposal				
Domestic waste disposal	%	90	90	100
Ind. waste comprehensive treatment	%	85	90	95
Hazardous waste treatment	%	—	100	100

Source:　Note 13.

Logic and experience appear to suggest that the previous recycling and end-of-pipe treatment approaches, because of their reactive nature, have their own limits. They are not the panacea to the problems at hand. In the last few decades, the paradigm of environmental protection in the Western world has evolved through a number of stages, focusing at different stages on dilution, recycling, treatment, pollution control, cleaner production and sustainable development. Seen in this perspective, the experience of Shanghai is only a mirror of what has happened elsewhere and Shanghai is only halfway on this evolving path. It is thus imperative that Shanghai acknowledge the intrinsic shortcomings of past strategies and explore other approaches. The Chinese leadership is not unaware of this need and has recently embarked on a campaign to make cleaner production its goal for combating industrial pollution.[30]

The ideal of cleaner production, which is now firmly established as the cornerstone of environmental management in the Western world, is gaining increasing acceptance in China. This has come with the realization that waste recycling, treatment and pollution control are merely "add-ons" to the manufacturing process. They incur significant capital, operating and transaction costs, and do not always bring desirable results. The solution lies in the integration of waste minimization with the production process. Cleaner production stresses pollution prevention rather than control. It internalizes pollution within the production system rather than externalizing it. A feasibility study undertaken by the United Nations Environment Programme (UNEP) for China suggests that there is plenty of scope for cleaner production in China. Cleaner production not only reduces pollution at its sources, but it is also a cost-effective way to operate industrial processes.[31]

It would, however, be too simplistic to assume that cleaner production can be implemented without making any adjustment to the current system. There are "hard" and "soft" obstacles to overcome. On the "hard" side, not all of the state-of-the-art clean technologies are available in China, and the main weakness of this strategy is its reliance on foreign technology and capital. At a time when the nation is low on foreign currency, it would be unrealistic to expect technological renovation to be adopted across the board overnight even though such investment can be paid back in a relatively short period of time.[32] Because of the lack of funds, technological renovation has only been completed in about 20% of the enterprises during the past decade. It is estimated that for the whole nation, at least RMB200 billion are needed to renovate the entire industrial sector.[33] At the moment, neither the central nor the municipal government has adequate capital to embark on such an ambitious programme.

Removing the "soft" hurdles is an equally formidable task. The introduction of modern clean technology requires an institutional setting that tips the balance away from outdated industrial processes. Operators should have basic skills to run modern production lines and management should be rewarded for the conversion process. In a system in which some enterprises are still heavily subsidized by the state, there is as yet an inadequate incentive in the system to phase out the old and usher in the new. An appropriate enterprise management regime will have to be instituted to reward those who convert it and to maximize the return from the conversion.

The greatest obstacle to technological renovation in China is still the lack of adequate capital resources. The problem faced by Shanghai is also the most acute because the majority of the major polluters are state enterprises which are currently beset by a host of other problems, in addition to the problem of technological renovation. It has been reported that one-third of the state enterprises are incurring losses and some are sinking deeper into debt.[34] Many have little funds to keep the enterprises running, let alone to invest in technological renovation and environmental protection. In the wake of the current economic reform, state enterprises will face even greater hardships because the level of protection afforded by the existing system will be gradually reduced.

The outdated state-owned industries can, of course, be gradually phased out in the course of industrial restructuring, something which has been discussed for some years.[35] However, restructuring will inevitably result in the laying off of employees and this will require commensurate social security and welfare measures which are currently not adequately provided for. Without the restructuring, the most urgent task is to revitalize and acclimatize the industries to the development of a market economy.[36] This necessitates the introduction of a new managerial system to run enterprises. Hopefully, these managerial skills will be readily acquired with the opening of Shanghai to foreign investment.

A discussion of industrial pollution in Shanghai is not complete without reference to the recent development of massive areas on the outskirts of the city. The opening up of these areas, such as Pudong 浦東 , can, of course, help to relieve some of the development pressures on the city.[37] However, one should not overestimate their effect in improving the environment in the city core. Up to now, Pudong has largely attracted new industries, rather than relocating industries from the old city core. Moreover, the industrial assemblage in Pudong is quite different from that of the city.[38] High land costs are also a deterrent for the relocation of industries already established in the city.

Thus, the key to curing pollution problems in Shanghai rests on restructuring the industries in the already developed areas rather than developing industries in new areas. Industrial development in new areas does not necessarily encourage the relocation of industries from the city core. Environmental improvement is urgently needed in the old areas where the population is most concentrated and pollution is the worst.

Although the task of improving Shanghai's environment is going to be long and arduous, the opening up of Shanghai is likely to enhance the process. The accelerated pace of development will bring in not only new technologies and resources, but also managerial skills and an economic climate which will help shake long existing industries out of their status quo. There are already proposals to change the industrial structure of Shanghai in the medium and long term. Heavy industries will play a less significant role, technological renovation will be expedited and older industries will be shifted out of the city core. Together with the increasing significance of the tertiary sector, all these changes will have beneficial impacts on the environment.

Conclusion

In spite of the municipal government's strenuous efforts in pollution control, the environmental quality in Shanghai is still far from satisfactory. Most of the pollution can be linked to outdated industries, although the problem is exacerbated by the high population density and the lack of environmental planning which results in the intermingling of industries with residential areas. Pollution control at its sources is the only effective way to improve the existing situation.

Previous strategies for environmental management were inadequate because they were end-of-pipe processes rather than waste minimization measures. In the wake of the rapid development in recent years, it is argued that a fresh approach is needed and the adoption of cleaner production technologies is the only viable solution. However, technological renovation of the major pollution sources, which are mostly state-owned, has been hampered by the lack of resources. Moreover, the opening up of new areas for development does not directly alleviate the pollution problems in the city core.

The rapid development that has taken place in Shanghai in recent years poses challenges and provides opportunities for environmental managers. Accelerated growth is expected to boost the demands for energy, iron and steel and other construction materials, and hence increase the amount of waste generation. On the other hand, it will also provide the much needed technology, resources and managerial skills for environmental improvement.

Economic reform will hasten the quest for development and exert even greater pressure on the environment. It will also create a milieu which places greater emphasis on economic efficiency and provides more incentives to adopt advanced technologies and cleaner production. Shanghai is currently undergoing a phase of rapid transformation. It is imperative that the changes bring in not only investment and technologies, but also managerial skills which are pressingly needed in the new production setting.

Notes

1. *Zhongguo huanjing nianjian* bianji weiyuanhui《中國環境年鑑》編輯委員會 (ed.), *Zhongguo huanjing nianjian 1990* 中國環境年鑑 1990 (Yearbook of the Environment in China 1990) (Beijing: Zhongguo huanjing kexue chubanshe 中國環境科學出版社, 1990), pp. 115, 311. See also *Zhongguo huanjing nianjian* bianji weiyuanhui (ed.), *Zhongguo huanjing nianjian 1994* 中國環境年鑑 1994 (Yearbook of the Environment in China 1994) (Beijing: *Zhongguo huanjing nianjian* she《中國環境年鑑》社, 1994), p. 124.

2. Guojia gongye wuranyuan diaocha bangongshi 國家工業污染源調查辦公室 (ed.), *Quanguo gongye wuranyuan diaocha pingjia yu yanjiu* 全國工業污染源調查評價與研究 (An Assessment and Investigation of Industrial Pollution Sources in the Whole Nation) (Beijing: Zhongguo huanjing kexue chubanshe, 1991).

3. The major findings were given in the following reports: Meng Zhihong 孟志虹 and Zhang Bingheng 張秉衡, "Woguo daqi TSP wuran xianzhuang ji qushi fengxi" 我國大氣TSP污染現狀及趨勢分析 (The Current Status and Trend of TSP in Our Country), *Shanghai huanjing kexue* 上海環境科學 (Shanghai Environmental Science), Vol. 8: 5 (1989), pp. 19–23; Yang Xiangwei 楊向偉, Shi Jide 史濟德 and Chen Cong 陳琮, "Shanghaishi quanqiu daqi jiancedian de wuran qushi fengxi" 上海市全球大氣監測點的污染趨勢分析 (Analysis of the Pollution Trend of the Shanghai Global Air Quality Monitoring Programme), *Shanghai huanjing kexue*, Vol. 8: 7 (1989), pp. 6–8.

4. Shanghaishi huanjing baohu ju 上海市環境保護局, "Shanghaishi huanjing yu shehui jingji xietiao fazhan" 上海市環境與社會經濟協調發展 (The Complementarity of Environmental and Socioeconomic Development in Shanghai), in *Maixiang 21 shiji de Shanghai* 邁向21世紀的上海 (Shanghai: Striding towards the 21st Century), edited by Shanghaishi "Maixiang 21 shiju de Shanghai" keti lingdao xiaozu 上海市"邁向21世紀的上海"課領導小組 (Shanghai: Shanghai renmin chubanshe 上海人民出版社, 1995), pp. 461–78.

5. Qiu Xinyan 裘鑫炎, "Shangyou yinshui baohu shuiyuan" 上游引水保護水源 (Why Transferring the Water Intake Points to the Upper Reaches of Huangpu River), *Shanghai huanjing kexue*, Vol. 5: 7 (1986), pp. 6–9; Dai Weiming 戴維明, "Linjiang qushuikou shuiyu shuizhi xianzhuang he wuran qushi" 臨江取水口水域水質現狀和污染趨勢 (Water Quality Conditions and Pollution Trend of Linjiang Intake," *Shanghai huanjing kexue*, Vol. 6: 3 (1987), pp. 27–29; Qiu Xinyan, "Guanyu Linjiang qushuikou ji qi shuizhi baohu" 關於臨江取水

口及其水質保護 (Linjiang Intake and Water Quality Protection), *Shanghai huanjing kexue*, Vol. 7: 9 (1988), pp. 8-10; Zhao Bingkui 趙炳魁 and Tang Xinyi 唐新益, "Huangpujiang shangyou shuiyuan baohuqu xiangzhen qiye huanjing baohu duice" 黃浦江上游水源保護區鄉鎮企業環境保護對策 (Environmental Protection Measures for the Rural Enterprises in the Protected Water Sources Areas of Upper Huangpu River), *Shanghai huanjing kexue*, Vol. 8: 8 (1989), pp. 6-8.

6. The survey results were taken from the *Zhongguo huanjian nianjian* bianji weiyuanhui (ed.), *Zhongguo huanjing nianjian 1993* 中國環境年鑑 1993 (Yearbook of the Environment in China 1993) (Beijing: Zhongguo huanjian kexue chubanshe, 1993), pp. 264-67.

7. See note 4.

8. For a description of the problems arising from sewage irrigation in China, see Shao Yilong 邵義隆, "Woguo wushui guangai wenti" 我國污水灌溉問題 (Problems of Sewage Irrigation in China), *Zhongguo huanjing kexue*, Vol. 3: 3 (1984), pp. 53-56. The soil pollution problem in Shanghai was discussed by Wang Yage 汪雅各 et al., "Shanghaishi nongye turang zhong ge gong xin tong qian ge shen he fu de hanliang ji beijing shuiping" 上海市農業土壤中鎘汞鋅銅鉛鉻砷和氟的含量及背景水平 (Levels and Concentrations of Cd, Hg, Cu, Zn, Pb, Cr, As and F in Agricultural Soils in Shanghai) which appeared on pp. 23-27 of the same volume and the same journal.

9. See note 2.

10. The mix of residential and industrial land uses has been described in detail in Chapter 9: Industrial Location by Rupert Hodder. The situation is best illustrated in Figure 9.1 of his chapter.

11. Shanghaishi tongjiju 上海市統計局 (ed.), *Xin Shanghai gongye tongji ziliao 1949-1990* 新上海工業統計資料 1949-1990 (New Shanghai Industrial Statistics 1949-1990) (Beijing: Zhongguo tongji chubanshe 中國統計出版社, 1992), p. 77. See also similar statistics produced by Shanghaishi tongjiju (ed.), *Shanghai tongji nianjian 1994* 上海統計年鑑 1994 (Statistical Yearbook of Shanghai 1994) (Beijing: Zhongguo tongji chubanshe, 1994), p. 195.

12. See note 9.

13. Chen Yuqun 陳予群, "Shanghaishi huanjing baohu de zhanlüe mubiao he cuoshi" 上海市環境保護的戰略目標和措施 (The Goal, Strategy and Measures of Environmental Protection in Shanghai) in *Shanghai jingji fazhan zhanlüe yanjiu* 上海經濟發展戰略研究 (The Strategy of Economic Development in Shanghai), edited by Chen Minzhi 陳敏之 (Shanghai: Shanghai renmin chubanshe, 1985), pp. 334-42.

14. Wang Shudao 王樹道, Jia Kai 賈楷 and Chen Dedong 陳德東, "Shanghai faxue gongye de huanjing wuran ji qi zhili celüe tantao" 上海化學工業的環境污染及其治理策略探討 (Environmental Pollution of the Chemical Industries in Shanghai: Problems and Counter Measures), *Shanghai huanjing kexue*, Vol.

5: 9 (1986), pp. 6–12.

15. The technological backwardness of Shanghai's industry in the 1980s is best exemplified in the two volumes of book edited by Li Boxi 李伯溪, *Zhongguo jishu gaizao wenti yanyiu* 中國技術改造問題研究 (Study of Problems of Renovating Chinese Technology) (Shanxi: Shanxi renmin chubanshe 山西人民出版社, 1983) pp. 631–39; 806–24.

16. Lam Kin-che, "Environmental Management in Developing Countries: Some Lessons from China and Hong Kong," *Asian Geographer*, Vol. 2 (1983), pp. 67–79.

17. This point can be substantiated by the statistics given in *Zhongguo huanjing nianjian* bianji weiyuanhui (ed.), *Zhongguo huanjing nianjian 1993* (see note 6), p. 214 and *Zhongguo huanjing nianjian 1994* (see note 1), p. 282.

18. Eleven years after the first National Industrial Pollution Conference held in 1982, the second conference was held in Shanghai in 1993. The conference was attended by a number of prominent Chinese leaders including Premier Li Peng 李鵬. The most important papers can be found in a special section of the *Zhongguo huanjing nianjian 1994* (see note 1).

19. See note 2.

20. See note 16 and also FAO (1977) *Recycling of Organic Wastes in Agriculture*. *FAO Soils Bulletin*, No. 40 (Rome: FAO).

21. The industrial pollution control policy of China was first spelled out in 1981 in a popular environmental magazine, *Huanjing baohu* 環境保護 (Environmental Protection), Vol. 6. The same article, written by Qu Geping 曲格平, director of the State Environmental Protection Bureau (國家環境保護局), was reproduced in *Zhongguo huanjing wenti yu duice* 中國環境問題與對策 (Chinese Environmental Problems and Countermeasures) (Beijing: Zhongguo huanjing kexue chubanshe, 1984), pp. 116–30.

22. Qu Geping, *Zhongguo huanjing wenti yu duice* (see note 21).

23. This system, which is better known as *San tong shi* 三同時, has been the cornerstone of the Chinese environmental management system.

24. See note 16.

25. Zhang Mingyu 張明裕, "Guanyu guolu gaizao gongzuo zhi qianjian" 關於鍋爐改造工作之淺見 (Views on Renovating the Boilers and Furnaces), in *Zhongguo jishu gaizao wenti yanjiu*, edited by Li Boxi (see note 15), p. 693.

26. This was the theme emphasized in a number of papers presented at the Second National Industrial Pollution Workshop. These papers, collated in the *Zhongguo huanjing nianjian 1994* (see note 1), were written by the Chinese Premier, Li Peng; chairman of Environmental Protection Committee, State Council (國務院環境保護委員會), Song Jian 宋健; chairman of the 8th National People's Congress Environmental Protection Committee (第八屆全國人民代表大會環境保護委員會), Qu Geping; director of State Environmental Protection Bureau, Xie Zhenhua 解振華; and vice-minister of State Economic

and Trade Commission (國家經濟貿易委員會), Shi Wanpeng 石萬鵬.

27. *Zhongguo huanjing nianjian 1993* (see note 6), p. 257.

28. See note 4.

29. See note 4.

30. The importance of cleaner production was repeatedly underscored at the Second National Industrial Pollution Workshop 1993. See note 18 and note 25.

31. S. de Hoo and John Kryger, "Cleaner Production: An Opportunity for Industry," paper presented at the Workshop on Green Productivity in Small and Medium Enterprises: The Role of Professional Service Organization, Hong Kong, 1994.

32. *Zhongguo jingji nianjian* bianji weiyuanhui《中國經濟年鑑》編輯委員會 (ed.), *Zhongguo jingji nianjian 1984* 中國經濟年鑑 1984 (Almanac of China's Economy 1984) (Beijing: Beijing jingji guanli chubanshe 北京經濟管理出版社, 1984), pp. v–281–82.

33. Anonymous, *Zhonghua renmin gongheguo huanjing yu fazhan baogao* 中華人民共和國環境與發展報告 (Report on Environment and Development in the People's Republic of China) (Beijing: Zhongguo huanjing kexue chubanshe, 1992).

34. The problems faced by state enterprises are described in Chapter 8: Industrial Development by Victor Mok.

35. The need for economic and industrial restructuring has been emphasized in a number of papers. See, for example, Chen Yuqun, "Shanghaishi huanjing baohu de zhanlüe mubiao he cuoshi" (see note 13). This was also highlighted in *The Comprehensive Plan of Shanghai* prepared by the Bureau of Shanghai Urban Planning and Building Administration in 1992.

36. See note 33.

37. It was suggested that the development of Pudong could help alleviate the pollution problems in Shanghai through economic and industrial restructuring and reducing the pressure of development in the city core. This view is quite prevalent; an example is a commentary of the work in Shanghai which appeared in the *Zhongguo huanjing nianjian 1993* (see note 1).

38. Shanghaishi Pudong xinqu guanli weiyuanhui 上海市浦東新區管理委員會, "Maixiang 21 shiji de Shanghai Pudong xinqu" 邁向21世紀的上海浦東新區 (The Pudong New Area: Striding towards the 21st Century) in *Maixiang 21 shiji de Shanghai* (see note 4), pp. 537–52.

19

The Shanghai Model in Historical Perspective

Kerrie L. MacPherson

Shanghai, whether viewed from Chinese or foreign perspectives, has long been perceived as a "special" or "model" city (*tebie shi* 特別市). This was true of the original foreign settlements in the half century following its opening as a treaty port in 1843. It was a view subsequently shared and extended to the Chinese city during the Nationalist era 1927–1937, and to the entire collection of communities that comprised a unified Shanghai from 1949 to the present.[1] But these views themselves must be placed in a broader context.

It is axiomatic that the nineteenth century constituted "the age of great cities."[2] That expression embraced the expansion of liberal politics, the sloughing off of vestigial feudalism and aristocracies, the provision for the elevation of personal and public standards of living within environments which, to an unprecedented extent, were man-made. The principal monuments to this elaborate and pioneering process were London, Paris and New York in the Western world, or within the ambit of its influences, and many other cities such as Berlin, Chicago, Vienna, Tokyo or Shanghai, were close behind. Moreover, throughout the first thirty years of this century, abundant reflections upon the vast potentialities of these major metropolises, as well as refined assessments of their transparent shortcomings, proved to be the inspiriting force that underlay a redefinition of great cities. It was also a major source of encouragement for the planning or replanning of their futures.

Redefinition was essentially a political, juridical and administrative development, one which differed from place to place, that eventuated in the transformation of each of them. In the case of London, for instance, prior to 1888 the metropolis was an inchoate urban entity, entrusted with only a modestly prototypical municipal government. This was the metropolitan Board of Works, that was soon replaced by an administrative county — a first step in an ineluctable migration towards regionalization. Similarly, the consolidation of New York City into Greater New York by the City of Brooklyn and other contiguous areas in 1898 represented another step in the same direction for a community that would shortly supersede London as the world's foremost metropolis. Destruction of Parisian fortifications, circumvallations that girdled the city in the 1860s

---

I wish to dedicate this chapter to the memory of Gorden E. Cherry, honoured town planner and distinguished planning historian. His scholarship, friendship and encouragement remain an inspiration to my work.

and the concurrent Haussmannization of the city represented a quintessentially French variation on the same theme. Edo, arguably Asia's greatest metropolis at the beginning of the nineteenth century, in a like manner was transformed from a feudal administrative centre into a national capital of a modernizing state by the close of the century. And while other world cities lagged somewhat in redefining their bailiwicks, they, too, were headed towards their own versions of regionalization.[3]

Coincident with this urban redefinition, the first third of the century also brought forth an effusion of plans and planning, which extended beyond administrative alterations to include greater emphasis upon social amelioration or the enhancement of the quality of metropolitan life. Among the most notable of the planning impulses — many of them to become international in their influences — were Ebenezer Howard's Garden City concepts, Patrick Gedde's broad urban progressivism, the "City Beautiful" movement inspired by the Chicago World's Columbian Exposition and, in Europe, the pragmatic translations of the conceptions, amongst others, of Tony Garnier and Arturio Soria y Mata.

These heralds of the new urbanism were accompanied by a host of supportive municipal, architectural and planning publications, which provided fresh lines of communication about urban proposals and problems, while broadening forums for their intelligent description and discussion. And, as planning activities climaxed, almost in consonance with the last bursts of nineteenth century confidence in progress, they were both incorporated in and lent further expression by a number of internationally influential organizations or gatherings: the New York Bureau of Municipal Research, launched in 1906; the Berlin–Charlottenburg Seminar on City Planning and a similar Paris gathering that drew nearly 4,000 participants in 1908; the first national Conference on City Planning in Washington, D.C.; the British Parliament's sanction of the initial Town Planning Act; Tokyo's City Replanning Committee commencing work in 1888, using Haussmann's Paris reforms as a model; and, not least, the integration of city planning with leading university departments or programmes.[4]

Such, briefly, was the international matrix within which Shanghai commenced the development of its own municipal government and modern identity. A context in which the planning and replanning of the role of China's major cities has absorbed the immense energies of successive Chinese regimes despite differing ideologies and, since 1949, periodic ideological campaigns and policies designed to weaken them.[5]

Shanghai in the Traditional Urban Hierarchy

Shanghai's ascent as a world class city, in company with London, Paris, New York or Tokyo in the nineteenth and twentieth centuries, was not a story of a past foretold. There was little in its origins in the mid-thirteenth century as a *xian* 縣 -level city in China's traditional hierarchy of urban places that could account for its dramatic growth and subsequent rise to pre-eminence commencing in the latter half of the nineteenth century. Yet qualifications are in order. Unlike Japan's two great ports of Yokohama and Kobe that attained importance only after the opening of Japan to foreign trade in the 1850s, Shanghai was already functioning as a modest agrarian based regional commercial port and entrepôt.[6]

Water and man's intervention in the natural environment were key physical factors in Shanghai's positioning in China's traditional reticulation of urban places. Extensive hydraulic engineering, the extension and then maintenance of waterways for irrigation and commerce, as well as the construction of a seawall along the eastern coastal reaches of Shanghai's hinterland, created viable agricultural land out of a swampy peninsula south of the Yangzi River (長江) (Figure 19.1). Between the eleventh and fifteenth centuries, the silting and shrinking of the Wusong River (吳淞江) and Qinglong River (青龍江) doomed Qinglong 青龍 , the major commercial town of the region, but dredging and canal construction helped to expand the Huangpu River (黃浦江), raising the prospects of Shanghai sited on its west banks, twelve miles from its confluence with the mighty Yangzi and the sea.[7] Even its name changed in the local chronicles, symbolizing this transformation — Hudu 滬瀆 or "fishing stake river [landing]" to Shanghai, "up from the sea."[8]

Proximity to more economically and administratively favoured cities during what Mark Elvin calls "the medieval urban revolution in market structure and urbanization" from the second half of the eighth century to the southern Song 宋 — cities such as Suzhou 蘇州 , Ningbo 寧波 , Guangzhou 廣州 , Fuzhou 福州 or Jinjiang 晉江 (China's chief seaport during the southern Song) — also guaranteed Shanghai a place in the rapidly developing hierarchy as a marketing town of some note, specializing in cotton textiles.[9] One measure of its economic growth was its inclusion in the periodic despoliation by ostensibly "Japanese" pirates on coastal cities during the sixteenth century. Another was the periodic redistricting and containment of Shanghai's immediate hinterland by central governments not prepared to award its economic success with administrative status.[10]

Figure 19.1 Maps Illustrating the Successive Administrative and Geographical Changes to the Shanghai Region from the Song to Qing Dynasties

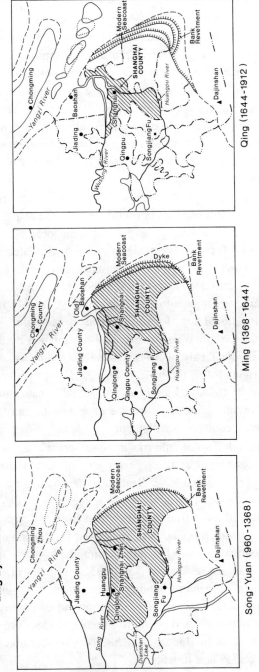

Song-Yuan (960-1368)

Ming (1368-1644)

Qing (1644-1912)

Source: Wang Xiaojian 王孝俭 (ed.) *Shanghai xianzhi* 上海縣志 (Shanghai County Gazetteer) (Shanghai: Shanghai renmin chubanshe, 1993). Adapted with the help of John Bradford, School of Architecture, University of Hong Kong.

By the mid-sixteenth century, partly for defense, and partly in recognition of its growing importance, Shanghai gained its massive walls, a symbol of administrative rank, approximately three and one half miles in circumference, enclosing a moderate sized city of approximately 252.5 ha of land.[11] From that time on, Shanghai was fixed politically, as a mere *xian*-level city subordinate to its administrative superior, Suzhou, the *fu* 府, or prefectural city in eastern Jiangsu 江蘇. It was to be contained politically by a failure to promote it in the administrative system, and economically subordinated by a substantial transfer of payments to its regional superior and the state, until a major redefinition of the role of cities commenced with the republican revolution in the early twentieth century.[12]

In reality, this was the Chinese context in which Shanghai interests fought their way to a position of prominence on the maps. Indeed, struggle was essential. For originally, its geographical location, a location which after the fact of its growing significance was touted widely by city "boosters," by tradespeople and enamoured transients, by historians and geographers as critical to its rise, at the very least proved more of a distinct handicap rather than an automatic advantage. Certainly in the 1830s and 1840s, its locational superiorities seemed to be slight. And, at the conclusion of the Opium Wars, its eventual designation by the Qing 清 as a treaty port by the Treaty of Nanking of 1842, with British and American settlement rights following in 1843 and the French concession five years later, cannot be construed glibly as an official bonanza dispensed for the benefit of foreign interests or for the expectant Chinese merchants who sought to conduct business with them.

Well enough if some enthusiastic observers wished to gild Shanghai's future by depicting it as the gateway to China, as the entrepôt for the abundance of the Yangzi River Basin, and as a natural magnet for international commerce. Such attributions before the first decades of the twentieth century stemmed more from romance than from realism. There was scant sustenance for such prophesies to be derived for Shanghainese or foreigners over a century ago dwelling amidst sinuous, regularly silted watercourses, settled upon the residues of 750,000 square miles of interior drainage on mud flats more than one hundred metres deep, living an uncomfortable distance from the open sea in an area devoid of readily accessible industrial raw materials, and trying to prosper in close proximity to established competitors in Hangzhou 杭州, Ningbo, Suzhou, Nanjing 南京, Jingdezhen 景德鎮 and Jinjiang.[13]

Foreign Shanghai as a Model

Shanghai's impressive economic growth during the latter half of the nineteenth and early twentieth centuries, the magnetism that it exerted upon hundreds of thousands, eventually millions of Chinese, as well as upon smaller but important numbers of foreigners, as well as its basic political establishment, were the direct consequences of British, American and French settlement after 1843. Against the old walled city that had remained virtually in stasis during the first half of the nineteenth century, these foreigners constructed the medical topographies requisite to medical and sanitary progress which, in turn, were prerequisite to converting an otherwise unpromising, if not forbidding, site into a healthy and habitable place even by relatively modern criteria. They furnished the nucleus of Shanghai with what passed eminently well through the last century for a modern urban infrastructure: raised, broadened and paved streets; a tram system; a pure and continuous water supply system; a bunded foreshore; extended and improved drainage; adequate sewage disposal; eleemosynary and charitable institutions; a constabulary and a fire brigade. In order to finance and advance such work, a fairly open, voluntary, and insofar as foreigners were concerned, judicially equitable, liberal government was created, epitomized by the Shanghai Municipal Council[14] (Figure 19.2).

For these reasons, foreigners within the settlements viewed what they had created as a "Model Settlement." One that was exemplary, unique and worthy of emulation. Indeed, comparisons were readily made between the estate of the settlements' populations and those of the great classical republics: Periclean Athens, Republican Rome, even fifteenth century Venice. However, extravagant and historically glib such allusions may have been, they nonetheless were commonly espoused. In short, as perceived, the settlements were a remarkably free and viable polity, utterly unindebted for its existence, as Justice Feetham would later acknowledge, to any state, to any legislature, or to any government.[15]

Between 1904 and 1914, when Shanghai's Chinese initiated and devised their own instruments of municipal self-governance, they were openly praised by the Settlement foreigners for their electicism. That is, on the face of it, the Chinese seemed to be following the same evolutionary steps earlier traced by the Shanghai Municipal Council and its antecedents: from a "General Works Board," to a "Self-government Office," to a "Municipal Government Hall." Furthermore, the functional responsibilities of those fledgling institutions intimately resembled those of the

**Figure 19.2   Map of the Foreign Settlements of Shanghai,
Including the French Concession and the Walled Chinese City, as of 1881**

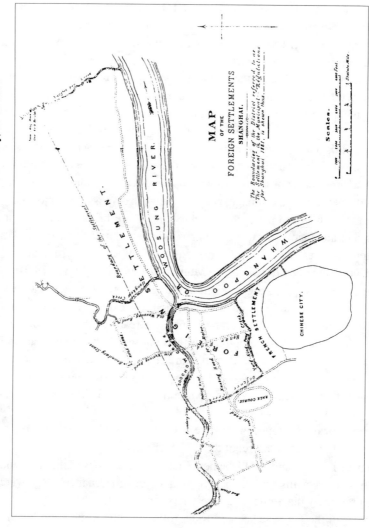

Source: Shanghai Municipal Council. *Report for the Year Ended 31st December 1881* (Shanghai: Kelly and Walsh, 1881).

Settlement's Council: namely, the fielding of a constabulary (or militia); constructing or improving roads and bridges; seeing to the disposal of garbage, refuse and night soil, as well as to the adequacy of drainage and sewerage; overseeing schools, charities and the licensing and inspection of retail shops; and of course, the assessment and collection of taxes.[16] As one British observer concluded in the *Municipal Gazette*, the Chinese, as evidenced by the aggregate of these municipal enterprises, were paying:

> the highest compliment possible, for in this (Shanghai) and other centres of industry she (China) appears to be anxious to adopt our form of government, our legal practice, our police procedure, our municipal methods, and even those minor social matters, our food and clothing.[17]

The intertwining of patronizing views, pride and conceit in this observation were manifest. Certainly, it belied any grasp whatever of the fact that the genesis of Chinese municipal government at Shanghai, as Mark Elvin has noted, was the product of "a steady evolution in local administration" well prior to 1905. And while the comment carried in the *Municipal Gazette* had no claims to profundity, it ignored the many skills gained by Chinese in bureaucratic management, in the oversight of water conservancies, notably provision made for the Huangpu Conservancy in 1905, which were revised and extended in 1912, in the essentials of taxation, and in the planning and direction of rudimentary public works by Shanghai's gentry over preceding centuries.[18]

However, even with the lengthy experiences garnered in local administration by the gentry being fully granted, there was truth, nevertheless, inherent in foreigners' conceits about Chinese mimesis in regard to the Settlement's municipal institutions and civic life. Although leading elements of the Kuomintang (Guomindang 國民黨) were no more comfortable with the urbanity, cosmopolitanism, or "foreignness" of Shanghai than was more recently to be the case with Mao Zedong's 毛澤東 regime, they were fully cognizant of the Settlement's inescapable influences. For instance, Marshal Sun Chuanfang 孫傳芳 in the mid-1920s, overlord of Jiangsu, Jiangxi 江西, Zhejiang 浙江, Anhui 安徽 and Fujian 福建, in addressing the Chinese General Chamber of Commerce in Shanghai, conceded the importance of the Model Settlement: first, because of the usefulness of the lessons learned there over the previous seventy-five years; and second, because the Settlement's achievements afforded a benchmark for Chinese municipal and democratic aspirations.

The Greater Shanghai Plan

Sun's immediate objective in his May 1926 speech was the unification of all administrative powers pertinent to Shanghai into "one centre so that it might have the authority to improve municipal government." Given a more mundane translation, this meant the development of a new port, resolution of animosities endemic to the existence of extraterritoriality — the so-called "long standing diplomatic disputes" (as they were courteously phrased), and the conversion of "the area outside of the foreign settlements into a model city." More importantly, it meant the eventual abolition of the foreign concessions themselves.

A nationalist by self-proclamation, Sun, of course, spoke to his country's exuberant nationalism. "Whenever I come to a treaty port," he declared, "I feel thoroughly humiliated ... because the treaty port is a long standing reminder of our loss of sovereignty." But, having reaffirmed his patriotic credentials before his audience, Sun then invoked the foreigners' municipal accomplishments the more vigorously to inspirit civic and democratic sentiments among his compatriots.

For as it transpired, his "humiliation" when in Shanghai had a dual provenance. It was foremost, a loss of Chinese sovereignty. In addition, however, as he instantly indicated, there was another source of his mortification:

> Whenever we pass from the concessions into Chinese, we feel that we are crossing into a different world — the former is the upper and the latter is the underworld, for nothing in Chinese territory — roads, buildings, or public health — can be compared to the concessions.

That stark contrast in Sun's judgment, constituted "the greatest of our national humiliations, much greater," he emphasized, "than our loss of sovereignty."[19]

In this regard, Sun differed little from his predecessors. In 1912, General Chen Qimei 陳其美 impressed by the "prosperity and efficiency" of the Settlement, used his authority as Military Governor of the Port to embark upon innovative administrative reforms in the Chinese city. Reputedly, the attempted reformation failed to generate more than tepid public enthusiasm which, in part, certainly revealed a general refusal to yield up the essential revenues. Destruction of the old city's walls and their replacement by the circular Minguo Road 民國路 represented the sole "permanent" results of what for a time had been a flurry of proposals.[20]

Yet, Shanghai's difficulties in this respect were strikingly similar to the vexations experienced in other world cities — London, Paris and New York — both in terms of their inner political necessities and their relationships to surrounding polities and to the state. Moreover, the imperatives that underlay visions of a Greater Shanghai, that is, of a Chinese metropolis, persisted: those imperatives being the dissolution or absorption of the foreign concessions and their simultaneous substitution by Chinese municipal institutions that were at least equally as effective as organizations like the Settlement's Municipal Council. Thus, in this light, it is not difficult to account for Sun Yatsen's (孫逸仙) 1921 plan for a "Great Port of Pudong 浦東," Zhang Jian's 張謇 Wusong 吳松 scheme, or Sun Baochi's 孫寶琦 plans for the creation of a "special area" status for the city, each of which foundered on the shoals of Jiangsu's official indifference and the plans dependent upon it.[21]

The marking of these administrative wrecks provided ample warning to Marshal Sun that he would be obliged to chart a municipal course of his own. Above all, he sought to avoid lodging his plan in the vise of conflicting administrative authorities. It was to escape such entanglements that he decreed the establishment of a unified organization charged with the preliminary development of Greater Shanghai. Prior consultations with the Civil Governor lent a harmonious cast to Sun's creation of a directorate of the Port of Shanghai and Wusong and his personal assumption of the office of director general. Unable to reside in Shanghai, Sun deputed responsibility for execution of his plan to Dr. Ding Wenjiang 丁文江. At thirty-nine, two years junior to Sun, Dr. Ding brought impressive training and experience to his position. Basically a geologist and mining engineer, he had studied in Cambridge, Glasgow and Freiburg. With his formal education completed just before the Nationalist era dawned, he served subsequently as the director of the Agriculture and Commerce Ministry's Geological Survey (中國地質調查所), as general manager of the Beipiao Coal Mining Company (北票煤鑛公司), as trustee of the China Foundation for the Promotion of Education and Culture, and simultaneously with Sun's selection of him, he sat briefly as one of the three Chinese members of the Anglo–Chinese Boxer Indemnity Commission. Whereas Sun, a native of Shandong, could claim extensive administrative and military experience within China, Ding complemented him with his Western background and his knowledge of the Settlement's most numerous foreigners — the British. Indeed, his stated task was to overcome foreign as well as domestic opposition to Sun's project.[22]

The Directorate of the Port of Shanghai and Wusong was not a municipality. Sun and Ding acknowledged its transitional character. Ideally, as they well understood, a Greater Shanghai would have to embrace Nanshi 南市, Pudong, Zhabei 閘北 and Baoshan 寶山, along with many villages and smaller towns, any number of which possessed their own jurisdictions, officials, gentry and local interests — not the least of them agricultural. And there were additional complexities that suffused the region encompassed by these bodies. Through the north and west of the area, for example, ran the disputed "extra-concessional" roads (*yujie malu* 越界馬路) built by the Settlement under the Yangjingbang Land Regulations (洋涇浜章程). By 1926, 170 miles of road had been constructed, every mile replete with actual or potential friction with foreign perspectives and interests (Figure 19.3). These highways were of no small concern, for their total extent of 6,666 2/3 acres was larger than the foreign settlements themselves, hence they posed serious practical questions. Did the Settlement's Land Regulations extend to these sectors? Who was responsible for policing them? What authorities controlled the utilities above and below such streets? How and by whom were taxes or licensing fees to be levied? And so on. Similarly, Nanshi and Zhabei, even as the Directorate was being formed, were already municipalities, the latter having just been taken over by the provincial government. Both municipalities, furthermore, were adjacent to the foreign settlements, again with the usual blurring of mutual interests and authorities, while Pudong was studded with scores of foreign industries.[23]

Worse yet, within the Directorate's ambit, sources of revenue were not forthcoming. Nanshi and Zhabei together raised less than RMB1 million annually from taxation; even their police salaries were unsecured. Pudong and Wusong, indeed, most of the localities lying west of the settlements, suffered from a total deficiency of municipal income. Preliminary estimates of the Directorate's areal responsibilities revealed, in fact, that the vast bulk of taxable properties unfortunately lay within the foreign settlements.[24]

Sadly, too, Shanghai harbour, a world class port and, according to Marshal Sun, "China's greatest source of revenue," as well as the master key to unlocking the potentialities of Greater Shanghai, was itself a fiscal oasis greatly in danger of dessication. Trade's reliance on the harbour, reduced to basics, meant reliance upon "a stretch of the muddy and erratic Huangpu River." But the natural vagaries of the River were only slightly more troublesome than the eccentricities of the governments charged with its mastery.

Figure 19.3 Map Showing the Regional Development of Shanghai as of 1926, Highlighting Land-use Patterns

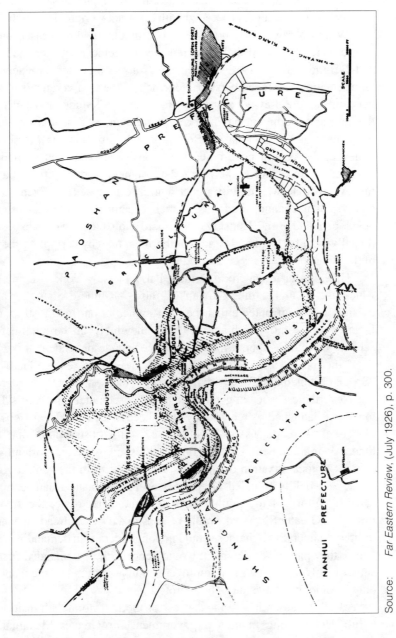

Source: *Far Eastern Review*, (July 1926), p. 300.

In 1905, cognizant of the River's vital importance, the Treaty Powers and the Chinese government established the Huangpu Conservancy which, reasonably well funded, proceeded with essential work to deepen the channel. Within a few years, however, government funding ceased and the Conservancy operations halted. A renewed agreement between the Powers and Beijing 北京 in 1912 revived the Conservancy and broadened the representation of its membership. Nonetheless, the Conservancy's revenues henceforth were drawn exclusively from the port's trade, assistance from the central government having been withdrawn. Withdrawal of funding, however, was not a signal of Beijing's neutrality. For, as Marshal Sun believed, the central government had consistently pursued a "policy of obstruction" in regard to the Port's development — obstruction at a juncture when trade was rapidly outstripping Port capacities. Even landfills composed of channel dredgings, which became valuable real estate, as developed under the Conservancy Board's auspices, were disposed of illegally both by local and central authorities, thereby "crippling the work of the Board."

Thus, not different from London, Paris, or New York — company in which the Shanghai of 1926 ranked third — Chinese Shanghai almost continuously confronted either the indifference or outright hostility of the larger polities into which it fitted and, inevitably in the administrative scheme of things, upon which it had been made dependent. Like other great metropolises, it was always to be viewed as "exceptional," as a "Special Municipality" (特別市), in effect as a case without precedents.

Nevertheless, cleaving through a sea of conundrums, Sun's Directorate was launched by remarkably clear-headed leaders. Expositions of its objectives were discussed openly, along with obstructions that could hinder their attainment. Lacking financial resources, that is, without viable sources of local taxation or financial sustenance from the central government, Sun boldly founded his project on the ultimate urban reality. He candidly informed the public that while the Directorate, the first step towards a Greater Shanghai, would be subsidized by an already inadequate military budget, Shanghainese could no longer persist in demanding results before they paid taxes. Payment would henceforth be demanded first and, subsequently, if there was no improvement in government, "then, and then only" would they have the right to protest.[25]

Of all the essentials to the success of the Directorate's transition into a fully functioning municipal government for Greater Shanghai, this forthright claim to revenues was the most fundamental. Indeed, Dr. Ding's attempt to marshal a host of disparate localities and administrations under one rubric may legitimately be perceived as a campaign to gain a secure fiscal base. By implication, it also posed a lesson in the burdens of democratic citizenship in a metropolitan setting. That is, if and when semblances of democracy reappeared. For, the Directorate, as well as what followed it, represented an imposition of municipal authority, not a return to the singular, albeit only marginally democratic "Regulations for Local Self-Government" which had evolved under the Council and its Assembly between 1909 and 1912 — a development that has been described as "the apogee of ... Shanghai self-government."[26]

Authority, percipience and realism, consequently, marked the transformation of the Directorate, between June 1926 and July 1927, into a Special Municipality, into the City Government of Greater Shanghai (大上海特別市政府). The new entity was at once severed from any dependency on either the Shanghai district or Jiangsu provincial government. Rather, by 1930 it was directly subordinated to the Executive Yuan in Nanjing. Less than two years later, with Wu Tiecheng's 吳鐵城 installation as mayor, his position in the Executive Yuan, as well as his membership in the Kuomintang's Central Executive Committee, effected a direct link between Shanghai and the central government. Here, of course, structural comparisons of Greater Shanghai and the government of the International Settlement (the Shanghai Municipal Council) failed. For the Settlement was politically independent; whereas the City Government of Greater Shanghai could, in many regards, be seen as a colonial dependent of the Chinese central government, of the Kuomintang Party. In that sense, the "model" was Chinese, closer to French and German practice than to British or American.[27]

The structure and basic functioning of Greater Shanghai's municipal government, briefly described, included ten separate bureaux, as well as a Secretariat and a Counsellors' Office modelled on the previously established city government of Guangzhou. Fiscal reforms were promptly initiated under the short-term mayoralties of Huang Fu 黃郛 , Zhang Dingfan 張定璠 and Zhang Qun 張群 . Taxation was extended and made more equitable and, as a result, revenues rose dramatically. Close attention was paid to urban fundamentals: in order of importance, expenditures went to extraordinary constructions, to police affairs, to ordinary construction, education and culture which, for example, took about 20% of budgeted spending, and to public health, an area in which favourable comparisons were made with Western cities. More importantly, measured against those in other major Chinese cities, these expenditures appeared impressive.[28]

However singular the foregoing accomplishments were, they none-theless constitute the basics of urban life. However, the retention of an urban vision was by far the most interesting and unique aspect of the municipality's agenda. This was particularly true under the administration of Mayor Wu Tiecheng, which began 1 January 1932, after the swift departure of three earlier mayors. Although born in Jiangxi, Wu's family was native to Guangdong, hailing from the same district as Sun Yatsen. He was educated briefly in Japan at Meiji University, enjoying a career that carried him through important police and military positions, magistracies, counsellorships, and when just forty into the Legislative Yuan and the Ministry of Interior as a vice-minister. Wu was the first to give official public voice to the conception of Shanghai as the urban expression of a "Chinese Renaissance." Furthermore, the impressive municipal construc-tion and urban development during his tenure (1932–1936) was ac-complished despite Japanese military operations in the area.[29]

The Plan, which included not only the redevelopment of the older districts now comprising Greater Shanghai, but also the building of a new city centre, evolved from the work of the City Planning Commission, which commenced its work in 1929. Dr. Shen Yi 沈怡, Commissioner of Public Works for ten years, lent continuity to the Plan's execution, though the political and military turmoil in China prevented its successful comple-tion. A German-trained engineer, with expertise in hydraulic engineering, in which he would later gain renown, Shen gave able direction to the Planning Commission.[30]

The City Planning Commission of Greater Shanghai was charged with the goal of creating a comprehensive plan that would represent a broad spectrum of community interests as well as provide for the much needed physical expansion of China's largest city. The Commission was com-posed of eleven technical experts drawn from the various city departments, as well as national and international advisors. Dong Dayou 董大酉, a native of Hangzhou, for example, though only in his thirties, had earned B.S. and M.S. degrees from the University of Minnesota and had worked for the Shanghai architectural firm of Suenson and Company, before be-coming the chief architect of Greater Shanghai's proposed Civic Centre. He would later enjoy a bright career in the Society of Chinese Architects as a secretary and editor.[31] Somewhat older, the foreign consultants who reviewed and critiqued the Plan included a past president of the American Society of Civil Engineers, Carl E. Grunsky, a German-educated Califor-nian, who had served as one of the seven original engineers on the Panama

Canal and who enjoyed an international reputation as an expert on hydraulics. Another American, Asa Phillips, a respected city planner, and University of Berlin, Professor Herman Jensen added their own weight to the consultancy.[32]

Basically, what was proposed was a new central city located in the Jiangwan 江灣 district between Wusong (the site of the new port) and the International Settlement, close to the Yangzi River on more than a thousand acres of land that were to be embanked and zoned. Rail and future extensions of Port facilities were carefully considered in relation to the site, as well as a proposed system of broad, rectilinear streets designed to alleviate Shanghai's already enormous congestion and frighteningly high rentals. Roughly 15% of the area was designated for parks and open spaces, including land on both sides of the numerous waterways that cut through the area (Figure 19.4).

A geographically determined zoning system was to be utilized, in contradistinction to the system whereby a series of concentric circles governed building regulations. Cognizance of the prevailing wind patterns also decided the location of industries. Indeed, the Commission adduced a myriad of beautifully integrated detail just in fleshing out the project's groundwork.

Most dramatic and imaginative of all, however, was the planned Civic Centre, the architectural and spiritual heart of the "new" city. Occupying about 333 acres, it evinced a style and scale reminiscent of Haussmann's Paris, even to its provision of a "grand croisee," intersecting right angle roads (up to 60 m wide) on east–west and north–south axes. The main intersection of these axes was to be "known henceforth as the Centre of Shanghai." A 50 m pagoda was planned as the centrepiece of a 170 m tract, with a 600 m, Washington style, reflecting pool. Nearby sites for major government buildings, a library, art gallery, additional, if smaller, reflecting pools, a Municipal Auditorium seating 3,000 people and a comprehensive Medical Centre. The landscaping was to complete the ensemble with extensive gardens, traditional style bridges and a memorial *pai lou* 牌樓 as a gateway to the complex[33] (Figure 19.5).

Although much of the complex remained unbuilt and what was constructed was almost entirely demolished during the Sino–Japanese War, a few obvious generalizations are in order. Its conception was eminently Chinese. If there were impressions of Paris, or Washington evoked by it, the closest comparisons, nevertheless, were most aptly applied to traditional Beijing. But with this difference. Though its execution was to be under

Figure 19.4   Planning Map Showing the Civic Centre and Road System of Greater Shanghai at Jiangwan

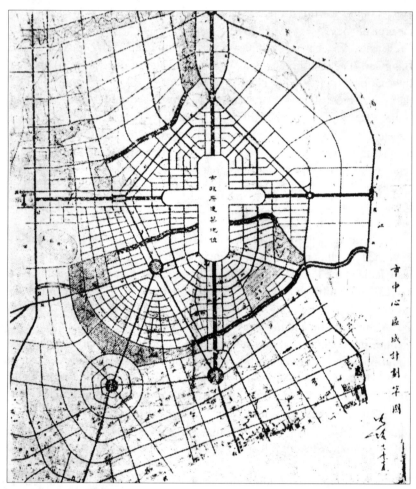

Source: *Far Eastern Review*, (June 1930), p. 296.

authoritarian auspices, its representations, its architectural statement, was clearly open and, in that sense, unlike the forbidden City, democratic. Its aesthetics were far superior to the bland utilitarianism, the cottage coziness, of a Garden City. It was, on the drafting boards anyway, less overwhelmed by monumentality than Washington and, considering provisions for the port and rail connections, it was at once more practical in a functional economic sense. On paper, it escaped being tarred with the worst

Figure 19.5 The Greater Shanghai Municipal Administration Building at Jiangwan, Formally Occupied on 1 January 1934

Source: Dayu Doon [Dong Dayou] "Architecture Chronicle," *T'ian-hsia Monthly* (1936), plate following p. 360.

criticisms of Haussmann's Paris: its development was not at the expense of tradition encrusted neighbourhoods, nor did it suffer from lengthy boulevards, sided with uniform, rather monotonous structures, designed like the Opera, for example, to lead the eye to monumental architecture that many felt was not worth viewing anyway. If comparisons are in order, they would seem to pertain to the more imaginative urban plans of the 1950s to the 1980s — Rome's EUR, for instance, or Montreal's Olympic City; or, on a smaller scale, the Civic Centre projects spotted across the Western world, mostly as part of urban revitalization. Redesigned Greater Shanghai, as far as can be presently determined, was sufficiently bold and inventive to have been decades in advance of anything else in the world.

Perhaps more critically, Greater Shanghai, in the context of this century's planning enthusiasms, spoke to a vision of a modern China that was at once pragmatic, in developing the infrastructure of the various areas comprising greater Shanghai, as well as achieving the political goal of uniting all the areas comprising Shanghai into one unified administrative whole, that would encompass and eventually absorb the foreign settlements with minimal disruption to foreign trade and investment. Civil unrest and war prevented its realization as originally planned, yet contrary to the assertion that "after the war Municipal Officials abandoned the idea of Greater Shanghai," the abrogation of foreign treaty rights and concessions during the war helped pave the way for more concerted planning, and the Greater Shanghai Plan (as well as its predecessors) formed the basis for fresh initiatives.[34]

Post-War Master Planning and the Greater Shanghai Model

In 1946, the Shanghai City Planning Board was created, composed of foreign and Chinese technical experts, to draft a "Master Plan" for Shanghai to be implemented in successive stages over a 25-year period, with a 50-year planning of the entire region as the final goal. This move towards regional master planning, embracing the physical structure of municipal development, as well as regional economic growth with co-ordinated development of transportation and industry that emerged from the wartime imperatives of national defense, was in consonance with post-war regional planning elsewhere — for example, Abercrombie's Greater London Plan, or the activities of the National Resources Planning Board in formulating new urban strategies for major American cities.[35] Shanghai was to remain a "special" city, that is, directly under the control of the central government, and the pre-war experience of planning "Greater Shanghai," as well as a refined assessment of its shortcomings, provided the basis of the Master Plan. In the words of Mayor Wu Guozhen 吳國楨 in a public speech delivered before the fifth meeting of the Board, "parts of the Greater Shanghai Plan were successful" despite the obstacles to comprehensive planning posed by divided jurisdictions and civil unrest. With the liberation of China and Greater Shanghai after the war, planning at the regional level was crucial: "if we do not start planning now, 100 years of Shanghai's development will be lost."[36]

Drafting the Master Plan and amassing a statistical base proceeded apace. The Plan provided for functional zoning, the co-ordinated development of all communication and transportation lines, the dispersal of the exploding urban population in Shanghai's already congested districts by the establishment of "satellite towns," and the pivotal development of Pudong, the agricultural district east of the Huangpu River that had historically remained undeveloped because it lacked adequate cross-river connections (it was beyond the jurisdictional reach of the former foreign settlements and their development priorities), though it lay only 2,000 feet across the river from Shanghai's central business district. It was well understood by the planners that a balanced development of Pudong and Puxi 浦西 could only be accomplished by bridging the river (an unrealized feature of the Greater Shanghai Plan) and by the additional construction of a cross-river tunnel to facilitate traffic. The co-ordination of all rail junctions and deliberations over the feasibility of emplacing a subway or an elevated rail system to service the city further preoccupied the Board. Although urban planning was supposed to emanate from the national government, dispensation of resources was at a premium. Operating without large-scale funds, a seemingly chronic state of affairs for Shanghai's planners, the municipal government repeatedly petitioned the central government for fiscal relief, thereby eliciting approval for local reconstruction. In the meantime, the Board initiated the practical restoration and redevelopment of efficient ferry services across the Huangpu as part of the government's "First Five-year Plan."[37]

The redevelopment of the port, however, was of unparalleled importance and the Board scrutinized Sun Yatsen's scheme for the "Great Port of Pudong" and the pre-war plans of Greater Shanghai. The state of the Port and the Huangpu River had reached crisis proportions. During the eight years of occupation by Japan (1937–1945), the river remained undredged, and no harbour improvements were actualized, though by 1939,

43.79% of China's total imports and 57.72% of her exports figured in Shanghai's trade statistics.[38] The redevelopment of the Port and its efficient management were essential to Shanghai's present as well as its future role in national reconstruction. Therefore, two sites were proposed to service not only Shanghai's projected growth, but also to spur the development of the entire Yangzi River region. Finally, for the further processing of unfinished products (imported free of duty and intended for re-export), a "Foreign Trade Zone" along the lines of pre-war Hamburg or San Francisco was planned.[39]

Yet, however encouraging these modernizing efforts in the planning of Shanghai's future, the failure of the Nationalist government to cope with China's endemic problems, as well as the extraordinary burdens of post-war reconstruction, led to their unravelling. For example, although the reconstruction of the Zhabei district into a "model" community was continuously planned since the first Japanese attack decimated the area in 1932 — with a second attack eliminating 100% of its industrial and manufacturing base in 1937 — the project was hampered by galloping inflation and a scarcity of funds.[40] By 1947, the city government was running an estimated RMB92 billion deficit, without recourse to central funding, having been warned to balance its budget before any more funds would be forthcoming.[41] Amidst more pressing concerns of rice and wheat shortages, hoarding, lack of basic utilities, and the civil unrest engendered by corruption and mismanagement of relief efforts, as well as escalating civil war with the Communist forces advancing on Shanghai, the estimated cost of RMB500 billion needed to reconstruct Zhabei's "model" district was beyond the grasp of Shanghai's Municipal planners.[42]

China was increasingly beyond the grasp of the Nationalist Government. In 1949, after the retreat of the Kuomintang to Taiwan (principally through Shanghai), it was the commissioner of Public Works and executive secretary of the Planning Board, Zhao Zukang 趙祖康 , who acted as mayor of Shanghai during transfer to the new Communist regime. Zhao was reconfirmed in his position as commissioner of Public Works and, in 1954, became head of the Planning and Construction Bureau of the People's Government of Shanghai. All personnel, however, with "blotches" on their service records such as "corruption or reactionary inclinations and opposed by the people," would be cut from the payroll, and work was now to be prosecuted with a zealous regard for the "interests of the people" towards the goal of creating a "socialist" Shanghai.[43] The City administratively remained a "special city," under the direct control of the central government with little or no autonomy. Socialist construction during the period of 1949–1956, meant essentially the restoration of all utilities, communication and transportation lines and other basic infrastructural improvements, as opposed to building a few "foreign" inspired, or monumental buildings associated with the Kuomintang period. Yet, it also meant that some articulated vision of a "socialist city" would embellish such pragmatic labours.

Such a vision was conjured up in 1956. A massive urban renewal project was proposed for the Zhabei district, as well as the planned dispersal of population (and industry) through the establishment of seven satellite towns around Shanghai. Contrary to assertions that these plans represented, "the most daring departures from the pre-1956 trends" or that Shanghai's planners were "following the Soviet planner's lead in community design," they were important features of post-war 1946–1949 planning in which Commissioner Zhao had a primary role.[44] In that sense, they were representative of a more continuous course of urban planning and development in Shanghai than has previously been appreciated.

A Note on Shanghai's Post-1949 Deconstruction

The vision that informed pre-liberation Shanghai became its undoing in the period extending from the Great Leap Forward (1958) and the Cultural Revolution (1966–1976) to the fall of the "Gang of Four." Briefly surveyed, Shanghai's foreign (and capitalist) and Kuomintang roots were to be expunged, and all urban planning was to be subsumed under various ministries of the central government in conformity with national development priorities. Shanghai, to that end, was to be transformed from a "parasitic," or "consumer city," to a "socialist" and "producer" city. Socialism was to provide the answers to industrial and population concentrations in the cities through a policy of spatial "evenization," or the elimination of the distinctions between the countryside and the city, and the combination of industry and agriculture by collectivization. This included the elimination of private enterprise and property, the planned but unvoluntaristic dispersal of the urban population in satellite town development, and the urban manageability of potentially threatening social groups was to be accomplished by their forced removal to the countryside in the collectively termed "*xia fang* 下放 " campaigns including the transfer of urban youth in the "return to the villages" (*hui xiang* 回鄉) campaigns. These policies were heralded as a unique contribution to world urbanism:

> China's claim to a special place in the annals of urbanisation must rest on two pillars of political and social policy peculiar to its culture and polity. The first is an uncompromising and often painful command over human resources, which has allowed over-urbanisation to be temporarily overcome. The second is the achievement of substantial industrial growth without the urban misery which we commonly associate with industrial revolutions in their early stages.[45]

Even if so-called "over-urbanization" had been temporarily forestalled, in lieu of any definitional clarity of what that meant in the Chinese context, the price was a heavy one. Was the ruthless shifting and dumping of millions of ostensibly human commodities in the campaigns to depopulate the cities, or the brutal and long-term effects of the great famine, the result of the Great Leap Forward's collectivist industrial and agricultural reorganization, said to have affected over 100 million people during 1958–1965 in no way responsible for "urban misery"? The human costs had to be counted all along. Yet, despite the expansion to Shanghai's administrative boundaries in 1958–1959 when 10 *xian* of Jiangsu province were annexed by the city, Shanghai's population continued to grow at a phenomenal rate, from 5.03 million in 1949 to 11.86 million in 1982.[46] Other problems suffused Shanghai's socialist transformation, particularly central fiscal policies which drained Shanghai's revenues through unfavourable taxation, leaving little to fund improvements or even to maintain of existing facilities, the basics of urban life. During the years 1949–1984, the central government was said to have extracted 87% of the total local revenues, much higher than any other urban unit of a similar size. Ramifications of such "transactions of decline," and other anti-development policies pursued by the central government included the demise of Shanghai's volume of foreign trade to levels below comparatively underdeveloped Hong Kong by 1958.[47] As one analyst concluded:

> Only during the period of the First Five-year Plan (1953–57) was there even modest development of Chinese cities. For the rest of the period from 1949 to 1978, Chinese cities grew slowly or stagnated for want of consistent and rational development policies.[48]

The Pudong New Area and The Shanghai Model

As ample testimony to the failure of the policies pursued since 1958 to achieve acceptable levels of modernization, the Third Plenary of the Eleventh Party Committee initiated key policy changes redefining the role of cities on the agenda of national development and dramatically reversed the policies pursued over the previous twenty years. Shanghai assumed unprecedented importance as not only the premier "key-point city" (*zhongdian chengshi* 重點城市) — a revival of the urban policies of the 1950s that recognized the scale economies of great cities and their role as agents in the expansion of economic life — but also it became the largest area designated for development to date with the opening of the Pudong New Area (浦東新區) in 1990. It now became the model of a "socialist" city that the rest of China's cities were exhorted to emulate. In the spirit of the reforms set in motion in 1978, policies were formulated that allowed for the experimentation in market economies by the creation of "special economic zones," as well as recognizing that foreign investment was a powerful tool for development. Shanghai was regionalized, making it a provincial-like urban unit, specifically to obtain a wider tax base and to provide for some local autonomy in decision making for the region. Similarly, visionary planning was back on the agenda, and the State Council accepted the city's New Comprehensive Plan of Shanghai in October 1986 that bore remarkable resemblance to the pre-war and post-war urban plans described in this chapter. At the same time, the municipal government established the Consultative Small Group for the Development of Pudong. A prominent member ("old technical cadre") of that Committee was Zhao Zukang, former executive secretary of the post-war Master Planning Committee and commissioner of Public Works in Shanghai from 1945 to 1954.[49]

In April of 1990, Li Peng 李鵬 officially sanctioned the opening of the Pudong New Area project. This monumental and ambitious project will be the pivot upon which the redevelopment of the entire Yangzi River region will depend — the "head of the dragon." It will also anchor further up river, the controversial and massive "Three Gorges Dam Project" (三峽大壩工程) — a water control project that will reshape the geography and settlement patterns in the upper reaches of the Yangzi River Valley. Clearly influenced by the prominent features, priorities and perspectives of the 1946–1949 Master Plan, the initial development of Pudong peninsula, achieving a balanced mix of residential and manufacturing activities; the co-ordinated development of Pudong and Puxi by cross-river connections, two bridges completed as well as a cross-river tunnel; the emplacement of a underground rail system, the reliance on foreign investment, and so on, also reflects the steady evolution of planning incentives and processes in Shanghai over the last century.

Yet, Shanghai's role as an agent of modernization has at best been controversial and mirrors Shanghai's unique history in its rise as a world class city. That is, by virtue of the status the city has attained over the past century and a half, not only as the centre of China's industrial or financial capacity, but also as the locus of the country's most influential political and intellectual activity. It has been variously perceived as either a negative model from 1842–1945 (including the Japanese occupation of the city) and the failure of the purportedly corrupt Kuomintang to implement the "Greater Shanghai Plan" or to others, Chinese and foreign alike, the city represented a positive exemplar of Western inspired, but Chinese efforts at sustaining a liberal, if not democratic, programme of municipal progress. More recently, "learn from Shanghai" has deafened the ears of municipal officials and planners of other metropolises who have not evinced the same record of development or who have lacked the same monumental urban vision.

If we are to understand the growth of cities as the "turning point," or "watershed of human history" that provides us with a yardstick or a means of measuring society, the economy, as well as the political and cultural order, an historical examination of the Shanghai "model" may raise or resurrect vital questions as to the problems of metropolitan growth that have marked Shanghai's rise to pre-eminence. It may also yield insights into the genesis of modern urban planning — hence the evolution of an urban vision in China — a vision, that may confront us all.

Notes

1. Examples of foreign perspectives are: C. A. Montalto de Jesus, *Historic Shanghai* (Shanghai: Shanghai Mercury, 1909); I. Lanning and S. Couling, *The History of Shanghai* (Shanghai: Kelly & Walsh, 1921) which was commissioned by the Shanghai Municipal Council but never completed; Anatol Kotenev, *Shanghai: Its Municipality and the Chinese* (Shanghai: North China Daily News and Herald, Ltd., 1927); F. L. Hawks Pott, *A Short History of Shanghai: Being an Account of the Growth and Development of the International Settlement* (Shanghai: Kelly & Walsh, 1928); William Crane Johnstone, *The Shanghai Problem* (Stanford: Stanford University Press, 1937); Carl Crow, *400,000,000 Million Customers* (New York: Harper & Brothers, 1937); Robert W. Barnett, *Economic Shanghai: Hostage to Politics,*

1937–1941 (New York: Institute of Pacific Relations, 1941); Rhoads Murphey, *Shanghai: Key to Modern China* (Cambridge, Mass.: Harvard University Press, 1953); John King Fairbank, *Trade and Diplomacy on the China Coast* (Cambridge, Mass.: Cambridge University Press, 1964); Mark Elvin, "The Gentry Democracy in Shanghai, 1905–1914" (Ph.D. dissertation, Oxford University, 1967); Rhoads Murphey, *Treaty Ports and China's Modernization, What Went Wrong?* (Ann Arbor: Center for Chinese Studies, University of Michigan, 1971); Marie-Clarie Bergère, "The Other China, Shanghai, 1911–1949," in *Shanghai: Revolution and Development in an Asian Metropolis*, edited by Christopher Howe (Cambridge: Cambridge University Press, 1981); Christian Henriot, *Shanghai, 1927–1937* (Berkeley: University of California Press, 1993); Linda Cooke Johnson, *Shanghai: From Market Town to Treaty Port, 1074–1858* (Stanford: Stanford University Press, 1995). For Chinese perspectives before 1949, see Hsia Ching-lin, *The Status of Shanghai: Its Future Development and Possibilities through Sino-Foreign Cooperation* (Shanghai: Kelly & Walsh, 1929); *Shanghai gonggong zujie shigao* 上海公共租界史稿 (History of the International Settlements of Shanghai) (Shanghai: Shanghai renmin chubanshe 上海人民出版社, 1980), a re-publication of such works as, Xu Gongsu 徐公肅 and Qiu Jinzhang 丘瑾璋, *Shanghai gonggong zujie zhidu* 上海公共租界制度 (The Status of the International Settlement of Shanghai), pp. 1–297, originally published in 1933. From 1949 to 1981, there were more than 50 monographs, 30 collections of source materials and over 1,100 articles on Shanghai published in China (excluding Taiwan). From 1957 to 1965, research centred on the development of capitalism to undergird the campaign to expose the "evils" of that economic system. Collections of materials included the Small Sword Society, the May Fourth Movement and the 1911 Revolution, as well as on the development of business enterprises and the collection of historical materials, focused on politics, economics, culture and religion. During the Cultural Revolution (1966–1976), only 30 articles were published and research on Shanghai almost ceased. After the fall of the "Gang of Four" (四人幫) and the loosening of ideological constraints, Shanghai has once again become the focus of intellectual activity. In addition to collections of essays, such as the series, *Shanghai yanjiu luncong* 上海研究論叢 (Papers on Shanghai Studies) published by the Shanghai shehuikexueyuan 上海社會科學院 commencing in 1988, and their *Shanghai difang shi ziliao* 上海地方史資料 (Materials on the Local History of Shanghai), some recent book length studies include: Liu Huiwu 劉惠吾, *Shanghai jindai shi* 上海近代史 (History of Modern Shanghai), 2 volumes (Shanghai: Huadong shifan daxue chubanshe 華東師範大學出版社, 1985), Tang Zhenchang 唐振常 et al. (eds.), *Shanghai shi* 上海史 (History of Shanghai) (Shanghai: Shanghai renmin chubanshe, 1989); and Zhong Zhongli 張仲禮 et al., *Jindai Shanghai chengshi yanjiu* 近代上海城市研究

(Research on Modern Shanghai) (Shanghai: Shanghai renmin chubanshe, 1990).

2. The term is borrowed from Robert Vaughan, *The Age of Great Cities, or Modern Society Viewed in Its Relation to Intelligence, Morals and Religion* (London: Jackson and Walford, 1893). See also Adna Weber, *The Growth of Great Cities in the Nineteenth Century* (New York: Macmillan, 1899) for the first scholarly treatment of this phenomenon.

3. For example, see Steen E. Rasmussen, *London the Unique City* (London: Jonathan Cape, 1937); Clifford Patton, *The Battle for Municipal Reform: Mobilization and Attack, 1875 to 1900* (Washington, D.C.: American Council on Public Affairs, 1940); R. L. Duffus, *Mastering a Metropolis: Planning the Future of the New York Region* (New York: Harper & Brothers, 1930); Howard Saalman, *Haussmann: Paris Transformed* (New York: George Braziller, 1971); Shun-ichi Watanabe, "Metropolitanism as a Way of Life: The Case of Tokyo, 1868–1930," in *Metropolis, 1890–1940*, edited by Gordon E. Cherry (London: Munsell, 1985), pp. 403–29. On the move towards regionalization in Shanghai, see Kerrie L. MacPherson, "Designing China's Urban Future: The Greater Shanghai Plan, 1927–1937," *Planning Perspectives*, Vol. 5 (1990), pp. 39–42; and Christian Henriot, *Shanghai, 1927–1937* (Berkeley: University of California Press, 1993), pp. 168–84.

4. Dugald MacFaden, *Sir Ebenezer Howard and Town Planning* (Cambridge, Mass.: MIT Press, 1970); Patrick Geddes, *Cities in Evolution: An Introduction to the Town Planning Movement and the Study of Civics* (London: Williams and Norgate, 1915); William H. Wilson, "The Ideology, Aesthetics and Politics of the City Beautiful Movement," in *The Rise of Modern Urban Planning, 1800–1914*, edited by Anthony Sutcliffe (New York: Saint Martins Press, 1980), pp. 166–98; Arturo Soria y Mata, *La Ciudad Lineal, Antecedentes y datos varios acerca de su construcció* (Madrid: Est Tipográfico "Succesores de Rivadenegra," 1904).

5. See, for example, David Buck, "Directions in Chinese Urban Planning," *Urbanism, Past and Present*, No. 1 (1975–1976), pp. 24–35; L.J.C. Ma, "Counterurbanization and Rural Development: The Strategy of Hsia-Hsiang," *Current Scene*, Vol. 15, No. 889 (1977), pp. 1–11; Y. M. Kau, "Urban and Rural Strategies in the Chinese Communist Revolution," in *Peasant Rebellion and Communist Revolution in Asia*, edited by J. W. Lewis (Stanford: Stanford University Press, 1974), pp. 253–70; Chang Sen-dou, "The Changing System of Chinese Cities," *Annals of the Association of American Geographers*, Vol. 66, No. 3 (1976), pp. 398–415; Zhao Xiqing 趙錫清, "Wo guo chengshi guihua gongzuo sanshi nian jianji, 1949–1982" 我國城市規劃工作三十年簡記, 1949–1982 (A Brief Record of Our Country's City Construction Plans over the Past 30 years, 1949–1982), *Chengshi guihua* 城市規劃 (City Planning), Vol. 40, No. 1 (1984), pp. 42–48; Kerrie L. MacPherson, "The

Head of the Dragon: The Pudong New Area and Shanghai's Urban Development," *Planning Perspectives*, Vol. 9 (1994), pp. 61–85; Chen Jiangze 陳絳澤 "Shanghai yu Zhongguo" 上海與中國 (Shanghai and China) in *Shanghai yanjiu luncong*, edited by Hong Ze 洪澤 et al. (Shanghai: Shanghai shehuikexueyuan, 1989), vol. 2, pp. 24–27.

6. Shen Weibin 沈渭濱, "Shanghai zhi jueqi" 上海之崛起 (The Rise of Shanghai) in *Shanghai yanjiu luncong*, edited by Hong Ze et al. (see note 5), vol. 2, pp. 36–37.

7. Man Zhimin 滿志敏 "Shanghai dichu Song dai haitang yu anxian de jidian kaozheng" 上海地區宋代海塘與岸線的幾點考證 (Some Textual Researches into the Seawall and Seashore in the Shanghai Region during the Song Dynasty), in *Shanghai yanjiu luncong*, edited by Hong Ze et al. (see note 5), vol. 1, pp. 49–57; Mark Elvin, "Market Towns and Waterways: The County of Shanghai from 1480 to 1910," in *The City in Late Imperial China*, edited by G. William Skinner (Stanford: Stanford University Press, 1977), pp. 411–74.

8. Tang Zhenchang et al. (eds.), *Shanghai shi* (see note 1), pp. 12–14, 55–61; Qiao Shuming 譙楓銘, "Qinglong zhen de shengshuai yu Shanghai de xingqi" 青龍鎮的盛衰與上海的興起 (The Rise and Fall of Qinglong Zhen and the Rise of Shanghai), in *Shanghai shi yanjiu* 上海史研究 (Research on Shanghai History), edited by Wang Pengcheng 王鵬程 et al. (Shanghai: Xuelin chubanshe 學林出版社, 1984), pp. 37–50.

9. Mark Elvin, *Patterns of the Chinese Past* (Stanford: Stanford University Press, 1973), pp. 164–78; G. William Skinner, "Cities and the Hierarchy of Local Systems," in *The City in Late Imperial China* (see note 7), edited by G. William Skinner, pp. 275–352. On the cotton textile trade and industry, see Linda Cooke Johnson, *Shanghai* (see note 1), pp. 43–65; but for its limits in promoting development in pre-modern China, see Hanchao Lu, "Arrested Development: Cotton and Cotton Markets in Shanghai, 1350–1843," *Modern China*, Vol. 18, No. 4 (1992), pp. 468–99.

10. On pirate raids, see *Shanghai shi*, edited by Tang Zhenchang et al. (see note 1), pp. 70–75; no comprehensive study of the economic or fiscal and political implications of redistricting in the Shanghai region exists in English, but see Linda Cooke Johnson, *Shanghai* (see note 1), pp. 42, 72–73. See also Wang Pengcheng , "Songjiangfu zai Mingdai de lishi diwei" 松江府在明代的歷史地位 (A Local History of Songjiang Prefecture during the Ming Dynasty), in *Shanghai shi yanjiu* (see note 8), edited by Wang Pengcheng et al., pp. 51–76; and Zheng Zuan, "Pudong lishi fazhan gaishuo 浦東歷史發展概說 (Some General Remarks on the Historical Development of Pudong), in *Shanghai shi yanjiu* 上海史研究 (Research on Shanghai History), edited by Tang Zhenchang and Shen Hengchun 沈恆春 (Shanghai: Xuelin chubanshe, 1988), vol. 2, pp. 397–406.

11. Zheng Zuan , "Shanghai jiu xian cheng" 上海舊縣城 (Shanghai, Old *Xian*

Walled City), in *Shanghai shi yanjiu*, edited by Wang Pengcheng et al. (see note 8), pp. 80–81. By comparison, the walled area of Suzhou was approximately 1,480 hectares. See Chang Sen-dou, "The Morphology of Walled Capitals," in *The City in Late Imperial China*, edited by G. William Skinner (see note 7), pp. 90–91 .

12. This urban redefinition, begun in 1909, with the first regulations on local self-government, concluded with the promulgation of China's first municipal laws, creating a two-tier system of cities as well as defining the relationship between the city and the state. The Organic Law of 1930 also defined the concept of "citizen" in the urban context. See Jiang Shenwu 蔣慎吾, *Jindai Zhongguo shizheng* 近代中國市政 (Chinese Municipal Government in the Modern Period) (Shanghai: Zhonghua shuju 中華書局, 1937), p. 62. See also Christian Henriot, *Shanghai, 1927–1937* (see note 1), pp. 24–36 for a discussion of the evolution of the system.

13. Representatives of such views are: J. W. Maclellan, *The Story of Shanghai, From the Opening of the Port to Foreign Trade* (Shanghai: North-China Herald Office, 1889); C. E. Darwent, *Shanghai: A Handbook for Travellers and Residents* (Shanghai: Kelly & Walsh, 1920); Mary Gamewell, *The Gateway to China: Pictures of Shanghai* (New York: Fleming H. Revell Company, 1916); John Orchard, "Shanghai," *The Geographical Review*, Vol. 26, No. 1 (1936), pp. 1–31; Rhoads Murphey, *Shanghai, Key to Modern China* (Cambridge, Mass.: Harvard University Press, 1953); Linda Cooke Johnson, *Shanghai: From Market Town to Treaty Port, 1074–1858* (see note 1).

14. For the emplacement of Shanghai's nineteenth century infrastructure, particularly provision made for public health, see Kerrie L. MacPherson, *A Wilderness of Marshes: The Origins of Public Health in Shanghai, 1843–1893* (New York: Oxford University Press, 1987).

15. Richard Feetham, *Report of the Hon. Richard Feetham, C.M.G. to the Shanghai Municipal Council* (Shanghai: North-China Herald Office, 1931), vol. 1, p. 178; *Shanghai Past and Present and a Full Account of the Proceedings on the 17th and 18th November 1893* (Shanghai: North-China Herald Office, 1893), p. 19. See also Lynn T. White III, "Non-governmentalism in the Historical Development of Shanghai," in *Urban Development in Modern China*, edited by L.J.C. Ma and E. W. Hanten (Denver: Westview Press, 1981), pp. 19–57.

16. Mark Elvin, "The Administration of Shanghai, 1905–1914," in *The Chinese City between Two Worlds*, edited by Mark Elvin and G. William Skinner (Stanford: Stanford University Press, 1974), pp. 239–62. See also Wu Guilong 吳桂龍, "Qingmo Shanghai difang zizhi yundong shulun" 清末上海地方自治運動述論 (Local Self-government in Late Qing Shanghai), *Jindai shi yanjiu* 近代史研究 (Research in Modern History), No. 3 (1982), pp. 161–82.

17. Shanghai Municipal Council, *Municipal Gazette*, 22 March 1912, p. 81.

18. A seminal but unpublished examination of the evolution of local government in Shanghai is, Mark Elvin, "The Gentry Democracy in Shanghai, 1905–1914" (see note 1). For the Huangpu Conservancy, see Whangpoo Conservancy Board, General Series Report no. 8, *The Port of Shanghai* (Shanghai: Oriental Press, 1923, third edition). The Board was established and wholly financed by the Chinese government, although foreign engineers were in charge of the harbour improvements. On the origin of the *guandu shangban* 官督商辦 system (official supervision and merchant management), see Albert Feuerwerker, *China's Early Industrialization: Sheng Hsuan-huai (1844–1916) and Mandarin Enterprise* (Cambridge, Mass.: Harvard University Press, 1988), as well as Hao Yen-p'ing, *The Comprador in Nineteenth Century China: Bridge between East and West* (Cambridge, Mass.: Harvard University Press, 1970).

19. *Shen bao* 申報 (Shanghai Times) 6 May 1926. The speech is translated in *The China Year Book 1926–1927* (Shanghai: North-China Daily News and Herald, Ltd., 1927), pp. 1012–14.

20. For a brief biography of Chen, see *Biographical Dictionary of Republican China*, edited by H. L. Boorman (New York: Columbia University Press, 1967), vol. 1, pp. 163–65. On the destruction of the old city walls and the construction of Minguo Road, see Zheng Zuan, "Shanghai jiu xian cheng" (see note 11), pp. 96–97.

21. Sun Yatsen's programme for rebuilding the Shanghai port at Pudong entailed diverting the Huangpu River away from the Shanghai bund fronting the foreign settlement (the commercial heart of Shanghai), by cutting a canal between the mouth of the Huangpu, swinging round Pudong point and reconnecting with the Huangpu above the Lunghua railroad junction. See Sun Zhongshan 孫中山, *Guofu quanji* 國父全集 (Collected Works of Sun Yatsen) (Taibei: Zhongyang wenwu gongying she 中央文物供應社, 1957), pp. 529–34. For a discussion of the significance of this plan in the redevelopment of Shanghai, see Kerrie L. MacPherson, "The Head of the Dragon: The Pudong New Area and Shanghai's Urban Development," *Planning Perspectives*, Vol. 9 (1994), pp. 65–68. For a biography of Zhang Jian, see S. C. Chu, *Reformer of Modern China: Chang Chien, 1853–1926* (New York: Columbia University Press, 1965), and for Sun Baochi, see H. L. Boorman, *Biographical Dictionary of Republican China* (see note 20), vol. 3, pp. 169–70. See also *Shanghai yanjiu ziliao* 上海研究資料 (Research Materials on Shanghai) (Shanghai: Zhonghua shuju, 1936), pp. 75–78.

22. Hu Shih 胡適, *Ding Wenjiang de juanji* 丁文江的傳記 (Biography of Ding Wenjiang) (Taibei: Zhongyang yanjiuyuan 中央研究院 [Academia Sinica], 1956), pp. 27–31, 32–40, 59–70.

23. On the complex process of metropolitanization of Chinese administered

Shanghai, see Liu Huiwu, *Shanghai jindai shi* (see note 1), pp. 323–28. See, for example, *Shen bao*, 21, 23, 27 February and 1, 2, 3, 5, 7, 17, 19, 21 March 1926 on the takeover of the Zhabei city office by the provincial government; for Sun Zhuanfang's official activities after his assumption of the directorship of Song-Hu, see *Shen bao*, 6 and 10 May 1926; for opposition to new taxation, see *Shen bao*, 14 October (defense tax); *Shen bao*, 2, 6 and 7 November 1926 (riceboat tax); 2 December 1926 (residential land tax). On the problem of extra-concessional roads, see Hsia Ching-lin, *The Status of Shanghai* (see note 1), pp. 94–114, and Richard Feetham, *Report of the Hon. Richard Feetham*, part IV (see note 15). See also *Shen bao*, 8 October 1926 for the extension of roads beyond the settlements; for SMC taxation of extra concessional roads, see *Shen bao*, 17 March and for extension of SMC police powers on these roads, see *Shen bao*, 10 September and 9, 10 December 1930.

24. The imposition of new sources of taxation inspired local protest, see for example, the problems over the residential land tax in the *Shen bao*, 12, 13, 18, 22 May; 7 June and July 1926 when the regulations were revised. For land values in the foreign settlements (courtesy of the Asia Realty Co.), see *North-China Herald*, 17 March 1926.

25. Hu Shih, *Ding Wenjiang de juanji*, pp. 63–64 (see note 22). The quotes are from Sun's inaugural speech, see *Shen bao*, 6 May 1926 and *The China Year Book, 1926–1927* (see note 19), p. 1014. For the problems of river conservancy and port development, see V. Bryan and H. Von Heidenstam, *The Future Development of the Shanghai Harbour: Report to the Whangpoo Conservancy Board* (Shanghai: n.p., 1919), pp. 27–32. On the Zhabei government and problems of taxation, see *Shen bao*, 21, 24, 25 February and 17 March 1926.

26. Mark Elvin, "The Gentry Democracy in Chinese Shanghai, 1905–1914," in *Modern China's Search for a Political Form*, edited by Jack Gray (London: Oxford University Press, 1969), pp. 41–61.

27. *Shen bao*, 30 June and 5, 8, 9, 15 July 1927. On the Kuomintang in Shanghai's political reorganization in 1927, see *Shen bao*, 2, 3, 25 and 26 July 1927; and *North China Herald*, 9 July 1927. See also Henriot, *Shanghai, 1927–1937* (see note 1), pp. 19–23.

28. Shen Yi 沈怡, "Shanghai tebieshi gongwuju shi nian" 上海特別市工務局十年 (Ten years of Public Works in the Shanghai Special Municipality), *Zhuanji wenxue* 傳記文學 (Biographical Literature), Vol. 17, No. 2, pp. 11–18.

29. On Wu's inauguration as mayor, see the favourable report in the *Shen bao*, 6 January 1932. One of his first public speeches concerned public finances (*Shen bao*, 16 January 1932) which was misreported in the paper and subsequently rectified at a press conference and meeting at his home with representatives of the central government and the financial community, see *Shen bao*, 17 January 1932. For the record of construction, see Shen Yi,

"Shanghai tebieshi gongwuju shi nian" (see note 28), pp. 25-30. For the changes in government administration of the Shanghai "Special municipality," see *Shen bao*, 25 April 1928, and for policy outline, see Ibid., 29 and 30 July 1928. See also "Greater Shanghai," *North-China Herald*, 16 July 1927.

30. For a biography of Shen Yi, see *Biographical Dictionary of Republican China*, vol. 3, edited by H. L. Boorman (see note 20), pp. 115-16; and Shen Yi, "Shanghai tebieshi gongwuju shi nian" (see note 28), pp. 81-85.

31. For a brief biography of Dong, see George F. Nellist, *Men of Shanghai and North China* (Shanghai: The Oriental Press, 1933), pp. 105-6; for Dong's connection with the American Architect Henry K. Murphy, who was instrumental in promoting the "adaptive Chinese architectural renaissance," see Jeffrey W. Cody, "Henry K. Murphy, an American Architect in China, 1914-1935" (Ph.D. dissertation, Cornell Univeristy, 1989), pp. 2, 305-10; see, also, Dong Dayou, "Greater Shanghai — Greater Vision," *China Critic*, Vol. 10 (1935), p. 103.

32. Stuart Lillico, "The Civic Centre at Kiangwan," *The China Journal*, Vol. 22 (1935), pp. 225-28; Dong Dayou "Greater Shanghai — Greater Vision" (see note 31), p. 103.

33. Stuart Lillico, "The Civic Centre at Kiangwan" (see note 32), p. 227; "Building a New Shanghai," *Far Eastern Review*, Vol. 27, No. 6 (June 1931), pp. 348-51, 366; Dong Dayou, "Greater Shanghai's New Million Dollar Stadium will Incorporate Features of Finest Western Sports Arenas," *China Reconstruction and Engineering Review*, Vol. 4, No. 1 (October 1934), pp. 3-7; *Shen bao*, 16 January 1931. Zheng Zuan 鄭祖安 "Guomindang zhengfu 'da Shanghai jihua' shimo" 國民黨政府"大上海計劃"始末 (The Whole Story of the Guomindang's 'Greater Shanghai Plan'), in *Shanghai shi yanjiu*, edited by Wang Pengcheng (see note 8), pp. 208-27; and Kerrie L. MacPherson, "Designing China's Urban Future: The Greater Shanghai Plan," *Planning Perspectives*, Vol. 5 (1990), pp. 39-62; and, for a beautifully illustrated discussion, see Fu Chaoqing 傅朝卿 *Zhongguo gudian shiyang xin jianzhu: Ershi shiji Zhongguo xin jianzhu guanzhihua de lishi yanjiu* 中國古典式樣新建築：二十世紀中國新建築官制化的歷史研究 (China's Classic Styles and the New Architecture: Historical Research on the Canonization of China's Twentieth Century Architecture) (Taibei: Nantian shuju 南天書局, 1993), pp. 146-52.

34. Christian Henriot, *Shanghai, 1927-1937* (see note 1), p. 184. For the use of the Greater Shanghai Plan in the post-war period, see Kerrie L. MacPherson, "The Head of the Dragon" (see note 21), pp. 71-74.

35. For the setting up of the Planning Committee for Greater Shanghai, see *Shen bao*, 25 August 1946. See also Philip J. Fungiello, "City Planning in World War II: The Experiences of the National Resources Planning Board," *Social Science Quarterly*, Vol. 53, No. 1 (1972), pp. 91-104; and Gordon E. Cherry,

The Politics of Town Planning (London: Longman, 1982), pp. 33–54.

36. Shanghaishi gongwuju dushi jihua zhuanti yanjianghui di wu ci gongkai yanjiang 上海市工務局都市計劃專題演講會第五次公開演講 (The Fifth Public Lecture on Special Topics of Urban Planning of the Publics Works Department, 12 July 1946) (Shanghai: Shanghai City Archives Office 1946), pp. 1–2. The following discussion is drawn from Kerrie L. MacPherson, "The Head of the Dragon" (see note 21), pp. 61–88.

37. W. G. Hamburger, "The Work of the Shanghai City Planning Board," *The Far Eastern Engineer*, (March 1948), p. 126; *Shanghaishi dushi jihua weiyuanhui mishuchu huiyi jilu* 上海市都市計劃委員會秘書處會議記錄 (Minutes of the Second Meeting of 12 September 1946 of the Shanghai Urban Planning Committee) (Shanghai: Shanghai City Archives Office, 1946), pp. 22–23.

38. For statistics, see Robert W. Barnett, "Starvation, Boom and Blockade in Shanghai," *Far Eastern Survey*, Vol. 9, No. 9 (1940), p. 106.

39. Shi Konghuai 施孔懷, "Shanghai gangbu ying ruhe fazhan?" 上海港埠應如何 發展? (How should the Shanghai Port be Developed?), *Shen bao*, 2 June 1947.

40. Shen bao, 14 November 1946; Norman D. Hanwell, "Shanghai Worst Crisis," *Far Eastern Survey*, Vol. 7, No. 15 (1938), p. 168.

41. *Shen bao*, 15 May 1947.

42. *Shen bao*, 31 March 1949.

43. "Inauguration of Shanghai P.W.B. and P.U.B. Commissioners," *The Far Eastern Engineer*, Vol. 7, No. 8 (1949), p. 416; and "Engineers Facing Fresh Deal Under New Rule," *The Far Eastern Engineer*, Vol. 7, No. 6 (1949), p. 324.

44. Quotes are from: David D. Buck, "Policies Favoring the Growth of Smaller Urban Places in the People's Republic of China, 1949–1979," in *Urban Development in Modern China*, edited by L.J.C. Ma and E. W. Hanten (see note 15), p. 125 .

45. Richard Gaulton, "Political Mobilization in Shanghai, 1949–1951," in *Shanghai: Revolution and Development in an Asian Metropolis*, edited by Christopher Howe (see note 1), p. 46. For the *xiafang* campaigns, see R. W. Lee III, "The *Hsia-fang* System: Marxism and Modernization," *The China Quarterly*, No. 28 (1966), pp. 40–62. Quote is from: R.J.R. Kirkby, *Urbanisatism in China, Town and Country in a Developing Economy, 1949–2000 A.D.* (London: Croom Helm, 1985), p. 254.

46. Laszlo Ladany, *The Communist Party of China and Marxism, 1921–1985, A Self-portrait* (Hong Kong: Hong Kong University Press, 1992), pp. 262–63; Yan Zhongmin, "Shanghai: The Growth and Shifting Emphasis of China's Largest City," in *Chinese Cities: The Growth of the Metropolis Since 1949*, edited by Victor F. S. Sit (Hong Kong: Oxford University Press, 1988), pp. 106–108.

47. Lynn T. White III, *Shanghai Shanghaied? Uneven Taxes in Reform China* (Hong Kong: Centre of Asian Studies, University of Hong Kong, 1989), pp. 9–14; Jane Jacobs, *Cities and the Wealth of Nations: Principles of Economic Life* (New York: Vintage Books, 1985), p. 231.

48. Y. M. Yeung and Zhou Yixing, "Editor's Introduction" in *Urbanization in China: An Inside-out Perspective*, 2 volumes, edited by Y. M. Yeung and Zhou Yixing (Armonk, New York: M. E. Sharpe, Inc. 1987); *Chinese Sociology and Anthropology*, Vol. 19, No. 3–4 (spring–summer 1987), p. 3.

49. MacPherson, "The Head of the Dragon" (see note 21), pp. 61–85.

20

Shanghai as a Regional Hub

Shi Peijun, Lin Hui and Liang Jinshe

Under the reform and open policies, the development of Shanghai has depended upon changes in its internal factors and on its relationships with not only its neighbours but also with an even larger environment. Prior to 1949, Shanghai was the centre of China and the Far East in economics, trade and banking. Since then, it had been reconstructed as the leading industrial base and one of the centres of education, science and technology in China. After 1978, Deng Xiaoping's 鄧小平 reform and open policies were first experimented with in Guangdong 廣東 province, which brought to it rapid economic development and significant political and social changes, greatly stimulating modernization construction in southern China. Compared with Guangdong, Shanghai lagged behind. Nevertheless, in the 1990s Shanghai has been emerging as the hub of a key region for open economic development in China. This strategic transfer has greatly affected Shanghai and its economic hinterland. In this chapter, the analysis and projection of Shanghai's development are mainly based on its relationships with other regions, especially its hinterland and foreign countries.

Generally speaking, the geographic location of a city or a region constitutes one of the foundations for its economic existence and evolution. This chapter will first analyze the geographical importance of Shanghai. Then, the regional factors in the development of Pudong 浦東 will be discussed. Such development not only will be key to the transformation and modernization of Shanghai, but also will generate an extensive influence on the Yangzi River (長江) delta, the basin and beyond. These factors come from the demands of those regions on various functions of Shanghai. Third, this chapter examines the changes and consequences that will be brought by the transport connections between Shanghai and other regions (i.e., water transportation, railways, highways, air, etc.). Finally, future developments in Shanghai will be speculated on.

Geographic Location and Its Importance

Regionalism has been a major issue in world trade since the end of the Cold War in the late 1980s. A well-accepted view is that world trade is dominated by three major regions: the North America Free Trade Area, the European Union and a non-treaty association of most countries along the Western Pacific Rim. The first two groups are based on the integration of their trade systems, while the third has its basis on economic comparative advantages.[1] In the meantime, Pacific Rim countries and regions are seeking co-operation on a larger scale through the Asia Pacific Economic

Cooperation (APEC) and the Pacific Economic Cooperation Council (PECC), so as to form an Asia–Pacific economic unit. Shanghai, having long been the gateway to the outside world for China, is located on the western side of the Pacific Ocean and at the centre of China's "gold coast" (i.e., the southeastern coastal region) and the "golden waterway" (i.e., Yangzi River). It is the bridgehead of China to the world. Through water transport, Shanghai enjoys geographic advantages in trade with Japan (820 n.m. to Kobe and 1040 n.m. to Yokohama), South Korea (500 n.m. to Pusan), Hong Kong (960 n.m.), Taiwan (420 n.m. to Keelung), Vladivostok (990 n.m.) and Southeast Asia, such as Singapore (2500 n.m.). Shanghai is also close to major shipping lanes (see Figure 20.1).

Located at the middle point on China's coast, Shanghai is connected by coastal transport to other developed regions in China, such as the Greater Bohai Region (環渤海地區), the Pearl River Delta Region (珠江三角洲地區) and the southern Fujian 福建 province. At the vantage point of the Yangzi River mouth, Shanghai commands a direct hinterland that covers the developed delta region and the watershed of the Yangzi River. The Beijing–Shanghai Railway (京滬鐵路) is Shanghai's important channel to northern China. With Shanghai as the core, the Yangzi River Delta Region (長江三角洲地區) has been linked together by the Shanghai–Hangzhou Railway (滬杭鐵路), the Shanghai–Nanjing Railway (滬寧鐵路), the Shanghai–Hangzhou Highway (滬杭公路) and the Shanghai–Nanjing Highway (滬寧公路). Shanghai is also connected with central and southwestern China through the Zhejiang–Jiangxi Railway (浙贛鐵路), which stretches to Kunming 昆明 through Zhuzhou 株洲 and Guiyang 貴陽.

The Yangzi River is a transport artery in China with great potential. It runs through nine provinces, autonomous regions and the Shanghai municipality in the eastern, central and western parts of China. Being 6,380 km long, the Yangzi River is the world's third longest river, only after the Amazon in the Latin America and the Nile in Africa. Its watershed covers 1.8 million sq km, about one-sixth of the Chinese land area. There are over 530 navigable rivers in this watershed, totalling more than 70,000 km, carrying about 56% of inland water transport in China. In particular, 16,000 km of the water routes (or 53% of this system) are suitable for steamship navigation.[2] At the mouth of the Yangzi River, Shanghai, therefore, possesses a strategic position linking central China and the outside.

As mentioned above, there are three highly developed regions in

Figure 20.1   The Geographical Position of Shanghai

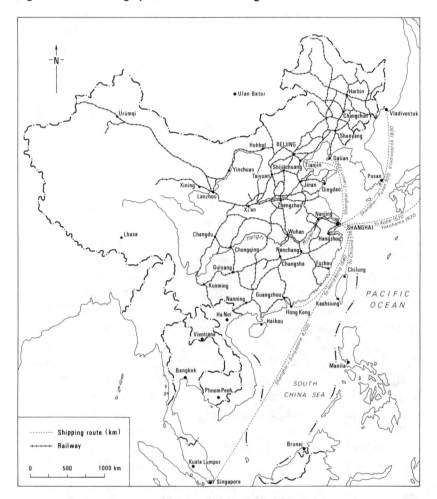

China: the Greater Bohai Region, the Yangzi River Delta Region and the
Pearl River Delta Region. Of these, the first region is close to the Korean
Peninsula. Historically, there were frequent contacts between the North-
east, Shandong 山東 , Beijing/Tianjin (北京/天津) of China and Japan.
Therefore, it is not unreasonable to expect the formation, from a
geographical point of view, of a Northeast Asia Economic Region, because
the establishment of the European Union and the North America Free
Trade Area will likely stimulate similar developments in eastern Asia.

Table 20.1 presents an assessment of the investment environment in

Table 20.1 The Investment Environment in Selected Regions in China
(Total 30 units, including all provinces, autonomous regions and municipalities directly under the Central Government, with 1 representing the highest score and 30 the lowest)

Region	Overall rank	Political base	Openness	Resource endowments	Economic power	Fiscal and trade base	Industrial ability	Fixed capital	Market scale
Beijing	1	5	1	26	2	2	3	2	1
Liaoning	2	15	3	5	4	3	1	6	3
Shanghai	3	11	2	29	1	1	2	1	2
Shandong	4	1	4	11	9	12	7	7	4
Hebei	5	8	8	9	12	7	5	5	10
Tianjin	6	14	5	27	2	4	8	4	6
Shanxi	7	9	16	1	10	6	6	3	22
Helongjiang	8	25	7	7	19	11	4	13	8
Jiangsu	9	6	9	24	3	8	9	8	9
Guangdong	10	7	6	19	11	5	17	11	5

Source: See note 3.

several cities and provinces of China by the Japan Association of International Trade Development.[3] It is obvious that Japanese businessmen favour the Bohai Rim Area. South Korea, inspired by a perspective of national unification, has also indicated its interest in this region. These factors are advantageous for forming a Northeast Asia Economic Region. It should be noted that the opening up of the Pearl River Delta was largely motivated by an effort to attract business from Hong Kong and Macau. Similarly, Xiamen's 廈門 opening was prompted by Taiwan. As a matter of fact, southern China, which includes Taiwan, Hong Kong and Macau, are geographically related to ASEAN. As Vietnam has joined ASEAN, ASEAN and China will have closer ties. Then, there will be an irresistible urge to form a South China Sea Economic Region. In this region, Japan, Taiwan and Hong Kong can have more scope for their economic activities — although this argument is only based on geographical accessibility considerations. The Yangzi River Delta Region, with Shanghai as its hub, will then have the advantage of accessing both the South China Sea Economic Region and the Northeast Asia Economic Region. In fact, the accessibility Shanghai will enjoy will be much better than other coastal regions in China. More importantly, since Shanghai has the biggest economic hinterland of China, the development of Shanghai inevitably will promote the development of the Yangzi River Delta Region, the Yangzi River Basin and, indeed, entire China. Therefore, Shanghai is so important that no other place in China can substitute for its functions. The economic evolution of the Yangzi River Basin led by Shanghai signifies the economic evolution of China. Shanghai obviously should open to the whole world. The geographical location of Shanghai has laid the foundation for it to become the economic, trading and financial centre of China.

The Emergence of Pudong and the Development of the Yangzi River Basin

Shanghai has an excellent geographic location to use fully domestic and foreign resources and to expand domestic and foreign markets. It evolved from a small fishing village to a modern industrial city, with a complete range of capabilities in manufacturing, high quality equipment, a strong base in science and technology, excellent technical facilities, developed trading and financial mechanisms and large consumer markets.

Shanghai was forced to open to foreign countries after 1843, and was forced to lease parts of its land to foreigners after 1845. It became a trading centre soon thereafter. In 1870, Shanghai was the premier port in China for import–export trade. Its importance in trading continued to grow after World War I. By the 1920s, Shanghai accounted for 40% of the total import–export trade of China, and this share grew to 55% by 1936. Meanwhile, trade stimulated the finance industry in Shanghai. The gold market in Shanghai was referred to as "the only gold market in the Far East" before World War II. Because Shanghai was the trading centre for domestic and foreign gold and silver, its volume of trade was higher than that of Japan, India and France, and was next only to that of London and New York. In the 1940s, many domestic and foreign banks, insurance companies, trust companies and other financial businesses moved into Shanghai. By the end of the Sino–Japanese War, 441 financial companies were located there. One-third of China's banks had their headquarters in Shanghai, and almost all insurance companies at that time were also head-quartered there. In a word, Shanghai was able to accumulate more than 40% of China's liquid capital. These financial companies had more than 600 branches and several thousand offices in over 20 provinces all over China. The Shanghai Stock Market was being prepared in May 1946 and opened for trading in September of the same year. More than 230 brokers were employed. It was China's only stock market, and the only one of import in the Far East. However, before 1949 Shanghai's manufacturing industry was weak and ill-structured. Most of the manufacturing business was in textile, flour, cigarettes, paper, rubber, leather, soap, matches, etc. In 1949, Shanghai's gross value of industrial output was RMB3 billion, where 88.2% was from light industry, with only 11.8% from heavy in-dustry. Moreover, the so-called heavy industries consisted of small-scale metallurgy, chemical materials, processing and mechanical manufacturing and repair shops. Since 1949, Shanghai has been rebuilt, reformed and redeveloped. The traditional manufacturing industries were strengthened, which included metallurgical, mechanical, chemical, shipbuilding, instru-ments, textile and other light industries. New industries were developed, including micro electronics, computer, fiber cable communication, laser, bio-engineering, molecular synthetic materials, precision instruments, etc. Shanghai also hosted large-scale electricity generators, special engineering facilities, ships, aircraft, automobiles, communication satellites and space shuttles that represented the most advanced technology in China. How-ever, because of the Cold War after World War II, and because of the limitations of China's planned economy, Shanghai's role as China's inter-national city was eroded. In particular, trade and financial industries declined. In 1992, Shanghai's GDP was RMB106.59 billion, where 33.1% was from the tertiary industry, and 66.9% from the primary and secondary industries.[4] The development of industry had some major problems, such as too much consumption of energy and raw materials, conflicts in raw material and energy supplies, out-of-date equipment and technology by international standards, and shortages of capital and land. These are some of the reasons that Pudong has emerged in the redevelopment of Shanghai.

The Yangzi River Delta Region is one of the most developed areas in China. It includes Nanjing 南京 , Suzhou 蘇州 , Changzhou 常州 , Zhen-jiang 鎮江 , Nantong 南通 , Yangzhou 揚州 and Wuxi 無錫 of Jiangsu 江蘇 province, and Hangzhou 杭州 , Jiaxing 嘉興 , Huzhou 湖洲 , Ningbo 寧波 , Shaoxing 紹興 and Zhoushan 舟山 of Zhejiang 浙江 province, with a total of 14 cities including Shanghai and an area of 100,000 sq km. In 1992, the region had a population of 72,722,200, representing 6.2% of China's population, and a GDP of RMB893.9 billion, or 19.37% of the total GDP in China. The GDP per capita in the delta region was RMB12,291, 3.12 times that of the country. Historically, the Yangzi River Delta Region had a close internal relationship. Shanghai, as the trading and financial centre of China and the Far East, had played an important role in the development of this region. However, because of the regional discontinuities of China's planned economy, and because of the erosion of Shanghai's role in finance and trade, the economic development of the delta region gradually became fragmentary. In the 1950s, the East China Bureau, as the representative of the central government, barely maintained the economic integrity of the Yangzi River Delta Region under its administrative authority. In the 1980s, when the central government decided to form the Shanghai Economic Region, conflicts in the existing distribution of interests and the lack of a leading development focal point aborted the whole project, except for its title. The Planning Office for the Shanghai Economic Region under the State Council also disappeared a few years later. The advantages of this most developed region in China as a whole were not fully utilized.

The Yangzi River Basin has a population of about 360 million, ap-proximately one-third of China's total population. Traditionally, this basin has a relatively high level in science, technology, education and culture. There are several major cities along the Yangzi River, including Shanghai, Nanjing, Wuhan 武漢 and Chongqing 重慶 . There are also 47 large and middle-sized cities, hundreds of small cities and many towns. It possesses very rich tourist and recreational resources, many famous historical sites, beautiful natural scenic areas, and several popular scenic tourist spots, such as the Yellow Mountain (黃山), the Lushan Mountain (廬山), the Three Gorges (三峽) and the Tai Lake (太湖). Countless domestic and foreign tourists have visited these sites.

The Yangzi River Basin is well known in China for its rich water resources. The water surface area in the basin accounts for 40% of China's total. There are four major fresh water lakes — Boyang Lake (鄱陽湖), Dongting Lake (洞庭湖), Tai Lake and Chao Lake (巢湖). The estimated hydro-electric potential is 197 billion watts, or 53.4% of China's total. There are also rich mineral resources in the basin, with 109 of the 139 on China's list of mining minerals. Thirteen have 60% of the total minable volume within the basin. Some rank high worldwide.

The Yangzi River Basin has a well-developed river-based transport system. There are 26 ports and more than 500 berths in the basin, some of which are open to the world, including Shanghai, Nantong, Zhangjiagang 張家港, Zhenjiang, Jiangyin 江陰, Wuhu 蕪湖, Jiujiang 九江, Wuhan, Yichang 宜昌, Wanxian 萬縣, Fuling 涪陵 and Chongqing. Some of the international ports along the Yangzi River have over 500 scheduled ships to and from Hong Kong, Japan, Singapore and the United States. Ships at the level of 1,500 dwt can reach Chongqing from Yichang while 1,500–3,000 dwt vessels can go to Hankou 漢口 from Yichang, and 5,000 dwt vessels can go to Nanjing from Hankou. During high tide, 25,000 dwt vessels can sail to Nanjing from the mouth of the Yangzi River. The clear height under the Wuhan Yangzi River Bridge (武漢長江大橋) is 18 m at the highest of the river water level, while the clear height under the Nanjing Yangzi River Bridge (南京長江大橋) is 70 m. Year round, ships smaller than 5,000 dwt can pass through the Wuhan Yangzi River Bridge and 10,000 dwt vessels can pass through the Nanjing Yangzi River Bridge. The number 1 and 2 shiplocks of Gezhouba Dam (葛洲壩) were designed for fleets of 10,000 dwt with the capability of 50 million tonnes per year. The capability of the shiplocks of the Three-Gorges Dam (三峽大壩) will be about the same as that of the Gezhouba Dam.

The Yangzi River Basin has a relatively developed economy, with a GNP accounting for 40% of the total in China. Both the per capita GNP and the per capita income are higher in the basin than the average in China. There are 370 million mu of farm land in the basin, a quarter of the country's total. Two-fifths of China's total grain production and one-third of its cotton production come from the Yangzi River Basin.[5] There are also many kinds of economic crops produced in the basin. China's metallurgical industrial bases (Wuhan, Baoshan 寶山, Panzhihua 攀枝花), colour metal industrial bases (Dexing 德興 of Jiangxi 江西 province, Tongling 銅陵 of Anhui 安徽 province), mechanical industry, light textile industry and petroleum chemical industrial bases can all be found in this basin.

However, compared with world class industries, the Yangzi River Basin suffers from major problems, such as backward equipment and technology, and the lack of capital and international connections. Within the basin, there are isolated economic blocks, without co-ordination or a leading development focus. Hong Kong and Macau played a very important role in the development experience of Guangdong province. For example, 80% of the total export goods from the Pearl River Delta went out through Hong Kong and Macau, and 70% of the import goods came in through the two regions. Some 80% of the total foreign investment capital in the Pearl River Delta came from Hong Kong and Macau, reflecting their importance as sources of capital investment. Hong Kong served as the "front line shops" for the "base line factories" in the Pearl River Delta; such a relationship closely tied the two regions' economies together. In Guangdong province, there are 3 million employees working in Hong Kong-invested factories, four times as many as there are workers in Hong Kong. Most of these employees live in the Pearl River Delta. In reference to its contribution to the development of Guangdong, the Yangzi River Basin badly needs a "Hong Kong" of its own, and the best candidate is Shanghai. However, Shanghai does not have financial and international trading capabilities as strong as those of Hong Kong. Thus, the development of Pudong must begin with attracting investments and expanding foreign trade. After accepting and absorbing advanced technology, efforts should be directed at reforming Puxi 浦西 (the western part of Shanghai), and extending reform towards the entire delta and the Yangzi River Basin. Therefore, the development of Pudong should attach priority to finance and foreign investment, high-tech industries and basic industries. In this way, Shanghai may gradually become an international metropolis, and be transformed from an industrial, science and technology, and education city to one which features finance, trade, industry, science and technology, and education. For this reason, it is necessary to readjust the industrial structure in China. This is to be accomplished mainly by moving some industries that consume too much energy and materials and that produce low technical products out of Shanghai to the Yangzi River Basin. The key to the development lies in the provision by Shanghai of high-tech products and rational co-operation among the cities in the Yangzi River Delta and the Yangzi River Basin, such as Nanjing and Wuhan.

Recent Progress in Transport

One of the important advantages of Shanghai is its location; but this advantage must be realized through its transport connections with other places. The geographical advantages of Shanghai can either be enhanced or weakened by the amount of its advancement in transport technology which, in turn, can change the economic role of Shanghai in the nation.

The Port and the Channels

The port of Shanghai, along with other ground transportation facilities around the port, have played a key role in the transport connections between Shanghai and other places. The port, which includes the south channel of the Yangzi River, Huangpu River (黃浦江), an auxiliary port at Luhuashan (綠華山) and its inland hinterland, is the largest seaport in China. It handles one-third of the total cargo tonnage of all major seaports in China and nearly one-fourth of the total international trade of China. In 1991, the port of Shanghai handled 147-million tonnes of cargo, among which 19.7% was related to international trade. This made the port of Shanghai one of the top ten ports in the world which have the capability of handling more than 10-million tonnes of cargo annually. One major change in the port of Shanghai during 1980s was the rapid growth of container ships. The number of containers handled at the port skyrocketed from about 2,000 in 1978 to 456,000 in 1990, which accounted for 29% of the container traffic in the nation.[6]

Two major problems associated with the port of Shanghai are the number of available berths and the shallow water channel due to the deposition of silt near the mouth of the Yangzi River. The current depth of the main channel is 7 m, which can only accommodate vessels smaller than 25,000 dwt. However, modern container ships, which make up the majority of the international container fleets, normally require at least 11.5 m of channel depth. This is an important reason why the port of Shanghai has been replaced by Hong Kong and Kobe in Japan as a major transfer point between European and the Mediterranean traffic and that from the United States and Canada.

Construction of the auxiliary port at Luhuashan was completed in 1979. The depth of its channel is 11 m to 12 m. Larger ships are docked at this auxiliary port to unload some cargo in order to bring their loads below the level of 25,000 tonnes. These partially unloaded ships then sail to the port of Shanghai during high tide. However, only six ships can be handled

in each direction during each high tide, which makes the port of Shanghai
less competitive than other major seaports in Asia, such as the port in
Singapore, which can accommodate large ships around the clock. This
major drawback of the port of Shanghai results in bottlenecks in meeting
the developmental needs of Shanghai, Pudong, and the Yangzi River Delta
and its hinterland. In order to overcome this disadvantage, the Chinese
government has announced a plan to invest over RMB10 billion to dredge
the main channel to 11–12 m deep and to construct an additional 40 berths
at Waigaoqiao 外高橋, Luojin 羅涇 and Jinshan 金山 to accommodate both
container and regular cargo ships. After the completion of these projects, it
is expected that the port of Shanghai will be able to handle 200 million
tonnes of cargo per year.

Another project related to the future growth of the port of Shanghai is
the construction of more berths and the dredging of the channel along the
Huangpu River. In 1990, there were 37 berths for ships smaller than
10,000 dwt along a 36 km segment of the Huangpu River. With the
completion of this project, the channel depth will be dredged to 7.5–8 m
deep to allow for the navigation of 58,000 dwt container ships directly to
this segment of the Huangpu River.[7]

Some experts predict that, even with the channel dredged to 11–12 m
deep, the port will still not be able to accommodate modern third- and
fourth-generation container ships. So, it is necessary to develop a long-
term plan of building other good ports around the mouth of the Yangzi
River.[8] Several ports around the Zhoushan Islands (舟山群島) are good
candidates for such projects. Some potential sites include Beilun Harbour
(北侖港) (10–20 m deep), Chengsi 嵊泗 (20–60 m deep), Dajishan 大衢山
and Zhoushan island. These sites can form a group of ports to accommodate various sizes of ships. Together they can serve as the nuclei for the
southeastern part of China and lead to further development of the region.
Since Beilun Harbour is under the jurisdiction of Zhejiang province, some
scholars in that province suggest that it may be more appropriate to shift
the jurisdiction of Beilun Harbour to the port of Shanghai.[9] These scholars
further suggest that it would be an even better plan to include the Lianyun
Port (連雲港) to the north of Shanghai and Wenzhou Port (溫州港) to the
south of Shanghai in the project. In this case, they could be connected by
the second Euro–Asia Continental Bridge to create a much larger hinterland for the port of Shanghai. This proposal is still at the discussion stage
at present. However, given the historical and economic ties and the
geographical proximity between these ports, it seems to be a logical

Figure 20.2   The Transport Setting of Shanghai and Northern Zhejiang

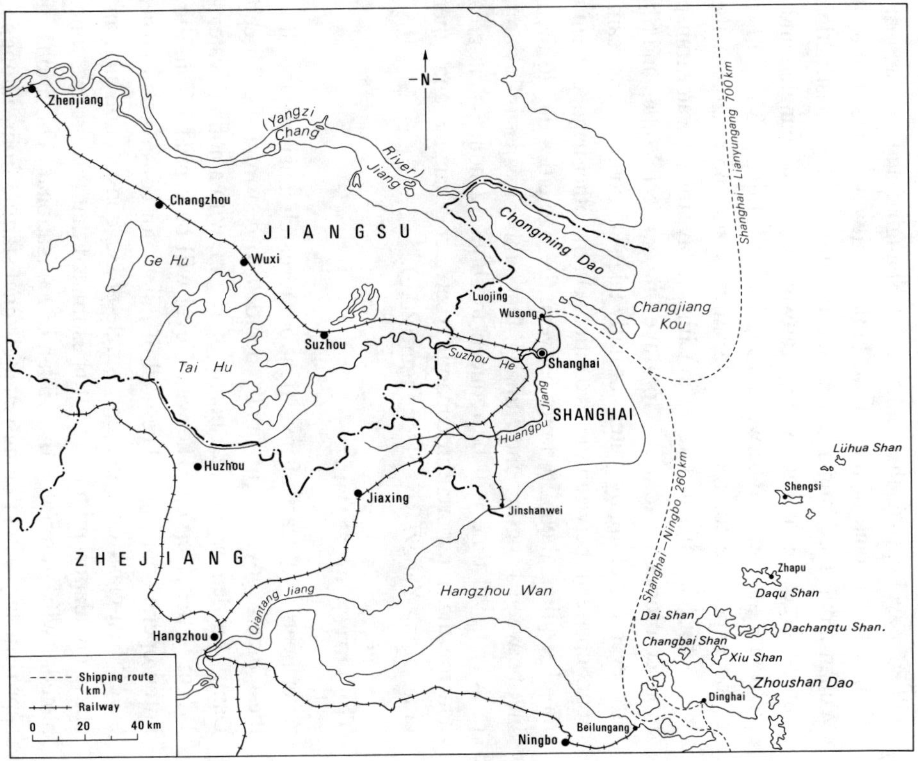

proposal to form a system of ports for the future development of the southeastern region of China. Such a project will definitely expand the field of influence of Shanghai (see Figure 20.2).

The Railways between Shanghai and Wuhan along the Yangzi River

Two recent important policy decisions taken by the Chinese government will greatly improve the transport of Shanghai and the area along the Yangzi River. One of them is to build a railway between Shanghai and Wuhan along the Yangzi River, and the other is the construction of the Three-Gorges Dam. The existing railways between Shanghai and Wuhan have a missing section between Tongling and Jiujiang. Since air transport is too expensive for most people, railway transport remains the major means for long-distance travel in China today. Inland water transport is a more comfortable alternative for travelling between Wuhan and Shanghai. However, travelling by water normally takes 45 hours downstream and 60 hours upstream between the two cities. On the other hand, current railway travel requires about 30 hours between the two cities due to the missing link between Tongling and Jiujiang. Once this missing link is completed, railway travel time will be reduced to about 12 hours, thus greatly enhancing the transportation capability between Shanghai and other major cities along Yangzi River (see Figure 20.3).[10]

The Three-Gorges Dam

After nearly 40 years of investigation, research, analysis and discussion, the Chinese government finally decided to construct the Three-Gorges Dam. This dam will have a height of 185 m, with a normal water level of 175 m in the reservoir. The water level will be kept at 156 m during the initial operational stage. The goal of this major construction project is to have "first-class development, single-phase construction and multiple-phase population migration." It is estimated that this project, when completed, will improve the inland navigational conditions for an approximately 600 km long water channel starting from Jiulongpo 九龍坡 in Chongqing, which is a major transfer point between water and railway transport. At the normal water level of 175 m, the channel will be deep enough for navigation of vessels up to 10,000 dwt. This will be a substantial improvement over current conditions which merely accommodate vessels up to 3,000 dwt. In addition, the water level can be kept at a higher level during the dry season for several segments along this 600 km water

Figure 20.3 Xi'an–Nanjing Railway and Wuhan–Shanghai Railway along the Yangzi River

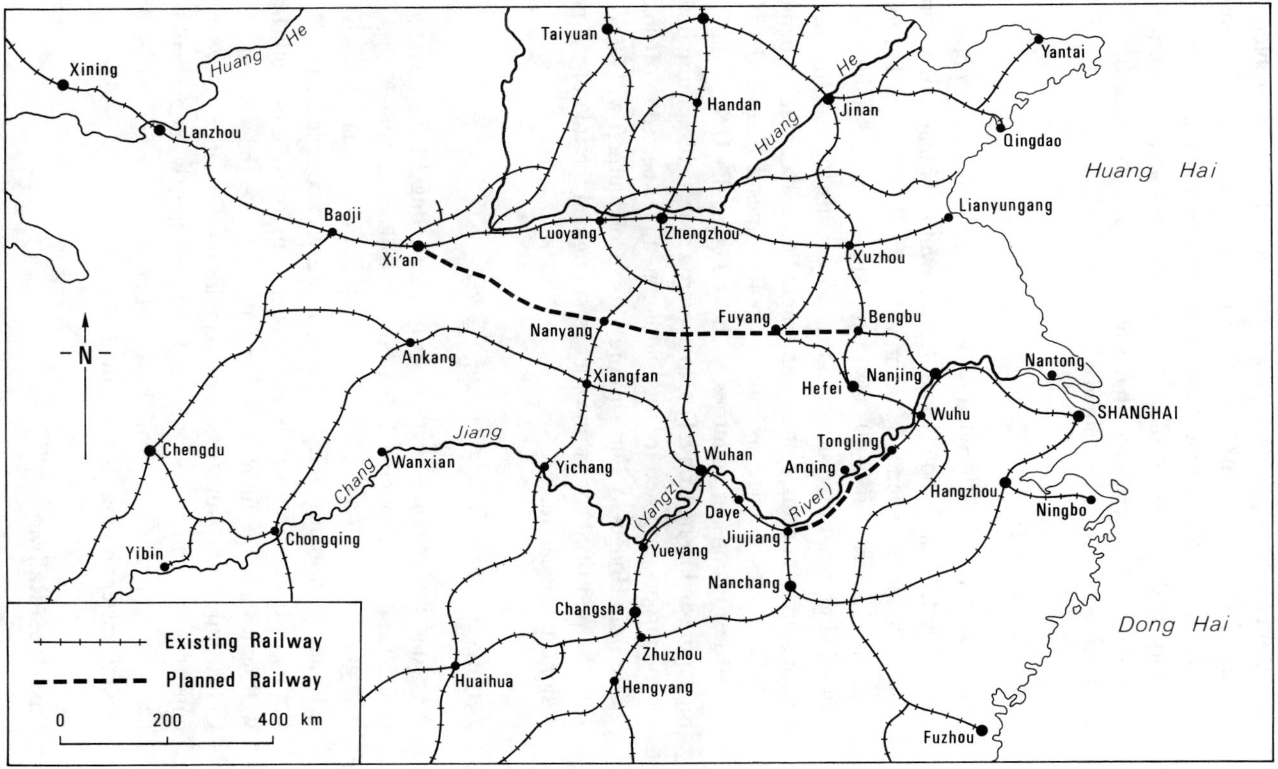

channel. This will provide a guarantee for 10,000 dwt ships to have a 45–50% chance of sailing through the channel without problems, which means a reduction of travel costs by 35–37%.[11] Such improvements will in turn introduce more efficient turn-around times of vessels and encourage the further development of ports and transport along the waterway. It, therefore, can be expected that water transport between Shanghai and Sichuan province will be enhanced.

Hongqiao Airport (虹橋機場)

Hongqiao Airport in Shanghai is one of the three largest airports in China. This airport, located about 13 km from downtown Shanghai, occupies 437 sq km. Its runway extends 3,200 m, with a width of 57.6 m. The total floor space in the terminal is 49,000 sq m. The airport is equipped with advanced flight control systems and runway lights for handling the largest civil jet aircraft during both day and night hours. It currently operates over 70 flight routes, connecting more than 40 domestic cities and 15 international destinations in countries such as Japan, the U.S., Canada, Paris, Singapore and Hong Kong. Due to overcrowding at this airport, however, a second airport proposed for the Pudong area is expected to off-load some traffic from Hongqiao. Furthermore, this second airport will be connected with the port of Shanghai in order to strengthen the role of the port as a major transfer centre.

Beijing–Kowloon Railway (大京九鐵路)

A second major north–south railway connecting Beijing, Tianjin 天津, Hengshui 衡水, Shangqiu 商丘, Fuyang 阜陽, Macheng 麻城, Jiujiang, Xiangtang 向塘, Ji'an 吉安, Ganzhou 贛州, Longchuan 龍川, Shenzhen 深圳 and Kowloon (九龍) in Hong Kong was completed in 1995. This Beijing–Kowloon railway is expected to improve north–south traffic as well as to help the future development of the central–eastern regions of China. Jiujiang is likely to become a major transportation centre due to the construction of this railway. Shanghai, through its water and railway connections with Jiujiang, will have better transportation links with the central–eastern regions (see Figure 20.4).

East–West Railway

The Ministry of Railways also plans to begin construction of a major

Figure 20.4 The New and Existing Beijing–Kowloon Railways

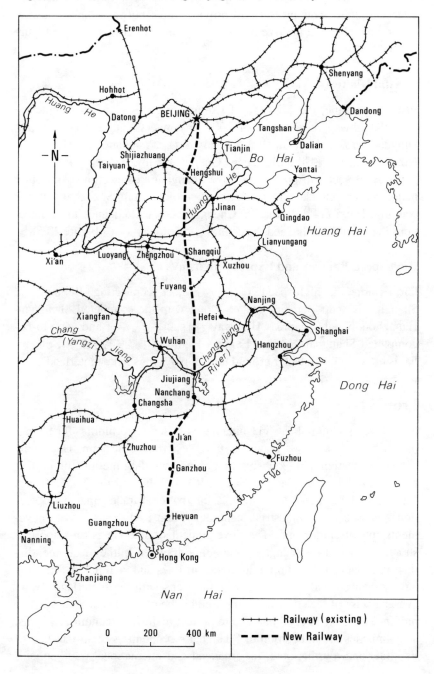

east–west railway connecting Nanjing and Xi'an 西安 sometime between 1995 and 2000. This project will provide direct railway connections between Shanghai and the five provinces in northwestern China (see Figure 20.3).

Coastal Highway

In the meantime, the Ministry of Communications plans to complete a coastal highway by the year of 2000 to connect Yantai 煙台 , through Qingdao 青島 , Lianyun Port, Huaiyin 淮陰 , Shanghai, Hangzhou, Ningbo, Fuzhou 福州 , Shenzhen, Guangzhou to Zhanjiang 湛江 . This highway project will greatly improve Shanghai's connections with other major coastal cities. Another highway project from Shanghai through Nanjing, Hefei 合肥 , Wuhan to Chengdu 成都 will enhance the connections between Shanghai and the central parts of China (see Figure 20.5).

High-speed Railway and Express Highways

Furthermore, a high-speed railway project connecting Beijing and Shanghai is at its planning stage. Along with the completed Shanghai–Hangzhou–Ningbo Express Highway (滬杭甬高速公路) and soon-to-be-completed Shanghai–Nanjing Express Highway (滬寧高速公路), Shanghai is building much better ground transport systems to its hinterland.

Prospects

New development policies in China have created opportunities for Shanghai to become a major player in the Western Pacific Rim. Due to its excellent location and extensive hinterland including the most important regions in China, such as the Yangzi River Delta and the Yangzi River Basin, Shanghai needs to further its international trade, financial operations, as well as its industrial technology, and to diffuse these achievements into its hinterland. The development of Pudong is an important strategy to speed up Shanghai's economic transfer. In the meantime, distinct improvements on important transport lines and facilities in Shanghai have enhanced wider and deeper connections with the hinterland. However, because of the constraints imposed by the planned economic system, provinces and cities in China tend to protect their own economic systems. This impedes the integration of Shanghai's economic system into that of its hinterland. Furthermore, the financial and international trade policies

Figure 20.5 Major Highway Networks in China

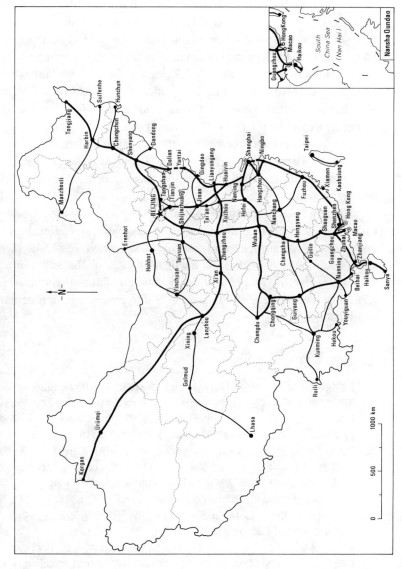

and management styles of the ports and other systems, which are part of the planned economic system in China, have negative impacts on the transformation of Shanghai. The construction of a system of harbours along the East China coast will have a great impact on Shanghai's external trade. If the problem of the sand bar at the mouth of Yangzi River cannot be resolved, it will limit modern container ships' access to Shanghai harbour. The main parts of the system of deepwater ports might be located at Beilun Harbour as the outport of Shanghai. Then the relation between Shanghai and Ningbo would be similar to that between Tokyo and Yokohama or that between Osaka and Kobe. This could weaken Shanghai's external relations. This kind of situation might be changed and improved upon if a huge amount of funds is used to dredge the mouth of the Yangzi River. However, it will be a long way before the Chinese government will make such a decision because of its complex decision-making system.

Shanghai has been one of the main doors to the outside world since China started its open policy. Changes in international relationships, especially in the relationships with Japan, the U.S., western and eastern Europe, and Taiwan, will certainly have major influences on the future of Shanghai. In other words, a successful transformation of Shanghai is also closely related to the progress of China's economic reform and its international relationships.

Notes

1. Sekigue Sueo 關口末夫, "Dongya jingji de xianghu yicun he shichang yitihua" 東亞經濟的相互依存和市場一體化 (The Interdependence of the East Asian Economy and the Market Integration), *Shijie jingji yicong* 世界經濟譯叢 (Translation Series of World Economy) (Beijing), 5 (1994), pp. 30–38.

2. Wang Baoyu 王保畲, "Changjiang hangyun yu liuyu jingji kaifa" 長江航運與流域經濟開發 (Shipping of Yangzi River and Economic Development of the Basin), *Jingji kexue* 經濟科學 (Economic Science) (Beijing), 3 (1991), pp. 1–6; Pudong kaifa yu Sichuan duice yanjiu keti zu 浦東開發與四川對策研究課題組, "Pudong kaifa yu Sichuan duice" 浦東開發與四川對策 (The Development of Pudong and the Strategy for Sichuan Province), *Quyu jingji yanjiu* 區域經濟研究 (The Study of Regional Economy), 3 (1993), pp. 1–24; Chen Youfang and Chen Yunlan 陳友放、陳雲蘭, "Rang Changjiang huangjin shuidao wei xiandaihua jianshe fuwu" 讓長江黃金水道爲現代化建設服務 (Using the Yangzi River Golden Water Channel for the Modernization Scheme), *Sheke xinxi* 社科信息 (Information of Social Science) (Nanjing), 11

(1990), pp. 21–24.

3. Chao Yung 曹勇, "Wo guo huan Bohai diqu maixiang 21 shiji mianlin de guoji jingzheng yu guoji hezuo" 我國環渤海地區邁向21世紀面臨的國際競爭與國際合作 (The International Competition and Cooperation faced by the Bohai Sea Greater Circle Area of China towards the 21 Century), *Dili xuebao* 地理學報 (Acta, Geographic Sinica), Vol. 49, No. 5 (1994), pp. 394–402.

4. Yang Wanzhong 楊萬鍾 (ed.), *Shanghai gongye jiegou yu buju yanjiu* 上海工業結構與佈局研究 (The Studies on Industrial Structure and Layout of Shanghai) (Shanghai: Huadong shifan daxue chubanshe 華東師範大學出版社, 1991), pp. 2–16.

5. See note 2.

6. Liu Kai 劉楷, "Jianshe Shanghai shenshui shuniu gang jingji lunzheng" 建設上海深水樞紐港經濟論證 (The Economic Discussion on Constructing the Deep Water Hub Port of Shanghai) (Master thesis, Department of Geography, Beijing Normal University [北京師範大學], 1993).

7. Ren Mei'e 任美鍔 (ed.), *Zhongguo de san da sanjiaozhou* 中國的三大三角洲 (The Three Largest Delta Areas in China) (Beijing: Gaodeng jiaoyu chubanshe 高等教育出版社, 1994), pp. 129–216.

8. Chen Fuxing 陳福星, "Shi lun Pudong, Ningbo kaifa de guanxi yu fazhan qianjing —— jian lun Beilun gang he Shanghai gang de guanlian zuoyong" 試論浦東、寧波開發的關係與發展前景 —— 兼論北侖港和上海港的關聯作用 (The Discussion on the Relationship and the Prospect of Developing Pudong and Ningbo: A Case on the Relationship between Beilun Harbour and Shanghai Harbour), *Ningbo daxue xuebao: Renwen kexue bao* 寧波大學學報：人文科學報 (Journal of Ningbo University: Social Science), No. 2 (1991), pp. 77–83; Huang Daming 黃大明 and Chen Fuxing 陳福星, "Pudong kaifang de gangkou ningjuli" 浦東開放的港口凝聚力 (The Centralization of Opening Port in Pudong), *Tuanjie bao* 團結報 (The United News) (Beijing), 6 November 1991, p. 2.

9. Tu Dewen 屠德文, "Chongpo xianyou geju, jishen guoji hanglie —— ba Ningbo gang jiashu jiancheng guoji maoyi da gang zhi wo jian" 衝破現有格局，躋身國際行列 —— 把寧波港加速建成國際貿易大港之我見 (Breaking through the Current Framework, Joining International Arena —— My Opinion of Constructing International Trade Major Port in Ningbo), *Zonghe yunshu* 綜合運輸 (Comprehensive Transportation) (Beijing), (1993), pp. 10–13.

10. Wang Hai 汪海, "Guanyu xiujian Wuhan zhi Shanghai yan jiang da tielu de shangque" 關於修建武漢至上海沿江大鐵路問題的商榷 (The Discussion on Constructing the Major Railway along Yangzi River from Wuhan to Shanghai), *Jingji dili* 經濟地理 (Economic Geography) (Changsha 長沙), No. 2 (1991), pp. 62–66.

11. Zhang Qi 張奇, "Sanxia gongcheng yu Changjiang hangyun" 三峽工程與長江航運 (The Three Gorges Project and Shipping of the Yangzi River), *Zhongguo heyun* 中國河運 (China Waterway) (Wuhan 武漢), No. 2 (1992), pp. 15–23.

Contributors

Y. M. YEUNG (楊汝萬) is professor of Geography, director of the Hong Kong Institute of Asia–Pacific Studies and head of Shaw College at The Chinese University of Hong Kong. His wide-ranging research interests have recently focused on China's coastal cities, South China, globalization and Asian cities. He has published extensively, including *China's Coastal Cities* (1992), *Urban and Regional Development in China* (1993), *Pacific Asia in the 21st Century* (1993), *Guangdong* (1994), *Emerging World Cities in Pacific Asia* (1996) and *Global Change and the Commonwealth* (1996).

SUNG YUN-WING (宋恩榮) is chairman and professor in the Department of Economics, and co-director of the Hong Kong and Asia–Pacific Economies Research Programme at The Chinese University of Hong Kong. He is associate editor of *Pacific Economic Review* and corresponding editor of *Asian Pacific Economic Literature*. He is working on the economic integration of China, Taiwan and Hong Kong, and also on a comparative study of the Yangzi Delta and the Pearl River Delta.

ANTHONY G. O. YEH (葉嘉安) is associate professor and reader of the Centre of Urban Planning and Environmental Management and director of the GIS Research Centre at The University of Hong Kong. He is a fellow of the Hong Kong Institute of Planners and the Royal Australian Planning Institute. His main research interests are in urban development and planning in Hong Kong and China, and applications of GIS in urban and regional planning. He has published extensively on urban development in China in international journals and book chapters, including *Special Issue of Asian Geographer on Spatial Development in the Pearl River Delta* (1989) (co-edited with K. C. Lam, C. M. Li and K. Y. Wong), *Reference Materials on Urban Development and Planning in China* (1990) and *Chinese Urban Reform — What Model Now?* (1990) (co-edited with R. Y. Kwok and W. Parish).

GRACE C. L. MAK (麥肖玲) is lecturer in Education at The Chinese University of Hong Kong and a free-lance education consultant for the World Bank. She has published on education in China and Hong Kong. She is editor of *Women, Education and Development in Asia* (New York: Garland, forthcoming) and co-editor of *Higher Education in Asia: An International Handbook and Reference Guide* (Westport: Greenwood, forthcoming).

GU XINGYUAN (顧杏元) is head of the Department of Health Statistics and Social Medicine, School of Public Health, Shanghai Medical University. Since his graduation in 1952 from Jiangsu Medical College, Dr. Gu has pursued an academic career. His main research interests include demography, health statistics, rural health and primary health care. He has published many papers on public health and several books on health statistics, family planning, health care management, medical insurance in rural China and primary health care.

HO LOK-SANG (何濼生) is university reader and head of the Department of Economics, Lingnan College. He is also an honorary research fellow of the Hong Kong Institute of Asia–Pacific Studies, The Chinese University of Hong Kong. A graduate of The University of Hong Kong and the University of Toronto, he writes on a wide range of subjects, including, among others, macroeconomic policy, urban economics, social security, labour market issues and health. Dr. Ho has served in the Ontario Government as an economist and has taught at The Chinese University of Hong Kong as well as at York University in Canada. Dr. Ho was recently appointed a member of the Hong Kong Committee for Pacific Economic Cooperation. He is also managing editor for *Pacific Economic Review*.

K. I. FUNG (馮家驤) is professor of Geography at the University of Saskatchewan, Canada. His major research and publications relate to Shanghai and urban China. Other academic interests and publications relate to cartography, such as *The Atlas of Saskatchewan* and *The Atlas of Saskatchewan Agriculture*.

KERRIE L. MACPHERSON (程愷禮) is lecturer in History and fellow of the Centre of Urban Planning and Environmental Management at The University of Hong Kong. She is a member of the Editorial Board of the *Asian Journal of Environmental Management*, as well as a Council member of the International Planning History Society. Dr. MacPherson specializes in Chinese urban history and planning history, particularly the history of urban public health which is the focus of her book, *A Wilderness of Marshes: The Origins of Public Health in Shanghai, 1843–93* (1987). Her recent publications on Shanghai include "Designing China's Urban Future: The Greater Shanghai Plan, 1927–37," *Planning Perspectives* (1990); and "The Head of the Dragon: The Pudong New Area and Shanghai's Urban Development," *Planning Perspectives* (1994).

KING K. TSAO (曹景鈞) received his Ph.D. from the Department of Political Science at the University of Chicago. He is currently an assistant professor in the Department of Government and Public Administration at The Chinese University of Hong Kong. Within the last three years, he has contributed articles in the journals of *Public Administration Review*, *Australian Journal of Public Administration, Hong Kong Journal of Social Sciences* (Chinese) and *Comparative Economic and Social Systems* (Chinese), along with a few book chapters. His research interests are on the relationship between the state and society, reform of the state-owned enterprises, and issues on Chinese public administration. He was a visiting scholar at the Fairbank Center for East Asian Research at Harvard University during January to June 1996.

LAM KIN-CHE (林健枝) is chairman of the Department of Geography at The Chinese University of Hong Kong. He has considerable field research experience in China, including environmental planning issues in the Special Economic Zones and ecosystem rehabilitation in the remote and hilly areas of Guangdong.

LAM TAO-CHIU (林道超) teaches in the Department of Management, Hong Kong Polytechnic University. He is also a doctoral student at the Contemporary China Centre, Australian National University.

LESLIE N. K. LO (盧乃桂) received his doctorate from Columbia University. He is dean of Education of The Chinese University of Hong Kong and past president of the Comparative Education Society of Hong Kong. He has authored numerous articles on educational development in East Asia. His recent research focus is on the implementation of "relevance education" and education and society in contemporary Chinese societies.

LIANG JINSHE (梁進社) graduated from Peking University and received his B.Sc. and M.Sc. degrees in Geography in 1982 and 1985 respectively. He has since been teaching and conducting research on economic geography in the Department of Geography, Beijing Normal University where he is an associate professor.

LIN HUI (林琿) graduated from Wuhan Technical University of Surveying and Mapping in 1980. He received an M.Sc. degree in Remote Sensing and Cartography from the Chinese Academy of Sciences in 1983, and M.A. and Ph.D. degrees in Geographic Information Systems from the University of Buffalo in 1987 and 1992, respectively. In 1992, Dr. Lin joined the Great Lakes Program of the University of Buffalo as a post-doctoral researcher for a US EPA-supported project in watershed water quality management. Dr. Lin joined The Chinese University of Hong Kong as lecturer in Geography in 1993. His research interests include GIS design, Remote Sensing, Investment Environment Information Systems and Spatial/Temporal Modelling Support Systems.

LYNN T. WHITE III (白霖) is professor of Politics and International Affairs at Princeton University. He has recently completed a book about the unintended and local causes of China's reforms since the early 1970s, entitled *Unstately Power*. He has also published many articles and books, including *Careers in Shanghai* and *Policies of Chaos* about the causes of violence during the Cultural Revolution.

NYAW MEE-KAU (饒美蛟) is vice-president of Lingnan College and honorary professor of Management, Faculty of Business Administration, The Chinese University of Hong Kong. He has authored and co-authored several books, including *Export-expansion and Industrial Growth in Singapore* and *Business Operations and Management: From West to East*. He has also contributed to *Asian Survey, Journal of Management Studies, International Studies of Management and Organization, Journal of Business Ethics, World Development, Euro–Asia Business Review* and several other international journals.

PETER T. Y. CHEUNG (張贊賢) is assistant professor in the Department of Politics and Public Administration at The University of Hong Kong. He holds a Ph.D. in political science from the University of Washington, Seattle, and he has published on various aspects of the political economy of development in South China. His current research interests include the politics of economic reform in Guangdong province, central–provincial relations, and the issue of leadership and reform strategy in post-Mao China.

REBECCA L. H. CHIU (趙麗霞) is lecturer at the Centre of Urban Planning and Environmental Management, The University of Hong Kong. She specializes in housing education and housing studies. Her research activities on various housing systems includes consultancy work on housing reforms in China for planning and international organizations.

ROGER C. K. CHAN (陳鎮江) is lecturer at the Centre of Urban Planning and Environmental Management, The University of Hong Kong. His current research projects include regional planning and development strategies and spatial transformation in large metropolitan regions in China.

RUPERT HODDER (郝德勇) is lecturer in the Department of Geography at The Chinese University of Hong Kong. His most recent book, *Merchant Princes of the East*, was published by John Wiley and Sons, Ltd., in 1996. His earlier publications include *The West Pacific Rim* and *The Creation of Wealth in China*.

SHI PEIJUN (史培軍) graduated from the Department of Geography, Inner Mongolia University of China, in 1982. Dr. Shi received his M.Sc. degree in Geography from Lanzhou Institute of Desert, Chinese Academy of Sciences, in 1984 and his Ph.D. in Geography from Beijing Normal University in 1989. In the same year, Dr. Shi joined Beijing Normal University as an associate professor of Geography. In 1994 he became professor and chairman of the Department of Resource and Environmental Sciences and associate dean of the School of Resource and Environmental Science, Beijing Normal University.

SUZANNE C. HO (何陳雪鸝) is associate professor in the Department of Community and Family Medicine, Faculty of Medicine, The Chinese University of Hong Kong. She obtained a Master of Public Health degree in the USA, a Ph.D. degree from the National University of Singapore and F.A.C.E. in USA. Her specialty is gerontology and the epidemiology of osteoporosis. An expert in these areas, she has published many papers on elderly health and chronic diseases.

TAO SHU (陶澍) is professor of Urban and Environmental Sciences at Peking University. He holds a doctoral degree from the University of Kansas and has published numerous books and articles on the mobility of heavy metals and environmental pollution in China.

TSUI KAI-YUEN (崔啓源) is associate professor of Economics at The

Chinese University of Hong Kong. His major research interests are regional development in China, theoretical issues with respect to the design of inequality and poverty measures. His publications have appeared in *Journal of Comparative Economics*, *Journal of Development Economics*, *Social Choice and Welfare* and *Journal of Economic Theory*.

VICTOR MOK (莫凱), Ph.D. from Michigan State University, is reader in Economics at The Chinese University of Hong Kong. His major research interests relate to international economics and economic development. He has published extensively on foreign trade, investment, industry and the economic development and structural change of Hong Kong.

WONG SIU-LUN (黃紹倫) is professor of Sociology at The University of Hong Kong. His recent research projects include Chinese entrepreneurship and economic development, emigration from Hong Kong and indicators of social development in Hong Kong. He is the author of *Emigrant Entrepreneurs: Shanghai Industrialists in Hong Kong* (Hong Kong: Oxford University Press, 1988) and the co-editor of *Hong Kong's Transition: A Decade after the Deal* (Hong Kong: Oxford University Press, 1995).

WONG TZE-WAI (黃子惠) is professor in the Department of Community and Family Medicine, Faculty of Medicine, The Chinese University of Hong Kong. He obtained an M.B.B.S. degree in Hong Kong, an M.Sc. degree in Public Health in Singapore, F.A.F.O.M. in Australia and M.F.P.H.M. in the United Kingdom. His research interests are diverse, ranging from the epidemiology of infectious diseases, occupational and environmental issues, to health services and administration. He has published extensively in medical and scientific journals and several books.

Name Index

Subject Index